THE COLLECTED LETTERS
OF JOSEPH CONRAD

VOLUME 3   1903–1907

EDITED BY

FREDERICK R. KARL

AND

LAURENCE DAVIES

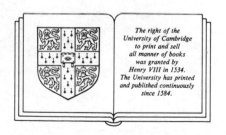

The right of the
University of Cambridge
to print and sell
all manner of books
was granted by
Henry VIII in 1534.
The University has printed
and published continuously
since 1584.

CAMBRIDGE UNIVERSITY PRESS

CAMBRIDGE

NEW YORK   NEW ROCHELLE   MELBOURNE   SYDNEY

Published by the Press Syndicate of the University of Cambridge
The Pitt Building, Trumpington Street, Cambridge CB2 1RP
32 East 57th Street, New York, NY 10022, USA
10 Stamford Road, Oakleigh, Melbourne 3166, Australia

Printed in Great Britain at
the University Press, Cambridge

British Library cataloguing in publication data

Conrad, Joseph
The collected letters of Joseph Conrad.
Vol. 3: 1903–1907
1. Conrad, Joseph – Biography
2. Novelists English – 20th century – Biography
I. Title   II. Karl, Frederick R.
III. Davies, Laurence, *1943–*
823'.912   PR6005.04Z/

Library of Congress cataloguing in publication data

Conrad, Joseph, 1857–1924.
The collected letters of Joseph Conrad.
English and French.
Includes bibliographical references and indexes.
Contents: v. 1. 1861–1897 – v. 2. 1898–1902 –
v. 3 1903–1907.
1. Conrad, Joseph, 1857–1924 – Correspondence.
2. Novelists, English – 20th century – Correspondence.
I. Karl, Frederick Robert, 1927–   .
II. Davies, Laurence, 1943–   .
PR6005.04Z48   1983   823'.912   82-14643

ISBN 0 521 24216 9 (vol. 1)
ISBN 0 521 25748 4 (vol. 2)
ISBN 0 521 32387 8 (vol. 3)

THE COLLECTED LETTERS OF
JOSEPH CONRAD

GENERAL EDITOR:
FREDERICK R. KARL

VOLUME 3

This volume is dedicated to the memory of
Ugo Mursia
un' uomo di virtù

CONTENTS

PLATES

between pages 180 and 181

These illustrations appear by kind permission of: The BBC Hulton Picture Library (3, 6, 7, 8, 9, 11, 13, 14); The National Portrait Gallery (1, 2, 12); Mrs C.E. Taylor (4); The Berg Collection, New York Public Library (10); Dartmouth College Libraries (5).

ACKNOWLEDGMENTS

We offer our warm thanks to the individuals and institutions listed as guardians of the letters.

Many of the people acknowledged in the first volume gave us assistance that benefits the entire edition; we render them all our redoubled gratitude. For particular assistance with Volume Three, we thank Professor Colette Gaudin, Professor David Leon Higdon, Professor Allan Hunter, Dr Owen Knowles, Professors Diana and Eric Manheimer-Taylor, Professor Sidney Reid, Professor Donald Rude, Professor J.H. Stape, Ms Bonnie Wallin, and Professor Cedric Watts.

The tireless help of Mr Hans van Marle, especially but not exclusively in the early stages of proofing, deserves a paragraph to itself. A discreet eminence, yet never a grey one, he has always been generous with his extraordinary fund of knowledge. Among Conradians, the question *quis custodiet?* has a clear and grateful answer.

Since we began our work, a new generation of senior librarians and curators has arrived. For their help with collections in their care, we thank William Cagle of the Lilly Library, University of Indiana, Philip Cronenwett of Special Collections, Dartmouth College, Anne Freudenberg of the Alderman Library, University of Virginia, Cathy Henderson of the Humanities Research Center, University of Texas at Austin, and Dr Susan Willis of the Rosenbach Foundation in Philadelphia.

The preparation of this volume was made possible in part by a grant to Laurence Davies from the Program for Editions (Division of Research) of the National Endowment for the Humanities, an independent federal agency.

HOLDERS OF LETTERS

Rosenbach   The Philip M. and A. S. W. Rosenbach Foundation,
             Philadelphia
Rothenstein Sir John Rothenstein
Sutton   Mr Raymond B. Sutton, Jr
Texas   Humanities Research Center, University of Texas at
             Austin
Trinity   Trinity College, Cambridge
UCL   The Library of University College, London
Vaugelas   Mme Charles Armand de Vaugelas
Wellington   The Honourable Company of Master Mariners, H. Q. S.
             Wellington, London
Yale   The Beinecke Rare Book and Manuscript Library, Yale
             University, New Haven, Connecticut

PUBLISHED SOURCES OF LETTERS

Baines	Jocelyn Baines, *Joseph Conrad: A Critical Biography*. Weidenfeld and Nicolson, 1960
Blackburn	William Blackburn, ed., *Joseph Conrad: Letters to William Blackwood and David S. Meldrum*. Durham, N.C.: Duke University Press, 1958
Curreli (1978)	Mario Curreli, ed., 'Una Lettera Inedita di Conrad a Ford', *Studi di Filologia e Letteratura* (Pisa), 1978, no. 2, 221–30
CWW	Norman Sherry, *Conrad's Western World*. Cambridge University Press, 1971
Danilewiczowa	Maria Danilewiczowa, ed., *Joseph Conrad: Listy do Johna Galsworthy'ego*. B. Świderski, 1957
G.	Edward Garnett, ed., *Letters from Joseph Conrad, 1895–1924*. Nonesuch Press, 1928
G. & S.	John A. Gee and Paul J. Sturm, trans. and ed., *Letters of Joseph Conrad to Marguerite Poradowska*. New Haven: Yale University Press, 1940
Goldring	Douglas Goldring, *The Last Pre-Raphaelite: A Record of the Life and Writings of Ford Madox Ford*. MacDonald, 1948
Guérin	Yves Guérin, ed., 'Huit lettres inédites de Joseph Conrad à Robert d'Humières', *Revue de Littérature Comparée*, 44 (1970), 367–92
Hunter (1985)	Allan Hunter, ed., 'Letters from Joseph Conrad, I', *Notes and Queries*, 230 (September 1985), 366–70
Hunter (1985, 2)	'Letters from Joseph Conrad, 2', *ibid.*, 500–5
J-A	G. Jean-Aubry, ed., *Joseph Conrad: Life and Letters*. 2 volumes. Heinemann, 1927
Keating	George T. Keating, *A Conrad Memorial Library: The Collection of George T. Keating*. Garden City, N.Y.: Doubleday, Doran, 1929
Knowles	Owen Knowles and G. W. S. Miskin, ed., 'Unpublished Conrad Letters: The H.Q.S. *Wel-*

lington Collection', *Notes and Queries*, 230 (September 1985), 370–6

Letters   Frederick R. Karl and Laurence Davies, ed., *The Collected Letters of Joseph Conrad*. Cambridge University Press, 1983, etc.

L. fr.   G. Jean-Aubry, *Lettres françaises*. Paris: Gallimard, 1929

Listy   Zdzisław Najder, ed., Halina Carroll, trans., *Joseph Conrad: Listy*. Warsaw: Państwowy Instytut Wydawniczy, 1968

Lucas   E.V. Lucas, *The Colvins and Their Friends*. New York: Scribner's, 1928

MacShane   Frank MacShane, ed., 'Conrad on Melville', *American Literature*, 29 (1958), 463–4

Marrot   H. V. Marrot, ed., *The Life and Letters of John Galsworthy*. New York: Scribner's, 1936

Najder   Zdzisław Najder, ed., Halina Carroll, trans., *Conrad's Polish Background: Letters to and from Polish Friends*. Oxford University Press, 1964

Najder (1974)   'Conrad's Casement Letters', *Polish Perspectives* (Warsaw), 17 (1974), no. 12, 25–30

Najder (1978)   *Congo Diary and Other Uncollected Pieces by Joseph Conrad*. Garden City, New York: Doubleday, 1978

Newbolt   Sir Henry Newbolt, *My World as in My Time: Memoirs of Sir Henry Newbolt, 1862–1932*. Faber and Faber, 1932

Rapin   René Rapin, ed., *Lettres de Joseph Conrad à Marguerite Poradowska*. Geneva: Droz, 1966

Ray (1983, 2)   Martin Ray, ed., 'Conrad to Wells: Yet Another Undated Letter', *The Conradian*, 8 (1983), 28–31

Ray (1985)   'Conrad to Wells: An Undated Letter', *English Language Notes*, 23 (1985), 48–61

Ruch   *Ruch Literacki* (Warsaw), 1927, no. 5

Scritti   Ugo Mursia, *Scritti Conradiani*. Milan: Mursia, 1983

Watts   C. T. Watts, ed., *Joseph Conrad's Letters to R. B. Cunninghame Graham*. Cambridge University Press, 1969

WR   Sir William Rothenstein, *Men and Memories, 1900–22*. New York: Coward, McCann, 1932

OTHER FREQUENTLY CITED WORKS

Busza, Andrzej   'Conrad's Polish Literary Background', *Antemurale* (Rome and London), 10 (1966), 109–255

Conrad, Borys   *My Father: Joseph Conrad*. New York: Coward, McCann, 1970

Conrad, Jessie   *Joseph Conrad and His Circle*. Jarrold's, 1935

Conrad, Jessie   *Joseph Conrad as I Knew Him*. Garden City, N. Y.: Doubleday, Page, 1926

Dupré, Catherine   *John Galsworthy: A Biography*. New York: Coward, McCann, 1976

Garnett, Edward, ed.   *Letters from John Galsworthy, 1900–1932*. Cape, 1934

Heilbrun, Carolyn G.   *The Garnett Family*. George Allen & Unwin, 1961

Holloway, Mark   *Norman Douglas: A Biography*. Secker & Warburg, 1976

Jean-Aubry, G., ed.   *Twenty Letters to Joseph Conrad*. First Edition Club, 1926

Karl, Frederick R.   *Joseph Conrad: The Three Lives*. New York: Farrar, Straus, Giroux, 1979

Ludwig, Richard M., ed.   *Letters of Ford Madox Ford*. Princeton, N.J.: Princeton University Press, 1965

Mackenzie, Norman and Jeanne   *H. G. Wells: A Biography*. New York: Simon & Schuster, 1973

Mizener, Arthur   *The Saddest Story: A Biography of Ford Madox Ford*. New York: World Publishing Co., 1971

Mottram, R. H.   *For Some We Loved: An Intimate Portrait of Ada and John Galsworthy*. Hutchinson, 1956

Najder, Zdzisław, ed., and Halina Carroll, trans.   *Conrad under Familial Eyes*. Cambridge University Press, 1983

Najder, Zdzisław   *Joseph Conrad: A Chronicle*. New Brunswick, N. J.: Rutgers University Press, 1983

Sherry, Norman   *Conrad: The Critical Heritage*. Routledge & Kegan Paul, 1973

Watts, Cedric, and Laurence Davies   *Cunninghame Graham: A Critical Biography*. Cambridge University Press, 1979

Unless otherwise noted, references to Conrad's work come from the Kent Edition, published by Doubleday, Page in twenty-six volumes (Garden City, N. Y., 1925). Books cited without place of publication originated in London.

CHRONOLOGY, 1903–1907

Unless otherwise shown, dates of book publication are for Britain rather than North America.

Christmas 1902	Began work on *Nostromo*.
March 1903	Attacked by gout; other episodes of pain and sickness in November 1903, August 1904, March and December 1905, May 1907.
22 April 1903	*Typhoon and Other Stories* published.
16 October 1903	*Romance* published.
17 January 1904	The Conrads took a flat in London.
Between 17 and 23 January 1904	Jessie Conrad injured both knees in a fall.
Late January–March 1904	Help from Ford, taking dictation and contributing to work in progress.
Late January 1904	Work on *One Day More*, stage version of 'Tomorrow'.
Late January or early February 1904	Began 'a series of sea sketches', later *The Mirror of the Sea*.
6 February 1904	Conrad's bankers failed.
2 March 1904	Finished 'A Glance at Two Books', published posthumously.
8 March 1904	'Missing' appeared in *Daily Mail*; other *Mirror* essays appeared in the *Mail, Standard, Pall Mall Magazine, Tribune, World Today, Blackwood's,* and *Harper's Weekly* between then and January 1906.
Between 15 and 20 March 1904	Conrad returned to the Pent.
May–June 1904	Wrote Introduction to Ada Galsworthy's Maupassant translations, *Yvette and Other Stories*.
16 July 1904	Review of France's *Crainquebille* in *Speaker*.

30 August 1904	At the Hopes' house in Essex, finished *Nostromo* (*T. P.'s Weekly*, 29 January–7 October 1904).
September or October 1904	Began the 'Benavides' stories, later 'Gaspar Ruiz'.
c. 10 October 1904	To London for treatment of Jessie Conrad's knees.
14 October 1904	*Nostromo* published as a book.
By 15 October 1904	Finished 'Henry James: An Appreciation' (*North American Review*, January 1905).
24 November 1904	Operation performed on Jessie Conrad.
13 January 1905	Departure for Italy.
20 January–12 May 1905	Residence on Capri; work on *Chance*.
Late March 1905	News of a grant from the Royal Bounty.
Early April 1905	Finished 'Autocracy and War' (*Fortnightly Review*, 1 July).
18 May 1905	Return to the Pent.
25 June 1905	First performance of *One Day More* in London.
15 July 1905	'Books' appeared in *Speaker*.
Autumn 1905	Parts of *Chance* written; work on it continued intermittently for the rest of the period.
26 October 1905	Jessie Conrad had a 'nervous breakdown of a sort'.
Mid November 1905	The Conrads went to London; Borys caught scarlet fever and was sent to hospital.
December 1905–January 1906	Wrote 'The Brute' (*Daily Chronicle*, 5 December 1906), 'An Anarchist' and 'The Informer' (both in *Harper's Magazine*, August and December 1906).
9 February 1906	Departure for Montpellier.
February 1906	Began 'Verloc', later *The Secret Agent*.
14 April 1906	Return to the Pent.
11–23 May 1906	The Conrads in Winchelsea; colla-

	boration with Ford on *The Nature of a Crime* (*English Review*, April–May 1909).
10 July–c. 2 September 1906	The Conrads in London.
2 August 1906	John Conrad born.
4 October 1906	*The Mirror of the Sea* published.
2 November 1906	Serial version of *The Secret Agent* finished (*Ridgway's*, 6 October 1906–12 January 1907).
Early December 1906	Finished 'Il Conde' (*Cassell's Magazine*, August 1908).
16 December 1906	Departure for Montpellier.
December 1906–January 1907	Revised Poradowska and Davray translations from *Tales of Unrest*.
January 1907	Wrote Preface to Jessie Conrad's *A Handbook of Cookery for a Small House* (published 1923). Began 'The Duel'.
Late February 1907	Borys seriously ill with measles, then with congested lungs: tuberculosis feared but not present.
11 April 1907	Finished 'The Duel' (*Pall Mall Magazine*, January–May 1908).
15 May 1907	The Conrads left Montpellier for Geneva. Both sons afflicted with whooping cough; Borys, who developed pleurisy and rheumatic fever, gravely ill until late June.
May–June 1907	*The Secret Agent* expanded for book publication.
12 August 1907	Return to the Pent; a search for new quarters began.
12 September 1907	Moved to Someries, near Luton. Book form of *The Secret Agent* published.
12 October 1907	'The Censor of Plays' in *Daily Mail*.
3 December 1907	Conrad's fiftieth birthday.
By 4 December 1907	Began 'Razumov', later *Under Western Eyes*.

INTRODUCTION TO VOLUME THREE

Both at sea and on land my point of view is English, from which the conclusion should not be drawn that I have become an Englishman. That is not the case. Homo duplex has in my case more than one meaning.

(To Waliszewski, 5 December 1903)

Conrad wanted to reassure Waliszewski, a compatriot living in France, that writing in English about English characters did not amount to spiritual secession from Poland. In a wider setting, Conrad's doubleness appears in the tensions (or harmonies) between sailor and author, moralist and sceptic, public man and private ironist, between the man who thinks with Abel and the man who feels for Cain. When we consider the letters written during the period of *Nostromo* and *The Secret Agent*, yet another reading of *homo duplex* comes to mind, a reading that returns the phrase not to its sources in Hermetic doctrine but to its uses in Buffon's *Histoire naturelle* and Baudelaire's *L'Art romantique*.

For Buffon, the human species differs from all others in its capacity for rational thinking. This difference confers privilege but also pain; thinking brings us to the edge of the gulf that separates what might be from what is. For Baudelaire, those who stand closest to the gulf, sensing its depth and its width, are artists and dreamers:

Qui parmi nous n'est pas un *homo duplex*? Je veux parler de ceux dont l'esprit a été dès l'enfance *touched with pensiveness*; toujours double, action et intention, rêve et réalité; toujours l'un nuisant à l'autre, l'un usurpant la part de l'autre.

Who among us is not a *homo duplex*? I mean among those whose soul has since childhood been 'touched with pensiveness' [De Quincey]; always double, action and intention, dream and reality; the one always damaging the other, the one encroaching on the other's place.   ('La Double vie', Pléiade edition, p. 658)

Such was Conrad's case. As he was only too well aware, his dreams of ideal and his situation in actual circumstances stood far apart.

In the summer of 1903, he reported progress on *Nostromo*:

I have never worked so hard before—with so much anxiety. But the result is good. You know I take no credit to myself for what I do—and so I may judge my own performance. There is no mistake about this. You may take up a strong position when you offer it here. It is a very genuine Conrad.

(To Pinker, 22 August)

Conrad knew he was writing *Nostromo* and *The Secret Agent* at the height of his powers. Finishing the serial version of both novels in a frenzy that, especially in the case of *Nostromo*, came perilously close to derangement, he wrote them too in a period of sickness, financial uncertainty and domestic worry. For all its risks of physical and mental collapse, the frenzy was characteristic; possibly Conrad in some measure needed the drama of telegrams to Pinker and sleepless nights in order to bring out his best, but that can only be speculation *post hoc* and *propter hoc*: crisis was his normal means of coming to an end. What looks more certain is that Conrad could not have worked at a more leisurely pace even had he wanted to. His circumstances did not permit. The meditative or con-templative quality of his work, his ability to find significance in the slightest gesture or the shortest utterance, was achieved in spite not because of the way he lived. The intricate architecture of *Nostromo* and the pure concentration of irony in *The Secret Agent* seem enabled by an unhurried, priestlike artistry, the perfection of modernist serenity, yet Conrad could afford neither the time to be a Rilke nor the funds to be a Proust. While aware that he had entered on a period of boundless creative possibility, he felt bound in by poverty and bad luck:

It is all very monotonous—my news is. I stick here fighting with disease and creeping imbecility—like a cornered rat, facing fate with a big stick that is sure to descend and crack my skull before many days are over.

(To Wells, 20 October 1905)

By the lights of Buffon and Baudelaire, Conrad was a *homo duplex* above all in his condition as an author.

Perhaps one can overstate the unpleasantness of his financial plight. As sub-tenant of Pent Farm he paid, when so disposed, £30 a year, about one tenth of his average income. Another twentieth went to the Inland Revenue. The unfortunate Mr O'Connor, whose services as secretary and tutor cost £14 a quarter all found, could be replaced by an even more unfortunate 'girl which* will have only 3 g[uinea]s per month and who they say can teach besides being a good stenographer' (To Pinker, 20 September 1905). Against this background of unintimidating rents, negligible taxes and cheap labour, Conrad's chronic shortage of cash might, to a censorious eye, seem related to a chronic failure of budgetary skills. So it must have seemed to Pinker. To us, without Pinker's stake in the issue, it might seem presumptuous to pass judg-ment. And in any case, to think in terms of balanced budgets is to think in terms of balanced lives; with their cross-rhythms of energy and torpor, Conrad's habits of work do not lend themselves to talk of balances – even had he not been subject to so many unpredictable and heart-wrenching disruptions.

Between 1903 and 1907, Jessie Conrad's knees suffered immobilizing damage and her heart caused general alarm, Borys Conrad's condition, true to previous form, ranged from mere delicacy to deathly illness, Joseph Conrad's health underwent assault by eczema, gout, neuralgia, severe toothache and malaria, and his banker failed. The record is a miserable one, cheered only by the arrival of John Conrad; luckily, and surprisingly, he turned out to be a sturdy baby. It was a costly period in time, in money, and in nervous strain – small wonder that Conrad occasionally sounded close to desperation:

I haven't the material time to be quicker. Borys is now powerless in both hands. He suffers a great deal. He's also very helpless as You may imagine. Can't even sit up without help. I've to look after him. I am having the ghastliest time imaginable. Nursing hinders me in my work not only intellectually but materially. I set down the pen in the middle of a phrase and have to go to him. And to look at him is not exactly composing to the mind. I come back to my paper as if out of a nightmare and don't remember what I wanted to say.

(To Pinker, 5 June 1907)

The misery goes on. Poor Jess had heart attacks the other day. Meantime the leg shows sign of athropy* but no improvement. I daren't even wish myself dead. At any rate dictation goes on every day since you left. 1600 words yesterday—and so on. (To Galsworthy, [1 April 1904])

The first passage refers to *The Secret Agent* and the second to *The Mirror of the Sea*. Few modern readers would want to take the latter work as seriously as the former, yet Conrad's contemporaries did. One might put their enthusiasm down to patriotism, to the special thrill of seeing a celebrated author move to a different and apparently more personal genre, or to the vogue for fine autobiographical prose epitomized by Turgenev's hunting sketches. One should remember, however, that although (or conceivably because) some parts of *The Mirror* were dictated at high speed for the *Daily Mail*, the *Standard*, and the *Pall Mall Magazine*, Conrad was furious when editors cut them about and touched when they won such a favourable reception. Quite untypically he kept admiring letters about them, even though the letters praised these sea-essays as his highest achievement just at the time when he was turning to novels set on shore. Thinking in Conrad's terms, it would be wrong to put up too absolute a barrier between his more and less serious work or to insist upon the absolute superiority of avowed fiction over everything else. He concerned himself about it all, hoping that the broth from the boiling pot would have some body to it.

Nevertheless, under easier circumstances, some at least of the essays in *The Mirror* and some of the stories from *A Set of Six* would not have been written at all. While insisting, in the Pinker correspondence, on the literary value of *The Mirror* papers, Conrad also dwelled on their value as commodities:

> Here is Conrad talking of the events and feelings of his own life as he would talk to a friend. They have been always asking for something of the sort and here it is with as little egoism and as much sincerity as is possible in a thing of that sort.
>
> (18 April 1904)

> And the stuff, I say it confidently, in literary merit and general interest is better than *Youth*. I suppose you'll smile at the 'literary merit' but I think we have the right to point it out as a Grocer points out the good condition of his cheese; and believe in it too in good faith as the Grocer believes in the good quality of his wares.
>
> ([12 October 1905])

Not many grocers sell a cheese of their own making.

For all its defensive ramparts of sarcasm and ironic reasonableness, this talk of offering his wares by the ounce or by the pound was new to Conrad's correspondence. He had always been a word counter, he had often wished for commercial success, but never before had he stood at such a distance from his work. 'They have been always asking for something of that sort and here it is.'

The detachment was not simply the consequence of taking a place amid the cheese-mongers. As the number of his books increased, his and the public's sense of Conrad's distinctiveness grew stronger. Thus he could refer to *Nostromo* as 'a very genuine Conrad' and, in connection with *Chance* and *The Secret Agent*, tell Pinker:

> One may read everybody and yet in the end want to read me ... For I don't resemble anybody ... There is nothing in me but a turn of mind which whether valuable or worthless can not be imitated.
>
> (30 July 1907)

A gap opened up between the Conrad who wrote and the Conrad who had written. His completed work had become a discrete phenomenon, charged with a life of its own. In its studies of loyalty, betrayal, braggadocio and delusion, *Romance* prefigures *Nostromo*, and *Nostromo* harks back to *Romance*; the texts resound with echoes. The greasy London around which Mr Verloc drags his bulk is not the imperial city that harbours the 'Narcissus'; the texts abound in differences. To see so much attainment under one's name would be gratifying, to acquire a loyal audience would be comforting – but the attainment and the audience had their price. The attainment had to be kept up: '14,000 words was all I could achieve. It's simply disaster and there's nothing in them, it seems to me, the merest hack novelist could not have written in two evenings and a half' (To Galsworthy, 9 April 1906). The audience had to be persuaded to change its tastes:

The S[ecret] A[gent] however has its importance as a distinctly new departure in my work. And I am anxious to put as much "quality" as I can in that book which will be criticised with some severity no doubt—or *scrutinised* rather, I should say. Preconceived notions of Conrad as sea writer will stand in the way of its acceptance. You can see this Yourself.   (To Pinker, 6 May 1907)

According to Baudelaire, the *homo duplex* cannot enjoy the ease of mere split-mindedness. The categories of action and intention, dream and reality overlap, 'l'un nuisant à l'autre'. The emphasis on infringement fits Conrad's case precisely. At one end of the scale he would rather contemplate stories than write them: 'I am sunk in a vaguely uneasy dream of visions—of innumerable tales that float in an atmosphere of volupt[u]ously aching bones' (To Ford, 9 May 1905). At the other end he wrote to keep his family alive and approximately healthy. In between, he shared a part in the same enterprise as Ford and James (later joined by Proust, Woolf and Gide), that of renewing the novel and the short story, of making fictions true to a vision of artistic necessity rather than economic need – and he also wrote to buy more time for writing. Conrad's approach to his work required fierce concentration: 'for me, writing—*the only possible writing*—is just simply the conversion of nervous force into phrases' (To Wells, 30 November 1903), while his life – his finances, his family's well-being, his own body – brought never-ending distraction. The complexities of his being as an author account for the constant strife between detachment and desperation that char-acterizes the letters in this volume.

The uncertainties of Conrad's career stand out at their clearest in the large and mostly unfamiliar correspondence with Pinker. As usual, only Conrad's half of the exchange remains; we can only guess at the precise tone of Pinker's replies to letters whose contents range from brisk professionalism through jocularity, affection, wheedling and importu-nity to contempt and downright outrage. Conrad was not rescued from his debts to Pinker (or, to state the other case, Pinker could not recoup his loans to Conrad) until the success of *Chance* in 1914. In the period of the present volume, Pinker settled the bills – for school fees, hats, railway tickets, furniture, and coals – while Conrad toiled away in a muddy no-man's-land somewhere between long-term plans and short-term deadlines. Quite understandably, the situation made Pinker impatient and Conrad resentful; the agent tried standing firm and the author dared him to do his worst:

A certain amount of pressure may do to bring a drunkard to his bearings but it must fail with my temperament. Kind regards
        Yours   Conrad.
PS Unless telegraphically don't trouble to answer.   (24 April 1905)

In 1910 came a rift that could not be easily mended, but until then Pinker would always relent, the necessary funds arrive by wire or post, and the cycle start again. 'Please send me a £10 note instanter because life without pocket money is not worth living' (25 January 1907). At times Conrad sounds like a schoolboy pleading with his elders. To some extent the dealings with his agent recapitulated those with his uncle and guardian, Tadeusz Bobrowski; once more the dreamer confronted a realist with a well-stocked but carefully monitored wallet. Pinker enabled Conrad's autonomy but also restricted it; inevitably, he had to bear the brunt of Conrad's rage at circumstances.

Similar questions of freedom, gratitude and obligation tint Conrad's response to two well-connected men of letters, Edmund Gosse and Henry Newbolt. In 1905, Conrad was delighted to hear of a grant of £500 from the Royal Bounty; apparently thinking this unexpected generosity reflected the king's or at worst the prime minister's personal tastes (Conrad understood the monarchy in somewhat feudal terms), he accepted in his courtliest manner. He was soon dismayed to find out, however, that the bounty had to be paid not in a lump sum but in instalments and for carefully specified purposes. The terms would curtail his independence and, moreover, make him look bad:

The whole affair has assumed an appearance much graver and more distressing than any stress of my material necessities: the appearance of 'Conrad having to be saved from himself'—the sort of thing that casts a doubt on a man's sense of responsibility, on his right feeling, on his sense of correct conduct.
                                                (To Gosse, 16 May 1905)

Practical considerations imposed a stricter deference than Conrad expressed to Pinker, yet that only strengthened the currents of frustration under the surface courtesy.

When, in 1902, he was nominated for a grant from the Royal Literary Fund, his backers stated that Conrad lived quietly in the country. After 1902, that became less the case; he left the 'green solitudes' of the Pent (as he called them in a letter to Henry James, 20 September 1907) in search of Mediterranean warmth or London company. The original attraction of visits to London was proximity to Galsworthy and Ford, but the accident to Jessie Conrad's knees was the first of a series of medical crises that overshadowed and protracted their stays. Conrad himself could take some consolation in the broadening of his acquaintance about town. He met Frances and Sidney Colvin, who became lifelong supporters. With their theatrical interests and their position as critics fortified by Victorian credentials and modern sympathies – intermediaries between old and new – the Colvins were valuable as well as good friends. The same could be said of Will Rothenstein and his wife, Alice; between them they knew 'everyone', artistic lawyers and doctors, the dissident painters of the New English Art Club, politicians and patrons. Typically, it was Will who instigated the award from the Royal Bounty. Beginning, as it did, with a series of sittings for a portrait in Kent, the friendship was by no means purely metropolitan, but it certainly helped Conrad to take his place in the salons of the capital. Increasingly, he was leading the public life of a professional writer, an agreeable life perhaps not always conducive to writing itself.

Although his visits there were of the briefest, Conrad was also becoming well-known in Paris. He continued to write informative letters to H.-D. Davray of the *Mercure de France*, was introduced by him to the de Gourmont brothers, and acquired a new enthusiast, Robert d'Humières. A figure from the world of Proust, d'Humières, like Davray, was a mediator between France and Britain; after many anxious delays, anxious that is on the author's part, he became one of Conrad's translators.

There were all sorts of motives for wanting to winter in the south, in Montpellier or on Capri: health, economy, diversion, even the search for new stories. When all went well, Conrad could write from southern France: 'I am better in this sunshine.... The beauty of this land is inexpressible' (To Ford, 8 January 1907). Sadly, with Borys's succession of dangerous ailments, the same journey became 'this damnable outing' (To Pinker, 30 July 1907). Earlier, the expected classical serenity of Capri had turned out to be

a sort of blue nightmare traversed by stinks and perfumes ... with a mad gallop of German tourists ... streaming, tumbling, rushing ebbing from the top of Monte Solaro (where the clouds hang) to the amazing rocky chasms of the Arco Naturale—where the lager beer bottles go pop. (To Ford, 9 May 1905)

This beautiful and absurd island was the perfect place to meet Norman Douglas, virtually but not virtuously its tutelary spirit. In *South Wind*,

Capri becomes Nepenthe; the island did not exactly heal Conrad's woes – he suffered among other afflictions from hammering toothache – but it did provide the solace of Douglas's conversation, a melange of gossip, wit, and erudition. In return, Conrad did what he could to place Douglas's essays, counselling meanwhile persistence and the philosophic mind:

> It is beastly no doubt; but if we once break the door open there will be no waste
> . . . .
> People don't want intelligence. It worries them—and they demand from their writers as much subserviency as from their footmen if not rather more.
>   (18 October 1905)

Kindness (sometimes a stern kindness) to promising authors often shines through Conrad's correspondence, not infrequently when he is in difficulties himself.

Kindness is also a feature of the correspondence with Elsie Hueffer and Ford Madox Ford, 'a sort of life-long habit of which I am not ashamed because he is a much better fellow than the world gives him credit for' (To Wells, 20 October 1905). The habit did not actually have many years to run, but the two were still close enough for Ford to stand by as a one-man literary rescue squad, ready to take dictation and, perhaps, even to fill gaps in the writing itself. The letters sent to Ford during his mental illness testify to the intimacy. Even when flattened by the exertion of finishing *Nostromo*, Conrad was able to post a long plea to Ford, who was in Germany terrified and incapable of work, to put his impressions into letters that might with a few Conradian splices be turned into saleable articles. 'And if you can write twaddle—so much the better. Directly I get something I shall make a sort of expedition—a crusade' (5 September 1904). The same tenderness comes through in the letters of that time to Elsie Hueffer and previously in his reactions to her Maupassant translations.

The friends, however, to whom Conrad turned most often were the ever-generous Galsworthys, who in 1905, liberated by the death of Old John the patriarch, could at last appear in public as a couple. To Jack and Ada, Conrad was consistently frank; the letter of 30 July 1907, for instance, makes a striking contrast with the sanguine projections of work and income offered Pinker on the same date. To Jack in particular, who was keeping up a steady output of fiction and drama, Conrad was ready to confess his guiltier feelings:

> I have always that feeling of loafing at my work, as if powerless in an exhaustion of thought and will. Not enough! not enough! And yet perhaps those days

without a line, nay, without a word, the hard, atrocious, agonizing days are simply part of my *method* of work, a decreed necessity of my production.

(9 April 1906)

Homo duplex again. And it was to Jack, the liberal who so often disagreed with him about politics and political literature, that he now expressed the kind of subversive thoughts he used to save for Garnett or for Cunninghame Graham, as when Conrad asked about the terrorist and the manufacturer of tainted meat: 'Query: Which is really more criminal?—the Bomb of Madrid or the Meat of Chicago' ([2? June 1906]).

With greater or lesser intensity, many other names from previous volumes recur: Marguerite Poradowska, Harriet Capes, Ernest Dawson, Arnold Bennett, Hugh Clifford, Neil Munro, Garnett, the Sandersons, Cunninghame Graham, and Wells. Wells was another person in whom Conrad confided, witness the candid letter, also dated 30 July 1907, announcing that *The Secret Agent* would be dedicated to him. As early as the three letters (and delightful diagram) about *Mankind in the Making*, September 1903, one can see the first cracks of the fissure that eventually separated them, but had the separation not happened, we might well take those cracks as evidence that the two men were close enough to stand a little friendly disagreement. A much more devastating letter than any to Wells is the critique of Garnett's doom-fraught play ([17 November 1906]) and yet, although more quietly than in the earliest years of Conrad's career, that friendship lasted.

The correspondence with Cunninghame Graham was also less intense. Its primary interest for a modern reader lies in its bearings on *Nostromo*, a novel written about Graham's terrain. The letters to him, to Roger Casement (on a brief visit from West Africa to Kent), and to several compatriots, Jasieński, Szembek, and Waliszewski, embody the strength of Conrad's political and historical feelings. Casement brought back Africa, Graham showed him Latin America, a continent and a half whose history could be represented either as a bloody but triumphant progress or as an endless spiral of futility, Poland was unforgettable.

When we think of Conrad's achievement between 1903 and 1907, we think above all of *Nostromo*, *The Secret Agent*, and the essay on 'Autocracy and War'; *Under Western Eyes* began as 'Razumov' at the end of the same period. The present volume offers some striking views of the maelstrom, filled with the uprooted fragments of Conrad's life, from which they rose. We find him adding 30,000 words to *The Secret Agent* during the two months of Borys's worst sickness; we find his sense of time dissolving as *Nostromo* comes to a close: '... the book is finished. It will be finished maybe ...' (To Pinker, [26 August 1904]). The three novels (his supreme fictions for many of us) are all intensely political. As already noted, political concerns thread through the correspondence but, not at all surprisingly, Conrad spends much of his time telling his friends, colleagues and acquaintances about the daily struggle of writing under the weight of crushing worries. The personal, the literary, and the political do, however, intersect. They do so most clearly in the campaign against theatrical censorship that involved Conrad and many other writers in 1907 and beyond. More pervasively but less obviously, the common subject is frustration. Conrad may have wanted an ideal world for himself in which he could imagine – and even write – fiction in his own time and on his own terms; he certainly did not want the ideal world for whose sake the conspirators foregather at Mr Verloc's. Yet the problem is the same in both cases: the conflict between the desirable and the possible. The Professor and the rest of them stand no chance of actually succeeding; London (a city which terrified Conrad as much as it attracted him) is too huge, too abundantly populated. The dislocated narration of *Nostromo* has a way of diminishing individual and even communal aspirations by framing them within the ironies of history and subjecting them to the power of material interests. The upheavals in Russia – incipient revolution and defeat by Japan – gave Conrad little hope that the autocracy would budge, unless to make way for another one at least as tyrannous. 'And it is the way of true wisdom for men and States to take account of things as they are' (*Notes on Life and Letters*, p. 110). 'Things as they are': the burden oppresses the whole correspondence. The political novels are not 'about' the condition of writing nor are they simply extensions of the letters, but they do speak of the same battle between will and circumstance, the same sense of the futility and the force of illusion. They were written, all of them, by the one *homo duplex*.

Dartmouth College   Laurence Davies

CONRAD'S CORRESPONDENTS
1903–1907

William ARCHER (1856–1924), a Scot, began his career as a drama critic in 1879, with the *London Figaro*. Later, he wrote for the *World, Nation, Tribune, Morning Leader*, and *Manchester Guardian*. An editor and translator of Ibsen, he fought to make the British stage more serious.

James Matthew BARRIE (1860–1937), the Scottish novelist and playwright. Conrad's earliest letters to him belong to the period of *Peter Pan*.

Enoch Arnold BENNETT (1867–1931), the prolific chronicler of Staffordshire, London, and cosmopolitan life. His Naturalist approach to fiction and his financial success made him the butt of Modernist writers such as Woolf and Pound, yet his taste in Conrad was impeccable.

George William BLACKWOOD (1836–1912), a friend of the great Victorian novelists and editor of *Blackwood's Edinburgh Magazine*, published some of Conrad's early work, including *Youth* and *Lord Jim*, in book and serial forms.

The Hon. Anne Elizabeth BONTINE (née Elphinstone Fleeming, 1828–1925) was Cunninghame Graham's widowed mother. Of Scottish Whig and Spanish ancestry, she lived in London and took a well-informed interest in politics and the arts.

Harriet Mary CAPES (1849–1936), who lived in Winchester, wrote inspirational stories for children. A great admirer of Conrad's works, she 'selected and arranged' *Wisdom and Beauty from Conrad* (1915); he dedicated *A Set of Six* to her.

Roger CASEMENT (born 1864; knighted 1911) had wide commercial and consular experience in southern and central Africa. He met Conrad at Matadi in 1890. In 1903, he asked Conrad's help in his attack on Belgian savagery in the Congo 'Free State'. Later, he exposed vile working conditions in the South American rubber trade. An Irish patriot, he was hanged in 1916 for his war-time dealings with Germany.

As a reader for Fisher Unwin, Wilfrid Hugh CHESSON (1870–1952) was among the first to see the MS of *Almayer* and appreciate its promise. As a newspaper reviewer, Chesson contributed several perceptive appraisals of Conrad's fiction.

Hugh Charles CLIFFORD (1866–1941; knighted 1909), a colonial administrator, was serving as British Resident in Pahang, Malaya, when he wrote one of the earliest general appreciations of Conrad's work. Later, he was appointed to the Governorships of Labuan and North Borneo, the Gold Coast, Nigeria, Ceylon, and the Straits Settlements. He published many volumes of stories and sketches, collaborated on a Malay dictionary, and produced a Malay translation of the colonial penal code.

Frances COLVIN (née Fetherstonhaugh, 1839–1924), after separation from her first husband, the Rev. A. H. Sitwell, made a living as an essayist; when she married Sidney Colvin in 1903, she had known him for over thirty years. Their friend Robert Louis Stevenson venerated her as his 'madonna'.

Sidney COLVIN (1845–1927; knighted 1911) became a good friend to Conrad, as he had been to Stevenson. Colvin had been Slade Professor of Fine Arts at Cambridge and director of the Fitzwilliam Museum; among his literary works were editions of Stevenson's letters and biographies of Landor and Keats.

Henry-Durand DAVRAY (1873–1944) encouraged French and British writers to know each other better. He appeared regularly in the *Mercure de France* and edited its Collection of Foreign Authors. Among those he translated were Kipling, Meredith, Wells, and Conrad.

Captain, later Major Ernest DAWSON (died 1960), brother of A. J., was introduced to Conrad by Henley and Wells. Dawson contributed reminiscences and stories of Burma and Australia to *Blackwood's*; he served in Burma as a magistrate and an officer in the Rangoon Volunteer Rifles.

George Norman DOUGLAS (1868–1952), traveller, polyglot, polymath, wit and former diplomat, started his long association with Capri in 1902 and had already published two of his monographs about the island. His oeuvre, ranging from 'The Herpetology of the Grand Duchy of Baden' (1891) to *Venus in the Kitchen* (1952), includes *South Wind* (1917) and *Old Calabria* (1915).

Robert P. DOWNES, Ll.D., edited *Great Thoughts from Master Minds*, a weekly compendium of reprinted stories, essays, and quotable quotations, price sixpence.

In his novels and his memoirs, Ford Madox FORD (1873–1939) created some of the best English fiction of the twentieth century. He was also a poet and an inspired editor. At the time of his collaborations with Conrad, however, his list of publications was still short. For consistency's sake, he is called Ford throughout this edition, even though he did not change his surname from Hueffer until 1919.

Ada Nemesis GALSWORTHY, born Ada Pearson (1864–1956), was adopted by Ernest Cooper, a Norwich doctor. As a teenager she studied the piano in Dresden; later, she wrote songs. Officially, she remained married to John Galsworthy's cousin Arthur until the end of 1904, when the death of John, Senior, eased the threat of family sanctions.

John GALSWORTHY (1867–1933) met Conrad in the *Torrens* in 1893. The early work was tentative, but in 1932 he won a Nobel prize (an honour denied his friend) for his fiction and his plays. Like the Forsytes, his family was well supplied with money, and he helped Conrad with many gifts and loans.

David GARNETT (1892–1981), the future author of *Lady into Fox* (1923) and many other novels, was the son of Constance and Edward.

Edward GARNETT (1868–1937), a publisher's reader and critic, was the husband of Constance, the translator. They lived at the Cearne, a meeting-place for writers, artists, anarchists, socialists, and Russian refugees. Edward's encouragement of Conrad was typical of his generous attention to new writers.

James Louis GARVIN (1868–1947), a vigorous journalist and crusading editor. He had charge of the *Outlook* (1905–6), the *Observer* (1908–42), and the fourteenth edition of the *Encyclopaedia Britannica* (1929).

Edmund GOSSE (1849–1928), poet, literary historian and biographer, had great influence in the literary world. His autobiographical *Father and Son* appeared in 1907; his critical enthusiasms included Ibsen and Donne. In 1894 he read the MS of *Almayer's Folly*, and in 1902 he procured Conrad's grant from the Royal Literary Fund.

Robert Bontine Cunninghame GRAHAM (1852–1936), socialist and (according to some scholars) rightful King of Scotland, had worked and travelled widely in the Americas. He drew on his experiences in many volumes of tales, sketches, and essays and also in his histories of the Spanish conquest. From 1886 to 1892 he represented North-West Lanarkshire in Parliament; he spent four and a half weeks in gaol for his part in the Bloody Sunday demonstration of 1887. His enduring friendship with Conrad began in 1897.

Howell Arthur GWYNNE (1865–1950), editor of the *Standard*, 1904–11, and *Morning Post*, 1911–37; formerly Reuters' chief war correspondent in China, Greece, and South Africa.

George Brinton McClellan HARVEY (1864–1928), president of Harper & Brothers from 1901 to 1915, edited both *Harper's Weekly* and the *North American Review*. From 1921 to 1923 he was ambassador to Great Britain; in 1924 and 1925, editor of the *Washington Post*.

William HEINEMANN (1863–1920) started his firm in 1890. He published *The Nigger* and *Typhoon*, and bought the book rights to *The Rescue*.

Dr Henry HICK (1853–1932) had been Gissing's boyhood friend in Yorkshire. During the last few years before Gissing's death in 1903, they corresponded frequently. Hick practised in New Romney, not far from the Pent; Conrad may have met him through Wells, another of Hick's friends.

Christina Margaret Madox HUEFFER, the Hueffers' first child, born 1897; in 1919 she became Sister Mary Matthew Hueffer of the Society of the Holy Child Jesus and devoted the rest of her life to teaching adult students.

Elsie HUEFFER (née Martindale, 1876–1949), married Ford in 1894, against her parents' wishes. She wrote several novels and published her translations from de Maupassant in 1903.

Aymeric Eugène Robert, Vicomte d'HUMIÈRES (1868–1915), an author and translator, active in the Théâtre des Arts and close to Marcel Proust, was to die in a hopeless charge on the German lines. Among the works he translated were Kipling's *Plain Tales from the Hills* and Lew Wallace's *Ben Hur*. His proposed translation of *The Nigger* took until 1909 to appear as a serial and 1910 as a book.

Henry JAMES (1843–1916): Conrad's friendship with the Master began with the presentation of *An Outcast* in 1896, reciprocated by a gift of *The Spoils of Poynton* in 1897.

Aleksander Marian JASIEŃSKI wrote a study of contemporary English fiction (Warsaw and Cracow, 1897).

Adolf Philip KRIEGER (c.1850–1918) became one of Conrad's first friends in England early in the 1880s. Krieger proved helpful in many ways, seeking out positions for Conrad and lending him substantial amounts of money. The friendship began to cool in 1897, apparently over Conrad's indebtedness to Krieger.

Edward Verrall LUCAS (1868–1938) was a critic, journalist, and surreal humourist who knew Conrad by way of Garnett. Lucas worked for Methuen for many years.

Miss MCANDREWS, evidently a neighbour at the Pent, but unlisted in local directories.

Mariah Hannah MARTINDALE (c.1841–1907), Elsie Hueffer's widowed mother; before marriage, she had been a nurse in Ireland.

David Storrar MELDRUM (1864–1940) was the literary adviser in Blackwood's London office; he became a partner in 1903 and retired in 1910. Among the first to recognise Conrad's talent, he published a novel himself in 1902.

Algernon METHUEN (originally Stedman, 1856–1924; baronetcy 1916) founded his company in 1889. Besides text-books, the source of the firm's prosperity, he published Kipling, Stevenson, and Maeterlinck; between 1906 and 1915 he brought out six Conrad titles.

Humphrey MILFORD (1877–1952; knighted 1936) worked in the London office of Oxford University Press. He was Publisher to the University from 1913 to 1945.

Neil MUNRO (1864–1930) was a Scottish poet, novelist, and critic.

Henry John NEWBOLT (1862–1938; knighted 1915) was a patriotic poet, naval historian, former barrister, and first editor of the *Monthly Review*.

T. F. O'CONNOR, an Irishman, served in 1905 as Conrad's secretary and Borys's 'governor'. Borys remembered him as 'a tall cadaverous person with lank black hair'.

Bryan PALMES (1851–1930) knew Conrad on Capri. He retired from the Somerset Light Infantry in 1891 with the rank of major.

Sydney Southgate PAWLING (1862–1922) was Heinemann's partner and one of Conrad's first admirers.

James Brand PINKER (1863–1922), a Scot, was one of the first literary agents in London. Over the years his clients included Ford, James, Crane, Wells, Bennett, and D. H. Lawrence. He began acting for Conrad in 1900 and helped him through many financial crises.

Marguerite PORADOWSKA (née Gachet, 1848–1937) was the widow of Conrad's cousin Aleksander, and thus his 'Aunt' – but also his good friend. Her novels of French, Belgian, and Polish life were well known in their day.

Alice Mary ROTHENSTEIN (stage name Alice Kingsley, 1867–1951), an actress, married Will in 1899. Her family, the Knewstubs, had ties with the Pre-Raphaelites.

William ROTHENSTEIN (1872–1945; knighted 1931), notable for his portrait graphics, paintings, and drawings. Max Beerbohm described him as a young phenomenon in 'Enoch Soames' (*Seven Men*): 'He wore spectacles that flashed more than any other pair ever seen. He was a wit. He was brimful of ideas.... He knew everyone in Paris.'

Agnes SANDERSON (born 1875) was Ted's second-oldest sister. The affectionate enmity between Conrad and 'Miss Agnes' began around 1894, the time of his first visit to the boisterous household at Elstree.

Edward Lancelot ('Ted') SANDERSON (1867–1939) took passage in the *Torrens* in 1893; on that voyage, Conrad read him a draft of *Almayer's Folly*. Sanderson taught at Elstree, his family's preparatory school in Hertfordshire. After service in the Boer War he remained in Africa, first in Johannesburg then in Nairobi, where he served as Town Clerk; he returned in 1910 to be Headmaster of Elstree.

Helen Mary SANDERSON (née Watson, c.1874–1967) married Ted in 1898. She was a Scotswoman full of moral and intellectual vigour.

Katherine Susan SANDERSON (née Oldfield, c. 1843–1921) was Ted's mother; according to the dedication of *The Mirror of the Sea*, her 'warm welcome and gracious hospitality ... cheered the first dark days' of Conrad's life ashore. As well as concerning herself with his well-being, she encouraged his development as a writer.

Count Zygmunt SZEMBEK (1844–1907), a Polish aristocrat, lived in Italy for his health. One of the Count's experiences in Naples gave Conrad the material for 'Il Conde' (*A Set of Six*).

Thomas Fisher UNWIN (1848–1935) published *Almayer's Folly*, *An Outcast of the Islands*, and *Tales of Unrest*. Neither his business practices nor his adherence to the Liberal party endeared him to Conrad.

Kazimierz WALISZEWSKI (1849–1935), a Polish historian living in Paris, wrote an article on Conrad. Some of Conrad's letters to him are in French, some in Polish.

Henry Brereton Marriott WATSON (1863–1921), born in Australia and educated in New Zealand, was an industrious novelist and journalist. He had worked for *Black and White*, *Pall Mall Gazette*, and Henley's *National Observer*.

Deshler WELCH (1854–1920), journalist and author, worked for the New York *Tribune* and founded *Theatre Magazine*.

Herbert George WELLS (1866–1946) began his friendship with Conrad with anonymous reviews of *Almayer's Folly* and *An Outcast*. They were good friends for over ten years, and Conrad liked the scientific romances such as *The Invisible Man* and *The Time Machine*, but their differing social, literary, and political ideas led to an estrangement.

Jane WELLS (née Amy Catherine Robbins, 1872–1927) had been H. G. Wells's student and became his second wife. A collection of her writings appeared posthumously.

EDITORIAL PROCEDURES

Hoping to balance the comfort of the reader against the requirements of the scholar, we have adopted the following conventions:

1. The texts stay faithful to Conrad's spelling, accentuation, and punctuation, but letters missing from within words are supplied in square brackets. Rather than use *sic*, we mark words that might be taken as misprints with an asterisk. Missing apostrophes are not restored.

2. Where absolutely necessary to the sense, missing pronouns and auxiliary verbs are also supplied in brackets. Gaps in the text, such as those caused by damage to the MS, appear thus: [...]. [?] marks a doubtful reading.

3. Again when sense dictates, full-stops are tacitly provided and quotation marks completed; words apparently repeated by accident have been deleted. A list of silent emendations will be found at the end of the volume.

4. Especially in pronouns, Conrad used capitals more profusely than English writers of his time. We preserve his usage, but distinguishing between upper and lower case must often be a matter of judgment rather than certainty. The same is true of locating paragraph breaks.

5. For the letters in French we observe the same conventions, but use square brackets and asterisks more sparingly. Conrad's erratic accentuation we leave as it is, except in texts from *L.fr.*, where some presumed misprints or misreadings have been changed.

6. For the convenience of those who do not read the letters in sequence, information in footnotes may appear more than once.

7. Although he kept the surname Hueffer until 1919, Conrad's collaborator is called Ford Madox Ford throughout the edition. His first wife (divorced before the change of name) appears as Elsie Hueffer, and the couple as the Hueffers.

8. American readers should note that Conrad used the British system of abbreviating dates; thus 3.6 would mean 3 June, not 6 March.

9. In this and subsequent volumes the Nonesuch rather than the less reliable Bobbs-Merrill edition of the letters to Garnett provides the copy-text when no manuscript is available.

10. This edition collects all available letters, but only the more interesting telegrams; references to most others appear in the notes.

11. In the provenance headings, letters that have appeared only in microfilmed dissertations or as disjointed fragments in books or articles are described as unpublished. Letters appearing in fuller but still incomplete form are described as published in part.

12. The heading TS/MS denotes a typed letter in which passages other than the salutation or farewell are handwritten.

Thanks to variations in wording and lay-out, headings on Conrad's stationery offer help in placing undated letters. The earliest Pent stationery associated with the present volume is type nine; for ease of reference, however, we list all the letterheads that include KENT in the address.

Type twelve was printed on paper measuring 260 × 230 mm and watermarked EXCELSIOR FINE; the paper for all other types measures 175 × 113 mm and is watermarked ORIGINAL ROCKLEIGH MILL.

Cancelled letterheads used on visits to London and after the move to Someries are not recorded in the text of the letters but have been taken into account when establishing the following periods:

Type nine: 5 November 1902 to late June or early July 1903

Type ten: 8 July 1903 to 31 December 1903

Type eleven: 21 March 1904 to 3 September 1904; 29 May 1905

Type twelve: 19 September 1904 to 15 July 1905; 20 and 22 October
    1905; 24? June 1906 to late September 1906

Type thirteen: 19 July 1905 to 2 November 1905

Type fourteen: 10 November 1905 to early June 1906

Type fifteen: 4 October 1906 to 10 October 1907

Someries letterheads can also be dated:

Type one: 24 October 1907 to March 1908 on paper watermarked
    LONDON CONQUEROR:

SOMERIES,

LUTON, BEDS.

In later types, SOMERIES is farther to the right, and the paper is water-marked J. S. & CO. ORIGINAL HARD SIZED

Type	Special features	Angle of STATION	Comma after STANFORD	Alignments: railway	Alignments: address
Six		60°	Yes	JUNCTION begins over stop between E and R	Comma over T of KENT, P over A
Seven		60°	Yes	ditto	Comma over N of KENT, P over A
Eight		50°	Yes	ditto	P over A
Nine		50°	Yes	J over R, under N	P over A
Ten		45°	Yes	J under O, above stop between E and R	P over N
Eleven		35°	Yes	ditto	ditto
Twelve	Larger paper, different watermark	25°	No	ditto	ditto
Thirteen	Address in large and small caps	45°	No	ditto	P over space between N and F
Fourteen	*Station* in italics	40°	No	ditto	ditto
Fifteen		45°	No	J under space between O and N	P over A

1903

To David Meldrum

Text MS Duke; Blackburn 175

[letterhead: Pent Farm]

1st Jan. 1903.

My dear Mr Meldrum.[1]

Your letter has been a rare pleasure. Indeed my dear Sir your message of good will would have been especially prized even if it had come in a great rush of congratulatory correspondence—which it did not. Only one other friend wrote.

And, believe me, there's no mans voice more welcome than Yours—from a perfect confidence in the genuine[ne]ss of your feeling and from the way your words go straight to the heart. I am touched by what you say and by your manner of saying it—and by the thought you've given me on the last day of the old year. And in return writing my first letter on the first day of the New Year I can find no better words than your own in wishing you both happiness: "in yourselves, in your children, in your work". There You have resumed all that may be found in life; and in the sincere desire that it should be Your lot for this year and all years, that other genuine friend of mine—my wife joins me with all her heart.

Believe me always yours

J Conrad.

To Ford Madox Ford

Text MS Yale; Unpublished

[letterhead: Pent Farm]

1903

2 Jan[y]. 1. AM.

Carissimo Ford.[2]

I've been very much so-so (like Kip[ling]'s stories really are) since my return.[3]—A start has been made with Nostromo.[4] I believe it will end in

---

[1] Meldrum (1864–1940) was the literary adviser in Blackwood's London office; he became a partner in 1903 and retired in 1910. Among the first to recognize Conrad's talent, he published a novel himself in 1902.

[2] In his novels and his memoirs, Ford (1873–1939) created some of the best English fiction of the twentieth century. He was also a poet and a brilliant editor. At the time of his collaborations with Conrad, however, his list of publications was still short. For consistency's sake he is called Ford throughout this edition, even though he did not change his surname from Hueffer until 1919.

[3] From a visit to the Hueffers (Elsie, Christina, Katharine, and Ford himself) in Winchelsea.

[4] Cf. *Letters*, 2, p. 448.

something silly and saleable.—As Youth seems to be in a measure.[1]—A letter from M[eldr]um contains the words "selling very well" and contains congrat's and proph's of mat'l pro'p'rity for the N[ew] Y[ear].

Imp[t] Note (And in this connection I would wish to inscribe on the portal of your Palazzo "Lasciate ogni dolore" etc,[2] with clamorous Felicità! for the Ill'ssimo Signore, the Ill'ssima Signora and the Ill'ssime Signorine Donna Cristina and Donna Catarina Del Fordo—together with many osculations for the latter two members of the Ill'ssima Famiglia.)

    Evviva! Evviva!!
    Hat in the air.
    (Intermezzo ends.)

By same post the Rescue[3] is dispatched into your friendly hands for the only real work of Rescue that will ever be found in its text. Our love

                                              Ever yours Conrad

To John Galsworthy
Text MS Forbes; Marrot 157

                                              [letterhead: Pent Farm]
                                              Friday. 2 Jan 1903
Dearest Jack.[4]

Do come. I've been rather seedy in W[inchel]sea and only so-so (like Punch's Kp'ng's stories)[5] since our return.

I hope and wish and believe that this year shall be memorable for all who love you by the triumphant progress of your story[6]—which is not so-so by any means. Certainly not. There's not an ounce of so-so in *your* composition; and out of *its* organism You've been chasing the so-so element in a manner compelling my most vivid admiration.

This feeble jocosity is meant to convey a profound and serious sense of

---

[1] *Youth* had been published on 13 November in an edition of 3,150 copies.
[2] A house as carefree as Dante's Hell is hopeless.
[3] The novel eventually published in 1919. Ford may have suggested some changes (Mizener, *The Saddest Story*, p. 81).
[4] Galsworthy met Conrad in the *Torrens* in 1893. The early work was tentative, but in 1932 he won a Nobel prize (an honour denied his friend) for his fiction and his plays. Like the Forsytes, his family was well supplied with money, and he helped Conrad with many gifts and loans.
[5] C. L. Graves and E. V. Lucas (Garnett's friend) wrote political satires for *Punch* in the manner of the *Just So Stories*; the most recent was in the 26 November issue, p. 365.
[6] A fresh draft of 'The Flying Goddess' (later *The Island Pharisees*).

the efforts you are making and of the results you are *achieving*. Because You *are* achieving. I wait with impatience.

> Best wishes and love from us all.
> Ever yours
> J. Conrad.

PS I leave my little news for viva voce.

To J.B. Pinker
Text MS Berg; Unpublished

> [letterhead: Pent Farm]
> 1903.
> 5th Jan

Dear Pinker.[1]

I am sending you here P's letter.[2]

He evidently thinks of Falk; and if *he* can do something, it is obvious policy to let him have it. You are out of pocket by that story and the sooner you get back your money the better I shall be pleased.

You advanced me £60 for the 24 thou: words or a little more the story contains which is barely £2.10 per thousand; and I trust you can not fail to get enough to exting[ui]sh the ad[van]ce with interest and com[missi]on of 10%. I of course expect nothing more from the story.[3] You ought to get at least £80 for it which would repay you. But the story is worth a hundred—quite. And if so it may be made to cover the premium you have lately paid on my ins^{ce} policy. All I am anxious for is to follow up with Typhoon the success of Youth. For success it is. The West End booksellers are satisfied. I have had reports as to that from several sources. Last Saturday only, a friend going into Bumpus's[4] saw piles of the book on the counter. B[lack]woods wrote to me on N Year's day that it is selling "very well".

Without exaggerating the importance of these symptoms there is no denying that they are favourable; and that you all who have backed me up may yet have your confidence justified. You who came last in the

---

[1] Pinker (1863–1922), a Scot, was one of the first literary agents in London. Over the years his clients included Ford, James, Crane, Wells, Bennett, and D. H. Lawrence. He began acting for Conrad in 1900 and helped him through many financial crises.

[2] From S. S. Pawling, Heinemann's partner, offering to sell the serial rights of any unplaced story (TS Indiana).

[3] 'Falk' was never taken by a magazine; Heinemann published it in *Typhoon*, 1903. It then came to 30,100 words.

[4] J. and E. Bumpus, 350 Oxford St.

order of supporters[1] have the greatest weight to carry and the most considerable importance in my eyes even from a business point of view purely. Of my personal feelings I'll say nothing here except to remark that I am neither blind nor insensible, nor forgetful by nature.

Naturally we cannot expect a fortune out of *Youth*. Mudie and Smith[2] have not yet been captured; but a beginning has been made with the "Trade" and I look upon my position as distinc[t]ly improved.

Now for the immediate future:

1°   I've been turning around *Rescue* to do away with retrospect. A most bothersome task. You shall have the amended copy soon.

2°   Since Xmas day I've for relief been writing a story called (provisionally) *Nostromo* which will do for the Kendal people.[3] Half or so of the MS. you shall have by the 15th *inst* and the balance end of the month. About 35000.

They should pay the £150 offered against the MS. Out of that (after deducting your 10% on the whole) you must keep £30 against my debt and let me have the balance which I need very much. Of course if you can dispose of the thing better elsewhere I have no pretention to dictate to you. This work shall come to you quite clear of any sort of entanglement, as to serial and book rights.

My letters are long. Aren't they? But they don't come thick.

Sincerely Yours

Jph Conrad.

[1] After Garnett, Chesson, Pawling, Meldrum and Blackwood.
[2] Mudie's Lending Library and W. H. Smith's nationwide chain of bookstalls and shops.
[3] John Watson (1858–1928) and his Northern Newspaper Syndicate.

To Elsie Hueffer
Text MS Yale; *Listy* 201; Original unpublished

[Pent Farm]

Thursday. [8 January 1903][1]

Cara e Illustrissima Padrona![2]

It is very lovely to have you both here with the young woman. Jessie is off in ten minutes to Folkestone to get glamorous rubbish for the tree of knowledge which arrived in a small cart yesterday and makes a sort of dark, dismal bower in a corner of the dining room.

Sixteenth is the day, by the force of circumstances.

My suggestion is that you should come on that very day by the 1.6 pm train from W[inchel]sea arriving here in time for the festivities which will begin (with the feed in the Kitchen) at 3.45. This will enable the staff (Jess—Mrs Graham—Mrs Gates and Nellie) to devote all their energies (from 10 in the morning) to the preparations—(cutting of sandwiches, dragging about of tables etc etc)—the time I sit and scowl and the tree (dressed the day before) remains shrouded in the dining room.

Xna[3] to take the head, Borys the foot of the table each before a birthday cake bearing their joined names (But we won't look upon this as a definite engagement if you doubt the wisdom of the step owing to the youthfulness of the parties).

Meantime Ford and I shall light up the tree in the empty dining room.

On the stroke of 5 the portal is to be thrown open and the glory revealed.

Carriages at 5.30.

Then we—the house party shall have a quiet time on Sat: and Sund: while the young people shall fight, scratch, kiss, play and generally behave like an old married couple in the remoteness of the den-pantry. What do you say to the plan? Suggest any modifications you please

[1] This and the next letter refer to a party on a Friday the 16th. If the Delhi Durbar was the current sensation (second letter), the period must be late 1902—early 1903. The only match of day and date is Friday, 16 January; the occasion, a birthday party for Borys (five the day before) and, lest she feel neglected, for Christina—who would turn six in July. Since the 16th was only the 3rd by the Eastern calendar, this could also be a second Christmas party, complete with crackers and a tree. The first letter belongs to 8 January: neither too close to the 16th nor too far from it. (The envelope cited in *Listy* belongs to an earlier letter.)

[2] Elsie Hueffer (née Martindale, 1876–1949) married Ford in 1894, against her parents' wishes. She wrote several novels and published her translations from de Maupassant in 1903.

[3] Christina.

always with the proviso that you are to stay over Sunday. Love to the Padrone. Believe me most gracious Signora always your humble and faithful servant

J. Conrad

To Ford Madox Ford

Text MS Yale; *Listy* 202; Original unpublished[1]

[Pent Farm]
Sunday evening [11 January
1903][2]
The Protocol of the Celebration
(official).   1st Leaf.

My dear Ford

Thank Elsie for her letter which, for all she says, *was* charming.

It shall be as it must be then; it only emphasises your goodness, to consent to rush over for such a short time. The thing would be as nothing in our eyes if Xtina failed to appear with her two faithful attendants. But, indeed, its no lack of hospitable intention but sheer funk that prevents us asking you to come the day (or two) before. First there are the ungovernable passions of the young man which receiving fresh impulse from the proximity of Xtina's charms would make him utterly unmanageable (unless by the help of a leather strap–which is . . . fie!). Then: What would you eat? How would you be attended to? Where could you hide your distracted heads? Already I am warned that on Thursday at lunch time a hunk of bread and cheese shall be thrown out to me at the back door and that I am expected to devour the same in a distant part of the field. Under the circumstances I look to this with a pleasant emotion. There is peace in the field. Peace!—Vous comprenez?

This thing menaces to overshadow the Delhi Durbar. Durbar me no Durbars! What is a Durbar?[3] An imperceptible circumstance!

In the words of Flaubert (when Bovary is married)—"il eut donc une noce ou vinrent quarante-deux personnes".[4] Quarante-deux is too many: thirty two only shall riot inside the house; not counting Elsie, Jessie, Ford and Conrad who shall indeed be like straws in a tempest, and of no more weight, insistance*, importance, substance and significance. God help us all!

---

[1] Baines (p. 273) prints half the letter.   [2] Date from the sequence of events.
[3] A spectacular display of imperial power held in honour of the new king, 1 January.
[4] Actually, 43 guests came to the wedding (*Madame Bovary*, 1, 3).

I've ordered the Newingreen fly to meet the 2.47 at *Westenhanger*. C'est compris—n'est-ce pas? For I fear I won't be able to come and meet you in person. I shan't be back in time from meeting in Ly[min]ge a gross of sandwiches, a hundred and twenty cakes and a large case of chocolate creams. Je crois que je deviens fou ma parole d'honneur. Enfin![1]

Jessie directs me to tell you that you are to come right in (in overcoats) at *the front door* and walk into the parlour where there will be tea and something to eat laid out (I hope not on the floor but answer for nothing).

At 3.40 the Young Lady having had barely time[2] to smooth her plumes shall proceed (attended by the Lady Regent—the Lord Regent is at liberty to swoon for fifty minutes) shall proceed—I say—to the Baronial Kitchen (where the feast is to be engulphed) to receive the guests with the young Cavalier.

Then she takes her arm-chair
at the
High End.

Engulphing by the young princes and princesses of the name of Hopkins, Mills etc etc begins.

The Dames Graham and Gates would come over at two to help. They preside at the flow of tea. The Lady Regent, the Chatelaine and the Chatelain assisted by the Maid of Honour Nellie scout about more or less effectively. But it is *distinctly understood* that the Lady Regent is *not to tire herself out in any way*. What is wanted mostly of her is to shed extra radiance on the glory of her daughter.

Engulphing stops
in the
Natural course of things.
Then
The Young Lady
Arises from her armchair

and proceeding up the table on *her* right pulls a cracker with every feaster on that side. The Young Cavalier performs the same rite on *his* right side.

Feasters don caps out of crackers.
A Bell rings cheerfully!
(It is then Five of the clock)

[1] 'Word of honour, I think I'm going crazy. Not before time!'
[2] At the head of the page: '*Protocol* (official) 2d leaf'.

And the open door reveals tree which has been lighted up by the efforts of the Lord Regent (now recovered from the swoon) and the chatelain.

> Inspection of same—Feast
> for the eyes and Flow of Soul.
> A Bell rings imperatively!
> All sit down.

Whereupon the distribution of presents begins by the young Lady and Cavalier assisted by Nomenclators exclaiming in loud tones, Snippers (armed with scissors) harvesting the bough of the tree with dexterous snips, Burden-bearers carrying large packages with ease etc etc.

> 5.45 pm
> Feaster's* depart in batches per
> Hired wagonette
>   with
> The Young Lady and Cavalier
> speeding the parting guests at the door
> "The rest is silence".

Seriously we hope to have the kiddies in bed soon after seven. It will I guess tire Xtina not much more than just playing with Borys after a journey in the ordinary way of a visit to the Pent. We earnestly suggest that Elsie and Xtina at least should tarry over Sunday if you must go to relieve your sister-in-law in home duties. Our triple and inseparable love to you all, and kindest regards to Miss Martindale.[1]

Yours ever,

J Conrad.

To J.B. Pinker

Text MS Berg; Unpublished

[Pent Farm]

19 Jan 1903

My dear Pinker.

I return you the absurd agreement of the Kendal people. I won't touch it in any way. My position is this: Either they want J. Conrad or they don't want him. If they do they must take the trouble to look over the story which will be soon in your hands[2] and if it suits them they may have it if they stick to their terms as first offered in the communication I

---

[1] Elsie's sister Mary, who would stay in Winchelsea with the Hueffers' baby, Katharine.
[2] Conrad still thought of *Nostromo* as a story of 40,000 words.

forwarded to you some time ago.[1] Your judgment must decide in the last instance.

Let them also know that I will not bind myself in any way which will prevent me from publishing serially elsewhere when it is convenient for me to do so while my story is running in their papers. The clause is impossible. Practically it would tie my hands for nine months at least. It is not likely however that two of my stories would be serialized at the same time. I don't shake them out of a bag with such profusion.

And they mus[t]n't drop me notes asking for photos and biographical details either. I don't intend to furnish them.

Yes. I see that the length is 10000 words more; but I don't see why you say that it is I that *mention it in my letter*. I've sent You *their letter* whence you'll see that thinking they had got a bite from the fish they have sprung the extra 10000. These are business methods which I know well and don't like. 35000 words (to 40) is my length and £150 is the price.

Considering they want both E^{sh} and A[meric]an serial rights the offer is not so very good. B'wood would take it here I guess for £3.10 per thou: and McClure in the States would give a sixty for it serially. I've been in communication with Robert who seems eager to see anything I write. I had also a letter from SS.[2] They are very pleased with *Romance* as shortened for serial and also in its book form. And bye the bye how about the serial here.[3] Is it absolutely no go? *Youth* goes on selling satisfactorily.

Kindest regards
Yours Conrad.

PS As to the Germans make the best terms you can for as to me I had never anything worth mentioning from there.

---

[1] In November: *Letters*, 2, p. 455.
[2] Robert and S. S. McClure of the *Magazine* and the publishing syndicate.
[3] *Romance* never appeared as a serial.

To Ford Madox Ford

Text MS Yale; Unpublished

[letterhead: Pent Farm]

Wednesday [late January? 1903][1]

My dear Ford.

I send you this as directed by the author. Things are bad with me. A fortnight's work is destroyed. It was impossible. But no mattter. How are you? How's your health—how's the "London"[2] and is anything concluded with P.

Will you come to see me next week any day after Tuesday? I need your presence if for no more than 24 hours. Il faut me mettre du coeur au ventre.[3]

You've got a distressful friend; as to my own feeling I would cheerfully die if....

Love to you all

Yours,

Conrad.

To H.B. Marriott Watson

Text MS Rosenbach; *Listy* 207; Original unpublished

[letterhead: Pent Farm]

28 Jan. 1903.

Dear Sir.[4]

What answer can I make to your kindly worded request?[5] The Author's method of work should remain an intimate thing. It is the method of his very life, the concern of every waking moment. I would just as soon think of laying bare coram populo[6] my method of home life—which, I trust is based on nothing less than the sincerity of domestic affections—as my method of work which is based on truth too, of not a very different order: on fidelity—in the words of a writer now dead—"remorseless fidelity to the truth of my own sensations."[7]

---

[1] Type nine letterhead: The placing is most tentative, but in January or February Ford negotiated with Pawling and Pinker (a choice of 'P.'s'), and set about writing 'London' (*Letters of Ford Madox Ford*, p. 17, and Mizener, pp. 82–3); by 3 February, however, Conrad was again at work.

[2] Which became *The Soul of London* (1905).   [3] 'I need to be cheered up.'

[4] Watson (1863–1921), born in Australia and educated in New Zealand, was an industrious novelist and journalist. He had worked for *Black and White*, *Pall Mall Gazette*, and Henley's *National Observer*.

[5] For information about his methods: Marriott Watson intended a series of articles about writers at work (note by 'H. W. F.' on verso of MS).

[6] In the presence of the public.

[7] Unidentified, but echoed in the Author's Note to *Within the Tides*.

I lay no claim to intelligence and imagination, certainly not to the knowledge of the language, and least of all to any special achievement. I've published in the last eight years six books; from my point of view each of them is a bitter failure; but what I do lay claim to is this: that no one who, either in kindness or antagonism, has read any ten pages of my writing, intelligently, can fail to see what I am trying for. The indifferent don't matter.

My conviction is that the general reader does not care anything for method. And rightly so. Why should he (having his own heavy grindstone to turn) bother his head about what he cannot possibly understand—while, at all events there is before him a story which he may reasonably hope to comprehend; and that may even make him forget for a moment the backache of his own special grind.

The public must not imagine that it is a judge. It is nothing of the sort. It is a jury—and it cannot pronounce on the question of intellectual worth or artistic quality. It cannot say: well meant—ill meant; or: this is good—this is bad. It does not know. It has no means of knowing. The appeal is made to its feelings; all it can say is: I like, or I dislike: and give effect to its finding by which the work remains unaffected however the author may suffer.

The crowd, which never dies, is interesting perhaps as a political engine; it is certainly touching by the vast uncertainty of its future; but there can be no fellowship with a great multitude whose voice is a shout—whereas every mute individual of it can and does make his appeal straight to a heart aware of our common fate about which there is no uncertainty whatever.

Therefore the matter of the artists solitary thought cannot be imparted to a public which never dies. However insignificant it may be in the general scheme of existence it has the high power of a conscience and the dignity of an ever present sense of its evanescence. For the rest—one writes for oneself even when one writes to live and in the hope of being read by an immortal multitude.

I trust you'll take this letter as it's meant; as my way of showing my regard for the work of a writer whose name has been familiar to me since the New Review days.[1] I answer your signature—for obviously I could not answer your request. Believe me very faithfully yours

Jph. Conrad.

---

[1] When Conrad wrote *The Nigger* for Henley's magazine.

To S.S. Pawling
Text MS Indiana; Unpublished

[letterhead: Pent Farm]
1903
28 Jan^y.

Dear Sir[1]

Mr James B. Pinker has the sole and complete charge of all my work; therefore what you propose is impossible, especially as my relations with Mr Pinker are of the most friendly and satisfactory nature.

Thanking you for your offers I
am faithfully yours
Jph Conrad.

To Ernest Dawson
Text MS Yale; Unpublished

[letterhead: Pent Farm]
3^d Febr 1903

My dear Dawson.[2]

You must forgive me. I've been rather seedy and somehow very wretched. This means I haven't done anything till I made a start a couple of days ago. I daren't break the current. I really daren't.

Yours was a good letter; but I have [been] so tongue tied that I couldn't even tell you how much I liked it. As to the Ath: review F.M. Hueffer (grandson of Ford Madox Brown, and at times my collaborator) had an idea that it was your brother who wrote it.[3]

No review of any of my work has pleased me better. Fact is—I suppose—that I like to be taken seriously. And when the seriousness is of a laudative kind the effect upon my feelings is simply lovely.

In all seriousness many thanks to him for the good feeling of course but almost more for the wording.

I don't wish to compare myself to a mountain, but couldn't you two

---

[1] Sydney Southgate Pawling (1862–1922), one of Conrad's first admirers and Heinemann's partner. On 3 January he wrote to ask if he could have any unpublished stories (*TS* Indiana).

[2] Ernest Dawson (died 1960), brother of A. J., was introduced to Conrad by Henley and Wells. Captain, later Major Dawson contributed reminiscences and stories of Burma and Australia to *Blackwood's*; he served in Burma as a magistrate and an officer in the Rangoon Volunteer Rifles.

[3] His brother, A. J., indeed wrote the anonymous review of *Youth*, *Athenaeum*, 20 December 1902, p. 824 (reprinted in Norman Sherry, *Conrad: The Critical Heritage*, pp. 137–9). He praised Conrad as an artist whose 'methods command and deserve the highest respect'.

prophets (no harm in comparing you to prophets) undertake a small pilgrimage?

This is no cheek; it is inertia; a dam' bad trouble it is too—a compound of lurking gout and a strange intellectual sluggishness. The weather may be tolerable—some day soon. It would be like going aboard a small coaster moored in some lonely creek, for a yarn; and there is a pair of rooms, of a sort, where you could sleep at least one night.

The River of Cathay[1] is good; it is right; perfectly right; right in tone and in expression. It pleased me much.

Think of the above proposal; and if it does not appear too shocking to you drop me a word an early word. We could find something to talk about while we smoked. It would be remarkably nice of you not to be afraid of my bohemianism.

Anyway and in some way au revoir very soon.

Yours

Jph. Conrad.

To J.B. Pinker
Text MS Berg; Unpublished

The Pent.
Wednesday 4th Febr 1903

My dear Pinker.

I have communicated with you fully because I thought that as between us nothing should be kept back. The result would have been the same if I had answered the man and said nothing to you. It is true that you might have heard something indirectly—things do leak out—but I trust you do not suppose I could be influenced by anybody's offers and promises be they ever so seductive. Now you've got the information you may make whatever use you like of it—the more so that I repeat that I don't think P[awling] guilty of anything whatever except the desire of seeing my stuff placed serially without delays so that he can publish the book.[2] Of our relations probably all he had grasped was that you had these stories to place and that this one was unplaced. This is why I thought of an official notification as to moneys[3]—which will make the thing perfectly clear to the most inattentive.

---

[1] Dawson's evocation of the Irrawaddy: *Blackwood's*, Vol. 173, pp. 222–30, February 1903.
[2] *Typhoon*, which included the unpublished 'Falk'.
[3] Hence the letter to Heinemann, 16 February.

I would be glad to get a form from you. I expected that to reach me before this. Have you changed your mind?

I am writing the *Nostromo* story as hard as I can. I have been very low mentally. Many days have been wasted. The reaction after the awful grind over the End of the Tether was bound to come.

The worry as to what will happen to the *Typhoon* vol: does not help me much. I am anxious to have it out this spring so that the autumn should be clear for *Romance*. The failure of that thing too to be placed serially does not add to the cheerfulness of things. I can't shake stuff out of a bag—as I've said. *Life with, as one may say,* the halter round one's neck is a *well nigh intolerable trial*. I am tired of it.

Yes, I've the revised agreement. I shall send you four or five thous: words at once. Let them look at that.[1] It'll give them an idea of how the thing is being done; and if they condescend graciously to approve I'll sign if you advise me to. But will my signing *bind* these people to take the story when finished? I'll try and see you some day next week. Kindest regards

Yours

Jph. Conrad.

To J.B. Pinker
Text MS Berg; Unpublished

Pent Farm
[6] Feb 1903[2]

Dear Pinker.

Here's the thing. More I cannot say unless I take another day. But I fancy You'll think this sufficient.

I promise to do my level best. After all if the worst comes to the very worst I can always do say 8000 in a month; but I hope to and shall try dam' hard to have the story finished in June.

By end of march there will [be] about four instalments ready.

They must trust me and I shall take care to have a good capable writer (you guess who)[3] so well impressed with the story that even if a fatality occurred he could finish it in a way.

---

[1] A synopsis of *Nostromo* for Harper & Brothers.
[2] A telegram sent that morning (Berg) promises the synopsis of *Nostromo* by 4 p.m. The day before, another telegram announced that Conrad was on his way to see Pinker in London.
[3] Ford.

No doubt in that case there would [be] an abatement in the terms but still you would get *some* money.

But let us dismiss this gloomy view. I feel quite alive.

Yours

Conrad.

Private for J. B. P only.

The letter you could show to S[mith] & E[lder][1] but I don't know how you stand as to the agreement and you have been too decent in this and other transactions for me to do anything to imperil your transactions.

There if they are in a position to raise difficulties I will tell you what I will do:

if you send me the *bound* copy *and* the *short* copy together I will go over the full MS and piece up the *shortened* first part to the *full* MS and that will reduce the book somewhat. More I cannot do—and would not do *that* much for S & E—though I'll do it for you.

As to taking out the arrest of Kemp and Spanish prison part[2] (as they suggest) the notion is too absurd.

Always yours

J. C.

To John Galsworthy
Text MS Forbes; Unpublished

[letterhead: Pent Farm]
1903
16th Febr

Dearest Jack

I held my news just because the thing remains vague as yet tho' no doubt it is very good as far as appearance goes.

We wait for news from the States. Harpers want a serial of about 85 thou and offer about £7 per thou: for serial rights in both countries with £100 for book form in Am*ca* on a 15% royalty.

Nostromo's the thing if they like the synopsis. On the other hand they may not care to take (and begin to print) a story which is not finished yet. Not by a long chalk mark. But their man here[3] says they would risk it if otherwise fascinated.

---

[1] The publishers, who were negotiating a contract for *Romance*.
[2] The end of Part Four and the beginning of Five.
[3] Either McArthur or George Harvey. Conrad visited London on the 11th (telegram, Berg).

Of course I would share my best news with you first of all men, I only waited for their decision which will come by mail. Hueffer had to be told the idea being that he should stand by and save an instalment or two should I be suddenly laid out on my back by gout—say.

Voilà!

I do long to see you—and see you soon. Man[1] has had a beastly cold. It is better now. I have done little very little. I feel curiously unwell; no pain, nothing to lay hold of but a sort of constant bodily uneasiness. I try not to notice it.

If the affair comes off it means 4 months of high pressure—that is the regular production of say 5000 words every week—till the end. I rather think that with the inducement offered I could manage to keep at it. We would take a cottage in W'sea and shift from one place to the other—say twice in the 4 months. I would be afraid of getting stale here as it happened more than once during the Lord Jim trouble. And this thing is worth while taking precautions. It may—with the English book rights —figure up to a thousand pounds, or thereabouts. Pinker who has engineered the offer is more excited about it than I am. Cold resolve (with a vague sense, at bottom, of funk) is my mental attitude.

And so we are waiting. A week ought to do it one way or another.

The story is very thin for such a large scale. Still! I would be able to let myself go . . . But no more of this.

Sorry for poor Sauter[2] but I gathered that this was expected. Jess had a dear letter from Mrs Sauter and shall write tomorrow. Meantime thank her from me for the list of books. It is just like her to keep in mind so kindly what I had asked her for. My dearest old boy do come down when you can.

Always yours

Conrad.

---

[1] Borys.   [2] The painter Georg Sauter, Galsworthy's brother-in-law.

To William Heinemann
Text TS Heinemann; Unpublished

Pent Farm
Stanford, Nr. Hythe,
Kent.
16th. February 1903

Dear Sir,[1]

I desire to inform you that I have appointed Mr. James Brand Pinker of Effingham House, Arundel Street, Strand, W. C. my sole Agent for the conduct of all business relating to my literary work, and I have also for valuable consideration authorised him to receive all moneys due to me in respect of my works. I shall be glad therefore if you will account to him in due course accordingly.

Yours faithfully
Joseph Conrad.

To
   William Heinemann Esq.
21, Bedford Street
Strand, W.C.

To William Blackwood and Sons
Text TS NLS; Blackburn 175

16th. February 1903

[Except for the address, the same text as the letter to Heinemann]

To Smith, Elder & Co.
Text TS Murray; Unpublished

16th. February 1903

[Text as to Blackwood and Heinemann]

To J.B. Pinker
Text MS Berg; Unpublished

Pent Farm.
20 Febr^y 1903

My dear Pinker.

I am surprised at Messrs: Smith and Elder's demand. Anyway you know that were I willing I have no time to undertake a further mangling

---

[1] William Heinemann (1863–1920) started his firm in 1890. He published *The Nigger* and *Typhoon*, and bought the book rights to *The Rescue*.

of the book. Hueffer on his side is busy with his London for Hyde's illustrations.[1] We really cannot give any more of our time to Romance. In any case I would not consent to take out the part they mention. Frankly, it seems to me a very casual suggestion and one which I can not treat with any sort of respect. That part *must* stand in the book form. There's nothing wrong with it—not a bit. It does not drag; and as matter* of fact the whole book does not drag. It is long—which is not a crime—but it is swift enough in reading. Moreover the McClures[2] would not consent to *that part* being taken out and I do not wish to have two versions of our story in book form.

You may also point out the incontrovertible fact that successful novels have been the long ones—always.

The size of the book is no new thing for Messrs: Smith & Elder. They knew they were not going to publish a number of Tit-Bits.[3] I am afraid that our consent to alter the book for serial purposes has given a wrong impression of our attitude towards our work. I shall take good care that no cause for such misunderstanding arises in the future.

Pardon this scrawl. I am very busy on *Nostromo* and snatched the first piece of paper to save the post

Kindest regards

Yours

Jph. Conrad.

To Hugh Clifford

Text MS Clifford; J-A, 1, 309; Hunter (1985)

[letterhead: Pent Farm]

26th February 1903

My Dear Clifford.[4]

I ought to have thanked you before but I preferred to read the book[5] first. I've read it twice, with casts back here and there.

[1] Henry Hyde, who had illustrated Ford's *The Cinque Ports*. For the frenzied production of *The Soul of London*, see Mizener, pp. 82–3.

[2] The U.S. edition of *Romance* was published by McClure, Phillips & Co. (1904).

[3] The first magazine designed for the reader-in-a-hurry.

[4] Hugh Clifford (1866–1941), a colonial administrator, was serving as British Resident in Pahang, Malaya, when he wrote one of the earliest general appreciations of Conrad's work. Later, he was appointed to the Governorships of Labuan and North Borneo, the Gold Coast, Nigeria, Ceylon, and the Straits Settlements. He published many volumes of stories and sketches, collaborated on a Malay dictionary, and produced a Malay translation of the colonial penal code. At the moment, Clifford was on leave between appointments in Pahang and Trinidad.

[5] *A Free Lance of Today*, which Methuen was about to publish.

The book is remarkable—and that it will be very much remarked I have no doubt. For myself I've been immensely interested by that in the book which you alone could have told us. And you have told it excellently well, with vivacity, with admirable touches, with an ease I quite envy you. I should not be in the least surprised if the book did turn out to be a popular success—which as usual would be given to it for what is least valuable, for the mere 'Novel' side of it. Well! and that is an achievement too deserving a word of congratulation. Of course for me 'Since the Beginning'[1] is a much more significant work, of greater feeling, of greater intrinsic value, less of a 'Novel,' more of a creation, better worth presenting. Here on the other hand we have more skill in presentation. A distinct advance.

The fault I would find in a certain immaturity or rather superficialness in Maurice's character. That sort of romantic and adventurous impulse argues a certain depth of character a certain firmness of fibre, a resolution that will stand more than a shock or two—whereas that young man seems as nervous as a cat in his disappointment, in his horror. He is terribly unscrupulous and too emotional to be quite convincing in his emotion. It looks a little as though he were not quite responsible for his actions and his feelings. When one thinks of a Christian and presumably a gentleman, already disillusioned (for you do strike that note almost at once), for nothing as it were, for a half-faded whim, carefully shooting at the Dutch officers and then directly afterwards beside himself with horror at the mutilation of the dead bodies one mistrusts the genuine[ne]ss of both manifestations. In short it seems to me that you make him too savage and too squcamish, in particular instances and too unthinking in general.

Of course, I may have misunderstood your intention. The most intelligent amongst us are very stupid and I don't lay claim to an exceptional dose of intelligence. Moreover you know my opinion—that criticism is a vain thing against a man's conceptions as to life, character, morality and whatever else goes to make up the only truth that matters. Criticism can be only ap[p]lied usefully to facts—which don't matter. Thus I've offered these remarks upon Maurice Curzon (Maurice not Nathaniel) who is a creation (whereas Nathaniel is only a Viceroy)[2] in no cavil[l]ing spirit of fault finding but simply for your consideration as one friend speaks to another in the belief that in the most imbecile

---

[1] Published by Grant Richards in 1898.
[2] Lord Curzon, Viceroy of India from 1899 to 1905, notorious for his loftiness.

remark there may be found a particle of truth—else we had much better all have been born dumb.

There's much to say yet—if only to talk of the pleasure of reading whatever you write. And that's a truth too if rather stupidly put. But it is late (tomorrow in fact) and I am made stupid by ten hours of steady trying to write something that by no effort of vanity I can imagine as giving pleasure in the reading to anybody on earth.

Kindest regards
Yours
Jph. Conrad.

To J.B. Pinker
Text MS Berg; Unpublished

16 Mch 1903
Winchelsea

My dear Pinker

Your news had not improved the gout which has kept me here in a state of great suffering and unhappiness for the last 14 days.

However as to Harpers I don't care much. All I regret is that the bad fit has not allowed me to prepare for transmission to You a considerable batch of *Nostromo*. The Synd^{cte}[1] is out of the question. It is easier for me to make now a story of 75 to 80 thou, which will be I think as easy to place serially and shall make a volume. What I expect is that you will get for it at least as much as I had for Jim in Egsh rights alone viz £*500* (300 serial 200 book). Of course You shall have a free hand with that and most of the MS shall be in your possession by June.

But you must help me to pull through. I've been let in for a frightful expense here coming for a couple of days only and remaining for a fortnight with Doc's bill and so on.

Pray pay in £*30* about to Watson[2] and let me know by wire when the money is in. I am leaving here at noon to go home, the first day I can move for the last 10. I don't hesitate to ask you because under other circumstances I would have asked the B'woods for that much upon the vol of *Youth* for which I had only £150 ad^{ce} on a 1/- a copy royalty. Anyway as I can't ask them now I ask You.

Pardon this abrupt letter. I am still in pain and worried. I shall write

---

[1] In Kendal: cf. 5 and 19 January.   [2] His banker.

you fully and send Elder Smith agreement signed from the Pent in a day or two.[1]

I expect a good working time after the little hell I've been through. Nostromo shall be a first rate story. Hueffer is engaged on his London and sends you his complts. He thinks You've acted as well as could be in re Romance. Pray wire.

Kind regards

Yours J. Conrad.

To J.B. Pinker
Text MS Berg; Unpublished

Pent Farm.
17th Mch 1903

My dear Pinker.

I had your wire on my return home but did not answer till this morning.[2] I desired to consider my situation.

I think my dear fellow that it would not have been either to your advantage or mine that I should accept. I can't scatter my thought here and there. Now I am engrossed in *Nostromo* I ought to stick to it without further change of plan. To try *another* story at high pressure would be fatal to both.

Whereas now I hope to have a *vol* (worth surely some £200) ready in 3 months from to-day. You or yours will no doubt keep your eyes open for the chances of serialisation (worth perhaps in Eng and Am another £400) with my name kept before the public by the Typhoon which is to appear shortly. (I've passed all the proofs.) Then we shall have a sum of money worth having and worth the exertion on my part. I would be able to wipe off a part of my indebt[ed]ness to you, to my bank and have a little left. That I *will* work you need not doubt. I have no other interest in the world as you know.

Meantime, perhaps for better security in case of my death, I am ready to assign to you the future proceeds of *Youth*—formally, if the thing can be done; say for the next two years? As I had in advance the royalty on 3000 copies only, (£150) the book may be said to be worth another hundred, because it will run up to 5000 copies.[3] Anyway if I were to expire you would have everything in your hands.

---

[1] Smith, Elder agreed to a contract for *Romance* on 28 February (John Murray, Ltd, archives).

[2] 'Think it unadvisable to accept letter follows presume you got mine of yesterday' (Berg).

[3] See the PS to Meldrum, 23 March.

I reckon thus that I secure to you the £60 of Falk and the £30 I asked for yesterday.

But my dear fellow you must help me. Last year the "Literary Fund" grant has saved me—but it had just saved me for a time. The burning up of my MS of End of Tether put me back again.[1] It was a peculiarly unfortunate affair since it put an awful nervous strain on me. But enough of that.

However I have no other creditors, except my Bankers[2] who hold a policy for £500 and where my overdraft is now over a hundred. I can't expect them to let me go on for ever. That's why I asked you for the £30 because I must have money to meet my Winchelsea cheques for my attack of gout. I am much better today as you may see from the handwriting though I write this in bed. I am certain now of a good long spell of uninterrupted work. But isn't it awful that besides the pain and discomfort of illness one should have to bear up also against a terrible worry of mind.

What I want you to do is to subsidise *Nostromo* to the extent of £20 for the next three consecutive months. My wife shall start typing afresh tomorrow the batch of MS which is ready so far. As soon as I think that there's enough for a good sample I shall send it to you. There must be a good lot to show the style and the tone of the thing. I promise it won't be long now. The book is sure to come off. Hueffer who is in possession of my innermost mind (and of my notes) on that story is confident of his ability to finish it should something unforeseen occur; and in that case he would *not* expect his name to appear at all. Therefore you will risk but little—unless my reputation is of no value at all. Pray let me know categorically whether *75000* words are enough for a 6/- vol on which we could get a decent advance. For serial purposes I take it 75000 are as good as 80 or 90. I want to concentrate the story as much as possible.

Kind regards

Yours Jph. Conrad

PS From letters coming from the States I see that *Youth* is out there. Keep your eye on the book over there. With the chorus of praise here it may go off very well on the other side.

---

[1] See *Letters*, 2, pp. 428–34.   [2] William Watson & Co.

To R.B. Cunninghame Graham
Text MS Dartmouth; J-A, 1, 311; Watts 141

19 Mch 1903
Pent Farm.

Très cher ami.[1]

I hope you've forgiven my long silence.[2] It is not, on reflection, a very great transgression; seeing that the best of us have but a few thoughts and that of these the best worth saying have a trick of being unutterable—not because of their profundity but because there is a devil that tangles the tongue or hangs to the penholder making its use odious and the sound of words foolish like the banging of tin cans.

With this exordium—c'est le mot, n'est ce pas?—I approach you with the offering of my book whose title-page proof I've just sent back to the Yahudi.[3] It is to appear on the 22^d of April (not on the *first* as the War Office Army Corps do)[4] and the exordium above is a sort of explanatory note upon the brevity of its declaration.

I have been reading again the Vanished Arcadia[5]—from the dedication, so full of charm, to the last paragraph with its ironic aside about the writers of books "proposing something and concluding nothing"— and its exquisite last lines bringing out the all-resuming image of travellers "who wandering in the Tarumensian woods come on a clump of orange-trees run wild amongst the urundéys."

A fit beginning and a fit note to end a book for which I have the greatest admiration wherein profound feeling and the poor judgment of such reason as Allah deigned give me are in perfect accord. Not for me are such beginnings and such endings. I should like to draw your attention therefore to the austere simplicity of the "*To R.B. Cunninghame Graham*" and nothing more—if my conscience didn't whisper, what you will see without any pointing out, that this is not austerity—but

---

[1] Robert Bontine Cunninghame Graham (1852–1936), socialist and (according to some scholars) rightful King of Scotland, had worked and travelled widely in the Americas. He drew on his experiences in many volumes of tales, sketches, and essays and also in his histories of the Spanish conquest. From 1886 to 1892 he represented North-West Lanarkshire in Parliament; he spent four and a half weeks in gaol for his part in the Bloody Sunday demonstration of 1887. His enduring friendship with Conrad began in 1897.

[2] Since 29 November.

[3] Heinemann, about to publish *Typhoon* with its simple dedication to Graham.

[4] Lord Grenfell would take up his controversial appointment to the 4th Army Corps on the first (Watts, p. 142).

[5] Graham's evocation of the Jesuit missions in the 'Tarumensian woods' of Paraguay (Heinemann, 1901), one of the Latin American histories that helped shape *Nostromo*.

barrenness and nothing else—the awful lack of words that overcomes the thought struggling eagerly towards the lips.

Et voilà! It is poor, poor: the dedication saying nothing and the book proposing something, wherefrom no power on earth could extract any kind of conclusion; but such as they are, and worth less than one single solitary leaf in the wilderness of the Tarumensian woods, they are yours.

Je vous serre la main. Tout à vous.[1]

Jph. Conrad

To William Blackwood

Text MS NLS; Blackburn 176

[letterhead: Pent Farm]
19 Mch 1903

Dear Mr Blackwood.[2]

Thanks for your letter and the enclosure from Toronto which I suppose I may keep.

Not being a professional celebrity I am writing to say that if he will promise to send me his photograph, he shall have mine directly I get myself "taken".

I also say that I am gratified—which is very strictly true.

The "Mercure de France" notice is agreeable—and as he reproduces what I have been lately talking at him as to French fiction I am flattered.[3]

Your kindly expressed hope as to my wellbeing finds me alas! with my leg up and exhaling groans still—but getting better. I trust that you have passed unscathed t[h]rough this period of storms and floods and atmospheric horrors.

With kind regards to your nephews believe me dear Sir

very faithfully Yours

Jph. Conrad.

---

[1] 'I shake your hand. Devotedly yours.'
[2] William Blackwood (1836–1912), editor of *Blackwood's Edinburgh Magazine*, published some of Conrad's early work, including *Youth* and *Lord Jim*, in book and serial forms.
[3] The notice came from Conrad's friend Henry-Durand Davray: *Mercure de France*, Vol. 45 (March, 1903), pp. 830–1. Davray complains that too much French fiction is taken up with sexual activities; Kipling, Conrad, and Wells, however, offer 'quelque chose de nouveau, qui a l'attrait du lointain, de l'inconnu, le "frisson des îles"'.

To David Meldrum
Text MS Duke; Blackburn 177

[letterhead: Pent Farm]
23 Mch 1903

My dear M! Meldrum.

I am just emerging from an awful attack of gout. A state of extraordinary nervous irritation from which I have been suffering ever since the beginning of the year was bound to end in something of that kind. It was very bad, but now the worst is over I feel myself able to work.

I am now very busy with "Nostromo: a story" of which I have said a few words to you when we last met. It will grow to 60 or 70 thound words after all; and if the serialization can be detached from the book form, that last shall be offered to the Firm. Such is my wish and only hard necessity places any reservation on it. Indeed if I am ever to breathe freely this year I must squeeze the utmost of money out of that book. I hope I shall finish it about end June.

How is the world using you? The last time I saw You I could not have left a very favourable impression. Was I very mad? That sometimes I am mad there is not the slightest doubt of in my mind.

My wife joins me in kind regards

Always Yours

Jph. Conrad.

PS The act to end of year states 1200 copies of Youth sold here and 500 in the colonies. Is that good for an Author like me? Typhoon volume is coming out on the 22^d Ap: I'll send you a copy of course.

To Ford Madox Ford
Text MS Yale; Curreli (1978)

[letterhead: Pent Farm]
23 Mch [1903][1]

My dear Ford.

I just only begin to pick up. I had two days in bed.

As it was to be expected I found myself in a hole on my return, with a stiff letter from Watson—d'un ton très rogue[2]—indeed. However its no use; he must put up with me up to that point. I've no doubt he will take

---

[1] Contents and letterhead nine supply the year.
[2] A letter from his banker, in a very haughty tone.

good care I don't go beyond. Damn! Anyhow if I can finish N in 3 months I am saved for a time. And if then I can finish Rescue by Dec next I am saved altogether. The question is—can I make the effort. Is it in me.

I've begun to write at a good rate enough for a sick man and I shall improve on that no doubt. And I do not doubt of your assistance in my efforts. You must run down and see me soon.

How goes London?[1]

Pray, can you procure me a life of Garibaldi—a picturesque one? Didn't he write an Auto? I have a vague notion of something of the sort existing under the aegis of Dumas the father.[2] Perhaps your uncle Rossetti[3] may have the book or any book of that sort either in French or in English. Could You borrow it for me.

Love to you all big and little.

Yours Conrad

Oh! for some book that would give me picturesque locutions idioms, swear words—suggestive phrases on Italy. Giorgio[4] shall take a good space in the book. And then the girls too!

Jessie sends her best love. Was lame too for a few days with a slipped knee cap.

To J.B. Pinker

Text MS Berg; Unpublished

[letterhead: Pent Farm]
1st Ap. 1903

Dear Pinker

Many thanks for the cheque (*£20*) received safely to-day. I shall write you about Rossetti's books in a day or two. Kindest regard[s]

Yours

J. Conrad.

---

[1] Ford's manuscript.

[2] Alexandre Dumas the Elder went to Sicily with Garibaldi in 1860, bought guns for him, and edited his memoirs. For a discussion of editions, see Curreli, p. 227.

[3] William Michael (1825–1919), brother of Christina and Dante Gabriel, an authority on English and Italian literature, an art critic, and the former editor of *The Germ.*

[4] Viola, the old Garibaldino.

To J.B. Pinker
Text MS Lubbock; Unpublished

[Pent Farm]
2ᵈ April 1903.

My dear Pinker

Pray send a messenger with the enclosed letter. He is to bring you two books which I trust your kindness to pack safely and send on to me *by post*.

I am going on well.

Kind regards and thanks

Yours Conrad

To John Galsworthy
Text MS Forbes; Unpublished

[letterhead: Pent Farm]
2ᵈ Ap. 1903

Dearest Jack

Hurrah for the end of the book![1]

I am burning with anxiety to see it. Do not delay. I've had gout—it is true—and am still in a parlous state but the book can do nothing but good to me.

What I regret is that I cannot ask you to come with it next Sunday. Our girl Nellie is gone home ill, and Jessie is alone; for even the woman we got to come for part of each day does not come on Sunday; and poor Jess herself is not at all bright and slightly lame too. She would never forgive me if she knew I am holding you off on her account; but then I know how fagged out she is. She has been nursing me and doing the housework practically alone for the last 5 weeks.

All this is very wretched. My work is greatly crippled; on the other hand Harpers refused to accept my story: T.D. Watts (the "*Aylwin*" man)[2] having offered them a completed novel. However somebody else will be made to take it no doubt. I go on at high pressure and the result is atrocious in quality—insignificant quality. Our love

Ever your

Conrad.

---

[1] The MS published in 1904 as *The Island Pharisees*.
[2] Theodore Watts-Dunton, remembered for his Gypsy novel *Aylwin* (1898) and his friendship with Swinburne.

To John Galsworthy
Text MS Forbes; Marrot 158 (incomplete)

[letterhead: Pent Farm]
Tuesday [7 or 14 April 1903][1]

Dearest Jack

I've just finished the MS.

If I've always felt most affectionately towards you for what you are, now my affection is augmented by my feeling for what you have done. I seem to care for you more by all the extent of your fortitude, patience, and devotion you've put into this work of yours. I am proud to think it is you who have achieved such a sustained and singleminded flight of imagination, of feeling and of thought. My dearest fellow I am inexpressibly glad at the end of the reading just as I was continuously pleased as I read.

Don't misunderstand me if I allude to the promise contained in your pages; they are a distinct and undeniable achievement. No doubt of that; and the promise of something more, of something better (though nothing could be more genuine) is like an added charm, another seductive quality of the work as it stands.

Therefore the limited notion of national studies of character absolutely excites me. But of that I shall hear more from your lips soon I hope.

Returning to the Pilgrimage[2] in truth there is no criticism to make except maybe in matters of small detail—choses infinies—that you need not be troubled with—certainly not in writing.

Here's the postman. I am scrawling desperately fast. My love—our love—our congratulations—for you can not imagine how[3] Jess has been interested in the MS.

Ever Your

Conrad

PS Decidedly dear Jack I had better say, non possumus to the artist's dinner. Am sorry.

---

[1] The only MS received during the time of the type nine letterhead arrived after 2 and well before 22 April; 7, 14, and 21 were Tuesdays, but more than a day must separate this letter from the next.
[2] An interim title: Galsworthy also used it for a story in *A Motley* (1910).
[3] Cancelled: 'in her inarticulate way'.

To John Galsworthy

Text MS POSK; Danilewiczowa

[letterhead: Pent Farm]

22 Ap 1903

Dearest Jack

Will you come on Sat or Sunday. We must have a talk about all things.

I am a little better; we got a sort of female slave now in the house. Hueffer has turned up yesterday evening and we discussed *the book* far into the night. His observations were shrewd and his tone highly commendatory.

We are delighted to hear your father is better.

You *are* coming—are you not?

Our love

Allways* Yours

J Conrad

To Ford Madox Ford

Text MS Yale; Goldring 81

[letterhead: Pent Farm]

[April? 1903][1]

Dearest Ford

How are you? Have you slept?

I send you the proofs with my suggestions. Pray note and consider this: on p. 32 Kemp *overhears* Carlos & Castro talking. I've corrected the conversation which per se is perfectly good and proper for our purpose; but in what language are they talking? Surely not in English—and how comes Kemp to understand Spanish at this stage of his adventure? Mira Vd?[2] My opinion is that the thing may pass and will pass with the gen'l reader. But what about some private reader. Let it go—eh? Love from us to you all.

Ever yours

Conrad

---

[1] Letterhead nine: the collaborators worked on the proofs in April, and Ford was losing sleep over the demands of his complicated life (Mizener, p. 83).

[2] 'Do you see?' (familiar verb and formal pronoun). The scene occurs in I, 5.

To Edmund Gosse

Text MS Indiana; Unpublished

[letterhead: Pent Farm]
1903
2 May

Dear Mr Gosse.[1]

I beg you to accept a copy of my last work which I am sending by this post. You no doubt have forgotten, but it would have been exceedingly improper of me to forget, that it was you who have given me the two Scandinavian names I needed for one of the stories[2] the volume contains. And a man nominated by you to the Academy of Novelists[3] should avoid (like C[a]esar's wife) even the shadow of impropriety.[4]

But in sober earnest, that little thing—the little note you have found time to write for me—is remembered very seriously; since it has given me the first hint of a fact pleasurable and important—the fact of your interest in my work.

I am, dear Mʳ Gosse, very
faithfully yours

Jph. Conrad

To J.B. Pinker

Text MS Berg; Unpublished

The Pent 1903
7 May

My dear Pinker

I had no time to write you at length on account of trying to catch the post. But now returning to the Harpers it strikes me that they may yet be of some use for Nostromo *should your other negociation* fail.*[5]

Harvey[6] asked me if *that* story was placed. I said that I thought so but

---

[1] Edmund Gosse (1849–1928), poet, literary historian and biographer, had great influence in the literary world. His autobiographical *Father and Son* appeared in 1907; his critical enthusiasms included Ibsen and Donne. In 1894 he read the MS of *Almayer's Folly*, and in 1902 he procured Conrad's grant from the Royal Literary Fund.

[2] 'Falk': see *Letters*, 2, p. 319.

[3] Gosse was keen to set up a British equivalent of the Académie Française and looked on Conrad as a natural member.

[4] Caesar divorced Pompeia even though he knew she was innocent of the misdeeds alleged against her (Suetonius, *Julius Caesar*, LXXIV).

[5] Although Harper & Brothers were not ready for *Nostromo* in serial, they might be persuaded to take it in book form – as they were. Perhaps Pinker was negotiating with McClure? In any case, Conrad went to see Pinker on the 8th (telegram, Berg).

[6] George Harvey, president of Harper & Brothers and editor of *Harper's Weekly*, was just ending a visit to London.

did not know, you being in sole charge of my work. He said he would see you—(alluding to you in a very friendly manner)—to ascertain how the case stood. He protested a great admiration etc etc for my work. Whatever thats worth I tell you all this for the use of your diplomacy.

So if you should not come to terms here for *N* they may yet be made to take it. The whole thing will be in extracting some money from them regardless of the time of publication. You know what can be done and what we ought to get. I want enough to give *you too* something substantial. The only thing I would like to mention is this:—that for book form here I would prefer an English publisher. Heinemann for choice. Don't be angry at the suggestion. *1°* they did send off the Typhoon extremely well as you may have remarked. 5 reviews on day of pub^{on}. 2^d, and most important, I want to keep them in good humour anent the *Rescue* which, it can't be denied, is again delayed by this work. I feel rather bad about that interminable obligation.

I don't suppose you are uneasy at not receiving copy. Fact is I am going ahead without staying to correct. Directly I come to a check I shall leave off and devote 3 days to revision. Anyway you shall get 15000 very soon and more to follow. The story will be long—as you know—and it requires about 25000 to give a good idea. Believe me I am doing my damnedest to hurry up. Kindest regards

Yours Conrad.

To ? [an associate of George Harvey]
Text MS NYU; Unpublished

[letterhead: Pent Farm]
8 May 1903

Dear Sir.[2]

I beg to thank you for your kind note and at the same time to acknowledge the safe arrival of the History. It is an extremely fine and dignified edition.

By the same post I am sending a letter to Col. Harvey trusting that you will have the goodness to forward it on should he have left London already.

I remain, dear Sir, faithfully
yours

Jph. Conrad.

---

[1] Evidently an employee or friend of Colonel Harvey. (The colonelcy was granted for services rendered to the Governor of New Jersey.)

To R.B. Cunninghame Graham
Text MS Dartmouth: J-A, 1, 314; Watts 143

[letterhead: Pent Farm]
1903
9 May

Très cher ami.

Don't let your dedicatory obligation interfere with your peace of mind. Frankly, I am more than repaid by the satisfaction of seeing your name at the head of my book. It is a public declaration of our communion in more, perhaps, than mere letters and I don't mind owning to my pride in it.

And if you will mettre le comble a Vos bontés[1] you may render me a service by coming to see me here. (I speak not of heartfelt pleasure—cela va sans dire). I want to talk to you of the work I am engaged on now. I hardly dare avow my audacity—but I am placing it in Sth America in a Republic I call Costaguana. It is however concerned mostly with Italians. But you must hear of the *sujet* and this I can't set down on a small piece of paper.[2]

Shall I send your copy of *Typhoon* to the club at once or may I keep it here till you find time to run down to my wretched ranche in the wilderness. Tout a vous

Conrad.

To Edward Garnett
Text MS Sutton; G. 187

[letterhead: Pent Farm]
1903
13 May

Dearest Edward.[3]

Many thanks for your letter. I've read it with attention and I fancy I quite take hold of the thought enshrined therein. But may be I don't. I can be colossally stupid and without any great effort either—I am indeed in that way equipped to go very far.

The bicycle news *is* good news; don't wait for the distant date you fix

---

[1] 'Put the crown on your kindness'.
[2] Graham put Conrad on a course of reading, offered his own perspectives and plied him with reminiscences about Latin America: see Watts, pp. 37–42.
[3] Edward Garnett (1868–1937), a publisher's reader and critic, was the husband of Constance, the translator. They lived at the Cearne, a meeting-place for writers, artists, anarchists, socialists, and Russian refugees. Edward's encouragement of Conrad was typical of his generous attention to new writers.

but snatch a run when the spirit moves you with the shortest of wires for a herald. I am here fixed to slave and groan for months. Harpers got the book of which *not a quarter* yet is written. I am indeed appalled at myself when I think what rotten contemptible bosh it must and shall be. By Jove I am too tired and with a heart worn too threadbare to be honest.

Love from us all to You and your house. If the boy[1] cycles too *bring him along*.

Ever yours

Conrad.

To R.B. Cunninghame Graham

Text MS Dartmouth; J-A, 1, 314; Watts 144

[letterhead: Pent Farm]

1903

21 May

Très cher ami.

Thanks for your good letter. I am glad you like the shorter stories but je me berce dans l'illusion that *Falk* is le clou[2] of that little show.

Of course: Gambu*s*ino.[3] I ought to have corrected my proofs carefully.

The book (Maison du Peché)[4] has arrived and is now half read. Without going further my verdict is that it is good, but is not "fort". For that sort of thing *no matter how good* I always feel a secret contempt for the reason that it is just *what I can do* myself—essentielment. Fundamentally I believe that sort of fiction (I *don't* mean the *subject* of course) is somehow wrong. Too easy. Trop inventé; never *assez vécu*.[5] There is a curse on the descriptive analysis of that sort.

Kindest regards from us both.

Always yours

Jph. Conrad.

---

[1] Edward's son, David.
[2] 'I flatter myself with the illusion that *Falk* is the nail', i.e., the pivot.
[3] 'Fortune-hunter': spelled 'Gambucino' in 'To-morrow'.
[4] By Marcelle Tinayre (Paris, 1902). Watts points out that, as in *Chance*, there is a character named Barral.
[5] 'Too much from invention, too little from experience.'

To J.B. Pinker
Text MS Berg; Unpublished

[letterhead: Pent Farm]
1903
21 May

My dear Pinker

I send you this communication without comment.[1] You must decide and act as you think proper but I should like to know Your opinion.

In haste
Yours

Jph Conrad

To Hugh Clifford
Text MS Clifford; Hunter (1985)

[letterhead: Pent Farm]
24 May 1903

My dear Clifford

The books shall be sent off to morrow (Sat)[2] to Normanholt.[3]

Pray keep them as long as you like; and believe that it is I who think myself highly favoured by the thought and labour you are willing to expend on the appreciation of my work.[4]

I would be made still happier by Your friendly office if I could feel, au fond de l'âme,[5] that it is quite worthy of your generous recognition and sympathy.

Gratefully yours

Jph Conrad

---

[1] A letter from the publisher Eveleigh Nash asking if the rights to *Tales of Unrest* were available.
[2] The 24th was a Sunday.
[3] Tower Hill, Dorking, Clifford's home while waiting to take up his appointment as Colonial Secretary of Trinidad and Tobago.
[4] Clifford was perhaps the first person to write on Conrad's work as a whole (*Letters*, 2, p. 130).
[5] 'In the depths of my soul'.

To Elsie Hueffer
Text MS Yale; Unpublished

[letterhead: Pent Farm]
1903
26 May

My dear Elsie

Jess is gone to London, to see the last of her brother. Before she left she had asked me to write you her thanks for the hair washes which arrived from London, imposingly labelled, and seem to be a "very powerful white man medicine" indeed.

I am at work. Wish to do a little more yet before I descend upon you. Despair of ever accomplishing anything good has dulled my nerves and I plod on drearily hoping for nothing and caring but very little.

Our love to you all.

Always Your faithful and
obedient servant

Jph. Conrad.

To J.B. Pinker
Text MS Berg; Unpublished

The Pent
1903
27th May

My dear Pinker.

I accept your conclusion gladly. The idea did not commend itself to me either but I did not want to obtrude my opinion. I am by no means anxious to have my earlier books republished *just now*. But I would be very glad to get them out of F[isher] U[nwin]'s hands as soon as possible.[1]

The work goes on. You shall have my portrait of course out of the first copies received. Always sincerely yours

Jph Conrad.

PS I suppose that the agreement with Harper's is as firm as if the document were signed? There's no question of looking at the story first and so on. Is there? They must swallow Conrad whole. Isn't that your idea too?

[1] Unwin had the rights to *Tales of Unrest*, the book that attracted Eveleigh Nash.

PPS I hear from Ford M Hueffer this moment in the matter of Gillespie.[1]

Pray impress the interviewer that he should also get some details of *Hueffer's personality* for the better advertising of Romance. Whatever F. H. tells him of me will be authentic but he need not expect much for even vicariously I do not mean to encourage the absurd and debasing practice. On the other hand I want to keep McClures in a good temper. Typhoon sells. I've been shown quantities of repeat orders in the entry book at Heinemann's

To J.B. Pinker
Text MS Berg; Unpublished

[letterhead: Pent Farm]
1903
29 May

My dear Pinker.

I haven't got the agreements, and I am afraid they have perished; a box of charred papers having been thrown away after the lamp accident last year.[2]

Is this serious?

I want to take a reasonable and practical view of things. I recognise also that I am not quite at liberty to indulge my tastes—or rather distastes in the matter of publicity. In view of your effort and of what I owe you already in material help *and* moral support it would be not quite honest of me to refuse to conform to the conditions of the time in which we both are living and working

Kind regards
Yours

Conrad

---

[1] An unidentified journalist: the reference to the McClures hints at his being American.
[2] On 23 June, when part of 'The End of the Tether' was destroyed.

To Ford Madox Ford
Text MS Yale; Unpublished

[letterhead: Pent Farm]
[May or June? 1903][1]

Dearest Ford
I am sorry for your worries. Tell the Padrona I feel deeply for her and that I hate T.F.U. more than ever.[2]
I send you a lot of proofs and revises of Romance. Those Clowes people[3] are overwhelming.

Post here. Love

J.C.

To J.B. Pinker
Text MS Berg; Unpublished

[Pent Farm]
[early June 1903][4]

My dear Pinker
I suppose you'll attend to this. I find that I cannot do the story within their limits—or some other excuse, that will serve.

Yours

J. C.

To John Galsworthy
Text MS Forbes; Unpublished

[letterhead: Pent Farm]
4th June 1903

Dearest Jack
Your stanzas to hand; I am pleased with the news though I don't understand the metre.
For my own part I was just about to write you my not very cheerful news. Nice man Borys has been in bed with a bronchial catarrh which

[1] Ford and Conrad corrected at least some proofs in April; now they are coping with revises. This must be an early batch, however, for it coincides with Elsie Hueffer's publishing difficulties and the type nine letterhead.
[2] Fisher Unwin evidently rejected her translations of Maupassant. They were taken up by Duckworth, however, and the proofs had been read by 22 August.
[3] The printers in Beccles, Suffolk.
[4] This text is scribbled on the back of a note from the Northern Newspaper Syndicate dated 2 June. The note reads in part: 'We have no definite information as yet as to the character of the story [*Nostromo*] ... neither have we a provisional title, nor information as to its length.'

might have been something considerably worse—Hackney[1] says. Anyway he has been delirious for a night or two and has given us no end of anxiety. Jessie, who sends you her love, is very, very tired.

Nostromo grows; grows against the grain by dint of distasteful toil—but it cannot be said to progress. The pile of pages is bigger certainly by three or four every day; but the story has not yet even begun.

I am excited by the news of the novel you are hatching. It *is* good news; for you are a man of purpose and know what you want to do. But what is it that you exactly want to do? That is it—for me—the question. The name of the people suggests the moral shape of the thing; yet I would like to know—to know absolutely—to know as much as you know (or think you know) of what is going to happen to the doomed crew of Forsythes.[2]

I saw Garnett on the occasion of a rush to town a fortnight or more ago.[3] Why I rushed would be too long to tell by means of the hateful stylographic pen.[4] But I will tell You if you are good and come to us directly Borys is out of bed. It is midnight; I can hear the poor little devil coughing pitifully. Its wretched.

From Edward I heard of the new title.[5] I approve it not from taste but from conviction. It is right; by accepting it you are doing your duty by the book which must have every chance. And—a propos—Duckworth was hardly a chance. I am rather glad that some other pub*er* is to have a look in.

Here I break off short with our best love. That child is decidedly worse again to night—and Nostromo *can't* wait now for anybody.

Ever Yours

J. Conrad.

---

[1] Clifford Hackney (1874–1956), a doctor from Hythe.
[2] Galsworthy had already written a story about the Forsytes (published in *A Man of Devon*, 1901) and was now planning *The Man of Property* (1906).
[3] 20 May: *Letters from Galsworthy*, p. 49.   [4] A type of fountain pen.
[5] *The Island Pharisees.*

To J.B. Pinker
Text MS Berg; Unpublished

[Pent Farm]
1903
Saturday
June 6th

My dear Pinker

Many thanks for the cheque for £30 advanced by you for the June month.

You shall hear from [me] soon.[1]

Yours sincerely

Jph. Conrad

To R.B. Cunninghame Graham
Text MS Dartmouth; Watts 146

[letterhead: Pent Farm]
Tuesday. [9 June? 1903][2]

Très chèr ami.

Your Saturday Review fling is first rate.[3] Nothing I liked more since the gold-fish carrier story.[4]

As to Rothenstein's proposal I am infinitely flattered to be drawn by him—and to be drawn in such company.[5]

The question is whether he would find my personality sufficiently interesting.

Après tout, even admitting I *am* deserving, it is not every deserving person that is worth drawing from the artist's point of view—qui est sacré. The other question is: would he consent to come here for a day in a bohême spirit as a sort of wild pic-nic. May I venture to ask him? For—I appeal to our loved Hudson[6]—the wild beast should be studied and figured in its "habitat." Is it not so. Pray advise me on that point. My

---

[1] He went to see Pinker on 16 June (telegram, Berg).
[2] The type nine letterhead points to the first half of 1903, and the news of Borys's illness suggests a date close to 4 June. The meeting with Rothenstein did not take place at once.
[3] His only recent story was 'A Convert': Vol. 95, 30 May, pp. 677–9.
[4] 'The Gold Fish': *Saturday Review*, 18 February 1899; reprinted in *Thirteen Stories* (1900).
[5] Graham's friend since the mid-90s, William Rothenstein excelled at portraiture. Letters later in the year (e.g. 28 July, 11 September, 13 October) show the rapid growth of a friendship and the success of Rothenstein's proposal.
[6] W. H. Hudson (1841–1922) lived in Argentina until 1870. He wrote fiction and many studies of wild and rural life remarkable for their author's knowledge of animal behaviour. He had many contacts with Conrad's circle: Graham and Garnett were close friends; Ford admired him for the quality of his prose.

wife joins me in kind regards. Borys has been 7 days in bed but is up
now. Tout à vous.

Jph. Conrad.

To Hugh Clifford

Text MS Clifford; Hunter (1985)

[letterhead: Pent Farm]

14 June 1903

My dear, good and forgiving friend.

Of course I'll come—tho' God knows how I'll have the pluck to face
you. Sorrow does mend the fatal and ugly aspects of my long silence—
which pray do not take for forgetfulness. I've been in uncommonly
rough water for the last 2 years. So rough that I hadn't the heart to write
and chose to put up with daily remorse. Weakness no doubt—and also
perhaps a sort of "pudeur". But explanations are of no use; I can only
thank you for this proof of unwearied, unrebutted friendship. The rest
viva voce soon!

Yours gratefully and affect^{ly}

Jph Conrad.

To Christina Hueffer

Text MS Yale; Unpublished

[letterhead: Pent Farm]

[late June or early July 1903][1]

Dear Xina[2]

This purse is modest and suitable more to my modest means than to
your native splendour.

Accept it graciously with Conrad's love and his best wishes for your
happiness.

Your friend

J. Conrad.

---

[1] Letterhead nine, making the most likely occasion Christina's sixth birthday, 3 July. This
letter is written in block capitals, as to someone who is just beginning to read.
[2] The Hueffers' first child: in 1919 she became Sister Mary Matthew Hueffer of the
Society of the Holy Child Jesus and devoted the rest of her life to teaching adult students.

To H.G. Wells

Text MS Illinois; Unpublished

[letterhead: Pent Farm]

Saturday. [4 or 11 July? 1903][1]

My dear Wells[2]

The other day I met Edward Garnett who talked much of you: intelligently and appreciatively as to your work and its significance and with a very apparent and genuine liking for the man—invisible as you are in some of your aspects, to him. Still it's wonderful to note in how few aspects! You've conquered him!

He gave me his father's book[3] for You. He handed it to me because I wanted to look at some new stories in the vol: and I had also informed him that you were abroad.

I send it on now. E. G. thinks that the intelligence and irony of the book may appeal to H. G. I think so too. For myself I like these things and even admire them. I think they are distinguished in the right and proper sense. That sort of writing is not found knocking about under horses' feet every day.

Edward hinted (with clear intent) to me that if you could find anything to say of this collection *to the old man himself* any words of yours would be highly appreciated. If any body can speak of irony nowadays it is you; and Dr Garnett suffers from the feeling (true or not) that he is out of touch with the "moderns."—I am having an infernal time of it with my silly stuff. It *is* silly—and I am a fool and the feeling discourages me utterly. However!

Always your

Conrad.

PS Our love to you and your 'House'. Jess is going to write to the dear lady who owns you.

PPS Cunninghame-Graham has been inquiring about you and Your work

[1] A time early in the duration of letterhead ten is likely; this type was first used in dated correspondence on 8 July. A 'new and augmented edition' of Richard Garnett's book came out in May; Wells spent June in Italy (Mackenzie, *H. G. Wells*, p. 179): Conrad would have written on his return.

[2] Herbert George Wells (1866–1946) began his friendship with Conrad with anonymous reviews of *Almayer's Folly* and *An Outcast*. They were good friends for over ten years, and Conrad liked the scientific romances such as *The Invisible Man* and *The Time Machine*, but their differing social, literary, and political ideas led to an estrangement.

[3] Richard Garnett's witty *The Twilight of the Gods and Other Tales*. Garnett (1835–1906), formerly Keeper of Printed Books at the British Museum, was a scholar and writer of wide interests and stupefying erudition.

To John Galsworthy
Text MS Forbes; Unpublished

[letterhead: Pent Farm]
Tuesday [7? July 1903][1]

My dear Jack.

I am sorry to hear of Const[a]bles stupidity.[2]

I shall incontinently write Pawling asking him principally for quick decision. I shall of course say what I think of the book—tho' I don't know if my opinion'll have any weight. If so it would be with Heinemann rather than with P.

At any rate it will do no harm I think.

My dearest and kindest of fellows I am writing for dear life. Theres 23000 words ready and the story just commences! But I want to "faire grand" and meantime — — — — — — — —

I wish I could see you.

Our dear love

Yours Conrad.

To Elsie Hueffer
Text MS Yale; Unpublished

[letterhead: Pent Farm]
Wednesday [8 or 15? July 1903][3]

My dear Elsie.

I am sending You and Ford my caricature by Jacob of Sandgate Artiste Photographe[4]—with my humble apologies for the neglect of the conventional letter to the hostess which was due to you from my gratitude. The sin indeed is great but then the feeling of my gratitude is not conventional and the penitence, here expressed is profound.

Nostromo is the real culprit. I've sent off up to 25000 words yesterday in a storm of toothache. My very neck is stiff with it but I am going on without stoppage.

Writing like this is like riding the whirlwind. The world reels before my gaze. Enough.

---

[1] This must belong to the same period as the letters of [8 or 15?] and [10 or 17? July]; all three carry letterhead ten. By 22 August, Conrad had added 19,000 to the 23,000 words mentioned here; the earliest possible date is therefore the most likely.

[2] Constable had followed Duckworth in rejecting *The Island Pharisees*. The MS was now with Heinemann's.

[3] The day after the letter to Galsworthy, if the word count below is approximate; if the count is accurate, the difference of 2,000 words would require another week.

[4] William H. Jacob, of Sandgate and Hythe.

Our love to you all. Jess & Borys are out for a drive but I am the correct interpreter of their sentiments.

How you get on? You both? And when do You come here? Believe me always your most faithful and obedient servant

Jph. Conrad

To R.B. Cunninghame Graham

Text MS Dartmouth; J-A, 1, 315; Watts 145

[letterhead: Pent Farm]
8 July 1903

Très chèr ami

Your delightful enthusiasm for les Trois Contes[1] positively refreshed my mind jaded with a sort of hopeless overwork.

I forward you the effigy (executed by Jacob Artiste Photographe) of your humble friend and servant. You are not however expected to compromise yourself by keeping it in a prominent place.

Trèves des plaisanteries![2] I am dying over that cursed Nostromo thing. All my memories of Central America seem to slip away. I just had a glimpse 25 years ago—a short glance.[3] That is not enough pour bâtir un roman dessus. And yet one must live.

When it's done I'll never dare look you in the face again. Meantime (and always)

tout à Vous

J. Conrad.

Presentez mes devoirs a Mme votre femme.[4] What of the novel? When is it coming out? I admit I've been struck and excited by your mere hint of its subject.[5]

---

[1] Flaubert's volume (a shared passion) or Conrad's own *Youth*?   [2] 'No more jokes!'
[3] In the *Saint-Antoine*, August/September 1876: Frederick R. Karl, *Joseph Conrad: The Three Lives*, pp. 143–5.
[4] Gabriela Cunninghame Graham, poet, translator and biographer of Santa Teresa. The story of her Chilean origin was a pretence kept up to save embarrassing her family; she was born Caroline Horsfall in 1858, in the North Riding of Yorkshire (information from Lady Polwarth, 1986).
[5] For a taste of Mrs Graham's highly seasoned novel, turn to Watts, pp. 145–6.

To Helen Sanderson
Text MS Yale; Unpublished

[letterhead: Pent Farm]
8 July 1903

My dear Mrs Sanderson.[1]

I do care; and I have been extremely concerned at the news of dear Ted's illness.

I had no idea You were home. I imagined you both and all the children in Africa—for I have thought often of you all. Nothing proves this assertion and yet it is true. I've often thought of you, with shame and yet with confidence—and most of all with affection. The wire 'recovered' is good. But am I to understand that he is coming home for good?[2]

This portrait which, if it had not been for your letter, would have gone to Africa, I send now to You. It is nearer; and if dear Ted comes I shall be there in effigy to meet him.

Thanks for your kind words about the book. If I tell you that I haven't had time, I will not say: to look round, but even to take one unanxious breath, you will understand me. It is the absolute truth; I haven't had the time even to think! And if the book is not utterly contemptible it is by God's grace alone.

Pray let me in your inexhaustible kindness know all the news and believe me, dear Mrs Sanderson,

always your faithful and obedient servant

Jph. Conrad.

My wife sends her kindest regards.

---

[1] Helen Mary Sanderson (née Watson) married Ted in 1898. She was a Scotswoman full of moral and intellectual vigour.
[2] For the sake of Ted's health, the Sandersons stayed in Africa until late 1910. They moved from Johannesburg to Nairobi in 1904.

To John Galsworthy
Text MS Forbes; Najder (1970)

[letterhead: Pent Farm]
Friday. [10 or 17? July 1903][1]

Dearest Jack

Sorry to say I am no better—or perhaps just a little better in mind but still most deplorably crippled in body.

I've been most dismally inefficient all this year. The book ought to have been finished by now. Had it been so I could have existed; now it seems as if the thing had gone too far to be retrieved. Well, if I can finish the 40–45 thou: words in the next six weeks I may yet save myself. The sight of the poor little chap[2] ought to nerve me to the effort. I exhort myself dishonestly to write anything—anything, any rubbish—and even *that* I cannot do just as if I were cursed with a delicate conscience. But no! It's powerlessness and nothing else alas! Let me know at once what you settle with P[awling]. I am anxious.

Ever yours

Conrad.

PS I can't find your new address.[3] Send it on to me on [a] little piece of paper. And pray don't distress yourself on my account—it is the destiny written within.

To Elsie Hueffer and Ford Madox Ford
Text MS Yale; Unpublished

[letterhead: Pent Farm]
Saturday [18 or 25 July? 1903][4]

Dearest Amigo and gracious Señora

At last I write because I am better; I hadn't the heart to write before. It would have been a dismal groan. And you know the tone of my groan too well. Hasn't its dull monotony worn down the edge of compassion yet?

In a day or two I shall write again. The only news now is that

---

[1] This letter must be close to that of [7? July], but a visit or a missing note may have intervened. Six weeks from 10 July, Conrad had indeed reached 42,000 words.
[2] Borys, who had been ill in June.
[3] Galsworthy had moved from Chelsea to Campden Hill to be near Ada, his lover.
[4] The date of Gissing's move suggests a date early in the period of letterhead ten; Conrad's improvement must have come after the toothaches of mid-July.

Gissing has left St Jean de Luz[1] but I shall get his address (he hasn't moved far away) and write to him for advice.

Meantimes our best love to you all

Ever yours

Conrad

How is Christina?

To William Rothenstein

Text MS Harvard; Unpublished

[letterhead: Pent Farm]

1903

28th July

My dear Sir,[2]

I dared not hope for this piece of luck. By all means pray fix on the week-end most convenient to you; the very next if you like. My wife suggests that you should come early; there is a decent train at 11 from Charing X arriving at Sandling 12.50. We only beg for an early notice.

I fear you will be frightfully bored. For reasons too long to explain I am just now more stupid than usual—perfectly *abruti* by the thing I am now writing. On the other hand I can promise to sit still because—like M[r] Joseph Chamberlain—I prefer a sedentary life.[3]

In this pleasant expectation I remain my dear Sir

faithfully Yours

Jph. Conrad.

---

[1] The ailing novelist left St Jean-de-Luz in June: Arthur C. Young, ed., *The Letters of George Gissing to Eduard Bertz, 1887–1903* (New Brunswick, N. J.: Rutgers U. P., 1961), passim. Gissing died at the year's end.

[2] William Rothenstein (1872–1945; knighted 1931), notable for his portrait graphics, paintings, and drawings. Max Beerbohm described him as a young phenomenon in 'Enoch Soames' (*Seven Men*): 'He wore spectacles that flashed more than any other pair ever seen. He was a wit. He was brimful of ideas. . . . He knew everyone in Paris.'

[3] Joseph Chamberlain (1836–1914), the Colonial Secretary, had recently begun his campaign to fortify the Empire with a wall of tariffs. In a speech at the Corona Club, Lord Selborne joked about Chamberlain's aversion to any exercise but the political kind (*The Times*, 20 June).

To David Meldrum

Text MS Duke; Blackburn 177

[letterhead: Pent Farm]
29 July 1903.

My dear Mr Meldrum.

I am neither dead nor as forgetful as it may seem. I have been—and still am—driving on hard with a story for the Harpers. The work may not be as congenial as some I've done before—but the terms are the best I've ever had.

I tell you this because I know You wish me well. Never before had I so much need of my friends' good wishes; for indeed, indeed, I fear this thing will turn out a very great trash!

That's in confidence; but the fact is I find it difficult to sit close just because of that suspicion.

Perhaps you will accept the photographic caricature of a man who however worried has a warm thought for you every day.

Our kindest regards to
Mrs Meldrum and yourself.
Believe me always yours
Jph Conrad

To Elsie Hueffer

Text MS Yale; Unpublished

[letterhead: Pent Farm]
[early August? 1903][1]

see pages: 2.3.6.13.17.21.23.24.28–9.31.34.35–6.38–9.40–1–2.44–5–6–.
Dear Señora.

I've 'suggested' *on the proof numbered 2* everything that occurred to me as improvement.

Your work and Your corrections are *all right.*

The preface is *extremely* good.[2]

I took a liberty with it on p xiii/ Really the second line of the french is not needed.

---

[1] Letterhead ten: the first of two letters about the proofs of Elsie Hueffer's Maupassant translations: by 22 August Conrad had seen the proofs and was ready to recommend the volume to Davray and the *Mercure.*
[2] It was by Ford.

Les hommes du port apercevant etc makes his point perfectly:—for that is the way in which a gossipy *conte* would have been begun.[1]

Also on pp xi & xii I fancy the lines marked should be deleted; it leaves his meaning unimpaired but does not give the story away—which is unfair to M'assant.

Then on pp viii & ix I would do away with the lines entre parenthèses. But if they remain the French reporter did not write *baisait* he wrote *embrassait*. For reasons which I am ready to explain to Ford privately he could not use *baisait* like this.[2] Anyway I think the illustrations unnecessary—même invisible.

We are waiting Your arrival with impatience. I am at work—too slow, too slow! Enough of that.

Our love to You all.

Yours J Conrad.

P S Preface p xv. Instead of *roturier* put *bourgeois*[3] for God's sake! I am anxious to these serious trifles because I want the vol to be noticed in the "Mercure". (or why not *business man* if the other is *man of the world*.)

To Elsie Hueffer
Text Copy, Lamb;[4] Unpublished

[Pent Farm]
[August? 1903][5]

Dear Señora

My sincerest congratulations. It is indeed a first rate translation. Your toil, a very honest and unselfish toil has not been thrown away. There are whole pages upon pages, rendered with an amazing fidelity of tone.

Your corrections are all *improvements* except the one in last batch, I pointed out and one in this p. 148 last par: where *served* is not so good as the erased phrase.

Why not say "carried passengers to" anyway it's of no importance.

Affectionately yours,

Jph Conrad

---

[1] Ford admired the start of 'The Field of Olives' for its careful pacing.
[2] Because *baiser* is much more strongly sexual than *embrasser*.
[3] Several steps up the social staircase.
[4] The original was sold in 1928; Mrs Lamb (the Hueffers' younger daughter) kept this copy.
[5] Written at a later stage of proofing: the book was published 1 October.

To H.-D. Davray
Text L.fr. 49

Pent Farm
22 aout 1903.

Mon cher Davray,[1]

Quelle idée! Fâché! au contraire, votre article dans la "Semaine Littéraire"[2] m'a fait un grand plaisir. Je vous remercie beaucoup.

Ce qui est arrivé est ceci: le journal a été mis de côté: c'est miracle qu'il n'a pas été égaré. Je reçois des envois de cette espèce assez fréquemment,—et généralement je ne les ouvre pas. Ils sont là: puis ils disparaissent. L'autre jour seulement ma femme m'a dit: "Mais c'est en français." Alors seulement je me suis rappelé votre intention d'écrire quelque chose sur moi dans un journal de Genève. Vous m'en avez touché un mot chez Wells.

Encore une fois merci: et merci encore pour la note,—une bonne note,—dans le "Mercure".[3] J'aurai dû vous écrire aussitot mais,—il y a de ces mais qui ne sont pas tout-à-fait ni paresse,—ni ingratitude,—ni insensibilité: mais plutot une stupeur de l'esprit, un invincible dégoût de la plume, une terreur de l'encrier, mon cher, comme si c'était un trou noir et sans fond où on pourrait se noyer.

J'étais en plein travail sur un roman assez long. Je me suis dit: Quand j'aurai fini la moitié du livre, j'écrirai à Davray.

Et voilà: la moitié est faite,—et je suis à moitié mort et tout-à-fait stupide. Je ne sais même pas comment vous dire combien j'apprécie vos bonnes paroles.

La solitude me gagne: elle m'absorbe. Je ne vois rien, je ne lis rien. C'est comme une espèce de tombe, qui serait en même temps un enfer, ou il faut écrire, écrire, écrire. On se demande si cela vaut la peine,—car enfin on n'est jamais satisfait et on n'a jamais fini. Puis arrive un beau jour, une phrase,—votre phrase: "Un écrivain absolument exception-nel." et le cauchemar devient un beau rêve. Puis le doute vient,—jamais le doute de votre parfaite bonne foi, ni même de votre sens critique; mais après tout, on se dit: Davray au bout du compte est humain (c'est dommage); il pourrait se tromper cette fois-ci,—par une exception fatale et unique. Et on rentre dans son cauchemar,—raffraichi, fortifié,—mais

---

[1] Henry-Durand Davray (1873–1944) encouraged French and British writers to know each other better. He appeared regularly in the *Mercure de France* and edited its Collection of Foreign Authors. Among those he translated were Kipling, Meredith, Wells, and Conrad.

[2] Année 11, 1 August, pp. 361–3 (published in Geneva).

[3] See letter to Blackwood, 19 March.

on rentre toujours. C'est comme ça. *Lasciate ogni speranza* vous qui, par amour et par haine, cherchez à donner un corps à quelques ombres sans conséquence.[1]

Assez de jérémiades.

Ecoutez! Il va paraître ici, dans un mois peut-être, une traduction de quelques contes de Maupassant. Ce sera un petit volume dans la bibliothèque verte de Duckworth (Greenback Library) je vais vous envoyer cela. Cela commence par *Le Champ d'Oliviers*, et finit par *Nuit*. Il y a *St Antoine, Mlle Perle, l'Epave, Menuet, La Relique, Le Retour, La Rempailleuse*. Je crois que c'est tout. Mais la chose a été faite avec amour—avec soin, avec dévouement,—et, je crois, moi,—avec un surprenant succès. Le traducteur E. M.[2] (une femme) m'a consulté sur le choix des contes. J'en suis un peu responsable. Vous concevez, il fallait de la prudence, ici! Enfin! *Entre nous*, j'ai vu les épreuves aussi,—mais *rien de plus*. Mon ami (et collaborateur) Hueffer a écrit une petite préface bien sentie, bien pesée, car enfin le public est si bête qu'il faut lui montrer le soleil du doigt pour qu'il puisse comprendre que cela luit. Si cela vous plait j'espère que vous voudrez bien faire remarquer, chez vous, cette traduction qui n'a été entreprise que comme hommage au grand talent, à l'art impeccable (presque) de Maupassant.[3] Et dites moi aussi ce que vous en pensez. Moi qui suis, sans me vanter, saturé de Maupassant, j'ai été étonné de l'allure maupassantesque que l'on peut donner à la prose anglaise. Vous qui connaissez la langue à fond vous verrez que l'anglais de la traduction est parfaitement idiomatique, tout-à-fait pur. Pardonnez cet affreux grimoire. Et croyez-moi toujours le vôtre

bien cordialement.

Translation

My dear Davray,

What an idea! Offended! on the contrary, your article in the *Semaine Littéraire* has afforded me great pleasure. I thank you very much.

What has happened is this: the journal was put on one side; it's a miracle it has not gone astray. I receive consignments of this kind quite often—and generally I don't open them. They are there; then they disappear. Just the other day, my wife said to me: 'But it's in French.'

---

[1] The Dantean resonance goes beyond the familiar words from *Inferno* III, 9.
[2] Elsie Martindale, her maiden name.
[3] The *Mercure* noticed Elsie Hueffer's translations on 15 January 1904.

Only then did I recall your intention of writing something about me in a Geneva journal. You mentioned it to me at Wells's house.

Once more thanks, and thanks again for the notice—a good notice—in the *Mercure*. I should have written to you at once but—there are some 'buts' which are not entirely either laziness—or ingratitude—or lack of feeling, but rather a stupor of the spirit, an insurmountable disgust with the pen, a terror of the inkwell, my dear fellow, as though it were a black and bottomless hole where one could drown oneself.

I was well under way on a passably long novel. I said to myself: 'When I have finished half the book, I shall write to Davray.'

And there: half is done—and I am half dead and wholly stupid. I do not even know how to tell you how much I appreciate your good words.

Solitude overpowers me; it absorbs me. I see nothing, I read nothing. It is like a kind of tomb, at the same time a hell, where one has to write, write, write. One asks oneself if that's worth the trouble—because in the long run one is never satisfied and never finished. Then a good day comes, a phrase—your phrase: 'An absolutely exceptional writer'—and the nightmare becomes a lovely dream. Then doubt enters—never the doubt of your perfect good faith, nor even of your critical sense, but after all, one says to oneself: Davray in the final account is human (it's a pity); he could have deceived himself this time—in a unique and fatal exception. And one returns to one's nightmare—refreshed, fortified—but one always returns. It is like that. 'Abandon all hope' you who, by love and by hate, seek to give body to a few inconsequential shades.

Enough jeremiads.

Listen! There is going to appear here, possibly within a month, a translation of some tales of Maupassant. This will be a little volume in Duckworth's Greenback Library—I am going to send you that. It begins with 'The Field of Olives' and ends with 'Night'. There are 'Saint-Antoine', 'Mademoiselle Perle', 'The Wreck', 'The Minuet', 'The Holy Relic', 'The Return', 'The Chair-Mender'. I believe that's all. But the thing has been done with love—with care, with devotion—and, I myself believe—with surprising success. The translator E[lsie] M[artindale] (a woman) has consulted me on the choice of tales. I am to a small extent responsible for them. You think there is a lack of prudence here! So! *Between ourselves*, I have also seen the proofs—but *nothing more*. My friend (and collaborator) Hueffer has written a brief preface, well-perceived, well-considered, for in short the public is so stupid that it doesn't realise the sun is shining unless you point it out. If you like it, I hope that in France you will call attention to this translation, simply in homage to a great talent, the (almost) impeccable art of Maupassant.

And tell me too what you think of it. I myself, who am, without boasting, saturated with Maupassant, have been astonished at the Maupassantesque style one can give to English prose. You who know the language thoroughly will see that the English of the translation is perfectly idiomatic, entirely pure. Pardon this frightful scrawl. And believe me always yours,

very cordially

To John Galsworthy
Text MS Forbes; J-A, 1, 317

[letterhead: Pent Farm]
1903
22 Augst

Dearest Jack.

The book is this moment half done and I feel half dead and wholly imbecile.

If you want to do your part by a man, for whom You have done so much already, then do not fail to come down here the first day you can spare.

To work in the conditions which are, I suppose, the outcome of my character mainly, is belittling—it is demoralising. I fight against demoralisation of which fight I bear the brunt and my friends bear the rest. All this is very beautiful and inspiriting to think about—and elevating and encouraging and—I can't think of any more pretty words.

Pawling if he's in London shall get my letter to him inquiring about *The Pharisees* on Monday next. I wondered too what was going on—

I didn't write to You because upon my word I am ashamed to write to anybody. I feel myself—strangely growing into a sort of outcast. A mental and moral outcast. I hear of nothing—I think of nothing—I reflect upon nothing—I cut myself off—and with all that I can just only keep going or rather keep on lagging from one wretched story to another—and always deeper in the mire.

We are so glad to hear Your father is really better. Remember us all round pray, as kindly as you know. And do come. The prospect of your going abroad fills me with dread. Why? Nerves?

Do you think I ought to apologise for this silly letter? I do! I do!

Ever Yours

Jph Conrad.

Love from Jessie. Borys expects you daily.

To J.B. Pinker
Text MS Berg; J-A, 1, 315

[letterhead: Pent Farm]
1903
22^d Augst
Saturday.

My dear Pinker.

This is half of the book about 42^{000} or so.[1] I send it as forming only one part, the First, entitled: the *Silver of the Mine*.

I suppose we will have to divide it in two somewhere to balance the other half planned in two parts II^d *The Isabels* and III^d *The Lighthouse*, which then would become respectively III^d and IVth. But where to divide and what title to give I don't know. It must first be typed clear and then we will consider. *Don't* let the typist *number* the chapters, on that account.

I have never worked so hard before—with so much anxiety. But the result is good. You know I take no credit to myself for what I do—and so I may judge my own performance. There is no mistake about this. You may take up a strong position when you offer it here. It is a very genuine Conrad. At the same time it is more of a novel pure and simple than anything I've done since Almayer's Folly.

Of the other half of the book a lot is done, written actually on paper; though not fit to be shown even to you. In fact it is not typed yet. My wife had a bad neuralgia (we suppose) in the right hand and it has delayed the completion of even this part; for as you know I work a lot upon the type.

If people want to begin printing (serial) say in Sept^{er} you may let them safely—for you know that at the very worst H[ueffer] stands in the background (quite confidentially you understand). But there's no reason to anticipate anything of the kind. If I am to break down it will be *after* this infernal thing is finished.

But it's a miserable life anyhow. Have you sent anything to Watson this month? I daren't draw a cheque. But I felt too sick of everything to write you before. Moreover my salvation is to shut eyes and ears to everything—or else I couldn't write a line. And yet sometimes I can't forget—I remember the tradesmen and all the horrors descend upon me. Damn! Try to help me out to the end of this and then we will see how we stand. If half the proceeds (which are yours) do not pay you back in full then I think that out of my half I will be able to pay say one third of

[1] About one quarter of the finished work.

remaining indebt[ed]ness and leave something for myself (after settling bills) to draw breath with. And then there will be nothing for it but to start at once on the Mediterranean story which is contracted for.[1] What will become of the Rescue then devil only knows! Enough. My head bursts with these silly worries. If you call on Wells do come and see me too.[2] Kind regards.

Yours

Conrad.

PS Do you know anything of the date for *Romance*? The proofs hang fire a good deal. And yet—who knows—the story seems very promising. It may do the trick.

To William Rothenstein

Text MS Rothenstein; Unpublished

[letterhead: Pent Farm]
25 Augst 1903

My dear Sir.

Delighted to hear you are coming on Friday.

There are three trains from Char^g X which you may be disposed to take—the 3.22 arr^g Sandling 5.15—the 4.28 in which carriages are detached at speed[3] in Ashford (so be careful what part of train you get in) and arrive at Sand^g 6.9. and the 4.36 which arrives at Sandling 7.6 not a very good train as you can see. I would recommend the first but whichever you choose from let me know and I shall meet you. I conclude of course you are going to stay till Monday. My friend and (sometimes) collaborator F. M. Hueffer (grandson of Madox Brown[4] etc) the heir of all the preRaphaelites (as I nickname him) would be very glad to meet you and may turn up on Sunday.

Au revoir then,
Yours sincerely

J. Conrad

---

[1] With Harper & Brothers: letter to Pinker, 29 March 1904.
[2] Wells lived in Sandgate, close by.
[3] Slip-carriages, detached from a moving train.
[4] Ford Madox Brown, the painter (1821–93).

To the Hon. A.E. Bontine
Text J-A, 1, 317

Pent Farm
26 August 1903

Dear Mrs. Bontine,[1]

I venture to send you this copy of the book dedicated to your son,[2] as a tribute—very inadequate, alas!—to his great gifts which I am proud of being able to understand and appreciate.

Pray accept it as a sign of my affectionate admiration for him and of my profound respect and my gratitude for the interest you have been good enough to manifest in my work.

I am, dear Mrs. Bontine
your most faithful and obedient
servant.

To Ford Madox Ford
Text MS Beyer; J-A, 1, 318

[Pent Farm]
[late August or early September?
1903][3]

My Dear Ford.

Here's the end of Romance. I beg to recommend to you earnestly the alterations and additions suggested in my set of proofs.

From about half of p. 460 I have written on embodying my conception of the end, which, you'll see, is exactly yours with some alterations.

Jack (who leaves to-night) has read with enthusiasm the whole (uncorrected) part. He absolutely admires the whole of the prison scenes and especially the trial. I am of his opinion. He has said several quite intelligent things in appreciation.

I won't bother you with my reasons for what I have done; I have done nothing hastily—and the intention is obvious in every case. Jessie suggested that the reunion with S[eraphina] should be made plain— and (as for the temper of average readers) her opinion may be allowed some weight. As she has volunteered it I must suppose that she had felt

---

[1] The Hon. Anne Elizabeth Bontine (née Elphinstone Fleeming, 1828–1925) was Cunninghame Graham's widowed mother. A descendant of Scottish Whigs and Spaniards, she lived in London and took a well-informed interest in politics and the arts.

[2] To complement the printed dedication, this copy was inscribed 'Avec les hommages respectueux de l'Auteur, 1903' (Jean-Aubry).

[3] Probably after the letter of 22 August (with the PS complaint about proofs and the invitation to Galsworthy), but clearly before the letter about dating *Romance*.

the necessity very strongly. Upon the whole I urge upon you to accept my version, or rather some, version to that effect.

Jack begs that the opening of par^{ph} "*It was rather tremendous*" should be eliminated. His very words are: that the Judge's speech per se, coming at the end of the admirable trial scene has a tremendousness which is diminished by being pointed out. I propose in case you would consider that change that the par: should begin straight away with—"*My dignity*" etc. However, that is an important point. I don't know quite how I feel. I am sure your feeling will be right. Be careful. The thing is too emphatically good to be pulled to pieces casually.

I repeat: I've only written the final scene because it would have not been quite fair simply to write you that something had to be done. This is a suggestion—the shadow of a suggestion.[1] *You* must do the thing yourself.

My love to you all.

Yours

J. Conrad

P S Be assured that I've done nothing casually. I've kept this two days. There's no use delaying any longer. I am sure you will not think that I've been wantonly interfering with quite a remarkable piece of work. Quite remarkable in execution, in conception and still more distinguished in its suggestiveness. I congratulate you.

To Ford Madox Ford
Text MS Yale; Goldring 74

[Pent Farm]
[early September? 1903][2]

My dear Ford

I am sending the revise on to Beccles[3] by this same post. You are right. The awful *it* (which I never saw) vous donne froid aux os![4]

The text goes. Your last alterations are all first rate and perfectly satisfying to my sense of fitness of things.

But there are the dates! Here my dear boy you've not to deal with my denseness. I understand perfectly the feeling which induced you to put

---

[1] The 'reunion with Seraphina' was 'made plain'; the reference to 'My dignity' went; the phrase describing the judge's speech stayed.
[2] The final letter about proofing *Romance*. Since the book, which appeared in mid-October, had yet to be bound, the date must be early in the month.
[3] Home of the printing-works.   [4] 'Chills one to the marrow.'

them there. But you have to deal with the stupidity which will never understand that a mere work of fiction may remain six years in the making. Anybody disliking the book would jump at such an unguarded confession. Make no mistake; no one will understand the *feeling*; they will only see the fact and far from taking it as imposing they will seize on it for a sneer. It opens a wide door to disparagement to anybody minded for that game. I don't care for the best criticaster of them all—but I don't want to see their ugly paws sprawling over the book (for which I care) more than is absolutely unavoidable. In figures it is the obvious that strikes; and I imagine them—some one of them—saying—but you can imagine yourself what a reviewer could say. The apparent want of proportion will be jumped upon. Sneers at collaboration—sneers at those two men who took six years to write "this very ordinary tale"—whereas R.L.S single handed produced his masterpieces[1] etc etc—and Mr So and So can write in a year a romance which is more *this*, less *that*, more *t'other thing*. Moreover we did not collaborate six years at that. We began in Dec: 1900 and finished in July 1902 really. The rest is delay; horrid delay—because we could not get ourselves printed sooner. Why intrude our private affairs for the grin of innumerable swine? And don't forget that they also may say: surely those men have not worked six years at that book! Six years of actual time! Then why this parade of dates? And if they did, well frankly, there's nothing to be proud of: it is well enough—but it is not an epoch making volume. Even Flaubert was not six years writing Mme Bovary[2] which *was* an epoch making volume.

Mettez vous au point un peu.[3] You can't express a *feeling* in two dates. I understand them in the light of your note which truly is not meant for reviewers. It had brought much doubt and some remorse to me; and it has touched me. What do you know,* mon très cher, that I also don't regret that *Seraphina* of the year 1896 which has become the *Romance* of the year 1903.

Il faut garder une certaine mesure.[4] Let it be a 20th century book. *Dec 1900—Sept 1903* it's imposing enough. Too much! Dec 1900—July 1902 is much better for it is long enough for an artistic conscience. And as it is no one will believe that we worked together all of 3 years at this tale. Besides it is pretty well known that the book had been ready for some time. Proof correcting is not *writing* in the sense a critic would look at it.

---

[1] Conrad was very touchy about Stevenson's reputation for effortless adventure stories; see *Letters*, 2, p. 371.
[2] He took four-and-a-half.   [3] 'Get down to brass tacks.'
[4] 'One should keep within bounds.'

I would not object to an explanatory note—This novel written from another point of view by F.M.H in 1896 under the title of Seraphina— became the subject of collaboration with J. Conrad at the end of 1900 after much preliminary discussion and was finished in its present shape in July 1902.[1]

                in italics on the fly leaf at end.

That's one way. But of course it does away with our theory of *welded* collaboration. The dates *1896–1903* also do away with that. That's a trifle. But to put six years to it is meaningless by its very magnitude. Consider the discretion of the *note* or accept my proposal Dec 1900—July (or Augst) 1902. Or nothing at all peut-être.[2] A quoi bon?[3] I've done it once—and nobody cared because nobody's native stupidity was provoked[4]—Ceci est une autre affaire.[5] Let us be even absurdly careful.

                        Yours affectionately

                             J. Conrad

PS   I return the revise after all, to you.

To William Rothenstein
Text MS Harvard; Unpublished

                        [letterhead: Pent Farm]
                                1903
                             11th Sept

My dear Rothenstein.

    I need not tell you what a great, a very great, pleasure your letter has given me. I ought to have answered it sooner; I held my hand however till I had seen Pinker. I hold that an artist should obtain the uttermost farthing that can be got for his work—not on the ground of material satisfaction but simply for the sake of leisure which, it seems to me, is a necessary condition of good work.

    Pinker professes himself delighted at the opportunity of handling your work, and I've no doubt that, so far, he is sincere. What is more to the point however is that he is confident of being able to handle it

---

[1] The chronology is complicated. The collaborators discussed Ford's original MS in autumn 1898; in September they offered Pinker a substantial 'specimen'; 'the last of *Romance*' went to London in March 1902; by 26 November, they had cut 'nearly half of the book' (*Letters*, 2, pp. 107–8, 262, 294, 387, 456).

[2] Such was the outcome.   [3] 'What's the good?'

[4] *Lord Jim* ends with the dates 'September 1899–July 1900' – rather an understatement of the time it took to change from story into novel.

[5] 'That's another matter.'

successfully. He proposes that you should write to him appointing a meeting in his office *Effingham House, Arundel Street Strand WC* on any day convenient to You (except a Saturday).

I would take the liberty to advise that if you have not signed anything with Duckworth you should hold off till you have had your talk with P. It is important that P should have his hands free to deal with the portraits in Eng*^{d}* as well as in the States.[1] For instance—were he to go to Harpers—they would probably wish to publish you in both countries. I am speaking from experience.

Do not think me a vile and base-minded fellow. Pence would not be respectable if they did not help *good* work; and I do not see why astute humbugs should have all the loaves and fishes. Obviously a *worker* can not (ought not) waste his time in being merely astute; but if there be a man who volunteers to be astute for us, why should we stand in the way of such a sound ambition. After all we (and the next rag-picker as well) must justify our existence in some way. Well, let us help Pinker to justify his, in his own way.

Voilà!

I am too busy, too absolutely overwhelmed with the atrocious misery of writing, just now, to come and see You as soon as I wish; but directly I get my head above that sea of troubles then ... Meantime pray gardez moi un bon souvenir. My wife joins me cordially in the expression of my great regard for you. Tout à Vous

J. Conrad.

To H.G. Wells
Text MS Illinois; Unpublished

[letterhead: Pent Farm]
Sat. [19 September 1903][2]

My dear Wells

There is any amount of *masterly* pages. I have not read all of them as you may imagine; and in any case a piece of paper of letter size is not a place, I won't say for discussion, but for even a single remark. Good many observations & remarks one would wish to make crowd upon the

---

[1] A series of lithographs in progress.

[2] One of three letters about *Mankind in the Making*, all of them with letterhead ten. As first in the sequence, this one must have been jotted down very soon after Conrad received his copy. Hans van Marle notes in *The Conradian*, 9 (1983), p. 44, that this copy was inscribed on 18 September.

mind—such is the real "virtue" of the book. I am glad you have written it—uncommonly glad.

Yes—the 'virtue' of the book is great. I feel it even where the force of dissent is strongest within me. Our differences are fundamental but the divergence is not great.—Graphically our convictions are like that

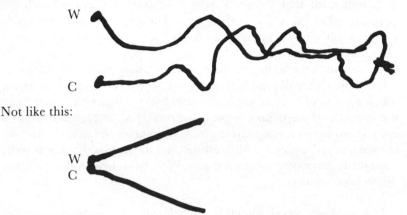

Not like this:

and I cant express better my great respect for Your thinking than by saying that I never feel more satisfied and certain than at the points of contact. We must talk soon. Always yours

Conrad.

To H.G. Wells

Text MS Illinois; J-A, 1, 328; Facsimile, Ray (1985)

[letterhead: Pent Farm]
Wednesday to Friday.
[23–25 September 1903][1]

Dearest Wells.

It was not likely to occur to a daily reviewer who would be more concerned with the text and not critical as to the attitude of the writer. Moreover it is absurd to suppose that the best of daily reviewers could possibly feel the interest I have in the book, a jealous care, as it were, that its appeal should not appear narrowed by any chance phrase.

Practically, for the moment, the thing is without importance. People

---

[1] The letterhead confirms Martin Ray's argument (based on internal evidence) that the book in question is *Mankind in the Making*. Since 2 October, the final date in the sequence, was also a Friday, Conrad must have finished this critique a week earlier.

are concerned with your views and your suggestions—to approve or to combat. I however (with my man in view) have looked at the *tactics* of what seems to me the opening of a campaign on your part. For this is what in the last and most general prono[u]ncement the book amounts to. It is—and as a matter of fact the whole tone of it implies that—it is *a move*. Where the move to my apprehension seems unsound is in this that it seems to presuppose—or even to establish a sort of select circle to which you address yourself leaving the rest of the world outside the pale. It seems as if they had to *come in* into a rigid system whereas I submit that Wells should *go forth* not dropping fishing lines for particular trout but casting a wide and generous net where there would be room for everybody, where indeed every sort of fish would be welcome, appreciated and made use of. Your first few pages proclaim an intellectual exclusiveness—and also an exclusiveness of feeling which (legitimate as it may be) can only serve your sincerity at the expense of truth. However this [is] a larger consideration which I do not wish now to pursue. But practically from the point of view of efficiency an exclusive attitude is always a disadvantage; and in social work especially, since it leads straight to clique'ism to the formation of a select circle of disciples, to a fatal limiting of influence.

Why should you say that you write only for people who think this or that? Who feel this or the other thing? And if you even think so—and so intend—there is no necessity to *say* so. That's what I mean by saying that such a declaration serves your sincerity at the expense of the truth—which is in you to expound and propagate. After all why should you preach to people already convinced.[1] That sort of thing leads only to a sort of high priesthood in a clique and it should be left to people who seek simply the satisfaction of their vanity. It is just to the unbelievers that *you* should preach; and believe me that no one is too benighted (emotionally or rationally) to be spoken to with some effect by him who *can* speak. And that you *can* speak is a fact that can not be questioned. No one's position is too absurd to be argued with. An *enlightened* egoism is as valid as an *enlightened* altruism—neither more nor less. The principle of absolutism did not fail to maintain itself because there is anything absurd in absolutism, but because autocrats had made themselves unbearable through a sheer want of intelligence. And that is the danger. However I am going off the line here. The immediate practical danger of which I am thinking is lest it should suddenly be said: "Ah! yes, the New Republicans—these are the people who look at the world as a breeding

[1] A question also asked of Cunninghame Graham: *Letters*, 2, p. 69.

place". Each System runs that sort of danger and my idea is that it should be minimised by an initial reticence. Generally the fault I find with you is that you do not take sufficient account of human imbecility which is cunning and perfidious. You see this is not criticism; indeed it has nothing to do with the book. This view occurred to me and I put it before you rather obscurely because upon my word I am not well enough to think in an orderly way.

So here I end trusting that your feeling won't be that I had better mind my own business.

I would dearly like a talk with you. If you come (as I hope you will) on Monday or Tues: come to lunch. If you want to be met say so by postcard or wire. And I would like the sight of a few representative cuttings if you don't mind bringing them in your pocket. Jess sends her love to your wife whom she could not visit because she has been nursing me ever since her last call.

Affectionately

J Conrad.

To Elsie Hueffer

Text MS Yale; Unpublished

[letterhead: Pent Farm]
1 Oct 03
Thursday

My dear Elsie

I have been ill—and feeling ill—too. I feel ill yet though I've managed to hobble down stairs. I can not shake off the horrible mental depression.

Many thanks for the book. It is done. No doubt it could have been better done; but that can be said of anything that was ever done— including the creation of the world and the scheme of salvation which last is dramatic enough but sins by excess of ferocity and generally "manque de vraisemblance."[1]

However you've come close to our M'ssant's vérité. What does Ford mean in the preface about Maupassant being or even seeming a rhetorician in the *last sentences* of the chair-mender?[2] It is either perverseness or carelessness—or I don't know what rhetoric is. To me its

---

[1] 'Lacks probability'.

[2] In his Preface, Ford wrote of Maupassant: 'It is an obvious defect of his qualities that at times he is to English tastes (I am thinking of the last sentences of "The Chair-Mender") a rhetorician.'

sheer narrative—sheer report—bare statement of facts about horse, dogs the relations of doctor to chemist and the tears in the Marquise's eyes. If its only one of his little jokes I am sorry that he let himself become folâtre[1] before the high altar. Its the sort of thing that hardly pays. C'est une triste passion. Did he mean the last par of Mlle Perle —by chance?

But any way the suggestion is de trop. The stupid reader will fasten on it—the intelligent reader (if such exists) will think that the limpid expression of (an even exaggerated) feeling is not rhetoric.

The above shows then I think the preface important.

Pray dear Elsie send me a copy for Davray to whom I've promised it. I am shut up or else I would get it here—somewhere.

I can't write any more. I am overwhelmed by the sense of our mortality and it is that—not death—that kills us.

Love to you all. Yours
J. Conrad

Don't let Ford be angry with me for anything. Did I tell you that the 16[th] is the date for Romance?

To H.G. Wells

Text MS Illinois; J-A, 1, 319

[letterhead: Pent Farm]
2[d] oct 1903

My dear Wells

I have neither appeared nor written because I have been gouty for the last week. The attack is not very severe, but I have *felt* start[l]ingly ill with it. Absolutely knocked over. Why? I don't know. It used not to be so.

Drop me a line and tell me how you are. Jessie made a cheery report as to your wife's appearance; at the same time she says she has heard the ominous name of Hick[2] pronounced in reference to something you must not do—or must do. This makes me wonder whether you did not bring from Your holiday some beastly cold or some beastly little ache—as so often happens.

I would like to know that you are in your best form whether you are working or not.

Now I've lived with your book for some days I like it more. What

---

[1] 'Frivolous'.   [2] Henry Hick, Gissing's old friend, and Wells's doctor.

surprises me is to find you so strangely conservative at bottom. In the end I don't discover more points where we are in contact. I felt all these as I went along on my first reading. The divergences which arise from the dissimilar sides of our natures become more definite in the process of thinking as was to be expected because one does not profoundly examine where one cordially agrees. Generally the impression of *soundness* is strong all through.

I must stop. If I were not so depressed generally I would try and write on but I am afraid in my present state to say something too stupid while meaning something tolerably reasonable. There are really one or two points I would like to talk over with you seriously. One of them would be on a matter of tact, or rather discretion in the attitude you take up, which to me seems incomprehensible on *your* part and generally disadvantageous to you. But enough. Most affectionately your

Conrad

To John Galsworthy
Text MS Forbes; Marrot 159

[letterhead: Pent Farm]
2ᵈ Oct 03

Dearest Jack

Do come. I want to see you very much. I have been gouty for a week now; and not only that but I have *felt* ill out of proportion to the attack which was not very severe. It has flattened me down start[l]ingly. This explains why I have not written to you following my wire with a letter as I ought to have done.

The very morning your letter came I was going to wire Sauter[1] inquiring the date of your return. This was because I had just seen Pawling just back from Switzerland. I was delighted to find him extremely well disposed towards the book. Heinemann himself I understand was doubtful not of the value but of the expediency.[2] However that's his usual attitude towards every new work and in Your case is no obstacle to publication by them. Well, I am glad! I am anxious to hear of your interview. P. himself seems to think that a hit is by no means impossible. But we will talk. All our love. Ever your

Conrad.

PS Write or wire train. Can't you arrive on Sat. evening?

---

[1] His brother-in-law.   [2] He did publish *The Island Pharisees*, in January 1904.

To J.B. Pinker
Text MS Berg; Unpublished

[letterhead: Pent Farm]
Wednesday. [7 or 14 October?
1903][1]

My dear Pinker

Can you get me over this. I reckoned upon the American money to save this worry and I still hope the Am^{can} money will not fail us. Meantime it is as you see. I would be worried out of my wits with these things if the great work were not going on steadily. I passed the other week through a period of depression but I am all right now; but anyhow the thing went on. I suppose it's good for me to be in a hole. That I shall afterwards pay for it in one way or another there's no doubt.

I don't send you P II^d yet. I simply can't spare time to look it over; the drama of the P III^d filling my mind. I don't like to send P II^d uncorrected if I can help it. When it appears I *must* then I shall I suppose, but I hang on yet on the chance of getting hold of a day or two. Six weeks ought to see the end of this terrible time. Let me know whether you will (or can) do anything in this case.

Would you like me to make over to you my right in my ½ proceeds of Romance (formally) till my debt to you is paid? I mean any future proceeds. If the thing does well that may be worth something. I see the 20th is the date.

Pawling makes no secret of Typhoon having had a sale, and declares himself very pleased. So much the better since I am afraid they will have to wait for *Rescue* another year. Damn! Kindest regards

Yours Conrad

To William Rothenstein
Text MS Harvard; WR 42

[letterhead: Pent Farm]
13th Oct 1903

My dear Rothenstein.

You are exceedingly kind. My wife is delighted with her Hudson both as to work and the inscription. You have got the man there in a

---

[1] The only October Wednesdays before the publication of *Romance* ('the 20th is the date'). 'A period of depression' looms over the correspondence earlier in the month.

striking way.[1] We are impressed for as it happens we have both seen him in just that way; or, may be, the force of the rendering imposes your conception of the personality. Anyway it is triumphant. Of myself in black and white (I mean without colour) I do not speak.[2] Hueffer prophesied to me how effective it would be—and it is. I am so profoundly satisfied that I cannot help fearing you've flattered me—not in feature Vous concevez—but in the suggestion. At any rate I accept your vision of that head eagerly. The contemplation of it m'a remonté le moral: for you must know I have been tormented by gout for three weeks and brought morally, intellectually, temperamentally to the lowest ebb.[3]

PS/   Have you found that Pinker can be of any use to you? Or is he no good?

To H.-D. Davray
Text MS Yale; *L.fr.* 52

[letterhead: Pent Farm]
24 Oct 1903

Cher Ami
    Voilà la chose.[4] Vous jugerez si cela mérite une ligne ou deux dans le Mercure.
    J'espère que vous allez bien. Moi je travaille—et la goutte me travaille.

Tout à vous

Conrad.

Translation

Dear friend,
    Here's the thing. You can judge whether it deserves a line or two in the *Mercure*.

---

[1] A trial pull of the lithograph published in 1904, or one of the four drawings of Hudson done in 1903. See John Rothenstein, *The Portrait Drawings of William Rothenstein: An Iconography* (Chapman & Hall, 1926), nos. 173–7.
[2] Rothenstein had drawn Conrad twice, once in chalk and once in pastel: *ibid.*, nos. 178–9.
[3] Part of this letter has disappeared: the surviving text (including the PS) is written on a sheet numbered 1.
[4] Elsie Hueffer's Maupassant—or *Romance*?

I hope you are well. I work—and gout works on me.

Yours truly,

Conrad

To Kazimierz Waliszewski

Text L.fr. 52; Najder 235

Pent Farm

27 octobre 1903.

Cher Monsieur,[1]

Pawling vient de m'envoyer votre lettre et je m'empresse de vous dire que je suis tout-à-fait à votre disposition; mais j'ose vous prier de me donner une idée exacte du genre d'information que vous désirez. J'imagine que les détails de ma vie *"avant les lettres"*, si je puis m'exprimer ainsi, ne pourront guère intéresser le public d'élite à qui vous parlez. Elle fut mouvementée, mais obscure. Et puis, franchement, je n'aime pas à paraître comme une espèce de phénomène des lettres. Ma vie littéraire commence en 1895. Elle est honnête, j'aime à le croire, quoique difficile. Cependant, cher Monsieur et compatriote distingué, veuillez croire que pour vous je saurai vaincre mes petites répugnances à l'endroit de la publicité. Le sacrifice d'une lubie sans importance est bien peu de chose à donner pour une étude de votre main!

Veuillez recevoir, cher Monsieur, aussi amicalement que possible, l'assurance de ma profonde estime pour votre personne et de mon admiration la plus vive pour votre oeuvre.

Joseph Conrad.

(Korzeniowski).

P.S.—Je rouvre ceci car je viens de recevoir votre bonne et aimable lettre. J'explique que je ne suis pas en ce moment chez moi (à l'addresse d'en tête) mais chez un ami[2] ou votre lettre m'a suivi avec un retard d'un jour.

Je vais donc vous envoyer dans la huitaine une page de notes. Quand* à la bibliographie, le plus court, si vous le permettez, serait de vous faire parvenir les volumes dont vous manquez. Ci-jointe une petite liste de la grrrande! oeuvre. Biffez les titres des volumes que vous connaissez et renvoyez moi ce bout de papier. Oui! Heinemann est charmant; et dans

---

[1] A Polish historian (1849–1935), living in Paris, who wanted to write an article on Conrad. Some of Conrad's letters to him are in French, some in Polish.

[2] He returned from a visit to the Hueffers c. 2 November.

leurs relations avec moi, ils ont été d'une délicatesse hors du commun.[1]
J'aime à le dire. Bien à vous.

J. C. K.

Translation

Dear Sir,

Pawling has just sent me your letter, and I hasten to tell you I am
entirely at your disposition; but I venture to ask you to give me an exact
idea of the kind of information you want. I imagine that the details of my
life 'before literature', if I may express myself thus, can scarcely interest
the elite public to which you speak. My life was eventful, but humble.
And then, frankly, I do not like to appear as a kind of literary
phenomenon. My literary life begins in 1895. It is respectable, I like to
believe, yet difficult. However, dear sir and distinguished compatriot,
please be assured that for you I shall learn how to conquer my slight
repugnance where publicity is involved. The sacrifice of an unimportant
whim is a very little thing to give for a study from your hand!

Please, dear sir, accept as amicably as possible the assurance of my
profound regard for you and my most lively admiration for your work.

Joseph Conrad.
(Korzeniowski).

P.S.—I am reopening this for I have just received your kind and good
letter. I must explain that I am not home now (at the above address),
but at a friend's house where your letter has been forwarded with a day's
delay.

In about a week, then, I shall send you a page of notes. As for the
bibliography, the shortest way, if you will allow it, would be to forward
to you the volumes you lack. Herewith is a brief list of the grrreat! work.
Cross out the titles of the volumes you know and return this scrap of
paper to me. Yes! Heinemann is charming; and in their relations with
me, they have been unusually delicate. I am pleased to say it.

Yours truly,
J. C. K.

---

[1] William Heinemann (1863–1920) started the firm in 1890; Conrad usually dealt with
S. S. Pawling, his partner.

To John Galsworthy
Text MS Forbes; Unpublished

[letterhead: Pent Farm]
1st Nov 1903.

Dearest Jack

You are very good to all my neglects omissions and abominations.

I think that the terms arranged with P[awling] are fair. The royalties are decent; but the best feature is the limit of time. That is really a master-stroke on which I congratulate You. It may save no end of worry in the future—that *certain* future which you *are* to have.

All our loves to you. We think of you standing before a desk in an immense room with a lot of glass panes all round—creating creating. O! lucky youth!

I grow more and more funky but there grows also the courage of desperation within me. No more now.

Ever Yours

Jph. Conrad.

Reviews of R. coming in. The Daily News is really yum-yum! The Man^ㅜ Guardⁿ heavenly![1] Even the Times is as friendly as Short & Codlin rolled into one.[2]

Later.

PS Pray tell Mrs Galsworthy that I am simply delighted to hear of Yvette in English.[3] Can I have a sight of her? I ask it as a favour with great earnestness and infinite curiosity. I leave the request however to Youre* discretion. I am glad to hear you've dropped the nom de guerre.[4] Very glad! The manner of doing it highly approved. I am anxious to see *The Pharisees* in print. You are quite right. The book *is* done. No doubt about it.

---

[1] The *Daily News* (30 October) offered just what Conrad wanted: the reviewer laid the ghost of Stevenson, who 'would have rejoiced at the skill with which the old properties are again handled', yet recognized a serious purpose— the 'analysis of moments of great trial ... as we found in "Typhoon" and "The *Narcissus*"'. The *Manchester Guardian* (28 October) called *Romance* 'a very fresh and beautiful story'.

[2] 'Codlin's the friend, not Short': *The Old Curiosity Shop*, ch. 19. The reviewer for *The Times Literary Supplement*, 30 October, p. 312, expressed 'heartfelt gratitude' for the authors' powers of entertainment.

[3] In a purely legal sense, Ada was still married to John's cousin Arthur Galsworthy. Her translations from Maupassant appeared in 1904, with a preface by Conrad.

[4] 'John Sinjohn': Galsworthy had now started to write under his own name.

To Elsie Hueffer
Text MS Yale; Unpublished

[letterhead: Pent Farm]

2 Nov. 1903

My dear Elsie

I trust You were not too tired, and that you did not get wet. I arrived home just as the first drops began to fall.

Found waiting for me the Ac^y and the Times notices. That last is I guess perfectly satisfactory to Ford. The Academy man has made up his mind I should not collaborate.[1] He must be one of my correspondents in the time of the Inheritors. Enfin!

The visit to You has started me off again with my stuff. Many thanks for all your kindnesses. Pray tell Ford that I remember the N[orth] A[merican] Review and shall send it with the clippings this afternoon. Our love.

Yours most faithfully

J. Conrad.

To J.B. Pinker
Text MS Berg; Unpublished

[letterhead: Pent Farm]

1903

Wednesday. [4? November][2]

My dear Pinker.

A thousand apologies for not answering Your two notes sooner.

As to account rendered by McClure—that is correct.

As to *N*. Yes. I feel that another six weeks will do it. Still; could you wait another week before giving positive assurance to Harpers. I intend to be done with it all by Xmas if possible.

Are you very sick of me?

I assure you I am half off my chump sometimes with the pressure of the thing.

We must have a talk soon.

Yours ever

Jph. Conrad.

---

[1] *Academy*, 31 October, p. 469. The *TLS* described Ford as 'a poet, and, therefore, something of an idealist'.
[2] After the appearance of several warm reviews, and seven weeks before Christmas.

Nothing I ever published had such enthusiastic reviews as Romance!!
Have you seen any cuttings? What do you think of the book's
chance?

To Ford Madox Ford
Text Copy, Cornell;[1] Unpublished

[Pent Farm]
[early November 1903][2]

My dear Ford,
Thanks for your wire which has to some extent relieved our anxiety.
Poor Elsie! What an abominable thing to happen to one. Do my dear
fellow give us some details as to the injury. Does it mean the arm in
plaster and other horrors? Is it the right or left arm? Has she got over the
shock? Pray write.

I quite understand that the universe does not wear a smiling aspect
for you just now. As to the silence about *"Romance,"* I fancy you take a
gloomy view. A good batch of reviews came in to-night I think. And all
good including even the Athe'um. I had also the Sketch and Vanity Fair
cuttings. And all the notices are of the selling sort.[3] I do not see that we
can complain very much. The thing is not treated as epoch-making, of
course, but then il me semble we did not pretend to make an epoch.
Buck up. I haven't by any means given up the hope of the thing soaring
into the lofty altitudes of popularity—say 10,000 or so.

The most amusing person is Waliszewski. We conduct a correspondence in three languages. Last note (received to-day) says:—"Il me
semble que je vois de que vouler* faire; je comprends les Tales of U. etc.
etc.: je comprends les *Inheritors* mais je ne comprends pas de que vient
faire *Romance* dans votre oeuvre. Je sens qu'il doit y avoir une expli-
cation; qu'une raison existe—je vous prie instamment de me la com-
muniquer."[4]

---

[1] Made by Violet Hunt.
[2] Conrad cites reviews dated between 4 and 7 November, but, with magazines, official
and actual dates of publication often differ. Waliszewski's plea arrived on or before the
8th.
[3] *Sketch*, 4 November, p. 95; *Vanity Fair*, 5 November, p. 608; *Athenaeum*, 7 November,
p. 610. The *Sketch* applauded *Romance* as 'a stirring sensational story in the fashion
demanded by the hour'.
[4] (The French of the copy is garbled.) 'I think I see what you want to do; I understand the
Tales of Unrest, et cetera: I understand *The Inheritors*, but I don't understand what *Romance*
is doing among your works. I feel there must be an explanation: that a reason exists—I
beg you to tell me what it is.'

It is perfectly serious—but what is one to say? Mind he does not judge, criticise, or disapprove—he simply wants to know. The thirst for the Unknowable (and the Useless) seems to be inherent in man's mental organisation. One would not be far wrong if one wrote—*"Ne voyez vous pas que c'est une bonne farce!!!"*[1] But that would not do perhaps. Also one could write: "Le besoin de manger, de fumer, de boire, de porter une culotte comme tout le monde."[2] But he is not the sort of person to believe in the Obviousness of the Incredible. I suppose the aest[h]etic racket is the practicable answer, satisfying if incomplete. I should think that with the other two we cover the whole ground of our motives. I have been worried with tooth-ache ever since last Sunday.[3] The end of all things is not far off for me. Our best love to you all.

Ever yours,

Conrad

To John Galsworthy
Text MS Forbes; Unpublished

[Pent Farm]
Friday. [6, 13, or 20 November
1903?][4]

Dearest Jack.

Send on the MS as soon as you can and I shall make McClure give it a serious consideration. Of course there's no saying what he may do.[5] I wired yesterday so that there should be no time lost. You must hurry up Your typewriter people. To wait for proofs would not've been expedient.

Ever so many thanks for exerciser w^h arrived this morning. In haste to catch the post.

Ever Yours

Jph Conrad.

---

[1] 'Don't you see that it's a big joke?'
[2] 'The need to eat, smoke, drink, have clothes on one's back like everyone else.'
[3] 1 November.
[4] A speculation: if the MS in question is *The Island Pharisees* (handwriting and the interest in McClure suggest the period), a likely date would be 6, 13, or 20 November, after the book's acceptance, but before proofs were ready. Publication came on 28 January.
[5] A cancelled passage follows: 'Publishers *are* fools. We must bear that in mind always.'

To Kazimierz Waliszewski
Text L.fr. 54; Najder 236

Pent Farm
8 Nov. 1903

Cher Monsieur et Confrère,

Il y a des choses difficiles à expliquer, surtout après coup. Je regarde *Romance* comme une chose sans aucune importance: j'ai collaboré pendant qu'il m'était impossible de faire autre chose. Il était facile de raconter quelques événements sans me préoccuper autrement du sujet. L'idée que nous avions était purement esthètique: rendre quelques scènes, quelques situations, d'une façon convenable. Puis il ne nous déplaisait pas de montrer que nous pouvions faire quelque chose dans le genre fort en vogue avec le public en ce moment-ci. L'évangile héroique de St Henri,[1] cher Monsieur, règne sur la terre entière, et,—vous savez,—il y a plus d'une manière de s'en moquer. Il y a eu des moments où nous étions fort gais, Hueffer et moi, en faisant cette machine. Mais on soignait la technique tout de même. Avouez que c'est bien écrit. Flaubert (un vrai saint, celui-là) s'est bien mis à faire une féerie.[2]

Et la presse y a donné en plein! Le *Times* qui a daigné étendre sur mes deux derniers livres (*Youth* et *Typhon*, les autres "lui pas connaitre") une protection méfiante et grincheuse, en pousse un cri de soulagement et de gratitude. Je dis *gratitude*. Le mot y est. L'article du *Daily News* (special: une colonne presque entière) commence par la phrase: *This is the real thing.*—et ainsi de suite.

Enfin, dernière raison, H et moi nous avons voulu nous faire la main en vue d'un roman sérieux que nous voulons écrire un jour. Il s'agirait d'un tableau comme pivot de l'action d'un peintre vieux et célèbre et des intrigues basses et perverses dans l'entourage d'un grand homme qui a eu son succès, mais qui—justement parce qu'il était un artiste suprême,—est resté incompris. On peut "faire grand" dans un sujet comme cela, dire ce que l'on pense sur l'art qui plane et sur le matérialisme qui rampe dans la vie. Pour cela H est bien documenté par tradition de famille, par ses recherches et aussi *de visu* car il fut le compagnon bien aimé de Ford Madox Brown pendant les six dernières années de sa vie.[3] Tout ceci, cher Monsieur, sous le sceau du secret.

---

[1] A literary evangelist: Andrzej Busza ('Conrad's Polish Literary Background', p. 185, n. 327) identifies him as Henryk Sienkiewicz (1846–1916); in the context of *Romance*, Conrad would be thinking of his historical novels.

[2] In his collaboration on the satirical fairy-play *Le Château des coeurs*?

[3] Ford Madox Brown, his maternal grandfather, also painted him in the guise of William Tell's son.

Probablement le livre ne sera jamais écrit.[1] J'ai voulu être tout-à-fait
franc avec vous.

> Mille amitiés.
> Tout à vous.
>   J. Conrad K.

Translation

Dear Sir and Colleague,
    Some things are difficult to explain, especially after the fact. I look on
Romance as something without any importance: I collaborated on it
while it was impossible for me to do anything else. It was easy to narrate
some events without otherwise bothering myself with the subject. The
idea we had was purely aesthetic: to render certain scenes and situations
in an appropriate way. Besides, it didn't displease us to show we could
do something in the genre that is currently very much in vogue with the
public. The heroic gospel of St Henry, dear sir, reigns over the entire
earth, and—you know—there is more than one way to make fun of it.
There were moments when we were indeed gay, Hueffer and I, while
assembling this contraption. But we were careful with technique all the
same. You must admit it is well written. Flaubert (a true saint, that
man) did set about writing a pantomime.
    And the press has played it up! *The Times*, which condescended to
extend to my last two books (*Youth* and *Typhoon*, the others 'not being
recognized') a cautious and testy patronage, lets out a cry of relief and
gratitude. I say *gratitiude*. The word is there. The article in the *Daily
News* (special: almost an entire column) begins with the phrase: 'This is
the real thing'—and so on.
    Then, the final reason: H. and I wanted to try our hand with an eye to
a serious novel we intend to write one day. As a pivot for the action, it
will deal with a picture of an old and famous painter and the low and
perverse intrigues among the entourage of a great man who has been
successful but who—precisely because he was a supreme artist—has
remained unappreciated. With such a subject, one can work on a large
scale and say what one thinks about the art which soars and the
materialism which creeps through life. For that, H. has a detailed
knowledge, by family tradition, by research, and also by experience, for

---

[1] The novel went nowhere, but the hero of Ford's *The Benefactor* (1905) has written the
biography of a 'great portrait painter'.

he was the intimate companion of Ford Madox Brown during the last six years of his life. All this, dear sir, under the seal of secrecy. Probably, the book will never be written. I wanted to be entirely frank with you.

A thousand regards.

Yours truly,

J. Conrad K.

To J.M. Barrie
Text MS Berg; Unpublished

[letterhead: Pent Farm]

14 Nov 1903

Dear Mr Barrie[1]

You certainly handle my horrid funk with a tender hand. It is only on reading your letter that I feel how sore I was all over, how the least rough (and well-meaning!) touch would have put an end to my ailing resolution. But, unless I am hopelessly incurable, Your words are the right magic to make a whole man of me again.

That's what your letter has done. And now let me thank you for the sum of £150 which, in the sacramental phrase, is safely to hand by to-nights post: as if you had tried to overwhelm me in every way—even to that promptitude which doubles the amount; only that I need have been obviously blind and wooden not to see the care you take that I should not feel squashed.[2]

I would, of all things, like to call and be allowed to extort personally from You the promise that You will not expect too much from my work. You have done so much, understood so much, that you must now continue the same large indulgence to my never-ending attempts to justify the audacity of my existence.

To-night my foot twinges with what the doctors (I suppose ironically) call my gout. I rather welcome these little reminders because they often clear the muddle out of my head. This however is a half hearted sort of affair and will be over in a day or two. Meantime, perhaps, you will just tell me at what time, on what days, one could call for a whole hour, without being in the way? That is now the question for me.

The old time regard could not be augmented, but there is added now

---

[1] The Scottish novelist and playwright (1860–1937): he started writing *Peter Pan* on 23 November.

[2] In 1905, Barrie helped with the staging of 'One Day More', but the present transaction remains mysterious.

to it a feeling not to be expressed in a hurry—or ever; and with that, dear Mr Barrie,

I am most sincerely and gratefully yours

Jph. Conrad.

To Kazimierz Waliszewski

Text Ruch; *Listy* 216; *L.fr.* 55; Najder 237[1]

Pent Farm

15th November 1903.

Dear and Honourable Sir,

I am writing today to all my publishers, and as you have already procured the *Typhoon*, Heinemann will be sending you the *Inheritors* and the *Nigger*, while Blackwood will send *Lord Jim* and *Youth*. I am afraid it is not going to be easy to get my first book, *Almayer's Folly*, because the edition was not big and was sold out long ago. At home we have only one copy of it, and my wife—to whom I presented it, even before our marriage—naturally cannot part with it. I intend to try the publisher. Du reste mes relations avec celui-là sont assez tendues.[2]

I have pricks of conscience at showering my books on you in this way. However, a few pages of each volume will suffice to give you an idea of what I was aiming at and what I managed to achieve. At any rate, be so kind as to accept them as the only testimony that I can give you of my true admiration for your work—which unfortunately I do not know well and which I am certainly unable to appreciate as I should, but which I believe that I have been able sympathetically to understand.

I consider it a great happiness and honour to return to my home country under your guidance (if I may express myself thus). And if you are prepared to take my word for it and say that during the course of all my travels round the world I never, in mind or heart, separated myself from my country, then I may surely be accepted there as a compatriot, in spite of my writing in English.

Please accept, my dear Sir ... etc.

Konrad Korzeniowski.

---

[1] The original was in Polish with a French PS. In the present text, the PS comes from *L. fr.*; Halina Carroll's translation of the Polish comes from Najder. All Najder texts appear by permission of the publisher, Oxford University Press.

[2] 'What's more, my relations with that person [T. Fisher Unwin] are quite strained.'

P.S.   Non! Non! Ne dites pas phénomène. Ça sent le Maxime Gorki[1] à plein nez. Ils sont étonnants ces braves Russes: All their geese are swans. Enfin, c'est leur affaire. Pour ma part, je n'ai jamais été ni vagabond ni aventurier de profession, ni une espèce de sauvage converti. Les notes et la photographie suivront dans peu de jours.[2]

To H.G. Wells

Text MS Illinois; J-A, 1, 310; Ray (1983, 2)

[letterhead: Pent Farm]

Thursday. [November–December 1903][3]

Dearest H G.

An excellent volume.[4] Last time I saw you, you spoke of it slightingly—and this only adds to my envy of your astounding gift—for if this is the sort of thing you throw off while you whistle!—well!

Your power of realisation of whatever you choose to imagine is astounding. The *force* of your imagination is even more surprising than its extent. The visual aspects in the Accelerator, the absolutely convincing effects in the *Spiders* fill me with admiration. You know what I mean exactly.

Filmer strenghtens* my conviction (derived from W of C and L & Mr L)[5] that at bottom you are an uncompromising realist. There is a cold jocular ferocity about the handling of that mankind in which You believe that gives me the shudders sometimes. However as you do believe in them it is right and proper and excellent that You should get some fun in making their bones rattle. And can't you do it too! Well more power to you. I'll do the sighing and slobbering and lamenting and sneezing—or whatever it is I am trying to do—and never getting done; which last is the only irony I've been able to achieve.

[1] The pseudonym of Aleksey Mikhaylovich Peshkov (1868–1936), known at this period for his short stories and plays; he was already identified with the cause of Russian revolution and had been arrested for seditious writing in 1901.

[2] 'No, no! Don't say phenomenon. That reeks of Maxim Gorki. They are amazing, these good Russians. All their geese are swans. Anyway, that's their business. For my part, I have never been either a tramp or an adventurer by trade—or a kind of converted savage.
The notes and the photograph will follow in a few days.'

[3] The stationery confirms Ray's dating: the period runs from the birth of Frank Richard Wells (31 October) to the last use of letterhead ten (31 December), 5, 12, and 19 November being the most likely dates.

[4] *Twelve Stories and a Dream*, published in October.

[5] *The Wheels of Chance* (1896); *Love and Mr Lewisham* (1900).

The ghost story is very good. As a matter of fact *in execution* You never falter. Of conceptions, of course, in the mass and variety of your work, some *must* be slighter than others. The fat man is good fooling dam' good—and quite sufficiently ferocious. The Rome business is by no means bad—but I understand *that* being thrown off. However in some strange way it does not read like Wells at all. The fairy story is the weakest I fancy. The last thing is in the tone of the *Sleeper*[1]— absolutely—with all the high qualities—and that something subtly wanting—that one felt in the big book.

Your wife looked delightfully well. Is the baby better? Has he got reconciled to his milk?

I my dear Wells am absolutely out of my mind with the worry and apprehension of my work. I go on as one would cycle over a precipice along a 14 inch plank. If I falter I am lost. Ever your

Conrad.

To Arnold Bennett
Text MS UCL; J-A, 1, 320

[letterhead: Pent Farm]
19th Nov 1903

My Dear Bennett[2]

You must think me a brute. I don't even attempt to palliate an inexcusable delay in thanking You for *Leonora*.[3] Still when I tell you that I am some four months behind with a wretched novel I am writing for Harpers You'll understand the state of my mind.

Yes. You *can* do things; you present them with a skill and in a language for which I wish here to thank you as distinc[t]ly as possible, and with all the respect due to such a remarkable talent.

Remains the question of conception; the only one in which discussion as between you a[n]d me is possible. And here the first criticism that occurs is that there is not enough of Leonora herself. The pedestal is, as it were, too large for the statue. And thats about the only objection that can be made to the book as a *work*. With the sheer pleasure of reading it, that—say—defect does not interfere. It is only in thinking it over that

[1] *When the Sleeper Wakes* (1900).
[2] Enoch Arnold Bennett (1867–1931), the prolific chronicler of Staffordshire, London, and cosmopolitan life. His Naturalist approach to fiction and his financial success made him the butt of Modernist writers such as Woolf and Pound, yet his taste in Conrad was impeccable.
[3] Bennett's novel, the second of a trilogy, published in October.

the objection arises. And it is impossible to read Leonora without afterwards thinking it all over—with great satisfaction, undoubtedly, and yet with some regret also.

You see I am frank with you; and I am frank because I have a great regard for your high ideal of workmanship, and for the ways of your thought. But one would need to talk it over with you to make one's meaning clear. Discussion alone could do that; for you must not imagine that I am trying to pick holes; I am too much fascinated by your expression, by the ease of your realisation, the force and the delicacy of your phrases. Whether you obtain them by hard toil or by an amazing inborn ability, does not matter: these qualities are there. That you can also go to the bottom of your subject "Anna"[1] proves sufficiently well; though even in that book, perhaps?...

However, don't mind me. It is very possible that I am too romantic and don't seize quite your true intention.

I trust that when you come over here[2] we may meet. You really ought to spare me an evening and we can put you up for the night—after a rough and ready fashion.

> Believe me dear Bennett always
> sincerely yours
> Jph. Conrad

To Kazimierz Waliszewski
Text L.fr. 57; Najder 238

> Pent Farm
> 20 Nbre 1903.

Cher Monsieur,

Mille fois merci pour votre bonne lettre. Le livre est arrivé aussi. Ma femme est touché par votre promptitude.

J'ai été fort occupé: je le suis encore, car voici l'année qui touche à la fin et mon misérable roman n'est pas près d'être terminé. Le pire est que je me sens découragé, fatigué par les efforts qui n'aboutissent à rien.

J'ai commencé à écrire *Almayer's Folly*, comme ça, sans penser à mal, pour occuper mes matinées pendant un séjour assez long que je fis à Londres au retour d'une campagne de trois ans dans les Mers du Sud.[3] Voilà la vérité vraie. J'avais 32 ans. Je ne savais rien de rien. Je n'en sais pas davantage aujourd'hui.

---

[1] *Anna of the Five Towns* (1902), first volume of the trilogy. [2] From Paris.
[3] He had left Europe in February 1887 and returned in June 1889. For Conrad's story of his start in literature, see *A Personal Record*, pp. 9–10 and 68–74.

Je ne puis vous en dire rien de plus pour le moment. Il est tard. Le sommeil me gagne. Je me sens bête plus que de coutume.

Sans doute, cher Monsieur, nous ne manquerons pas de nous présenter chez vous si nous venons à Paris l'année prochaine, comme c'est notre intention. Veuillez présenter mes hommages les plus respectueux à madame Waliszewska et croyez-moi toujours à vous bien sincèrement.

Translation

Dear Sir,

A thousand thanks for your good letter. The book has also arrived. My wife is touched by your promptness.

I have been very busy: I am still at it, for here is the end of the year and my miserable novel is not nearly finished. The worst is that I feel discouraged, tired by efforts which lead to nothing.

I began to write *Almayer's Folly* like that, without bad intentions, to occupy my mornings during a rather long stay I made in London upon returning from a three-year voyage in the South Seas. That is the real truth. I was 32 years old. I knew nothing about anything. I don't know anything more about it now.

I can tell you no more for the present. It is late. Sleep overcomes me. I feel more stupid than usual.

Without a doubt, dear sir, we shall not fail to present ourselves at your door if we come to Paris next year, as is our intention. Please give my most respectful greetings to Madame Waliszewska and believe me always, sincerely yours.

To J.M. Barrie
Text MS Berg; *Listy* 217; Original unpublished

[letterhead: Pent Farm]
23ᵈ Nov 1903

My dear Mr. Barrie.

I've been too optimistic as usual. Your good letter found me in bed, and though I've crawled out of it to-day I remain still recumbent and am writing this on a pad with a horrid fountain pen. Another week lost out of the few left to me for the silly book I am writing now—if the thing can be called a book at all. I am afraid it shall be more in the nature of printed matter. A certain amount of cheap sincerity there is in it, some shadow of intention too (which no one will see), and even an "artistic!" purpose—but all this makes for failure, since I've never felt that I had my subject in the palm of my hand. I've been always catching at it all along; and I shall be just catching at it to the end. That state of feeling leads one to sheer twaddle. I've already suspected that there was a lot of twaddle in the thing; and, since I've heard, the other day, that Harpers' people are very pleased with the part they have got, I am perfectly sure there is. I am trying to persuade myself that the other two parts may fill them with dismay. But I doubt it. I doubt it very much: I am too full of dismay myself.

All this year, practically, I've been hopping on two sticks—ever since March in fact. No doubt I've been sitting too close and what's worse with the feeling that for all my close sitting I've not been doing well. It was that feeling which helped the gout as much as insufficient exercise.

Thanks very much for the "boat-case". Anything may happen in an open boat. This instance is credible enough per se. But it presents some psychological difficulties. For, sailors would not have acted in that way towards their officer qua *officer*. There would be some previous ground of dislike. But a man of the sort to inspire such a dislike would have been of a character to bring the situation to an issue at once at the risk of getting himself flung overboard. On the other hand if they hated him to that extent they would have knocked him on the head rather than starve him in the boat, a course of action which I consider somewhat incredible for a lot of average sailors. It is too inhuman and not enough brutal. There is a subtle confusion of motives and action in the anecdote which makes me think that it is invented by a landsman with imagination but without sufficient knowledge of details that cut the ground from under his fundamental assumption. But I am very grateful to you for mentioning it since it contains a suggestion for something really credible. A short story will come out of it—when God wills it.[1]

Directly I am able I shall come to London—which just now is you—not to dinner yet (since it would mean a night in town) but for that hour—after four which, I consider, Your letter authorises me to rob you of almost any day. But I'll write once more to ask whether the day is convenient.

> I am, dear Mr Barrie most
> sincerely yours,
>
> Jph. Conrad

[1] The parallel is distant, but the fugitive of 'The Secret Sharer' is an officer who has killed a rebellious sailor.

To John Galsworthy
Text MS Forbes; J-A, 1,322

[letterhead: Pent Farm]
1903
30 Nov

My dearest Jack.

I've been ill again. Just got down, shaky weak, dispirited. No work done. No spring left to grapple with it. Everything looks black; but I suppose that will wear off, and, anyhow, I am trying to keep despair under. Nevertheless I feel myself losing my footing in deep waters. They are lapping about my lips.

My dear fellow it is not so much the frequency of these gout attacks, but I feel so beastly ill between, ill in body and mind. It has never been so before. Impossible to write—while the brain riots in incoherent images. It is sometimes quite alarming.

I've just written refusing Mrs Hoare['s] invitation for an evening function on the eight[h]—and also a dinner of Smith's for the 10th.[1] I got a card the other day and meantime advt[s] are appearing of the first ed[on] being exhausted just one month after publication. That is better than anything of mine has ever done. Et voilà! What a Romance!

I've been trying (lying on my back in bed with one knee and one ankle swollen) to think of a title. But I've been unable to think of anything better than the *Phylacteries*. In fact if *Pharisees* is impossible then the other is the right title, it seems to me. Does P object to it on 'popularity' grounds? Or what? Why don't you let them try their hand themselves at a name if they are so mighty difficult to please. There was some bother of that sort about the *Nigger of the N.*[2] I remember. But whatever the name that book my dearest Jack shall lay solid ground under your feet. With the next you shall begin to climb—and build. I am glad I've lived long enough to see and with wits enough left to perceive that You've found Yourself. Do come my dear Jack as soon as you can and help me through a day or two. Bring what you've written to the very last word. I *want* to see it all.

All our love to you. Ever yours
Conrad.

[1] Reginald Smith of Smith, Elder? Mrs Hoare is unidentified.
[2] Called in the first North American edition *The Children of the Sea*.

To H.G. Wells

Text MS Illinois; J-A, 1, 321

[letterhead: Pent Farm]
30 Nov 03

My dear H. G.

Indeed I did not expect You in this awful weather, especially as Jessie reported you with a cold.

I was laid by the knee (this time) the day after we travelled up together. I did not feel particularly bright even then, or else I would have succumbed to Your blandishments and stayed for a dinner and a chat in town.

Things are bad with me—there's no disguising the fact. Not only is the scribbling awfully in arrear but there's no 'spring' in me to grapple with it effectually. Formerly, in my sea life, a difficulty nerved me to the effort; now I perceive it is not so. However don't imagine I've given up, but there is an uncomfortable sense of losing my footing in deep waters.

Rce's gone into 2ᵈ ed: I hear. That, no doubt, does not mean much but still it is better than any of my other books did do. Is *M[ankind] in the M[aking]* doing well for you—I mean *really* well? After all, my dear boy, for all our faith in our good intentions and even in our achievement a paper-success (as I call it) is not a strong enough tonic. I say so because for me, writing—*the only possible writing*—is just simply the conversion of nervous force into phrases. With you too, I am sure, tho' in your case it is the disciplined intelligence which gives the signal—the impulse. For me it is a matter of chance, stupid chance. But the fact remains that when the nervous force is exhausted the phrases don't come:—and no tension of will can help.

Don't imagine I am grumbling. I had ten times the luck I deserved. All this talk is very stupid but it comforts me to worry you a little.

Ever Your

J Conrad.

Our love to all your house. I am touched by Archer's Repentance[1] (would do as title for short story). It strikes me my dear Wells that in your quiet almost stealthy way you are doing a lot for me; if it were not for you a lot of people would not know of my existence anything palpable, and still less of my involved form of narrative. I will be

---

[1] William Archer (1856–1924), the Scottish critic and playwright, who translated Ibsen and campaigned for a national theatre.

delighted to know Prof: York Powell.[1] Don't forget to send me Metchnikow's book.[2] I am really curious to see that.
PS   I am out of bed but haven't yet ventured out. I *feel* a perfect wreck.

To Kazimierz Waliszewski

Text L.fr. 63; Najder 241

[Pent Farm]
[early] décembre 1903.[3]

Cher Monsieur,
    Voilà. Cela ne me ressemble pas du tout. Je suis plus vieux, plus maigre, pas si léché. Et l'imbécile retoucheur s'est avisé de retoucher le bout de mon nez, d'où son apparence israelite qu'il ne possède pas dans la nature.
    Ci-joint quelques criticismes de mes livres. N'allez pas au moins me croire un mégalomaniaque. Je voulais vous donner une idée de ce que l'on dit de moi ici. Les journaux sont bêtes!

Bien à vous.

Translation

Dear Sir,
    Here it is. It doesn't look like me at all. I am older, leaner, not so polished. And the imbecile retoucher took it into his head to redo the end of my nose, whence the Israelite appearance it does not in fact possess.
    Enclosed are some reviews of my books. At least don't think me a megalomaniac. I wanted to give you an idea of what they say about me here. The newspapers are silly!

Yours truly.

---

[1] Frederick York Powell (1850–1904), Regius Professor of Modern History at Oxford and one of the founders of Ruskin College.
[2] Ilya Ilyich Mechnikov, *Etudes sur la nature humaine: Essai de philosophie optimiste* (Paris, 1903). Mechnikov (1845–1916) was a pioneer immunologist.
[3] The photograph was promised 'in a few days' on 15 November.

To Roger Casement

Text MS NLI; Najder (1974)

[letterhead: Pent Farm]
1903
1st Dec

My dear Casement.[1]

If you are the man I knew in Africa[2] you shall not shirk coming all the way here to see a more or less lame friend. Since we foregathered last I've married, got a boy, become a victim of gout—"poor man's gout" if acquired; and if not acquired then hereditary in a legitimate way. No doubt some of my ancestor[s] drank deep, after the manner of their time.

This year has been very bad for me.

We live here; it is a sort of one-horse existence. But we can put you up after a fashion. Besides you are used to hardships.

There is not a bad train on Sunday morning from Charing + to Sandling. I would ask You for a Sat to Monday stay only I am afraid you will get bored all that time with us only. We are dull people; we know no one to meet you in the neighbourhood and for want of accom[m]odation can't ask more than one man at a time.

It is a farmhouse life with a vengeance.

Still you may have the pluck to face the longer period. I have always had a great opinion of your courage. In that case leave Char + on any Sat (but the very next) by 4.28 pm. Only let us know by letter or wire. Any *Sat* or *Sunday* after the next—I repeat. There is an evening service in the village church (14th centy) less than ten minutes walk from here.[3]

But no doubt your time will be very much taken up. Perhaps you could more easily spare a weekday. In that case you have only to write and follow your message for an evening and the night. The smallest visit thankfully received.

Always my dear Casement,
sincerely yours

Jph. Conrad.

---

[1] Roger Casement (born 1864; knighted 1911) had had wide commercial and consular experience in southern and central Africa. As British Consul at Boma, he had just written a report on Belgian savagery in the Congo 'Free State'. Later, he exposed vile working conditions in the South American rubber trade. An Irish patriot, he was hanged in 1916 for his war-time dealings with Germany.

[2] Their first meeting was at Matadi, June 1890. See Najder, *Congo Diary*, p. 7, and the letter to Graham, 26 December.

[3] Casement was a fervent churchman.

I need not tell you there's no more ceremony than if we asked you to step under a tent on the road to Kinchassa. I am glad you've read the Heart of D. tho' of course it's an awful fudge.

To Kazimierz Waliszewski

Text Ruch; *Listy* 221; Najder 239

Pent Farm,
5th December, 1903.

Dear Sir,

A thousand thanks for the friendly letter which has just reached me. I shall begin by apologizing for the thin paper, which is what I am using for my manuscripts. It is late now and I have no other paper handy; so, removing the 567th page of the novel I am now engaged on, I address myself to you.

The weekly *Kraj* to which you refer is probably the one that comes out in Petersburg.[1] In this case you probably know Mr. Włodzimierz Spasowicz, a friend of my late Uncle Bobrowski, who wrote a preface to my Uncle's memoirs (published in 1900 in Lvov).[2]

After his marriage, my Father, Apollo Korzeniowski (son of Teodor, a captain in the Polish Army), leased a farm on the estate of Mrs Melania Sobańska. I was born in December 1857. Subsequently my parents moved to Warsaw. In 1862, my Father was imprisoned in the Warsaw fortress and after a few months was transported to Vologda. I accompanied my parents in their exile. Later they were moved to Chernikhov and there my Mother died. I can hardly remember her, but judging by what I heard about her and by the letters she wrote to her brothers— which I read later—she must have been a woman with uncommon qualities of mind and spirit. Her young brother, Stefan Bobrowski, was a well-known personality in 1863.[3] After my Mother's death, I stayed with my Uncle Tadeusz in the country. In 1867 my Father was released and he took me with him to Galicia. He died in Cracow in 1869. Mr. Stefan Buszczyński (a man of letters who was well-known in his day) wrote a short biography of him entitled 'A little-known poet'.[4] My Father's funeral was the occasion for a demonstration by the students of

---

[1] Rather than the Cracow newspaper of the same name.
[2] He also wrote Tadeusz Bobrowski's obituary for *Kraj*.
[3] The year of the rising against foreign occupation and of his death in a duel rigged by political opponents.
[4] Published in 1870: Buszczyński (1821–92), was a poet, dramatist, critic, and historian.

Cracow University. Cracow was also the place where I went to school, but in 1874 I left my country to go to sea.

I cannot write about Tadeusz Bobrowski, my Uncle, guardian and benefactor, without emotion. Even now, after ten years, I still feel his loss. He was a man of great character and unusual qualities of mind. Although he did not understand my desire to join the mercantile marine, on principle, he never objected to it. I saw him four times during the thirty* years of my wanderings (from 1874–1893) but even so I attribute to his devotion, care, and influence, whatever good qualities I may possess. The last two occasions on which I visited him were in the Ukraine (as a British subject)[1] in 1890 and 1893.

Everything about my life in the wide world can be found in my books. I never sought for a career, but possibly, unaware of it, I was looking for sensations. Now it is all over. With no connexions, contacts, or influential friends, I can nevertheless look upon the past with satisfaction. I managed somehow. During my life as a seaman, though mainly prompted by curiosity (as well as by a genuine liking for the profession), I was conscientious, passing all the necessary examinations, winning the respect of people (in my modest milieu) who, certainly not out of sheer affection, attested to my being a 'good sailor and a trustworthy ship's officer'. In what it seems to me were pretty difficult situations, I think I always remained faithful to the traditions of the profession I had chosen.

I received my first command of a ship at the age of 29, which, you must admit, was not bad for a foreigner without influence.[2] That I never sought, and I have to give the English their due, they never made me feel a foreigner. I consider myself to be the last seaman of a sailing vessel. Anyway, no one will be writing any more about that old sea-life. As a work of fiction *The Nigger* puts a seal on that epoch of the greatest possible perfection which was at the same time the end of the sailing fleet. I feel that deeply each time I look at the British* Channel where nothing but smoking funnels are to be seen nowadays.

Both at sea and on land my point of view is English, from which the conclusion should not be drawn that I have become an Englishman. That is not the case. Homo duplex has in my case more than one meaning.[3] You will understand me. I shall not dwell upon that subject.

Apparently, so far as writing is concerned, I have some sort of a

[1] And thus protected against Russian officialdom.

[2] That he was actually 30 when he took command of the *Otago* is scarcely less impressive.

[3] The phrase occurs in *Asclepius* VII (formerly attributed to Apuleius), it is the title of an essay in Vol. 4 of Buffon's *Histoire naturelle* (1753), and Baudelaire takes it up in 'La Double Vie' (*L'Art romantique*: Paris, Calmann-Lévy, 1880), p. 423.

talent. That is no merit of mine. You may judge if I make use of it conscientiously. All I know is that I am striving after a writer's honesty. But that is not a great merit either. Am I achieving anything? I do not know—or rather, I know I am not. It is difficult to depict faithfully in a work of imagination that innermost world as one apprehends it, and to express one's own real sense of that inner life (which is the soul of human activity). However, absolute sincerity is always possible—I mean sincerity of intention. One does what one can.

I shall finish now, apologizing for the alarming dimensions of this letter. Here are some dates. My wife, thanking you for your kind regards, expresses her readiness to lend you her copy of *Almayer's Folly*. I expect, however, to hear any day from the publishers. *Almayer's Folly* was begun in 1889. It was written bit by bit all round the world. It was finished in 1895.[1] *Outcast of the Islands* 1895.

Lagoon, Outpost of Progress, Idiots—1896; *Nigger of the 'Narcissus'*— September 1896—February 1897; *Karain, The Return* 1897.

Youth, Heart of Darkness 1898; *Lord Jim* October 1898—July 1899.[2] Simultaneously with my collaboration in the writing of *The Inheritors*.

The Inheritors and the beginning of the collaboration on *Romance* 1900, *Typhoon, Falk, Amy Foster* 1900–1.

To-morrow January 1902, *Romance* finished April 1902. *The End of the Tether* November 1902.

Since that time I have not worked well. I was ill and lacked inspiration. The circle of my readers is very small. Life has now become much harder. I write with difficulty, slowly, crossing out constantly. What a foul profession! 'This craft is exacting'—as dear and good Henry James repeats, whenever we meet, throwing his arms up to heaven. It is touching to hear that coming from the lips of a man who is approaching sixty[3] and who has to his credit forty volumes practically free from imperfection.

PS.   That is so, my dear Sir! A lot could be said and certainly there would be a lot for me to listen to. May it be granted to us that we meet again soon. Do you ever visit England? I live only about 5 English miles from Folkestone. You could call on me on your way from Paris to London—even if only for one night. Do not forget, please!

---

[1] Submitted to Unwin in July 1894 and published the following year.
[2] Finished July 1900.
[3] He had turned 60 in April.

To J.B. Pinker
Text MS Berg; Unpublished

[letterhead: Pent Farm]
9th Dec 1903

My dear Pinker

Thanks very much for the cheque (£15) safely to hand with your interesting letter.

Of course I rejoice at escaping the ordeal of serializing in Am:—as long as Harpers pay the agreed amount. The terms of their declaration are very nice; but don't you think that, in reality, they are vexed with the *form* of the tale?

Anyhow your news is good. Mine is not so. I've been laid up with severe gout. The fact is I am run down—stale. It's about time I had a radical change. The writing of this book is anxious work. Let us hope it will repay the trouble—to us both.

Always my dear Pinker sincerely
Yours

Jph. Conrad.

To J.B. Pinker
Text MS Colgate; Unpublished

[Pent Farm]
12 Dec 1903

My dear Pinker.

I have no objection to the compression of the story for the purpose of serial pub^{on} in T. P's Weekly[1]—as long as I am not called upon to do the compressing myself. I am willing to trust in that matter M^r O'Connor's judgment, the skill of his staff and, most of all, *his supervision* of the process. I would stipulate also that no proofs should be sent to me. On those conditions I am ready to let M^r O'Connor have an absolutely free hand in making the story acceptable to his large public.

I work as I can. Not very intelligently perhaps; but I trust I have enough intelligence to understand his point of view; and frankly, looking at the conditions of publication (short instal^{ts} and so on) it seems to me wise generally and of advantage even to myself. There's

---

[1] Founded in 1902 by T. P. O'Connor (1848–1929), Irish M.P., journalist, and humourist. The *Weekly* expressed his literary tastes; his other creations, the *Star* and the *Sun*, were committed to the causes of radical Liberalism and home rule. He represented the Scotland division of Liverpool for more than 40 years.

nothing I desire less than to appear as a portentous bore before so many readers.

Yours sincerely

Joseph Conrad.

To J.B. Pinker
Text MS Berg; Unpublished

[letterhead: Pent Farm]
1903
Tuesday 15th Dec

My dear Pinker

I have no other copy of the book. I am sorry the thing gives you so much bother in one way or another.

Whatever happens I *must* have proofs of the book. They[1] can't do better than send them out to me from N. York. I can't let a book of mine go into the world without a careful personal revision. Let them pull off galley slips in the US—or else here if they are going to set it up here. And I *will not* put up with the American spelling in the *English* edition. I would rather—and I will too—fling the thing into the fire. Till I am sure of that they shan't get a page more out of me. Let it be clearly understood.

Yours cordially

Conrad.

PS I need not tell you how much I am sensible of your good and successful care of my interests.
PPS I am working desperately to catch up the gout delay. Horrors!

To Kazimierz Waliszewski
Text Ruch; *L.fr.* 63; Najder 242

Pent Farm
16 Dec 1903

Cher Maitre,

Merci mille fois pour l'article que vous me consacrez dans la Revue.[2] Je l'ai lu avec un vif intérêt, une attention profonde et beaucoup de gratitude.

---

[1] Harper & Brothers, still the publishers in book form although they had decided against a serial.
[2] 'Un Cas de naturalisation littéraire: Joseph Conrad', *Revue des Revues* (Paris), vol. 47, pp. 734–48, 15 December.

Vous êtes sympathique et indulgent. La justice en souffre, mais ce n'est pas à moi de m'en plaindre. Du reste, je me flatte d'avoir compris votre article mieux que personne n'est en état de le comprendre. Vos paroles ont pénétré dans ces plis profonds de l'âme où l'homme cherche à cacher ses faiblesses même à ses propres yeux.

Après tout on travaille comme on peut, non comme on veut,—surtout quand on se donne sans réserve aucune à son travail. C'est une réflexion que n'excuse rien, aussi je l'avance d'une façon désintéressée, comme je le ferais en causant avec vous, en général, de la manière dont on exerce son art.

Quand* à 'l'infériorité des races',[1] je me permets de protester,— quoique évidemment la faute est à moi si je vous ai donné une fausse idée de mon intention. C'est la *différence* des races que j'ai voulu indiquer. Si je dis que le navire qui bombardait la côte était français, c'est tout simplement parce que *c'était* un navire français. Je me rappelle son nom: le Seignelay. C'était pendant la guerre (!) du Dahomey.[2] La réflexion qui suit s'apppliquerait à un navire de toute autre nationalité. Je prends mes personnages où je les trouve. Hermann est un Allemand, mais Stein l'est aussi.[3] J'ai pris grand soin de donner une origine cosmopolite à Kurtz. Quand* à mes deux bonshommes qui se poursuivent avec des revolvers dans l''Outpost of Progress', je m'insurge. Kayerts n'est pas un nom français. Carlier peut l'être, mais aussitôt que je le nomme, je m'empresse de dire qu'il est un ex-sous-off de cavalerie d'une armée *garantie de tout péril par plusieurs puissances européenes*. Je me suis donné la peine de faire un militaire de cet animal là exprès. Ils sont de braves Belges.—Dieu les bénisse: et on les a reconnus comme tels ici et à Bruxelles quand le conte a paru en 1890 dans une Revue (défunte à présent) 'Cosmopolis'.[4] Assez de radotage. Je vous serre les mains bien affectueusement.

Tout à vous.

---

[1] Waliszewski observed that he was unduly lenient towards the English.
[2] The first French attempt to conquer the Kingdom of Dahomey, February–October 1890. Stripped of its official purpose, the shelling incident appears in 'Heart of Darkness'.
[3] The sea-going shopkeeper from 'Falk' as opposed to the oracular student of nature and humanity from *Lord Jim*.
[4] June and July 1897.

[Alternative ending, from the Polish][1]

But that's enough of idle prattle! I send you a hearty hand-shake and the expression of my deep respect for Mrs Waliszewska. I really must visit you soon in order to thank her personally and to apologize for having taken up so much of your time and thought.

Translation

Dear Master,
  A thousand thanks for the article you devote to me in the *Revue*. I read it with lively interest, profound attention, and much gratitude.
  You are sympathetic and indulgent. Justice suffers by it, but I mustn't complain about that. Anyway, I flatter myself for having understood your article better than anyone else could do. Your words have penetrated into those deep recesses of the soul where man seeks to hide his weaknesses even from his own eyes.
  After all, we work as we can, not as we wish, especially when we give ourselves without any reservations to our work. This is a reflection that excuses nothing; besides, I offer it in an impartial way, as though I were chatting with you, in general, about the way we carry on our art.
  As to the 'inferiority of the races', I mean to protest—although, if I gave you the wrong idea of my purpose, the fault is obviously mine. It's the *difference* between the races that I wanted to point out. If I say that the ship which bombarded the coast was French, it is quite simply because *it was* a French ship. I recall its name—the *Seignelay*. It was during the war (!) with Dahomey. The ensuing commentary could be applied to a ship of any other nationality. I take my characters where I find them. Hermann is a German, but Stein is too. I took great care to give Kurtz a cosmopolitan origin. As to my two fine fellows who chase each other with revolvers in the 'Outpost of Progress', I rebel. Kayerts is not a French name. Carlier perhaps, but as soon as I name him, I hasten to say that he is a former cavalry n.c.o. of an army *protected from all danger by several European powers*. I took the trouble to make a soldier out of that animal deliberately. They are gallant Belgians—God bless them: and they were recognized as such here and in Brussels when the tale appeared in 1898 in *Cosmopolis*, a now-defunct review. Enough twaddle. I shake your hand very fondly.
                                             Always yours.

[1] This paragraph, which appeared in *Ruch*, must have been a Polish supplement to the now lost French original: Najder, p. 243, n. 2.

To Roger Casement

Text MS NLI; Najder (1974)

[letterhead: Pent Farm]
1903
17th Dec^{er}

My dear Casement

During my sojourn in the interior, keeping my eyes and ears well open too, I've never heard of the alleged custom of cutting off hands amongst the natives; and I am convinced that no such custom ever existed along the whole course of the main river to which my experience is limited. Neither in the casual talk of white men nor in the course of definite inquiries as to the tribal customs was ever such a practice hinted at; certainly not amongst the Bangalas who at that time formed the bulk of the State troops. My informants were numerous, of all sorts—and many of them possessed of abundant knowledge.

I have to thank you for Morel's pamphlet[1] which reached me from L'pool a few days ago. There can be no doubt that his presentation of the commercial policy and the administrative methods of the Congo State is absolutely true. It is a most brazen breach of faith as to Europe.[2] It is in every aspect an enormous and atrocious lie in action. If it were not rather appalling the cool completeness of it would be amusing.

My best wishes and cordial regards

Yours

Jph. Conrad.

To Roger Casement

Text MS NLI; Najder (1974)

[letterhead: Pent Farm]
21st Dec 1903

My dear Casement

You cannot doubt that I form the warmest wishes for your success. A King, wealthy and unscrupulous, is certainly no mean adversary; for if the personality in this case be a rather discredited one,[3] the wealth, alas, has never a bad odour—or this wealth in particular would tell its own suffocating tale.

---

[1] *The Congo Slave State* (Liverpool, 1903), 'to be distributed gratis'. E. D. Morel (1873–1924) was Casement's ally in starting the Congo Reform Association.
[2] In flouting the stipulations of the Conference of Berlin (1885).
[3] Leopold II (1835–1909), King of the Belgians and proprietor of the Congo 'Free State': portrayed in *The Inheritors* as the Duc de Mersch.

It is an extraordinary thing that the conscience of Europe which seventy years ago has put down the slave trade on humanitarian grounds tolerates the Congo State to day. It is as if the moral clock had been put back many hours. And yet nowadays if I were to overwork my horse so as to destroy its happiness of physical wellbeing I should be hauled before a magistrate. It seems to me that the black man—say, of Upoto—is deserving of as much humanitarian regard as any animal since he has nerves, feels pain, can be made physically miserable. But as a matter of fact his happiness and misery are much more complex than the misery or happiness of animals and deserving of greater regard. He shares with us the consciousness of the universe in which we live—no small burden. Barbarism per se is no crime deserving of a heavy visitation; and the Belgians are worse than the seven plagues of Egypt insomuch that in that case it was a punishment sent for a definite transgression; but in this the Upoto man is not aware of any transgression, and therefore can see no end to the infliction. It must appear to him very awful and mysterious; and I confess that it appears so to me too. The amenities of the 'middle passage' in the old days were as nothing to it. The slave trade has been abolished—and the Congo State exists to-day. This is very remarkable. What makes it more remarkable is this: the slave trade was an old established form of commercial activity; it was not the monopoly of one small country established to the disadvantage of the rest of the civilized world in defiance of international treaties and in brazen disregard of humanitarian declarations. But the Congo State created yesterday is all that and yet it exists. This is very mysterious. One is tempted to exclaim (as poor Thiers did in 1871) "Il n'y a plus d'Europe."[1] But as a matter of fact in the old days England had in her keeping the conscience of Europe. The initiative came from here. But now I suppose we are busy with other things; too much involved in great affairs to take up cudgels for humanity, decency and justice. But what about our commercial interests? These suffer greatly as Morel has very clearly demonstrated in his book. There can be no serious attempt to controvert his facts. Or [it] is impossible to controvert them for the hardest of lying won't do it. That precious pair of African witch-men seem to have cast a spell upon the world of whites—I mean Leopold and Thys[2] of course. This is very funny.

---

[1] After failing to involve the European powers in the Franco-Prussian war.
[2] In 1889, as deputy director of the Société Anonyme Belge pour le Commerce du Haut-Congo, Albert Thys (1849–1915) had interviewed Conrad as a prospective employee.

And the fact remains that in 1903, seventy five years or so after the abolition of the slave trade (because it was cruel) there exists in Africa a Congo State, created by the act of European Powers where ruthless, systematic cruelty towards the blacks is the basis of administration, and bad faith towards all the other states the basis of commercial policy.

I do hope we shall meet before you leave.[1] Once more my best wishes go with you on your crusade. Of course You may make any use you like of what I write to you. Cordially Yours

Jph Conrad.

To Ernest Dawson
Text MS Yale; J-A, 1, 323

[letterhead: Pent Farm]
21 Dec 1903

My dear Dawson.

Perfectly correct. The Chief mate on the forecastle head takes charge of all the operations connected with the raising and securing of the anchor; and generally when getting under weigh the chief officer takes charge forward and the second mate aft, where he is under the eye of the captain (or rather Master) who is in command of the whole thing.

This is the absolute practice in sailing ships and steamers of the merchant service. There may be a special routine and different "stations" in large mail-boats, perhaps. But I doubt it; and in any case it cannot be very different. The chief officer even there is, I am pretty sure, responsible for the efficiency and correct handling of what is called "ground tackle" chains, anchors fish and cat davits and all purchases appertaining thereto, windlass etc etc. When a steam windlass is used the carpenter is driving it. This is his work even in steamers. The boatswain is with the mate to carry out orders.

I think I have answered fully your question.

I was glad to hear from You. Yes my dear fellow; we shall meet before you leave. I shall make it my pleasurable business to see you and A.J.[2] directly the thing is practicable. My wife sends her kind regards and joins me in most cordial wishes for your happiness and prosperity. I am delighted to hear B'wood is hospitable to your stuff.[3] Don't talk of

---

[1] He visited the Conrads on 3 January (Watts, p. 151).
[2] Ernest's brother (1872–1951), traveller and author.
[3] His next signed piece, an Australian story, came out in April; a story and an essay had appeared in 1903; an unsigned contribution about Burma and South Africa, February 1904, may be his as well.

potboilers. We are all writing potboilers. The best work of the best men has gone into potboilers. I had an awful year of it. Never mind.

Yours

J Conrad.

To Harriet Mary Capes
Text MS Yale; Unpublished

[Pent Farm]
26th Dec 1903

My dear Miss Capes.[1]

It was very dear of you to send your own book[2] inscribed to Borys. The reading thereof began yesterday and proceeds but slowly because Jessie is far from well—chilly and languid, a most unusual thing with her. I fear she is very much run down.

She sends her love. Your friendship, your kindness, are, without a shadow of exaggeration in the term, very precious to us both. Whatever happens pray believe that always.

I never thanked You for your last letter. Really I am lost to all sense of shame; but believe me laziness had nothing to do with my reluctance to write; neither had indifference. All your words were—and always shall be—most welcome to me.

My mind struggles with a strange sort of torpor, struggles desperately while the sands are running out. That is the most terrifying thought of all. They are running out—and there is nothing done; nothing of what one desires to do.

I am glad you find *Romance* tolerable. The book has been hammered at with infinite industry and is but little the better for it. The dedicatory verse is Hueffer's of course. He's the poet of the team. And yet I too have seen visions. Anch'io son[o] pittore![3] But they fade, they fade, quicker, alas, than life itself. Still while there is life there is hope.

Believe me, dear Miss Capes
affectionately yours
Joseph Conrad.

---

[1] Harriet Mary Capes (1849–1936), who lived in Winchester, wrote inspirational stories for children. A great admirer of Conrad's works, she 'selected and arranged' *Wisdom and Beauty from Conrad* (1915); he dedicated *A Set of Six* to her.

[2] Her most recent book was *The Lucky Sovereign* (The Sunday School Union, 1899).

[3] 'I too am a painter!' – Antonio Correggio on seeing Raphael's 'St Cecilia', c.1525.

To Mariah Hannah Martindale
Text MS Yale; Unpublished

[letterhead: Pent Farm]
26th Dec 1903

Dear Mrs Martindale.[1]

Our gratitude for the pencil case You and Miss Martindale[2] have been kind enough to send to Borys is the greater because the recipient has declared his intention to let his mother and his father use it, sometimes. It is very convenient for us and also shows that he is extremely gratified at your present, since it is only his especially precious possessions that he offers thus formally to share with his parents.

Jessie sends her best love to Yourself and Miss Martindale. I regret to say she is not very well. I fear she is run down and requires a thorough change. Meantime we or rather I cannot as yet fix a date for that long-looked-for holiday abroad. It is a pity; but this year has been bad for me as far as my work is concerned and I am ending it under a crushing load of arrears of 'copy'.

We had a letter from Ford (from W[inchelsea]) with good news of Elsie. This has cheered us not a little. But what has come to Ford? He declares he has hired a palace in London on Campden Hill.[3] Has he suddenly grown extravagant and reckless—or is it only that the letter was written after a festive dinner when the world is seen through a rosy flush of wine? However as he states his intention to entertain us there I've no objection to a palace. I hope the palace exists; and I have a good mind to accept his and Elsies gracious invitation to share their splendour for a couple of days at some early date. In that case we promise ourselves the very real pleasure of seeing You and Your daughter before very long.

Beli[e]ve me, dear Ladies, Your
very faithful and obedient servant
Joseph Conrad

---

[1] Elsie Hueffer's widowed mother; before marriage, she had been a nurse in Ireland (Mizener, p. 27).

[2] Elsie's sister, Mary.

[3] 10 Airlie Gardens, Kensington, a 'very large, absurd house' (Ford, quoted by Mizener, p. 85), in a quarter occupied by prosperous Bohemia.

To David Meldrum
Text MS Duke; Blackburn 178

[letterhead: Pent Farm]
26th Dec 1903.

My dear Mr Meldrum.

It was very good of all in Muswell Hill to remember Borys. Nothing could have pleased him better than the gift and his excitement at seeing "how Betty looked" was very great.

They are dear delightful children, with lots of individuality in their faces so different and yet so subtly alike. And there does not seem to be anything the matter with their health. That you may watch through long years their unclouded happiness and prosperity is the best wish I can send you and your Wife in this season of wishes.

Borys sends his love to Betty and Jan.[1] He is extremely anxious to see them; and we hope that he may have that pleasure before long—not to speak of ours. The Hueffers have taken a house in London for a few months and ask us to stay with them for a few days early in January. If that comes to pass we shall appear in a body on your doorstep before the new year is many days old.

Of myself I have a dread to speak. It has been a most disastrous year for my work. If I had written each page with my blood I could not feel more exhausted at the end of this twelvemonth. And the tale of pages is not yet complete!

My wife joins me in kindest regards and love for the children from their unknown friend Borys' father and mother. Pray express our most friendly sentiments to Mrs Meldrum—and believe me always yours with the most cordial regard

Joseph Conrad.

To R.B. Cunninghame Graham
Text MS Dartmouth; J-A, 1, 324; Watts 148

Pent Farm.
26th Dec 1903.

Cher Ami.

I snatch this piece of MS paper first of all to thank you for remembering the boy at this festive (?) season. Next to tell you that H. de Soto[2] is most exquisitely excellent: your very mark and spirit upon a

---

[1] Betty was six, Jan four, and Borys five.

[2] *Hernando de Soto*, just published by Heinemann. Its narrative of exploration and conquest in Peru and around the Gulf of Mexico had a special interest for the author of *Nostromo*.

subject that only *you* can do justice to—with your wonderful English and your sympathetic insight into the souls of the Conquistadores. The glamour, the pathos and the romance of that time and of those men are only adequately, truthfully, conveyed to us by your pen; the sadness, the glory and the romance of the endeavour together with the vanity of vanities of the monstrous achievement are reflected in your unique style as though you had been writing of men with whom you had slept by the camp fire after tethering your horses on the t[h]reshold of the unknown.

You have an eye for buried jewels! The Pizarro going about mournfully with his hat pulled down on his ears after the death of Atahualpa is new to me. He is made unforgettable at last. "C'est *énorme* d'humanité" as the great Flaubert would have yelled to the four winds of heaven. What a touch. Behold in this Conquistador my long lost brother together with those others: the Indio gentile hombre shouting insults underneath his tree and the thirty lances riding on to the sea, some of them already with death sitting on the pillion behind; to be received with the question: "Have you seen any signs of gold in the country?" One seems to hear the very voice. C'est la verité même! It's the most amazingly natural thing I've ever read; it gives me a furious desire to learn Spanish and bury myself in the pages of the incomparable Garcilasso[1]—if only to forget all about our modern Conquistadores.[2]

Their achievement is monstrous enough in all conscience—but not as a great human force let loose, but rather like that of a gigantic and obscene beast. Leopold is their Pizarro, Thys their Cortez and their "lances" are recruited amongst the souteneurs, sous-offs, maquereaux, fruit-secs[3] of all sorts on the pavements of Brussels and Antwerp. I send you two letters I had from a man called Casement, promising that I knew him first in the Congo just 12 years ago. Perhaps you've heard or seen in print his name. He's a protestant Irishman, pious too. But so was Pizarro. For the rest I can assure you that he is a limpid personality. There is a touch of the Conquistador in him too; for I've seen him start off into an unspeakable wilderness swinging a crookhandled stick for all weapons, with two bull-dogs: Paddy (white) and Biddy (brindle) at his heels and a Loanda boy carrying a bundle for all company. A few months afterwards it so happened that I saw him come out again, a little

---

[1] Garcilaso de la Vega, el Inca (1539?–1616), the son of a conquistador and an Inca princess: his *Commentaries* on Peruvian history served as one of Graham's main sources.

[2] Graham's histories of the conquest challenged the 'black legend' of uniquely Spanish depravity; he argued that the modern conquerors of Africa were no less brutal and considerably more devious.

[3] 'Ponces, N.C.Os, pimps, and losers.'

leaner a little browner, with his stick, dogs, and Loanda boy, and quietly serene as though he had been for a stroll in a park. Then we lost sight of each other. He was I believe Bsh Consul in Beira,[1] and lately seems to have been sent to the Congo again, on some sort of mission, by the Br Gov^t. I have always thought that some particle of Las Casas'[2] soul had found refuge in his indefatigable body. The letters will tell you the rest. I would help him but it is not in me. I am only a wretched novelist inventing wretched stories and not even up to that miserable game; but your good pen, keen, flexible and straight, and sure, like a good Toledo blade would tell in the fray if you felt disposed to give a slash or two. He could tell you things! Things I've tried to forget; things I never did know. He has had as many years of Africa as I had months—almost.—

Another small matter. S. Perez Triana[3] heard from Pawling of my longing to get away south (when possible) and has written me the kindest letter imaginable, offering information and even introductions. I am quite touched. But pray tell me whether he is Colombian Minister in Spain and if it behoves me to *lui donner de l'Excellence on the envelope*. I don't want faire une *bévue*[4] and after all I know him very little. And à propos what do you think of the Yankee Conquistadores in Panama?[5] Pretty, isn't it? Enfin. Veuillez presenter mes dévoirs les plus respectueux à Madame Votre Femme. Borys Instructed me to send his love to you. Jessie's kind regards. Tout à vous

Jph Conrad.

---

[1] Casement served at Lourenço Marques (now Maputo, Mozambique), Luanda (Angola), Durban and Capetown, and in the Congo at Kinshasa and Boma.

[2] Bartolomé de las Casas (1474–1566), missionary and historian, whom Graham revered for his defence of the Indians.

[3] Santiago Pérez Triana (1860–1916), Colombian Envoy Extraordinary in London and Madrid. For a full account of his influence on *Nostromo*, see Watts, pp. 206–8.

[4] 'To make a blunder' by failing to address Triana by the correct title. Conrad was always scrupulous in such matters.

[5] Mindful of the canal about to be dug, the U.S. government had encouraged the province of Panama to secede from Colombia. On 18 November, the Hay–Bunau-Varilla Treaty gave the U.S. permanent control over a ten-mile-wide Canal Zone and the right to intervene anywhere else in the new country. Meanwhile, in *Nostromo*, Conrad was telling the story of a secession prompted by 'material interests', whose ultimate beneficiary lives in San Francisco.

To Roger Casement
Text MS NLI; Najder (1974)

[letterhead: Pent Farm]
29 Dec 1903

Private and Conf[identi]al

My dear Casement.

I am overwhelming you with my scrawls! The cause of this one is that my friend R.B. Cunninghame Graham writing in answer to a letter of mine in which I'd mentioned Your presence in London wishes to communicate with you in person.

The man is able and more than willing to help in your noble crusade; and you may safely give him your confidence. No doubt You have heard of him—in one way or another. Do not let his reputation for socialism influence your judgment upon the man. It has never been anything but a form of his hate for all oppression and injustice.[1] His character is upright and unselfish; his talents (with the pen too) are great; he knows everybody worth knowing, and his social relations extend from Dukes to Labour-members. He may be of use to you, if only with his pen; and perhaps in other ways as well. Whatever may be the difference of Your political opinions I am sure that you will understand each other perfectly on humanitarian grounds.

He has heard of you from me years ago and he is anxious to know you. His actual words which I transcribe are:

"I think I could help. I would call in Chester Square or meet him at his club or mine (Devonshire)."

There is more but the above is sufficient for practical purposes. His address is 7. *Sloane Street*. He has not been very well of late but is better now and thinks of going to Spain soon for a month or so. If you want to enlist him there is no time to lose. Drop him a line. He is by some years your senior,[2] so that there is no impropriety in you taking the first step—for which he is quite prepared. I honestly think that it would be worth your while, from the point of view of the *great Cause*. Besides he is a charming and in many ways an unique personality. Well; no more. God bless you and your work in the new year and in long years to come.

Yours cordially

J. Conrad.

[1] Graham had associated with Engels and quoted Marx in Parliament.
[2] A difference of twelve years.

To J.M. Barrie

Text MS Berg; Unpublished

[letterhead: Pent Farm]

31 Dec 1903

My dear Mr. Barrie.

I am coming in with my best wishes for yourself and Mrs. Barrie on the t[h]reshold of the New Year. I would have liked better to come in person after the rather good French fashion; but I daresay I would not have been much more expressive. Expression just now seems to have gone away from me completely. You must try to think the very best you can of the intention; of the thought and the feeling that remain mute in their fulness.

The reading of the *White Bird*,[1] apart from the sheer pleasure Your work always gives, had a special interest for me as demonstrating once more your wonderful power to deal with fanciful and delicate conceptions; something much too perfect to be called skill. It is rather an amazing continuity of felicitous inspiration.

My work which has no delicacy, no felicity, no inspiration has gone on lamely—but still it has gone on; and I've learned during the last disastrous Year to be very thankful for small mercies. As long as something gets itself written one needn't grumble.

Believe me dear Mr Barrie

always faithfully yours

Jph. Conrad.

To John Galsworthy

Text MS Forbes; Unpublished

[letterhead: Pent Farm]

31st Dec 1903

Dearest Jack.

I want to get in on New Years day with my answer to your Christmas letter. I wish you peace of mind, grasp of Your subject, a continuous flow of inspiration. Everything in short, in the way of alleviation of the unavoidable burden each passing years* lays upon our shoulders. Your road is open. May you travel it as lightly as possible and mark with success each place of rest.

---

[1] *The Little White Bird* (1902), a novel about rather than for children: it includes the first version of *Peter Pan*.

I have been doing a little for the last day or two. It isn't much to boast of.

Jessie's and Borys' love. Ever
Yours

Jph. Conrad.

To R.B. Cunninghame Graham
Text MS Dartmouth; Watts 168

[Pent Farm]
[1903–1905?]¹

Très chèr ami

What a pity this cannot be published. The story has all the character-istic excellence of your work, and the missionary is elaborated with judicious effect.² Clearly this was the only way; but this is a way nobody has except you.—

I send it back regretfully; I should have liked to freeze to it. Don't destroy the copy. The time may come when the good lady could be induced to take off the embargo. Her objection is inept. The man is your creation and an entity while the person she imagines she has met somewhere is probably nobody at all.

Toujours a vous

Conrad.

PS My wife's kindest regards. Don't spoil her with books—tho' she is on ne peut plus fière of your attention. Borys had the grammar read to him. Listened with attention and went away thoughtfully to dig. Not a word of comment.

---

¹ During these years Conrad used the stationery (Rock Bros English Made Bank) for MSS and informal letters (e.g. 27 June 1904). He had also used it before 1903, but Graham, who was kind to children, would not have inflicted a grammar-book on Borys quite so prematurely. On 7 July 1906, his father described Borys as a competent though unenthusiastic reader, but the boy had been slow to learn.

² It is not known whether this story was ever allowed to join Graham's many published studies of missionary eccentricities.

1904

To John Galsworthy
Text MS Forbes; Unpublished

The Pent
Thursday. [7 or 14? January 1904][1]

Dearest Jack

It is a fact that we are coming up to London for a time. It is a sort of desperate move in the game I am playing with the shadow of destruction. In other words, and as it would appear to a dispassionate observer the Hueffers have taken a house in Airlie Gardens (it's Oliver[2] Hueffer's wife's house—*they* live in Manchester now) for three months and have invited us to come for a fortnight—to see how I get on. Anyhow I shall soon explain to you how it came about. As a matter of fact we shall take a couple of rooms on some terrace near by,[3] round the corner, as we used to do at Winchelsea.

I am coming up tomorrow by the midday train, and want to see you first of all if possible. I arrive at Cannon St at 2.5 and would go on at once to Notting Hill Station (by tube) if you can give me audience sometime before three. As to the Monday evening Inter[l] festivity I am your man unless the Heavens fall on my head meantime.

I am in a state of nervous excitement or rather tension which may carry me through the next four weeks of work either all in London or partly in London and partly here. And if it were not for Jessie and the boy I wouldn't mind it killing me at the end.

Yours ever

Conrad.

PS If you can't see me to-morrow (Friday) afternoon pray wire here in the morning. I shan't leave home till 11.30.

To Alice Rothenstein
Text MS Harvard; Unpublished

17 Gordon Place
Kensington. W
23 Jan[y] 1904

Dear Mrs Rot[h]enstein[4]

I am writing for my wife to express our thanks—and our profound regret at our inability to accept your kind invitation for next Tuesday.

[1] The Hueffers moved early in January (Mizener, p. 85).   [2] Ford's brother.
[3] They found rooms at 17 Gordon Place, just off Kensington Church St.
[4] An actress, she married in 1899; née Knewstub, she came from a family with ties to the Pre-Raphaelites.

My wife had an extremely nasty fall and she is now laid up for a few days in a state of utter lameness and profound desolation.[1] She thanks you for Your good and charming letter—in which I join her with all my heart. We, I assure you, have been extremely anxious to make your acquaintance and to be introduced to the children. As soon as my wife can walk more or less upright she shall write asking you to name a convenient day for a call. We are made sorry more than we can say by this horrible contretemps which delays the pleasure we have promised ourselves from being made known to you. With our kindest regards to your husband and Yourself believe me dear Mrs Rot[h]enstein Your most faithful obedient servant

Joseph Conrad.

To J.B. Pinker
Text MS Berg; Unpublished

17. Gordon Place
Kensington W.
Jan. 26. 1904

Continuation of "Nostromo"
more to follow tomorrow.

J. Conrad.

To Sidney Colvin
Text MS Rosenbach; Lucas 302 (in part); *Listy* 230

10. Airlie Gardens.
Tuesday. [2 or 9 February 1904][2]

Dear Mr Colvin.[3]

Many, many thanks for your letter. I am really distressed to think how much of Your valuable time You are, most generously, giving up to that trifle.

---

[1] She hurt both knees; one of the knees, already weakened by an accident in her teens, was damaged for life: Jessie Conrad, *Joseph Conrad as I Knew Him*, pp. 50–1.

[2] Conrad claimed to have written his adaptation of 'To-morrow' in six days (letter of 28 April 1905), but the date of this effort is uncertain. By 7 February, however, he had finished the first version. Among Tuesdays early in the year, 2 and 9 February were by far the most 'beastly as to weather'.

[3] Sidney Colvin (1845–1927; knighted 1911) became a good friend to Conrad, as he had been to Stevenson. Colvin had been Slade Professor of Fine Arts at Cambridge and

As a matter of fact I *feel* on the subject with you. And this is not because I've no conception, no general *idée a moi*, of what I'd like to do on the stage. I have that. But I have also a very clear perception of my innate clumsiness in carrying out anything, unless with much toil and trouble. Work has never been to me a feast of cakes and ale.

In this case I've been hampered also by the particular ignorance of the craft. Therefore I went straight ahead catching the inspiration of the moment as it came for fear that a more careful reflexion would bring me to absolute inaction. The only thing I've consciously looked to was verisimilitude of dialogue. And even there I've an uneasy suspicion of having failed.

Not altogether, however, I suppose, since you think the thing worth talking over. I assure you that if there were no such thing in the world as a theatrical manager I would still be most eager to hear (and absorb) Your criticism.

It occurs to me that the day being very beastly as to weather and one likely to keep people at home I could perhaps see you to-day. I sit to Sauter[1] till a little after 4—and at about a quarter to five I could be at the museum[2]—if you wish to give me an hour to-day. The messenger has orders to wait if you are at home.

But if not pray be good enough to indicate the day and hour. No appointment of mine—unless absolutely par force majeure—shall be allowed to stand in the way.

> With kindest regards I am very
> faithfully yours
> Jph Conrad.

To H.G. Wells
Text MS Illinois; J-A, 1, 326

> 7th Febr. 1904
> 17. Gordon Place
> Kensington
> London W.

My dearest HG.

I am a kickable person for not letting out a squeak about myself to you. But we've been in a sort of a tempest ever since our arrival here.

Director of the Fitzwilliam Museum; among his literary works were editions of Stevenson's letters and biographies of Landor and Keats.
[1] Galsworthy's brother-in-law Georg (1866–1935), a painter born in Germany.
[2] From 1884 to 1912, Colvin was Keeper of Prints and Drawings at the British Museum.

Jessie fell in the street and wrenched both her knees. No joke to her and an awful anxiety to me. However she gets on very well but no doubt expensively. Then Watson & C⁰ failed and I've lost a good friend for he did back me up through all these six years.[1] Of course I shall be bothered now about my overdraft and so on.

No matter. I've been working on Nostromo besides writing a play in one act[2] (based on my To Morrow story) on the suggestion of S: Colvin who has been very friendly. Another acquaintance which I owe to you my dear fellow in the long list of your good offices.

I've started a series of sea sketches and have sent out P on the hunt to place them. This must *save* me. I've discovered that I can dictate that sort of bosh without effort at the rate of 3000 words in four hours. Fact! The only thing now is to sell it to a paper and then make a book of the rubbish. Hang!

So in the day *Nostromo* and from 11 pm to 1 am dictation. No more just now.

We trust that You both and chicks are well. Our dear love

Always Your

Conrad.

To J.B. Pinker
Text MS Berg; Unpublished

17 Gordon Place
Kensington W.
[early February? 1904][3]

My dear P.

Watt's answer abridged runs: offer £40 *but if refused McC[lure] desires time to consult Harmsworth*[4] *and settle matters end this week or the next one way or another.*

My reply runs:

Don't mean to haggle. Conrad's stuff of that sort not difficult to

---

[1] Adjudication against the banker William Watson and his partner Paul Pfeiderer was announced in the London papers on 6 February.

[2] Since he is now occupied with a mere two projects, *Nostromo* and *The Mirror of the Sea*, Conrad must mean that he has finished the play.

[3] On 7 February, Pinker was 'on the hunt to place' the proposed 'series of sea sketches'.

[4] These negotiations involved Alfred Harmsworth, proprietor of the mass-circulation *Daily Mail*, and Robert McClure, who represented the London interests of his brother Sam. The third person may have been A. P. Watt, a long-established agent and Pinker's rival.

place—as man of his experience knows well—besides being capable of expansion.

My reply continued

If in earnest D. M. ought to have been prepared to accept my terms. Refuse further personal correspondence.

Am fully advising my very good Friend and agent Mr J. B. Pinker of understanding as to Mr Watt acting on this occasion for me.

Beg him communicate with Mr Pinker if desires to carry matter further.

My Reply ends.

I suppose he will. If so please take line as follows: Conrad annoyed. £60 the price. Cash on delivery. (2500 to 3000 words.[1] serial rights) Book rights reserved strictly. _____

Of course my dear fellow you'll use your own judgment but try to avoid climbing down. Still it may be worth while to take something less and reserve Am^{can} serial rights. But avoid it if possible. DM ought pay sixty for English rights alone. Try that. _____

As to series which my dear fellow are of vital importance to me and my work. Pray start the business *at once* where and how You like. I engage to furnish one a week [for][2] either six or ten.

Also pray fix book with option of short vol: at 3/6 (or illustrated at 5/-) or with added matter to 50000 in 6/- form, or illustrated at 10/6.

Proposed title.

The Mirror of the Sea _____

I forward you here a list of contents as I have them in my mind.[3]

> Gales of Wind
> Up Anchor
> Yards and Masts
> The Cut of the Sails
> The Web of Ropes
> Old Timbers.

_____

optional

> Round the Compass.
> The Chance of Landfalls

---

[1] Per essay? Or a mistake for 25 to 30 thousand?
[2] Cancellation restored for clarity.   [3] These titles were soon changed.

The Run of the Seas
etc   etc.

Essays—impressions, descriptions, reminiscences anecdotes and typical traits—of the old sailing fleet which passes away for good with the last century. Easy narrative style.

Work it for all it's worth! If you can do better for the series as a whole drop D.M. completely. Perhaps the DM itself may take up the idea. In that case Watt must not be let in beyond the first. Matter of life and death to me. You shall get the stuff this week. Yours

Conrad.

PS Pray find out how much TP's W[eekly] will pay for F. M. H[ueffer]'s article.

To Frances Colvin
Text MS Rosenbach; Unpublished

17. Gordon Place
[London] W.
Sunday [February 1904][1]

Dear Mrs Colvin.[2]

Thanks very much. As you may imagine I shall be delighted to avail myself of your kind invitation for Wednesday.

I take this opportunity to say that I went about the mending of the little play at once, with Mr Colvin's remarks fresh in my mind, and keeping strictly to the line of alterations indicated by him. The pages are being typed now.

My wife who is improving slowly sends her kind regards. She rejoices to know, on my report, that, in the matter of briskness, she is being hopelessly outdistanced by Mr Colvin.

I am, dear Mrs Colvin,

Your very faithful and obedient
servant

Jph. Conrad

---

[1] After the visit proposed to Colvin on 2 or 9 February, and before 4 March, when Tree was looking at the play, presumably in typescript: 7, 14, 21, or 28 February.

[2] Née Fetherstonhaugh (1839–1924). After separation from her first husband, the Rev. A. H. Sitwell, she made a living as an essayist; when she married Colvin in 1903, she had known him for over thirty years. Their friend Robert Louis Stevenson venerated her as his 'madonna'.

To the Chairman of the Provisional Committee of the Henley Memorial

Text MS Berg; Unpublished

> 17. Gordon Place.
> Kensington. W.
> 17th Febr^y 1904

Dear Sir.[1]

I accept with great pleasure the invitation of the Provisional Committee of the Henley memorial. I never met Mr Henley[2] and I regret bitterly now the putting off of that great pleasure and privilege—which after all was never to be realized in the end.

Though, unfortunately, remaining without the circle of his personal contact I've like many others, felt his influence. His lamented death has left me under the painful sense of unexpressed obligation. His admission of a story of mine to the pages of the National Review[3] was the first event in my writing life which really counted. And I don't know when—if ever—there will be another of the same intrinsic value, as encouragement and recognition. The two or three letters I wrote him[4] seem now miserably inadequate as the expression of a very genuine feeling of gratitude. It seemed impossible to tell him on paper that the story he accepted for the Review was written with an eye on him[5]—and yet with no idea whatever that it would ever meet his eye. And that is the strict truth. At the time he was to me but an inaccessible name—so widely did he cast abroad the spell of his individuality, the beneficent white magic of his masterful temperament working for the truth, vigour, for the right expression and the right thought in literature.

I remain, dear Sir, very faithfully Yours,

Jph Conrad.

---

[1] As a result of the Committee's work, Rodin's bust of Henley was unveiled in St Paul's Cathedral, 11 July 1907. The Chairman was then George Windsor-Clive (1857–1923), newly created Earl of Plymouth; the identity of the Chairman in 1903 remains hidden.

[2] Poet, critic, and editor (1849–1903): the patron of Wells and many other promising authors.

[3] *The Nigger* in the *New Review*; Henley had also edited the *National Observer*.

[4] Only the letter of 18 October 1898 survives.

[5] The paean to England and the excoriation of sentimental 'pity' would have pleased Henley—without betraying Conrad's own position.

To J.B. Pinker

Text MS Berg; Unpublished

[London]
Wednesday [24? February
1904][1]

My dear Pinker.

I send you the D. M. article—about 1000 words.[2]

I also send you the cheque which turned up last night. I think that is the last which has not been presented in time. I sent it on to Miss Hills the postmistress[3] in payment of taxes. Pray write out a cheque for the amount to *Mrs E Hills* and put it into the open letter which I send on to you—in time for the country post.

The 4th paper (of 3000 words) is finished. You shall have it in a day or two. Also 37 pages of Nostromo which is going on well.

To J.B. Pinker

Text MS Berg; Unpublished

[London]
Thursday. [25? February 1904][4]

My dear Pinker.

I intend to call on you to morrow bringing No 4 of the *Mirror of the Sea* and a letter I've received in connection with Watson's failure.

Everything is progressing steadily. Will you find out if the D.M. is likely to want the other two 1000 word papers to follow "*Missing*". I would propose to call them II[d] "*Overdue*" and III[d] "*Stranded*".[5]

Eventually they would go to swell the volume of the others. It is really the same sort of thing only done short.

I've plenty of material.

Yours truly

J Conrad.

I would come about 3 unless you are engaged at that hour.

---

[1] By Wednesday 2 March, the fifth paper was 'half done'.
[2] 'Missing': *Daily Mail*, 8 March, p. 4; *Mirror of the Sea*, XVI.
[3] Mrs Emma Hills, sub-postmistress and shopkeeper at Stanford, Kent.
[4] Another letter about the fourth paper.
[5] *Daily Mail*, 16 November, p. 4, and 2 December, p. 6; *Mirror of the Sea*, XVIII–XIX and XX–XXI.

To Kazimierz Waliszewski
Text L.fr. 65; Najder 243

17 Gordon Place
Kensington
London W.
fev[rier] 1904[1]

Cher Monsieur,

Mille remerciements pour le don de votre livre,[2] que je me prépare à lire avec joie.

Nous sommes depuis un mois au milieu de toutes sortes d'avantures. Ma pauvre femme s'est démise un genou en tombant. Donc médecin, chirurgien, masseuse et tout ce qui s'ensuit. Là-dessus mon banquier fait faillite et je me trouve soudain sans banque, sans argent, sans carnet de chèques,—sensation atroce dont je frémis encore. Evidemment la chose à faire était d'écrire un drame en un acte. C'est ce que je me suis empressé de faire. La lecture de la pièce a déjà épouvanté un de nos directeurs,—les autres sans doute partageront sa frayeur. Puis je viens de signer un contrat pour une série d'esquisses de mer (un journal quelconque): mon roman que l'on a commencé en feuilleton[3] n'est pas encore terminé (il reste une douzaine de chapitres à faire) et dans mes moments perdus je cherche un banquier naif et bienfaisant qui veuille bien me fournir un carnet de chèques,—par amour du prochain sans doute, car je ne possède pas de fonds à lui offrir. Voilà.

J'espère, cher Monsieur, que vous voyez la situation nettement. Il ne me reste donc qu'à ajouter que je suis à la page 24 de *Ivan le Terrible*, c'est à dire que j'ai été 24 fois consolé par l'oubli complet de mes embarras.

D'ailleurs ma femme se tirera fort bien d'affaire quoique nous avons eu les plus graves inquiétudes. Aujourd'hui même elle a traversé la chambre en marchant avec une canne. Ce petit fait vous explique le ton de cette lettre qui aurait dû être lugubre.

Kozakiewicz est bien bon de penser à me traduire,[4]—ou c'est peut-être votre idée amie, n'est-ce-pas. Puisque vous indiquez la possibilité de votre concours je n'ose pas soulever la question de mon mérite. Reste donc: *l'affaire.* Eh bien, j'ai peur que l'affaire sera mauvaise! Ceci est mon sentiment vrai.

---

[1] Evidently before Jessie Conrad's journey to the Pent on 4 March. The 'directeur' in the second paragraph cannot be Tree, therefore, but some member of the 'provisional Committee' (4 March to Colvin).
[2] *Ivan le terrible* (Paris, 1904).   [3] 29 January.
[4] Bronisław Kozakiewicz (died 1924): nothing came of his plan.

Veuillez présenter mes hommages à madame Waliszewska et croyez,
cher Monsieur, toujours bien à vous.

Translation

Dear Sir,
    A thousand thanks for the gift of your book, which I am gleefully
preparing to read.
    For the last month we have been in the midst of all kinds of surprises.
My poor wife has dislocated her knee in falling. Then, doctor, surgeon,
masseuse, and all that entails. On top of that, my banker failed, and I
found myself suddenly without a bank, without money, and without a
cheque-book—a dreadful feeling which still makes me tremble. The
obvious thing to do was to write a play in one act. It is what I hastened to
do. Reading the piece has already terrified one of our directors—no
doubt the others will share his terror. Then I have just signed a contract
for a series of sea sketches (a journal of sorts): my novel, which has
started in serial, is not yet finished (a dozen chapters remain to be done)
and in my spare moments I look for an ingenuous and charitable banker
willing to supply me with a cheque-book—for love of his neighbour no
doubt, for I have no funds to offer him. There it is!
    I hope, dear sir, that you see the situation clearly. It only remains for
me to add that I am on page 24 of *Ivan the Terrible*; that is to say that I
have been comforted 24 times by complete forgetfulness of my difficulties.
    In any event, my wife is recovering fully from this business, although
we have had the gravest anxiety. Today she has even crossed the room,
walking with a stick. This little fact explains to you the tone of this letter,
which should have been doleful.
    Kozakiewicz is very good to think of translating me—or is it perhaps
your friendly idea? As you indicate the possibility of your cooperation, I
dare not raise the question of my merit. There remains, then: *business*.
Well, I am afraid that the business will be bad! This is my true
sentiment.
    Please convey my regards to Madame Waliszewska and believe me,
dear sir, always yours.

To J.B. Pinker

Text MS Berg; Unpublished

Wednesday.
2 Mch. [1904]
17 Gordon Place
Kensington W.

Dear Pinker.

I send you the Causerie for the *P.M.M.*[1]

My wife is leaving to morrow morning for the Pent and I want you to send me £10 to day that I may send her off. Could you give it to the boy, and also instruct him to pass at* your bank and get cash for the cheque. *Two £5 notes.*

Pardon me worrying about all this but if I were to attend to all these things my morning's dictation would go to pot. You'll get the 2^d D Mail paper to morrow. The 5th paper of the M of the Sea is half done. When there are six I shall devote myself exclusively to Nostromo.

Another idea for more work has occurred to me. I shall call in to morrow about that, in the afternoon.

Yours sincerely

Jph Conrad.

To Sidney Colvin

Text MS Duke; Lucas 302 (in part)

17 Gordon Place
Kensington W.
4th Mch 1904

Dear Mr Colvin.

Indeed your patience and interest in the play seem inexhaustible; and if anything may make me think better of the tribe that certainly will do it.

I am very sorry to hear Mrs Colvin is not well. Pray thank her from me for her kind words. I needed no reminder of her graciousness which has produced a deep impression on myself and my wife. She sends her sympathetic regards on leaving (to-day) for the country, to pick up the dropped threads of our life there. I remain here bound fast by the necessities of dictation which is the only way, as I discover, to breast the high wave of work which threatens to swallow me up altogether.

[1] 'A Glance at Two Books' reviewed Galsworthy's *The Island Pharisees* and Hudson's *Green Mansions*. This 'Causerie', which did not appear in the *Pall Mall Magazine*, was printed posthumously in *Last Essays*. The MS is dated 2 March.

Reverting to the play. I imagine that the provisional Committee (including Miss Constance Collyer) is much too indulgent. Mr Tree[1] no doubt will show himself more severe; and I am willing (quite honestly) to admit the justness of all his remarks—beforehand. I do not, even in my thoughts, question your judgment and experience. The only questions that arise are: Is the thing (so slight) worth the labour—which is partly answered by the fact of your interest; next: what of the Time (with a cap: T). I am by no means sure that there is a playwright (let alone a dramatist) in me. But let us wait for M[r] Tree's verdict which it occurs to me may settle the matter beyond any question. Believe me dear M[r] Colvin yours very gratefully

                                                                    Jph. Conrad.

To J.B. Pinker
Text MS Berg; Unpublished

[letterhead: 10, Airlie Gardens,
Campden Hill Road, W.]
Monday [7 March 1904][2]

Dear Pinker.

Don't be alarmed; but my doctor advises me to go for a day to Deal[3] in order to get rid of a certain nervousness which has been bothering me since Saturday.

He sounded me. Everything is right. Only nerves—just a bit on the stretch. Ford is going with me and we shall finish the sixth paper there.[4] We start now and are returning on Wednesday night.

The 5th paper as You know is ready but can not be dictated into type this afternoon as we intended.[5] This morning I did 5 pp of *Nostromo*. There is no question of a breakdown. Batten[6] simply wants me to pause for 48 hours. He is quite aware of the situation. The 3[d] Dy Mail paper is

---

[1] Herbert Beerbohm Tree (1853–1917), one of the great actor-managers, had presided at His Majesty's Theatre since 1897. Constance Collier was a leading member of his company between 1901 and 1908; among her famous roles were Cleopatra, and Nancy in *Oliver Twist*. In *One Day More*, she played the daughter.

[2] The progress of the sea sketches (fifth 'ready', sixth to be finished, third *Daily Mail* paper all but finished) suggests a place between the letters of 2 and '4' [=14] March.

[3] On the Kentish coast, about 85 miles from London.

[4] Although its extent is debatable, Ford had a hand in the sketches composed before his nervous breakdown (letter of 19 September and Mizener, pp. 88–9); he also took some of them down in shorthand at Conrad's dictation.

[5] To judge by the letter of 29 March, Pinker did not have number five until late in the month.

[6] Rayner Derry Batten, a Harley Street physician and surgeon.

ready all but the last par—or two. Send me £5 to the ad[d]ress I am going to give you in the postscript. On Thursday you shall get about *50* pp of *N* and probably the 3^d Dy Mail.

I depend upon you in that little matter.

Yours Ever

J. Conrad

The Royal Hotel.
Deal.

To J.B. Pinker

Text MS Berg; Unpublished

[London]

4th [14th?] March 1904[1]

My dear Pinker.

I found I've left myself literally without any money. Pray send me a sovereign by the boy.

I am afraid I must ask you to let me have a lot of money this week Fifteen pounds at least; Jessie discovered another returned cheque for *£4 10/-* in the country. The people did not want to bother us about it and waited for our return. As they are rather small people I must settle with them; otherwise I was going to ask you for only ten.

Tree is now considering the play, and Colvin takes an immense interest in my development as dramatist. Without entertaining undue hopes I may say that if I once get in something may be achieved. The principal thing is to make such originality as I possess, *acceptable* to the public. That is really the crux of the matter. But a man who has invented five headlines for an article of 1000 words to please the Dly Mail (and I've done that very thing) is capable of sage compromise, I should think.

N° 6 of the *M^{or} of the Sea* finished last night.

Yours

Conrad.

---

[1] Apparently later than the 'Monday' [7 March] letter: '4th March', therefore, is likely to be wrong; a forgotten stroke of the pen is a common error. Unless she sent a telegram, his wife could not have told him about the returned cheque on the day she arrived.

To Adolf Krieger

Text MS Ogilvie; *CWW* 395

1904
15th March
17 Gordon Place,
Kensington W.

My dear Krieger.[1]

Pardon the delay, but now you may take this bill as absolutely safe. In fact I shall take it up before it matures. It is made payable at Pinker's office because I've no banker after Watson's failure. Two fifty[2] gone in one fell swoop. I am nearly out of my mind with worry and overwork. My nerves are all to pieces. On top of all that my wife had a nasty fall in the street and wrenched both her knee-caps. There was an awful business with doctors nurses, massage, surgical implements and all that. She just can crawl about now, and is gone back to the Pent; but I am afraid that for all practical purposes she will remain a cripple.

Yours affectionately,

Jph Conrad

To Edward Garnett

Text MS Sutton; G.191

Pent
Saturday [March 1904][3]

Dearest Edward.

I am very sorry but I had a distinct impression of having written to say we were coming to London. Please forgive me this time.

If I haven't seen You I've seen no one else either. Dawson[4] did turn up once for an hour and, yes—Cunninghame Graham who invited himself to the Pent and had to be told we were coming up on the very day he proposed for his visit.

I tried to write (and finish) an imbecile sort of story in that time. It is indeed very imbecile but it isn't finished yet.

If I did better work, more of it and a little easier you would see me

---

[1] Adolf Philip Krieger (c.1850–1918) became one of Conrad's first friends in England early in the 1880s. Krieger proved helpful in many ways, seeking out positions for Conrad and lending him substantial amounts of money. The friendship began to cool in 1897, apparently over Conrad's indebtedness to Krieger.

[2] The approximate size of his overdraft.

[3] The contents confirm Garnett's dating; Conrad returned to the Pent between 15 and 20 March.

[4] Ernest or his brother A. J.

often enough. As it is I am shy of inflicting myself upon my friends. I go about oppressed, secretly irritated against my works, never free from it, never satisfied with it. Not a man of profit or pleasure for his friends.

But it's too difficult to explain. I can only ask you to believe in my very steady affection for you and all yours. You are much more with me than you suspect. All unconscious you check and sometimes urge my pen. It's a fact.

Ever yours
Conrad.

To Arnold Bennett

Text TS/MS UCL; J-A, 1, 327

Pent Farm,
Stanford, near Hythe,
Kent
[late March or early April?
1904][1]

My dear Bennett

Excuse typing.[2] I haven't got into the way of writing after a bout of gout yet. As it happens I have dramatised "To-morrow" myself and I leave to your unbiassed judgment to say which version—the English or French[3]—is the more individual and artistic. Both MSS go by book post.

Tree has my play to look at through the agency of Sidney Colvin. Frankly, in my opinion, the French dramatisation has for its only merit the evidently good knowledge of the English language. It is too long in exposition (and so is mine I fear), and for the rest lacks force in dialogue. I think I could write something much more striking in French myself; but if, on reflection, you think it feasible to show my rendering to your friend, and he would like to translate it, accepting the spirit of my conception and letting me see the MS, I would of course agree to his terms, he working the French end of the business while I shall try to do something with it here, if no more but to secure a performance by the Dramatic Society.[4] Colvin takes a great interest in the thing.

[1] Jean-Aubry has February, but Conrad was in London until mid-March. Around 4 March Colvin had sent the play to Tree; on 5 April, Conrad was recovering from an attack of gout.

[2] The salutation, 'just now', and the PS are in holograph.

[3] A version by P. H. Raymond-Duval opened at the Théâtre des Arts in Paris on 14 April 1909.

[4] *One Day More* was mounted by the Stage Society in June 1905.

We have had a rough time of it generally, serious misfortunes hindering my work and destroying the peace of my soul, but I shall say nothing of them, just now.

Many thanks for the trouble you have taken and apologies for suggesting more.

> Believe me, my dear Bennett,
> With great regard,
> Joseph Conrad

You will notice my play has full stage dir[ecti]ons. It makes it long in reading, rather.

Tree has a slightly shortened version and therefore an improved one—but there was only one copy of it. The fishman is cut down considerably, also old Carvil at the very beginning. A situation or rather action which repeats itself is eliminated in one place. That one would be the version to translate. But in essentials *this is* the play.

To John Galsworthy

Text MS Forbes; Unpublished

> [letterhead: Pent Farm]
> Monday. [21 March 1904][1]

Dearest Jack

Yesterday the doctors did not leave till they had seen Jessie in bed where she must remain for three weeks.

It's her only chance as they tell me; both however think that the chance is good. Tebb[2] told me plainly that this was 'not a thing to play with'. He believes that if she were to remain about exerting herself in the usual way all the ordinary symptoms of heart disease would develop themselves in less than six months. On the other hand he has a *very good hope* that the treatment upon which he and Hackney have agreed will prove successful.

She is very cheerful and very amused at being put to bed. Miss Hallowes[3] is behaving very kindly and for a few days Nellie[4] can manage alone, while I try to get some help for her.

---

[1] The day after the joint consultation, which Conrad described on 29 March as happening 'Last Sunday week'. This is the first use of letterhead eleven.

[2] Albert Tebb, a London physician, attended the Hueffers among other families in the worlds of literature and painting.

[3] Lillian Mary Hallowes (1870–1950) had been hired for a month. With substantial interruptions, she remained Conrad's 'typewriter' and secretary for the rest of his life.

[4] Nellie Lyons, the maid.

As to myself—well. I did no dictation on Sunday but am going to begin this morning at ten. You must come and see me soon. Yours ever

Conrad.

To Alice Rothenstein

Text MS Harvard; Unpublished

[letterhead: Pent Farm]

Tuesday [22 March 1904][1]

Dear Mrs. Rothenstein

I behaved badly in not writing to you before; but the fact is I was feeling far from well. Besides the anxiety till Dr Tebb came was so great that I could not concentrate my thoughts upon anything whatever. The dear man has comforted me greatly. He and young Hackney[2] (who liked him at first sight immensely) sent Jessie to bed, instantly, for 3 weeks. As to myself I went to bed too yesterday with headache and high temperature wondering dismally enough what was coming. However I am better to-day, and *must* get well by to-morrow. Illness in the present circumstances would be utter ruin and desolation.

This afternoon I shall begin to dictate again. Too many days have been wasted already. Miss Hallowes (the typewriter) turns out to be a most good-natured, useful girl.

Your affectionate interest and true friendship are most precious to us both in this time of difficulty.

I am too dull and heavy just at this moment to find any sort of expression for our feelings or even to go on writing words that mean so little; but we send our best love to you four. I dont enlarge upon the state of the patient as I've asked Dr Tebb to tell You everything.

Believe me dear Mrs Rothenstein most affectionately and gratefully Yours

J. Conrad

To J.B. Pinker

Text MS Berg; Unpublished

[letterhead: Pent Farm]

29 Mch 1904

My dear Pinker

Last Sunday week the local doctor and the man I got to come from London sent my wife to bed for a month; not only on account of her knee

[1] The day after the letter to Galsworthy: the envelope is postmarked 22 March, and the letterhead is type eleven.

[2] Clifford Hackney rather than John, his partner.

but as her only chance to get her heart right. The treatment promises well and that is all I can say for the present. You can easily understand my anxiety and worry.

The worst is that a beastly attack of influenza laid me out in bed too. No use repining. I went in just a week to-day with temperature above 104. No joke. But since last Saturday[1] I've commenced dictating again, the first two days from under the blankets and now (since yesterday) from a couch in the sitting room.

I wonder I don't go mad with despair and apprehension. However I feel fairly sane yet. Galsworthy has been here to see me on Sunday and I have arranged with him to correct for me the MS of Nostromo should I have no time myself. It is a great relief indeed. I am sending him a batch to-day, which we shall forward direct to you.

I trust you have now paper V of the Mirror of the Sea. That was all I was able to do during the height of my influenza. Except paper VI which is ready but not typed I have nothing more in that way done. But I've in my head a 2500 paper about a voyage with a cargo of explosives[2] and shall try to get it ready at odd times.

It's no use mincing matters my dear Pinker. In order to exist here I want £45. There are my taxes £8.17. and I must distribute a few pounds amongst my tradesmen, or my position shall become untenable. I am too weary to say more than this that I must hang on here till Nostromo is finished. And I haven't but 2/- in the house. It's awful! If I were to think of it all too much all the sand would run out of me.

As to the typewriter young Lady it occurs to me that the month I arranged for at the office is running out. Their charge is too heavy. But as obviously I would want her after Nostromo to complete the Mirror vol: and so on I don't know whether it would not be better to make some arrangement with her direct. I've a machine and the girl would stay for 25/- per week I fancy: if I could guarantee her 6 months' work.

It strikes me that if you could make a contract better than the Harpers for the next novel—the one based on the blo[c]kade of Brest you are at liberty to do so, since their agreement says *Mediterranean** novel. I thought of giving them the Bay of Biscay instead but after all there's no time limit to their agreement and I've a Meditt: story (of another kind) up my sleeve.[3] But I don't feel disposed to write it—not till I've seen two

[1] The 26th.   [2] Raw material for *Chance?*
[3] Conrad's interests in the Mediterranean and the time of Napoleon later converged in *The Rover* and *Suspense*. The great Atlantic naval base at Brest was blockaded from 1793 to 1801.

or three places. When that'll happen devil only knows unless Nostromo makes a hit—I mean a real money success.

For goodness sake don't drop me now I am just hanging on by my teeth.

Always yours

J. Conrad

To John Galsworthy
Text MS Forbes; Unpublished

[letterhead: Pent Farm]
Good Friday. [1 April 1904][1]

Dearest Jack

The misery goes on. Poor Jess had heart attacks the other day. Meantime the leg shows sign of athropy* but no improvement. I daren't even wish myself dead. At any rate dictation goes on every day since you left. 1600 words yesterday—and so on.

Is it all well with You?

Ever Yours

Conrad.

To John Galsworthy
Text MS Forbes; Unpublished

[letterhead: Pent Farm]
5th April 1904.
2 am.

Dearest Jack.

I am sorry to hear that all is not well with you. It fills me with vague uneasiness, which I can not define. I can't think though I can feel—and only by that I know I am alive! Pain and trouble are the only incontrevertible* realities of existence. Happiness can be controverted and ease denied—even if it existed!

Jessie's nerves are giving way. She is lying now light-headed and groaning with the pain of neuralgia all over the body. And I sit here writing to you at her dressing table with a sort of notion in my head that this is hell. I suppose I am near enough to insanity. She has been suffering all day like this. I do not see the end. And how am I to write fiction to-morrow?

[1] Letterhead eleven suggests the year; the miserable news confirms it.

Never mind. My dearest Jack can you let me have a cheque for 5gs to send to Dr Tebb. I just had a little from P but people came around with their little bills and got it all from me. I am ashamed to keep the man waiting any longer for his fee. By Jove this existence is like a horrible nightmare in which one sits and dictates with one's heart in one's mouth all the time. Yours ever

Conrad.

To David Meldrum
Text MS Duke; Blackburn 179

[letterhead: Pent Farm]
5th Ap. 1904

Dear Mr^r Meldrum.

We came to London end Jany for a fortnight and before we had been there a week my poor wife had a nasty fall in the street putting out both knee caps.

This was bad enough, to be laid up in London lodgings with the bother and expense of doctor, nurse, massage, surgical appliances and so on—not to speak of the pain to the patient and the anxiety for me. I was far from well myself after a year of ill health and making desperate efforts to get on with my story. On the top of that came the failure of my bankers (Watson & Co).

This is not the worst however. My poor wife who has been complaining of not feeling very well ever since last Oct was found to have a valvular defect of the heart. After nearly two months of worry in London (I going on working all the time to stave off utter annihilation) I got her down here. The doctors in consultation have sent her to bed for six weeks both for her heart and her knee. She certainly can't walk and it looks bad; it looks as if she were to be a helpless cripple. The words as I write give a shudder. There is something seriously wrong with the left leg which she had injured in the same way many years before. It is obviously wasting. She has (even in bed) surgical appliances on both.

She has been now laid up for 3 weeks. Her heart seems better; but now, after all her anxieties and shocks she had, her nerves are giving way and as I write to you in her bedroom she is lying lightheaded and groaning with neuralgia in all the limbs.

I myself have just got over an attack of gout. I stiffen my back but I feel the tension nearing the breaking point. I've here a typewriter to whom I am dictating the last part of Nostromo. What the stuff is like

God only knows. Half the time I feel on the verge of insanity. The difficulties are accumulating around me in a frightful manner. Pardon this dismal letter following on such a long silence. I had not the heart to write; and I may just as well have kept silent now but for my desire to assure You of my great and unalterable regard.

I can write no more.

Kindest messages from us both to Mrs Meldrum and the children

Yours

Conrad.

To J.B. Pinker
Text MS Berg; Unpublished

[letterhead: Pent Farm]

1904

5th April

Dear Pinker.

By this post I am sending you (regd) a batch of Nostromo. The next set to follow in a few days shall contain the end of P. II. Part Third will not take long.

Thanks for the cheque for twenty safely to hand. But my dear fellow pray make the next (which you promised for this week) for 25. I've to pay Dr Tebb's fee for coming here and I [am] ashamed to keep him waiting any longer.

I am informing the Typing office that I bring my arrangement with them to an end.

Miss H of course remains with me. She will be necessary for I mean to write a lot of stuff of all sorts after finishing Nostromo. Pray my dear Pinker send her salary directly to her as long as she remains with me—25/- per week.

I shall return those people's machine on Thursday or Friday at latest; and on that day the arrangement with Miss Hallowes shall begin.

If you should place the papers as a series let me know and in [a] fortnight you shall get two more. Meantime I don't bother finishing them. It is a dismal time with me here and I require all my energies for *N.*

Kindest regards

Yours Conrad

To John Galsworthy
Text MS Forbes; Unpublished

[letterhead: Pent Farm]
Wednesday [6 April 1904][1]

My dearest Jack

No end of thanks. Jessie is better to-day and sends her love. It was an awful neuralgic bout which I am glad to say has done her no harm according to Hackney. He made a thorough examination to day. Of course she feels weak. I bear up extremely well, but mentally I feel languid. Even writing this letter is a terrible effort.

Lots more to do. Still with Miss Hallowes here, I think I can manage to pull it all off in a month. She is now taken over by me for six months.

I shall try to work late to night at correcting.

Haven't heard from the H[ueffer]s. Are they all right?

With love my dear Jack

Always Yours

J. Conrad.

To J.B. Pinker
Text MS Berg; Unpublished

[letterhead: Pent Farm]
Friday [8 April 1904][2]

My dear Pinker.

Many thanks for last cheque.

The enclosed is for your information; and in this matter I want you to tell me whether I may talk to Harvey about the Sea papers.

Next: whether I ought to tell him of another plan for a book I have in my mind.

I ask you because I want to be guided by you so as not to traverse any line you have taken or intend to take in the disposal of my work.

Of course I would not touch upon terms and conditions.

I don't attach much importance to this invitation. Still out of a conversation over a table cloth something might arise which you could convert into satisfactory business.

---

[1] Letterhead eleven, Mrs Conrad's sufferings, and Miss Hallowes' re-engagement suggest a date in late March or early April. Galsworthy must have sent the £5 requested on 5 April by return post; Stanford had two collections and two deliveries a day.

[2] The lunch with Harvey (of Harper & Brothers) took place on 14 April; this is the Friday before.

Write me what you think and on Thurs: next I intend to call on you before proceeding to the lunch. (about 12.45)

Nostromo goes on.

Yours cordially

J. Conrad

To William Rothenstein

Text MS Harvard; Unpublished

[letterhead: Pent Farm]
[10] April 1904[1]
Sunday

My dear Rothenstein

I find I must come up to town on Thursday next, and I am bold enough to ask whether You would put me up for a night.

I ask because I don't imagine myself spending a night away from home under any other roof, just now.

But pray, do not on any account let me make myself a nuisance to your wife and yourself. I could get back here by the last train if necessary. Good Dr Tebb turned up unexpectedly to day cheering us both up immensely. He's pleased with the patient's progress.

Jessie sends most affectionate messages

Yours always

Jph. Conrad.

To John Galsworthy

Text MS Forbes; Unpublished

[letterhead: Pent Farm]
Sunday evening. [10 April 1904][2]

Dearest Jack

We do grieve for Mrs Galsworthy's loss.[3] But you are right. It was a good merciful death; merciful to the departed and to the living too.

I must come to town this week, and would lunch with you on Friday if the thing is feasible, if you feel disposed to put up with my depressing

---

[1] 'Thursday next' would be 14 April; on 18 April Conrad thanked the Rothensteins for their hospitality.

[2] Letterhead eleven gives the period and the resemblance to the Rothenstein letter the precise date.

[3] Of her brother, Arthur Charles Cooper, who had just died: R. H. Mottram, *For Some We Loved* (Hutchinson, 1956), p. 22.

presence. But I beg You insistently not to alter any of Your arrangements for that.

Dr Tebb came to day to see Jessie. It seems that this rest has done a
lot of good. They wish to keep her in bed for another fortnight. Our love

Yours ever

Jph. Conrad

No end of thanks for the three vols of Navy Rds[1] Don't mention my visit
to London anywhere.

To George Harvey

Text MS Harvard; Unpublished

[London]
15th Ap. 1904

Dear Sir.[2]

I have a book which is nearly ready, a volume of Sea-sketches,
something in the spirit of Turgeniev's *Sportsman's Sketches*,[3] but
concerned with ships and sea with a distinct autobiographical and
anecdotal note running through what is mainly meant for a record of
remembered feelings. It is, before all, a temperamental work which I
consider of importance for my literary reputation. For title I thought of:
A Seaman's Sketches or if a more general effect is desired *Mirror of the Sea*. I
would like it serialized about the time when Nostromo appears in book
form—especially in the US, to be of course published later on as a
volume.

I of course don't know how far you desire me to be "Your"
author—and of course also I am not asking that question. My feeling is
that I would not like to see my future work scattered amongst various
publishing firms—as it had been in the past. I have therefore asked Mr.
Pinker to approach you in the matter before taking any steps elsewhere.
I am, dear Sir, Yours faithfully

Jph Conrad.

---

[1] *Publications of the Navy Records Society.*

[2] George Brinton McClellan Harvey (1864–1928), president of Harper & Brothers from
1901 to 1915, edited both *Harper's Weekly* and the *North American Review*. From 1921 to
1923 he was ambassador to Great Britain; in 1924 and 1925, editor of the *Washington
Post*.

[3] A book much admired in Conrad's circle, especially by Garnett and Ford.

To J.B. Pinker

Text MS Berg; Unpublished

[letterhead: Pent Farm]
18 Apr 1904.

My dear Pinker.

I did write to Col: Harvey, before I left the club to go home,[1] in the sense indicated by your note for which thanks.

I suppose you will be seeing him on Mond: or Tuesday for I fancy I heard him say something about Wednesday being his last day for engagements.

May I suggest to you to say that a book like the *Mirror* would appeal to all who like Conrad as much as a novel and that even the general public may take to it; for, its interest is not exclusively maritime but largely human. It is not the sort of book a professed sea-writer would produce,[2] the *intention* being literary and the *expression* by no means exclusive or precious, but, within its limits, popular. Moreover those who want to know something of Conrad (the individual) shall find it there, and the serialisation being commenced at the right time may help the vogue of Nostromo. Here is Conrad talking of the events and feelings of his own life as he would talk to a friend. They have been always asking for something of the sort and here it is with as little egoism and as much sincerity as is possible in a thing of that sort.

Pardon this suggestion. I don't doubt in the least that you *do* know what to say; but this is a so confoundedly anxious time for me!

What would you think of letting the Harpers have the book outright for a price? Would it be an inducement? The sample you've got is good enough and if [I] don't send you more it is simply because I wish to give all the time to *N*—a much more difficult thing to write. The MS notes of papers 6. 7. 8. 9 are ready. The thing is to get a contract signed. I can't exist like this.

Pray let me know what happens, good bad or indifferent. And don't get exasperated with me.

Miss Hallowes initials are L. M. A cheque was due to her last Thursday for £1.5.

Kind regards

Yours Conrad.

---

[1] The letter was written on Junior Carlton Club stationery—with the address crossed out.
[2] He was eager not to be typed as a marine writer.

To Alice Rothenstein

Text MS Harvard; WR 66

[letterhead: Pent Farm]

18 Ap. 1904

Dear Mrs Rothenstein

Just a word of thanks from myself and of love from Jessie who, You may be sure, is as grateful as I am myself for all your kindness to us.

Notwithstanding my half-dead condition I went to see the pictures[1] and was recalled to life in all its fullness and force. What, in art, could do more! I felt myself in the presence of something profoundly significant and wonderfully comprehended. I wonder what people write about him? What ineptitudes they find to say? I would be sorry to parade my own; I only know that standing before the work I felt a profound pity for all the shams and pretences struggling for a place in the sun—for all of them, including myself.

I looked at nothing else whatever and went out even without trying to see Mr John's drawing. I have been very powerfully affected; it was so much more than I expected—and yet you know my opinion of him. C'est un artiste hors ligne,[2] affirming himself as such in his very promise. And now my expectations shall be boundless.

I must come up again to look my fill once more. In my present state I was not worthy. Art and such art is an august thing and should be approached with a free mind since true appreciation lies just in the surrender of that freedom to the artist's triumphant power. It was terrible to get out into the street. Awful! our best love. Affectionately yours,

Conrad.

To Ford Madox Ford

Text MS Yale; Unpublished

[letterhead: Pent Farm]

[25? April 1904][3]

My dear Ford.

I did not write because I did not have your address. It may be You've sent it in Your last note. I can't lay my hands on it.

---

[1] Rothenstein's 'The Talmud School' and 'A Corner of the Talmud School', hung in the New English Art Club's spring exhibition.

[2] 'He is an artist out of the ordinary.' Augustus John (1878–1961), a close friend of the Rothensteins and an ally in the N.E.A.C., had several drawings in the show, among them 'La Joconda'.

[3] Date from envelope, confirmed by the contents.

Jack said you were in Hampshire and I expected to hear from you.[1]

I am sorry for Your news—glad that you are better and I hope that Elsie and the chicks are flourishing.

Jessie has been carried downstairs yesterday—for the first time. She is so far a cripple. Massage, electricity and so on they say may restore her walking. I trust she will get all that but I don't *see* it. I have been bad all the time. 2^d part of *N[ostromo]* finished yesterday. It seems that I must give up but I suppose I won't.

Harpers are inclined to take the papers. Expect to hear from them next week. Of course I've done nothing more. 40 000 would be required. Our love. Yours always

Conrad

To J.B. Pinker
Text MS Berg; Unpublished

[letterhead: Pent Farm]
3^d May 1902 [1904][2]

Private

My dear Pinker,

Thanks for paying up the premium of the £600 policy. Upon my word I think I've forgotten to acknowledge safe receipt of cheque for £5 last week. My apologies.

In a day or two I'll be sending you the first 30 pages of p^t III. Nostromo. I see my way clear to the end now; it is only a matter of sitting close. Miss Hallowes is a great help; and by the bye a cheque for £1.5 is due to her since last Thursday. She's well worth the money.

Speaking of money: there shall be but little or nothing from Nostromo for me when I've finished. I shudder to think how deep I am in Your debt. But Nostromo ought to put me right even if I must call upon you again before the end which is near.[3] As to the immediate 'afterwards' the book of sketches must be made to provide for that. Is Harvey going to take it? Should he do so and (the contract being signed) should I take out another policy on my life (for six months say) I suppose you could raise some money for me on it at once. This is a case where one misses poor Watson.[4] I can't exist very long in this penury. I've some small

---

[1] On the brink of a nervous breakdown, Ford had gone down to the New Forest.
[2] Conrad wrote 1902, but the stationery and contents indicate 1904.
[3] Part Three, 'The Light-House', grew much longer than Conrad had envisaged.
[4] The broken banker.

liabilities to meet which must be attended to. As things stand now, involved as I am here, I cannot even begin to economise though I don't see really where I could do so. And besides my wife will have to get a change directly she can be moved by rail without risk of undoing all the good the six weeks in bed have indubitably done to the limb. To prevent her becoming a cripple is worth any sacrifice even from the point of view of my peace of mind. The thought of her being left permanently disabled adds another terror to death. That may be unreasonable since I feel as yet tolerably alive; but if I were not imaginative I could not write—don't you know. And writing, writing, is the only radical, sound remedy for all the worries and difficulties.

I am confident that from the word *go* I could get the Mirror of the Sea ready in six weeks.

N.B.   Serialisation in both countries is absolutely necessary—is it not?

I have a feeling that the book would do me no harm in my struggle to a decent popularity.

In reference to the enclosed note I wish you to tell me whether it would be proper for me to attend a dinner of the R. L. Fund. You know I had a grant from them 2 years ago.[1] Isn't it a dinner of *Grantors* where a *grantee* would be out of place? I am ignorant and want to know. Again: why this sudden cordiality on the part of F. Unwin,[2] and why *this particular* invitation. I wonder whether I ought to accept it since I know that he cannot get from me what he perhaps wishes to get. Tho' that too seems strange because I am not such a valuable author—not yet. Anyway if you have any advice to offer I would be obliged. Post it before 5 so that I can get it on Thursday and answer him on that day. Best regards

Your

Conrad.

---

[1] In July 1902, the Royal Literary Fund granted Conrad £300: *Letters*, 2, pp. 433–4.
[2] On Conrad's part, at least, relations with his ex-publisher had been strained.

To T. Fisher Unwin
Text MS Colgate; Unpublished

[letterhead: Pent Farm]
4 May 1904

Dear Sir.[1]

I am sorry I cannot accept your invitation. My wife has been ill for some time and I cannot leave the house for the night; besides having, under the circumstances, very little indication* for festivities of any kind. Many thanks for the friendly wording of your note. Let it be a pleasure deferred to better times.

Yours faithfully

Joseph Conrad

To J.B. Pinker
Text MS Berg; Unpublished

[letterhead: Pent Farm]
Saturday [7? May 1904][2]

My dear Pinker

Here first batch of Pt III.

Pray let my type copy go to the printers because it is carefully corrected; whereas if you have it retyped a new set of errors creeps in such as:

nothing for *hiding*
slip for *ship*
etc etc.

I have been appalled by the galley slips. But I've no time to correct.

Even if my type copy is somewhat interlined it is better to let it go to press right away—as it is.

I verily believe that N. has elements of success in book form. I've never written anything with so much *action* in it. The thing is not half bad upon my word.

Yours sincerely

Conrad

[1] T. Fisher Unwin (1848–1935) published *Almayer's Folly*, *An Outcast of the Islands*, and *Tales of Unrest*. Neither his business practices nor his adherence to the Liberal party endeared him to Conrad.

[2] On 3 May, Conrad promised the first 30 pages of Part Three 'in a day or two': on Tuesday, 17 May, he had 'dispatched yesterday N. pt 111ᵈ up to p 51'. 14, then, is less likely than 7 May, but not impossible.

To John Galsworthy
Text MS Forbes; Unpublished

[letterhead: Pent Farm]
16th May 1904.

Dearest Jack.

Imagine I, like a fool, mislaid your last letter with the Devon address, and therefore could not answer You. As soon as I found it I sent off a wire to Manaton[1]—which may or may not reach you.

I do not know that Jessie is so much better. She walks with difficulty. Massage now is being applied, a Miss Madden coming from Hythe 3 times a week. I struggle on. But that's an old and sickening story. Harvey has given no sign of life in relation to sea papers.

I get on slowly with the Maup^t preface.[2] Why should You be apologetic at all? The preface shall be ready by the seventh next. And there shall be nothing in it—alas. I am too far run down, for anything worthy of the translation. Still there is a 1000 words on paper now. But like old Cato with Carthage I end by: Delenda est[3]—preface. It should be destroyed rather than printed—as a matter of policy. Our love

Ever yours

Conrad.

To J.B. Pinker
Text MS Berg; Unpublished

[letterhead: Pent Farm]
17 May 1904.

Dear Pinker.

I'm inclined to accept the proposal for *W's W*. I know that H Norman is really well disposed towards me;[4] and if it is material to keep one's name before the public this is as good a way to do it as any.

C. Graham could meet me, say in Deal,[5] for a days sail. My wife

---

[1] On the edge of Dartmoor: Wingstone, an old farmhouse, was to be the Galsworthys' country home for many years.

[2] His Preface to *Yvette and Other Stories by Guy de Maupassant*, translated by A[da] G[alsworthy] and published by Duckworth in July. The Preface later appeared in *Notes on Life and Letters*.

[3] 'Delenda est Carthago' ('Carthage must be destroyed'): Cato the Elder's contribution to Roman foreign policy, the exhortation with which he ended every speech to the senate.

[4] Henry Norman (1858–1939), traveller, industrialist, inventor, former journalist, and founder of the *World's Work*; he took Conrad's 'London River' for the December issue.

[5] About 20 miles east of the Pent.

wants a change badly and if the damned thing pays the hotel bill for 3 days it's worth while doing.

I propose writing to Pawling for fuller particulars[1]—as to lenght* and so on. For myself I am inclined to *see* the article done in an anecdotal mood, rather than in a descriptive one. If I write that sort of thing I want it to strike a favourable note with the general reader.

What do you think?

Anyway it can do no harm.

Thanks ever so much for the £6 received lately. I dispatched yesterday N. pt III^d up to p 51.

Returning to P. Shall I attend to this personally or through you *strictly.* Tell me too whether an article of that sort for magazine publication could be made of use for the M of the Sea papers? Shall I reserve it for book form?

What I think should be done is this. I arrange with P. (his autograph letter being of a friendly nature); but the MS shall go to him through you and cheque for pay^t to be made out in your name. Don't forget I want to keep P in his good disposition since I owe them a book—there is no shirking the fact. Money has passed[2]—alas!

I am doing a preface to a vol of Maupassant translation which Duckworth is to publish; the translator, a lady, being a great friend. I think it is likely to be noticed (the preface I mean), by the press generally. Otherwise its done for love you understand.

I feel most damnably stale but the work goes on.

Kind regards

Yours J Conrad.

To R.B. Cunninghame Graham

Text MS Dartmouth; J-A, 1, 329; Watts 152

[letterhead: Pent Farm]
18 May 1904

Très cher ami.

It is only from Pawling's letter today that I learn you are here. And first my thanks for the brass censer-cup (I call it) which I received some time ago. It is a thing I like—first with affection as coming from you and next from taste because it is brass for which I have have a fondness. The

---

[1] Of the collaboration he had proposed between Conrad and Graham: Heinemann, Pawling's firm, published *World's Work*.

[2] In June 1898, for *The Rescue*.

form is good too. Is it meant for embers to light one's pipe? Or is it for burning perfumes? Anyway it contains cigarettes now and stands at my elbow as I write or read.

Pawling's proposal of a joint article is fascinating. Whether it is practicable that is another affair. I desire it to come off. The question hangs on your inclination and leisure. It would be jolly to have a day's sail, and a talk between sky and water: say starting from Deal in one of their galleys through the Downs and round Nth Foreland to Margate Roads. But I am afraid it would bore you to death. And in such promenades there is always too much sun—or not enough: too little wind—or else a confounded, unnecessary blast. And yet, now and then, one falls upon a perfect day. Is your luck good? I mean that propitious fortune of which Sylla the dictator was the spoilt child.[1] As to my luck I prefer to say nothing of it. I am absolutely ashamed to mention it; because if "Fortune favours the brave"[2] I must be about the poorest sort of coon on earth. Enfin.

Do let me know how you are. I presume you've been in Morocco. Rothenstein could not tell me—only the other day. Il est artiste celui là—et pas bête. N'est ce pas?[3]

> Kindest regards from us
> all   Tout à vous
>
> J Conrad.

PS m'est avis qu'il faut nous faire payer bien par ces gens là. Moi parc[e]que j'en ai besoin et Vous par principe. Ce brave P. est vague sur ce point là.[4]

---

[1] In Plutarch's *Lives*, Lucius Cornelius Sulla, dictator of Rome 81–79 B.C., is celebrated for his streak of good fortune.

[2] A Roman commonplace, occurring, e.g., in Terence, *Phormio*, 203, and Vergil, *Aeneid*, x, 284.

[3] 'He's an artist, that one – and not stupid. Isn't that so?'

[4] 'I think we ought to be paid well by those people. I because I need it and you on principle. The good Pawling is hazy on that point.'

To S.S. Pawling
Text TS Heinemann; Unpublished

[letterhead: Pent Farm]
May 27. 1904

My dear Pawling.

Being in town on Wednesday I tried to see you twice but as, to my great regret, I failed, I must write once more on the subject of that paper.

First of all, the collaboration with Cunninghame-Graham, the idea of which did not originate with me, must be put an end to by yourself.

Next my dear Pawling, answer me categorically whether the article is sure of acceptance. I could not spare the time to write on the mere chance. I am very hard at work now. Why I insist upon this point is because something about the commercial aspect of London has been suggested. Obviously I could not write anything upon that, except the mere statement, which is neither interesting nor instructive, that the port of London is doing a very large trade; but I have not the slightest interest in the commercial aspect of the port of London, nor any knowledge of facts of that description upon which I could write. The fact is I think my prose would cut a strange figure in the World's Work, which I admit to be an admirable publication, well planned and excellently conducted. Besides you have not answered my questions as to the length of the article, which it is necessary for me to have some idea of; nor yet as to whether my terms are acceptable. You say something very kindly about getting for me the best terms possible in America, but the terms in England you do not mention. Upon the whole I think I would prefer, as I have said before, to get £50 for serial rights in both countries, the article being between four and five thousand words in length. And I would ask for the money on delivery of the manuscript.

To save you the bother of correspondence upon this small matter I suggest that if I do not hear from you by Thursday next I shall consider the thing off.

Kindest regards.

Yours sincerely
Joseph Conrad.

To Ford Madox Ford
Text MS Yale; Unpublished

[letterhead: Pent Farm]
1904
29th May

Dear Ford.

I am awfully grieved to hear of your state.[1] Mine though not identical is just as bad in its way and surely less excusable.

I struggle on. I see the end of the trouble but there's many a slip.—
I've heard that your poems[2] are being well reviewed. Do You think so? I've seen nothing of course. Je vis ici comme une taupe[3] and my daily post consists mostly of bills.

I saw Pinker the other day. No word yet from Harvey as to sketches. Halkett[4] offered to take *six* at £5.5 per thou: *Eng rights* but is being held off and meantime somebody else (?) is looking at them (here) with a view of trying for better terms. Halkett really is a last resource and I told P not to throw the thing away in haste. But still Halkett's proposal means 90 g[uinea]s of which (I told Pinker again) I must have 30 when—and if—the affair is concluded, pour votre seigneurie.[5] As to the book form (which Harvey already is ready to take) a small calculation will fix our proportions; for I suppose we can not finish the whole together.[6] Can we?

Anyway so far nothing is fixed.

I spoke to P of the *London*.[7] He protested that he has not in the least slackened his efforts. He believes that the time will come for it, is sure of its coming, but can not command it. You know how he failed with Falk and yet managed to do a stroke of business afterwards.[8] Not that he apprehends failure in this case but, says he, patience is necessary.

I tell you this for what it is worth.

I am making strenuous efforts and shall persevere therein till I am able to send you quelque monacos[9]—not the whole hundred as yet but some appreciable part at least.

---

[1] Nervous exhaustion, fear of open spaces and of writing.
[2] *The Face of the Night*, published in April.
[3] 'I live here like a mole.'   [4] George R. Halkett, editor of the *Pall Mall Magazine*.
[5] 'For your Lordship' – as part payment of his debt to Ford.
[6] As well as taking dictation, Ford seems to have acted as midwife for some of the early papers, and did so again the following year: Mizener, pp. 88–9.
[7] One source of Ford's misery was his current failure to place *The Soul of London*.
[8] 'Falk' missed magazine publication but appeared in *Typhoon*.
[9] 'Some cash.'

J'ai la cervelle en compote, les bras cassés, tous les nerfs a nu, et (as Flaubert says of Matho, in Salammbo) "il marchait toujours."[1]

I share in toto your opinion as to the use of electricity. Hackney thinks likewise. However Jessie gets massage three times a week from Miss Madden out of Hythe whom I knew as passenger on board the Torrens in 1892. She (out of pure friendship) has carted up here a battery—so we let her play with it. Massage is to all appearances doing good.

Your friendly words as to N'mo did do me good. Quelle machine![2] Bon Dieu! Enfin! Distractedly yours, a Vous tous

Conrad.

To Ada Galsworthy

Text MS Forbes; J-A, 1, 339 (incomplete)

[Pent Farm]
[June 1904][3]

My dear Mrs Galsworthy.[4]

This preface is not worthy the excellence of your translation. Really it is not. I am quite miserable about it. However I've expanded a couple of paragraphs, whether for better or worse I don't know. I was struck with dismay at the horrid barrenness of the thing. I don't suppose D[uckwor]th will object. After all it makes no difference to him if I drivel for a few lines more—and the very first paragraph may be taken out if that's any help towards squeezing the thing in the allot[t]ed space. Pray tell them that; and I trust you will do me a comrade's favour by seeing the revise for punctuation and grammar and sense. I never thanked you for your letter but Heaven's my witness I was ashamed to take it unto myself. Jessie sends her love. *She* thinks you write beautiful letters. She's dead to all sense of shame and proportion. I am always your most faithful friend and servant.

Jph Conrad.

---

[1] 'My brain is pulp, my arms are smashed, all my nerves are raw and ... "he kept on walking"'—as, although horribly tortured by the Carthaginians, the rebel leader does at the end of Flaubert's novel.

[2] 'What a contraption!'

[3] On 16 May, Conrad promised the Preface to *Yvette* by 7 June; the volume appeared at the end of July.

[4] Born Ada Pearson (1864–1956), she was adopted by Ernest Cooper, a Norwich doctor. As a teenager, she studied the piano in Dresden; later she wrote songs. Technically, she remained married to John's cousin Arthur; divorce and remarriage waited on the death of John's father, at the end of 1904.

To William Rothenstein
Text MS Harvard; Unpublished

[letterhead: Pent Farm]
9 June 1904.

My dear Rothenstein.

Rather sooner than I expected I found at home a certain "Sommation à payer."[1] So if the arrangement you mentionned* can be carried out now as to a hundred or so I shall be glad because those people are becoming restive slightly.

Quelle sacré misère[2] having to think of these things which interfere with ones mind in a sort of sterilising way driving all images and expressions clear out of it.

I have looked up my memoranda and see that the policies now in force (tho' charged to Pinker to secure his advances) would still be sufficient to cover that new liability (say 100 to 150) too, (provisionally) should a sudden extinction overcome me before I've finished *Nostromo*. For the time being I shall send you an I.O.U for the amount. Afterwards I shall take out a further policy for £500 and make it over to my friends the creditors; but just now I could not spare the year's premium.

I don't know whether I have made myself clear, in my hurry but I trust to your intelligence.[3]

Our best love

Yours Conrad.

To William Rothenstein
Text MS Harvard; Unpublished

[letterhead: Pent Farm]
10 June 1904

My dear Rothenstein.

Many thanks for everything, promptness included, which is like that last touch which distinguishes art from amateurishness in the matter of friendly offices.

I enclose here an I.O.U for your fifty. As to the other hundred I do not know what I ought to do; but meantime *I acknowledge formally here the receipt of a sum of £100 from you.* I shall get* about effecting an insurance for 500 and I thought that I would come to town next week for that purpose,

---

[1] 'Demand for payment.'   [2] 'What a damned nuisance.'
[3] Rothenstein not only responded at once to Conrad's latest scheme for raising money on his life; he wrote by the same post to Henry Newbolt, a move that led to the Royal Bounty grant awarded in 1905 (Najder, *Chronicle*, pp. 301 and 556, n. 169).

as I want to see the secretary personally. If you name the day we could meet then as You suggested and I would even stop the night providing you allow me to get a room somewhere; for I could not think of inflicting myself upon your dear wife who has a houseful as it is. It is of course understood that your £50 is to [be] repaid at the *first opportunity* and in no case later than four months from to day.

I end in haste to catch post from Hythe with our love to you all

Yours ever

Jph Conrad.

I think that the policy for £500 should be deposited with Mr Hammersley[1] as securing the loan of all the contributors. And perhaps he would consent to the same being made out in his name should the other lenders agree. I intend to pay one years'* premium at once.

To John Galsworthy
Text MS Forbes; Unpublished

[letterhead: Pent Farm]
Sunday evening [12? June 1904][2]

Dearest Jack

My trouble simply *won't* leave me. Hackney was here on Friday on his final visit to Jessie, at any rate for a time. Again there is a lot of fluid in the knee and he gave me to understand that she won't be able to walk (to any purpose) for a long time—if ever. Massage however is doing some good to the muscles. What is worst, from the point of view of her heart, is the strain which moving about puts on her. The valvular noise is still there. What Hackney wants is either a new left leg-machine or the alteration of the one she wears now to make it lighter and enable her to sit down with comfort which she can not do now.

I would write to Ernst[3] at once. Those damn things she is wearing now cost £14 which I haven't paid yet. I've been paying other people. I don't know whether I've told you that I've accepted a proposal from H. Norman to write something for the World's Work about the Thames estuary. However that is not written yet, as I've made a start with N and don't want to check it. If you can let me have a ten I possess here enough

[1] Hugh Hammersley (1858–1930), a Hampstead banker and patron of the arts.
[2] Between 27 May, when Norman's proposal was still too vague to accept, and [15 June], when Conrad gave Galsworthy further details. If the letter of the 15th offers prompt gratitude for a speedy loan, the 12th is the likely Wednesday.
[3] Friedrich Gustav Ernst, a maker of surgical appliances.

to make up Ernest's* bill without leaving myself utterly stranded. He would put the thing in hand and to go up for that fitting I could call upon Pinker by and bye.

The other day she had a fit of oppression, alas, not very severe but still disheartening. I believe she does not always tell me though. And I watch but do not ask. A quoi bon? Love

Your Conrad.

To John Galsworthy
Text MS Forbes; Unpublished

[letterhead: Pent Farm]
Wednesday [15 June 1904][1]

Dearest Jack.

Thanks ever so much. I am a miserable person. I don't know what to say.

Of further fate of Sea Papers I know nothing as yet. The paper for H. Norman is to be about the lower Thames and I shall try to make it fit into the Vol of Sea Sketches by and by. It is to be 4500 words. So far I've no conception of it; do not *see* it in the least. I doubt whether I'll ever begin it—tho' of course I shall. But this is my state of mind.

Our best love. Sorry to see the weather go to pieces just as you start; still you may have the fine overcast sort of weather good for walking though otherwise untrustworthy.

My greeting to Edward and good luck to you both[2]
Yours Ever

J. Conrad.

To William Rothenstein
Text MS Harvard; *Listy* 232; Original unpublished[3]

Pent Farm
27th June 1904

My dear Rothenstein.

You have evidently made up your mind to save me. Thanks seem out of place. But I acknowledge here formally the receipt of another £50.

Pray tell me my dear fellow if I am supposed to know *all* the sources of this most timely help? If I am some expression of feeling would be decent; and it would also be very difficult. I express nothing to you

---

[1] The holiday with Garnett was to begin on the 18th: *Letters of Galsworthy*, p. 53.
[2] Galsworthy and Garnett were off on a hike through Wales.
[3] Jean-Aubry (1, p. 330) printed about a third of the text.

because you know, and because I am overwhelmed by my good fortune.

Jessie is writing to your dear wife in a day or two. My dear good fellow I am afraid that the journey to Yorkshire would be too much for her. She gets awfully tired by the very slightest amount of knocking about. Dearly as she would love to be with you she confessed to me that the railway journey and all the small efforts it would necessitate fill her with dread. I dare say it is the consequence of her nervous state which is not very good. For myself I work desperately but slow—much too slow for the situation. I am unable to say whether moving from home would put me off or not. I fear it would. I don't know. I dare do nothing. Either my soul or my liver is very sick. If it is the liver then the cold shall make it worse. Even here I go about shuddering when a cloud passes over the sun. And I am tired, tired, as if I had lived a hundred years.

Reverting to the matter of that salvage you are conducting to preserve a rather rotten old hulk (but full of the best intentions)—I think You ought to take charge of my debt in the sense that the policy shall be made over to you and the repayments also shall be made to you. I shall take three years for it—no less. I don't think I could take less unless something very fortunate in the way of book sales were to take place: a contingency not worth reckoning upon. Je n'ai pas le don terrible de la popularité.[1]

I cut this letter short here. It is late—and to morrow is another dread day. C. Graham has been here for the Sunday and we talked much of you. He was in very good form and very friendly but the episode of his visit has not refreshed me as much as I expected. I am not myself and shall not be myself till I am born again after Nostromo is finished.

Our dear love to you four people. Je tombe de fatigue.[2]

Always yours

Jph. Conrad.

To John Galsworthy
Text MS Forbes; Unpublished

[letterhead: Pent Farm]
2ᵈ July 1904

My dearest Jack.

Glad you had a good time and are ready for work.

I drag on my appalling length as it were a bullet rivetted to my leg. I sit up o' nights and go to bed sick and get up disgusted.

I daren't look anybody in the face. And there's no one to look at.

[1] 'I don't have the dreadful gift of popularity.'   [2] 'I'm collapsing with tiredness.'

C Graham came and went last Sunday leaving a legacy of Brazilian cigarettes which have scraped my throat like unto rusty knives. I preserve a packet of same for your edification.

So encouraged you ought to come over soon. Come and write in the wooden house and see nothing of us *if you like* except at meal times. You could even sleep there if the weather continues like it is now.

I am anxiously waiting for the sight of the Saga.[1]

Thanks for reading the preface. You are chaffing me about it in a manner so agreeable that I haven't the heart to be angry. But really if Mrs A. Galsworthy is pleased then I have not lived in vain.

Arrived: A book with a Chinese title of Scandinavian authorship translated by Mrs Reynolds.[2] I am touched and pleased indeed by the kind attention. Have looked into it already with the translator alone in view. *And that is all right.* That's all I've to say. If I were to talk of skill and fluency and mastery and the rest of the journalese bosh you would not believe me and you would be right. But the thing *will do* and that's the most an honest man may say of *any* writing. (I only wish mine would *do*!) Pray mention the above criticism with my thanks in 10 Tor Gardens.[3] I shall read on Sunday and write on same day for Monday's post—unless I am dead or otherwise disabled.

Our usual miseries are pursuing their course. And that is the exact truth.... Borys sits the mare "like a centaur" barebacked with the anxious parents hanging onto the bridle. But his reading is a matter of terrible difficulty. He applies himself with great determination however and that is good. Our love to you.

Yours ever

J Conrad.

To R.B. Cunninghame Graham

Text MS Dartmouth; J-A, 1, 331; Watts 154

[letterhead: Pent Farm]

2 July 1904

Très cher ami.

Cigarettes came first and the two books followed. You are very good. Your too short visit has been a god-send. You've left me believing once more in the reality of things.

---

[1] Early work on *The Man of Property*, the first Forsyte novel.

[2] Henri Jean François Borel, *Wu Wei. A Phantasy based on the Philosophy of Lao-Tse* (Luzac & Co, 1903), translated by 'Meredith Ianson' (Mabel Reynolds, Galsworthy's sister). Borel (1869–1933) was Dutch.

[3] Home of the Reynolds.

Hudson's "Sparrow"[1] is really first rate and just in the tone I expected. C'est une belle nature, which never falls short in its domain. One can depend upon him.

The other volum[e] I've been reading with a surprised admiration.[2] It shall be an abiding delight—I see that much. But I don't pretend to have seen *everything* as yet. The sheer interest in themes and bookmanship stands as yet in the way of deeper appreciation. One must read oneself *into* the true quality of the book.

And so poor Watts[3] is coming to the end of his august career. What a full and rounded life. And yet it seems poor in stress and passion which are the true elixirs against the majestic overpowering tediousness of an existence full of allegoric visions. Dieu nous preserve de cette grandeur![4] Better be born a lord—a king—better die Arch priest of an incredible religion!

My wife sends her kind regards and Borys his love. The Cricket set is a great and solid success

Tout à Vous

Jph Conrad.

Veuillez me rappeler au gracieux souvenir de Madame Votre Mère dont je n'oublierais jamais le bienveillant accueil.[5]

To William Rothenstein

Text MS Harvard; Unpublished

[letterhead: Pent Farm]

3^d July 1904.

My dear Rothenstein.

I think that my answer ought to be yes, for reasons which you will see without my pointing them out. And since you are in touch with that matter then go on with it in the name of Allah!

I asked you to take charge of the debt in the full confidence that you would not refuse me that service. It need not be a matter of great worry.

---

[1] 'The London Sparrow' appeared in *Kith and Kin: Poems of Animal Life*, ed. H. S. Salt (Bell, 1901).

[2] Watts surmises Hudson's South American fantasy *Green Mansions*, published in February.

[3] George Frederic Watts (1817–1904) specialized in vast allegorical paintings and massive sculptures.

[4] 'God save us from this magnificence.'

[5] 'Please remember me to your mother, whose kind welcome I shall never forget.'

You were quite in accord with my innermost feeling in not writing to C Graham or Garnett. Garnett is poor as a church mouse!

I feel an extreme load of obligation to You—I don't say irksome, mind—but e[x]treme to that extent that it is only your personality that makes it so easily bearable. Meantime I go on working slowly.—

We shall meet soon. I am glad you have found inspiration for your work. Our deep love to you all.

In haste to catch Sunday post

Ever Yours

J Conrad

To Edward Garnett
Text MS Sutton; G. 192

[Pent Farm]
6th July 1904

My dear Edward.

Ecco-la. Here's your A.F. in proof of my affection.[1] Two nights and the morning of to day. Isn't it miserable! Isn't it miserable to have to work in fetters and bound and gagged as it were by the irresolution and sluggishness of one's intellect, by a difficulty of saying the simplest thing.

Measure then my affection for you. But how to give you an idea of my disaffection towards the whole body of Editors I am at a loss. The best way would be to suggest that the malefactor conducting the *Speaker*[2] should give me 5 g[uinea]s for these pages. Explain to him that this is the price of my conscience for abetting him in his weekly crime. Had his crime been daily £10 per thou: would have been my figure. Console him by the remark that he shall not have J.C. in his page in the future at that or any other conceivable price. Strenghten* his faint soul by pointing out that the thing is low down and commonplace enough to please the divine mediocrity of the only god he knows—his public. Tell him these wholesome and fortifying truths in order that his constitution should be braced up for the extraction of 5 gs. Comprenez-Vous? This is a matter of principle.

For the rest I won't insult your intelligence by stating in too many words that the thing is yours and wholly yours, written for you, meant

---

[1] 'Anatole France', *Speaker*, 16 July, pp. 359–61; reprinted in *Notes on Life and Letters*, pp. 32–41. Garnett was a regular contributor to this Liberal weekly.
[2] The historian J. L. Hammond, editor from 1899 to 1906.

for you to sell, or give away, or light a fire with. Comprenez-Vous? This is a matter of fact.

Other things I would like to stipulate are: that my heading should be preserved and if possible the article billed on posters. This is a matter of fancy.

Our best love to you in your domestic solitude.[1] You should run down here for a night—for several nights. Who knows how long I shall last. The sands O Brother are running out.

Ever Yours

Conrad

To J.B. Pinker

Text MS Berg; Unpublished

[letterhead: Effingham House,
Arundel Street,
Strand, London W.C.]
Monday July 11th [1904][2]

My dear Pinker.

I thought I would not come to see you till I had the balance of N[ostromo] ready. However I had to.

Have You closed with Harvey's offer for the two papers (serially)? He offered a hundred as far as I remember. If you have not pray do so and let me have £70. I am being just a bit dunned. And I don't want to be worried just now as I am finishing N. A fortnight ought to do it.

The Thames paper is 2/3ds done (for W[orld's] W[ork]). But everything is laid aside for *N*. If you see a short paper of mine in the *Speaker* you ought to know it was done at Ed. Garnett's special request and I get 3 gs for it. I shall come in again about five. If you go home before leave me a note on the subject—as I am anxious—and also a *sov[ereign]* to get home by.

Yours very tired

J. Conrad.

---

[1] Constance Garnett was travelling in Russia.
[2] Just before the *Speaker* article appeared: written on Pinker's office stationery.

To Ford Madox Ford

Text MS Yale; *Listy* 233; Original unpublished

[letterhead: Pent Farm]

29 July 1904

My dear Ford.

Of course I shall write to Uncle Dunn[1] tomorrow Saturday.

I have been half dead. I am now in the night and day writing stage. I am simply in despair. Nothing matters.

You do not say anything of the Señora and the chicks. Why? But I suppose that they are well.

Jessie's a complete cripple. To walk as far as the orchard is a great undertaking. She lies down half the day.

By same post with Your letter comes the enclosed.[2] I was going to fling it into the paper basket. Still—If you have something written that you do *not* care for *in the least* send it on. I'll put in a few of my jargon phrases and send it on. As I remarked: nothing matters—and we are intimate enough to say anything to each other. You may as well have their modest cheque. If the thing shocks you tear the sweet note up. Our love to you all if you can bear the mention of it.

Ever yours

Conrad.

To William Rothenstein

Text MS Harvard; Unpublished

[letterhead: Pent Farm]

Monday. [Summer? 1904][3]

My dear Rothenstein

We are both delighted at the possibility of seeing you. Do come and see for yourself how we are any day this week up to Saturday; to stay for the night that is. From Sat till Monday an aunt of Jessies[4] is coming to occupy our only spare room.

It would do me no end of good to see you. I am making superhuman

---

[1] James Nicol Dunn (1856–1919), editor of the Conservative *Morning Post*. The letter to Elsie Hueffer of 2 September mentions a plan to get work from him.

[2] A letter from the Northern Newspaper Syndicate asking: 'Will you kindly say if you have an early story, which has not been published serially, and which we could have at a modest sum?'

[3] Letterhead eleven: the 'superhuman efforts' on *Nostromo* and Jessie's ability to receive visitors suggest the summer rather than the spring.

[4] Probably Miss Alice Sex, a favourite with the Conrads.

efforts to get on with that cursed book and want badly a moment of relief.

Jessie is going to write to your dear wife. Meantime our love to you all

Yours

Conrad

To J.B. Pinker

Text MS Berg; Unpublished

[letterhead: Pent Farm]

Tuesday. [16? August 1904][1]

My dear Pinker

Here's my letter to G[osse].

Also this morning I've received a letter from TP's Weekly[2] which I send you. I haven't read it. I am afraid of being upset. Don't laugh at me. If I *must* know what it is about I [would] rather hear it from you. Otherwise it may go to the devil.

Am hard at it.

Yours

Conrad

PS If anything displeases You in G letter pray say frankly what? Any change shall be made or another written send it back to be posted here.

To Edmund Gosse

Text MS Yale; J-A, 1, 331

[letterhead: Pent Farm]

19 [or 18] Aug 1904[3]

My Dear M[r] Gosse.

It has come to my isolated ears that it is given out at large, that it is said—in what exact words I don't know, but said in effect—that: "Pinker deals harshly with Conrad". Such a statement, injurious to Pinker, becomes by implication an aspersion upon Conrad in a way which I need not point out to your insight. I suppose that anything may be said (and even believed) of a man who has not a large balance at his

---

[1] After Pinker had seen it, the letter exonerating his treatment of Conrad went to Gosse on 18 or 19 August.

[2] About the serial of *Nostromo*, under way since 29 January?

[3] See the dating of the next letter: Gosse replied on 19 August.

bankers. The only thing worth consideration is: who says and who believes.

Without troubling to trace what is said to its source, I am extremely anxious that you should not believe it. Therefore were it to reach You (as it well may, since it has reached even me) je vous prie de n'en rien croire. *Cela n'est pas!*[1]

I have no taint in my character either of vice, indolence or sub-serviency which could ever make me the victim of such a situation as is implied in that piece of baseless gossip. And on the other hand, my good friend Pinker—tho' he does not advertise himself by a volume of nauseous adulation from 'men of letters!'[2]—is neither stupid nor a man without a conscience: as that same gossip would imply also. For it would be a very stupid move to "deal harshly with Conrad". His conscience I'll leave in his hands where I think it is in good keeping.

He has known me for six years. He has stepped gallantly into the breach left open by the collapse of my bank; and not only gallantly, but successfully as well. He has treated not only my moods but even my fancies with the greatest consideration. I would not dream of wearying you with details and figures; but his action, distinctly, has not been of a mercenary character. He can not take away the weariness of mind which at the end of ten years of strain has come upon me; but he has done his utmost to help me to overcome it by relieving the immediate material pressure—and the even more disabling pressure of human stupidity. But let that pass! How much can he expect in return for these services? I don't know. But I fear I am not a 'profitable man' in anybody's speculation.

I venture to write this openly, because the world is aware of the benevolent interest you take in my work.[3] As to my personality I am quite conscious of its insignificance but very little concerned as to what it is. But I may say that much for it: that any sort of underhand dealing is utterly revolting to it by tradition, by training and by nature.

I ought to apologise for troubling you with my handwriting: but as it is a question of sentiment turning on loyalty to a man and on fidelity to the truth of facts I am sure not only of your indulgence but of your approval.

---

[1] 'I beg you to believe none of it. *It isn't so!*'

[2] Starting in 1893, Pinker's rival A. P. Watt had published an annual volume of testimonials from grateful clients.

[3] And Conrad was aware of the interest Gosse took in literary gossip.

Believe me, my dear Mr. Gosse, with many feelings of which the note is sincerity very faithfully yours

Joseph Conrad

To J.B. Pinker

Text MS Berg; Unpublished

[Pent Farm]
Thursday [18 or 19 August
1904][1]

Dear P.

I posted the letter to Gosse this moment.

Am glad you are satisfied with the tone. I thought it better to bring myself in—rather well forward too; since nothing would prevent some liar saying that the letter was written under pressure from you! I suppose G. will be angry.

Brothers Dawson been here. A. J. brought your name up himself saying that on two occasions you have behaved to him extremely well. It was easy then to mention the matter of our relations and ask him to contradict the Calumny.

Yours

Conrad.

To J.B. Pinker

Text MS Berg; Unpublished

[Pent Farm]
[c. 20 August 1904][2]

Dear Pinker

Here's Gosse's answer which is satisfactory as far as it goes. You note he disclaims all knowledge; and after all we couldn't expect more.[3]

Yours

Conrad.

---

[1] The letter to Gosse, sent 'this moment', is dated 19 August – a Friday.
[2] Written on the verso of Gosse's letter dated 19 August.
[3] He told Conrad that he knew neither Pinker nor the rumours about him. 'It is pleasant to learn that you have in Mr Pinker so valuable an ally.'

To J.B. Pinker

Text MS Berg; Unpublished

[Pent Farm]
Wednesday. [24 August 1904][1]

Dear P.

I am coming on Friday with the book! Ended! Unless—Unless—

But I won't even contemplate a single day's delay.

I'll want to see you—probably about 12.30 or so unless I wire a later hour.

Pray send me *by return* cheque for £2 (two) or so, as I haven't the price of railway fare in the house.

Yours

Conrad.

PS I say by *return* because even so I shall just get it in time to catch my train.

To J.B. Pinker

Text MS Berg; Unpublished

[Pent Farm]
Friday 2.30 AM. [26 August 1904][2]

My dear Pinker.

I thought I would be done by Thursday but Miss Hallowes will tell you what a time I had.

The dentist came just 12 hours ago and mangled me terribly, and grubbed in my gum. However!—He made me unfit to work till about seven. Since then I've been at it. All Thursday was lost because in the morning I did nothing, either, but rave and tramp about.

Now the tooth is gone and the book is finished. It will be finished maybe by the time Miss Hallowes returns. She will then start to type and post the copy on Sat[y] morning. Without fail.

My dear fellow You and the book are safe. Pray then do what I ask you. Let me have *three* cheques. *One for _fifty_. (that one* you may date

---

[1] By the following Wednesday, *Nostromo* really had been finished.

[2] If this was indeed Friday rather than Saturday morning. The chronology of the next few days defies interpretation. The versions for Pinker (the middle-man between desperate publishers and yet more desperate author) and for Galsworthy (as at the finish of *Lord Jim*, the intended reader of a vivid and circumstantial narrative) do not tally, and the individual letters are dense with inconsistency. Conrad was closing an extraordinary novel in what was, even by his standards, extraordinary turbulence of body and mind.

on Monday. $\underline{30}^{th}$.[1]) and *two* for *twenty five*. I ask for two for a specific purpose.

I am off on Saturday to Essex by motor for three days' stay with my oldest friend.[2] On Tuesday we bring back his boy to finish his holiday with us. Some time next week I shall take him home and on that day shall come to see you and talk over matters—especially as to future work.

Pray note: I shall not send more copy to Harpers till I get slips to the end from T.P. and then you may tell them there will be no delay. No proof will be kept longer than 24 hours. There's no reason why they should not have all the slips by the 7th Sept. Ask T.P. to hurry up. I'll be ready for work by Wednesday next. Till then I shall do nothing.

Yours

Conrad.

PS Miss Hallowes will bring the cheques. She is going away on Sat. Pray pay her up the week.* She has been very good. I think I shall have her back for six weeks, on the 15 Oct. to dictate the remaining papers. You shall have book completed by Nov. 30th. Nevertheless try to ascertain Harpers' ideas as to the novel I've been telling you about last time we met. That one could be written by end of May.

To J.B. Pinker
Text MS Berg; Unpublished

Stanford le Hope

Essex

31st[?] Aug. 1904.[3]

4 am.

My dear Pinker

I could not resist the temptation of a Sunday intervening and kept the MS to work at it a little more. I corrected it to such a purpose that, as You see, I had to rewrite some thirty odd pages the typed copy being quite impossible.

---

[1] Monday was the 29th.

[2] The friendship with G. F. W. Hope, once a professional and still an amateur sailor, went back to 1880. It seems apt that Conrad should finish *Nostromo* in the house of a 'Director of Companies' who speculated, ruinously, in mining shares.

[3] A mystery: according to the PS, the day is Monday – the 29th; according to the next letter, Conrad wrote to Pinker towards four on the morning of the 30th. The 30th is the date at the end of the *Nostromo* MS, and Stanford-le-Hope is the place (facsimile, J–A, 1, p. 333).

Miss Hallow[e]s being gone you will have to get this typed if necessary. I believe I have not broken the spirit of my promise to you. In the letter you ought to have had this some time on Sat.; but you could not have dispatched it till Monday. I've tried to write as legibly as I can.

I may just as well thank you for this work being finished; for thanks are due to you undeniably. And if I don't say more it isn't that I grudge You the words but because I am tired—done up.

Yours very cordially and gratefully

J. Conrad

My friend takes this to town and shall send by messenger boy.—Give the lad a receipt.

PS If you have anything pressing to say writing before five today (Monday) c/o AJ Dawson You may catch me yet in Slinfold.[1] But a wire would be safer.

We shall be home on Tuesday.

To John Galsworthy

Text MS POSK; J-A, 1, 332

Pent Farm
1st Sept 1904

Dearest Jack!

Finished! Finished on the 30th in Hope's house in Stanford in Essex, where I had to take off my brain that seemed to turn to water. For a solid Fortnight I've been sitting up. And all the time horrible toothache. On the 27th[2] had to wire for dentist (couldn't leave the work) who came at 2 and dragged at the infernal thing which seemed rooted in my very soul. The horror came away at last, leaving however one root in the gum. Then he grubbed for *that* till I le[a]pt out of the chair. Thereupon old Walton[3] said: I don't think your nerves will stand any more of this.

I went back to my MS. at six pm. At 11.30 something happened— what it is I don't know. I was writing, and raised my eyes to look at the clock. The next thing I know I was sitting (not lying) sitting on the concrete outside the door. When I crawled in I found it was nearly one. I managed to get upstairs and said to Jessie: We must be off to-morrow. I took 30 drops of chlorodyne—and slept till 7. Sydney went off on his bike

---

[1] Near Horsham, about 40 miles south of London and far from any obvious route between the two Stanfords. The topography of this period is as enigmatic as the chronology.
[2] The 25th in the 'Friday 2.30' letter to Pinker.
[3] G. C. Walton, a Folkestone dentist.

to Ashford at 7.30 and at 10 the motor car was in the yard: a 12 hp Darracq. I sat by the man's side like a corpse. Between Cant[erbu]ry and Faversham he said to me You look ill sir; shall I stop? Sittingbourne I remember as a brandy and soda. Good road. Steady 24 miles an hour. In Chatham, street crowded, packed.[1] Going dead slow knocked down a man—old chap, apparently a bricklayer. Crowd around cursing and howling. Helped him to my front seat and I standing on the step got him to the hospital in 10 minutes. No harm. Only shaken. Saw him all comfy in bed for the rest of the day.

In Rochester Hope waiting for us. Had something to eat—and *tasted it too*, for the first time in 10 days. On crossing the river began to revive on the ferry. Jessie very good and Borys quite a man watching over Mama's 'poor leg' and warning off porters with luggage. At five, in sight of Stanford-le-Hope R^{wy} Station petrol gave out. Man ran on and ran back with a two gallon tin.

That night I slept. Worked all day. In the evening dear Mrs Hope (who is not used to that sort of thing) gave me four candles and on I went. Finished at 3. Took me another half-hour to check the numbering of the pages write a letter to P. and so on.

I had not the heart to write to you that same night nor yet the next day. Wasn't sure I would survive. But I have survived extremely well. I feel no elation. The strain has been too great for that. But I am quite recovered and ready for work again. There can be no stoppage till end of Nov^{er} when the Sketches'll be finished. And then, I fancy, something'll have to be done to get away.

I was with Pinker yesterday talking matters over. If I had known your Hampstead address I would have wired you. There is wanting to the finish of this undertaking the sanction of your presence and voice.

Drop me a line. Come down if you can! But I hardly dare to suggest that. I don't know how you are, how everybody is.

I'll write soon. Love from us all.

Ever Yours

Jph Conrad.

---

[1] Evidence of travelling on Saturday (27th) rather than Sunday.

To J.B. Pinker

Text MS Berg; Unpublished

[Pent Farm]
[2 September 1904][1]

Dear Pinker

This is all I have here. I send it specially.

This letter received this morning.[2]

Note.

If you ask them (TP's) how many words they have from slip *139* (and they are sure to have counted the MS) you will be able to soothe Harper's nervousness.

To Elsie Hueffer

Text MS Yale; *Listy* 235; Original unpublished

[letterhead: Pent Farm]
2 Sept 1904

Dearest Señora

I am so sorry you had to write. Well, I've done writing at last! N. is finished and in some fifteen days or so the money (what there's left of it) shall be coming in and I shall forward you £20 to begin with; in the hope that by some more desperate efforts I'll be able to set myself right all round in another eight months—more or less.

I would send at once but on delivery of MS (on the 31ˢᵗ Aug) Pinker had to pay off my overdraft at Watson's for which the Receiver in Bank^cy was pressing me. Nearly £200! in one fell swoop. I can't ask him (P) for anything more till both TP and Harper begin to pay the serial rights. Till then I've £3 in the house.

I am half dead. For three weeks I've been sitting up. The last few nights I felt my brain going—a delusion no doubt, but very awful.

Depend upon it that now and later as I go on (for go on I must) You shall be the first to be attended to.[3]

I've got a lot to do to the *book text* of N

A clear and fairly cheery letter from Ford arrived 2 days ago. I shall answer him to day. Yesterday I saw Pinker and we had a long conversation about F. P. has a clear notion of the system on which he

---

[1] Harper's wrote on 1 September; Conrad's note is on the back of their letter.

[2] Sent with the proofs of pp. 289–304, the letter reads: 'We must really ask you to let us have the completion of the "copy" at once, as the delay is getting very serious, as not knowing how much the book makes we cannot order the paper.'

[3] Conrad owed the Hueffers nearly £200 (Mizener, p. 96).

could go on hammering to get for F. the place which is due to him. Of course, now, Ford must not be worried.

Meantime P. says that should F. feel able to write anything on Germany[1] special efforts shall be made to place it to advantage. I could not see Dunn (of the M[ornin]g P[o]st) yesterday but shall write him a careful and cautious letter as to corr*ce* from G[erma]ny—(so, you understand, as not to engage Ford who may be as yet unable to write) but to prepare the way.

I look upon it in this way: he wrote me a good interesting, amusing letter. (He says that he wrote it without excitement). Well my dear Elsie 3 letters like that would make an article. And if it is easier for him to write in letter form we could (that is: I would be ready) to have them typed, then work on them a little (adding nothing) in the way of shaping and so on. Then P. would ram the product somewhere: M^g Pst for choice—but any periodical will do.

I cut off short here. There's a mass of corres*ce* in arrears as you may imagine.

Jessie has been in bed a bit seedy, for a day. She feels the stress too now. She sends her best love. We shall turn up for a day soon to see you and the chi[c]ks.

Ever Yours,

Conrad

To Roger Casement
Text MS NLI; Najder (1974)

[letterhead: Pent Farm]
1904
3^d Sept

My dear Casement.

Forgive my apparent brutality. Your letter had been a great and valuable pleasure. And I answer it now; the moment I've finished the book whose writing in illness and trouble I am not likely to forget in a hurry.

I am delighted to see You've accepted the Consulate in Lisbon; a post worthy of your usefulness. And I feel a great, strong longing to start and see you there. But at present I am only a half-liberated slave. I must not move away. A vague plan of leaving the Pent for the winter is in

---

[1] Where he had gone in June; he described himself as 'in a state of hourly apprehension of going mad' (Mizener, p. 94).

existence—and perhaps then! Meantime You will not, I am sure forget
me quite. The book appears end this month. I shall post you a copy.
Now I am sending you an inscribed copy of *Typhoon* my latest so far.

My wife sends her most cordial regards and I am

Always Yours

J. Conrad

To Edward Garnett
Text MS Free; J-A, 1, 335; G. 193

[letterhead: Pent Farm]
3 Sept 1904

My dear Edward.

I drop you these lines just to say that Nostromo is finished; a fact upon
which my friends may congratulate me as upon a recovery from a
dangerous illness. Therefore I am writing to dear Jack Galsworthy, to
you and—but there does* not seem to be any more friends whose
congratulations would be enlightened enough for such an occasion.

Your article in the Spectator in which you beat a dummy called
Benson with a stick called Rutherford is, as an exercise in whacking,
simply admirable.[1] It is something more too, since it has made me take
down from the shelf the Revol^{on} in Tanner's Lane.[2] Your stick my dear
boy has a queer aspect of a medieval staff already. But it's good and
more than good. It's precious wood of straight fibre and with a faint,
delicate scent. But I regret the dissipation of your energy, the waste of
vigour and the sound of divine blows lost in an unresonnant* medium.
No dust is seen to fly. There is no dust, even, in the dummy; not so much
truth as there would be in a handful of dust. Nothing! For I have looked
at the dummy too with a malicious pleasure and a melancholy curiosity.
Alas. This is what we are all coming to—at least what I am coming to.
A few days later I saw (and read) in the 'Standard' a warm and
gentlemanly appreciation of the dumminess of your dummy. Amen!
And I beheld the bald summit of my ambition. Some day I shall write a
thing that'll be reviewed thus and not otherwise. Then in the dead of

---

[1] *Speaker*, 16 July, pp. 361–2: Garnett's review of E. F. Benson's *The Challoners* and a new
  edition of *The Revolution in Tanner's Lane* by 'Mark Rutherford' (William Hale White).
  Garnett finds *The Revolution* a classic, while *The Challoners* is cheapened by the 'sham
  "drawing-room" aestheticism' of an author who ignores the need for 'a remorseless
  analysis of life'.
[2] Originally published in 1887, a novel about early nineteenth-century radicalism.

night, in the woods about the Cearne,[1] wearing the cope and the pointed mitre of a High Priest, in the secrecy of a persecuted faith, by the light of a torch held by David[2] clad in white vestments—you shall bury my lame and impotent soul. You'll bury it alive—by God!—and go home smiling ironically, and sleep no more that night.

Meantime what do you think of the subject on the enclosed piece of paper?[3] Will the public stand it? Can my tact and sense of proprieties be trusted on that classical theme?

My love to you all

Yours ever

J Conrad.

PS Send me back the scrap please—with a word of how you are.

To William Rothenstein
Text MS Harvard; J-A, 1, 336

[letterhead: Pent Farm]

1904

3^d Sept

My dear Rothenstein.

The book is finished; it has been finished for a couple of days now, but I have been too tired too flat to write to you at once. The last month I worked practically night and day; going to bed at three and sitting down again at nine. All the time at it, with the tenacity of despair.

What the book is like I don't know. I don't suppose it'll damage me; but I know that it is open to much intelligent criticism. For the other sort I don't care. Personally I am not satisfied. It is something—but not *the* thing I tried for. There is no exultation, none of that temporary sense of achievement which is so soothing. Even the mere feeling of relief, at having done with it, is wanting. The strain has been too great; had lasted too long.

But I am ready for more. I don't feel empty, exhausted. I am simply joyless—like most men of little faith. To see you would do me good. I count the days. I must take Jessie to London to see Walton Hood.[4] I am sorry to say that her heart seems to be troubling her again of late.

---

[1] Garnett's secluded house in the country.   [2] Edward's son, the future novelist.
[3] 'This was a sketch of a Napoleonic subject' (Garnett's note).
[4] Wharton P. Hood, an authority on the treatment of injured joints.

She is very cheery however. Your dear wife's letter has brightened her up.

   Plans of work with ideas of getting away for the winter jostle in my head. I won't say anything more now. Only our dear love to You four people with the hope of meeting soon for a day or so.

Ever yours

J. Conrad.

To Ford Madox Ford
Text MS Yale; Goldring 124

The Pent
5th Sept 1904

My dear Ford

   Don't imagine I have not been thinking of you in all the concern of the sympathy and affection which exist between us. Four days ago I finished the book. I wrote to no one—except to Elsie in answer to a letter I had from her. I spoke of Your last missive to me favourably. That was the true impression. Distinctly favourable. I received it just as I was starting to see Pinker about my own deplorable affairs. I was unable to see Dunn that day. Perhaps its just as well. The idea of a correspondence from Germany has been very much in my mind even in my half delirious state of finishing Nmo. I have meditated upon it since. Out of evil, great evil, some little good may spring. To expect much good out of anything is useless; tho' cases have been known. . . .

   Of course your illness is a serious matter. You must not be worried. But I've been struck by your letter. It contains much promise. Why not correspond in that tone? And even correspond with me—if you like; if You think that the idea of a concrete recipient of your prose may help you in the least. Write currente calamo.[1] Trust me to have the thing properly typed: and if joints are to be made I'll attend to that. In the state of nerves from which you suffer any mention of Pinker may be exasperating. But it is unavoidable. So I'll only say that the man says and repeats that he has always been, still is, and intends to continue in a state of readiness to handle your stuff. He says he will make special efforts. The fact is my dear boy that without understanding you in the least the man likes you personally. He also nurses in his mind a by no means irrational idea of Your usefulness. You are for him the man who can write anything at any time—and write it well—he means in a not

---

[1] 'Off the top of your head.'

ordinary way. His belief in you is by no means shaken. He admits in effect that he has failed both with the *London* and the *Novel*.[1] But he does not admit that he has failed finally. The things are not topical. They exist. They are not lost.

Write then (if you can and only when you can) the German correspondence, with remarks on authors, landowners, officers officials—and the language. Write down what you see; and if you are well enough to put your tongue in your cheek, put it there and fire off a general consideration or two upon the role of Germany in the future of Europe. Raise a whisper of German peril—or German blessing—what you will. Something for the Great Stupid. But mainly describe. And if you can write twaddle—so much the better. Directly I get something I shall make a sort of expedition—a crusade.

Phoo! I am weary. For more than a month I have been sitting up till three am—ending with a solid 36 hours, (in the middle of which I had to wire for the dentist and have a tooth drawn. It broke!!. . !!) till at 11.30 *I* broke down just after raising my eyes to the clock. Then I don't know: two blank hours during which I must have got out and sat down—(not fallen) on the concrete outside the door. That's how I found myself; and crawling in again noted the time: considerably after one.

But I've finished. There's no elation. No relief even. Nothing. Moreover I've yet a good fortnight's work for the book form. The miserable rubbish is to be shot out on the muck-heap before this month is out.[2] I'll send you the book. I'm weary! weary!

As soon as I recover I shall try and write something sensible to you. If this letter irritates you you must forgive me. My mind runs on disconnected like the free wheel of a bicycle. I feel going down hill as it were. Love from us all

Ever Yours

Conrad.

---

[1] *The Soul of London* and *The Benefactor*, both published in 1905.
[2] 14 October was the actual date.

To H.G. Wells

Text MS Illinois; Unpublished

[letterhead: Pent Farm]
Monday. [12? September 1904][1]

My dear Wells.

I've at last finished.

After writing these words there does not seem much else to say. On Friday I saw Pinker who told me You looked well at the first night of Jacob's play.[2] When is *your* first night to come off?[3]

Are you very busy? If not I would come to see you in a day or two.

I am confoundedly tired but not so empty as I feared I would be. There is no sense of relief of course. The strain has been too long. But I feel ready for more.

Yours affectionately

Jph. Conrad.

PS A fortnight ago or so M[r] and Mrs Bowkett[4] appeared walking from Dymchurch where it seems they've been staying. As I was then in my usual half-delirious state (when finishing a book) I have no clear notion of what B. said. He seemed effusive. She, as usual, looked nice and good.

To Elsie Hueffer

Text MS Yale; Unpublished

[letterhead: Pent Farm]
Wednesday [14 September? 1904][5]

Dear Señora

Thanks for your letter. Do please send me Ford's present address. I have mislaid his letter for the moment.

Our visit to Winchelsea cannot take place as yet. I've a fortnight's

---

[1] Letterhead eleven: type twelve begins on 19 September. 5 and 12 are the Mondays after the end of *Nostromo*, but Conrad is unlikely to have seen Pinker on Friday the 2nd.
[2] *Beauty and the Barge*, by W. W. Jacobs and Louis N. Parker, first given at the New Theatre on 30 August.
[3] Wells had turned his bicycling novel *The Wheels of Chance* into a play, *Hoopdriver's Holiday*.
[4] Nell de Boer and Sidney Bowkett: Bowkett, one of Wells's oldest friends, was the model for Chitterlow in *Kipps* (Mackenzie, p. 27).
[5] Apparently after *Nostromo* was finished, but within the bounds of letterhead eleven. On 5 September, Conrad had a current address for his peripatetic friend; 14 is thus more likely than 7 September.

work on proofs and so on. Hope is coming to day till Sat: and then his daughter Muriel'll come for a week.

I feel very tired now. Jessie sends her love.

Yours,

J. Conrad

To Elsie Hueffer
Text MS Yale; Unpublished

[letterhead: Pent Farm]

19 Sept. 1904

Dear Señora.

Pardon the delay. I've not yet delivered the book form. Again I've been sitting up nights trying to make something of the tale—the turn of the screw that's to hold everything together. Another night'll finish it.

Cheque (endorsed) enclosed here is for Ford's proportion of Sketches[1]—nothing to do with the loan. Please do not trouble with a receipt. Perhaps you will just note it in some small book and I shall make a note on my side. Mark: on act/ of two sketches disposed of up to now. (serial).

You understand I've been very hard at it. The finishing for T P 's horror[2] was no end at all in *any* sense. 'Twas a necessity. I am sick and tired to death.

Had letter from dear F. Seems improving. Don't be disheartened at the unavoidable sets back—if they do come.

Jessie's and Borys' best love to You three women.[3] Of course we shall dash over—if only for a day as soon as her worries give me a week's respite. I've given up hoping for more. Your[s] affect^{ly}

J Conrad.

To John Galsworthy
Text MS Forbes; Unpublished

[letterhead: Pent Farm]

23 Sept 1904

Dearest Jack.

I am glad to hear from you. Won't you come this Sunday with the MS. I am all impatience to hear what You've done. We can't come up

---

[1] His work for *The Mirror of the Sea*: see the letter of 29 May. [2] *TP's Weekly*.
[3] Elsie, Christina, and Katharine.

yet—at any rate not till I've had the last proofs which I expect every day. I have been seedy—not gout however.

I want to bring up Jessie to see Walton Hood or his chief disciple. You could arrange perhaps an appointement* with the prophet himself. And we long to behold baby Reynolds[1] of whom we know nothing—not even his name.

Mogador[2] may be our place of refuge for the winter. Mr Pépé Ratto of the Palm Tree House[3] says that *by special favour* he will do for us (3 adults and one boy) for about a pound a day. So that, if only you will promise to come out after Xmas to see us (and shoot some partridges which I hear infest the coast) there does not seem to be anything against the flit. Only don't tell anyone how cheap Mr Ratto is going to feed us because—he says: "it will detriment my business".—Jack dear I want to see you and your Saga. Ever Yours

Conrad

Nmo is to be dedicated to you as life is uncertain and am not sure of ever finishing something more worthy of your affection.

To William Rothenstein
Text MS Harvard; Unpublished

[letterhead: Pent Farm]
24 Sept 1904

My dear Rothenstein

Thanks for the card. Don't think can get to town for the first. Have just finished and sent off copy of book form and now am waiting for proofs—which are due any day.

Of course we are all impatience to see you both and the chicks.

I feel utterly done up. No more just now. Our dear love to all your house

Affectionately Yours
J. Conrad.

---

[1] His sister's son, Owen Blair Reynolds.
[2] Now known as Essaouira, on the Atlantic coast of Morocco.
[3] Well known to Cunninghame Graham, who describes it in *Mogreb-el-Acksa* (Heinemann, 1898), pp. 53–5. The proprietor spoke 'Spanish, English, Arabic, and Shillah quite without prejudice'.

To R.B. Cunninghame Graham

Text MS Dartmouth; J-A, 1, 336; Watts 155

[letterhead: Pent Farm]

7th Oct 1904

Très cher ami.

I forgive you (generously) the treacherous act of looking at a fragment of Nostromo. On your side you must (generously) forgive me for stealing and making use of in the book of* your excellent "y dentista" anecdote.[1]

The story comes out on Thursday next.[2] Don't buy it. I'll send you a copy of—and in due—course. I expect as of right and in virtue of our friendship an abusive letter from you upon it; but I stipulate a profound and unbroken secrecy of your opinion as before everybody else. I feel a great humbug.

I am glad to hear you are in possession of your new house.[3] I wondered where You were. Hudson imagined you in Morocco. I met him the other day; dear as ever but a little depressed.

I notice there is no date yet to the adv^{ents} of your next (Duckworth) volume.[4]

I don't suppose you'll remain very long now in the "black North". We are contemplating a flight somewhere for the winter. Capri perhaps? Quien sabe? Don Pietro Canonico Ferraro,[5] I hear, lets half his house and terrace with a south exposure above a grove of orange trees—and so on. It may be worth trying.

Our kindest regards. I am on the point of taking Jessie up to London to the doctors. C'est triste.

Ever affectionately yours

Jph Conrad.

---

[1] An old soldier describes Sotillo as an 'hombre de muchos dientes' – 'a man of many teeth': III, 7, p. 444.

[2] On Friday the 14th.

[3] Ardoch, overlooking the Clyde, his Scottish home for the rest of his life.

[4] *Progress* (1905): Heinemann published the histories, Duckworth the collections of stories, essays, and sketches.

[5] Davray's friend.

To Ford Madox Ford
Text MS Yale; Unpublished

99^B Addison R^d,[1]
Kensington. W.
15 Oct 1904.

Dearest fellow.

The news in a nutshell is: *Nmo* appeared Yesterday in a strangely shy and obscure manner; and we are in London in the hands of the doctors. We did see Elsie just for a couple of hours and have had a glimpse of the chicks looking pretty and good in a striking degree. I've just done a 2.500 words thing on H James for the *Nth Am^{an} Re^w*;[2] the Strand Mag. has asked me for a story (short).

Borys was immensely pleased at the postcard. He carried it about in his pocket till it resembled nothing in the world.

I am now going to start upon the sketches. Three more are wanted for the P[all] M[all] M[agazine]. Two for B'wood to pay off an old debt.[3]

This is all. As to writing anything inspiring to you that's impossible. I am too shaky in mind and body. Our best love to You; and may the stars be propitious to your efforts to get well. Yours always

Conrad.

Vous me manquez, mon cher.[4] I daren't say more.

To J.B. Pinker
Text MS Berg; Unpublished

10 Prince's Sq.
18 Oct 1904

My dear Pinker.

It is atrocious that the Albemarle Street people[5] should keep back the whole amount because of the acc/ for corrections. I have never been treated like this before and I've had to do with publishers and had corrections on proofs. I do know something about it. There is not if I am to judge by former experience more than £7 worth of corrections. They are on the whole less than the *R[oman]ce* corr^{ons}. It's a fact. Half at the

---

[1] Conrad's address as of 20 October; any reply from Ford in Germany would take a few days.
[2] 'Henry James: An Appreciation', *North American Review*, vol. 180, January 1905, pp. 102–8; reprinted in *Notes on Life and Letters*.
[3] The *Pall Mall Magazine* published six of the sea papers, January–June 1905; *Blackwood's* took 'Her Captivity' and 'Initiation', September 1905 and January 1906.
[4] 'I miss you, dear fellow.'   [5] Harper & Brothers.

most I think. They are all in the last 8 pages. In the bulk of the book they are simply verbal alterations that should not be charged to me.

My insistence makes me appear more of a contemptible nuisance than I am really; but I have promised to settle with various people and I am anxious to do so. Be good enough to let me have a cheque for £20 which I want to send to the country to night. I will call about three and would like to see you. Miss H has started typing *Benavides* (Strand Story).[1] I'll finish the thing by Thursday. Then on Fri: will begin dict^g a sea-paper. It's impossible to dictate here. Dined with Prothero[2] Sund[ay]: He wants a critical Paper for the Quar^{ly}.

Always yours

Jph. Conrad

To J.B. Pinker
Text MS Berg; Unpublished

10 Prince's Sq
Bayswater
19th Oct 1904

My dear Pinker

Pray don't forget that I am taking over the flat to morrow at eleven and that I want to leave 10 Prince's Squ^{re} for good by nine or half past; and that from being a stranger to all these people I must display cash. Very sorry to be a worry but I don't see how it can be helped just now. I don't want to be involved in any difficulties to morrow. The people of the flat wish to catch some eleven forty five train or other as the letter from the man (received to day) states.

When deducting what I had from the amount agreed upon (370) you will not, of course take into account the last £25 (Henry James paper) cash in hand and the £10.17 to pay the Standard Life. I am going to call on their West End office and instruct them to send the policy on receipt of cheque from you. You ought to have it at once in case of some accident—Quien sabe? as the Spaniards say.

I am disgusted at the slovenliness, meanness of the book's get up—the horrid misprints, the crooked lines, the dropped punctuation marks. By

---

[1] The origin of 'Gaspar Ruiz' (*Pall Mall Magazine* and *A Set of Six*). Conrad had been intrigued by the doings of a pirate, Vicente Benavides, as narrated in Captain Basil Hall's *Extracts from a Journal Written on the Coasts of Chili, Peru, and Mexico in the Years 1820, 1821, 1822* (letter to Graham, 30 March 1923; see Watts, pp. 197–8).

[2] George Walter Prothero (1848–1922), a distinguished historian and editor of the *Quarterly Review*.

Jove a fourth of the pages slants! I've never seen anything like this! It's painful! I have imparted the facts to two business men—one a civil engineer used to the ethics of large contracts, the other a partner in a banking house—a well known house. They were both surprised and amused. The proper thing of course was to pay on date keeping back a fifty or less. Jack Galsworthy who is a director of two companies thinks so too. What amazes them is that not even a date was mentionned* apparently. As the banker man remarked: the printer's acct may be quarterly! It's either smartness or damned cheek.

Always yours

Conrad.

To William Rothenstein
Text MS Harvard; Unpublished

99 Addison Rd.[1]

24 Oct 1904

My dear Rothenstein.

I am going to take Jessie to see B Clarke[2] to day at 11.30. What he will say God only knows—something very beastly no doubt.

I have been quite unwell with something resembling asthma. 3 days ago I had a very bad fit of it; took me in the street; I thought I would never get home. And on Sat. I took Borys for a walk when it came on again and in less than a quarter of an hour I had to come home in a cab with the child who most tactfully seemed not to notice my gasps and chokings on the way. It's perfectly miserable. I feel done up, unable to work after it. And yet every day is of supreme importance!

I am so glad You find a good word for *Nmo*. No reviews appeared yet as far as I know.

I'll write you this afternoon to say what Clarke thinks and advises.

Our dear love to you all

Yours

Conrad.

---

[1] Written, like several other letters from the London visit, on Pent stationery with the letterhead (twelve) crossed out.
[2] Bruce Clarke, a surgeon attached to St Bartholomew's Hospital.

To *The Times*

Text Times, 26 October 1904, p. 10; Najder (1978), 78–81

[London]
25 October [1904]

Sir,[1]

The position of the fishing boats, victims of the outrage on the part of the Russian fleet, is beyond doubt, but the accounts of the courses steered and the manoeuvres—save the mark—of the squadron appear to me confused. The point, however, which I would raise does not depend upon the correctness of the statements published in the Press.

The firing upon the fishing fleet is an outrage no doubt so extraordinary, so amazing, that it passes into the region of fantasy which borders upon the incredible; for it is hard to believe that even the extreme of nervousness would make a man forget the ABC of his profession in a case so obviously simple.

I know nothing about the handling of a fleet, which is a knowledge appertaining to naval officers and to one or two landsmen—writers who apparently have made a speciality of seamanship *en chambre*. But this is not a question of manoeuvring; it is a simple matter of safe navigation upon which any seaman is competent to speak.

After nearly a quarter of a century of sea service in all sorts of craft, upon seas both narrow and wide (and in the North Sea itself), and in command of both sailing and steam ships, the point I would raise is that the mere taking of a squadron through a fishing fleet is such an outrage, from the seaman's point of view, as any act wantonly courting an accident is bound in conscience to be.

A large fishing fleet can be seen at least at a distance of three miles; it is impossible to mistake the nature of its lights: they blaze at one like a town upon the water. It is an effect of multitude perfectly unmistakable, and the proper and seamanlike practice followed both in sailing and steam ships of the merchant service is to go outside such a fleet; at night always, without exception, and in the daytime almost invariably, unless, indeed, a clear way can be seen between the different clusters of boats with their nets down. In that principle of sea conduct I was brought up by men who certainly were not afraid of handling their ships. To act against it except in case of absolute necessity is nothing short of criminal

---

[1] On 21 October, en route for the war in Asia, the Russian navy's Baltic fleet opened fire on a supposed pack of Japanese torpedo-boats. It was really the Hull fishing-fleet going about its lawful business on the Dogger Bank. One trawler was sunk, two men died, and a score were injured. Conrad's protest was one of many.

recklessness. Even in broad daylight the taking of one ship through a fishing fleet is a matter of great care and special vigilance.

As I said, I know nothing of handling a fleet. But naval officers are seamen, and, speaking simply as a seaman of some experience, I make bold to say that no commander of a British squadron, on a passage, would, without necessity and when not engaged in warlike operations, take his ships through a fishing fleet at night. He would not do it on the ground of professional skill and common humanity out of regard for the fishermen's lives and property. The thing is not done. In every ship I have been in, and men I know have been in, the distinct standing order is to go outside all fishing fleets. An officer of the watch disregarding it, especially at night, would lay himself open to a severe reproof from his captain. Fishing boats engaged in their avocations are not fully under command; that is why an international agreement has provided them with lights whose meaning is perfectly clear. Neither are they completely stationary; the fleet drifts as a whole, with variations in the drift of individual boats which causes a constant shifting and shuffling, as it were, of the units composing its body. For this reason, the taking of a ship through a fishing fleet is an operation requiring special vigilance, and involving a risk—a risk which is absolutely useless. I see from the Press that Russian officials in St. Petersburg, with a characteristic impudence, charge the fishermen with falsehood (a charge of lying occurs naturally to the Russian mind), and talk airily of collisions; but my contention is that, even if the boats had been sunk and damaged by collision, it would have been no usual accident, but a wanton outrage. Ships have collided with each other and single fishing smacks have been run down by men who have been made to suffer for such an accident. But no lubber upon the seas has ever gone, as far as I know, into the middle of a fishing fleet, sinking and damaging boats. Such a proceeding passes beyond the limits of accident; it is nothing short of a crime. Stupidity can hardly explain it, unless a stupidity of colossal proportions fit to match the size of the Empire that produced those extraordinary naval officers who are supposed by their countrymen to have done that very thing of steaming a whole fleet through boats at work upon their fishing-ground. How this exploit can be reconciled with the fear of Japanese laying floating mines passes my comprehension. The obvious thing would have been to give that illuminated, blazing mob of deadly engines as wide a berth as possible. If the diagrams I have seen are true, it is nothing short of a miracle that a round dozen of the boats had not been sunk.

But, colossal stupidity or inconceivable malevolence, I am heartily thankful that I am not master of a ship homeward bound in the chops of the Channel in the way of the Russian fleet. To be rammed by a cruiser or a battleship of the Second Pacific Squadron, and then to be left to sink or swim upon the wide sea, is not an enviable fate.

Joseph Conrad

To R.B. Cunninghame Graham
Text MS Dartmouth; J-A, 1, 337; Watts 157

99^B Addison R^d
London W.
31 Oct 1904.

Très cher et bon ami.

Your letter was indeed worth having and I blush deeply as I re-read it both with pleasure and shame. For in regard to that book I feel a great fraud.

What is done with can not be mended. I know that you have made the most of my audacious effort; but still it is to me a comfort and a delight that you have found so much to say in commendation. Your friendship and good nature, great as they are where my person and scribbling are concerned, would not have induced you to accept anything utterly contemptible—that I know. It is a great load off my chest. Now as to an explanation or two.

I don't defend Nostromo himself. Fact is he does not take *my* fancy either. As to his conduct generally and with women in particular I only wish to say that he is not a Spaniard or S. American. I tried to differentiate him even to the point of mounting him upon a mare which I believe is not or *was not* the proper thing to do in Argentina; though in Chile there was never much of that nonsense. But truly N is nothing at all—a fiction—embodied vanity of the sailor kind—a romantic mouthpiece of "the people" which (I mean "the people") frequently experience the very feelings to which he gives utterance. I do not defend him as a creation.

Costaguana is meant for a S. Am^{can} state in general; thence the mixture of customs and expressions. C'est voulu.[1] I remembered but little and rejected nothing.[2]

---

[1] 'It's intentional.'
[2] Of his extensive reading or of his limited experience in Latin American affairs?

Mi alma is a more serious mistake.[1] I've heard a little girl so address a pet small dog as they swung in a hammock together. What misled me was this that in Polish that very term of endearment: "My soul" has not the passionate significance you point out. I am crestfallen and sorry.

Pasotrote I've heard somehow, somewhere, from someone—devil knows where. But the mistake is in the word *canter* which I wrote persistently while I really meant *amble*, I believe.[2] I am appalled simply.

I am compunctious as to the use I've made of the impression produced upon me by the Ex[im] Sr Don Perez Triana's personality.[3] Do you think I have com[m]itted an unforgivable fault there? He'll never see or hear the book probably.

I end with a general apology for ever attempting a tale of this kind; and with the renewed assurance of the great pleasure your good long letter has given me. It is a very magnificent sign of forgiveness on your part.

Tout à Vous de coeur

J. Conrad.

PS. My wife sends her kind regards. She is not at all well and I am very anxious. Borys too has been in bed a week now. Tonsilitis. The temperature went up to 103° on two nights. But he is mending I am glad to say. Rothenstein likes the book. He got hold of the inwards with an amazing intelligence. E. Garnett likewise wrote me a most appreciative letter. As to the public it will turn its back on it no doubt. Ce sera un four complet.[4] I don't care.

P.P.S. Are you likely to come to town this year? We are here till end of Nov[er] at least.

---

[1] Don José Avellanos twice calls Mrs Gould 'my soul' (pp. 86 and 141) – an expression too passionate for the circumstances.

[2] On p. 48, Conrad describes Gould as he is 'when cantering ... to the mine ... at his easy swift *pasotrote*'. Watts hears an echo of Ramon Páez, *Wild Scenes in South America* (1868).

[3] The Excelentísimo Señor Santiago Pérez Triana (1860–1916), Colombian Envoy Extraordinary to London and Madrid, influenced the portrayal of Avellanos and, arguably, the design of the whole *Nostromo* canvas. The 'liberal, rhetorical, and optimistic side of Triana's nature' (Watts, p. 208) appears refracted in Avellanos's political behaviour; his pessimistic side, alert to the abuses of wealth and power, in the vision of the book itself. Such contrasts are general in Conrad's work, but Triana's example—in the story of his political triumphs and misfortunes, and in his analysis of political dilemmas—helped to place them in a Latin American context.

[4] 'It will be a total failure.'

To J.B. Pinker

Text MS Berg; Unpublished

99 Addison R^d. W.
31st Oct 1904

My dear Pinker.

Imprimis I am no end sorry to be worrying you again as to the money you promised (and partly performed) to lend me out of the proceeds of Nostromo. I am really concerned at my insistence which is forced upon me by the entreating letters of people who have trusted me without any other security but my word and their reliance on my promise to settle before the end of October. This thing robs me of my sleep. Of the sum I asked you for I have had already £*20* (E. Hueffer); two fives and one ten in cash=£*20*; and a £*100* lately (of which I sent away eighty). Then £*50* goes or is gone to Keen.[1] Together then, since the account has been squared to within a few pounds as per your account I've had (*borrowed from you*) £190. I think that in this reckoning I am not very wrong. I think also that in my letter from the Pent I asked you for £370. I have no copy but you have the original. Can you then let me have the balance now? I know I am a heavy individuality to carry through and that no one would be anxious to undertake the task. I haven't the slightest illusion on that score. Therefore my dear Pinker pray don't allow yourself to misunderstand what I may happen to say. After all a man's words must be judged upon his whole character. If I were a person of placid disposition I would not write as I am (for better or worse) able to do.

If You could let me have a cheque for £60 made out to *Richard Hogben*[2] to morrow it would take a load off my breast. This is the most pressing. I will ask you by telephone tomorrow (Tuesday) about 11. Perhaps you will be kind enough to leave instructions if you go out. I can't leave the house for any time as I have two invalids to look after just now. The boy has been in bed for nearly a week with tonsilitis; temperature reached 103° on two nights. He is mending now. And my wife is laid up too but I trust she will be up to morrow. This is why I write to night and propose to telephone to morrow instead of coming to see you.

I paid Miss Hallowes last Wednesday £*1.5*. Will you please send her a cheque for next Wednesday addressed here.

As to work. One paper is far advanced; another can be finished in 24 hours if needed; and also the short story. What is *quite ready* is the paper

---

[1] One of the receivers winding up the affairs of Watson's bank: William Brock Keen, accountant, 3 Church Court, Old Jewry. See also the letter of 30 December.

[2] Who had let the Pent to Ford, who in turn let it to Conrad.

on *London River* for H. Norman agreed for with Pawling. It will do for the
Mirror of the Sea. Vol.

They are to pay £50 ser rights both countries. They wanted it for
August summer N° but Pawling tells me that it will do for the Xmas N°.[1]
Do you want it to go there from your office? You'll let me have ½ the
amount for current expenses here which are no joke! And generally I
mean to come to you not otherwise but MS in hand for such advances as
I may need leaving the proceeds of the sea papers intact as much as
possible towards the extinction of my debt (as distinguished from
advances). The short story will be next out of hand to live on—while the
papers go on and the M of the Sea vol will be done by the end of this
month. The London River is really an extra paper written to order, but
it will serve to swell the book.

I am afraid Nostromo had a bad sendoff. I receive magnificent letters
from unexpected quarters; I know well enough that the book is no mean
feat—but what about the public?

Yours always

Conrad

To William Rothenstein
Text MS Harvard; Unpublished

[London]
3^d Nov 1904

My dear Will:

It strikes me that perhaps you may think I've forgotten the *£50* You've
lent me. I think You said at the time you would want it before Xmas.
Will next week be soon enough for repayment of £30 and the week after
for the balance? Or are you, perchance, very pressed?

Pray tell me at once. Because after all the whole thing could be
managed within the week; only I don't want to do any "flying around".
You know what I mean. Whereas by taking a fortnight a short story will
be ready—and paid for.

But don't think of me. The thing's provided for anyhow. It's a mere
question of method.

Our best love to you all

Jph. Conrad.

---

[1] *World's Work*, vol. 5, December 1904, pp. 19–32.

To Alice Rothenstein
Text MS Harvard; Unpublished

99 Addison R^d
Friday. [4? November 1904][1]

Dear Mrs. Rothenstein.

Borys has been ill in bed and Jessie has been upset; but Dr Tebb has been putting them right with great success. Now they are both better we venture to ask whether you would come to dine to morrow (Sat)—if it is not too much to ask; for there can be not much pleasure in associating with such broken-down crocks as we turn out to be.

I would have turned up but I had to stand by. In fact Jessie was not fit to be left alone in the nervous state she was in. She would love dearly to see you; but go alone I won't let her and we can not both leave the boy.

His trouble was tonsilitis with a high temperature. Since dear Will has been here (we treated him abominably) I haven't been out of the flat till this evening when I took the poor Missus for a short drive about the outlying streets.

A postcard would reach us in time to let us know whether we are to be made glad by seeing you both.

Will had excited me with his generous praise of the poor, clumsy book. For hours I could not go to sleep going over, in my mind, the precious things he said of what at best was only well meant, not well executed.

Our very best love to you both and the dear chicks. Yours affectionately and obediently

J Conrad.

PS Jess wanted to write to you herself but I drove her off to bed. She had no sleep to speak of for two nights.

To J.M. Barrie
Text MS Berg; Unpublished

99 Addison R^d W.
Saturday. [5 November? 1904][2]

Dear Mr Barrie.

The missis has unexpectedly produced the play[3] from somewhere amongst her skirts in the trunk. So I send it on at once; for I am anxious

[1] The address gives the general period, and the convalescents' progress a likely date.
[2] Just before the letter to Pinker of 8 November?
[3] *One Day More*, the adaptation of 'To-morrow'.

to know whether there is in me the "sense" of the stage in any degree that could be turned to a practical advantage. And you are the only man whose Yes or No (qualified or unqualified) I could implicitly believe.

With many thanks for the permission

Always yours,

Jph. Conrad

To Elsie Hueffer
Text MS Yale; Unpublished

99 Addison R^d
(Holland Park Avenue end)
Sund: 6th Nov. 04

My dear Elsie.

Do come to lunch if you can. We'll wait till *1.30* unless you wire the hour; but come as early as you can manage it. It would be delightful to see Miss Martindale too[1] if you are going about together—which strikes me as possible. It is such a business to get poor Jessie along any distance that we could not yet call on your mother. Please give her our very best regards. We would have turned up before anyway but Borys immobilised us by going to bed for a week with tonsilitis or something of that sort. Temp: up to 103°. It looked alarming. But he has been up and out three days ago.

Your letter got here by the 10 o'clock post. Too late to wire. Our nearest station is Shep[he]rds Bush (Tube) or Holland Pk Av^{ne} (Tube) 3 and 5 minutes walk. Also Uxbridge R^d Station of the West London Ry. (3 minutes). The Add[is]on R^d Station is to be avoided as it is on the other end of the long, long Add^{on} Av^{ne}. Flat on first floor.

With this topographical information I close, leaving all news for tomorrow's talk. Our dear love to you.

Yours always

Jph Conrad

---

[1] Her sister Mary.

1 Joseph Conrad: pastel by William Rothenstein, 1903

2　William Rothenstein: lithograph by John Singer Sargent, 1897

3   Sir Roger Casement on trial for his life, 1916

4 Mrs Sanderson with her sons and daughters, *c.* 1895, Ted standing at the
far right, Agnes third from the right

5 The Hueffers and a German cousin, *c.* 1904

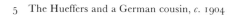

6   J.M. Barrie and Henry James in London, 1910

7   Ada Galsworthy with Chris, *c.* 1900

8 E.V. Lucas

9   Henry Newbolt, *c.* 1900

10 The Hôtel Riche, Montpellier: the Conrads stayed on the top floor

11 Capri

12   Sidney Colvin, by William Rothenstein, 1897

13   Constance Collier in 1907: she acted in *One Day More*

14　Anarchist rendezvous, Windmill St, London

To J.B. Pinker

Text MS Berg; Unpublished

[London]
8th Nov 1904

My dear Pinker.

This is the letter from *Paw[lin]g*. I neither saw him nor wrote to him. Why he should talk to me of Am^{an} rights I don't know. If my memory serves we agreed for £50 ser: rights, *both* countries. However there's no need to trouble; but I think that (publication being now assured) I may ask you for £*15* in advance which, with the £5 I had lately, makes £*20* on *that* product of my genius.[1] By the by. Have You seen the consecration of my aforesaid Genius in the Dly Mail of yesterday? It was too laudatory by far, but what pleased me was the decency of tone.[2] Barrie got hold of my play. He requested me to let him see it. I asked him for a critical, instructive, opinion. For I've not given up the idea of perpetrating 3 acts some day. And he is a good craftsman.

Please give Miss Hallowes a sort of cheque she can cash at your bank.

Yesterday a lot of people invaded us all day long delaying the story for the *Strand*.[3] I am at it since 8 this morning. It'll be done typing this afternoon I hope.

Could you ask the World's Work by telephone for early slip of the *Thames*. It's awful to think I can't, simply *can't* work any faster. Give them my address here or it will go to the Pent.

Yours always

J. Conrad.

To J.B. Pinker

Text MS Berg; Unpublished

[London]
[mid November 1904][4]

My dear Pinker.

Here's the story. Credit me with it for as great a sum as you can squeeze out of some discriminating editor. Sorry I've been so long about it. Two more (if you can place them) would make a Benavides cycle. I

---

[1] 'London River'? As well as the British publication in the *World's Work*, it appeared in the American *Metropolitan Magazine* in February 1905.

[2] 7 November: the review, by 'C', ends 'If Poland gave us Mr Conrad, did he not pay us the superb compliment of choosing as the medium of his art our English tongue?'

[3] A Benavides story, later incorporated into 'Gaspar Ruiz': it was turned down.

[4] Soon after 8 November, judging by the evidence of the finished story and the proof of 'London River'.

can't pretend I care for the writing of them much. But I am ready to go on.

'Tisn't a startling one but it has a quality.

Pray send me now a cheque on *Nmo* acct/ for £30. Date it on Monday next if you like. It's to be sent away. Now the Pres^al election is over I trust Harp^s will sho[o]t the book out in Am^a, at once.[1]

I've got proof of *River*. Seems all right. Man going down the Thames to take a few photographs for it. I've consented to my portrait appearing in the W's Work Birthday-Xmas N° along with the article.

Am told (in two places and also at Mudies (City)) that Nmo's doing well. Also that there is some demand for Lord Jim since the other was published

Shall call on you soon.

Yours always

Conrad

To Alice Rothenstein

Text MS Harvard; Unpublished

London
17th Nov 1904

My dear Alice.

The thing is over;[2] and to hear Bruce Clarke talk one would think there is nothing the matter with the knee. Anyway there will be no operation.

The examination went off beautifully.

Report: No disease. No fracture. General athropy* of muscles and tendons—and the prospect of a long treatment.

She's to remain at the house for another 5 or six days. 13 Bulstrode Street Cav^dish Sq^re. W.[3]

I am relieved in a way but the prospect is not all smiles as I don't put much faith in massage and in "treatment". It's, to speak politely, a form of the all prevailing bosh. In the name of Allah—figs![4]†

But I trust Dr Tebb implicitly and he seems to think the diagnosis right.

B. Clarke is to see her several times in the course of the next 4 days.

[1] *Nostromo* appeared on 23 November, three weeks after the election of Theodore Roosevelt, apostle of intervention in Latin American affairs.
[2] The inspection of Jessie's knee under anaesthetic.
[3] A nursing-home run by Miss Elizabeth Ellis.
[4] Originally 'the Prophet—figs!': James and Horatio Smith, *Rejected Addresses* (1812).

Borys (asleep now) is going out to morrow for the day to see some friends of his (and mine) at Muswell Hill.[1] He has been very manly in the whole of this affair.

Jessie's dear love to You and Will, in which I may be permitted to join. Always affectionately Yours

Jph. Conrad

† This opinion need not to be communicated to the lady when you see her.

To Elsie Hueffer
Text MS Yale; Unpublished

99 Addison R[d.] W.
Tuesday [22 November 1904][2]

Dear Elsie

Pray read this letter before You send it to Ford.

On my word of honour I am for the present ruined as poor Jessie's business can not be seen through for less than a hundred. Clarke's fee alone is 58 gs. She will have to remain in that nursing home a month in all at 8 gs per week. I am a miserable creature, I know.

No more just now except my very useless love to You and the dear chicks

always yours

J. Conrad

PS But I am working and contriving to raise something before middle December.

To Ford Madox Ford
Text MS Yale; Goldring 126

22 Nov 1904
99 Addison Road W.

My dearest Ford

I am bitterly ashamed of my criminal remissness in writing to you; but you know me enough à fond to understand my state of utter exhaustion after finishing the accursed *Nmo*. Do you know my dear fellow that the almost full half of that book has been written in 5 months.

---

[1] The Meldrums. [2] The same date as the letter to Ford.

From end Mch to end Augst. All Sep^{ler} was taken up in revision and 'writing up' at high pressure. And what energy was left after that bout had to be used for writing on and on infernal things for sale. And still it has to go on tho' I feel half dead mentally and very shaky physically with a sort of choking fit every day which I hope is nothing worse than asthma.

We came here about 5 weeks ago. Got into this flat. Then the doctors got to work upon Jessie. Her general state is not satisfactory but the great matter was the knee. And the matter has dragged. She has been a week now in a nursing home near Harley Street with Bruce Clarke the joint specialist surgeon, lecturer at Barts, in charge of the case. Various rather horrible things have taken place. The examination under chloroform was made four days ago, and would you imagine?, the mischief was not located—it was not even found. As a matter of fact B Clarke (as good a man as there is, I suppose) took his patient for a pampered, silly sort of little woman who was making no end of fuss for a simple stiff joint. You may imagine to what horrible pain he put her acting on that assumption. I daren't trust myself to write of it. Assez!

The long and the short of it is that he found his mistake. The cartilage *is* displaced and must have been so for thirteen years since her first accident when she was seventeen. That no disease of the bones was set up Tebb† (and also Clarke) accounts for by the large quantity of fluid always present which prevented the displaced cartilage from granulating and, as it were, infecting the bones.

Clarke owned up his mistake the day before yesterday, like a man. Yesterday he wired for me and told me he had no doubt now; he could *feel* the displacement now; had felt it on three separate occasions. "I can put my finger on it every time" he said. (I felt as if I could strangle him) His compunction was very visible. What would you have! He is a good operator with a great reputation for carrying his cures through. The operation is fixed for the day after tomorrow, Thursday at noon.

Voilà. And all this time I've been writing! I've written since we came here a thing on H James, a paper on London River (for the World's Work), an imbecile short story (2500 words) for the *Strand*. To-day even I did 500 words dictating to Miss Hallowes. But I could not muster courage enough till now to sit down and write you a letter, though there is not a day You haven't been in my thoughts.

This is all for to-day or rather for to-night. I shall write you a *real* letter in a few days. I've been meeting a few men lately. The sound of Your name is not allowed to die out of the land. But I can't enlarge just now;

the natural egoism of a suffering man will not allow it at present. Jessie and Borys, your great friends send their love. As to mine it is always with you. Yours ever

Conrad.

† The doctor, friend of Will R, admirer of Your grandfather.[1]

To David Meldrum
Text MS Duke; Blackburn 180

[London]
Tuesday. [22 November 1904][2]

My Dear Mr Meldrum

Many thanks for your good letter. I don't answer it at lenght* just now. I want only to tell you that an operation is fixed for Thursday midday.

There is every reason to expect a complete success; and the poor woman is extremely anxious to be carved for no other reason but that she would be more useful to me and the boy in the future. We must put off naming the day for your dinner (which I am loth to forego) till that business is over.

Please assure Mrs Meldrum of my grateful regard for her genuine kindness to us all. Love to the dear chicks

Always Yours
J. Conrad

To William Rothenstein
Text MS Harvard; Unpublished

[London]
25th Nov 1904

Dearest Will

Yes. The fees and so on have exhausted my cr^dt at Pinker's for a time. Still I was not quite desperate, but only nearly so.

You my dearest boy ought to have £15 out of that amount which would still leave me Your debtor for a balance of £5.

I'll send on directly I get it changed. Thanks dear boy.

Jessie's better to night. Pain subsiding at last. Going on very favourably upon the whole. Never had fever at all.

---

[1] The painter Ford Madox Brown.   [2] Two days before the operation on the 24th.

Our best love
                                        Yours
                                                    Conrad.

I acknowledge formally on the next page.
    I.O.U Thirty (30) pounds
                                                    Jph Conrad.

To Alice and William Rothenstein
Text MS Harvard; Unpublished

                                                    [London]
                                        Sat ev^g [26? November 1904][1]

Dearest Alice and Will
    Thanks for your letter. Jessie is going on excellently and there is every
prospect of her having a serviceable stiff limb and a life free from pain.
    The reaction has left me a little flabby; but I shall soon get hold of my
work again, but now I spend every moment I can spare with Jessie.
    She sends you her dear love and says she will write to Alice directly
she can sit up in bed with any comfort.
    I shall drop You a line soon with a further report.
    Borys sends his most affectionate regards. He has supported me
nobly.
                                        Ever Yours
                                                    J. Conrad

To William Rothenstein
Text MS Harvard; Unpublished

                                                    [London]
                                                    Tuesday
                                                    30 Nov 1904.

Dearest Will
    I've been seedy myself yesterday with a sort of chill which kept me
indoors.
    This letter *acknowledges the £25 loaned by Kerr*.[2] Would you mind my
dear Will to bank it for me?

---

[1] Two days after the operation?
[2] Probably W. P. Ker (1855–1923), Professor of English at University College, London,
    author of *Epic and Romance* (1897) and *The Dark Ages* (1904). In *Men and Memories* (2,
    p. 61), Rothenstein lists him as one of those who came to Conrad's aid.

I send the cheque back. Let the amount remain in your acct/; and as to *£10* of it I'll ask you for a cheque for part or the whole according as necessity may arise. *£15 must* go towards extinguishing my indebt[ed]-ness to you.

I beg your pardon for bothering in this way but as you know I've no banking acct/ and don't see my way to opening one just now.

We stand then thus: I owe you still £5 and have in Your hands a sum of *£10* which You hold at my disposal.

I've made application for a life policy but must see You before settling details.

Jessie goes on well. My love to you all

Yours ever

Conrad

To Mariah Hannah Martindale

Text MS Yale; Unpublished

99 Addison R^d
1st Dec 1904

Dear Mrs Martindale

Just a word to thank you very much for calling and cheering up Jessie. In her own words, You have done her a lot of good.

Pray rest assured that your kindness i[s] appreciated as it should be by the two people concerned.

If I do not come to thank you in person it is because I am simply overwhelmed with work which ought to have been done weeks ago; and besides I am feeling extremely seedy at the present moment having caught some sort of chill. This in fact is the true reason; because from one's work one may get away but from a chill one cannot.

With most friendly regards to Miss Martindale I am dear Mrs Martindale your most faithful and obedient servant

Jph. Conrad.

To E.V. Lucas
Text MS Indiana; Unpublished

99 Addison R^d
1st Dec 1904

My dear Lucas[1]

I've informed Pinker of the desire which the Firm of Methuen misled deplorably by You manifests for what your blind partiality is pleased to call Essays (save the mark!).

Also it's likely that there will be a 6/- story ready by June or so. Quien sabe?

If they get to talking the firm, you are doing youre* best to ruin, may be let in even for that too.[2]

But all this is left in P's hands as is only just and proper under the peculiar circumstances. I don't know whether he has done anything.

Jessie's making a swift progress. She's already moving the limb in bed. Clarke thinks that she may walk across the room on Saturday. If so I'll have her moved here on Mond: or Tuesday. I am anxious to have her under Tebb's care as soon as possible.

With my humble duty to the Ladies of Your House

Yours affectionately

Jph. Conrad

To J.B. Pinker
Text MS Berg; Unpublished

[London]
Thursday. [1 December 1904][3]

My dear Pinker.

I am still seedy but keep at work, which is the great affair just now. Of course I don't get on as fast as I ought to or rather need to—but still.

On the other hand my wife gets on much faster than we dared to hope. She has now begun to move the limb in bed and Clarke told me to day distinctly that there is no chance of any complications arising. That stage is past. He would not be surprised if she walked across the room by Saturday. In that case she could be moved to the flat on Mond. or Tues:

---

[1] Garnett's friend, Edward Verrall Lucas (1868–1938), author, critic, journalist, and surreal humourist. He worked for Methuen for many years.

[2] Over a period of ten years, beginning with *The Mirror of the Sea* (1906), Methuen published most of Conrad's books.

[3] The contents match those of the letter to Lucas.

next. Thus the drain of 8 gs p week for the Nursing home will be stopped after one more payment.

Meantime I ought to pay the balance of rent for the flat up to 22 Dec. The man reminded me by a letter to-day. It is ten pounds. Also I must pay Dr Tebb for the two special attendances on my wife, for examination and for the operation: Four guineas. For his attendance on Borys and further visits on my wife he will send his acct/ later on which I firmly believe I'll be able to discharge without coming to you for that specific expense.

For the household expenses I can go some way into the next week, yet.

So please send me the *two* cheques. I would like to send them away to morrow (Friday).

E.V. Lucas writes me that *Methuen* is anxious for a vol: of criticisms. Thus there are two publishers after the thing. The game is in your hands. As to me when all this strain that has been on since January last is off I've no doubt I will be able to sandwich critical papers between the slices of the novel.[1]

Each of them when once begun is no trouble to finish. I may yet perpetrate one or two before leaving London—I mean without interfering with the sea papers. Please ask Halkett[2] to let me have slips of the other 3 papers as soon as possible.

Yours always

Jph Conrad.

To David Meldrum

Text MS Duke; Blackburn 181

[London]
[2? December 1904][3]

My Dear Mr Meldrum

Just a word to say I am still somewhat seedy, and apologise for my behaviour on Mond: evening.

My wife is getting on famously. I went out yesterday to see her. She wishes to be remembered to you with thanks for the flowers ... Her

---

[1] The '6/– story' dangled in front of Methuen? The Mediterranean novel for Harper & Brothers? *Chance*? Over the next few months, Conrad's plans were volatile.
[2] Of the *Pall Mall Magazine*: six *Mirror* papers appeared there between January and June 1906.
[3] Conrad is suffering from the 'seediness' regretted in the letters of 1 December. Their contents imply that he had seen Jessie (and her surgeon) on that day, 'yesterday'.

kindest and most friendly regards to Mrs Meldrum and love to the little ones.

Always yours

J. Conrad

To ?
Text MS Yale; Unpublished

[London]
12 Dec 1904.

Dear Sir
  Here's my precious signature

Yours faithfully

Jph. Conrad

To H.-D. Davray
Text MS Yale; *L.fr.* 67

15 X^{bre} [décembre] 1904
London
99 Addison R^d. W.

Cher ami
  Je vous envois l'edition Américaine.[1] Celle d'ici est trop villaine. Ma femme vient de subir une operation serieuse au genou. Elle est encore au lit. Elle rêve de Capri. Moi aussi du reste. Je vais vous envoyer un petit mot dans peu de jours. Mes devoirs à Madame. Mille amitiés.

Tout à vous

Conrad.

Translation

Dear Friend,
  I send you the American edition. The English one is too wretched. My wife has just undergone a serious operation on her knee. She is still in bed. She dreams of Capri. So do I. I shall send you a short note within a few days.
  My regards to Madame. A thousand greetings.

Always yours,

Conrad.

---

[1] Of *Nostromo*.

To Marguerite Poradowska

Text MS Yale; Rapin 182; G. & S. 104

99 Addison Road.
London. W.
15 Dec. 1904

Chère et bonne amie.[1]

L'année dernière j'ai été malade tout le temps. Cinq accès de goutte en onze mois! En Decembre dernier c'est Jessie qui sans être precisement malade nous a donné des vives inquietudes a cause de son coeur. Pouvant a peine marcher moi même je l'ai amennée a Londres (en Janvier) pour consulter les medecins. Ils m'ont un peu reasuré mais juste comme nous nous preparions a retourner chez nous a Pent Farm elle a eu un horrible accident, une chute dans la rue demettant les deux genoux! Après six semaines d'angoisse a Londres nous avons passé un été miserable a la campagne elle pouvant se trainer a peine, moi écrivant nuit et jour, pour ainsi dire, pour finir mon malheureux bouquin. Car il faut vous dire que pour completer la situation mon banquier fit faillite en Fevrier de cette année-ci.

Enfin en Septembre le livre etant fini nous sommes arrivés a Londres. J'ai transporté Jessie aussitot dans un hopital privé (Nursing Home) ou il y a 3 semaines elle a subi une operation sur le genoux gauche (l'autre etait gueri). Bruce Clarke un de nos distingués chirurgiens etait l'operateur. C'est un succès complet autant qu'on peut en juger en ce moment. Aucune complication n'est survenue, et je viens de la mouvoir du Nursing Home a notre appartement ici.

Je l'ai là depuis hier. Elle vous envoit mille baisers. Elle est au lit encore mais, je le repète, en bonne voie de guérison *radicale*. Je respire librement pour la première fois depuis deux ans! Et tout de suite je vous écris.

Tout ce temps là j'ai été dans un état moral pitiable. Incapable de travailler pendant une année entière, plein d'angoisse quand* a l'avenir, me debattant contre les difficultés materielles, je ne voulait pas, je ne pouvait pas, Vous attrister par mes gémissements. A quoi bon! Enfin j'en sors, secoué, ébranlé mais ayant ressaisi un peu d'espoir. J'ose enfin lever les yeux. Et c'est vers Vous que je regarde.

Au millieu de tout çela ma santé c'est rétablie comme par miracle. Je n'ai eu qu'un accès de goutte cette année, fort leger du reste. Il s'agit

---

[1] Marguerite Poradowska (née Gachet, 1848–1937), the widow of Conrad's cousin Aleksander, and thus his 'Aunt' – but also his good friend. Her novels of French, Belgian, and Polish life were well known in their day.

maintenant de rattraper le temps et l'argent perdu. On nous ordonne a tout deux (Jessie et moi) de passer l'hiver dans le midi. Nous pensons aller a Capri pour quatre mois aussitot que Jess pourra supporter le voyage. Peut-etre dans une quinzaine—qui sait. Nous passerons par Paris! Y serez-vous en Janvier? Aussitot assuré de votre pardon je Vous ferais connaitre la date de notre depart.

Toujours à Vous de tout mon coeur

Conrad

Translation

Dear and kind friend,

Last year I was constantly ill. Five attacks of gout in eleven months! Last December it was Jessie: without being exactly sick, she made us most uneasy on account of her heart. Hardly able to walk myself, I took her to London (in January) to consult the doctors. They reassured me a little, but just as we were getting ready to go home to Pent Farm, she had a terrible accident, a fall in the street dislocating both knees! After six weeks of anguish in London, we spent a miserable summer in the country, she hardly able to drag herself around, I writing night and day, so to speak, to finish my hapless book. Moreover, I must tell you that, to crown the situation, my banker failed in February of this year.

At last, in September, with the book completed, we came up to London. I brought Jessie at once to a private hospital (Nursing Home) where three weeks ago she underwent an operation on her left knee (the other had healed). Bruce Clarke, one of our most distinguished surgeons, operated. As far as one can judge at present, it was a total success. No complications followed, and I have just moved her from the Nursing Home to our rooms here.

I have had her here since yesterday. She sends you many kisses. She is still in bed, but, I repeat, well on the way to a complete recovery. I breathe freely for the first time in two years! And I write to you at once.

During this time I have been in a pitiable mental state. Incapable of working for an entire year, full of anxiety about the future, struggling against financial difficulties, I did not want to, I could not, trouble you with my complaints. To what use? I am finally coming out of it, shocked, shaken, but having regained some hope. At last I dare to lift my eyes. And I look towards you.

In the middle of all this, as if by a miracle, I have regained my health. I have had only one attack of gout this year, a fairly mild one, moreover.

Now I must make up for lost time and lost money. Both of us (Jessie and I) have been ordered to spend the winter in the south. We are thinking of going to Capri for four months as soon as Jessie can stand the journey. Perhaps within a fortnight—who knows? We shall pass through Paris! Will you be there in January? Once assured of your forgiveness, I shall let you know the date of our departure.

Ever yours, with all my heart

Conrad

To William Rothenstein
Text MS Harvard; Unpublished

[London]
16 Dec 1904

Dear Will.

I intend to drop on you on Sat: next having permission to that effect from the gracious Lady Alice. But if you have something to do or if You want to be left alone just stop me by a note.

By the same token send me a £5 cheque to replace the lost one from which I think no danger is to be apprehended now.

What's this lecture? I want to see your notes of it. I am strongly interested. I am also pleased to understand that You are writing it out apparently in full.

Please hold the document at my disposition when I come.

Our love to you all

Yours ever Conrad.

To J.B. Pinker
Text MS Berg; Unpublished

[London]
21 Dec 1904

My dear Pinker

I had a fit of gout, not very severe it is true. It is now over and I'll be able to go out to-morrow.

I regret to have no MS to send you. There is half of a story written and also half a paper (M[irror] of the S[ea]). I turned to a paper not being able to get on with the N° 2 Benavides while in pain.

Miss Hallowes is going to stay in London till the first week in Ja*ny*, so that I shall be dictating to the last minute as it were.

Pray send me funds to get over this confounded festive season. I have 2 weeks to pay for flat from to-morrow. There will be the gas and water bill. Also I must make some return to people by sending things to their kids. And there's ten of them! The nurse too will have to be paid—and so on. Altogether I must ask you for £*30*. But you may depend on getting MS to that amount (at least) before I go.

I wish I were gone. Wife is getting on very well but she is still in bed.

I am glad the gout has come and gone. It was due and hanging over me. Now the worst is over and it was by no means as bad as I feared. I feel well in myself now.

By the bye. Halkett spoke to me with great enthusiasm of *The Rescue*. Could you on resuming after holidays find out whether he would serialise it in *P*[*all*] *M*[*all*] *M*[*agazine*]? It would be worth doing then. More than half is done. And (confidentially) I can get Ford to help me in it a little—block out things and so on.[1] He is here and getting better. However nothing must be allowed to interfere with the new novel which is simmering within me all the time. I'll bring it all complete from Italy I do believe. My mind is freer than it has been for years and a little sunshine will get my steam up—I know. Look how (in adverse circumstances) I managed to write half of Nostromo in less than five months during the fine summer we had. Kindest regards and best wishes

                                                    Yours

                                                    J Conrad.

To David Garnett
Text G. 195

                                                    [London]
                                                    23rd Dec 1904

My dear David,[2]

A man who makes maps[3]—even in imaginary countries—should have a compass; a pocket-compass to show him the way of his exploring.

The lenses are not first rate but Borys (whom you perhaps remember) got them specially for you. They may serve to examine a casual beetle or a blade of grass or a bit of moss that you may pick up in your wanderings in the woods—the deep woods of an imaginary country.

And with these insignificant tokens of our love we send you our best

---

[1] Ford probably made some suggestions about the structure of the long-delayed novel (Mizener, p. 81) – which appeared in serial in 1919.

[2] David (1892–1981), the future author of *Lady into Fox* (1923) and many other novels, was the son of Constance and Edward.

[3] He had drawn a map for a new Duckworth edition of Richard Jefferies' *Bevis*.

wishes for that uncertain and hazardous journey upon which you are
engaged now.[1]

Your friend

Joseph Conrad

To H.-D. Davray
Text MS Yale; *L.fr.* 67

99 Addison Road

London. W.

28 Dec 1904.

Cher Davray.

Quelle douleureuse fin d'année pour Vous! Soyez assuré de notre vive
sympathie. Le plus précieux de notre passé—les affections que rien ne
peut remplacer—s'émiettent entre nos mains a mesure que nous
avançons dans la vie.

Vous êtes bien de penser a nous. Ma femme s'essaye a marcher avec
des béquilles. C'est lent mais le progrès e[s]t visible.

J'écris au Canonico[2] demain car jusqu'a présent je n'osais faire
aucune demarche. J'espère que nous pourrons quitter Londres le sept
du mois prochain. Mais je ne sais pas encore pour sur.

Avec nos meilleurs souhaits pour Votre prosperité je Vous prie de
nous rappeler au bon souvenir de Mme Davray.

A vous bien cordialement

Joseph Conrad.

Translation

Dear Davray,

What a painful end of the year for you! Be assured of our ardent
sympathy. The most precious part of our past experience—the affections which nothing can replace—crumbles away in our hands as we go
on through life.

You are kind to think of us. My wife tries to walk on crutches. It is
slow, but her progress is visible.

I shall write to the 'Canonico' tomorrow, for up to now I dared not
make a move. I hope we can leave London on the seventh of next month.
But I'm not sure yet.

---

[1] With his mother, he was going go Russia – on a journey made all the more dangerous by
    her revolutionary connections.
[2] Canon Pietro Ferraro, Davray's friend on Capri.

With our best wishes for your well-being, I beg you to give our regards to Madame Davray.

Very cordially yours,

Joseph Conrad.

To J.B. Pinker

Text MS Berg; Unpublished

[London]

Friday 30th Dec 1904

My dear Pinker

I've heard from Keeen* again. I don't think it is an attempt to put pressure on. He appeals to me to make some sort of definite proposal to him† as he has got to face his Committee[1] on Monday at *10.15* and wishes to show them he has been doing something. Keen understands the position pretty clearly. What he asks me to do specifically is to get You to write something offering *him* some terms—any terms he says— with which he can meet the questions of his committee who are under the influence of Rising—the solicitor.[2] That beast is likely to make trouble. His textual words are that: *personally* he does not wish to press me in the least. A suggestion for any sort of arrangement from you to *him* is all he advises us to make. I rather think it would be worth while writing him a letter for I have had, in many Years, several proofs of his general good feeling towards me. I can't believe this is mere sham. Even if you were to write—he thinks—that the unforeseen expenses connected with my wife's illness prevent anything being done at present—it would facilitate his task of keeping Rising from taking legal proceedings.

With this faithful report I leave the thing to you merely remarking that there's always time to "burst" if it has to come to that. I own that I don't want to figure in a cause célèbre in B[ankrupt]cy Court from the natural shyness of my disposition and also from other reasons which'll occur to you so readily that I refrain from stating them here.

Pardon me chasing you with my affairs in the very precin[c]ts of Your home. I've just heard from K this afternoon. Kind regards

Yours Conrad.

† Not to Rising the solicitor.

---

[1] The committee winding up the affairs of Conrad's former banker.
[2] Robert Watts Wellington Rising, 9 King William St.

1905

To J.B. Pinker

Text MS Berg; Unpublished

[London]
Wednesday
4th Jany 1905.

My Dear Pinker

You won't take it amiss if I try to refute the charge of mad extravagance which your perfectly friendly remarks as to my expenditure did in fact contain. As a matter of fact the extravagance—(I don't defend myself here—I simply rectify a statement) was not so mad as all that.

If my recollection of the words you said is correct they amounted to the positive statement that in this (1904) year I drew £*1050* and that last year (1903) I drew something like £1200. I can't be altogether mistaken as to your meaning, since I remember perfectly the staggering impression received. Moreover I have a vivid recollection of you saying that I spent at the rate of 1200 a year on a rough estimate. As I went along the street the thing began to appear impossible upon the basis of fact. For, my dear fellow, reckless in my demands as I must have appeared to You pray believe me that I've never asked for any given sum without the question of repayment being present in my mind. In fact that question is present in my mind always.

Our financial history begins (on the debit side) in October 1900 with the item of £1.13.1 "for typing Seraphina".[1] From that date to June *31st 1904* I drew (or was otherwise debited) the sum £*1352*; from July *first* to Sept *First* 1904 (when *Nostromo MS* was delivered to you and the contracted amount *secured*) I drew £*245*.

Therefore from *Oct 1st 1900* to Sept *1st 1904* say in 3 years and ten months you have advanced me the sum of £*1597*.

In the same time I earned or have been credited otherwise with the sum of £*1578* in which the MS of *Nmo* (delivered tho' not paid for by Harper at that precise date) enters for £*900* (contract price) and the other items are taken from Your acct as delivered to me up to 1st Sept 1904.

_____

That is the position established from my memos and which your books will confirm I am sure within a limit of say £5 either way.

It may be extravagance but not *mad* extravagance even taking into consideration my overdraft with Watson which I am sorry to say falls

[1] The original form of *Romance*.

now upon you. *That* included I've spent in 3 y & 10 m. £1778 roughly speaking. I don't deny it is too much especially looking at the rate of earnings. But pray consider that in that period I had against me a lot of illness which acted adversely both ways, checking production and increasing expenses. The fact however remains that in 1904 on the 1st of Sept. I owed you about £17 to £19, and there was a certain amount of MS in hand, that is: 5 papers of the *M of the S.* series. Since that time I've written (as against money drawn) the H. James paper the Thames paper. 3 M of the S papers.

Besides 2/3ds of Benavides tales[1] are written, and I hope to finish to morrow another sea paper.

A beggarly account I don't deny especially when contrasted with the advances you've made in that time. *Why* they are so large, you know. They certainly haven't been spent on beer and skittles. I am perfectly certain you judge me with fairness. I've spent as little as I knew how and produced as much as I could. I hope to do better both ways in the future. As I said before I am well aware that to keep me up is a heavy undertaking but I argue that it is not a hopeless one.

Then in considering the future you may take it from me that some money up to 140 to 150 will turn up within this quarter. Nothing but the extinction of the vital spark will prevent me from bringing a good 2/3ds (at least) of a novel from Italy. The vol of *MS* M of the Sea is practically ready and as to that I have an original idea which I would mention to you. It is this: To include all the Sea Sketches and all the literary papers now ready in *one* vol giving both sides of Conrad—seaman and artist.

The vol could have a general title and contain two parts:

The M of the Sea Pt Ist

The Mirror of Life P IId

the mirror of life being fiction—of course.

It would be a new sort of audacity; but I would like to try. General Title could be something like *Action and Vision* do you see my point?

I'll be with you at *12*.

I trust You will see Your way to send me off but whatever happens I am Yours

Conrad.

---

[1] The tales of piracy that became 'Gaspar Ruiz'.

To J.B. Pinker
Text MS Berg; Unpublished

[London]
Monday [9 January 1905][1]

My dear Pinker,

I send you the acct from Cooks. Pray let me have the cheque as I ought to get hold of the tickets by to morrow or else there may be some trouble with the sleeping car berths for which there is some competition. I send you the corr^ted proofs of the last papers for the PMM.[2]

Tomorrow I expect to see you with the Harvey Paper N° 2 ready[3] and perhaps some *MS* as well.

From some advert^mt slips sent me from Harpers Am^an House I see *Nmo* has gone into a second edition 3 weeks after publication. Do you think the first Ed does amount to 4000 copies?[4] I should think it must since that number of copies would just cover the adv^ce on the other side. They would hardly print less than that. Upon my word I need all the good news I can get just now for a while. I've an awful choking cold and am very depressed. The reaction after the last 2 months I suppose. Nothing but sunshine will set me right.

Besides the cheque for Cook please send me another for £7, as I must settle up here; the time is getting short. The balance of the journey money I must ask You to let me have Thursday morning at latest.

Kind regards

Yours Conrad.

To J.B. Pinker
Text MS Berg; Unpublished

[London]
Tuesday. 10th *Jan^y* 05

My dear Pinker

Please read the enclosed letter. The man who writes is a Swiss of good family[5] who two years ago was staying in England with some friends of mine. He is all right and knows the right sort of people here.

---

[1] The closest Monday to the 13th, the day of departure.
[2] 'The Rulers of East and West', Parts One and Two, *Pall Mall Magazine*, May and June 1905.
[3] George Harvey's *Harper's Weekly* published two sea papers, 'The Tallness of the Spars' and 'The Weight of Her Burden', 10 and 17 June.
[4] *Nostromo* appeared there on 23 November in an edition of 3,000 copies.
[5] The Zwingli discussed on 5 February?

His proposal is worth considering. Moreover every little helps. If it were but three pounds I would let him translate.

I am writing to him suggesting *The End of the Tether* which may be considered a short novel. *Ld Jim* & *Nmo* are too long I fear. The *Typhoon* Vol does not belong to me. The "*Nigger*" would not be suitable. I really see nothing else but the *E. of the T.* because *H of D* in the same Vol would be too short.

Will you make an appointement* for him to see you?

I've settled with Cooks. The doctor has seen Jessie for the last time. The wound is all but closed. No complication is to be feared. She is however rather low generally which can not be much wondered at after her experiences of the last 7 weeks.

Please send me the cheque (dated on Thursday) so that it reaches me by first post as I will have to go to the bank with it, to get cash. I had £55 therefore I am to get 75. Most of it has to be distributed before I leave. I shall try to arrive in Capri with as much in hand as possible. But when one leads a caravan of four it mounts up in a terrific way. Paris with hotel and carriages will cost me £3. Naples is sure to cost as much. The passage to Capri alone will amount to more than a sov[ereign]. And I must have carriages at every step. I shudder. I won't feel easy till I sit down to write.

Yours

Conrad.

To J.B. Pinker
Text MS Berg; Unpublished

[London]
11th Jan 1905

My dear Pinker

Thanks very much for the money (£75) and your good letter.

I don't think that Keen takes you either for a donkey or a rogue (using your own words). And I dare suggest that he did not put his back up—or at any rate not voluntarily. There is that brute of a solicitor and I know there is a beast or two on the committee.[1] The Secretary of the Standard Life for one. Keen has been appointed in opposition to these people's wishes. As he is well disposed to me (has been so for many years) I am sure that the difference arises from a misunderstanding as to what You

---

[1] Charged with clearing up the affairs of Watson's bank, among them Conrad's overdraft.

or he have said of which the others will make the most. I need not tell You I have had no communication with him.

I am inexpressibly sorry to be such a worrying client to you in so many ways. All I can do is to shut my ears to everything and write— write. And that's not so easy as it looks.

Kind regards

Yours

J. Conrad

I will write you on arrival in Capri.

To H.-D. Davray
Text L.fr. 68

Jeudi 14 [12] Janvier 1905[1]
99 Addison Rd
[London] W.

Cher ami,

Votre canonico[2] est charmant. Je vous envoie sa lettre. Voyez vous-même.

Tout ça à cause de vous: le nom magique de Davray!

Nous partons demain le quinze[3] et nous passerons la nuit à Paris à l'Hotel de St Pétersbourg: rue Caumartin où nous arriverons vers 7 heures. Rien que la nuit. J'ai hâte d'arriver à Capri pour des raisons que vous comprendrez facilement sans que je les mette tout au long ici. Pas moyen de vous voir donc et de saluer madame Davray. Veuillez bien nous rappeler tous les deux et même tous les trois à son bienveillant souvenir.

Nous quittons Paris le samedi par le *sleeping-car train* à 11.30 du matin.

Pourriez-vous me faire parvenir un petit mot à l'hotel? J'ai besoin d'un livre sur la Russie—récent—sérieux. Leroy-Beaulieu[4] a-t-il du bon?

Vous me rendrez un grand service.—Je ne suis pas au courant. Je veux quelque chose sur l'aspect politique et social de l'Empire Blanc, au point de vue français. J'aurais bien le temps de sortir pour trouver une librairie, dans la soirée ou le matin.

---

[1] Thursday was the twelfth; from the course of events, it is clear that the date rather than the day is wrong.

[2] Canon Ferraro   [3] On the fifteenth, the Conrads were travelling through Italy.

[4] Anatole Leroy-Beaulieu, *L'Empire des Tsars* (2 vols., 1881–2), and *Etudes russes et européennes* (1897). Conrad's main achievement over the next few months was 'Autocracy and War'.

J'ai l'idée d'écrire 3 articles sur l'avenir du susdit Empire—pour la marmite, vous comprenez.

Parole d'honneur quand on se met à écrire on donne son âme au diable—le diable de l'économie domestique.

Quel sale métier! Enfin!

A propos de l'économie domestique. Peut-être madame Davray aura la bonté de me dire si "la serva" (qui fera la cuisine à l'italienne—et un poco alla Caprese) *se charge du marché*; et quelle est la somme qui doit lui être confiée à cette fin. Moi je ne suis pas pratique. Je redoute d'effrayer cette brave femme par la profusion de l'or Anglais! Nous sommes quatre. J'ai une garde-malade diplomée avec nous—fille d'un officier supérieur de l'armée, tout comme l'ancienne cocotte, maitresse du ministre dans "Nostromo".[1]

Au revoir; car au retour en mai à moins que le diable ne s'en mêle, je ne manquerai pas de vous serrer la main.

Mille amitiés.

Tout à vous.

Translation

Dear Friend,

Your 'Canonico' is charming. I send you his letter. See for yourself.

All this because of you: the magic name of Davray!

We leave tomorrow, the 15th, and shall spend the night in Paris at the St Petersburg Hotel, rue Caumartin, where we shall arrive towards 7 o'clock. Only the night. I am in a hurry to arrive in Capri for reasons that you easily understand without my putting them at length here. No chance, then, of seeing you and greeting Madame Davray.

Please remember both of us and even all three of us to her.

We leave Paris on Saturday by the sleeping-car train at 11:30 a. m..

Could you forward a little note to the hotel? I need a book on Russia—recent—serious. Is Leroy-Beaulieu any good?

You will do me a great favour. I am not up to date. I want something on the political and social aspect of the White Empire, from the French point of view. In the evening or morning, I would certainly have the time to go out to find a bookshop.

I have the idea of writing three articles on the future of the said Empire—to keep the pot boiling, you understand.

---

[1] 'A stout, loud-voiced lady of French extraction, the daughter, she said, of an officer of high rank' (p. 55).

Word of honour when one takes up writing one gives one's soul to the devil—the devil of domestic economy.

What a dirty profession! So!

On the subject of domestic economy: perhaps Madame Davray will be kind enough to tell me if 'la serva' [the maid] (who will cook in the Italian style—with Caprese touches) will take charge of the shopping; and how much should be entrusted to her for this end. I myself am not practical. I am afraid of scaring this worthy woman with the profusion of English gold! We are four. I have a certified nurse with us—daughter of a senior army officer, just like the old harlot, the minister's mistress in *Nostromo*.

Until next time; for on returning in May, unless the devil interferes, I shall not fail to shake your hand. A thousand regards,

Sincerely yours.

To H.G. Wells
Text MS Illinois; J-A, 2, 8

[London]
13 Jan 1905
2 am.

My dear Wells

I kept quiet imagining You to be very busy; and only now I intrude just to say goodbye—and no more.

We are off to-day. A mad extravagent thing to do but if I bring a book back from Capri it will be some justification. Jessie must have some change and I myself feel at the end of my tether.

Your first inst^t in the PMM[1] is jolly *good*. It turns up* remarkably well. Coming upon it unexpectedly (the N° of PMM was sent to me) I gave a great gasp to see the story of which I had heard first so long ago here beginning at last. I don't know that I will read the other instalments. I should think *not*. I'll refrain. I've been pleased and now I can wait. There is in that opening, my dear boy, a *quality*. You will smile scornfully if I name it: a sympathetic quality. Well, it *is* a bad definition but I can't think of anything nearer. I like the treatment itself (of these early episodes) and also the temper of that treatment. To begin in the way you do is generally dangerous. Often it kills all interest. In this case I think you come off wonderfully well. There's no taint of triviality. The interest is kindled.

---

[1] Of *Kipps*, which began in the January *Pall Mall Magazine*.

Upon the whole I think I'll read the second inst[t].

I had a rough time of it my dear Wells this last month or two. Well that's over. The success of the operation is beyond doubt. Now the great thing is to recover the use of the limb. It's slow. Her nerves are gone now.

Change will help her. Our love to you all.

Your

Conrad.

PS I'll send you my address in a week or so. What are you writing? How do you get on.

To John Galsworthy
Text MS Forbes; Unpublished

[letterhead: Hotel St. Petersburg,
33 & 35
rue Caumartin]
14 Jan 1905

Dearest Jack

Jessie had a sweet dear letter from your wife for which I send her my thanks; for you know how much I appreciate and prize every mark of her good will and friendship towards us both.

I hope You are in a state of peace wherever you are, inward peace I mean to say. Outward worries, I know, there must be for a few days;[1] I wish you well through them: but really all these forms of "human wisdom" though odious enough in their way, need not disturb the serenity of your souls.

We got here last night with no end of labour and an expense which makes my hair stand on end when I think of it. I try not to. Jess stood the journey very well but she is awfully helpless. What will happen at the end of the journey when landing in a small boat in Capri has to be faced I don't know.

We leave in an hour.

Love to you both

Yours ever

Conrad

---

[1] Now that Jack's father was dead, he and Ada had made their liaison public; they could not marry, however, until Ada's divorce became final in September. To escape the 'outward worries' of scandal and ostracism, they were off to the continent for several months.

To J.B. Pinker
Text MS Berg; Unpublished

16 Jan 1905
Hotel Isotta & de Genève
Naples.

My dear Pinker

We arrived here at 1.50 *am* without accident but two hours late on the whole journey. I've had a most anxious time but on Sat and Sund: managed to scrawl something in the nature of a political article, with which I am not very satisfied.

However my mind was anything but free. The whole proceeding has been very ruinous up to now and to put the finishing touch on it we found the north wind blowing; Naples bitterly cold and the Steamship C° refusing positively to land my wife in Capri till the weather changes and their boat can approach the Marina Grande. I am quite powerless in the matter as the landing takes place in small boats at Capri and the arrangements must be left in their hands. For the last three days this norther has been blowing, and may last another three. It is sheer bad luck to be let in for that expence* as the hotel for our party of four will come to more than £2 a day I fear. I had to go to it because it had a lift. It is the most modest of the few that have. But it is possible that the wind may leave off to morrow. I earnestly hope it will do so. The Steamboat C° will telefone (It^an spelling) me on the morning of the first day that their boats resume calling at Marina Grande; so that I may get away by the afternoon.

All this is atrocious. The arrangements for landing will cost me about 20 frs apart from the price of tickets which come to as much more. Pray open me a credit with Tho: Cook & Sons, just ten pounds or so, which you can do through their office in London of course. I ask you to do this for I see clearly I shall not have enough to do that myself as I intended. A few days in this hotel will ruin me effectively. Still, there can be no going back on this experiment. Otherwise when once settled I still think it will work for economy. If so You won't see me again till the novel is done—quite done! I feel well only tired. My wife making great progress every day. Kind regards

Yours

Conrad

PS When paying the money to Cooks please ask them to *wire* their Naples office. I own I am nervous though really I hope to get through the first month comfortably with the add[ition]al £10 I am asking for.

To John Galsworthy
Text MS Forbes; J-A, 2, 9[1]

21ˢᵗ Jany. 1905
Villa di Maria
Isola di Capri.
(Napoli).

Dearest Jack

We've just got in here—seven days out from London! From Sunday night till Friday noon we have been weather bound in Naples it being impossible to land Jessie at Capri if the sea was at all rough as the steamer does not come alongside the jetty; and the transfer from steamer to small boat and from boat to shore required smooth water for safety. Perhaps the difficulty was not so great as all these people—hotel keeper, the steamboat officials and the head man at Cooks tried to make me believe. The weather was indeed very bad. I had foreseen everything in planning that voyage but that, and the delay of all these days in the hotel has utterly ruined me. In fact to be able to get over to Capri I had to leave a 150 frcs unpaid on my bill and am beginning life here in charge of a party of four with 30 frcs in my pocket. My dearest Jack can you come to the rescue by sending me a cheque for £*10*? I've written to Pinker but that unforeseen demand not backed by any MS will receive a cold and languid answer I guess. Some answer there will be of course but I am anxious being at the mercy of the good man. The nervous irritation of these days in Naples prevented me doing anything. I got 1000 words of a political article written (and thats all) during the voyage. Here the outlook is very promising; the rooms good, the terrace on the south side. Through the good Canonico we have fallen into the hands of priests. There were three of them waiting on the marina grande for our arrival which took place on a moonlit evening about 7. The whole population surged and yelled round poor Jessies chair while we waited on the quay for the large carriage which was ordered but did not turn up in time. I think we will be very comfortable here. But the whole expedition is a mad thing really for it rests upon what I am not certain of—my power to produce some sixty thou: words in 4 months. I feel sick with apprehension at times. Jessie tired but progressing all the time. Do forgive me my odiousness dear Jack. Our very best love to you both.

Yours ever

J. Conrad.

---

[1] Omitting the section from 'My dearest Jack' to 'of the good man'.

To David Meldrum
Text MS Duke; Blackburn 181

22 Jan 1905.
Villa di Maria.
Isola di Capri
Napoli.

My dear M\ :sup:`r` Meldrum.

I waited to thank You for Your wire till I could send you my address. We have been infinitely pleased and touched by your kind message which was put into my hand at the moment Jessie was being carried down the gangway on board the boat in Dover. They did it in the most lubberly and dangerous manner I must say; but the arrangements in France from Calais onwards have been most excellent good men and well devised carrying chairs being in waiting in Paris at stations and in the hotel where we spent the night. From there to Rome we had no trouble; but in Rome where we had to change trains with only 15 minutes to do it in they nearly dropped my poor wife off the platform of the car in their excitement and hurry. She was the only one not to be frightened. My hair stood on end and the nurse nearly fainted. However a miss is as good as a mile. We arrived in Naples 2½ hours late at 2 o'clock in the morning—snow on the ground and a bitter North wind blowing. The Cook's interpreter waiting for us with the chair and carriers looked the very picture of misery. As to the carriage which was ordered it had gone home simply. Fortunately, we were able to capture the only hotel omnibus in waiting; and the hotel captured us to some purpose—for we had to remain weather-bound in Naples for five solid days. On two of these the boat for Capri never left at all and on the others the weather was still too boisterous to admit of landing an invalid. I thought I had foreseen everything but I had not foreseen that. This waiting was a most wretched business—apart from being atrociously costly. At last, taking the first chance, we got landed here yesterday by moonlight the whole population (I should say) of the Marina turning out on the jetty to see the fun. The Captain took his steamer in as close in as he dared and a special big rowing boat came off to do the trans-shipping. The uproar was something awful; but I must say that for all their yelling these Italians did their work extremely well; and though the thing looked (and to my wife must have felt) dangerous I had not a moments uneasiness. The whole affair which had afforded the population of Capri so much innocent enjoyment cost me 40 frcs or so—and I don't grudge them. To feel settled at last and able to go to work was well worth the money. Today the sun shone and Jessie has been resting on a warm terrace.

She has stood the journey perfectly well and looks as fresh as paint. I feel rather limp now. But the best of the joke is that the nurse has gone to pieces completely. She went to bed directly we got into the house and remains at the time of writing. That's my usual luck; and it is serious enough because every day is of extreme importance for massage and the bending of the knee. I can only hope she will get up tomorrow—but who knows?

Such is the history of our voyage. And if I can only get to work in earnest nothing else matters much.

Jessie sends her love to all your house. I can't tell You how pleased she was at Your kind wire. She wanted to write to Your wife this evening but I dissuaded her, tho' I admit she did not look tired. In Naples the anxiety about the landing and the fretting over the delay had kept [her] nervous all the time.

To morrow I take up the task again. I know I have your good wishes and I can assure you that no man's good will and friendship is more prized here than yours. Believe me most cordially yours.

Jph. Conrad.

To J.B. Pinker
Text MS Berg; Unpublished

Villa Di Maria
Isola di Capri.
Napoli
22^d Jany 1905

Dear Pinker

Many thanks for your wire which reached me by post to day only—from the hotel. We managed to get off by Friday afternoon (by the usual steamer) and landed here by moonlight with some trouble but without mishap. I had a special rowing boat here and a chair with carriers from Naples.

If you have written to me through Cook I haven't got Your letter yet. Neither have I heard from them. But I write you at once to catch the morning post from here, which means the evening mail from Naples. When you will get this devil only knows.

On reflexion I've held back the MS in order that my wife should type it. I will make my corrections and in that way may at a pinch do without proof. She has begun to day. I've commenced the second pol*cal* paper to day also. With the novel I shall go on steadily from to morrow giving an hour or two to the papers every afternoon. As the TS will be very much interlined you will oblige me if You give such retyping as you consider necessary to Miss Hallowes who has got a machine of her own now. The novel most likely will come to you in MS.

I am well but feel very tired just now the result of the journey which was anxious as you know. My wife stood it very well. She's quite fresh—but the nurse, Miss Jackson, has gone to pieces. She went to bed on Sat afternoon and remains there at the time of writing. Its real dog gone luck, this is. The weather has improved. I am sorry to have bothered you so abominably.

Yours

Conrad

PS I got off here rather cheaply the usual fare and special arrangements together coming to £5. I left about that amount undercharged on my hotel bill in Naples (damn it) and landed in Capri with 15 frcs. In a week's time I'll have a clear notion of my living exp*ses* here.

To John Galsworthy
Text MS Forbes; Unpublished

Villa Di Maria
Capri
29 Jan 1905

Dearest Jack

Thanks a thousand times. I breathe freely a bit. You are good!

Lovely news this of the chance (if ever so remote alas) of seeing you two dearest people here walking the earth in happy serenity. I haven't got into my working stride yet. Not yet! Its awful.

I think of the end of the Saga[1] with a much greater composure and certitude than of any of Your other books. I feel somehow certain that you are *working well*. I am happy to hear that You are working steadily. Do bring the MS when you come. It seems to[o] good to ever come to pass.

---

[1] *The Man of Property*, first novel in the Forsyte Saga: Galsworthy finished revising it late in March.

No more just now. Just now I feel as if I could cry a bit
Yours

Conrad

Jessie says she wrote to you both the other day. What audacity! Give my dear love to your wife—qui est mon confrère[1]—don't forget. Is An[atole] France shelved quite??!

To Robert d'Humières
Text MS Vaugelas; Guérin

29 Janvier 1905
Villa Di Maria
Is: di Capri
(Napoli)

Cher Monsieur[2]

Votre lettre si aimable et si flatteuse vient de me parvenir ici ce matin même.

Je veux commencer par Vous remercier du plaisir que Vous m'avez donné. Votre nom cher Monsieur e[s]t loin de m'être inconnu comme vous paraissez le croire. La preuve que vous me donnez de Votre appréciation est une charmante surprise. Je ne me permets pas de mettre votre jugement en question; si Vous croyez que le public français voudra accepter une oeuvre ou votre pénétration (et surtout Votre bienveillance) a decouvert quelques qualités d'art et de vérité je ne puis que dire oui de tout mon coeur—en Vous assurant que je suis on ne peux plus sensible a l'honneur que Vous me faites. Aimant la France et les Français d'une affection héréditaire et personelle je désire vivement leur être connu. Ce serait un vrai bonheur pour moi que d'être interprété par Vous qui avez si bien compris (votre lettre le prouve) la simple âme de ce petit livre.

Voici cher monsieur mon sentiment. Le côté *affaire* devra être reglé avec l'editeur qui dans notre contrat c'est réservé les droits de traduction. Je ne crains aucune difficulté de ce côté. M. Heinemann est un charmant homme et un homme raisonnable. Il ne se fait pas une idée exagerée de ma valeur commerciale. Je lui écris par cette poste même

---

[1] Because of her Maupassant translations and her songs.
[2] Aymeric Eugène Robert, Vicomte d'Humières (1868–1915), an author and translator, active in the Théâtre des Arts and close to Marcel Proust, was to die in a hopeless charge on the German lines. Among the works he had translated were Kipling's *Plain Tales from the Hills* and Lew Wallace's *Ben Hur*. His proposed translation of *The Nigger*, the subject of this letter, took until 1909 to appear as a serial and 1910 as a book.

pour lui donner l'autorisation de traiter avec Vous—(car, de mon côté, je me suis réservé le choix du traducteur)—donc il sera préparé a recevoir la communication que Vous voudrez bien sans doute lui addresser directement.

Merci bien, encore une fois, pour tout ce que Vous avez dit et pour ce que Vous voulez faire. Croyez moi le votre bien cordialement

Joseph Conrad

addresse. M^r Wm: Heinemann. 21 Bedford Street
Covt Garden
W. C.

Translation

Dear Sir,

Your letter, so friendly and flattering, has just arrived here this very morning.

I would like to begin by thanking you for the pleasure you have given me. Your name, dear Sir, is far from being unknown as you appear to believe. The proof you give me of your appreciation is a charming surprise. I do not allow myself to question your judgment; if you believe the French public will want to accept a work in which your penetration and, above all, your good-will have discovered some qualities of art and truth, I can only agree with all my heart—in assuring you that I could not be more sensible of the honour you afford me. Loving France and the French with an hereditary and personal affection, I eagerly wish to be known to them. It will be a real joy for me to be translated by someone like you who have so well understood (your letter proves it) the simple soul of this little book.

Here, dear Sir, is my feeling. The *business* side must be settled with the publisher, who by our contract has retained rights of translation. I do not fear any difficulty on that side. Mr Heinemann is a charming man and a reasonable man. He does not have an exaggerated sense of my commercial worth. I am writing to him by this same post to authorize him to negotiate with you—(for, on my part, I have kept the choice of translator)—so he will be prepared to receive the communication that you undoubtedly will want to send him directly.

Thanks indeed, one more time, for all that you have said and for what you want to do. Believe me, very cordially yours

Joseph Conrad

To R.B. Cunninghame Graham
Text MS Dartmouth; J-A, 2, 10; Watts 160

Villa Di Maria
Isola di Capri
(Napoli)
3ᵈ Febr 1905

Très cher ami.

This moment I receive Progress,[1] or rather the moment (last night) occurred favourably to let me read before I sat down to write. Nothing in my writing life (for in the sealife what could approach the pride of one's first testimonial as a "sober and trustworthy officer"!) has given me greater pleasure, a deeper satisfaction of innocent vanity, a more distinct sense of my work being tangible to others than myself—than the dedication of the book[2] so full of admirable things, from the wonderful preface to the slightest of the sketches within the covers.

My artistic assent the intellectual and moral satisfaction with the truth and force of your thought living in your prose is unbounded without reservation and qualification.[3] And with every masterly turn of phrase masterly in picturesque vision and in matchless wording my pride in the dedication grows, till it equals—nay—almost surpasses— the pride of that long ago moment, in another existence, when another sort of master of quite a different craft vouched with his obscure name for my "sobriety and trustworthiness" before his fellows well able to judge and amongst whom I believed my life was destined to run and end.[4] Tout a vous, de coeur.

Jph. Conrad

PS Jessie who is progressing favourably sends her kindest regards.

---

[1] *Progress and Other Sketches*, newly published by Duckworth.
[2] The dedication reads 'To Joseph Conrad'.
[3] Commas supplied after 'assent' and 'your prose' would clarify the sentence but lessen its spontaneity.
[4] That 'moment' was on 25 April 1881, when Captain Stuart signed the papers discharging Third Mate Korzeniowski from the *Loch Etive*.

To J.B. Pinker
Text MS Berg; J-A, 2, 10

5 Febr 1905
Villa Di Maria
Capri.
Italy.

My dear Pinker

I send the form filled up at the earliest possible moment.

Imagine Miss Jackson[1] had influenza & pneumonia—quite an illness. She's just convalescent. It's perfectly awful. My wife had to nurse her and so on; and I who now if ever wanted peace to concentrate my thoughts after all the anxieties in London could not achieve it (as you may guess) in these lodgings. I have worked but badly—there's no use disguising the truth. I've been in a state of exasperation with the eternal something cropping up to distract my mind. Of course Jessie did not get the attention which was necessary; but nevertheless she's progressing slowly.

I had to take another room (in the same house) to do such work as I was able to achieve. It's mostly the *novel*. However when I get at last into the stride I shall sit night and day and something considerable (I still trust) will come of it. Of course You may say that I ought to disregard all the complications and peg away with my eyes shut to domestic affairs. I know some men are capable of that sort of thing; and with an organised household one could perhaps abstract oneself for six hours per day. It's another matter with me. You understand that my wife was pretty helpless and required some attention; the child too. For me to have to lay down my pen ten times in the course of the day is fatal. I wish there had been something of a hack-writer in my composition.

The copy of *Tallness of the Spars* I've sent you last Dec[er] I think needs no revision.[2]

R. D'Humières a French man of letters of some distinction asked me for permission to translate the *Nigger*. In view of your action in the matter of the Scandinavian proposal[3] I referred him direct to Heinemann. Is that right?

What about the Germans?

Zwingli[4] wrote me that if you came to terms with the Ill[te] Ber[ner]

---

[1] The nurse.   [2] For *Harper's Weekly*.
[3] *Tales of Unrest* appeared in Swedish in 1903; its translator, Karin Hirn, must have been told to deal directly with Unwin.
[4] Cf. 10 January.

Zeitung they would pay his expenses down here so that he could work under my eye.

That is all. Better news next time.

Yours ever

J. Conrad.

To John Galsworthy
Text MS Forbes; Marrot 164

[Capri]
12th Febr
05

Dearest Jack

I doubt whether this will reach you but I can't refrain from a shout at the news.[1] How You must have worked! I only regret that the publication is to be delayed till Xmas season—which is crowded as you know. Of course Your motive is unanswerable. I wonder if letting it go over the New Year say and Jan 06 will not be good policy. The book to my mind is so considerable that no circumstance of its pub[on] should be disregarded—I fancy I'll *have* to review it—anonymously. A good place for that review will have to be found. But there's plenty of time. We are waiting with the greatest impatience You[r] arrival here. Our deep love

Always yours

Conrad.

To Agnes Sanderson
Text MS Lubbock; Unpublished

15 Febry. 1905
Villa di Maria
Capri.

Dear Enemy.[2]

Pardon this delay in answering your letter and also in my writing to Barrie. However a letter to him—as warm as I know how to make it—goes by this post. A card of introduction would not meet the

---

[1] That Duckworth was taking *The Man of Property*: it appeared in March 1906.
[2] Agnes Sanderson was Ted's second-oldest sister. The affectionate enmity between Conrad and 'Miss Agnes' began around 1894, the time of his first visit to the boisterous household at Elstree.

requirements of this case, to my mind. He will write to me and then you may go to see him—*or* the thing will have to be dropped; for I am not intimate with B. and I don't know how he will take this request.[1]

Let us hope for the best. You know I have the success of all the Sandersons at heart; and this case on account of our especially inimical relations enlists my warmest sympathies.

No more at present on account of the post. Pray give my best love to Your dear mother[2] and to as many Sandersons as you have within reach of the voice.

My work here goes on very lamely and I don't feel happy—in that respect at least.

Believe me my dear Agnes your affectionate and obedient servant

Jph. Conrad

To R.B. Cunninghame Graham
Text MS Dartmouth; J-A, 2, 12; Watts 161

16 Febr. 05
Villa di Maria
Capri.
Italy

Cher Ami.

Your letter is delightful. As to your sea people and their manoeuvres (in *Progress*)[3] You've confounded nothing either in form or in the substance. You seem to know more of all things that* I thought it possible for any man to know, since the Renaissance swells (who knew everything about everything) perished by sword, dagger, poison pest (and too much 'doune') in the glorious yesterday of the world.

Vous—Vous êtes né trop tard.[4] The stodgy sun of the future—our early Victorian future—lingers on the horizon, but all the same it will rise—it will indeed—to throw its sanitary light upon a dull world of perfected municipalities and WC's sans peur et sans reproche. The grave of individual temperaments is being dug by GBS and HGW with

---

[1] For a part in one of his plays: letters of 1 and 2 March.
[2] Katherine Sanderson, the mother of twelve children, took a warm and intelligent interest in Conrad's career. He dedicated *The Mirror of the Sea* to her.
[3] In 'M'Kechnie *v.* Scaramanga', a satirical tale of a Scottish ship-owner.
[4] 'You—you were born too late': *Progress* bristles with asides against 'the modern world . . . and the immeasurable meannesses which we have deified' (p. 185).

hopeful industry.[1] Finità la commedia![2] Well they may do much but for the saving of the universe I put my faith in the power of folly.

Do come over if you go south our way. A steamer leaves Naples at 9 am and 3 pm every day. Arrives at Capri noon and six pm. We can't, Alas! offer to put You up as we are pigging it in 3 rooms of an inferior villa. But the Hotel de Capri is a place where one can hang out well enough for a small ransom. Of the questions you start in your "Polish" letter I'll talk—but I don't trust myself to write. It would scandalise you if I did. Jessie and Borys send their regards. Tout à vous

Jph. Conrad.

To J.B. Pinker
Text MS Berg; J-A, 2, 12

23^{d} Febr 1905
Villa Di Maria
Isola di Capri
Italy.

My dear Pinker.

It's lucky that your letter re ins^{ce} reached me when it did. A day or two after sending the answer I got influenza with bronchitis and so on: a terrible time. I've been in bed of course. Now I suffer from insomnia and nerves for which I am being stuffed with strychnia and other drugs. I won't tell you what I think—or what I feel—at seeing days slipping away from me in that miserable fashion. A whole month is gone since we settled here!

Whatever was written of my political articles needs recasting in view of the events in Russia.[3] I've been trying to do that when in bed, dictating to my wife. I've 4000 words ready of an article which I call "The Concord of Europe". It is a sort of historical survey of international politics from 1815 (The Vienna Congress)—with remarks and conclusions tending to demonstrate the present precarious state of that concord and bringing the guilt of that precariousness to the door of

---

[1] Although the friendship had not yet cooled, Wells's shift from scientific romance to scientific assertiveness clearly worried Conrad; of Shaw he once said 'The fellow pretends to be deep but he never gets to the bottom of things' (Garnett, p. xxx). Graham was a socialist, yet shared Conrad's opinion of the Fabians.

[2] 'La commedia è finita!' ('The comedy is over'): the last words of Leoncavallo's *I Pagliacci* (1892).

[3] During January, strikes, riots, and repression in St Petersburg and also in Russian-occupied Poland; on 17 February, the assassination of the reactionary Grand Duke Sergei.

Germany or rather of Prussia.[1] There are other things too—but I won't
enlarge here. 6000 words will be the length I suppose. If the monthlies
are shy of it I fancy Prothero (Quar^ly R) will take it.

There may be something in it. At any rate the question is treated
largely. Perhaps it would be better to publish without signature. It'll be
for you and the eventual Editor to consider that.

Impossible to say yet how the novel will shape itself out. I am too
weak physically and mentally to think much about it.

On the other hand I've found here the subject of my Mediterranean*
novel—or indeed rather the subject has found me. It is the struggle for
Capri in 1808 between the French and the English. I have access here to
the collection of books and MS belonging to Dr Cerio.[2] There are
letters—songs—pamphlets and so on relating to that time.

A book treating of the bay of Naples, Capri, Sorrento etc—places
visited every year by the English and Am^can tourists—stands a better
chance of popularity. That is what I must aim at in the measure of my
forces. There is not a bad story too in that episode, or at least the
elements of a story. A hermit used to live in the grotto near the ruins of
the villa of Tiberius at that time and tradition mixes him up with the
military events in a rather queer way. I haven't yet of course examined
my material but if there is any inspiration for a sea and land tale in it the
working off of my second cont[ra]ct with Harpers will be a much easier
matter than I dared to hope.

The weather is impossible. Rain hail, thunder—thats what we've had
for the last 4 days. But the air is getting warmer.

Pray send me £25 by post in notes—if possible. A cheque would have
to be sent back to Lond: before Cook would give me money for it—a
delay of another 3 days and I am now utterly without cash.

I hung back hoping to send you *MS* but this horrid influenza came
and I can wait no longer.

Kind regards

Yours always

Jph. Conrad.

[1] A theme prominent in the closing pages of 'Autocracy and War'.
[2] Dr Ignazio Cerio (1840–1921), a doctor who devoted his life to the study of Capri and
the welfare of its inhabitants.

To Agnes Sanderson
Text MS Lubbock; Unpublished

[Capri]
1ˢᵗ March 1905

My dear Miss Agnes

Barrie writes that certainly he will see you tho' he fears he can do nothing for you just now. None of his plays are coming on at present. That is the sense and even the whole text of his short note in answer to my letter.

I should think that You ought to see him anyway. But you know best.

Pardon this short and abrupt communication. I've had influenza and feel quite unable to write any sense.

I think no further introduction is necessary now but the sending up of your name. But I am always at your disposition.

Yours affectionately
Joseph Conrad.

To E. V. Lucas
Text MS Wellington; Knowles

Villa di Maria
Isola di Capri
Italy
2ᵈ Mch 1905

Dear Lucas.

I've been in correspondence with Barrie about an actress—a friend—who wanted an introduction to him. He has been very good about it. I should like however to know his mind about something much more personal—that is about a one-act play of mine. I sent it to him last Novᵉʳ on his own demand.—Now I would like to know what he thinks of it; but I don't want to give him the grind of writing his opinion. As you see him pretty often You could perhaps ask him what may be his opinion —that is if the thing is worth any sort of opinion. Very likely it is not. But it would be something to know even that for certain. Mainly I would be glad to hear if that first essay shows any vestige of scenic sense which would be worth cultivating.

If You were just simply to mention when opportunity offers— "Anything in Conrad's play?" or words to that effect You could tell me whether he grinned or grunted or said something. A word so obtained would be enough; whereas if I wrote to him it would take up his time unnecessarily and perhaps he would try to gild the pill for me or do something in the way of kindness. You understand me. You know me well enough also to know I've no susceptibilities that can be hurt. And I am quite ready to take his verdict as final. Our love to your two ladies

Yours always

Jph Conrad

To H.-D. Davray
Text MS Yale; *L.fr.*70

Villa di Maria

Capri

12 mars 1905

Cher Ami

Votre bonne lettre m'a fait du bien.

C'est malheureux de Vous avoir manqué a Paris. Mais bien sur nous nous verrons a notre retour, a moins que le diable ne s'en mêle. A ce propos je Vous dirai que je commence à croire au diable. Je vois trop de traces de son travail sur la terre. Il s'impose—l'animal! Et il manque de dignité: il s'occupe de l'infiniment petit. Par exemple il s'est amusé a me donner l'influenza. J'en sors faible de corps et imbecile d'esprit. Ce n'est pas que je tienne tant que cela a être vigoureux de mes membres et rempli (comme un vase précieux) de pensées sages; mais pour le moment l'impossibilite d'inventer une bêtise quelconque (qui vaille la peine d'être ecrite) est désastreuse.

Le charme de Capri m'engourdit je crois. Je n'ai rien fait. Absolument rien. C'est délicieux mais cela devient dangereux. Le maitre des postes et toute sa famille vous envoient leurs salutations. Je n'ai pas vu le bon Canonico encore.

Ainsi Vous avez eu l'idée d'infliger Nostromo a Madame Davray d'un bout a l'autre! Pourquoi avez-Vous risqué la paix de Votre ménage par cet inqualifiable abus du pouvoir marital. Mon cher vous n'êtes pas prudent. Presentez mes hommages les plus respectueux a votre patiente Victime avec l'assurance de ma profonde sympathie.

Tout à Vous bien cordialement.

J. Conrad.

PS—Merci bien pour votre offre amicale des journaux et livres. Oui envoyez-moi quelque chose. Il me semble qu'il y a des années que je n'ai rien lu. Ma femme se rappelle a votre bon souvenir.

Translation

Dear Friend,

Your kind letter has done me good.

A pity to have missed you in Paris. But of course we shall see each other on our return, unless the devil interferes. On that subject, I should tell you that I'm starting to believe in the devil; I see too many traces of his work on the earth. He imposes himself, the animal. And he lacks dignity; he occupies himself with infinitely small things. For example, he has amused himself by giving me influenza. I am coming out of it feeble in body and imbecile of mind. It's not that I require all that much to be energetic in my limbs and filled (like a precious vase) with wise thoughts; but for the moment the impossibility of making up any stupidity whatsoever (that might be worth the pain of being written) is disastrous.

The charm of Capri makes me languid, I think; I have done nothing. Absolutely nothing. It is delicious, but that becomes dangerous. The postmaster and all his family send you their greetings. I haven't seen the good Canonico yet.

So, you have had the idea of inflicting *Nostromo* on Madame Davray from beginning to end. Why have you risked your domestic peace with this unspeakable abuse of marital power?

My dear fellow, you are not prudent. Present my most respectful regards to your patient victim with the assurance of my profound sympathy.

Very cordially yours,
Joseph Conrad

P. S. Thanks very much for your friendly offer of books and newspapers. Yes, send me something. It seems to me years since I read anything. My wife wants to be remembered to you.

To Neil Munro
Text MS NLS; Unpublished

> Villa di Maria
> Capri
> Italy.
> 13 Mch 1905

My dear Munro[1]

Of course, with the greatest pleasure; tho' to tell you the truth that note is by no means a cool and pondered opinion as to what the Art of Fiction is or should be.[2] I've grown older since.

Only one condition I stipulate for. This is that you should look the proof over, not for misprints of course, but for the soundness of the text. I haven't seen the thing for years, but I hope there isn't anything outrageous in it. Still!

One par: (relating directly to the novel for which the note was first written) will have to come out in any case. You will spot it at sight. For the rest the matter is left in your hands to excise or arrange as you think best. The Art of Fiction would be a good title.

Ask the Ed^{or} to send me a *money order* to address as above instead of cheque.

My wife has been operated 3 months ago for damage to knee joint. Her general state was not good either. So we had to come here for recovery. All this nearly broke my back or I would be ashamed to accept payment.

I read you and take delight in you. As to my last book it seems a sort of frost.

> Yours always
> J. Conrad

---

[1] Neil Munro (1864–1930), the Scottish poet, novelist, and critic.
[2] Munro wanted to reprint the Preface to *The Nigger* in the *Glasgow Evening Herald*. Originally an 'Author's Note' to the serial (*New Review*, December 1897), the Preface was not included in the book form until the Doubleday edition of 1914. In 1902, however, Conrad published it as a pamphlet (100 copies printed by J. Lovick of Hythe and Cheriton). As 'The Art of Fiction', the Preface also appeared in *Harper's Weekly*, 13 May 1905.

To Edmund Gosse
Text MS Yale; J-A, 2, 14

Villa di Maria
Capri.
Italy.
23 Mch. 1905.

Dear Mr. Gosse.

I have received to-day a communication from W. Rothenstein the answer to which is due to you directly and without delay.[1] Acutely conscious of being neither the interpreter in any profound sense of my own epoch nor a magician evoker of the past either in its spirit or its form I have often suffered in connection with my work from a sense of unreality, from intellectual doubt of the ground I stood upon. This has occurred especially in the periods of difficult production. I have just emerged from such a period of utter mistrust when Rothenstein's letter came to hand revealing to me the whole extent of *Your* belief and the lenght* to which you have taken the trouble to go to prove it—even to the lenght* of making another mind share in your conviction. I accept this revelation with eagerness. I need not tell you that this moral support of belief is the greatest help a writer can receive in those difficult moments which Baudelaire has defined happily as "les stérilités des écrivains nerveux".[2] Quincey too I believe has known that anguished suspension of all power of thought that comes to one often in the midst of a very revel of production like the slave with his *memento mori* at a feast.[3]

For that kind of support my gratitude is due to you in the first instance. It can, properly speaking, hardly equal the obligation. The material outcome of your active belief I accept, sans phrases which I am sure you do not desire either for yourself or the Prime Minister.[4] I know too that you will be good enough to express the perfect sincerity of my sentiments in the proper quarters with greater tact and juster measure than I, in my inexperience could command.

The feeling of pride is not perhaps one to entertain in this connection.

---

[1] Conrad had been told of a grant of £500 from the Royal Bounty Special Service Fund. In the correspondence, this is also called a Civil List grant (to be distinguished from a pension, paid recurrently).

[2] Echoing the comments on Flaubert's 'style nerveux'? ('Madame Bovary', *L'Art romantique*).

[3] In Part Three of *Confessions of an English Opium-Eater* (1821), 'The Pains of Opium', Thomas de Quincey (another victim of toothache and gout) describes the freezing of his creative powers. For the slave at the feast, Petronius, *Satyricon*, LXXVII–LXXVIII.

[4] Arthur James Balfour (1848–1930), Prime Minister 1902–5, leader of the 'Souls', a coterie of Conservative intellectuals.

It is the one however that comes to the surface at the end of this letter. It cannot be but a matter of pride for me that two minds like yours and the Prime Minister's, which it has never entered into the compass of my hopes to reach, have been moved by an acquaintance with my work to a friendly interest in my mere personality.

Believe me, dear Mr Gosse,
very faithfully yours
Joseph Conrad

To Norman Douglas
Text MS Texas; Unpublished

[Capri]
Sunday ev. [2 April? 1905][1]

My dear Douglas[2]

I've had a hell of a time. It's no use shortening it. We are off to Naples tomorrow morning all of us. We return Tuesday evg. Yours,

J. Conrad

I haven't looked at MS as yet.

To J.B. Pinker
Text MS Berg; Unpublished

[letterhead: Hôtel Isotta &
Genève, Naples]
[c. 6 April? 1905][3]

My dear Pinker.

£30 received safely. I wired you for them as I felt I would have to go to Naples soon to see a dentist. And so it turned out. I had to go over after 3 nights without sleep. There is no dentist in Capri.

My wife, Borys and Miss Jackson went over with me for a 24 hours change. The dentist however kept me over another night here for

---

[1] For the date of the visit to Naples, see the next letter.

[2] (George) Norman Douglas (1868–1952), traveller, polyglot, polymath, wit and former diplomat, started his long association with Capri in 1902 and had already published two of his monographs about the island. His oeuvre, ranging from 'The Herpetology of the Grand Duchy of Baden' (1891) to *Venus in the Kitchen* (1952), includes *South Wind* (1917) and *Old Calabria* (1915).

[3] The Galsworthys' travels give the approximate date. On 20 March they were in Amalfi; after a week in Sorrento, they spent a week on Capri with the Conrads and were seen off from Naples. By 9 April they were in Florence (Dupré, *Galsworthy*, p. 101). The previous note to Douglas puts the start of the expedition on a Monday, presumably 3 April; events then took their miserable course.

another appointement*. So we went to see Pompei[i] and somehow during that excursion poor Borys got a whiff of tainted air and in the course of about three hours sickened for a most awful sore throat with very high temperature. For a night and day he was delirious. He's still in bed and must not be moved for another two days at least.

No luck at all!! I can't write at length now tho' I have a good few things to say. Galsworthy is here—You remember him I suppose—with his novel finished.[1] For that one he is under a sort of moral obligation to let either H[einemann] or D[uckworth] have it. But he will be worth getting hold of in the future. He's on his way to a no mean place. You'll see!

All my fine plans are knocked on the head; but of one thing you may be sure. There will be a novel for the winter season's publication.

                                                   Yours always
                                                           J. Conrad.

To Norman Douglas
Text MS Texas; Unpublished

                                                           [Capri]
                                              [early April 1905][2]

My dear fellow,

I am rushing off at 4 to Naples. Dentist! I had a fiendish night. Are you coming over with me as you hinted the other day you thought of doing. Yours

                                                           Conrad

To Edmund Gosse
Text MS Yale; J-A, 2, 15

                                                   Villa di Maria
                                                           Capri.
                                                   11th Ap. 1905

Dear Mr Gosse.

I don't know what I appreciate most:—the trouble you've taken in this matter, which, depending from first to last on your influence, has matured so generously in the warmth of your active good-will—or the delicate consideration for one's anxieties and feelings proved so clearly by the letter I've just received.

---

[1] *The Man of Property*, whose revision was completed in Amalfi.
[2] The time of his unrelenting toothache.

My thanks go out not so much to the facts and figures (unexpected as these are) it contains as to the friendly insight which has put the pen into your hand so promptly. I must thank you too for consenting to make yourself the interpreter of my feelings in a manner so acceptable to the Prime Minister. For the rest I may say that the way of return having been so unexpectedly made smooth I am more anxious than ever to get back to Pent Farm, under whose lowly (and imperfectly watertight) roof five volumes had the audacity to get themselves written. I've done very badly here. It's all very well for Englishmen born to their inheritance to fling verse and prose from Italy back at their native shores. I, in my state of honourable adoption, find that I need the moral support, the sustaining influence of English atmosphere even from day to day.

In the matter of the confidential treating of the transaction, I conceive that there's no option for me but to extend the rule of absolute discretion even to such friends as H. G. Wells and Hugh Clifford?—since the most innocent confidence could be, by some accident, made to look like a wilful disregard on my part, of the King's distinct wish. I suppose that the view I take of the injunction conveyed in Your letter does not appear exaggerated to you. My feeling is that your tact and experience are the best judges in what direction (if at all) the letter of that injunction may be overstepped consistently with the respect of its spirit.

Believe me, dear Mr Gosse with the greatest regard
very faithfully Yours
Joseph Conrad.

To J.B. Pinker
Text MS Berg; Unpublished

Villa di Maria
Capri
12 Ap 1905

My dear Pinker.

I had this letter warning me of Keen's next move.[1] I don't know what you will do. Of course you've the right not to believe a single word I say now after the miserable failure I've made of these last 3 months. But if you can't save a public exposure otherwise than by letting Keen have something I promise to raise £50 from Jack Gals^y by the 15th of May. I can't get at him just now. They have left Rome hurriedly for the Tyrol

---

[1] On behalf of William Watson's creditors.

and I may not get his address for a month or so. As to his ability and readiness to help me there can be no doubt.

I write with a raging tooth-ache. I've had a swollen face for the last fortnight. There is no dentist in Capri. I've been to Naples twice and had two teeth dragged out. Now a third is going. I seem to have been out of my mind for days and days together. The doctor here says this is the after effect of the influenza. I don't know. I am feverish now. This place is a curse to me—but a blessing to my wife. I have a great mind to clear out at once for the Pent where I am sure to get a grip on things. Head simply teeming with ideas—but what's the good of them!

Of course I've a MS copy of the article.[1] But this is incredible! You have it no doubt by now. I did not send it on the day I named. There was a delay of a week. However such as it is it is not lost and Jack while here read it and was quite impressed by it. He saw me post it. Damn! Apart from that thing all you can expect from me before we see each other is a short story something in the style of Youth—about a dynamite ship.[2] That's nearly done but is now hung up with everything else. It's a hard matter with one thing and another to look calmly at the situation. Of course there will be the novel by Oct or Nov. But when I think of what I meant to do and have not done it is enough to make me doubt the evidence of the pages written and done with, of which there are a good few anyhow. ——————

13th Ap //

I have had a better night and resume this morning with a calmer mind. As far as my plan of keeping the pot boiling is concerned the last three months are gone to waste in a way which would be nothing short of miserable if it were not for the very great advantage to my wife's health. Here she thinks all the good we could expect is done, and for the rest she urges me to cut the losses, as it were, by leaving the place which obviously is unfavourable to me. I desire that she should finish her course of electricity (another ten days or so) and then I would clear out of this before the term fixed originally for our return. I do believe that in that way I would save the best part of the May month for some work that would tell. My idea is to send Miss Jackson off home alone (she's entitled to 1st class travelling) as soon as possible. A couple of days afterwards we would leave too travelling second of course. We would go third if it weren't for the little chap and the fear of vermin in Italian carriages. Perhaps we may take steam by one of the cheap lines from Naples to Marseilles where we could stay *one day* with my relative Mme

[1] 'Autocracy and War'.   [2] The ancestor of *Chance*.

Poradowska who has hired a villa there till June next. She's very anxious to see us and I would be glad to meet her too if only for a few hours. D'Humières also is there or there abouts; who says he would like to see me for the translation of the Nigger. By going that route by the "Florio" or "Adria" Company the cost of our return would not be increased as one saves a lot on the luggage which is charged for heavily on Italian Rways. Coming here I had to pay over £4 from the frontier to Naples for our 3 trunks.

From Marseilles we would go without stoppage via Boulogne to Folkestone in the decent French 2^d class carriages. I want about £120 no less to clear me out from here, paying the doctor, the last month's stay, a balance to Miss Jackson of £15 and her travelling exp^{es} which amount to nearly as much more. If you send it to me by the 25 inst we will clear out at once. I've had my change and God save me from such another holiday.

At the Pent I expect to pick up. After all my mind must have been refreshed by new sights and impressions. I may feel some of its good afterwards. In the country I owe nothing except a few pounds to Hogben the Farmer[1] and that is no anxiety. He could not let the house to anyone anyhow. Nobody would look at it even. Now my wife is so much better she does not care where we hang out and how. We can put up with anything where there is a quite* room for me to write in. We can make a start without any particular anxieties. At any rate it can be no worse than before when a few books *did* get written anyhow. Here—nothing, try as I will. But anyway before you send the money most likely you will have received the confounded political article and the Dynamite Ship story. That ought to bring a few pounds because even in 1897 B'wood gave me £50 for *Youth* serially.[2] From US I had nothing for it, I remember, as it wasn't copyrighted at all.

A most damnably beggarly tale of copy this!

If I get Miss Hallowes (I think she would come) from June to say Sept, I will produce a few papers (by the way, as I go on with the novel.) on sea subjects or literature. The series of political articles could be carried out too. Or finish the second and third Benavides. Meantime my dear fellow if you must have some of your money back then pray consider again the suggestion I made once to you of having the *M of the S* published in a volume with such literary papers as are ready for a sort of II^d part. It would be always something and the very originality of it—the *whole* Conrad as it were between the covers—may make it a

---

[1] Owner of the Pent.   [2] £35, in 1898: *Letters*, 2, p. 67.

better move than we think. Of course it is an act of courage on my part to lay myself so provokingly (almost) open to two-sided criticism. But I have good friends in the press here and there. In this connection I must tell you that the Glasgow Ev: Herald has asked me (through N. Munro) for permission to reproduce my preface written for the Nigger (and not published in book) as a special article on the Art of Fiction. I did give it and have received a M[oney] O[rder] for 3 gs the other day; so pray debit me with your lawful com[missi]on on that large amount.

And here's the end of this interminable scrawl. My very handwriting is gone to pieces in this Capri air. Too much ozone they say: too exciting and that's why no lung patients are allowed to come here. You must be heartily sick of my epistles. It isnt the sort of MS that I want to write or you to receive. Kindest regards

Yours

Conrad.

To J.B. Pinker
Text MS Berg; Unpublished

[Capri]
22 Ap. 1905

Dear Pinker

I wrote you last week about Douglass[1] whose MS specimens of work are going with my scurvy contribution of an article.—I apply this epithet to the *quantity*. The *quality* is all right. And as long as *quality* keeps up *quantity* will have to come somehow. I've been able to sit very close with my dynamite ship but had to turn my attention to correcting new typescript of the article—a damnable work as I can not remember how it ran. Else I would have had nothing ready. However here it is ready to go off registered this time.

Please try Murray with it first—for Quart.^ly Rev. They ought to do it justice if they take it. First place and so on. Signature I suggest is C. *at first*.[2] Either it has effect or it has not. If it has and controversy (if any) had its say then the authorship may be disclosed—if it passes unnoticed, why, then, it does not matter in the least one way or another whether C is identified or not with me.

As swiftly as possible the *D.S.* story shall follow. The missus is beginning to type, but the whole thing must be worked over of course. Badly as I feel the need to get on I can't let things go out *anyhow*.

[1] Probably by accident, Conrad often used the original spelling of his friend's surname.
[2] The essay appeared in the *Fortnightly Review* (1 July, pp. 1–21) under the author's full name.

I am anxious to be away from all this here and come to terms with myself, as H. James says. Never more will I leave England while the necessity to *keep at it* lasts. It's an utter failure both as regards work and play.

Kindest regards

Your Conrad.

PS Douglas here with his MS and I write a note you'll find amongst his stuff in his presence.

To J.B. Pinker

Text MS Berg; Unpublished

[Capri]
22 Ap 1905

My dear Pinker

Here you will find together with my MS the three papers announced in my letter. My view of Mr Douglass' future simply as a magazine writer you know. Of the rest we will talk when we meet. Here I'll only add that I think that the handling of his stuff you will find easy and so far profitable. I'll expect you to do your very best amongst the magazines to introduce him properly. I know that you, if anybody, can do that thing both at home and in America. I've taken this matter to heart, you understand and I know that it may suit Your purposes as well. I am authorised to tell you that he is open to write on suggested subjects—or at least to try to. Of course it will be no hack work as a glance at the pages I send will make clear to you.

In the course of the next 2 months he'll have ready a paper 2–3 thou: on *Nelson in Naples* and another on *Emperor Tiberius* in the light of modern criticism both suitable to magazine readers tho' the last ought to be tried on a Review.[1]

It's understood that *all business* is put into your hands without reserve. When I get back I'll be able to facilitate perhaps the placing of one or two papers by going to Prothero, Edward, Lucas etc.[2] I am confident that after the first start he will do well.

Yours ever

J. Conrad

---

[1] 'Nelson' became 'Blind Guides' (*English Review*, 1913, collected in *Experiments*, 1925); *Tiberius* was published as a pamphlet (Naples, 1906).
[2] G. W. Prothero of the *Quarterly*, Garnett, and E. V. Lucas.

To J.B. Pinker

Text MS Berg; Unpublished

[Capri]
Ap 24 1905

Dear Pinker

The MS of Autocracy & War went off last night in a box insured for 1200 frcs Gov^t ins^{ce}; so if that don't make it safe nothing will. This morning's post brought me your letter.

I don't know what to say for if your position is difficult in the face of my exigencies, mine in the face of Your Non Possumus[1] is absolutely without issue.

I propose that you should send me *telegraphically to Capri* on receipt of MS. £40 at least to get Miss Jackson off. The article (10000 words) ought to be worth that. She expected to be able to leave here on the 28th. She won't now if ever she does unless at her own cost I suppose. For I am shaken and do not know whether You will do anything. Your right in the matter is undeniable. The question is whether you will exercise it now. What I feel is the suddenness. It seems to me you might have given me a warning with the last remittance. For even from the point of view of the business that concerns us most, the prospect of being abruptly chucked out (in debt) into the street in Capri (our rooms are let to an Italian Family from the 19th I believe) is not likely to get the story finished in time. Not in the least. I won't say anything as to the probable time of its termination. It will be done when it is done and if you think that *I don't care* you are mistaken. On the other hand if I know by the 28th that it is your intention to leave me here you can't blame me if I devote my energies to getting away and to that exclusively. You can my dear fellow put me in a hole but I won't be kept there. In what state of mind do you think I'll be able to approach the work lying before me and to which I shall turn directly this writing is done?

Yesterday I heard from Sydney* Colvin. The Stage Society[2] want to perform Tomorrow this very season; early in June. I ought to get back at once to attend rehearsals for it is a chance. In another year I won't care for it—if it returns then. And I am invited by Sec[retary] Matthews and Granville Barker[3] to return in order to settle certain alterations. Both

---

[1] Refusal: literally 'we cannot'.

[2] Founded in 1899, the Stage Society mounted small-scale professional productions of valuable but uncommercial (and often daring) plays. Among the authors already performed were Ibsen, Tolstoy, Maeterlinck, and Shaw.

[3] W. Lee Mathews, Chairman of the Society's Producing Committee, and Harley Granville-Barker (1877–1946), playwright, actor, director, and critic.

these men and G. B. Shaw seem to attach much more importance to the thing than I do myself. However all this is not worth talking about now. Had You warned me six weeks ago all this would have been in order. I fail to comprehend the policy of Your action. Till the 28 inst. I shall do my best to sit tight and work. After that date I shall consider myself "left" and what I will do, where I will go and how is a mystery even to myself—and not worth much considering anyhow.

Finally you will remember that there was a time when I submitted to you the expediency of cutting short off* the peculiar relation.[1] It was possible for me then to arrange it. I did throw out the suggestion knowing myself and thinking you knew me too. I am not particularly conceited but in this last transaction I think (and I think others may think so too) that I was entitled to the ceremony of a warning the more so that I am abroad—and absolutely in your hands.

Don't imagine I beg you to reconsider it; I am only waiting till the 28th to see whether you will do so before I answer S. Colvin and take measures to get out of here. A certain amount of pressure may do to bring a drunkard to his bearings but it must fail with my temperament. Kind regards

Yours

Conrad.

P.S. Unless telegraphically don't trouble to answer.

To Aleksander Marian Jasieński

Text Ruch; *Listy* 242; Najder 244

Capri, Italy.
25th April, 1905.

Dear Sir,[2]

I was born on the 3rd December 1857 at Żytomierz.[3] In no way am I related to Józef Korzeniowski.[4] Our coat of arms is that of Nałęcz. My Father, Apollo Korz., was a son of Teodor, a former colonel in the Polish Army and a landowner in Volhynia; for a time he was an administrator of one of Mrs. Melania Sobańska's estates. My Father was, however,

---

[1] 8 January 1902 (*Letters*, 2, p. 370).
[2] A. M. Jasieński had written a study of contemporary English fiction (Warsaw and Cracow, 1897).
[3] At Berdyczów, about thirty miles away: for details, see Najder, *Chronicle*, p. 10.
[4] The nineteenth-century novelist.

also a man of letters; he was brought up first at Niemirów and then at Żytomierz. He graduated at the University of Petersburg.[1] Together with Adam Pług[2] he translated *La Légende des siècles* (in 1852). Both his comedy in verse *Dla miłego grosza*[3] and his translation of *Chatterton* (Alf. de Vigny) were published at Żytomierz in 1856–8. Later, when exiled, he translated comedies of Shakespeare and dramas by Victor Hugo; as well as *Les Travailleurs de la mer* by the latter.[4] He was freed in 1868 and died in Cracow in 1869. Stefan Buszczyński, his closest friend, published a biographical pamphlet entitled *A Little-Known Poet*.[5]

My Mother, née Bobrowska (from Oratów in the Ukraine), was the sister of Stefan Bobrowski who played a considerable role in Warsaw during the years 1862–3 as a member of the National Government; she died in exile.[6]

I am writing all this not for publication but so as to acquaint you with my Polish origin.

I remain, dear Sir, respectfully yours,

Konrad Korzeniowski (Joseph Conrad)

To H.G. Wells
Text MS Illinois; J-A, 2, 15

Capri
Italy.
25 Ap. 1905

My dear Wells.

I was trying to get something off to Pinker for dear life and that's why I did not write sooner to acknowledge the book's most welcome arrival.[7]

You know—I had rather talk than write. Words do chill the warmth of thought whether it is set down in a book or in a letter. At least so it is in my case. All I can say to begin with is that I am quite enthusiastic about the work. From the first line of the preface to the closing sentence I feel in touch with a more accessible Wells—a Wells mellowed, as it were, in

---

[1] According to a letter to Garnett that surveys the same territory, Apollo did not graduate (*Letters*, 2, p. 246).

[2] The pen-name of Antoni Pietkiewicz, another radical nationalist.

[3] *For the Love of Money.*

[4] *Chatterton* aside, the only published translations were *The Comedy of Errors* (1866) and parts of Hugo's *Légende* (1874, posthumously).

[5] Cracow, 1870.

[6] In 1865: her brother, a leading figure of the resistance to foreign rule was killed in a politically motivated duel in 1863.

[7] *A Modern Utopia.* The inscription was dated 10 April: Hans van Marle, *The Conradian*, 9 (1984), 44.

the meditation of the three books[1] of which this last one is certainly the nearest to my understanding and the most commanding to my assent.

It is a quality not easily defined; but since O Brother! I am but a novelist I must speak in images. Thus I say it is not Wells merely talking to us; it is Wells extending a hand. No civilized man in his infinite variety, need, when reading that book, feel "left" for a single moment. Helpful would be a word to use if it had not been desecrated in connection with infinite rubbish. And of course this helpfulness should be defined. And the definition is that [it] is just indefinable; that what is so really helpful in your last book is as difficult to seize as the quality of light in the landscape which at certain times appeals to us—invigorates our thought by the way of emotion (I suppose)—more than at others. I would call it the intellectual kindliness characterising your development of the idea. This is the nearest I can come to expressing that something which differentiates the thought of this book from the two preceeding* vols. And don't think for a moment that your thought lost anything of its force. It lost nothing. I know two men here, fellows by no means contemptible; and since the book came we have met 3 times and each occasion was a "Wells" sitting. They are much better fit to judge your calibre than I am. Our discussions were infinitely varied and no doubt very vain. But afar here, away from all the petty clamour and clatter of criticasting pars we could agree on one point: that you were the one honest thinker of the day. I don't propound this as a discovery just made in history or ethics. It was just the form in which we found possible in perfect accord to express the high value of your thinking.

And one of these men was a Scot (born in Austria) once in our diplomatic service which he threw up I fancy in sheer intellectual disgust.[2] A man who can not only think but write. The other was an American with that peculiar vein of childishness and savagery which crops up so often from under the erudition culture and scientific knowledge of many US citizens. But I perceive this piece of paper is written over. I won't go on now. I'll in a day or two write more. I've been confoundedly tired here. Jessie got on wonderfully well.

Our love. Goodbye provisionally

Yours

Conrad.

[1] The sequence beginning with *Anticipations* (1901) and continued in *Mankind in the Making*, the volume that disturbed Conrad late in 1903.

[2] Officially, Douglas left St Petersburg, and the service, in order to study the question of Imperial tariffs; his unofficial purpose was to escape certain love-affairs that had become too nearly simultaneous: Mark Holloway, *Norman Douglas* (Secker & Warburg, 1976), pp. 95–102.

To Sidney Colvin
Text MS Yale; J-A, 2, 17

Villa di Maria
Capri
28 Ap. 1905

My Dear Mr Colvin.

I was waiting for Ford M. Hueffer's answer before writing to you. I hear he wrote you directly. The facts are that Hueffer a good and dear friend helped me by spending a whole day in taking out the dialogue of story in a typewritten extract for my use and reference. The play, as can be shown by the MS, has been written entirely in my own hand;[1] and I wrote it alone in a room lent me by an acquaintance[2] to ensure perfect quiet for the six days it took me to achieve that very small feat. In such matters however one cannot be too scrupulous. I won't say any more. You'll understand a demi-mot.[3] And of course now Ford has written to you You'll allow me to show you the MS. on my return. Five minutes' perusal will show you the exact value of the sample which caused me to refer to Hueffer at the last moment and the genuin[en]ess of his disclaimer. I've always looked upon the play as mine only till brought to terms—as it were—by the offer of the Stage Society for which—as for the very inception of the play I have to thank your unwearied interest. You may take it from me that no one collaborated in that play so much as yourself. But when actually pen in hand to accept eagerly the proposal conveyed in Your letter I felt that not even a shadow of ambiguity should be allowed to rest upon my action in the matter.

For the rest my dear Mr Colvin You can do no wrong in this affair. I don't think we can get back to England much before the 15th of May. I am ready to defer to the suggestions as to cutting out which our unique G. B. S will favour me with. The artificiality of the abominable fish-hawker has ever been an offence to me. In my unskilfulness I could not imagine anything else to "establish" the psychology of the girl. It is a gross artifice I own—and I am glad to be shown that I was mistaken.

Many thanks from us both to Mrs Colvin and yourself for the expression of your kind wishes. When in London before our departure I

---

[1] The question of Ford's links with 'To-morrow' starts with the original story, which Conrad described as '*Your* suggestion ... *my* conception' (*Letters*, 2, p. 372). There is noteworthy evidence of Ford's help with the adaptation too: 43 pages of MS in his hand (now at Cornell) and three undated letters to Pinker expressing Ford's willingness to let Conrad take all the credit for their work (Mizener, pp. 107–9). The letter of 9 May (paragraph four) also acknowledges Ford's proprietary interest in the play.
[2] Galsworthy: see *Laughing Anne* (John Castle, 1924), p. vi.   [3] 'You'll take the hint.'

was so wretched that I dared not intrude upon anybody whatever my abominable nervousness. I worked however. Here I have done very badly. Reaction (after those six weeks before and after the operation) with an attack of influenza superadded unfitted me for any sort of purposeful thinking. My wife however has made a splendid recovery and I am just beginning to scribble at some speed.

With kindest regards to Mrs Colvin and yourself believe me my dear Sir always faithfully yours

Joseph Conrad.

To Alice Rothenstein
Text MS Harvard; Unpublished

Capri.
1st May 1905.

Dear Alice.

You are very good; and being good you shall have your goodness taken advantage of.

As soon as Will returns do please ask him from me if the Civil List money is paid to send me *at once £150* in notes if possible.[1] I would not be bothering him so everlastingly: but that particular affair is in his hands.

If the money is not yet paid (and it won't be delayed very long now) I beg him most earnestly to raise that amount from some magnate of his acquaintance, and let me have it as fast as post will go. It is urgently necessary for me to get back home by the 15th at latest. First of all I am not working well here; but there is another reason which you will appreciate. It's this: the Stage Society offer to perform my little play *To morrow* in June this year. I think it is really a chance for me; it may lead to the end of all my financial troubles for if the play produces a good impression I may place the 3 acts I've been carrying in my head for the last seven years.[2] Now it is necessary for me to be back in *England as soon as possible* to carry out the alterations insisted upon.

As the Civil List money is a sure thing and bound to pass through Will's hands very soon I make bold (the transaction being quite safe) to appeal to that friendship and affection of which he has given me so many proofs, in this case also. It'll cost some time and some trouble but unless he gives me a shove in that way I am afraid to be sticking in Capri too

---

[1] Two trustees were to administer the grant: Rothenstein and Henry Newbolt.

[2] 1898 was the year in which Crane proposed and Conrad refused a theatrical collaboration (*Letters*, 2, p. 13). On 15 July 1905, Conrad told Douglas that he had 'a notion of a farcical comedy'.

long. I've, just at present, no story ready to send to Pinker in order to get
the cash for our return. One is in the making but I may be longer about
it than I expect. The Civil List grant and Will's inexhaustible devotion
are my only dependence.

Jessie (she'll write You soon) has made a splendid recovery. You
should see her walk! There's just a slight limp left. She looks in rude
health like a very milkmaid. It is the most delightful thing for me. I feel I
am beginning to live again.

Our dearest love to you all. In haste for post

Always most affectionately Yours

Jph Conrad

To J.B. Pinker

Text MS Berg; Unpublished

[Capri]
6th May
1905.

Dear Pinker.

Isn't it incredible! However here's my note about A.* Douglas. Age
35 or so a Scotsman born in Austria and educated partly there. Good
family. After 1895 in diplomatic Service Attaché in Const.*^{ple}* afterwards
in St Petersburg. Linguist Scientist. Wide information. A very good
style. A great range of subject. An originality in thinking. Published
once when very young a vol of stories with Fisher Unwin on comm:[1]
Swindle! 3 copies sold. Others stored with his lawyer in London. (NB
something may be done with some of them yet)

Causes of my taking him up: his intelligence and my belief he will do
something yet. Came to see me with introduction from the Bsh Cons:
Agent here. (NB both Bsh & Am^{an} colonies here made rather a set at
me). Directed him to You simply because thought it would be *business* for
you—not of the gold mine kind of course—but of an easy sort. I also
remembered You saying once that supply of Mag: art: of a superior sort
was desirable. He would be something of *new blood* to the better class of
Mag: and Reviews. I understood You had no objection to handle such
stuff. I saw that the quality was good—readable—accessible to public
and Editors (I fancy)—so directed it into your channel. At the start I

---

[1] *Unprofessional Tales* (1901), under the pseudonym 'Normyx', and written mostly by his
   then wife, Elsa FitzGibbon (Holloway, *Douglas*, pp. 129–31). Under the commission
   system, the author paid most or all publication costs.

will do what I can with men I know. We will see what comes of it. I believe he's promising. But anyhow he expects nothing wonderful; and if you can get him a few guineas it will be all in the course of Your business and you may rear up an author that will not discredit your connection. Why he left the diplomatic service is a longish story but does not bear upon his character.

Anyway he's a remarkable man in his way.—The Nelson paper and the Tiberius article are nearly ready.

Kind regards

Yours Conrad

To John Galsworthy
Text MS Forbes; J-A, 2, 18

Capri.
8th May 1905.

My dearest Jack

I own I expected good news from you. They are none the less welcome for that. I was more concerned than uneasy at your seediness which I seemed to know so well. It was like beholding ones own weird acquaintance in a looking glass; my own well known mysterious, disturbing sensations reflected in Your personality which is as near the inner *me* as anything not absolutely myself can be. I saw you depart from Naples with a feeling of confidence that no usual current mistrust of life could qualify. You were going off in good hands. And I returned tranquil as to your fate—to the tortures of my awful, overwhelming indolence the very negation of tranquil[l]ity—just as a cage is not a shelter, is the negation of a place of rest.

I would have beaten myself to pieces against the wires if I too had not been in good hands. But it's no use enlarging on one's evil or good fortune. I finished the paper which you have seen, then I rewrote it entirely and extended my worthless rhetoric to 10000 words. And I sent it off. It was a fine show of work to make—the work of one month in nearly four. My average has been just about that: 10000 a month. And it will *have* to be caught up. I put my trust in the Pent. This place here, this climate this sirocco, this transmontana,[1] these flat roofs, these sheer rocks, this blue sea—are impossible. But Miss Jackson is gone. That at least is removed. I sent her off—at last! She was impossible too. But this

[1] The hot desert winds made humid by the sea, and the cold northern winds from the mountains.

is unworthy talk. The only impossible fact to live with is the man who writes this himself.

The paper's called *Autocracy and War*. I don't know who will consent to print it—and with how much scorn and derision it may be received. It is however very likely it will not be noticed at all—a very good fate. Since I began a short story—something like *Youth*—but not at all like it. In the face of my situation it is mere trifling.

The grant of which I've told you is much better than I expected. It will be something like 300. It will get me out of here without further recourse to Pinker and set me going at the Pent. Another piece of news is that (would You believe it?) the Stage Society wishes to perform *To Morrow* next June. Colvin wrote me. Several men (whose names I can't recall just now) and amongst them G.B. Shaw profess themselves very much struck. But alterations are demanded and I don't know whether I can return in time. I've written to Lond: to hurry up enough pounds to take us home—but I don't know. I own I would like to secure that chance of the stage. I still cherish the hope of getting away by the 12 inst.

We go by Sea to Marseilles where I want to have a day with M^r d'Humières who's trans^g my poor *Nigger*. I fancy two days at sea will do me good. We would go by one small boats* of the Adria C^o or *Florio C^o*. I shall expect the run of the bridge. And in Marseilles I did begin life 31 years ago! It's the place where the puppy opened his eyes. Marguerite Poradowska is also there—who really seems to love us. With our best love to you both, always yours

J. Conrad.

PS This moment your letter arrives. Miss Hallowes is now in Paris for a few days, so impossible to say what she's prepared to do. I only know she returns to London this month.

PPS. Our congratulations on the real and true end of your labours.[1] Good luck to the book!

---

[1] After sending off the MS of *The Man of Property*, Galsworthy had continued revising another copy.

To Ford Madox Ford
Text MS BL Ashley 2922; J-A, 2, 19

[Capri]
9^h May 1905.

Dearest old boy.

Hurrah for the Soul of London![1] Brute as I am by nature and training I was touched by the sight of these pages so familiar in a way and so strange now, when far away from You. I went on following your thought over-leaf from page to page.

I went straight to the last Chapter (after reading the preface). If one could believe in the fate of books—this one deserves the blessing of a thing without sin. Of course it was not a surprise. I heard it was coming out. Still one had enough to be anxious about. The Editor—the format—the body for that soul—it was enough to speculate about. It is very dear and good of you to have sent it on without waiting for my return—which is now a question of days.

Vous m'avez manqué affreusement.[2] I've done nothing. And if it were not that Jessie profited so remarkably I would call the whole expedition a disaster. This climate what between tramontana and sirocco has half killed me in a not unpleasant languorous melting way. I am sunk in a vaguely uneasy dream of visions—of innumerable tales that float in an atmosphere of volupt[u]ously aching bones. Comprenez Vous ça? And nothing nothing can do away with that sort of gently active numbness. The scandals of Capri—atrocious, u[n]speakable, amusing, scandals international, cosmopolitan and biblical flavoured with Yankee twang and the French phrases of the *gens du monde* mingle with the tinkling of guitars in the barber's shops and the rich contralto of the "bona sera Signore" of the big Mrs Morgano as I drag myself in an inwardly fainting condition into the Café to give some chocolate to ma petite famille. All this is a sort of blue nightmare traversed by stinks and perfumes, full of flat roofs, vineyards, vaulted passages enormous sheer rocks, pergolas, with a mad gallop of German tourists laché[s] a travers tout cela[3] in white capri shoes, over the slippery capri stones, kodaks, floating veils strangely waving whiskers, grotesque hats, streaming, tumbling, rushing ebbing from the top of Monte Solaro (where the clouds hang) to the amazing rocky chasms of the Arco Naturale—where the lager beer bottles go pop. It is a nightmare with the fear of the future thrown in.

[1] Ford's just-published book.   [2] 'I've missed you terribly.'
[3] 'Let loose across it all'.

I hadn't the pluck to write to you—not even after the telegram about the play—not after your good letter which saddened me a little and augmented my desire to see you very much. And a propos de tout cela if I inquired what you wished done re *play* it was mostly from the feeling that You did *not* like the thing anyhow. And as I feel also it's going to fail in the end I could not without your distinct authorisation associate you with what I believe will be a sort of "four."[1]

We'll be at the pent about 16–17. Drop us a line there say in a week. I must make a colossal effort for copy. I must! Or die. The last would be the easier feat—and so beautifully final!

Love from us all to the House of Hueffer with many Compliments for La Señora (as warm as a Caballero may venture without absolute risk of sudden death) from me. Jessie with affectionate messages wishes you all to know that she is in rude health. She looks like a jolly milkmaid and it's balm to me. A vous de coeur.

                                                        J. Conrad.

To Bryan Palmes

Text MS NYU; Unpublished

                                                        [Capri]
                                                        Thursday
                                                        11th May. 1905.

My dear Sir[2]

We leave in a hurry to morrow (Friday) at 6 AM a full 5 days before the fixed time.

This explains why I have not called on you; and also why I cannot write as fully as I would wish of the high value I put on your appreciation of my work.

Keep a small corner of your memory for me till kind fates (who knows!) bring us together again.

With our kindest regards to Miss Palms and yourself believe me dear Colonel very faithfully Yours

                                                        Joseph Conrad.

---

[1] 'Bungle'.
[2] Bryan Palmes (born 1851) had retired from the Somerset Light Infantry in 1891 with the rank of major.

To J.B. Pinker
Text MS Berg; Unpublished

[Capri]
12 May
1905

My dear Pinker.

I feared it might be so. Obviously it would not do to hold the article[1] over 3 months or so even if Prothero approved its text and tone.

Try to do something with it—with the Monthly Reviews—so as not to lose whatever little money there may be in it.

Short stories—is the watchword now.

I won't worry you now till you get real *MS*.

We are leaving to day for Naples and catch steamer for Mars: to morrow ev^g.

I expect to call and face your anger and indignation on Friday next. If not there by noon then won't come up till Monday.[2] I've settled nothing with Miss Hallowes till I see you and hear your views as to what should be done to pick up the abominably lost time.

"Explosives" ready.

NB. What do you think (as idea for a series of short stories) of extracts from *private* letters of a war correspondent. Imagine him writing to his girl—the inner truth of his feelings—things that *don't* go into his war correspdence—that *can't* go into it.

They could each begin abruptly (being extracts). I've a sample blocked out—but you may test the ground meantime.

Kindest regards

Yours Conrad.

I've received wire money orders though, in the case of the second, post would have done.

I *am* glad to be off at last.

---

[1] 'Autocracy and War': by 21 May the *Fortnightly Review* had taken it.
[2] On the 19th, Conrad confirmed his intention of seeing Pinker on Monday, 22 May (telegram, Berg).

To Count Szembek

Text *L.fr*.71; Najder 245

Grand Hôtel de Genève
Marseille.
Mardi 16 mai 1905.

Très cher Monsieur,[1]

Je vous aurais écrit de Naples comme vous pouvez bien vous imaginer mais juste au moment où j'allais m'y mettre on est venu nous prévenir que le vapeur était prêt à partir à cinq heures au lieu de sept comme nous pensions.

Notre traversée a été peu agréable, pluie et grosse mer tout le temps presque. Mais Borys s'est bien amusé et ma femme aussi dit qu'elle ne regrette point l'aventure. Tout le monde a été d'une amabilité charmante pour nous. C'était des gens simples mais pleins de prévenances. Quant à moi j'ai été traité comme collègue—en homme du métier et cela certainement m'a fait plaisir.

Nous sommes arrivés ce matin ou plutôt dans la nuit d'hier. Nous avons dormis à bord. Nous partons demain matin pour Paris, où nous passerons la nuit pour arriver chez nous le jeudi à 3 h. 50 m. Autrement on arriverait ou trop tard ou trop tôt.

Ici il pleut à verse! c'est odieux le temps que nous avons eu cette année.

Je n'ai pas besoin de le dire que le vif souvenir que nous avons emporté de votre bienveillante amitié demeurera avec nous toute la vie. L'heure de la journée où nous avions le plaisir de vous voir arriver chez nous à Capri, a apporté le regret de votre absence. Borys a prononcé votre nom au moins trois fois par jour et a essayé d'expliquer aux officiers du navire la nature intime de ses relations avec "my friend Count Szembek". Cet enfant vous aime beaucoup ainsi que le font ses parents qui naturellement sont des personnes beaucoup plus humbles.

Le vendredi passé, sur le tard, à Naples, j'ai eu une soudaine inspiration et je me suis précipité dans un Banco Lotto qui allait fermer. Comme nous sommes partis avant le résultat du tirage fut connu, je me permets de vous envoyer ci-inclus le billet. On ne sait jamais quel peut être le caprice de la fortune. Qui sait! J'ai peut-être gagné et dans ce cas je ne doute pas que vous me ferez parvenir la nouvelle par télégramme. Ce que j'aimerais le plus cependant ce serait

---

[1] Count Zygmunt Szembek (1844–1907), a Polish aristocrat, lived in Italy for his health. According to Jean-Aubry (*L. fr.*, p. 71), one of the Count's experiences in Naples gave Conrad the material for 'Il Conde' (*A Set of Six*).

une petite lettre pour nous donner les nouvelles de votre santé et de l'état moral de Capri.

Toutes nos amitiés.

A vous de coeur.

J. C. Korzeniowski.

Translation

Very dear Sir,

As you might well expect, I would have written to you from Naples, but just when I was going to begin, someone came to warn us that the steamer was ready to leave at five o'clock instead of at seven as we anticipated.

Our crossing was not very agreeable: rain and a big sea almost all the time. But Borys enjoyed himself and my wife says she doesn't regret the adventure at all. Everybody was amiable and charming to us. They were simple people, but full of kind attentions. As for me, I was treated as a colleague—a man of the profession—and that certainly pleased me.

We arrived this morning, or rather last night. We slept on board. We leave tomorrow morning for Paris, where we shall pass the night in order to arrive home on Thursday at 3:50. Otherwise, we should arrive either too early or too late.

It is pouring here; the weather we've had this year is odious.

I don't need to tell you that the lively memory we have carried away of your kind friendship will remain with us all our lives. The time of day when we had the pleasure of seeing you arrive at our house on Capri has brought regret at your absence. Borys has said your name at least three times a day and tried to explain to the ship's officers the intimate nature of his relations with 'my friend Count Szembek'. This child loves you very much, as do his parents, who are of course much humbler persons.

Last Friday, in Naples, towards the end of the day, I had a sudden inspiration, and I rushed to a lottery agency, which was about to close. As we left before the result of the drawing was known, I allow myself to send you herewith this ticket. One never knows what the caprice of fortune can be. Who knows! Perhaps I have won, and in this case I've no doubt you will forward the news to me by telegram. What I should like most of all however would be a little letter to give us the news of your health and of the moral state of Capri.

All our friendship.

Yours most truly,

J. C. Korzeniowski

To Edmund Gosse

Text MS Yale; Unpublished

Tuesday.
16 May 1905
Hotel de Genève
Marseille.

Dear Mr. Gosse.

I am hastening home this way with feelings more akin to dismay than anything I've ever experienced in my life.

While expecting the communication which you were good enough to promise me, I received, almost at the eve of leaving Capri, the astonishing letter from Rothenstein, which I take the liberty to enclose here for your information; begging you to read it at this point.

I find it difficult to believe that the Prime Minister intended that or any other sort of curatelle to be established.[1] It seemed to me that the grant was offered without conditions;—else, I feel sure from the most considerate tact invariably manifested in all your communications with me You would have given me a hint beforehand of any such arrangement with all the delicacy displayed in your good works. It is therefore excessively startling to discover that a grant given (in the terms of your own letter announcing the fact) "in recognition of my talents and for my services to literature":—a grant therefore which however beyond one's deserts one could have imagined oneself to have, in a measure, earned—becomes converted into a bounty which has to be begged for; and this not once only but many times as it were: that it is a gift no longer conferred upon such merits as I may have but upon two men with power to control, grant and withhold, according to their will and judgment: and that power apparently unlimited in its discretion.

I trust you'll not think this view of the mere material position exaggerated. If R's letter (where he gives no authority for the decision) means anything in the world it means just that. On the face of it there is no earthly reason why a third, a half, or any other portion should not be kept back for a year, for three years—for any time—should my petition or application fail to carry conviction to the holder's minds.

This side of the case suggests itself to me only by the way. The whole affair has assumed an appearance much graver and more distressing

---

[1] 'Curatelle': a guardianship. Thinking of Conrad's temperament, Gosse and the two trustees, Newbolt and Rothenstein, felt it wise to disburse the money cautiously (Najder, *Chronicle*, pp. 311–12), but in any case, as Gosse at once told Conrad, such trusteeships were customary.

than any stress of my material necessities: the appearance of 'Conrad having to be saved from himself'—the sort of thing that casts a doubt on a man's sense of responsibility, on his right feeling, on his sense of correct conduct. How it has arisen since your friendly and considerate letter came bringing with it the regret of many imperfections and the comfort of your approving judgment—I can not tell. What indiscreet act or word of mine (or somebody else's) might have given cause for it I cannot tell! All I know is that I haven't been able not only to write a line since but even to think of one worth setting down.

I assure you my dear Sir that I write this after some days of anxious meditation, that I write in the spirit of the utmost deference where deference is due, and with an abiding feeling of gratitude, which nothing, that may or may not happen, can ever impair. Obviously incapable of asking the Prime Minister to rescind as an act of grace the conditions which to my mind amount to a withdrawal of the grant, I have always recognised and recognise now his absolute right to be fully informed if such be his pleasure. I know that he trusts your judgment; that the information given to you is at his disposal. And I, dear Mr Gosse, put my trust in Your sympathy so implicitly that I've no hesitation in asking you to give me an opportunity to see You at the hour and place most convenient to a man of Your many occupations and engagements. In less than half an hour I can give, without going into figures, a clear idea of my situation, together with the plain statement of the way in which I intended to avail myself of that proof of appreciation I have been honoured with at Your suggestion by the Prime Minister. I feel very strongly that You ought to know: in fact I feel it so strongly that the granting of my earnest request for an interview (however distasteful it may be to you) I shall look upon as the greatest practical proof of Your favourable regard for my work. The moral complexion of a situation like mine will be really of more importance in Your eyes than the exact enumeration of amounts and the mode of their distribution:—though of course, I am fully prepared to satisfy You on every point. There is nothing to conceal. The only thing I imagine that is wrong with me is that with infinitely more effort than most men I produce much less work than many of them are capable of doing in a given time.

As to the rest I am confident that giving me an unprejudiced hearing you will find nothing even unconsciously unworthy. *Hearing* I say— because to write I could not. And besides what more is there to write that your penetration has not discovered between the lines of this— shall I call it: appeal?

Believe me, dear Mr Gosse, with the greatest regard

Always yours

Joseph Conrad.

PS You will have noticed from R.s letter that a cheque (signed by him and Mr Newbolt) for money I asked for in ignorance of the conditions set out in his letter, has been sent to me. All my arrangements for leaving Capri being made on that basis I was absolutely compelled to make use of it; but in a fortnight or so should it be found necessary and proper I shall be in a position to refund to them the amount.

We arrive home (at Pent Farm) on Sat:[1] where I shall await your reply and hold myself at your disposition from next Monday. You understand of course that there is no question of personalities. For R. I have a strong and lasting affection; for Mr Newbolt whom I met only once a great regard and much sympathy with his ideas.[2]

To Edmund Gosse

Text MS Yale; *Listy* 245; Original unpublished

[letterhead: Pent Farm][3]

19 may 1905.

My dear Mr Gosse.

Your chiding letter reaches me this moment and I lose no time in expressing to you my profound regret at having laid myself open to an unfavourable impression. Pray, believe that, however mistaken my feelings are, my only wish has been and is, to *act correctly*.

Rightly or wrongly I thought that writing to You, whom, after all the marks of interest You have given me by word and deed, I cannot regard as a stranger, I could without offence disclose "le fond de ma pensée"— and of my perplexity. If I have presumed too far I owe You an apology for that presumption.

I had no means of knowing that the procedure was not exceptional in my case but usual in all cases. I own to a, not I hope very peculiar, dislike of falling, even by the remotest appearance, into the class of those

---

[1] Really Thursday afternoon.

[2] Henry Newbolt was famous for his patriotic poetry, but Conrad would have taken a special interest in his views on educating naval officers and on strengthening the Mediterranean fleet. They had met one Saturday at the Savile Club: Newbolt, *The World as in My Time*, pp. 253–5, 300–1.

[3] Conrad had a new batch of stationery printed in mid-July; until then he used odd sheets of types eleven and twelve.

disorderly talents whose bohemianism, irregularity and general irresponsibility of conduct are neither in my tradition and my training nor in my character. You will in all fairness to me remember that it is through you—and you alone—that I received the only intimation which I could regard as authoritative and official. Granting that I've been unspeakably stupid, to whom else, under my mistaken impression, was it proper for me to appeal for a hearing? It was asked for, in all deference, as a favour. I conclude with a perfectly unaffected regret, that it is refused. But is my readiness to throw myself unreservedly upon Your judgment to be counted a sin so grievous as to reflect on my character?

Your chiding—severe as it is—I take as meekly as if it were wholly deserved. Nothing could please me more than to discover that I've made a dense ass of myself. Remains the question of ingratitude which you touch upon so pointedly as to give a good deal of pain. All I can say is that if Will Rothenstein ever doubts or mistrusts my most affectionate sense of his friendship he is not the man I most firmly believe him to be.[1] As to M[r] Newbolt I venture to rely on his highmindedness which would not cast lightly the most odious of charges upon what at worst may be the blunder of a man overharassed by the sense of his own deficiencies—by searching doubts not of his aim but of his effort.

I remain, dear Mr Gosse, with the greatest regard,

always faithfully yours

Joseph Conrad

To Count Szembek
Text I.fr.73; Najder 246

Pent Farm,
Lundi 21 mai 1905.[2]

Très cher Monsieur,

Nous arrivâmes chez nous jeudi dans l'après-midi très fatigués au bout du compte, mais tous en bonne santé. Tout de suite j'ai été accablé par une masse de correspondance d'affaires de toute sorte, et même par des gens qui sont venus me relancer ici en personne. De plus j'ai trouvé mon article politique que le "Fortnightly Review" a accepté avec enthousiasme, mais avec demande de corrections ou plutôt de changement sur un point ou deux. J'en ai été occupé, car le temps presse.

---

[1] Rothenstein, the initiator of the plan to help Conrad, was in a painful situation: he knew as well as any one the extent of his friend's miscellaneous debts, but as a trustee he was obliged to use the money for Conrad's 'permanent benefit': Newbolt, pp. 301–6.

[2] The 21st was a Sunday.

Ceci pour vous expliquer pourquoi je n'ai pas envoyé tout de suite nos remerciements les plus sincères pour le plaisir de votre bonne, chère et gracieuse lettre qui nous attendait à la poste. Ma femme est on ne peut plus touchée par votre bienveillante pensée. Je ne parle pas de moi. Vous savez que je vous porte une vraie aff[e]ction et que je regarde toute marque de votre amitié comme un don très précieux.

Je finis en toute hâte, nous partons pour Londres dans une heure. Tout à vous bien affectueusement.

J. C. Korzeniowski.

Translation

Very dear Sir,

We arrived home on Thursday afternoon, very tired when all is said and done, but all in good health. Immediately I was overcome by a mass of business correspondence of all sorts, and even by some people who came to badger me here in person. What's more I found my political article, which the *Fortnightly Review* has accepted enthusiastically, but with a request for corrections or rather for the revision of a point or two. I have been busy with it, for time presses.

This is to explain to you why I have not immediately sent our most sincere thanks for the pleasure of your kind, dear, and graceful letter which was waiting for us at the post office. My wife couldn't be more touched by your friendly thought. I do not speak of myself. You know that I hold you in true affection and that I regard every mark of your friendship as a very precious gift.

I finish in haste; we leave for London in an hour. Very affectionately yours.

J. C. Korzeniowski

To Henry Newbolt
Text MS Mursia; Unpublished

9. Princes Sq.
Bayswater.
23 May 1905

My dear Mr Newbolt.[1]

I came to London for a couple of days or at least as few as possible the days in London being lost days as far as my work, of which I seem unable to do enough, are* concerned.

[1] Henry John Newbolt (1862–1938; knighted 1915), patriotic poet, naval historian, sometime barrister, and first editor of the *Monthly Review*, 1900–4.

Will you have the kindness to let me see you to-morrow (Wednesday). At 1.30 I lunch with Mr Colvin; but up to one and at any time after four I will be ready to meet you at any place you may appoint. Perhaps You would not mind wiring me in the morning the hour and the place— unless indeed you can not spare the time to morrow in which case you will have the kindness to name the day also.

I am my dear Mr Newbolt

very faithfully Yours

Joseph Conrad.

To Henry Newbolt
Text MS Mursia; Unpublished[1]

Pent Farm.
Stanford
N^r Hythe
Kent
25 May 1905

Dear Mr Newbolt.

In my view of the grant made to me I start from the principle that the first and main intention has been to procure for me the ease of mind necessary for tranquil and steady writing, in which—and in which alone—is to be found a radical and complete remedy for my difficulties.

It is this thought which emboldened me to urge so earnestly the advisability of allowing me the sum of £250 at once in order to pay certain very pressing debts. I trust that after our conversation you take the view that they have not been incurred recklessly; at most perhaps indiscreetly, and if indiscreetly then only in part so. The pressure of circumstances must be taken into account. Besides there is the fact that provision was made to meet them (not quite completely but in considerable proportion) at the end of last year, when the aggravated state of my wife's health necessitating an operation of a serious kind and a sojourn abroad under rather expensive conditions diverted the moneys destined for my creditors. In this I had but little option. Life is uncertain (mine from the actuarial point of view is not a very good risk)—and I admit that the dread of having to leave, perhaps, a woman completely and painfully crippled with a small child and with no means of support left but little inclination for the cool consideration of ways and means and consequences.

---

[1] According to Newbolt, who quotes about one third of the text (p. 304), this letter reiterates the points Conrad had made in their conversation that afternoon.

The detail of debts is as follows.

Wm Watson's overdraft

(£198)—instalment   £60—at least.

Landlord (arrears in six years)—	50	
Taxes due.	22.10	
Dr Hackney. (Hythe)—	20	
Dr Batten:—	14	
Dr Tebb	10	
Dr Cerio (in Capri)[1]		
for electric treatment (for my wife	18 (acct just received	
and attendance on our nurse)	from him)	

in Hythe	Lewis & Hylands.	30
and	Bushel	30
Folkestone	Ninnes	12
	Small bills about	20
	Convent	10 old debt.[2]

                                  298.

By sitting very close all the next month I think that with 250 I may be able to manage. Though of course it will be managed under stress.

With the sense of the responsibility weighing upon you and W.R. as trustees of the money I have cast about for some expedient to relieve You from the burden of immediate decision in that matter. The only one I see is to raise the money elsewhere—but as a matter of business I could not do that with a stranger. To demand that sum from Pinker is not practicable without disturbing our established relations on the basis of MS against money—the only really sound one. It would involve a full disclosure too—which I wish to avoid—and in the end it will mean writing for dear life and really I had enough of that for the last eighteen months. Remains a friend. Of moneyed friends I have only one to whom if desperately driven I could think of going.[3] He's ready enough to lend but of repayment he will not hear but in a dim and distant future. I know how it would be. He will never consent to be repaid by monthly or any other instalments. His generosity closes the door in a manner you will understand. I really don't think I could. Moreover he is abroad under

---

[1] Giorgio, brother of the scholar Ignazio Cerio.

[2] Lewis and Hyland, drapers; W. Bushell, outfitter; Frederick B. Ninnes, watchmaker and jeweller; the Bernardine convent in Slough (for the education of Jessie's youngest sisters).

[3] Probably Galsworthy.

circumstances which make me extremely unwilling to disturb him with my affairs. And the time presses, since under the impression that the grant was unconditional I promised all these people to settle with them on my return from abroad.

Besides, frankly, the idea of pledging the grant (in a manner) is distasteful to me. I could not have done it behind your backs. And the state of affairs being disclosed openly—as is due to you and W. R. as my friends and the representatives of the Prime Minister—I do not think that it would be to your taste to evade the responsibility. All these affairs are very miserable; but the point, as I venture to state it with all the deference and gratitude imaginable, is that if I have been judged worthy of that favour there can be no harm of* applying it in the way in which its beneficent effect will be most felt. Never perhaps an unexpected help had been more timely. The view also may be taken that more debts being for the *most part* the result of my wife's illness, the grant pays for her cure; which is in fact the feeling I first had when the news reached me. And what greater relief could be given to a man?

I trust you will forgive this interminable letter. I wished to state my case fully for the matter is of great and urgent importance to me. I can't thank you sufficiently for the sympathy with which you listened to me this afternoon. You have in that interview given me the great moral support of your commendation of my work heard from your own lips. It is a great thing. Sometimes a few words have a magical effect. I look forward with increased belief to my work.

I am, my dear Mr Newbolt, always Yours faithfully

Jph. Conrad.

I intended buying your latest book[1] to morrow before going home to the Pent; but I venture now to ask you to send me a copy—inscribed—à charge de revanche[2]—as the French say. I'll send you my Mirror of the Sea as soon as it comes out[3]—a pinch of my chaff for your solid grain—but one gives what one has.

---

[1] Probably *The Year of Trafalgar*; Murray brought it out in March.
[2] 'On condition that you let me do the same for you'.
[3] In October 1906.

To Norman Douglas

Text MS Texas; Unpublished

[letterhead: Pent Farm]
29 May 1905.

My dear Douglass*

I've just read Nelson. It is very good. Some criticism could be made mainly on the point that you presuppose too much knowledge of facts in Your readers. Still, we shall try to place it where it may be judged sympathetically.[1]

I didn't write sooner because a horrible fit of the gout laid me by the heels almost at the very moment of our arrival. We did go to London but I had to be brought back to the country almost immediately leaving every business unattended and the prospects of my play in jeopardy. I am indeed a broken reed to trust to; of my good intentions You need not doubt, but, so far, I've done very little for your copy not having been able to see anybody of much use.

The truth is I feel most confoundedly ill—tho' the pain is not so severe now. What's worse I feel dispirited by this bad beginning. Every day is of the utmost importance and I must be in bed and watch them go, irretrievably, to waste. It's bad. Don't imagine however I've lost all pluck. It is not so; but one can't defend oneself from some bitterness of feeling. Pardon this empty and unsatisfactory letter. I shall try to do better next time. Wife sends her kind regards and love to your kiddies.[2]

Always yours in comradeship of feelings and convictions.

Jph. Conrad.

PS I haven't even been able to order the book I promised you yet.

To David Meldrum

Text MS Duke; Blackburn 183

[letterhead: Pent Farm]
29 May 1905

My Dear Mr Meldrum.

We returned about the 20th and came to London where I fully expected and looked forward to the great very great pleasure of seeing you. But just note my luck. The second night in town a horrible fit of

---

[1] As 21 October, the Trafalgar centennial, approached, magazines were brimming with articles on Nelson.

[2] Archie and Robin: Douglas's marriage collapsed in 1903; the boys were placed in the care of friends in 1906.

gout came on and I could feel at once it was going to be no joke. So I got myself brought back here while I could yet stand being moved; and I've been groaning for 3 days and nights. To day, after having finished groaning, I am sitting up sufficiently to be able to scribble this to you.

Let me know by a word how you all are; and before everything give my wife's Love to Mrs Meldrum and the children. She has been so disappointed at not being able to see all your family! It is my fault entirely or rather the fault of my confounded infirmity.

As I still hope and look forward to seeing you soon I wont enlarge upon the story of our residence in Capri. It will be enough for your good and tried friendship to hear that my wife came back immensely improved. As far as she's concerned the whole cruel and expensive affair has been a success. For myself I must sadly confess that I've done nothing or next to nothing in Capri.

But of that later.

Jack Galsworthy (whom I saw in Italy) writes me asking whether the two little poems of Mottram[1] are going to find a place in Maga soon? It seems the poor youngster in whom we both take some interest is generally unhappy and to see himself in print would wind him up morally. So I venture to mention the matter, for I know your kindness is great and the little bits of verse are not so bad after all.

The news I have is that the Stage Society wishes to perform my little play "To-Morrow" next June.[2] I am rather glad of it for it will be instructive for me and besides may give me chance for something bigger by and bye. G. B. S. seems to think very well of my first essay in play writing.

Pardon this illegible scribble. Remember me kindly please, to Mrs Meldrum.

Always Yours

Jph. Conrad.

PS May I ask Messrs. B'wood to send me 2 copies of "*Youth*" which I want to present to some people abroad.

---

[1] Long a friend of Ada Galsworthy (his father had managed her business affairs after her guardian died), Ralph Hale Mottram (1883–1971) was beginning a career as a writer. His later books included the Spanish Farm trilogy and a memoir of the Galsworthys.

[2] I.e. the following month. Conrad sent the corrected version to Pinker (and so to Colvin) on 31 May (telegram, Berg). For Conrad's current attitude to the play, see the fragment of a letter [2? June 1905] quoted by Lucas, *The Colvins*, p. 303.

To Count Szembek

*Text L.fr.*74; Najder 247

Pent Farm,
29 mai 1905.

Très cher Monsieur,

Imaginez que me voilà cloué au lit par un accès de goutte. Nous sommes allés à Londres et c'est là que je fus pris. Je me suis fait transporter ici en toute hâte, car j'ai vu tout de suite que ce serait une longue affaire.

Quelle guigne! Enfin! Il faut prendre patience mais j'avoue que c'est dur de voir les jours glisser comme ça quand on est forcé de rester étendu sur le dos.

Merci mille et mille fois pour les livres qui sont arrivés à ma grande joie juste à temps pour m'aider à prendre patience et à oublier un peu la douleur. C'est un homme de talent et un homme d'esprit.[1] Il pense bien et il sait dire ce qu'il pense d'une façon intéressante. Ce qu'il imagine il le fait vivre pour nous d'une vie réelle et poignante. Et puis ses convictions me sont sympathiques.

Ici il fait très beau; le temps même est chaud. De mon lit je vois l'air ensoleillé et j'écoute les oiseaux chanter. Mais je ne suis pas gai!

Je ne veux pas vous attrister par ma lettre dolente, donc je finis ici. Ma femme et Borys se rappellent tendrement à votre bon souvenir. Croyez-moi, cher Monsieur et Ami, toujours à vous très fidèlement.

J. C. Korzeniowski.

P. S.—Je n'ai même pas encore commandé les livres qui vous sont dus. Pardonnez-moi. Ce sera mon premier soin.

Translation

Very dear Sir,

Imagine me riveted to bed by an attack of gout. We went to London, and there I was smitten. I had myself brought here in all haste, for I saw immediately that it would be a long business.

In a word, what bad luck! One must have patience, but I admit that it's hard to see days slip by like that while forced to rest flat on my back.

A thousand thanks and a thousand more for the books which, to my great joy, arrived exactly at the time to help me be patient and forget the pain a little. He is a man of wit and talent. He thinks well and he knows how to say what he thinks in an interesting way. He brings what he

[1] Identity unknown.

imagines to life for us with a genuine and poignant vitality. And then his convictions are congenial to me.

The weather here is very good; it's even warm. From my bed I see the atmosphere bathed in sunshine and I hear the birds singing. But I am not cheerful!

I don't want to sadden you with my doleful letter, so I finish here. My wife and Borys wish to be remembered to you affectionately. Believe me, dear sir and friend, always very faithfully yours,

J. C. Korzeniowski.

P. S. I have not yet ordered the books that are owed you. Forgive me. This will be my first concern.

To Henry Newbolt
Text MS Mursia; Unpublished

[letterhead: Pent Farm]
1st of June 1905

My dear Mr Newbolt.

Many thanks for your good and friendly letter. I have meditated upon it with all the regard due to your indefatigable kindness, to your position of responsibility—and to the generous intentions of the donor. I entreat you not to suspect me of stupidity, obstinacy or odious ingratitude. I have an unshaken belief in your open mind. (In all I say I include Rothenstein of course). You must also forgive me for writing very fully—since this correspondence—I take it—is to remain on record to justify your action (whatever it may be) and my view (whether sound or not) of my case.

My impression is that, in effect, your letter proposes I should consent to making a composition with my creditors: a step equivalent, in all but publicity, to declared bankruptcy. But leaving that truth aside I wish to submit that this particular case is not, and should not be treated as the case of a man having dealt with unconscionable usurers, or who has incurred extravagant debts with tradesmen giving reckless credit on the chance of making something good out of it in the end. The small tradespeople with whom I've dealt for nearly seven years now in the usual way, for the necessities of life, have treated me always very well and have lately behaved in a really considerate way—letting their accts stand over without a murmur (tho' they too, I dare say, wanted their money badly) in the full confidence that these liabilities would be settled as soon as I was able. The first consequence of what you propose would

be to destroy utterly my credit in the part of the country where I have
been favourably known for more than six years, where I wish to reside,
from which I could not remove myself to set up a household elsewhere
without trouble enough to unsettle me for months and without incurring
expenses which I cannot afford! I ask you my dear Mr Newbolt how
would you like such a proposal being made to yourself in relation to your
own tradesmen and generally to people who trusted your word? It [is]
an expedient for a hopeless situation, a calamitous sort of thing to which
in justice to myself as well as to the other parties I cannot consent. There
is no sentiment here whatever; I leave that out altogether; but from a
practical point of view it would be *bad business*, making my position much
worse for the future. I would repel the transaction as unnecessary and
practically discrediting; but the true point of my objection lies in this
that it is not applicable to my case. Can we send a solicitor to negotiate
with the Tax Collector (who has send* me a reminder yesterday)? Or
with Drs Hackney and Tebb for instance? or with Dr Cerio in Capri
whomI called in to apply the very much needed electric treatment—or
to Mr Hogben my friendly landlord who stands on my list for £50 (for a
year's rent, supplies of farm produce and keep of the pony—not an
extortionate amount) or the good nuns in Slough—and so on with the
others. I leave to your judgment how much that sort of thing would help
me to attain that peace of mind and serenity of thought necessary for
good work, how much it would make my position easier—or securer.

Generous help has been extended to me (through the exertion of
friends for whom my gratitude is great and lasting) in honourable terms.
I accepted it; and, since the question of practical application arose I say:
The way in which I can be helped is by the payment of my debts as far as
possible. They arose in such and such manner. Such and such amounts
are needed. I have explained I think everything. I can always go on
living; it is the necessity of earning besides the sum in which I am
indebted from causes stated that is the source of my anxiety—an anxiety
from which I can in this way be relieved. After having stated this I've
nothing more to say of practical import. Whether the arguments
contained in my previous letter to you cover your responsibility in the
administration of the grant it is obviously not for me to say. I think I
ought to be trusted after giving a very detailed statement. The grant
obviously can not secure my future permanently—but it can save the
passing hours for that work in which alone lies the final solution of all my
embarrassements*. Therein is the power to help. The decision rests with
you.

I am ashamed to beg again for a speedy conclusion—not from any unholy desire to lay hands on the cash but because having, in consequence of the grant, abandonned* the steps I was taking to raise some money against my return home I find myself placed in a damaging situation in regard to the people to whom I made definite promises; therefore in the case of your refusal it behoves me to bestir myself in order to provide what's needed as quickly as possible. If I must mortgage my future—why, I must; but the uncertainty is very trying and I ascribe to it the horrible fit of gout from which I have just, lamely, arisen. I will also beg from your friendship and kindness for a definite statement (should the eventuality arise) of the manner in which Your sense of your charge will permit You to dispose of the money. I ought, I think to know that exactly and definitely. Don't be angry my dear Mr Newbolt if I believe that a man to whom such a sort of "in extremis" suggestion has been made has a right to answer it by the fullest expression of his thought. Speaking with all deference and with the deepest sense of responsibility with which You have been saddled I feel compelled to say that a confession of insolvency in exchange for the assistance received would *not* carry out the intention of the grant—I mean always from the practical point of view—I don't mention my feelings which, after all, may legitimately be taken into consideration. I am no stranger to business, and know the meaning of things. I've had charge of valuable property and of conflicting interests beyond what falls commonly to the lot of commanders of ships. I look upon a composition with one's creditors as a *most* serious thing, worse than bankruptcy in some respects inasmuch as bankruptcy may be forced on by the stupidity or malevolence of a creditor whereas the other is a confession of absolute inability to meet one's engagements. I hope as long as I can sit a chair and hold a pen to keep it off. I am my dear Mr Newbolt with the deepest recognition of the thought and trouble you take about my wretched person always faithfully yours

Joseph Conrad.

To Henry Newbolt

Text MS Mursia; Newbolt 306 (with omissions)

[letterhead: Pent Farm]
5th June 1905.

My dear Mr Newbolt.

I am afraid you must have enough of me and my debts and my handwriting. Still as this grant is, as I easily understand, of exceptional magnitude, as the fact of its being made is sure sooner or later to come into public light and have its discretion questioned or at least discussed (you remember no doubt the Civil List Pension of M[r] Austin Dobson and the adverse comments thereon);[1] and as in the case of a writer such as I am, of unconventional origin, everything, literary achievement as well as personal character, may, and probably will be, scrutinised with no friendly eye, I felt bound to explain my position fully and state my arguments "in extenso" with the hope, I own, that some day, perhaps, you, a literary man of undeniable, distinguished and *national* position hearing some harsh opinion would be disposed to say: "It is not so. I knew the man and I know the facts." With most people (unless actuated by prejudice or malice) this would be a sufficient vindication of my character—and certainly it would be enough to satisfy my sensitiveness to the fullest extent. And I thank you for the patience, the indulgence, the friendliness you have displayed in hearing me out.

To the remarks in your last letter I will say in further justification that the appearance of a solicitor attempting to buy up my debts[2] would still have produced the disastrous effect I wished to avoid. For on what ground could he approach my creditors? Evidently on that of my utter hopelessness as a debtor and on that ground alone. But no more need be said since I have looked at your suggestion in every way with a sincere intention of deferring to your wishes as reason and gratitude dictated, have found it practically impossible—and have set out my objections as amply as was due to you, first as my friends—concerned in my moral and material welfare—and next as men selected for the discretionary dispensers of the Prime Minister's grant to—my merits!

It would have been easier to accept had I been a convinced believer in my merits. I assure You (and You won't misunderstand my sincerity) that the acceptance was a matter of some considerable heart searching. I did not feel worthy enough to take what was offered with a light and undoubting heart. In my grateful acceptance I own I was swayed by the thought of my wife and child, not because they were in any immediate want, but because I wished to give myself a chance of remaining with them as long as possible, for their sake:—for I know well that sitting for 10 or 12 hours on end not to waste a moment of a vein of facility, as I've done repeatedly; that sitting at work to catch up arrears till conscious-

---

[1] In 1904, Austin Dobson (1840–1921), poet, belletrist, and student of eighteenth-century literature, was granted a Civil List pension of £250 a year. Conrad's award was not renewable.

[2] Newbolt had proposed using a solicitor to ensure there were proper records of the debts' being settled (Newbolt, p. 305).

ness was lost (as happened twice to me last year) cannot be done without paying a price whose nature I need not hint at to you.

That I cannot work with the regularity and certitude of an Anthony Trollope[1] is a defect purely temperamental; but that I desire to avoid the most remote appearance of being the XXth century edition of Johnson's M[r] Savage[2] you cannot but understand and approve (even if you find my dread exaggerated) knowing as you do the irresponsible judgments passed every day upon the living and the dead alike. I have turned myself I think thouroughly* inside out before you as before good friends who would find it in their hearts to declare eventually: Conrad has been open with us. His position from the causes he stated and which we believed was worse than we thought. But his character is such that after a full explanation from him—in writing—as to what seems to him the most direct way of relieving the pressure of his liabilities we have given him that sum of money to be used in the manner made known to us beforehand in full detail. However what I ask for now is not quite as much as that. I simply ask whether You will consent to spare my feelings to the extent of allowing me to meet you once more in London either alone or with Will, seeing the documents I can produce, giving me the opportunity of answering any additional questions you may wish to ask; letting me arrange the amounts to the best advantage (taking of course your suggestions into account) and then give me for the various sums fixed in consultation cheques made out to me which I shall endorse and in your presence put into the envelopes already addressed which I shall bring with me?

I dont ask this because I believe for a moment that you suspect me of being capable of basely squandering the money instead of using it as stated. I am firmly convinced there is another quite valid reason for the procedure you wish to follow in the terms of your letter. But others may believe so and even say so without believing it very much. Everything gets known in the end and to answer them would be difficult. There would be the fact of two men whose good will proved to the hilt could not be questioned—one of distinguished and authoritative position in letters and in the world, the other younger it is true but well known and generally and justly looked upon as an intimate and devoted friend—

---

[1] According to his posthumous *Autobiography* (1883), he would begin the day by writing 2,500 words at 1,000 words an hour.

[2] The poet Richard Savage (c. 1697–1743) was pensioned by Alexander Pope and died in a debtors' prison. In the *Life* (1744), Johnson remarks that 'He appeared to think himself born to be supported by others'; moreover, 'he was very ready to set himself free from the load of an obligation'.

and yet both apparently unwilling in an important transaction where their responsibility is engaged to trust my veracity and conduct! For that could be said. Your own denials would be credited not to your conviction but to your compassion. I entreat you earnestly not to give to envy, malevolence or simple unadorned stupidity an opening to misrepresent what on your part is no mistrust but solicitude for the effective performance of the charge thrust upon you and on mine would be no tacit confession of unworthiness but the highest recognition of the obligation I am under to You both. Pray remember that from the nature of things I cannot count upon the moral support one's family, connections, the opinion of numerous early associates gives one against the hasty judgments of the world. Except for the woman who trusted me and the child not yet old enough—thank God—to understand all the uncertainty of his future, I am so alone that you two stand in virtue of your charge in the positions that only the nearest of blood could occupy with perfect safety to myself. From the inference drawn from your acts there is no possible appeal. Pray remember this if I appear to you unreasonable; and forgive this last of the three long letters written to you in perfect confidence and trust. Always sincerely yours

Joseph Conrad.

PS I beg for a wire if you grant the appointment asked for and also if you do not. If advised the day before I can be in London by noon on Wednesday and altogether at your disposal from that hour when most convenient to you.

To Henry Newbolt
Text MS Mursia; Unpublished

[letterhead: Pent Farm]
9th June 1905

My dear Mr Newbolt.

I send, as agreed between us, (page lettered A) an exact statement resuming in a precise form the subject of our conversation and of the letters we exchanged bearing upon the immediate employment of the grant.[1] This I see is the least amount I can do with. I see with regret that

[1] Newbolt had written to Conrad on 7 June, telling him that £250 would be applied to his debts, and agreeing to the suggestion (5 June) that the cheques be made out to Conrad, endorsed by him, and sent off in envelopes addressed in his hand. 'I think this plan with your letters, will effectually clear us from any suspicion of having paid away the money in a lump to save ourselves trouble' (Newbolt, p. 310).

it is greater than my first estimate by some £*20*. This arises from the fact that since our interview I had to expend out of the moneys I had in hand (including the balance of the money received in Capri) nearly £25 for furniture—since the books could not remain indefinitely on the floor and we also had to have something to sit upon downstairs and to eat our dinners off.

I enclose also here (on page lettered C.) a short note of the way the money sent to Capri had been spent. Miss Jackson's receipt I could produce; for the rest I have no vouchers but I trust the obvious reasonableness of the expenditure and my word will suffice to satisfy you that the money has not been squandered thoughtlessly.

Out of the grant therefore £*370* may be taken as expended. Had it not been for that generous help all that amount would have had to be borrowed and repaid with 'copy' written for dear life. If I own to you frankly that the mere thought of that escaped burden turns me chilly with apprehension even now you will not regret the infinite pains you have been good enough to take in order to investigate my affairs and to settle upon the most judicious use of the money.

On the page lettered B you will find a few remarks (relating to the list of payments to be made)—summarising as it were my views as to the advantages secured for me—which I have laid before you both as the basis for your decision.

I can not sufficiently thank you both for the inexhaustible patience, for the scrupulous care and the sympathy you have displayed in considering and concluding this business.

I am my dear Mr Newbolt very gratefully yours

Jph. Conrad.

PS Thanks, more than for anything, for the few heartening words as to my work in your good and friendly postscript.[1]
PPS The contents of the enclosed envelopes—ready for posting—are of course for your inspection.

A.   9th June 1905.   Pent Farm.
Please make cheques out in the names standing against the amounts as under.

1.   *Wm. Keen Esqre* £50 on acc/t of Watson's overdraft.   £50

---

[1] 'As to your work, I shall look forward to talking about it with you when we next meet. In the meantime do believe what I said: I have a plentiful knowledge of literature and in

2. *M*^{r}. *Richard Hogben* £45 on acc/t of his bill enclosed for
   your inspection.   45
3. *M*^{r} *C.R. Nelson.* Income tax & house duty due Jan^y
   1st 05.   20.3.4.
4. *Messrs: Lewis & Hylands* £30 on acc/t of their bill (for
   £58.2) 1904.   30
5. *M*^{r}. *W. Bushell* amount of his acc/t for 1904   24.11.10
6. *M*^{r} *B. Ninnes.* amount of his acc/t for 1904.   10.19.9
7. *Messrs: Hackney, Davis & Hackney.* on acc/t. (med^{cal}
   att^{ce})   20.
8. *Albert Tebb Esq*^{re} (no acc/t rendered as yet.) med^l att^{ce} 10.
9. *George Cerio Esq*^{re} amount of his acc/t lire 390
                      @ 25 lire=£1.   15.12.6
10. *Rayner D. Batten Esq*^{r} medical attdce Jan. Febr. Mch
    04   14
11. *Joseph Conrad Esq*^{re} for settling small bills left from last   20
    year in amounts from £1 to £3 for which I shall
    forward you receipts for inspection
                                                                  ─────────
                                                                  £270.7.5.[1]

B.   Referring to numbers preceding each item in the list
as to N° 1. That payment is a preliminary condition of a negociation* M^r
     Wm Keen is ready to open in order to effect a compromise as to the
     whole amount—which of course would be of immense advantage to
     me.
N° 2. I beg you will be good enough to send *me* the cheque *made out to
     Richard Hogben* as I see him every day. I shall forward you his
     receipt for inspection. I wish to hand him the cheque myself. He has
     been in his simple way kindness personified both to myself and my
     wife.
N° 3.* Can't lay my hands on Lewis & Hylands' bill. But shall send
     their receipt to you if desired. The payment made now secures for
     me the faculty of paying the balance (£28.2) by instalments at my
     leisure. No mean advantage for me.
Nos 5 & 6. Their acc/ts are disch^{ged} in full as I had nothing from them
     since 1904—being either in London or abroad. And that is absolute
     relief.

this case I feel no doubt about my judgment, especially since all my friends agree with it'
(*ibid.*).
[1] The total should be £260 7s. 5d.

N° 8 Would you kindly—if not too much trouble send Tebb's £10 in a banknote instead of cheque. I ask this for reasons Rothenstein will guess at once.[1] To send something to him at once is a great point with me. He's a man of such delicacy that I fear he would refrain from sending me his account being, as intimate friend, aware of my difficult position.

NS 9. & 10. Call for no comment. *Cerio's* bills for attendance on the nurse we had with us and later (when I learned of the grant) upon my wife (for electric treatment) are in the envelope addressed to him. *R. D. Batten* acc/t is for £*14* now outstanding for nearly eighteen months. As some of our papers are coming from Italy by sea with the heavy luggage I haven't his latest reminder. But I know the amount only too well! His receipt will, with the others, be forwarded to you in due course.

N° 11. I don't send you the batch of these little bills overlooked in the worry and anxiety at the beginning of this year. I will pay them in money and send them receipted for your inspection and return to me. They have to be settled for very shame. There's the laundry the chemist—the saddler, the stationer—etc etc and others of a few shillings only. If I had more *Copy* ready I would not have appealed to you. But I've done rather badly in Italy and I don't want to overstep my usual limit with Pinker keeping the proportion of MS furnished and money drawn within a defined limit. Though it is no matter of agreement I am not inclined to break the tacit rule I made for myself. Moreover he is now in the U.S. till the end of the month which would be too long to wait.

NB I beg to have the cheques made *to the order of the people named in the list* instead of to myself (for endorsement) as it will shorten the procedure.

Envelopes duly addressed enclosed.

C. Note as to the disposal of the £*100* received in Capri.
Miss Jackson (the nurse with us) salary (balance)

—   £19.10

One month: bills for rooms and household expenses in
Villa di Maria

(four persons)   28.

Return journey from Capri to Pent Farm—3

---

[1] As Tebb's friend, Rothenstein would know that the doctor was almost as poor as the artists he treated and admired.

persons—with one day in Marseilles and one night
in Paris

—   34
        ———
        81.10

The balance was used (with some other money) for journey to London
and to pay for some necessary furniture.

To Henry Newbolt
Text MS Mursia; Unpublished

Pent Farm
Stanford
N^r Hythe. Kent.
15 June 1905

Dear Mr Newbolt.

I'm so sorry to bother you again. I wished only to ask when the money
will be sent? Yesterday the tax collector absolutely came to see me here
and generally I would feel better with that load off my chest.

Is there any difficulty or any further explanation needed? I am of
course ready—tho' I don't see what more I could say. A thousand
apologies—but what with the promises I've (incautiously) made and
Pinker's absence in America I am in a very tight place, and especially
very helpless in regard to these small bills.

A thousand apologies with kindest regards. Always yours

Jph. Conrad

To Henry Newbolt
Text MS Mursia; Unpublished

The Pent.
16 June 1905

Dear Mr Newbolt

I am sorry I worried you; but as a matter of fact, having sent the
package by a lad across the fields to the rway station I began to wonder
whether it had reached you safely.

Many thanks for the cheques. One receipt has already reached me by
this morning's post. I'll hold the lot at your disposition whenever you
wish to inspect them—which I think you had better do as a matter of
form so that there should be nothing wanting in the admirably
conscientious care in the discharge of your trust. I am glad you do not

think I've failed in the duty of sincerity and clearness I owed you *on more than one ground* in this transaction.

Of course the position is not made perfectly sound, but short of that for which the only way is in steady work (which I don't fear as long as the physical and mental health lasts) you have afforded me the greatest amount of intellectual and moral relief possible under the circumstances. This is the feeling with me now! I will not however repeat my thanks here: but you may rest assured of my memory.

In haste for this post

I am, dear Mr Newbolt always faithfully yours

Jph. Conrad.

To Norman Douglas

Text MS Texas; Unpublished

Pent Farm

21st June 1905

Dear Douglas.

There's no denying the fact that I've been confoundedly ill. I'm just beginning to crawl; for I had a sort of 'rechute' after an imprudent visit to London—where all sorts of things have been and are still clamouring for me.

Sent: *Love* received.[1] I like it. But really everything's going askew just now.

While I was on my back Pinker cleared out to the States on Hy James' business, and is not coming back till first week in July. It's impossible to find out whether anything has been done for your stuff. I know mine is all hung up. Then H. G. Wells who was coming to lunch with Edward Garnett here, lost his mother a couple of days ago[2]—put off Edward and rushed away to stay with his father. I was going to open Your case to these two men and enlist their cooperation. Now that move too is put off to goodness knows what date. I worry rather about my inability to display any sort of activity. You must forgive me. There are runs of bad luck that no foresight and no incantation can turn away.

Believe in my fidelity quand même. Jessie's kindest remembrances.

Always Yours

Jph Conrad.

[1] Holloway (p. 153) suggests that 'Sentimental Love' might be the original form of 'Men and Morals' ('By a Father', *English Review*, August 1913), but the latter essay was written for the occasion.

[2] She died on 12 June.

PS Since the wretched Pinker cleared out so suddenly I am left rather short of cash. Could you *without inconvenience* pay for me frcs 126 to padre di Maria which I still owe him and I will remit to you in the course of the month. But *only if it's convenient* for obviously he can wait. And next time You write you can tell me what you have done. I am sorry You had to send away your little chap and are yourself adrift with Archie. Borys sends him his love. I'll write directly I get hold of life again.

To Ford Madox Ford
Text MS BL Ashley 2923; Unpublished

The Pent
21 June 1905

Dearest Ford.

Don't be angry with me. I did not get on as well as I expected and then to tell the whole silly truth I hung on to my few bawbees[1] in expectation of having to go to London for the rehearsals of *One day more* which is the new title of the play. It seems there's a To-morrow touring in the provinces.

And so it turns out. I am off on Thursday for the rehearsals on that and the following day. I am so weary that the idea of travelling fills me with dread and the prospect of seeing the actors overcomes me with dismay. Two days in town seem a terror. Really I'm not fit to live.

"Et le misérable marchait toujours" You remember that phrase out of Salammbo![2] Indeed I feel more miserable than Matho.

Don't count me not having been to see You yet for a sin. Il y a des circonstances ou tout est difficile même les choses les plus desirables.[3] And of my desire to see as much as possible of You and Yours you cannot doubt. Give our best love to Elsie and take to yourself your rightful half. If she is good enough to feel offended at what seems our want of "empressement" to return her good and kind visit tell her it isn't lack of "empressement" but lack of precious metals—simply. And another thing happened which would have been somewhat in the way of our leaving the house.

See! We took your sanction of our vague plan with lightning rapidity. I've already secured a quaint and subdued creature for *gouverneur* to

---

[1] Small coins: alleged to be wealth among the Scots.
[2] Conrad's favourite moment from the final chapter: the condemned rebel keeps on walking despite hideous torments.
[3] 'There are circumstances where everything is difficult—even the most desirable things.'

Mons. Borys—and secretary to myself.[1] I get him from the hand of Father O'Gorman in Hythe. He's been Sec[y] to Sir George Campbell[2] for 3 years. Nous verrons! He comes on Sat to begin on Monday.

Interviews and negociations* took up a good few days.

Voilà tout pour le moment.

Love from us all to you and your house.

Ever yours,

J. Conrad.

To Count Szembek

*Text L.fr.*75; Najder 247

Pent Farm,

21 juin 1905.

Très cher Comte,

Il n'y a pas à dire. J'ai fait une maladie. J'ai même eu une rechute. Ceci explique, et vous fera pardonner, mon long silence.

Vos lettres si généreuses, m'ont fait le plus grand plaisir. Quant à moi, vous concevez, j'ai forcément négligé toutes mes affaires et toutes mes promesses. Mais je n'ai rien oublié. Seulement je demande un peu de patience à votre affectueuse amitié.

Ma femme prépare un petit envoi à votre adresse qui contiendra aussi une petite boite à allumettes pour Luigi dont nous faisons cas à cause de son dévouement pour vous. J'ai écrit à Paris pour l'ouvrage dont vous parlez. Quant aux volumes de mes oeuvres ils vous seront expédiés d'ici une semaine au plus tard.

Veuillez avoir la bonté, si vous voyez Mr. Trower,[3] de lui faire part de ma mauvaise fortune depuis mon retour et lui présenter mes amitiés.

Ma femme, cher Monsieur, se joint à moi dans l'expression du sentiment de profonde et solide amitié que nous vous portons. Donnez-nous de vos nouvelles.

Bien à vous de coeur.

P. S.—Borys dort, donc je n'ai rien à dire de sa part—mais je puis vous assurer qu'il parle souvent de son "ami le Comte".

Ma pièce est en répétition—et moi je ne peux pas allez y voir! Quelle

---

[1] T. F. O'Connor: his governorship lasted until September.
[2] Retired from the Indian Civil Service, he lived in Wimbledon.
[3] Harold Edward Trower, British Consular Agent on Capri since 1900, the original of Freddy Parker in Douglas's *South Wind* (Holloway, p. 503).

malechance! La visite au personnage haut placé que vous savez n'a pas eu lieu non plus.

Mes compliments au Colonel Palms s'il vous plait. A bientôt!

Translation

Very Dear Count,

There is nothing to say. I have fallen ill. I have even had a relapse. This explains, and you will pardon, my long silence.

Your so generous letters have given me the greatest pleasure. As for me, you can imagine, I have perforce neglected all my affairs and all my promises. But I have forgotten nothing. I only ask of your affectionate friendship a little patience.

My wife is preparing a small parcel for your address which will also contain a little match-box for Luigi whom we esteem for his devotion to you. I have written to Paris for the work of which you speak. As to the volumes of my works, they will be sent from here in a week at the latest.

If you see Mr. Trower, please have the goodness to tell him about my bad fortune since returning and to offer him my friendly wishes.

My wife, dear sir, joins me in expressing the sentiment of deep and solid friendship which we bear for you. Give us your news.

Always yours.

P. S. Borys is sleeping, so I have nothing to say for him—but I can assure you that he speaks often of his 'friend the Count'.

My play is being rehearsed—and I can't go to see it! What bad luck! The visit to the highly placed personage, you know whom, hasn't happened either.

My compliments to Colonel Palms, please. Goodbye for the present!

To Ford Madox Ford
Text Violet Hunt's copy, Cornell;[1] Unpublished

[Pent Farm]
Saturday p.m. [24 June 1905][2]

Dearest Ford

I've obtained a Box for next Tuesday's performance 2.30. (the last and no doubt the best) expressly at Elsie's and your intention. We are coming up by the 9.50 train. Will you join us? The box holds four.

---

[1] The original was sold at Christie's, New York, 22 November 1985.
[2] Dated from the run of *One Day More*, 25–7 June.

As I said I asked for it with Elsie and you in view and no one else, but if both of you feel disinclined to travel up, pray let me know, as I feel morally obliged to fill the places up for the honour of the Stage Society.

I quite admit the game is not worth the candle and it is proposed to you in proof of our close comradeship. Only, My dearest boy, spend a sixpence on a wire "Yes or No," as I want to be fixed early on Monday.

I had two days of rehearsals. 'Twas an experience which I do not regret.

Our dear love.

Yours,

Conrad.

P.S. Suppose that you don't have the pluck, perhaps Miss Martindale[1] would come up with Elsie. Tell the Senora that there are three Acts by Miss Alma Tadema to begin with.[2] It may please the ladies. If 'yes' we ought to meet at Charing Cross, if not in Ashford. Or at the door of the "Royalty" perhaps?[3] But that's not so good. We are going home directly after the performance.

To John Galsworthy
Text MS Forbes; J-A, 2, 20

Pent Farm.
30th June
1905

My dearest Jack

Without vain apologies and explanations I proceed to make my report of such things as may be reported on less than 3 reams of paper.

We returned here on the 24th and since then the resumé of my activities runs as follows. Gout. Tinkering at the play. Worry. Two 'mirror' papers. Touch of gout. Rehearsals of the play, with going up to London for the purpose—(which is a game not worth the candle). Loss of time. Some experience (which may or may not be of use). Performance of the play on Evening of 25th (Sunday) and in matinées on two following days[4] as after-piece to Miss Alma Tadema's 3 act comedy *The*

---

[1] Mary, Elsie's sister (and Ford's lover).
[2] Laurence Alma-Tadema's *The New Felicity*.
[3] The Royalty Theatre.
[4] Stage Society performances could be given at unorthodox times because they were unlicensed and therefore 'private'.

Near* Felicity, a thing with some smart touches and some considerable folly.

As to the success of my thing I can't say anything. I've heard that some papers praised it and some ran it down. On Tuesday when we went (like the imbeciles we are) there was some clapping but obviously the very smart audience did *not* catch on. And no wonder! On the other hand the celebrated 'man of the hour' G.B. Shaw was extatic* and enthusiastic. "Dramatist!" says he. With three plays of his own running simultaneously at the height of the season,[1] he's entitled to speak. Of course I don't think I am a dramatist. But I believe I've 3 or even 5 acts somewhere in me. At any rate the reception of the play was not such as to encourage me to sacrifice 6 months to the stage. Besides I haven't the six months to throw away.

In the end: loss of time. A thorough unsettling of the writing mood. Added weariness.

On the other hand an American Manager has already written to G.B.S. asking him to procure him a prompt copy of the play which he has a mind to play as lever de rideau[2] for Shaw's *Candida* in US. But nothing's decided as yet. And anyhow it's all unsettling unsettling.

Clear product: in a month since our return, with the worry of gout and the disturbance of the play, 7000 words written—2 Mirror papers.[3]

To day the article Autocracy and War with the motto 'Sine ira et studio' appeared in the *Fortnightly*.[4] I *hope* for a sensation. I am reduced to that.

Jessie has been fairly well. Borys too. There would be lots to say but I've just returned from *W'sea* and feel half dead. Moreover not everything can be written. There are things which must be *said* to be bearable. I am looking forward to seeing you both. The only real good news I had was from you: the news that you are again thinking of writing. Our dear love to you both.

Ever Yours

Conrad.

---

[1] *Man and Superman, You Never Can Tell*, and *Candida*.

[2] 'Curtain-raiser'; the manager may have been Charles Frohman, active on both sides of the ocean, but there was no American run of *Candida* in 1905 or 1906.

[3] 'Her Captivity' was submitted to Blackwood in late May (Blackburn, p. 184); the MS of 'Initiation' is dated 4 July (Rosenbach). These pieces come to about 10,000 words.

[4] Vol. 84, pp. 1–21. The *Fortnightly* did not print the motto ('without anger or partiality'), which is the attitude Tacitus avows towards the viler Roman emperors (*Annals*, I, i).

To E.L. Sanderson

Text MS Yale; J-A, 2, 21

[letterhead: Pent Farm]
15 July 1905 [1901?][1]

Dearest Ted.[2]

You are always that to me—however unworthy I may be to address you thus.

But if you think of me as mentally bedridden you will find it easier to forgive me. I have not been unfaithful. I have been only paralysed.

Discontent—with myself, with my work, with my general ineffectiveness—has benumbed my hand but left my affection untouched. Often Thought went to sleep—but Memory never. And what could one say? All the words seemed lifeless and I had not the courage to bombard you with things that had lost their meaning. I'd rather be pronounced a pig than a bore (observe the pun "boar". I am indeed in a bad way)—and if optimism is often wearisome such pessimism as mine grows soon intolerable in expression. I didn't want to bore you and since I believe in your freindship* I did not want to sadden you—who had causes enough not to find life particularly joyful.

You my dear fellow have done so much for me—you have *given* me so much, simply by one day recognising my existence, that I feel ashamed to have never anything to give You—nothing but a book more or less inept now and then. I am sending you one to-day—to you and your dear wife to whom I wish to be remembered humbly and affectionately—as I think of you all.

Pray don't believe that the vol I am sending is aimed at individuals. It is in origin and conception directed against the tendencies of the time—more or less of every time. We did not want to attack these with a bludgeon and perhaps the blade of our rapier is a little thin. Otherwise I am not ashamed to stand up for the book, which has already brought me some abuse and perhaps shall bring more.

---

[1] A puzzle: Jean-Aubry was perfectly correct in reading the written date as 1905; both stationery and contents, however, place the letter in 1901. The letterhead type, seven, appeared from February 1901 to March 1902. The book 'directed against the tendencies of the time' was a collaboration ('We did not want', 'our rapier'); it must be *The Inheritors*, published 26 June 1901. Either Conrad was even more than usually distracted, or the date was inserted later, in the proper ink and an excellent imitation of his hand.

[2] Edward Lancelot ('Ted') Sanderson (1867–1939) took passage in the *Torrens* in 1893; on that voyage, Conrad read him a draft of *Almayer's Folly*. Sanderson taught at Elstree, his family's preparatory school in Hertfordshire. After service in the Boer War he remained in Africa, first in Johannesburg then in Nairobi; he returned in 1910 to be Headmaster of Elstree.

However such as it is—here it is—for you two. I haven't written it all by myself but I worked very hard at it all the same—and as is always the case when I work, Your personality, my dear Ted, with one or two more, has been invisibly at the elbow of my writing hand. Thus it shall always be to the end of time—my time.

Soon you'll hear from me again. Don't for a moment suppose that this is all I wanted to tell you. I want to tell You much more than I can just now express and so I stop.

Ever Yours

J. Conrad

PS Drop me a line on a postcard: the address of Your Mother. I've been hearing of You from Jack. Jessie sends her love to your wife and children.

To Norman Douglas
Text MS Texas; J-A, 2, 22

[letterhead: Pent Farm]
15 July 1905

My dear Douglass.*

I am surprised. I dropped you a letter card with acknowledgment of the £5 lent. At least I think I must have posted it since the search in the pockets of the clothes I wore in town that day reveals nothing. I repeat my thanks.

You wouldn't believe it! But it must be said. I've had three days in bed with influenza. I must have got infected in town the day we went to see the performance of the play. I really think I am accursed.

Garnett has got (since yesterday) the *Nelson* and *Sent: Love* papers. You may be sure that his interest will be genuine. Wells I haven't seen yet and no word came either from him or his wife. I don't know where he is. Pinker has returned from US. I did not see him yet and won't see him till the tale I've in hand just now is finished: a matter of a couple of days. When I go up I'll take with me Your vol and the Fisher Unwin agreement. In the letter I've had from him he doesn't say what he has done in America either with your stuff or mine. I fear therefore: not much.

Patience et Perseverance must be our motto.

Life is hard my dear fellow and not only hard. But I am not going to groan. We'll do something yet.

My play is not a success tho' good many kind things have been said and printed.[1] All the same I felt it did not get hold of the public. I am afraid it won't do much to open the door of fortune for Your humble servant. Still I've a notion of a farcical comedy in my head but I haven't either the time or the courage to tackle it now.

Kindest regards to Yourself and Archie from wife and Borys.

Yours always

Jph. Conrad.

To Henry Newbolt

Text MS Mursia; Newbolt 311[2]

[letterhead: Pent Farm][3]

19th July 1905.

Dear Mr Newbolt

Could you let me have or even borrow for a month or so £15 out of the fund? There's always the unexpected turning up. It would be (even in the form of loan) a great convenience.

I am asked for a short article on Nelson. I don't see very well what I could write—nothing of value I fear. My ignorance of the Admiral's career is appalling. I suppose you will let me ask you a question or two should I resolve to tackle the subject. For it *is* tempting!

Will you tell me whether it would be permissible and of any use for me to try the Monthly Review[4] now and then with an article upon politics (not 'home') something in the style of the article in the current Fortnighly only of course not so long. Now and then I feel a sort of stirring up of thought (probably worthless) a sort of inwards voice (probably silly).

Believe me my dear Sir always yours

Jph. Conrad

P. S.—The book arrived.[5] Some day I will bring it to London for you to write your name and mine on the flyleaf, thus making it specially valuable apart from its intrinsic worth, which I have been eagerly

---

[1] For example, Max Beerbohm's ironic but amiable notice in the *Saturday Review* of 8 July, reprinted in *Around Theatres* (Hart-Davis, 1953), pp. 384–7.

[2] Without the first paragraph, but with the PS, now missing from the MS.

[3] Type thirteen begins.

[4] Newbolt was the founder and former editor.

[5] Newbolt's *The Year of Trafalgar*, in which he compares Nelson's tactics with those of Collingwood.

absorbing. Of course, the tone, the expression, the feeling are all what we expect from you. To my mind (not skilled, of course, in these matters but still a seaman's mind) your discussion of the tactics seems to settle the question. And don't take for an impertinence my admiration (and wonder) of the truly seamanlike way in which you handle your unanswerable (I think) arguments. I have been absorbingly interested and, lying on my back unable to write, I could without any compunction give myself up to the enjoyment. Many thanks.

To Edward Garnett
Text MS Colgate; G.199

[letterhead: Pent Farm]
20th July 1905

Dearest Edward

I am rather ashamed of the silly thing I had to send to the Speaker;[1] tho' I think that to say it contains all my philosophy of life is a severe hit. But I suppose you know best. For myself I don't know what my philosophy is. I was not even aware I had it. Am sorry to think I must have since you say so. Shall I die of it do you think?

Your article on Sagas first rate[2] and extracts quoted are good. I quite see how one could get dramas out of that. I own I am much more interested in Your drama than in all the sagas that were ever written. I don't believe their merits are very peculiar but I do believe that You can make use of that quarry.

I am anxious to see if only one act of your play.[3] I would keep it only one day/return duly registered. Do let me have a look into the chamber of horrors of your brain.

I send you 2 papers by Norman. Pray do something[4]

---

[1] 'Books', *Speaker*, 15 July, pp. 369–70; reprinted in *Notes on Life and Letters*.
[2] 'The Icelandic Sagas', *Speaker*, 3 June, pp. 236–7. Garnett praises the sagas for their narrative terseness.
[3] *The Feud*, produced in 1909.   [4] The rest is missing.

To Henry Newbolt
Text MS Mursia; Newbolt 311 (with omissions)

[letterhead: Pent Farm]
Saturday [22 July 1905][1]

My dear Sir.

Many thanks for cheque (£15) received this morning.

At *your leisure* perhaps you will give me a word of advice as to what to read. I know Southey's 'Life'[2] and that's about all.

Has the Admiral's corresp[ce] with Collingwood[3] been published? You see I would never attempt anything historical. I know nothing except what every one knows. But of a life that in its whole was a Great Masterpiece something can always be said—something that would not be mere rhetoric since it would spring from deep conviction.

From a perusal of letters one could get the best impression of the man.

I've re-read your book on Trafalgar and I can only repeat that your argumentation is absolutely convincing.

Believe me dear Sir very sincerely yours

Jph. Conrad.

To Norman Douglas
Text TS/MS Texas; J-A, 2, 23

Pent Farm
Stanford nr. Hythe
Kent.
July 24th 1905

My dear Douglass.*

I enclose Edward Garnett's letter because it expresses exactly what I have felt on the subject of the two papers.

With the N[elson] I will try Lippincott certainly and that is the only opening. For—it is very true—I run the risk of being kicked downstairs by the average British Editor. You don't allow enough for the imbecility of human nature.

The objection to the Westminster Review is the one Garnett states. Moreover no one reads the thing.

As to S[entimental] L[ove] I do not know what to do with it. Hadn't you

---

[1] Three days after the letter of the 19th, according to Newbolt.
[2] His *Life of Nelson* (1813).
[3] A vice-admiral, he headed the lee line at Trafalgar and took command when Nelson died.

better have it back to reconsider and re-write on broader lines than an attack upon Finck implies?[1]

To introduce the thin end of the wedge you must give me acceptable stuff on other than literary grounds. You must get a footing before you can begin to hit. I beg you earnestly to finish your article on *The Russian* at once and send it to me. Don't be disgusted or discouraged.

> Kindest regards from us all
> Yours ever
>
> Jph Conrad.

PS   Depend upon it that everything possible shall be done. But I advise you to take Garnett's advice to heart.

When you are in Naples could you, when lunching at the Hotel de Genève ask the porter about my stick which I think I must have left there. Black with silver head. Would it be possible to send it by post wrapped up in paper? Or if not—please take charge of it for me for a time.

The address as the heading of this is the correct one. *Don't* put Ashford on the envelope because it sends the letter astray. Vale.

To William Blackwood
Text MS NLS; Blackburn 186

> [letterhead: Pent Farm]
> 9th Augt 1905.

Dear Mr Blackwood.

I was glad to get proofs for 'Maga' and it was kind of you to write the friendly note.[2]

I've returned the slips yesterday after making a few verbal alterations.

Thanks for your kind inquiries. My wife is fairly well now. We spent the winter in Italy, in Capri: but the weather was not favourable.

The other day I saw Mr Meldrum and heard from him with great satisfaction that you were enjo[y]ing fair health.

I am, my dear Sir, always faithfully yours

> Joseph Conrad.

---

[1] Henry Theophilus Finck, author of *Romantic Love* (Macmillan, 1887)?
[2] This note, sent with the proofs of 'Her Captivity' for the September *Blackwood's*, is given by Blackburn, p. 185.

To the Editor, *Temple Bar*
Text TS BL Add MSS 55264; Unpublished

[letterhead: Pent Farm]
Aug 19, 1905

Sir,

I am obliged for your letter of the 18th inst. with reference to the January issue of "Temple Bar".[1]

In regard to your kind invitation to contribute I have communicated the offer to my agent Mr. J. B. Pinker.

I am, Sir, yours faithfully
Joseph Conrad

The Editor,
The Temple Bar Magazine.

To J.B. Pinker
Text MS Berg; Unpublished

[letterhead: Pent Farm]
1905
20th Sept. Thursday.

My dear Pinker

You may laugh or not but that damned tax gatherer's letter cost me a fit of gout. I've been in bed a week. Everything is thrown back, but not so very much after all as I've been able to do a little except on 2 days when the pain was too great.

I am sending you one copy of my *Nelson* with the idea you will make use of it in America as a piece of writing.[2] At any rate the copyright there should be obtained. Perhaps Harper's Weekly may fire it off in the Trafalgar week? Or others or anybody.

Another copy is gone to the Standard with a demand for 25 pounds, I should think that twenty is sure—if they are not ashamed to haggle over a good piece of work done at their own demand. If any hitch occurs *you* will place it I am sure. Meantime please advance me the £20 now which I want much and which are safe in England. Besides please send a cheque for £14 to T.F. O'Connor 87 Sutherland Avenue. W. His three months are up and I am parting with him. He does the boy no good so it

---

[1] To the consternation of its habitual readers, the editor intended to cut the price of this sedate monthly from one shilling to sixpence, strengthen its fiction list, and seek a wider market (Macmillan archives, BL).
[2] No separate American publication of 'The Heroic Age' is known.

is better he should go. Next month I shall have a girl which* will have only 3 gs per month and who they say can teach besides being a good stenographer. We shall see. At any rate it will be cheaper. This £14 may not be covered by the problematical U.S. rights of the Nelson. Whatever is short you shall deduct from what I'll ask for the *Mediterranean* paper[1] which is in the oven and shall be served to you hot in a very few days. Meantime *Chance* simmers slowly on to be ready by the end of the year.

Will you be so nice as to take a year's subscription at Romeike[2] for 'Conrad's' cuttings as I shall want to know what will be said of the *Mirror* and other things. Also *most important* send me particulars for my income in the year 01/02 for the tax people with whom I am corresponding. A thousand apologies for all these demands.

Yours always

Conrad.

To John Galsworthy
Text MS Forbes; Unpublished

[letterhead: Pent Farm]

21 Sep^t 1905

Dearest Jack

Peace on your house and Allah's blessing. If I hadn't been so lamed and cowed by gout I would have asked permission to come and sign, since two witnesses a man must have. Better friends you two may have (indeed that's not difficult) but none that love you so much.[3]

I won't say here what I've done and undergone lately, leaving all that for viva voce. Are You beginning the domestic life to morrow in Addison Road?

I've just finished a Nelson—a 3000 words utterance for the *Stand^d*'s Trafalgar day number. Today I am doing nothing—just sitting still and thinking of you dear People.

Jess and Borys's dear love

Always Yours,

Jph. Conrad

---

[1] 'The Inland Sea': it later split into 'The Nursery of the Craft' and 'The "Tremolino"'.
[2] Romeike and Curtice, Ltd, press-cutting agents of Ludgate Circus.
[3] The Galsworthys were married on 23 September.

To John Galsworthy
Text MS POSK; Danilewiczowa

[letterhead: Pent Farm]
23 Sept. 1905

Dearest, best Jack

Your dear letter arrived just as my note went off.

I haven't the pluck even to *look* at a journey of any sort. And to start on a pilgrimage without faith is the worst thing one can do. Here at any rate I do some work. I've got into the gro[o]ve. A change would unsettle me I fear. Thank you my dear fellow for all you say; and no doubt you are right—but.......

Everything seems frightfully difficult and writing most of all.

Our best love to you both.

Yours ever

Jph. Conrad

To T.F. O'Connor
Text MS NYPL; Unpublished

[letterhead: Pent Farm]
1905
26th Sept

Dear Mr O'Connor.[1]

Many thanks for Your kindly missive. My wife who sends her kindest regards has prepared a parcel of your things, which will leave by tomorrow's morning post.

I need not take advantage of your truly friendly offer which you may be sure I appreciate in the spirit in which it was made. I've arranged for my typing to be done in London; and Borys will be provided for by the end of the week.

Pray receive the cordial assurance of our best wishes for your health prosperity and happiness. I trust that whenever You come this way You will not pass us by. We think alike on many points; and during our short but close intercourse I've learned to appreciate the worth of Your character, tact and kindliness.

I trust Nice will suit your health. It looks here as if we were to have a horrid wet autumn.

---

[1] Conrad's Irish sectetary, Borys's 'governor', at the end of his three months' service. Borys remembered him as 'a tall cadaverous person with lank black hair, a quantity of which appeared to have migrated to his upper lip, from which it drooped like a forgotten garment on a clothes-line' (*My Father*, p. 41).

Believe me, dear Mr O'Connor, always faithfully yours

Jph. Conrad

PS   I enclose a letter which arrived on Saturday.

To J.B. Pinker
Text MS Berg; Unpublished

[letterhead: Pent Farm]
6th Oct 1905

My dear Pinker.

I had a letter from Methuen in which he said that he made you a proposition as to the *M of the S* papers. He suggested further his desire to have *three* novels from me under some sort of contract ('eminently satisfactory' he says) and explained the publisher's point of view in such a transaction.

I acknowledged his letter with thanks and on both points answered, that: "Mr Pinker had a free hand in dealing with all my work for which he was qualified in every way and mostly by this that he understood me thoroughly". This is the gist and almost the textual wording of my reply which was very civil but quite short. You *do* by this time know me thoroughly. I didn't write to you, first, because I didn't think you wanted to hear my views in this matter which is eminently one for Your judgment, and, next, because I expected to come up to day to see you, when, I thought, you could mention the proposal to me if you wished.

I'll be with you on Monday but meantime I may say this much as to the *M of the Sea* that I want you to squeeze out every penny there is in the book form on this side; for I am anxious to see my indebt[ed]ness to you beginning to be reduced. On the other hand it would be of undoubted advantage to both of us if the book had a good send off. The public taste being in some sort unac[c]ountable a success may lurk in the most unlikely stuff. I don't in the least care who has it. I venture to suggest however that the season announces itself as very full, all the lists seem to be made up, and that it would be good perhaps to hold the vol: over till after the new year?

The "Inland Sea" paper completing the series is ready and typed. I'll bring it with me on Monday my intention being to give it a final look over on Sunday afternoon.

As to Methuen's larger proposal you know best what to do with it. All my energies and all my thoughts are taken up with writing as it is proper they should be. But as you have asked me, I'll put down here some considerations which occur to my mind. And first: Harpers. How will it affect our position towards them—in this country and perhaps also on the other side? They have been on the whole very decent, taking my stuff at fair prices—(H James, 2 sea papers, Autocracy). Methuen has no periodicals, has he? How if being bound to him should make it difficult to serialise my copy?

I don't mind being bound to him myself; what I am anxious for is that *you* should keep a free hand, because I've a greater confidence in your skill than in any arrangement with a publisher. Harpers is not perfection but I think we ought to keep in with them. It is quite possible I may catch on in the States if they work me well there.

But you being 'inside' know best what to do. For the rest we may have a talk on Monday.

———— You will be glad to hear that the income-tax people have abandonned* the claim for £50 *completely*. It seems a sort of miracle. You said it would be so. A man who can read the mind of a tax-gatherer fills me with astonishment and respect. I begin to be positively afraid of you. Many thanks for your advice which guided my correspondence and for the accts which backed up my case. For current year I am assessed with full deductions at £389 which is considerably less than the 800 they tried on at first.[1]

Miss Wright[2] has taken up duties from the 1st Oct. at £3 per month, the first month being on trial. It looks like a success with Borys. Her stenography is good; her typing so far very slow if correct. But she is new to the machine it must be said. I am having a carbon copy made now of everything.

Proof of my *Nelson* has come and gone back to the Standard. As I distinctly stated my price (£25) that affair seems all right. I don't suppose I'll get the cheque much before the end of this month when I shall send it on to You. I am rather glad this is settled. The Nelson is quite fit to go into the *M of the S* volume—is it not? As you may have remarked I've put the personal note in that too since all the papers have it thus making the unity of the book as a set of autobiographical recollections.

The 'Inland Sea' paper (the last) is discursive, with classical allusions and really not so bad. You might suggest to Harpers that they ought to take it as it deals with the Mediterranean.[3] If you hold the book over till Jan[y] there will be plenty of time.

[1] In the 1904–5 fiscal year, income was taxed at one shilling in the pound (5%).
[2] Jessie's cousin.
[3] And Conrad had promised them a Mediterranean novel.

I have been much interrupted in Sep[t]. Gout. Two sets of 4 days' guests: the Hopes first and then Jack Galsworthy with wife. Shaw has been writing urging me to a play and practically guaranteeing acceptance somewhere. Altogether I feel more alive. I've done a fair bit of *Chance* and shall devote myself to it exclusively, now.

I am much steadier in mind and I feel more on terms with my work than I have done for the làst 12 months—or even 24 for that matter.

I am however worried a little with the balance of my debts. I wish you would help me out there. It is a thing quite apart and not depending on MS at all. As you know I have £*115* to draw but I can't dispose of it in bulk and the country people at this time of the year want their money. If you lend it to me I would repay you in 7 months by monthly instalments of say £15 for which You would get cheques signed by Newbolt and Rothenstein, beginning in December—or perhaps I could arrange to begin in Nov[er]. I don't see any other way to get rid of the only uneasiness that is worrying me now. Do my dear fellow help me out in this for I really need it for my peace of mind; and the transaction is not really very gigantic. The relief however would be immense. I don't, you understand, ask you to stretch our arrangement as to MS and supplies. It is quite a special service I ask you to render me for the good of the cause.

Kindest regards

Always Yours Conrad.

To J.B. Pinker
Text MS Berg; Unpublished

[letterhead: Pent Farm]

Thursday [12 October 1905][1]

My dear Pinker

Chance TS (*50* pp) received but by the mark on my MS I am under the impression that you have some 20 pp more. I[f] not, then you ought to have them. But please make inquiries of your staff and I think You will find that the whole lot has *not* been sent back to me. Of course I have it here in *MS* but should like to have the TS too if possible.

No doubt you have discovered that *Inland Sea* is not 5 but pretty near 12 thousand words in length and certainly no less than eleven. As *Youth*

---

[1] Soon after the delivery of 'The Inland Sea', promised for Monday, 9 October, but seemingly handed over on a Wednesday. The letter of 20 October shows (a) that Pinker now had the essay, (b) that Conrad was too 'absorbed' on Thursday the 19th to write a letter himself.

(14000 w) fetched £50 (serially) in '98 Eng'sh rights alone I don't think I 'skinned' you very much by taking an advance of £30. It seemed to me, yesterday, you thought I rather did. And the stuff, I say it confidently, in literary merit and general interest is better than *Youth*. I suppose you'll smile at the 'literary merit' but I think we have the right to point it out as a Grocer points out the good condition of his cheese; and believe in it too in good faith as the Grocer believes in the good quality of his wares. One thing is as absolutely real as the other—and both are just a question of taste. If you get more for it I'll expect to be credited with the excess for the purposes of drawing. You must, my dear fellow, allow me *all* my serial prices (less interest, and commission of course) in full for this year and the next and be content with being reimbursed mainly from proceeds in book form.—What about the *Initiation* paper? When you have time to scribble me a word you may tell me whether it's placed and where.[1]

Always yours

Jph Conrad

To Norman Douglas
Text MS Texas; J-A, 2, 24

[letterhead: Pent Farm]
18th Oct 1905

My dear long suffering Douglass.*

You must have thought me a conscienceless brute. Alas! I have been an overworked one. I may safely add that I haven't had more than 3 weeks of decent health in the whole time since I left Capri.

I enclose here a note for £5 and have wired Green to draw on me. Thanks my dear fellow, ever so much.

I am afraid you are bitterly disappointed at the slowness in placing your articles. My dear Douglass believe me that all that could be done has been done and is being done. The first campaign failed but I am going to open the second when we go to London for a week end Nov. Even the Nelson may be rammed in somewhere after the heat of the centenary is over. I don't see what good it would do to you to get the stuff back. I have talked of it in many places—and if suddenly anybody were to ask me for it I would not like to have to say I hadn't got it.

---

[1] Blackwood had offered £22 for this piece on 22 September (Meldrum, pp. 186–7). For whatever reasons, Pinker was still keeping Conrad in the dark about the offer in early November.

Hueffer's work was kept off for 3 years and now it is all going as easy as can be.[1] Some of my stuff has been in Pink[er]'s drawer two years now. It is beastly no doubt; but if we once break the door open there will be no waste.

Even if you do go to India leave the articles behind You here. Don't forget my dear fellow that your point of view in general is the unpopular one. It is intellectual and uncompromising. This does not make things easier. People don't want intelligence. It worries them—and they demand from their writers as much subserviency as from their footmen if not rather more.

I trust you are not angry with me. I have had a deucedly hard time of it lately. I am just just keeping my head above water.

Good bye for the present. I'll write again soon. Kindest regards from my wife. Always Yours

Jph. Conrad

To J.B. Pinker
Text MS Berg; Unpublished

[letterhead: Pent Farm]
20 Oct. 1905

My dear Pinker.

Yesterday after getting up very early to work at Benavides I asked Miss W[right] to answer your letter. To day being less absorbed I wish to supplement what she has written by the remark that the *In^d Sea* as it stands summarises a certain individual view of the Mediterranean—with facts to back up its authenticity. It is in truth much more of a revelation of a personality than I, perhaps, meant it to be. I thought that as a piece of feeling and a piece of writing some review would print it on its merits. On the other hand I am not in a position to pick and choose; and I am perfectly confident that you are doing what is best under the circumstances.

Nevertheless I can not but feel acutely the necessity of an action which destroys whatever merit there may be in the paper, and takes from me the only ground of distinction between myself and a hundred story tellers all very excellent and infinitely better than I can ever hope to be. I do not say this in affected modesty. If I do assert any sort of value for my work (and evidently I do assert since I publish) it is not on the ground of

---

[1] *The Soul of London* was a critical and financial success.

superiority but on that of distinction—or say *distinctiveness* rather, to avoid all offence.

This being so the question suggests itself whether as a matter of policy it were not better to work Conrad on his own ground instead of, in a manner, trying to pass him off for something he can never be in a truly satisfactory manner? There is a certain strength to be derived from the nature of things *as they are*—not from what we would like them to be. You are Scots enough to understand both my sentiment and my argument. As to what is feasible, practicable or expedient it is for You to judge in the circumstances.[1] These too must be looked at *as they are* not as we would like them to be.

Kindest regards
Yours always

Jph Conrad.

To H.G. Wells
Text MS Illinois; J A, a, a5

[Pent Farm]
20 Oct 1905
evening

Dearest H. G.

All luck to Kipps! I've just seen that he came out today.

I suppose A J Dawson told you he has seen me down—very much down. I got up and went down again some four distinct times since that time; having nevertheless managed to do some 13 thousand words—the last paper of the Mirror of the Sea vol. It won't appear till after the New Year but anyhow it is off my chest.

It is all very monotonous—my news is. I stick here fighting with disease and creeping imbecility—like a cornered rat, facing fate with a big stick that is sure to descend and crack my skull before many days are over. If I haven't been to see you (which I admit is beastly and ungrateful) I haven't been to see anyone else—except Ford and, of course, the indispensable Pinker, but that only officially—in his office. As to Ford he is a sort of life-long habit of which I am not ashamed because he is a much better fellow than the world gives him credit for. After pulling off with an awful effort the first 15000 words of a thing

---

[1] The complaints may refer to the essay's division into 'The "Tremolino"' and 'The Nursery of the Craft'.

which is supposed (for trade purposes) to be a novel[1] I took an afternoon's rush to Winchelsea and back letting the air blow through me: a silly, perhaps, and expensive restorative but the only one left to me. As to working regularly in a decent and orderly and industrious manner I've given that up from sheer impossibility. The damned stuff comes out only by a kind of mental convulsion lasting two/three or more days—up to a fortnight—which leaves me perfectly limp and not very happy, exhausted emotionally to all appearance but secretly irritable to the point of savagery. You understand that in either condition I am not very fit to show myself to my fellow creatures.

Jessie begs you to explain to your wife that the only reason she has not yet put in an appearance is simply because she has no longer the pluck to drive herself or even to be driven by the lad. The mare is not very good with motors it is true but there's no danger really. However I don't insist because with a defective heart any sort of emotion is certainly not good. So she walks to and fro on the sheltered bit of road near the farm to the amount of about a mile per day.

Perhaps You've heard that my little play was performed by the S[tage] S[ociety] under Colvin's wing as it were. Complete failure I would call it. G.B.S thinks I ought to write another. That luxury is out of my reach however. Yet the temptation is great.

I[f] you don't know already it may interest you to hear that in Anatole France's last book there are two allusions to you.[2] Whatever may be the differences of opinion it cannot be denied that A F apart from being a great master of prose is one of the finest minds of our time.[3] If he has not understood you completely he has certainly apprehended your value.

One passage begins: "They are few who have tried to penetrate the future from pure curiosity, without moral intention or an optimistic bias. I know only of H. G Wells" etc etc. (allusion to Time Machine) the other, only two lines, runs: "A naturalist philosopher who never quails before his own thought, H. G Wells has said: 'Man is not final.'"

Those things read in their proper place demonstrate that you have produced a strong impression upon a man who anyway is far above the common in his intelligence and his sympathies.

Can you tell me if the *Invisible Man* is out of print? I want to have it.

---

[1] *Chance?* Cf. letter of [12 October].

[2] 'Last' in the sense of 'latest': *Sur la pierre blanche* (Paris, Calmann-Lévy, 1905), an assembly of philosophical discussions and tales; the allusions come on pp. 186–7 and 319.

[3] Conrad wrote short pieces on France in 1904 and 1908; they are collected in *Notes on Life and Letters*.

Are you going to arrange soon for a uniform edition? There are a good many volumes already to make a fine backing for *Kipps*. I wonder what criticism he will get. I fear that whatever he gets will be unsatisfactory. The worst of our criticism is that it is so barren. Most of our reviewers seem absolutely unable to understand in a book anything but facts and the most elementary qualities of rendering. Thus Wells gets reviewed on the same plane with X.Y.Z and a hundred others; whereas the whole point is that H.G. Wells is unique in the way he approaches his facts and absolutely distinctive in the way he leaves them.—Our love to you all

Yours ever

J Conrad.

To Ada Galsworthy
Text J-A, 2, 26

Pent Farm.

Stanford, Near Hythe, Kent.

21 Oct., 1905

My Dear Mrs. Galsworthy,

Pardon the blotch!

Jessie being laid up quite with an atrocious headache it falls to my lot to express our pleasure at Chris's noble feeling and behaviour.[1] We have, as you may have casually remarked, a dog ourselves, whose mental and moral disposition under the trials of this imperfect world is a source of never ending concern and pride.

I don't know whether I ought in the same breath to mention my delight at your approval of "Abeille."[2] I put it in your hands with confidence and trust—but one never knows. Henceforth I shall dismiss all unworthy fears. I must tell you in confidence that, some time ago, dear Jack sat upon me so heavily for my admiration of *Thaïs*[3] that I promised to myself to walk very delicately in the way of recommending books for the future. I mention this because this very morning I came upon his letter. Its tone of lofty disapproval filled me again with renewed dread and astonishment. I can do the lofty disapproval myself pretty well, but Jack is simply perfect.

Your welcome note contains nothing but good news—it is exactly what we would like letters from people we love always to be. We rejoiced

---

[1] He was the Galsworthys' spaniel.
[2] 'Honey-bee', a fairy-tale by Anatole France, 1883.
[3] France's novel (1890), the story of a courtesan who turns into a desert saint.

to hear that the little house[1] has been tamed at last and brought to know its masters. But is it tamed enough for the reading of "Abeille" to be accomplished decorously within its doors? It wouldn't be a bad test. I entreat you not to relax your vigilance. Houses are naturally rebellious and inimical to man. As to dear Jack, I picture him to myself outwards, as impassible as fate, facing the loose pages of MS. in the solitude and silence of the dining room. I don't envy him his talent—the great gift which grows more apparent with every line he writes—for that would be a sin, but I do envy him the quiet force of his determination, for that is power, a human thing which it is not in human nature to behold without envy.

Our dear love. Always, dear Mrs. Galsworthy, affectionately and obediently yours.

To H.A. Gwynne
Text TS Yale; Unpublished

[letterhead: Pent Farm]
October 22nd. 1905.

Dear Sir.[2]

I have some readers of my own; not so many as the Standard but still too many to be individually and privately addressed with an explanation. I trust that, in fairness to a man who has always treated the intelligence of his public with respect, you will find room in your next issue for a note of two lines or so to the effect that: "At Mr. Conrad's desire we state that in his contribution to the Nelson number we have taken out carelessly a material passage, thus destroying the sequence of thought and rendering unintelligible the opening sentence of the next paragraph.[3]

This being a mere statement of fact I leave it in your hands with perfect confidence.

But further you will allow me to make one or two simple remarks. Had the article been 'edited' with proper respect for another man's work I would have said nothing. But that sort of suppression in defiance of

---

[1] 14 Addison Road, Kensington.
[2] H. A. Gwynne (1865–1950), editor of the *Standard*, 1904–11, and *Morning Post*, 1911–37; formerly Reuters' chief war correspondent in China, Greece, and South Africa.
[3] The essay known as 'The Heroic Age' appeared under the title 'Palmam qui meruit ferat' (Nelson's motto, 'Let him who merits bear the palm') in a Trafalgar Day supplement to the *Standard*, 21 October, p. 13. The excised paragraph, restored in *The Mirror of the Sea* (XLVIII), begins 'Never more shall British seamen'.

simple sense (I say nothing of feeling) is not editing—it is mangling. In the face of my offer to shorten (if needed) the article it is unjustifiable.

It would have been so even if applied to the merest hack work; but that a piece of writing, which—whatever its value—has been deeply felt and meditated with care, should receive such treatment, makes me wonder why on earth you wanted to print it at all? I beg to remind you that though asked to write I have never considered you as bound to take the thing. I said so emphatically in my letter when sending you the M.S.

And the paragraph was material. It rounded my view of the memorable day as the last great action of sailing fleets and linked the past to the present in the allusion to the old auspicious names of ships and men keeping watch to day over that inheritance of glory your number was intended to celebrate.

I am, yours obediently,

J C

To J.B. Pinker
Text MS Berg; Unpublished

[Pent Farm]
22^d Oct 1905

My dear Pinker

This is a true copy of the letter I've forwarded to the Ed^{or} of the Standard. You will gather from it what has happened to my Nelson, the only piece of individual writing (with the exception of W. Sichel's contribution) in that number made up of the cheapest sort of hack work and utterly insignificant documents(?)[1]

You know (at least I hope so) that I am not inclined to hold a fancifully high opinion of my work. The thing may be rubbish, I trust it is not so. The point however is that it has been *asked for* 3 times and that they were at liberty to decline it. I also did say clearly that I could shorten it by 2 to 5 hundred words tho' I was not anxious for the job.

I do not know what you may think; as to myself without attaching too much importance to a piece of contemptuous stupidity (it looks like it) I felt I could not pass it altogether in silence. Literary sensitiveness has nothing to do with it. I think the line should be drawn at botching not the spirit or sentiment of the work but the mere *literal sense*. The preservation of that last the least conceited man may justly claim if not from

---

[1] Walter Sichel wrote on Lady Hamilton; the issue also included a paper by Conrad's admirer A. J. Dawson.

self respect then from respect for his readers. And as I know enough of
my public to be aware that it contains a certain proportion of men of
intelligence I think I've done the right thing by asking the Standard to
insert the note. If no notice is taken I shall do my very best to get the
letter published in some other daily. What do you think?

Yours

Conrad.

To H.A. Gwynne

Text TS Yale;[1] Unpublished

[Pent Farm]
October 24th, 1905

Two literary men are not enough to destroy a glaring fact. It may be
remembered that I too can read large print and, so far at least, am a
literary man myself. Neither am I easily dazzled by a display of their
anonymous authority—especially as it goes just a bit too far. Had they
simply said: Conrad ought to be told he's making a fuss over a very small
matter—I would have allowed to such an opinion all the moral weight it
deserves.

But they have overshot the mark. They affirm there is nothing wrong
whatever with the 'editing'. That the meaning is clear. Is it? The
opening lines of the par. immediately following the suppressed passage
run: "This the Navy of the Twenty Years War knew well how to do, and
never better—etc—etc." . . . This—what? I defy any one uninformed by
the sight of my copy to discover any sort of meaning in those lines as they
stand in print. I defy the two literary men. Can they tell me what the
Navy of the Twenty Years War knew well how to do? They cannot tell.
No one can tell. The opening as you have printed it has no sense and no
connection with anything that goes before. This being so what, pray, is
the word untrue doing in your letter?

But as it is there, I meet it with the direct re-assertion of the charge of
mangling. The journalistic routine has nothing to do with it. You had
my article three weeks together with my offer to shorten it. And I would
not have objected to justifiable editing. If the word careless displeases
you I am ready enough to confess that I don't like it either. It has not
enough force in this connection.

As to the elementary routine of journalism I admit I am ignorant of its
mystery—yet not so ignorant as to mistake the letter I received from you

---

[1] A carbon-copy without salutation and farewell.

for a part of its usual practice. To meet a remonstrance by giving one the lie in the face of a patent fact is not the routine of journalism. It cannot be! That sort of thing has another name.

To Ada Galsworthy
Text MS Forbes; Unpublished

[letterhead: Pent Farm]
31 oct. 05

My dear Ada.

I receive the privilege conferred upon me to address you thus with delight and gratitude.

We are sorry to hear your news about Jack.[1] And he writes! He's wonderful! The reading of Your good letter inspired me with a great desire to come up at once and see you. I would have done so too but for the unhappy fact of Jessie being in bed ever since Thursday last.

She had a violent fit of palpitation in the morning which alarmed me to some extent. I sent off for the doctor. His verdict is nervous breakdown of a sort; nothing dangerous in itself but with a defective heart most undesirable and needing to be watched. Absolute rest was the prescription.

To tell you the truth I saw it coming for the last month but hoped it would pass off. Fact is our life or else life in general is beginning to tell on her. The sameness of existence varied by nothing but anxiety during my fits of gout is I suppose proving a bit too much. And as I don't see any end to it or way out of it I don't feel over happy. There's no doubt that the ordeal she went through *after* the operation has shaken her up considerably. But, as Bruce Clark said, she made a record recovery— and that is all he cared about. For my part I always felt that the wonder would have to be paid for sometime or other.

As you know her you will not be surprised to hear she has picked up considerably and is now looking very good and bright sitting up in bed dressing dolls for the village children. At first she was exceedingly tired—quite done up. But after slumbering for[2]

---

[1] A heavy cold, in spite of which he was working on 'Danaë', later known as *The Country House* (Dupré, pp. 118–19).

[2] MS incomplete; Conrad must have mentioned plans to visit London – see the next letter.

To Ada Galsworthy
Text MS Forbes; J-A, 2, 27

[letterhead: Pent Farm]
2 Nov 1905

My dear Ada.

No doubt I wrote stupidly of our coming up. I don't think we can come up before the 15th and I meant to say so. Our most affectionate thanks to you and Jack for inviting us. We will come but not to stay. We could not think of inflicting ourselves upon You while you are still busy 'tuning up' the little house.

Jessie is better but of course she remains under the impression of the scare still. Of myself I won't speak. I am writing, like dear Jack, but unlike him I am writing a worthless sort of stuff.

What does Jack think of that political article of mine in the Fortnightly? As a piece of prophecy both as to Russia and Germany I think it comes off rather.

I am greatly moved by the news from Russia.[1] Certainly a year ago I never hoped to live to see all that. It's just ½ a century since the Crimean war, forty two years since the liberation of peasants—a great civic work in which even we Poles were allowed to participate. In the words of my uncle's memoirs this great event opened the way to a general reform of the state.[2] Very few minds saw it at the time. And yet the starting point of orderly rational programme in accord with the national spirit was there!

Jessie sends her dear love. I think I will run up next week for a day and knock at the fierce little house's door if I may at about one o'clock.

With love to dear Jack I remain always most affectionately Yours

Jph Conrad.

---

[1] The decree of 30 October announced an extension of civil liberties, a strengthening of the Duma (the new national assembly, elected by limited franchise), the restoration of the Finnish constitution, and the resignation of certain particularly obscurantist ministers.

[2] In his *Memoirs*, Tadeusz Bobrowski (1829–94) also observed that 'the greater the scope of the first reforms, the slower would be the pace of the subsequent reforms' (Najder, *Familial Eyes*, p. 36). The Russian serfs were emancipated in 1861; those in Russian Poland, in 1864.

To J.B. Pinker
Text MS Berg; Unpublished

[Pent Farm]
[early November 1905][1]

My dear Pinker.

I answered this saying that You may still have a recent piece of my writing unplaced and that I would ask you to send it on, and that its title was *Initiation*.[2]

Of course you will do what you'll think fit; but in any case please drop a line to Gibbs.

Yours

Conrad.

I suppose you have had the Standard cheque all right?

To Ada Galsworthy
Text MS Forbes; Unpublished

[letterhead: Pent Farm][3]
10 Nov 1905

My dear Ada.

Let me congratulate you and Jack on having escaped my visit. I came along feeling so miserable that my call would have poisoned the rest of the day for you. J'avais la mort dans l'âme and a gout-boot on my right foot. After leaving your doorstep I trudged down Add[is]on Rd with a lamentable limp and feeling that if a policeman spoke to me I would burst into tears. Poor Sauter[4] had no luck. I wonder what he thinks of my apparition. He was very good but he must have been bored half to death. I owe him a visit of apology. To you two, since You've escaped the infliction, I'll not apologise because my intentions were really good.

Jessie is not quite well yet. She sends her love and a[n] Xmas pudding. Her intentions are good too; and I hope the pudding will not depress you very much.

I am ashamed to say I am in bed with gout. Still we expect to be in London on Wednesday to stay a week or so.

---

[1] Philip Gibbs, editor of the *Tribune*, a new penny paper starting in January, asked for a 5,000 word story on 2 November; Conrad wrote on the back of this request.
[2] Already placed: see p. 285, n. 1. Gibbs took 'The "Tremolino"', publishing it on 22 January.
[3] Letterhead fourteen begins here.   [4] Galsworthy's brother-in-law, the painter.

Borys after giving me a hurried message of love for you has rushed downstairs to pack up the pudding himself for Mrs Jack.

Au revoir donc very soon. Our best love. Very affectionately and obediently yours

Jph Conrad.

To William Rothenstein
Text MS Harvard; Unpublished

36 Princes' Square.
22^d Nov
1905

Dearest Will.

Borys is ill. All our arrangements are knocked on the head.

It's obviously something more than a sore throat and it would be as well if You kept away till You hear from me.[1]

Don't for goodness' sake alarm Alice unnecessarily. We here are not alarmed but of course greatly put out. I won't be able to get away to call on you just yet.

Would you be good enough to sound Newbolt whether the balance of the Grant money could be paid to me in monthly instalments of £20 or if that's too much of £15—beginning say on the first of Dec*er*?

It would be a great convenience.

Our best love to you all.

Yours in haste
J. Conrad.

To H.G. Wells
Text MS Illinois; J-A, 2, 28

32 St Agnes' Place
Kennington Park
28th Nov. /05

Dearest H G.

We came to London, after my last fit of gout, for a few days; but last Sat. week Mr Borys became seedy and by Monday developed scarlet fever. We came over here to be near him. He's shut up in a nursing home the London Nurses' Association has in Kennington Pk Rd for infectious cases. The Lond: Fever Hosp: was full.

---

[1] The Rothensteins had young children.

I don't see him now, but Jessie helps to nurse him relieving the professional for 3–4 hours every afternoon. The case is not particularly severe. The temp: never went above 100.5 and for the last two days has been normal. But the poor little devil is very weak and unfortunately since yesterday dysenteric symptoms appeared—as I feared they would. I own that this worries me considerably.

This closes the account of the current calamities. What's to come next I can't imagine and don't try to. No doubt it will be bad enough when it does come. Meantime I've been writing silly short stories in which there is no pleasure and no permanent profit. But for temporary purposes they come handy. All the same I am sick of them.

Drop me a line to say how *Kipps* goes off. The few reviews I've seen were practically good tho' not shining with intelligence. Upon a mental review of your career, my dear Wells, I am forced to the conclusion that both kinds of your work are strangely and inexplicably underestimated. Praise of course there is in plenty but its quality is not worthy of you. And even the attacks of which one would expect more comprehension do nothing but nibble at the hem of the mantle. The cause of this (setting aside the superiority of your intelligence) it would be curious to investigate and on those lines a fundamental sort of study upon HG Wells could be written. I wish I could liberate my tongue-tied soul. But perhaps what I could find to say if it ever came out would be as disappointing to you as it would be to myself.

Coming to the particular case of the latest book I must say here this at least: that the high expectation roused instantaneously as it were by the sight of the 4th or 5th instalment in the P. M G.[1] is fulfilled to the very limit of possibility. The book my dear fellow is simply admirable in its justness and its justice in its human and humane quality. Nothing You have written before has approached such perfect proportion or revealed the delicacy of treatment of which you are capable, so well. I would say infinitely more but must end now with most affectionate congratulations.

Ever Your

Conrad.

PS. Our love to you all. Tell me how you are in health and when you come to town. Jessie (after disinfecting herself) intends to write to your wife soon.

---

[1] Conrad saw the first instalment of *Kipps* in the *Pall Mall Magazine*, not the *Gazette* (letter of 13 January).

To William Rothenstein
Text MS Harvard; Unpublished

2^d Dec 05
32 St Agnes Road.
Kennington Pk SE

My dear Will.

Many thanks. Cheque safely received.

Borys is rather better. The beastly thing was complicated by dyssenteric* symptoms which have yielded to treatment. Yesterday a slight kidney trouble developed itself. So far it seems very mild, and both heart and lungs do not seem in the least affected.

But it'll be a long and ruinous job—I can see.

I've been thinking and even dreaming of the picture. Hueffer whom I met yesterday told me he has seen it and seems pretty near as full of it as myself. The effect of that painting is profound and memorable. Nothing modern that I can remember has interested me so strongly on the technical side and made such a strong emotional appeal to my artistic sense.

Our dear love to you all. We have been in a state of the greatest anxiety about your chicks. I conclude with relief they are well. Drop me a line.

Yours ever

Conrad.

To Sidney Colvin
Text MS Duke; Unpublished

32 St Agnes' Road
Kennington Pk. SE
26 Dec. 05

Dear Mr Colvin.

You cannot imagine our regret on missing the delightful opportunity of seeing you under our roof.

We came to London in Nov: for a week or so; mainly to let the doctors see my wife who showed some symptoms of nervous break down. Thereupon poor Borys developed scarlet fever. You may imagine the worry and the scare in the 'high class' boarding house! However we got him moved swiftly to a nursing house and have taken up our quarters in this delectable neighbourhood[1] to be near him.

---

[1] As a bachelor, Conrad had lived on modest streets in Pimlico, but his recent visits had taken him to comfortable areas of Bayswater and Kensington. Kennington, south of the river, had kept its Regency houses, but not its good name; it was now famous for

Our* wife has helped to nurse him in the daytime, and we had a rather anxious time; every possible complication (kidneys, heart etc) having a lunge at him. But it seems these were all feints and none, thank God, got home. He has been up for the last three days. An hour ago I saw him at the window looking much better than I expected. We trust we shall be allowed to move him to the Pent on Saturday next.

Of course we would not have failed to call; but under the circumstances there was nothing left for us but absolute isolation. I ought to have written perhaps; yet after we went into exile I own I had not the heart to write. Fact is I am getting ashamed of my calamities of which my gout is not the least. Ever since July I had an attack every month. Today I came out after nearly a fortnight of seclusion and torture. My poor wife had a joyous time of late between the two of us.

The feeling of disappointement* at not having seen you this time is intensified by your wife a hundredfold. My wife is very sorry too. She joins me in the expression of most sincere regards to Mrs Colvin and yourself with the best wishes for an uninterrupted peace and happiness for many years to come. Believe me always very cordially yours

Jph Conrad.

To John Galsworthy
Text MS POSK; J-A, 2, 29

[London]
1905
26th Dec.

Dearest Jack.

I've been abominably ill. Abominably is the right word.

Ada's letter found me in bed. I thank her very much. I would like to say something nice, but I have got up empty headed, shaky, and so weak that I can't make the smallest mental effort.

And to morrow I must start another short story. And I shall of course; but I dread the to morrow all the same. And in another 20 days or so the same thing shall turn up again, the same powerlessness of body, the same anguish of mind—I don't say anything of actual bodily pain for God is my witness I care for that less than nothing. It is the helplessness with the bitter sense of the lost days that I stand in fear of.

'hooligans' and overcrowding. In less than two months, Conrad was at work on 'Verloc', ancestor of *The Secret Agent*; in Chapter Eight of the latter, he evokes 'the sinister, noisy, hopeless, and rowdy night of South London' (p. 159).

And you know well that I don't want these days for myself and that each, each is of the most vital importance.

Our loving thanks for the postcards which Borys treasures; but I am afraid they shall have to be burnt when he leaves.[1] We expect to move him to the Pent on Saturday.[2] Jessie goes on Friday. The nurse is to take him down and I'll come too probably—unless I stay in London for a few days with Dr Tebb, to get a little mended. I had a good deal of fever with my third relapse and ugly internal symptoms. I must try to get up some strength, mental and physical, before the next attack comes. Likewise I must write some 20 000 words.

Jessie keeps up pretty well. I've sent her to bed. The poor woman had a particularly joyful time this last fortnight.

Our dear love to you both.

Ever Yours

J. Conrad

To John Galsworthy
Text MS Forbes; Unpublished

32 St Agnes Place

Kennington S.E.

29th Dec. 05

My dearest Jack

I have your letter. You are good. Indeed my dear boy I could and have somehow kept up—I don't mean to say without effort—but still I have. You ease me immensely though I know I am doing a perfectly immoral thing in taking that cheque. I hope you do not think—but it's impossible!—that my jeremiad had any indirect purpose! What cuts me to the quick is the forced deterioration of my work produced hastily, carelessly in a temper of desperation. There is no remedy for that.

Ada of course is an angel. I am quite excited at the news of the "great massacre". Upon the whole I feel this is an occasion for congratulations of the most unaffected kind. But is it possible that You did really go so far wrong?

Yes I wrote the Anarchist story and now I am writing another of the sort. I write these stories because they bring more money than the sea papers. A sea paper *Initiation* is to be seen in Jany N^o of B'wood Maga. The anarco story (N° 2) is entitled *The Informer*.[3]

---

[1] As a sanitary measure.   [2] The 30th.
[3] 'An Anarchist' and 'The Informer' both appeared in *Harper's Magazine* and then in *A Set of Six*.

The 3 Benavides have been taken by the PM Mag: I believe.[1] I get about £90. Pays, all but, for Mons: B luxurious scarlet fever interlude. Ada's (who *is* an angel) cards are gone to be disinfected somewhere Putney way. And, by the bye, Batten[2] won't let him go till Wednesday next as his peeling is not over. The Pent is being fired up *now*. The Vol. shall be sent to the L Ly[3] on Tuesday without fail. Jessie's dear love and mine to you both   Yours ever

Conrad.

To J.B. Pinker
Text MS Yale; Unpublished

[letterhead: The District
Messenger
and Theatre Ticket Company]
[1905?][4]

My dear Pinker.

I've had to buy such a lot of things that I must ask you for another £4. Please send under cover of Hueffer Nat: Lib Club where I'll be lunching with them I hope from 1 to 2.30. I shall be detained another night here I fear which is a ghastly nuisance.

Yours,

Conrad

---

[1] As 'Gaspar Ruiz', the stories were serialized in the *Pall Mall Magazine* between July and October 1906 and collected in *A Set of Six*.

[2] Rayner Derry Batten, who had also attended Jessie Conrad.

[3] The London Library on St James's Square, a private lending and reference library founded and much patronized by authors.

[4] Ford joined the National Liberal Club in 1905 (Mizener, p. 107). The stationery comes from a batch printed 10 September 1904; this batch is unlikely to have lasted much beyond 1905.

1906

To J.B. Pinker
Text MS Berg; Unpublished

[London]
Monday
1st Jan. o6

My dear Pinker

Happy New Year to you and yours.

Miss Wright brings You double copy of just half of the *Informer*. The story is finished but the second half (which is not typed yet) I like to keep for another 24 hours to look at and improve. I may just as well do that as I feel incapable of beginning another story till I get to the Pent. I shall be too busy dispatching wife home to morrow and taking Borys there on Wed^y.

———————

I shall bring the end of *Informer* myself tomorrow. Meantime, owing to my wife going to morrow early I ask You to let me draw money as if you had the whole. I want £30 for Hogben[1] (which exhausts *Anarchist* balance) and £20 on acct/ Informer—in two cheques—for other people. And £5 in open cheques for my wife's travelling, which will be covered yet by the Gaspar Ruiz[2] credit. I mention all this to let you see that I am scrupulously keeping count.

I think it would be simpler if you just gave Miss Wright an open cheque for £55 instead of making them out separately. My wife shall go round in Hythe and pay the people in cash.

———————

I would like the *Informer* to be entitled *Gestures* instead. I am thinking of the book form, You see. On looking at story you will see why that title is the proper one as bearing not on the facts but on the moral satirical idea. But of course don't let my wish interfere with the demands of serialisation.

I'll bring you the Author's note for best story tomorrow.[3]

Kindest regards Yours always
Jph Conrad

---

[1] The owner of the Pent.   [2] The new and final name for 'Benavides'.
[3] 'My Best Story and Why I Think So', a note on 'An Outpost of Progress', published in the *Grand Magazine*, March 1906 (reprinted in Najder [1978], pp. 82–3).

To J.B. Pinker

Text MS Berg; Unpublished

[letterhead: Pent Farm]

Thursday. [4 January 1906?]¹

My dear Pinker

Here you are. It's probably too long and if so it may begin just as well at the par: marked thus ÷ or if that also appears too long, then let it start at par: marked * (*page 3.*), and it'll be under a 100 words then.

Anyway I think it is wrong for me to have anything to do with these, say, exhibitions. I am lumped there with a lot of people of whom I don't express any sort of opinion but from whom I am *fundamentally different*. It isn't I who say so but *G. B. Street* who made that point in a critical article last year—in the P.M.M. I think.²

If there's one man who wrote that, there are a good many who think so.

As to me I think that since it is a point of view which can be taken then it is as good a point of view to take as the other one. And I believe without undue vanity that the position is *tenible**—at least.

Having done what You wished me to do I feel free to say what I had on my heart.

Always yours

Conrad.

Balance of story shall be posted this evening.

---

¹ Letterhead thirteen, not found on dated correspondence after 2 November; the other [4 January] letter uses type fourteen. The circumstances, however, match those of the first week in 1906: a story ('The Informer') has been finished, and a note (160 words as published in the *Grand Magazine*) must keep unsuitable company.

² G. S. Street, 'About Our Fiction', *Pall Mall Magazine*, vol. 34, September 1904, p. 136: 'Mr. Conrad is a man whose genius of intuition and whose extraordinary eye for the colour and fire of life might well be seen in a clearer perspective by our critics, might well be distinguished from the facile, respectable qualities of the writers with whom he is commonly placed on a level.' Conrad's precursors in the 'Best Story' series were H. B. Marriott Watson, Morley Roberts, Robert Hichens, Jerome K. Jerome, and W. Pett Ridge.

To John Galsworthy
Text MS POSK; Danilewiczowa

[letterhead: Pent Farm]
Thursday. [4 January 1906][1]

Dearest Jack

We brought him down yesterday. And to day he is down with a severe heart attack hands and feet swollen and the pulse simply terrific—130 or very near that. I am down here hunting up doctors. God knows how it will end.

Our very dear love to you both
Conrad

To David Meldrum
Text MS Duke; Blackburn 187

[letterhead: Pent Farm]
5th Jan. 1906.

My dear M[r] Meldrum.

Many thanks for your kind thought of Borys and your good letter to me. I don't know what you may think of my silence? Nothing very hard I hope.

I spent Xmas in bed. I had fifteen days of most horrible gout in these awful lodgings. I could not write to you. I am getting ashamed of my constant invalidism and of my persistent calamities.

I got up on New Year's eve and on the 3[d] I took Borys down here with the nurse. We arrived at noon without mishap but by midnight the poor little devil developed a most alarming heart attack with swelling of hands and feet and a terrific pulse. Half the day yesterday I was hunting up doctors in torrents of rain. To-day I am just told he has got over the worst of it. So be it; but to look at him is not very reassuring. His face is twice its normal size. He's propped up with many pillows and has the lighthouse on his knees. He wishes me to tell you that he will call it Skerryvore,[2] and that it works very well. I must tell we didn't let him have it in the nursing home. It is difficult to disinfect toys and he would have had to leave it there most likely.

Here's the whole story.

---

[1] The subsequent letter to Meldrum fixes the date.
[2] After the deep-sea light off western Scotland built by Alan Stevenson, Robert Louis' uncle; R. L. S. wrote poems about it (in *Underwoods*, 1887) and borrowed its name for his house in Bournemouth.

Our most affectionate regards to you all with best wishes for your peace and happiness.

Always Yours

Jph Conrad.

To John Galsworthy
Text MS Forbes; Unpublished

[letterhead: Pent Farm]
11 Jan. 06

Dearest Jack.

The long and the short of it is the child was poisoned (through the skin) with the new disinfectant *Lisol* a most damnable stuff.—Nurse put too much of it in the last bath at the Nursing Home. He was swollen all over with a head like a balloon and purple spots all over him. He was a sight to terrify a rhinoceros let alone his thin-skinned parents. He was cold and clammy and horrible but the purple spots put Hackney[1] on the track—and the nurse said: "I am really afraid I did"—And now this adventure is over I may reasonably expect a 15 minutes entre-acte at least.

The second 'Anarchist' story title *Gestures* is finished. How is it with you?

I suppose You will be returning to town soon. I don't know what we'll be able to do. I long to get away for a bit where it is dry and warm.

Jessie has been a brick all through; but all this tells on her naturally.

She sends her dear love. Ever Ada's and Yours

Conrad

Benavides sold to PMM (serially) to begin in June.[2] *£126* for all rights except in the U.S. That is confoundedly little really because the US rights are not worth much. I worry about my prices not because I am greedy but because I am weary.

---

[1] The doctor from Hythe.
[2] 'Gaspar Ruiz' ran in the *Pall Mall Magazine* from July to October.

To J.L. Garvin

Text MS Texas; Unpublished

[letterhead: Pent Farm]
11th Jan 1906

Dear Mr Garvin.[1]

Pray believe that the delay in answering your letter arose from no negligence of mine—still less from want of appreciation for its contents and tone.

I have a very great regard for the *Outlook*[2] and I thank you very sincerely for the offered hospitality of its pages. Whether I am worthy of it is another matter. The offer as you put it is indeed fascinating. It is indeed true that I've had sometimes thoughts upon the current questions of our time which have been checked by the incertitude of finding an outlet for them. And perhaps it was just as well: for, putting aside the question of intellectual value, I very much doubt whether I could have expressed them in a journalistic way.

The highest journalistic quality I take to be the gift of bringing out concisely the *practical* bearing of a given idea (or even of a simple emotion) upon the course of contemporary life. And this gift I haven't got. I've a natural bent to express myself theoristically;* in other words I fall into rhetoric; in other words I provoke the reader to exclaim 'bosh' as he runs. It may be very wrong of the reader but the mere idea of a reader of the Outlook being provoked to such an exclamation is intolerable to my loyalty.

I've set down my scruples in order that you should not suspect me of stupidity or indolence. But the first time I manage to throw my scruples to the winds I shall take good care that you get the first sight of my effort.

Believe me, my dear Sir, very sympathetically and faithfully Yours

Joseph Conrad

---

[1] James Louis Garvin (1868–1947), a vigorous journalist and crusading editor. He had charge of the *Outlook* (1905–6), the *Observer* (1908–42), and the fourteenth edition of the *Encyclopaedia Britannica* (1929).

[2] A weekly, it argued for tariffs, suspicion of Germany, and military readiness; its great rival was the *Spectator* – also Unionist, but supporting free trade.

To David Meldrum
Text MS Duke; Blackburn 188

[letterhead: Pent Farm]
11 Jan 06.

My Dear Mr Meldrum

Now the little boy is better I have in a certain measure regained my wits: and I perceive I've utterly forgotten to refer to the Whitefriars Club[1] invitation.

I have once already declined one with profuse thanks. As a mat[t]er of fact I am always either desperately gouty or desperately busy. Moreover that sort of thing is not in my way. I've systematically declined all such invitations from various quarters and therefore can not in logic and decency accept this one—tho' I am very sensible of the honour.

Perhaps You could say that nicely for me.

I long for a talk with you but can't get away from here just now. Our kindest regards and love to your House.

Always yours

Jph Conrad.

To William Rothenstein
Text MS Harvard; Unpublished

[letterhead: Pent Farm]
11th Jany 06

Dearest Will.

We had another scare with Borys after he had been brought down here. But it's all right now.

We do think of you all with affection and regret of the lost opportunity of seeing a little of each other. I have had a desperate fit of gout end Dec^er in London. Now I am driving hard to make up time.

Thanks for cheque to hand safely. Our dear love to You all. Jessie has been a bit seedy.

Yours ever

Conrad.

---

[1] Located close to Fleet Street, in an area frequented by journalists, editors, and publishers.

To J.B. Pinker
Text MS Berg; Unpublished

[letterhead: Pent Farm]
16th Jan 1906

My dear Pinker.

I return you the story ready for the printer. I wish this text to go to America as it would require no correction except for typographical errors.

I have begun the other story[1] and hope to have it done in a week.

Please settle this last acct/ from the Nurses' Association. Also send me one cheque for £2.8 and another for £2.10.

I write some alternative titles for the story. I would prefer any of them to the *Informer*.

Henry James seems in very good form and interested in correcting his earliest novels for the collected edition.[2]

Thanks for your last letter with enclosures. After I've done a little more copy I'll want to get away before the next fit of gout nabs me here.

Kindest regards Always yours

Jph Conrad.

PS H. J. was loud in your praises and in admiration of your '*perfect tact*'

To J.B. Pinker
Text MS Berg; Unpublished

[letterhead: Pent Farm]
18 Jan 1906

My dear Pinker

Thanks very much for the cheques.

I return the *Nelson*. It must go either first or last in the volume and quite apart from the *Mirror of the Sea* papers, having its own independent place in the Contents table.

The arrangement of these papers is worth careful consideration. If we could manage it so as to produce the effect of a contin[u]ous book— would it not be better? Is it worth while bothering about it? I mean from the *selling* point of view. With some little trouble the thing could be done—except as regards the *Port of London* perhaps. My idea is of a sort of reminiscent discourse running on like this: I. II. III IV etc etc XX XXI

---

[1] 'The Brute'?
[2] The New York Edition, 1907–9. The first volumes were *Roderick Hudson* and *The American*.

and so on, with no titles or blank or half blank pages between; something, in short, like poor Gissing's Ryecroft papers;[1] and only the headings at the top of pages being changed according to the matter treated. The changes of these headings could be tabulated nevertheless in the table of contents under the general name *Mirror of the Sea*. Then at the end separated by a blank page we would have *Trafalgar* and I am afraid the *Port of London* too, as additional to the long book *M of the S*. But perhaps even the *P of L* could be squeezed into the body of the work.[2]

Would talk it over with the publisher.[3] They don't like short stories or sketches. Well let us make it a long book.

In any case I would want badly to see the whole lot of copy. And for that I depend upon you as I have nothing by me. Kindest regards

Your Conrad.

The table of contents would look something like this.

Contents

THE MIRROR OF THE SEA: —				Page
—————————————	—	—	—	3
—————————————	—	—	—	
—————————————	—	—	—	and so on
—————————————	—	—	—	
—————————————	—	—	—	
—————————————	—	—	—	
THE PORT OF LONDON———————	—	—	—	(say) 245(?)
TRAFALGAR———————————	—	—	—	(say) 267(?)

(But I would try to do my best to melt in the port of London thing. As to Trafalgar the vol may even be advertised as containing in addition to the *M of the S*. the commemorative paper on Nelson)

All allusions to the Mirror of the Sea *papers* should be dropped in preliminary notices

Simply: *M of the Sea* a vol of memories and impressions of which some have appeared already in periodicals under various titles.

---

[1] *The Private Papers of Henry Ryecroft* (1903).
[2] As 'The Faithful River', it became sections XXX–XXXI; 'The Heroic Age', the Trafalgar essay, ends the volume.
[3] Methuen.

To William Archer

Text MS BL Add MSS 45291; Unpublished

[letterhead: Pent Farm]
23ᵈ Jan '06

My dear Sir[1]

I would not presume to thank You for a conscientious expression of opinion; but You will permit me to tell you how deeply touched I am by the generous tone of your utterance.[2]

You certainly reward me with a lavish hand. In the face of your written and signed words whose authority stands established by a long record of fearless and impartial judgements any sort of protestation of unworthiness on my part would savour of impertinence.

But this much I may say; Your words made valuable by having been weighed in the scrupulous balance of your critical insight have been scanned by many men's eyes; but mine alone can detect how large a part your generous sympathy with honest endeavour has played in shaping Your judgement. And for this sympathy I may well express my gratitude without breaking any rule of propriety or decency.

Believe me dear Mʳ Archer

always faithfully Yours

Jph Conrad.

To J.B. Pinker

Text MS Berg; Unpublished

[letterhead: Pent Farm]
23ᵈ Jan 06

My dear Pinker.

Thanks for the papers. There's nothing wanting as far as I can remember. The *Port of London* paper shall be melted in all right; and you may be sure that in the process of arrangement the book shall gain somewhat in length.

By fairly careful counting and including *Trafalgar*, I make *58,867* words. By the time I am done with it it won't be far short (if at all) of 60,000—which is a perfectly adequate amount I fancy for a book of that

---

[1] William Archer (1856–1924), a Scot, began his career as a drama critic in 1879, with the *London Figaro*. Later, he wrote for the *World, Nation, Tribune, Morning Leader,* and *Manchester Guardian*. An editor and translator of Ibsen, he strove to make the British stage more serious.

[2] In the 20 January number of the *Tribune*, Archer devoted two columns to praising Conrad as 'a poet of the sea'. Publication of 'The Sea of Adventure' began on the 23rd.

sort. Couldn't you when arranging with Methuen stipulate for some extra advertising? Yesterday Wells was telling us that Kipps hung in the balance till he tackled McMillans* and got from them another £100 worth of advertising.

Is *M of the Sea* to count as one of the three books contracted for?

I send you my idea of the title page. Make it a condition. I want my name at the top of page because *Memories and Impressions* cannot be *by* anybody. You see my point?

Now after Archer's trumpet call in the Tribune the sooner the book's out the better.

I trust You got some decent terms from *M*.

The story is not quite ready yet. Meantime please send me 3 small cheques *£2.12.7*—*£4.3*—*£1.18* because the bills keep coming in all the same.

I shall tackle seriously the papers tonight. If I am away Ford'll see the proofs through.

—————————

Please complete address on letter to Archer which I enclose here and send it on.

Kindest regard[s]

Yours always

Conrad

PS Can you give me the address of *Beresford* the photographer?[1]

To John Galsworthy
Text MS Forbes; Unpublished

[letterhead: Pent Farm]
1906:
31 Jan

Dearest Jack.

The book is in parts marvellously done and in its whole a piece of art—undubitably* a piece of art. I've read it 3 times. My respect for you increased with every reading. I have meditated over these pages not a little. I want to know when it is going to be published.[2]

Let me know of your return at once. I want to run up and say a thing or two—if you can spare me the time and, perhaps, put me up for one

---

[1] George Charles Beresford, Yeoman's Row, Brompton.
[2] *The Man of Property* was published 23 March.

night. But that last as Ada thinks fit. We think of going away on the 7th Febr.

Our dear love to you both.

Yours ever

Conrad.

I keep the book yet. By Jove its admirable in at least *three* aspects. But, I say, the socialists ought to present you with a piece of plate. Enfoncés les Bourgeois.[1]

To William Rothenstein

Text MS Harvard; Unpublished

[letterhead: Pent Farm]
7 Febr. 1906.

My dear Will.

Thanks very much for the cheque.

I am glad You work. I've been working too; hardly lifting my nose off the paper. The trouble is that there's so little to show for all this toil.

We are going off on Friday to Montpellier for the end of the winter. 'Tisn't a luxury. It's a necessity of life. I particularly don't want to go to pieces just now. Jessie is writing the particular reason to Alice;[2] so I won't say anything about it except that I feel very shy and blushing at being let in for that thing at my venerable age.

In the witching month of august (damn it) we shall be in London I suppose; but April May, June, we shall try to hang out[3] at the Pent.

Give my dear love to all your house

Ever Yours

J Conrad

---

[1] 'The bourgeois are sunk'—thanks to Galsworthy's assault on their good name.
[2] A second pregnancy.
[3] I.e. to hang on.

To J.B. Pinker
Text MS Berg; Unpublished

[letterhead: Riche Hôtel &
Continental Montpellier]
13 Febr 1906

My dear Pinker.

We've got fixed in this imposing edifice which looks a jolly sight better on the picture than in reality.[1] Anyway the sanitary arrangements are just tolerable.

I spent the whole of yesterday hunting high and low for rooms, lodgings, anything—in the midst of a most extraordinary uproar reigning over the whole town an amazing mixture of carnival and political riots going on at the same time.[2] In the same street troops, infantry and cavalry drawn up in front of churches, yells, shrieks, blows—people with broken heads carried into chemist's shops, and through it all bands of costumed and masked revellers pushing with songs and ribald jokes. It's extremely curious and very characteristic. A very brilliant sunshine lighting up all that with a rather sharp wind blowing down certain streets.

I think that as far as work is concerned the place will be a success. But to find a home was a great job. I had to look out for sanitation and there was a question of stairs for my wife—no end of difficulties.

However after some negociations* I have arranged the business with this hotel. They have taken us in for 5/6 per day all round. We have two rooms with five windows on the top floor, which I've marked on the picture for your information. Anyway it's the only house in town with a lift and there was no prospect of getting anything suitable. The only other place which might have done at a pinch was in a ramshackle old house where they would have taken us for a pound a day. But the sanitation was so suspicious and offensive that I dared not risk it with Borys.

We both feel infinitely better already. The air is splendid. In sheltered places the sun is positively hot. As soon as I've posted this letter I shall climb up to our tower and sit down to work at the story which is provisionally called *Verloc*.[3] The prepared text of M of the S you'll get in a few days. Kindest regards

always your Conrad.

---

[1] See Plate 10.
[2] The riots, which had spread right across France, were over the separation of church and state (*The Times*, 22 and 23 February).
[3] *The Secret Agent*, at first a short story.

To J.B. Pinker

Text MS Berg; Unpublished

Hotel Continental
place de la Comedie
Montpellier
21st Febr '06

My dear Pinker.

I send you the first 13 pp of Verloc partly that you should see what the story is going to be like and partly as evidence that the Capri fatality is not likely to overcome me this year. After all, considering that we have been just a week here and that it takes some time to feel settled I haven't done so badly. There is a good bit more MS actually written but I can't part with it yet. I've also worked at the text of the M of the Sea. That and the balance of *Verloc* you'll get in the course of a week. Meantime I hope you won't think I am stretching the point unduly if I ask you to send me £20 on the day you receive this—which I imagine will be Friday—either in English notes or by draft on the Credit Lyonnais who have a house here—whichever is less trouble.

Don't imagine that the story'll be unduly long. It may be longer than the Brute[1] but not very much so. What has delayed me was just trying to put a *short turn* into it. I think I've got it. I haven't done anything to Chance of course. I imagine it would go easiest at the Pent. But that or some other MS you are sure to have from here. I feel well and have a few ideas.

Yours always

Conrad.

PS Would you have the extreme kindness to buy for me and send out by parcel post a fountain pen of good repute—even if it has to cost 10/6. I am doing much of my writing in the gardens of Peyron under a sunny wall and the horrible stylo I've got with me is a nuisance.

To J.B. Pinker

Text MS Berg; Unpublished

[letterhead: Riche Hôtel]
27 Febr. 1906
8 am.

My dear Pinker

You have been very good. The pen was already here on Saturday.[2] It is excellent. The money arrived on Monday.

---

[1] Around 8,200 words.   [2] The 24th.

Many thanks!

I've had a heavy cold for a couple of days but its better to day. I am going to work now with the new pen.

Yours always

J. Conrad.

To J.B. Pinker
Text MS Berg; Unpublished

2 Mch 1906

Hotel Continental

Montpellier

My dear Pinker

I send you in this envelope 17 pages of typed story and the first part of Gaspar Ruiz proof duly corrected. Also the Methuen agreement for M of the S.

Verloc is extending.

It's no good fighting against it. It would take too much time. Any way I think the story is good. And you may tell people also that it is authentic enough.[1]

Please send for me a cheque for 5 gs to Dr Albert Tebb. 226 Finchley Road NW. A typed line on a half sheet *From M^r J Conrad* will do to enclose it in. Also pray send £*4.10* to *Miss Nellie Lyons*. Mill Cottage. Sturry. Near Canterbury. The girl is leaving us and this settles for some bills she has paid and her month's money. Likewise £*1.9* to Alfred Richards High Street. Hythe.

Many thanks and apologies for these unceremonious instructions.

The M of the S text will reach you in the course of a few days.

Yours always

J. Conrad.

To J.B. Pinker
Text MS Berg; J-A, 2, 30 (incomplete)

[Montpellier]

Monday. 5th Mch

1906.

My dear Pinker

Here's the text of the M of the Sea ready at last. It is surprising how much time was taken up in putting it into some shape; but any rate the

---

[1] As Norman Sherry demonstrates in *Conrad's Western World*, *The Secret Agent* draws heavily on the deeds of contemporary militants.

proof corrections are not likely to go beyond the limit fixed by agreement. There will be no printer's bill for me to settle.

With the copy there is a loose leaf containing instructions which should be attended to.

I breathe a prayer for the book's success—the best success a book of that sort can reasonably expect. I'll put in motto and dedication[1] on the first proof of title page, when I get it.

When you get the money from Methuen I trust you will be able to settle for me the bill for £3.6.5 which I forward to you here and let me have the following amounts:

W. Powell. £10.5.3

B Ninnes £10.10

Those two on acct of the furniture I had to buy when we came back from Italy. Another twenty later on will settle it.

also to

W. Bushell £16.10

T. Divers £*10*

If you can spare me that fifty from the book advance you'll be working towards a happy release from worries. It isn't quite all that is necessary but it'll go a long way towards it. By and bye when I've sent you a short story (to follow Verloc) there will be an amount of 16 another of about 20 and the income tax to pay. Meantime they must wait.

Verloc has been delayed rather by this Mirror. I sat up 3 nights. To have all my stuff in bits and scraps of print like this confused my mind in a perfectly ridiculous manner. But it's over!

I would be glad if notwithstanding that I do not send you any fresh copy in this packet you were good enough to send me £20 at once. For all my efforts at economy I find the money goes quicker than I expected. The only luxury I have allowed myself is to get riding lessons for Borys. I have taken a series of twelve tickets which cost me 25/–. It's wonderful what good they are doing him; he looks a different child already; he was very white and peaked after his scarlet fever, with defective circulation too. Now all this is changed and I credit the horse with this improvement. As the father of a fine boy[2] and a horseman Yourself you'll understand my satisfaction at his shaping extremely well. From the very first day he had an excellent seat and a most amusing assurance on horseback. I daresay he inherits the instinct from his Polish ancestors.

---

[1] A motto from Boethius and a dedication to Katherine Sanderson, Ted's mother.

[2] Eric, who later joined his father's business.

This week you'll get a further batch of Verloc. I don't like to say the final batch—but it's possible. Alas it'll be a longish story 18000 or so—I fear. On the other hand it is not a bad piece of work. We will see.

Kindest regards Yours always

Jph Conrad.

I give you here the names and address.

W. Powell. 11 *Rampart R^d Hythe Kent*

B. Ninnes. *High Street* same

W Bushell. High Street *same*

Thomas Divers. Newingreen N^r Hythe Kent

A line "to the credit of Mr J. Conrad's acct/" with each cheque will suffice. Rowlstone's bill I enclose.[1]

To William Rothenstein

Text MS Harvard; J-A, 2, 31

[letterhead: Riche Hôtel]

11 Mch 1906

My dear Will

Many thanks for the cheque which came extremely handy indeed.

I am glad to hear that Balfour[2] really likes my work. After all one writes for the intelligence. As to Your wonderful picture whose memory abides with me forever the hanging back of buyers distresses me of course but does not astonish. There is a vigour a vitality, an energy of conception and execution which naturally scares the usual sugar-stick bourgeois. I flatter myself that my *Typhoon* story is *as art* somewhere near—(if not *very* near)—your admirable picture—in *intention* I mean to say, for to your mastery of technique I can't pretend—even to myself. Well, Pinker had the greatest difficulty in placing that story and ultimately had to let it go for a few pence so to speak; and a *really* friendly critic writing of it absolutely raised the question whether it was a "fit" subject. Voilà.

But neither praise nor blame can affect your undeniable achievement. No doubt you will do better—do greater. But all the same there is in that

---

[1] The creditors included William Powell, furniture dealer, T. Divers, coal merchant, and Rowlstone & Co., china and glass dealers.

[2] The ex-Prime Minister.

work a finality of expression which will mark an epoch in your artistic life.

> Our dearest love to you all
>
> Yours Conrad

We are sending some goody-goodies to Alice by tomorrow's post. They are a speciality of this town.

To J.B. Pinker

Text MS Berg; Unpublished

> [Montpellier]
> [mid March ? 1906][1]

My dear Pinker.

Please attend to this without if possible breaking its neck. The offer seems fair,[2] and at any rate I've not given up the idea of writing a play or two yet.

I think you have a copy of the play in Your possession. Mss is in a drawer at the Pent and it would not be easy to get it out before my return. I'll* hear from me soon.

> Yours always
>
> Conrad.

To J.B. Pinker

Text MS Berg; Unpublished

> [letterhead: Riche Hôtel]
> [mid March ? 1906][3]

My dear Pinker

A very poor lot I am sending you, but the next will be better.

I've been hindered by the necessity to write *at once* a review of Galsworthy's book for the Outlook.[4] Still I am not doing badly.

In this packet you will find fifteen pages of *Verloc* and corrected proof of 2 Ruiz.

Send me some money. I had the misfortune to lose my pocketbook the

---

[1] Written on the back of a letter from Frank E. Washburn Freund dated 11 March 1906.

[2] Freund, the London representative of the Anstalt für Aufführungsrecht dramatischer Werke of Berlin, wanted to arrange a German production of *One Day More*; he offered Conrad 60% of the gross.

[3] The review of *The Man of Property* went off on Tuesday, 20 March (letter of 22 March).

[4] 'A Middle-Class Family', 31 March 1906, pp. 449–50; reprinted in *Last Essays* as 'John Galsworthy'.

other day when gambol[l]ing with Borys I suppose along a country lane. However there was only 100 frcs in it. Send me £25 at least.

When the end of Verloc reaches you and also perhaps the first half of the next story we will arrange for our return.

The next story is begun.

I have a beastly cold.

Kindest regards Yours always

Conrad.

To John Galsworthy
Text MS Forbes; Marrot 187 (in part)

Riche Hotel
Place de la Comédie
Montpellier
22^d March 1906

My dearest Jack

The article—the thing—the inept and benighted attempt at appreciation of *M of P* left on Tuesday. Before your letter arrived I had arranged with the *Outlook*. I am appalled at the bad use I've made of the opportunity; but the thing is done; it is the best thing I was capable of doing. That I know you will believe; and as for the rest You need not look at it. What I tried to do was to interest the readers of the Outlook —send them to the book.

I have hinted to Garvin that about a fortnight after publication would be the best time to shoot off that poor bolt. I hope you'll approve of this arrangement which no doubt shall be carried out by the amiable Garvin.

I have written a good many thousands of words but havent finished anything. I am delighted and excited to hear of the play.[1]

I am trying to put off this horrid dread of the future which oppresses me. I am dispirited by that feeling of mental exhaustion of which I cannot get rid at all now. I have learned to write *against* it—thats all. But you may imagine that effort of will—the sense of failure!

Jessie is getting on remarkably well upon the whole. Borys slaves at his reading. The weather mostly fine and Montpellier has done *him* good. I've invested 30 frcs in riding lessons for him, I am a frivolous person—ain't I? This is my only comfort so to speak. It is the most amazing success. You should see him sit the 14 hands mare of the

---

[1] *The Silver Box*, recently finished (Marrot, pp. 190–1).

Tarbes breed (looks like Arab) which is the smallest they could give him. His legs don't reach much below the saddle straps and the riding master[1]

To J.B. Pinker

Text MS Berg; Unpublished

Montpellier.
28 Mch 1906

My dear Pinker

My apologies for not acknowledging the £25 received two days ago.

I am sorry I am doing no better; but I tell you frankly I refrain deliberately from forcing myself on. The time for the great pull will come on our return when *Chance* is taken in hand *exclusively*. I've been nibbling at it a little.

I hear that The Fifth Queen[2] is a *really* remarkable success (selling one I mean). Please drop me line to say whether it is really so. I would take it as a favour. I had a depressed letter from poor Ford and do not know what to think.

If that's the case (the success) allow me then to congratulate You upon Your judgment and insight. You remember the conversation we had in Jany about Ford's chances. I am rather excited, the letter I got shadowing something really big—first edition gone in three days and so on.[3]

I also hear that Jack Galsworthy's book attracts quite a considerable amount of attention ("The Man of Property")—in journalistic circles. So much the better. He will be a good author for you to handle tho' his output will never be very great. I wrote an appreciation of that book for the Outlook. It put me off my stride for 3 days.

The time has now come to confess to You our expectation of a new arrival. We await him—it—in August. Jack Galsworthy has offered us his house; for obviously the Pent is not a quite safe place with the nearest doctor 4 miles off. We shall come to London last week of July.

If you should happen to get proofs of *Mirror* from Methuen soon please send them on to Hueffer who in his letter asks to be allowed to see them through for me. It's very good of him because proofs do worry and

---

[1] The MS breaks off.

[2] Ford's historical novel about Katharine Howard, dedicated to Conrad and the first part of a trilogy.

[3] Author and publisher were over-sanguine (Mizener, pp. 117, 132).

disturb me. All the same I must see them too before they are returned to Methuen because there are things which I must do myself to them.

I had a sort of influenza last week. Better now.

Kindest regards

Yours always

J. Conrad

To Ford Madox Ford
Text MS Yale; Unpublished

29 Mch. 1906

Riche Hotel, Montpellier

Dearest Ford.

Your *most* welcome letter this moment to hand. I can not express to you my delight, my pride, in the success, that has come to you. I wanted good news and I could hardly have expected anything better—seeing that no book of mine is out.

The blessed vol: arrived about 4 days ago—or is it a week? I've read it twice—that's all. I know. You cannot say that I have waited for the way the "cat of a public" was going to jump before expressing my opinion on the score of mere selling success. I've (prudently) foretold it. This passes my expectations—but does not surpass my opinion of the book. I fancy I've already told you my feelings as to that piece of work. Here I'll add one more phrase bearing upon the most 'sensible' general effect. And that is this, that: *The Pictorial impression of the whole is positively overwhelming*. A triumph: my dear boy, a triumph!

What your modesty and tenderness prompt You to say of myself I reject utterly in its literal sense. It is a delusion of your affection—and as a delusion I accept it with a melancholy eagerness; for it is a delusion which, for me, is of infinite "douceur". And precisely after reading it once more I shall burn Youre* letter. If you wish to repeat that thing after I am dead I shall not come out of my grave to protest. Alas! Les morts ne retournent pas. But I may smile in the midst of the torments that await my sins.

What you say of Your health worries me considerably. We had half a hope you would turn up here. The weather was rather beastly for the last week. We think of getting back middle April

Jessie (who has for You more affection than she knows how to express) has shed a tear over Your success. She sends her love and Borys too. Express with my duty to your mother my sincerest congratulations on the vogue of the Vth Queen and also to Mrs Martindale. But before all to Mary[1] in special termes* and with very special regard.

Yours ever

Conrad.

To William Rothenstein

Text MS Harvard; Unpublished

[Montpellier]
29 Mch 1906

My dear Will

I am thinking of coming back and before I make my arrangements I would like to know whether I may expect anything more from the fund. Not having by me my note of payments received I am not certain whether there is anything more left. In any case it cannot be very much, alas!

Do let me know my dear Will and if there is a balance you could manage perhaps to let me have it before the 6th of April.

I have been* from gout but I had something very much like influenza. Worked all the time but not well.

Hueffer's book I hear has an enormous success. I am very very glad, and as I prophesied it to him months ago I am also proud of my penetration.

Our dear love to you all

Yours

Conrad

To J.B. Pinker

Text MS Berg; Unpublished

[Montpellier]
4 Ap 1906.

My dear Pinker.

The £5 received to day.[2] Many thanks.

I am sending you only 13 pages of Verloc with regret but without shame, considering that the conduct of such a story requires no small amount of meditation—not upon questions of style and so on—but simply upon what is fit or is unfit to be said. It is easy with a subject like

---

[1] Mary Martindale, Ford's sister-in-law and lover.
[2] The result of a telegram (Berg) sent 2 April: 'Please send five pound note today letter with MS on Wednesday'; Wednesday was the 4th.

this to produce a totally false impression. Moreover the thing has got to be *kept up as a story* with an ironic intention but a dramatic development.

Altogether it is a damnably complicated job. I trust you will like it when it is done. You'll find it dramatic enough. Anyway I hope You are not angry with me for embarking in that enterprise. I must let myself be carried away, sometimes. I should like it to appear somewhere where it would be read. Do You think it would be worthwhile to try the *Tribune*? They run stories in there—don't they?[1]

That and a short thing (about a bomb in a hotel)[2] will be ready this month. Meantime please send me £30 now and by next week you'll get either a considerable lot of *Verloc* or the *hotel* story complete. By the bye *Verloc* is *not* a good title. We'll have to invent something. Length of *Verloc* will be about 18[000] words I think.

With that and the *hotel* story we shall have another vol ready to stand by with. But *Chance* must be the next to come out. Kind regards

Yours always

Conrad.

To John Galsworthy
Text J-A, 2, 32

9th April, 1906,
Riche Hôtel,
Montpellier.

Dearest Jack,

My prevision is accomplished. Only yesterday talking with Jessie of your play, I said confidently "Barker'll take it!"[3] And lo and behold! the thing has arrived! I feel quite warmed up by the news. As poor Hope's expression is: "You are a made man."[4]

Garvin notified me of the appearance of the article. He professes himself highly pleased with it, which naturally made me feel very uncomfortable. However, as your letter does not seem to display a deadly animosity, I hope to live it down in time. Seriously, my dearest fellow, my very great regard for that piece of work has stood in my way. I could have written 10,000 words on it. But I had to consider space. I

---

[1] The editor had asked him for one in November.
[2] A piece which has not survived.
[3] Harley Granville-Barker took *The Silver Box* within 48 hours of submission (Marrot, p. 191).
[4] Unlike G. F. W. Hope himself; his experiences as a 'director of companies' had been unlucky.

took an unnatural attitude towards the book, for if I had followed my
bent I would have required lots of room to spread my elbows in. My
natural attitude would have been of course literary,—and perhaps I
would have found something not quite commonplace to say,—a critical
tribute not unworthy of you. But there was the risk of being misunderstood. So I simply endeavoured to send people to the book by a sort of
allusive *compte-rendu*, a mere "notice" in fact. How much it cost me to
keep strictly to that is a secret between me and my Maker.

I have also heard that directly on its appearance the book began to be
talked about in "journalistic circles." I confess that I felt slightly sick at
that, till I reflected that the *quality* of your book was too high to be
affected by false admirations. And take it from me, my dear Jack, that
the *quality* of your work is very high,—the sort of thing that cannot in
good faith be questioned, but that cannot be conveniently expressed in a
letter,—and not even in talk, however intimate. Because that last is
bound to swerve into considerations of a subject and method fascinating
to the limited nature of the human literary mind: whereas that quality is
something altogether more subtle, more remote, whose excellent and
faithful unity is reflected rather than expressed in the book, yet is as
absolutely, deeply and unavoidably present in it as the image in the
mirror. And there are a very few books only that have this quality. *Don
Quixote*, for instance, is one of the few: and you may tell dear Ada that no
book of Balzac had that: which is perhaps the reason she has her knife
into the poor man,—a sentiment which (however shocking to me) does
her definite honour by its mental insight and instinctive delicacy of
taste.

The above developed, made as intelligible as can be in the way of
feeling and conviction, should have been the fundamental theme of the
article I would have liked to write on the *Man of Property*, but I have been
wise with a worldly and journalistic wisdom. Perhaps it is only because I
mistrusted myself,—who knows? But here you have the shadow of
what might have been written in all truth and justice.

As to myself, my dear Jack, I have always that feeling of loafing at my
work, as if powerless in an exhaustion of thought and will. Not enough!
not enough! And yet perhaps those days without a line, nay, without a
word, the hard, atrocious, agonizing days are simply part of my *method* of
work, a decreed necessity of my production. Perhaps! But if it is so, then
nothing can repay me for such a sombre fate—not even Pinker's
satisfaction with the stuff I send to him. 14,000 words was all I could
achieve. It's simply disaster and there's nothing in them, it seems to me,

the merest hack novelist could not have written in two evenings and a half. I doubt not only my talent (I was never so sure of that) but my character. Is it indolence,—which in my case would be nothing short of baseness,—or what? No man has a right to go on as I am doing without producing manifest masterpieces. It seems I've no excuse under heaven or on earth. Enough!

We shall be starting off for home in a week or so and then I shall run up at once to see you. I must see you both and get braced up in the contact of your sure friendship and affection. And I must read the play,—must.

Our collective love to you both.

To Henry Newbolt
Text MS Mursia; *Scritti* 53; Original unpublished

Montpellier.
10 Ap. 1906.

Dear Mr Newbolt.

Many thanks for the last cheque—and infinitely more for the patience kindness and sympathy You have proved up to the hilt in the administration of the grant. I won't say more. Words which are the common property of mankind are but fit for common occasions. As the notions of truth, justice and beauty are clear enough as long as we abstain from definitions whose intellectual effort only blurrs* and diminishes the mental image, so I think that gratitude too is fated to remain unexpressed. It is a feeling which to keep its warmth must perforce remain (in the phrase of our forefathers) locked in one's breast. Searching for adequate expression is a too coldblooded proceeding to be possible for a writer whose daily task is just this deliberate turning over of the awful formless heap of words. It would seem odious to attempt writing to you in the same mood in which I sit down to write a page of fiction.

Thus a simple word of thanks is all [I] send for all Your thoughts, words and acts in this connection. I wish it were in my power to make you look back upon the episode with some very special satisfaction— with something more than the bare consciousness of having done good to a fellow creature. But that, I fear, is beyond my strength. Pray do me the great favour of saying a few words in that sense to Mr Gosse when you meet him: and I would be happy to learn that Mr Balfour is well assured of the permanence of my feelings.

Money is easily reckoned and I hope that you will believe in reckoning

this amount that it has done the utmost possible good in the circumstances. But what I would like is to give to all concerned with the grant
some faint idea of the magnitude of moral support derived from such a
testimony. But that can not be reckoned up. It is immense—and it is of
so intimate a nature that it must be left to Your sympathetic insight.

Believe me dear Mr Newbolt always cordially yours

Joseph Conrad.

To William Rothenstein
Text MS Harvard; Unpublished

[Montpellier]
10 April 1906

Dear Will.

Many thanks for the last instalment. We start for home on Monday
Jessie keeping well and Borys greatly benefitted* by this outing.

After all I myself need not complain. The gout has kept off. I've
worked a little and doing fairly good stuff, I feel sufficiently hopeful to
keep me going. Et voilà.

Our dearest love to the whole crowd of you

Ever yours

Conrad.

To John Galsworthy
Text MS Forbes; Unpublished

[letterhead: Pent Farm]
Wednesday ev^g [18 ? April 1906][1]

Dearest Jack.

We are home and very concerned to hear of Ada's rheumatisms. Let
us know by a PC directly you get this whether Ilkley[2] has done good.
Where's that place?

My dearest boy I am delighted to find that Pawling the mercantile is
making use of my review. It is quite a compliment. If he judges it good
for his purpose then indeed for once I've done what I meant and tried to
do.

I burn to see these 'mirobolantes'[3] reviews. Your consecration as a

---

[1] On the 10th, Conrad predicted a departure from Montpellier on Monday the 16th.
[2] The moorland resort in Yorkshire.   [3] French: 'astounding'.

dangerous man by the Spectator fills me with a pure and extatic* joy.[1]
I quite understand you're cheered.

I found a pile of proofs M[irror] of the S[e]a and am going to sit up
with them. Rot.

Jessie's dear love to you both. She stood the journey excellently and is
as cheerful as possible. Regular brick—for she has atrocious back aches
a couple of hours every day. I feel a bit tired. Borys long and thin rushes
round the fields. House dry. If only one could work at twice one's
natural speed all would be well.

Ever Yours

Conrad.

I've a couple of books of which a few pages may interest Ada. Tell her so
with my beso manos.[2]

To Miss McAndrews
Text MS Trinity; Unpublished

[letterhead: Pent Farm]
[Spring 1906?][3]

Dear Miss McAndrews[4]

Would you have the kindness to lend me one* your small bicycle
spanners, to lower Borys' saddle. I'll send it back at once.

Apologies and many thanks

faithfully yours

Joseph Conrad

To John Galsworthy
Text MS Forbes; Unpublished

[letterhead: Pent Farm]
1906
11 May

Dearest Jack

We are delighted to hear the cure has done good to Ada. I had an idea
that such was the case and was on the lookout for a letter from
You—from London.

---

[1] 14 April, pp. 587–8: the reviewer found *The Man of Property* 'so able that it cannot be
overlooked, and so ugly in places that it cannot be recommended without a serious
caution'.

[2] Spanish: 'I kiss hands'.

[3] Letterhead fourteen, used briefly in autumn 1905 and then from April to June 1906.

[4] Evidently a neighbour, but unlisted in local directories.

We are going this very evening to Winchelsea for a week in the Bungalow.[1] Ford would have it so. *The Heart of the Country*[2] is out to day and a very charming piece of writing it is.

We talked of You much and admiringly last week in the Nat: Lib:[3] trying conscienciously* to pick holes in *the M of P* after the manner of workmen all the world over: for no greater compliment can be paid to a Mate. And it is a wise procedure too, since in no other way can one get the full flavour of a job well done.

I've been loafing at mine—mostly because of the proofs which came in a lump. I am done now with *The M of S*. Verdict: neither pleasure nor profit.

Jessie's going on well; but I am worried about her heart. That does not seem to be well. Still her appearance does not show any serious advance in whatever lesion there may be.

Our tenderest love to You both. I do want to set eyes on you. Talking of *the* play with Hueffer we agreed that it must be *hit or miss* but if 'hit' then sure to be a knock down one. However I ought to see *the* play. H. says: dialogue admirable in places. Three cheers. Ever Yours

Conrad.

PS Jessie begs me to say to Ada that she feels so lazy and restless that *impossible* to write a letter just now. No doubt that phase will pass off soon.

To Messrs Methuen & Co.
Text J-A, 2, 33

Pent Farm,
30th May, 1906.

Dear Sirs,

Thanks for your letter with the two missing sign[ature]s: 9 & 10 and suggestion for title page.

As regards that last my feeling is against half measures. My idea being rejected let us have the usual form. *OF* will not do.[4] I thank you for the attention paid to my remark; but it was only a remark. *OF* is logical no doubt but it is not expedient. In this connection it is distinctly aggressive and that apparently insignificant departure from the usual is likely to

---

[1] Jessie Conrad gave an account of the visit in *Joseph Conrad and His Circle*, pp. 112–16; Ford's trick of drying his panama above the noon-tide roast did not endear him to her.
[2] Ford's rural sequel to *The Soul of London*.   [3] Ford's club, the National Liberal.
[4] After 'Memories and Impressions'.

provoke more remark than the radical rearrangement of title page suggested by me. So let us have *BY* and shock no one's preconceived notions.

My feeling is against a red title. Black, providing that the lettering can be made a little heavier, is more to my taste. I leave the final decision to you. Couldn't the words *Mirror of the Sea* be printed in Gothic type? It rests with you.

You ask me for something very difficult. Any definition of one's work must be either very intimate or very superficial. There is only one man to whom I could open my confidence on that extremely elusive matter without the fear of being misunderstood.[1] The intention of temperamental writing is infinitely complex, and to talk about my work is repugnant to me—beyond anything. And what could I say that would be of use to you? I may say that the book is an imaginative rendering of a reminiscent mood. This is a sort of definition and it is true enough in a way. But the book is also a record of a phase, now nearly vanished, of a certain kind of activity, sympathetic to the inhabitants of this Island. It is likewise an attempt to set down graphically certain genuine feelings and emotions born from the experience of a respectable and useful calling, which, at the same time, happens to be of national importance. It may be defined as a discourse (with a personal note) on ships, seamen, and the sea.

All this and much more may be said of it; and pray believe that I regret not being able to answer your demand in a more liberal spirit. Whatever I've written above is in strict confidence. Mr. Conrad *must not be quoted* as having said this or that about his book. But I hope it will be of some use for the note in your catalogue.

[1] Garnett?

To John Galsworthy

Text MS POSK; Danilewiczowa

[letterhead: Pent Farm]

Saturday *8 am* [2? June 1906][1]

Dearest Jack

Borys has developed high fever on Thursday night, I wired for a nurse, and so on:—I am getting an expert in managing the beastly and the unexpected.

This morning fever slightly less no signs of any rash so far. It may be only a very sharp attack of influenza.

I'll let you know how the case develops on Monday: now I'll merely remark that this thing is getting monotonous. This puts me off the end of my long Anarch: Story which is becoming topical anyhow.

Query: Which is really more criminal?—the Bomb of Madrid or the Meat of Chicago.[2] But "in all these tales"—as I remark a propos of Falk's cannibalism "there is always a great deal of exaggeration."[3]

Give my beso maños to dear Ada—Jessie's dear love. Can't say we are cheerful here but anyway we are making a stand.

Ever yours

Conrad.

Jerrold[4] called here cycling and for a good hour talked with admiration of the *M[an] of P[roperty]*—with some intelligence too.

---

[1] This letter and the next four (all five bear letterhead fourteen) are linked by a web of allusions to current events, domestic and political, but dating the others is contingent upon dating the first. Although later Saturdays would be possible, the most likely date is 2 June, two days after 'the Bomb of Madrid', hidden in a bouquet and hurled by an anarchist, almost killed the newly married King and Queen of Spain – making Conrad's work on *The Secret Agent* eerily topical.

[2] The attempted assassination, which killed twelve courtiers and bystanders, or the tainted meat which endangered the lives of thousands? President Roosevelt's commission of inquiry confirmed the findings of Upton Sinclair and other 'muck-rakers': American packing companies produced adulterated food under filthy conditions.

[3] *Typhoon*, p. 237.

[4] Ford's friend Walter Copeland Jerrold (1865–1929), the author of a vast number of popular biographies, an editor of standard authors, and an employee of the *Daily Telegraph*.

To J.B. Pinker
Text MS Berg; Unpublished

[letterhead: Pent Farm]
Sat: [2? June 1906][1]

My dear Pinker

Please make out the cheque for which I asked you on Wednesday to Mrs Ada Galsworthy, and forward to 14 Addison R^d. W.

Jack to whom You are very sympathetic (is it mutual?) wants to ask you to lunch at 14 Addison R^d. for a confidential talk. He asked me whether you would mind and I said that you would not. You know each other already.

But perhaps the evening would be more convenient to you. If so please tell me (if the invitation has not reached you yet) and I'll give him a hint to that effect.

Your tact will get over his shyness and scruples. As far as I can see he's under no engagement to anybody except a verbal promise to let H[einemann] have the refusal of his next book.

He's scared of dates, engagements and 'pressure' of any kind. I've talked with him for hours; but 10 minutes with You'll do more no doubt. It is not that he would think for a moment of any other literary agent. It is the propriety of having a literary agent at all that he must be made to see. And that is indubitable. His future present[s] itself much better than Hueffer's or mine. He may be the Coming Man indeed! And in view of that possibility I think it is important that his future should be taken in hand on its practical side as soon as possible.

Your[s] always

J Conrad

To John Galsworthy
Text MS Forbes; Unpublished

[letterhead: Pent Farm]
Monday night [4? June 1906][2]

Dearest Jack.

All is well. It was not measles as we feared. Must have been influenza. He had 36 hours of fever rising on Sat to 103. To-day he has begun to mend—nearly normal at 9 pm. We are in luck and the nurse will leave at the end of the week.

[1] References to Ada Galsworthy's cheque and the Pinker lunch place this letter in the sequence.
[2] The Monday after the letter of [2? June].

I am weary of these scares.

Nothing else to say. Am still toiling at *Verloc* part IV. I am weary of that too. But the end is in sight.

How goes your work?

I should like to write something nice but I am too stupid just now. Midnight. It is cold. No ideas—and what's worse no words. So with my blessing to your slumbers—but *are* you slumbering? Or on the contrary are the sounds of revelry issuing from 14 Add^{on} R^d? I wish I were living in an old Abbey and drank sham out of dead men's skulls and woke to find myself famous![1] I wish! I conclude P sent the cheque to Ada but I don't know. That slave obeys my behests in profound silence as a rule. I wish he would say sometimes: "Hakem![2] On my head be it" or some words to that effect. I feel disenchanted—dreary. Our civilisation is like the potted chicken of the U.S.A.[3]—corrupt sir!, Corrupt. It is announced in the press that a play is going to be written upon it.[4] A tragedy I suppose. I mean upon the chicken. Astonishing! Our love

Ever yours

Conrad.

To J.B. Pinker

Text MS Berg; Unpublished

[Pent Farm]
Wednesday. [6? June 1906][5]

My dear Pinker.

I send you 13 pages p[art] IV of *Verloc*.

I am really doing my best and my quickest—tho' you may not think so.

Borys got very ill suddenly last week. We thought at first it was going to be measles of a severe type. However we are in comparative luck. It's nothing but influenza. I got a nurse down here but she is going back this Friday.

I am weary of all these scares.

I'll direct the Bond Street Nurses Association to send their account to

---

[1] As Byron did. 'Sham' was a nineteenth-century abbreviation of 'champagne' (OED).

[2] Arabic: 'Excellency!'

[3] The Brighton magistrates had condemned a shipment of tinned but putrid American poultry (*The Times*, 1 June).

[4] Upton Sinclair's novel *The Jungle* had already appeared – and forced Congress into action.

[5] Dated by Borys's illness.

you. It won't be much *3 to 4* g[uinea]s. Meantime send me a £5 note here to-day if possible.

I hear you have lunched with Jack and that you are pleased with each other. That's good. You'll hear from me soon.

Kindest regards Yours
Conrad

To John Galsworthy
Text MS Forbes; Unpublished

[letterhead: Pent Farm]
Wednesday [6? June 1906][1]

Dearest Jack
Ecco-là the Press cuttings.
Thanks very much for letting Pinker into the sacred precincts.

I hear he is quite delighted and has expressed his appreciation of you by telephone in one or two directions. The above is a sort of joke.

Our thanks for Ada's dear letter. You two dear people hate the Pent so that one dares not ask you to come down even for a few hours. And the journey is such a grind too! But the Missus is wondering when she will see you two—this Year or the next!

The above is a sort of exaggeration.

I am struggling since last night with p. 198. It's disgusting.

Our love
Yours ever Conrad

To William Rothenstein
Text MS Harvard; Unpublished

[letterhead: Pent Farm]
[24?] June [1906] Sunday[2]

Dearest Will.
Our heartfelt sympathy goes to Alice. Jessie has been uneasy for some time and wrote for news only a day or two before your letter came.

Sorry you could not come. Any day would do. We want to see You—and also we have a proposal to make. It would have been made before only we were under the impression that you considered this part

---

[1] Soon after the lunch: the same Wednesday as the letter to Pinker.
[2] By [29? June], the Rothensteins had replied to Conrad's proposal. From now until mid-September, letterhead twelve reappears.

of the country unsuitable to your art—upon the whole. Also we doubted whether Alice liked it. Moreover we had a notion that your plans were fixed already.

For all these reasons we *naturally* offered this home to the Tebbs[1] for the time of our stay in London—that is from the 11th July to about the 10th of Sept^{er}. But the Tebbs can not come. Unless then you do come to the dear old hovel it shall stand empty because Jessie (nor I) won't hear of letting it out to anybody. It's a matter of sentiment. But it would be a real joy for us to think of you being here. I submit the idea to your favourable consideration.

As to details: there is church quarry and barn right in your pocket as it were. There is within three miles a magnificent aspect of the marsh—the great Romney marsh; a miracle of colour at times. There are nooks in the folds of the Downs that wait for a 'seeing' eye—little lost homesteads, stackyards around churches and the beautiful lines of the uplands. And within the house there is one well lighted room with a northern exposure where you could set up your easel for indoor work.

The house itself you know. Five bedrooms above, two and the long kitchen below—with everything needful in it except *the bed sheets* which we take up to London. Stove's in good order—water first rate and no possible smells to affect the chicks; with the wooden house (where you worked at my head)[2] for them to play in when they are tired of the fields.

A good-natured ass called Andrews[3] stays in *our* service to clean knives boots, light kitchen stove in the morning, fetch water from well, give information, and drive the trap which holds four with a kiddy or two thrown in.

I think that with one servant Alice could do but there's plenty of room for two girls. Andrews has a sort of cubicle for himself downstairs. The two front bedrooms communicate; each has a double bed. In the other 3 rooms there are four single beds in perfect working order.

We would expect you to adopt the kitten. The dog is going to have bachelor lodgings in the village.

There would be no difficulty to provision the ship. We would warn our tradespeople and leave you their address. Moreover Andrews knows where to go for things.

The sanitary arrang^{ts} are primitive as you know:[4] and there is no

[1] Albert Tebb (doctor to the Hueffers and the Rothensteins) and family.
[2] In August 1903.
[3] Walter Andrews, the cheerful young man whom Conrad once thought to be suicidal (Jessie Conrad, *Joseph Conrad and His Circle*, pp. 109–10).
[4] A three-seater privy in the garden.

bathroom—but the good natured ass above mentioned is trained to carry hot and cold water upstairs and in due course to empty the sponge baths. There is also a tin bath suitable for baby.

Could not Alice run down here? Either for the day or for the night. Jessie is *most anxious* to see her here. I would of course meet her with a suitable conveyance. Or come both together. Or perhaps young Mr John could spare the time to bring his mother down here. Borys would be beside himself with delight only I won't say anything till I hear from you.

You do say nice things. Fancy you taking up *Falk* again! Well perhaps the thing's not so bad but it stank in the nostrils of all magazine editors.

I work hard but, as usual, not hard enough. Subject: Anarchists. One longish tale and two short ones will make a special volume by and bye.

Our love to you all big and little

Ever your

Conrad.

To Alice Rothenstein
Text MS Harvard; Unpublished

[letterhead: Pent Farm]

Friday. [29? June 1906][1]

Dear Alice.

We are glad to hear that there is the prospect of you finding something suitable in France. I am sure it would be much better both for you and Will not to speak of the dear chicks.

We only wished to convey the idea that there *is* a house at your disposal. Nobody's coming here if you do not so there's no time limit for your decision; except in so far that if you do come we want to instruct the farmer (our landlord)[2] to send here from his other farm another milch cow. The one kept for our use has reached the limit of her usefulness in the honourable career of a milk-giver. That's all.

Jessie is extremely anxious to see you before the event. Do you think you will be in London on the 10th?

We are much concerned to hear that Rachel is not very well. Nothing to give you serious anxiety—is there? It's almost unthinkable that this vivacious, fairy like and wholly admirable young person should be out of sorts.

Jess will drop you a line in a day or so. She goes on wonderfully well,

---

[1] The nearest Friday to 4 July, date of the next letter.   [2] Richard Hogben.

cooks and runs the house with energy but has developed a morbid aversion to writing anything whatever. Our dear love to you all.

Yours affectionately

Conrad.

PS I suppose Will can't come down here?—And you? But I suppose its a wild hope.

To Alice Rothenstein

Text MS Harvard; Unpublished

[letterhead: Pent Farm]

4 July 1906

Dear Alice.

Decide absolutely in your own time. At all events we got the new cow in, so that should you come, there will be plenty of milk for the chicks.

I am doubled up with lumbago or I would have taken a run up to town to see you this week. I hope you won't be away by the time we arrive.

This month begins badly as to weather. I think France would be the best thing for you. It costs me something to write this.

Our dear love to you all big and little

always affectionately Yours

Conrad

To John Galsworthy

Text MS Forbes; Unpublished

[letterhead: Pent Farm]

4 July 1906

Dearest Jack

I had a letter from Chme Graham extremely appreciative of the *M of P*. He's in London and wanted to come here but I had to hold him off.

I see Barker gets into Balloons.[1] What does he mean by it! He's endangering the future of British Drama.

I am positively doubled up with atrocious lumbago.

I will send our two trunks by rail on Monday.[2] I myself shall appear

---

[1] A honeymoon diversion? Granville-Barker and Lillah McCarthy had been travelling in Austria and Germany.

[2] 9 July, for the two-month stay at 14 Addison Rd: the Galsworthys were leaving for the continent.

on Tuesday about 11 am. Would you ask Mrs Hempson to provide lunch on that day for herself and the maid I will bring, and dinner (out of her own head) for the full gang of four. Jessie will arrive at about five.

I am weary and sick of things in general. My work drags badly. I have at last settled up with the Watson C⁰ Estate and shall lay hold of my £600 policy which was pledged to them. Borys is exhibiting signs of melancholia at the thought of leaving the Pent. Jessie alone is very perky and if it were not for the heart trouble in the background I would feel very confident. Beso los manos de la Excelentissima Señora. Our best love

Ever yours

Conrad.

To John Galsworthy

Text MS POSK; Danilewiczowa

[letterhead: Pent Farm]
7th July 1906

Dearest Jack.

I don't eat strawberries because by a merciful dispensation of Providence I detest the things. My lumbago is quite insignificant now.

We shall try not to burst the house asunder by the quantity of the luggage. It, (the house) being given up to the purposes of true charity we propose to stand the two trunks (small—or comparatively small) on the landing. They will disfigure but they will not damage the prospect. Jessie begs Ada not to give herself the trouble to clear out any wardrobes of* cupboards in Your room. The trunks will serve, and if there is an empty drawer or two in the spare-room so much the better. The trunks being scientifically packed will answer the purpose of sheltering the 'dry goods' the dear woman feels herself obliged morally and physically to take with her. You understand I've no voice in those matters. At the least word I've *two* children flung at my head which has a surprisingly weird effect on my feelings.—

How nice and dear of Ada to think of providing for Tues: and Wedʸ to spare Jessie. As a matter of fact that person is perfectly capable of taking care of us all as is daily demonstrated here. In the spirit of the cook of the *Narcissus* she says: 'As long as I stand I will cook'[1]—and does it. At his last visit Hackney declared himself very pleased with her general state and advised me not to check her activity. But she nurses pleasant anticipation of being really lazy for a few days under your roof. All the

---

[1] The cook of the *Narcissus* says: '"As long as she swims I will cook!"' (pp. 81 and 84).

authorities agree on the last week in July on or about the 28th. I hope they are right because waiting gets on my nerves.

Our tenderest love and thanks to you both—and au revoir.

Yours ever

J. Conrad.

PS Borys is taking leave of his moorhens, stack-yard mice and the two white owls he discovered to be our neighbours 3 weeks ago. He reads with ease now but shows no taste for books. It's a long time now since you saw him last.

PPS Ada's letter this moment to hand. Jessie repeats her request not to "*scurry things out of the way*" most emphatically. The trunks are packed, she says on purpose to be used all the time. Borys is having his afternoon lesson but his delight'll be great to have a charge of trust from Mrs Jack.

To Ada Galsworthy

Text MS Forbes; J-A, 2, 34[1]

14 Addison Rd

25 July 1906

My dear Ada.

Your most satisfactory letter delighted us immensely.

We on our part are doing well under your roof. One hot day we have had but no more; and the attentions of your faithful retainers make life easy for us all. I don't know that I am writing much in the little wooden house, but I smoke there religiously for 3½ hours every morning with a sheet of paper before me and an American fountain pen in my hand. What more could be expected from a consciencious* author I can't imagine. Personally, I would prefer to hold in my hand a Tirolese flower in a landscape of mountains at 7 am after breakfast. How delightful it sounds. A breath of cool pure mountain air comes from the pages of your letter and makes me dissatisfied with the pure (but inferior) fragrance of cheap cigarettes.

The temple of Your domestic gods is not profaned by sounds of revelry, but still we have visitors. Mrs Sauter[2] was good enough to come twice, bringing with her the second time Agnes Sanderson, who is said to be enamoured of a son of some High Priest but does not put on insufferable side on that account.

---

[1] The MS is incomplete; after 'Your domestic gods', the text comes from Jean-Aubry.

[2] John Galsworthy's sister Blanche Lilian.

Ladies turn up daily and are taken upstairs to inspect the dry goods store. They come from town and country, from Winchester, from Essex, from Capri and even from Battersea. It is my impression that Jessie has never had such a good time in her life. And they all exclaim at our great luck in such a dear home. It is luck indeed! Too great for words.

Between whiles we live with your portrait pretty considerably. It is a remarkable piece of work. It presides silently at our meals and overlooks Borys' studies. But we discuss it no longer. The last word has been said and it was my boy who said it after a period of contemplation. "How like Mrs. Jack this is, and I hope she will never look like that." Here you have the truth straight from the heart of your admirer.

Pray remember us to your mother.[1] I've read Jack's article in the *Speaker*.[2] Hum! Hum! He had better be careful.

Yours most affectionately.

To Marguerite Poradowska
Text MS Yale; Rapin 183; G. & S. 106

14 Addison Road
London. W.
2 Août 1906

Chère Marguerite.

Un autre garçon dont les noms sont Jean Alexandre Conrad, et pour qui je demande une petite place dans Votre coeur.

Il n'est pas bien gros mais il est bien bâti. Tout c'est très bien passé. A six heures je me suis levé pour aller chercher le medicin et a 9.30 j'ai fait la connaissance de mon second fils. Il m'a regardé avec bienveillance et a cette heure ci (4ʰ de l'après midi) je me sens déjà beaucoup d'amitié pour lui. La maman qui va très bien Vous embrasse bien fort. Elle est très calme et très heureuse. Il n'y a rien a redouter aucune complication. Elle se sent parfaitement bien.

Borys a été fort surpris mais il a fait le meilleur accueil possible a son frère. Il a fait déjà un juste partage de ses joujoux et lui a donné aussi la moitié de son chien—ce qui est une preuve d'affection je Vous assure. Donc la plus parfaite harmonie régne dans la famille.

Quand* a moi après la semaine d'énervement qui a précédé le grand jour je me sens mou comme une loque.

[1] Jack's mother, that is.
[2] 'Wanted—Schooling in Fiction', 14 July, pp. 340–1. Galsworthy attributes the abundance of bad fiction to commercial pressures, particularly the author's need to publish rather than revise and the critic's failure to discriminate.

Comme naturellement j'ai commencé par Vous j'ai quatorze petites notes a écrire cette après midi.

Donc je termine ici en Vous embrassant de tout mon coeur et pour toute la famille.

Toujours le votre

Conrad.

Translation

Dear Marguerite

Another boy, whose names are John Alexander Conrad, and for whom I ask a small place in your heart.

He is not very big, but he is well-built. Everything has gone off well. At six o'clock I got up to look for the doctor, and at 9:30 I became acquainted with my second son. He looked at me with goodwill and now (at 4 o'clock in the afternoon) I already feel a good deal of friendship for him. His mother, who is very well, hugs you warmly. She is very calm and very happy. There is no reason to fear complications. She feels perfectly well.

Borys has been very surprised, but he has given his brother the best possible welcome. He has already made a fair division of his toys and has also given him half of his dog—which is a proof of affection, I assure you. Thus the most perfect harmony reigns in the family.

As for myself, after the week of nervous tension which preceded the great day, I feel limp as a rag.

Since naturally I began with you, I have fourteen notes to write this afternoon.

So I close here, embracing you with all my heart, and for the entire family.

Ever yours,

Conrad.

To Ada Galsworthy

Text MS Forbes; J-A, 2, 35

14 Addison R^d. W.

2 Aug. 1906.

My dear Ada.

I have lately made the acquaintance of a quiet, unassuming extremely ugly but upon the whole a rather sympathetic young man. A lady I like very much introduced him to me and I am very anxious to secure Yours and Jack's friendly reception for him when you return. His name is John Alexander Conrad and he arrived here at 9.30 am today in a modest and unassuming manner which struck me very favourably. His manner is quiet—somnolent; his eyes contemplative, his forehead noble, his stature short, his nose pug, his countenance ruddy and weather-beaten. Altogether I think already that he will be quite a valuable acquisition for our little circle. I feel already (9 pm) a good deal of affection for him.

Borys was extremely surprised. He calls him Brother Jack. His mother whose behaviour is jocose sends her dear love to you both and her very kind regards to Mrs Galsworthy, and I join her with all my heart.

From the remark I have heard: "Escamillo will have to be taught that he has two masters now" I conclude that the harmony of the family is not likely to be disturbed. As a matter of fact besides half of his dog Borys has been busy making over a large share of his property to Brother Jack. I have (as head of the family) sanctionned* all these arrangements which come into force immediately.

Feeling now that you are sufficiently re-assured I refrain from further details for the present. All is well.

Your affectionate friend and servant

J. Conrad.

To Count Szembek
*Text L.fr.*76; Najder 248

14, Addison Road,
London. W.
2 aout 1906.

Très cher Monsieur et Ami,

Juste un petit mot pour vous annoncer l'heureuse arrivée de Jean Alexandre Conrad Korzeniowski à 9 h. 30 ce matin. La maman qui se porte très bien se recommande cordialement à votre bon souvenir.

Borys qui a été fort surpris a fait un excellent accueil à son petit frère. Donc une parfaite harmonie règne dans la famille.

La dessus, Cher Monsieur, je vous serre les mains bien affectueusement car j'ai encore une dizaine des lettres à écrire et il se fait tard.

Tout à vous.

Translation

Very dear Sir and Friend,

Just a little note to announce to you the happy arrival of John Alexander Conrad Korzeniowski at 9:30 this morning. His mother, who is in good health, cordially asks to be remembered to you.

Borys, who was very surprised, has given his little brother an excellent welcome. Thus, perfect harmony reigns in the family.

With that, dear Sir, I shake your hands very affectionately, for I still have a dozen letters to write and it is getting late.

Always yours.

To Jane Wells
Text MS Illinois; Unpublished

14 Addison R*d*

W.

2 August. [1906]

Dear Mrs. Wells[1]

Another boy.

Jessie sends her best love to you all in which I join. I have not written to H. G. having a notion he is absorbed in his American book; and I myself am trying desperately to finish some thing ever since June last.

In haste for post

Yours most faithfully

J Conrad

To Norman Douglas
Text MS Texas; Unpublished

14 Addison Rd

W.

3d Augst. [1906]

Dear Douglass*

Just a line to let you know we have another son and that everything is well so far. What are You thinking of doing in the near future and what are You doing meantime.

We often think and talk of You. My wife sends her cordial regards.

Yours always,

J. Conrad

---

[1] Jane Wells (née Amy Catherine Robbins, 1872–1927) had been H. G. Wells's student and became his second wife.

To Jane Wells
Text MS Illinois; Unpublished

14 Addison Road. W
4ᵗʰ Aug. 1906

Dear Mrs. Wells.

I write for Jessie who wishes to thank you at once for your friendly letter. She seems very well and so is the new boy whose names are John Alexander Conrad—otherwise 'Brother Jack'.

Borys' astonishment was very great but he has welcomed the new-comer with boundless cordiality. In fact we are all very much pleased with Brother Jack who is very red and ugly, but is of an amiable and unassuming disposition. Since last night he has developed an enormous appetite which there is nothing to prevent him from gratifying to the fullest extent.

So much, with her love, I am commissioned to give from Jessie.

For myself I anticipate a sort of moral bucking up which will enable me to finish quickly the story I am engaged upon at present. It is an Anarchist story, rather long, which with two others (short) is to form a special volume. Ever since I turned to that subject I've cherished the notion of dedicating the special volume to H. G. Now I have my doubts as to its worthiness. As *stories* these things seem to me to lack 'quality', and as *view* and *feeling* I fear they are but superficial. If this dismal opinion is confirmed on further examination H. G. will have to wait till *Chance* (a book already begun) is finished.[1] Of that I am (just now) a little more sure.

I got an impression from Hueffer that H G. is plunged deep in his American book.[2] I imagine confidently something clear, cutting sparkling—the real Wells brand of intellectual stimulant which will do us no end of good all round.

We will be back at the Pent about middle of September.

Believe me dear Mrs Wells with our love to H. G. always yours most faithfully and obediently

Jph. Conrad.

---

[1] *The Secret Agent* was, in the words of the dedication, 'affectionately offered' to Wells.
[2] *The Future in America*, serialized in *Harper's Weekly* between July and October.

To Alice Rothenstein
Text MS Harvard; Unpublished

14 Addison R^d W.
4th Augt 1906.

My dear Alice.

John Alexander Conrad—otherwise Brother Jack—arrived on the 2^d at 9.25 am looking very flushed but amiable. I waited till to day as I wished to be able to tell You distinctly that all is well with mother and child.

Borys most cordial to "Brother Jack". He has made over to him a considerable part of his personal belongings including motor cars, baby chair some tools and half his dog. As head of the family I have confirmed these arrangements which are to come into force on our return to the Pent.

Brother Jack weighs 6 lbs 4 oz. His stature is short, his nose long, his hair very dark, his manners quiet and unassuming. We are all very pleased with him. His appetite since last night is enormous but not beyond the means of his mother.

Jessie who is calm and cheery sends her dear love to Your wandering tribe in which I join with all my heart. We are so pleased to hear you are comfortably located. Is your great man at work? More power to his genius. Always dear Alice yours affectionately and obediently

Jph Conrad

To Harriet Mary Capes
Text MS Yale, Unpublished

[London]
4 Augt 1906

Dear Miss Capes.

Many thanks for Your dear friendly letter which I read to Jessie last night.

Everything goes on as well as possible. John Alexander Conrad— otherwise 'Brother Jack' is a very amiable and unassuming person with a pug nose and dark hair. His appetite is good but not beyond the means of his mother.

Borys (who was extremely surprised) is displaying the greatest cordiality towards 'Brother Jack'. He has already made over to him a considerable part of his personal property including half of his dog. You may judge from that last item that the cordiality is unfeigned.

All these arrangements (which have my approval as head of the family) are to come into force on our return to the Pent which will take place about the 15th of Sept.

Jessie sends her dear and grateful love, which expresses exactly my sentiment towards your infinitely valued friendship.

Always dear Miss Capes, your affectionate friend and obedient servant

Joseph Conrad.

To Elsie Hueffer

Text MS BL Ashley 2923; Unpublished

14 Addison R^d W.

8 Augt 1906

Dear Elsie.

We were delighted to get your PC from the Channel. We hope the passage was good and pleasant.[1]

I beg to report in our joint names the happy arrival of John Alexander Conrad—otherwise Brother Jack. He is extremely small but very sound (Tebb says) with a lot of dark hair, long eyelashes and a flushed countenance. His character is amiable and we are all very fond of him. I forgot to mention that his nose is pug.

He was born on the 3^d*—but as you were then at sea I did not hurry on the news. Moreover at that distance I was anxious to be able to tell you positively that everything is as well as can be. The awful heat has tried Jessie a little but she's very cheery and very satisfied with the new boy.

NB We have forgiven him for not being a girl, within the first hour of his existence.

I have been more or less paralysed in my head on account of the heat and other worries. Tebb has tinkered me up a bit and I have begun to write again after a long and dreary pause.

The best of luck dear Padrona, to you and the Illustrissimo Sposo. Incite him all you can to astonish the unpainted savage of the great Republic. What he wanted to get there (where you are) is a succès d'ébahiss[e]ment.[2] Let him deliver up all the glass beads of his intellect and keep the precious stones for a select band on this side of the pond. Has he attended yet any scalp dances at young men's lodges (vulgo

---

[1] The Hueffers left Hamburg for the United States on 3 August and returned at the end of September (Mizener, pp. 123–4).

[2] 'An astonishing success'.

Clubs)? They will feed him there on intellectual roast dog no doubt (NB. this letter is not for publication). Let him try to bag a grizzly editor or two. Always your[s] devotedly

Conrad.

PS Jessie's dear love to you both.

To Mariah Hannah Martindale
Text MS Yale; Unpublished

14 Addison R^d
8 Aug. 1906.

Dear Mrs Martindale

I beg to report in our joint names the arrival of John Alexander Conrad (otherwise Brother Jack) who is very small but very sound and as far as I can judge of a most worthy and amiable character.

I have waited a few days so as to be able to tell you positively that everything is as well as can be. My wife wanted as a matter of fact to write to you herself but we have persuaded her not to sit up to-day. She has felt the awful heat rather but otherwise she is very cheerful, and pleased with the new boy—tho' it ought to have been a girl. However we have forgiven him for not being one.

Jessie's love to yourself and Miss Martindale.

Believe me dear Mrs Martindale of both you ladies the most faithful and obedient servant.

Jph Conrad.

To Ada and John Galsworthy
Text MS Forbes; J-A, 2, 36 (with omissions)

[London]
14 Augst 1906
(it's the 15th really)

Dearest Jack & Ada

Thanks for your letters. We are so glad you approve of the name. Everything is going on very well; Brother Jack thriving exceedingly and his mother all smiles. She has been up for 2 hours to day over the confounded phenomenon.

I manage to write something nearly every day but it is like a caged squirrel running in his wheel—tired out in the evening and no progress made. It's very mysterious that thing. I feel as if I should like to sit down for a couple of years and meditate.

Sisyphus was better off. He did get periodically his stone to the top. That it rolled down again is a mere circumstance—and I wouldn't complain if I had his privilege. But I roll and roll and don't seem to gain an inch up the slope. And that is distinc[t]ly damnable.

Ford I guess is being now entertained in the skyscraping wigwams of the unpainted savages of the grrreat continent. I hope he'll find the war-dances agreeable and soothing to his nerves. No doubt they'll feast him on intellectual roast dog, too. Perhaps his next book will be written with an eagle's feather.

I take note with immense approval of what you say as to your next book.[1] I should love to have a couple of hours tête-a-tête with your copy. A word in your ear: Give up pulling your stuff to pieces over much.

This is my last word for the present.

Many thanks with our deepest regards to Your mother. Jessie's love. I kiss the hand of the gracious lady and shake Your horrid, inky literary fingers. You should see mine! The beastly american fountain pen has gone back on me.

Ever yours

Conrad.

To Harriet Mary Capes
Text MS Yale; Unpublished

14 Addison Road, London
15 Augst
1906

Dear Miss Capes.

We were delighted with your letter. Everything is going on extremely well here Brother Jack thriving exceedingly and his mother all smiles.

I am the only painful person of the crowd. But that is my usual state which is a natural one for a man trying to squeeze some trickle of silly fiction out of a dry, sawdusty brain. It is, I assure You, a very horrid operation which should be forbidden by law on humanitarian grounds.

But if the brain is dry the heart is not sawdusty yet, and cherishes much affection for you. We would be so glad to see you! So glad!

As Jessie nurses the precious baby I can't snatch her away for a dash

---

[1] *The Country House.*

down to Winchester for fear of Brother Jack yelling the roof off the house—and a house that is lent to us too. It would not do. But surely the time will come—it must come soon.

And till it comes we recommend ourselves with our children to your good and precious friendship. Always yours

Jph. Conrad.

To Mariah Hannah Martindale
Text MS Yale; Unpublished

[London]
16 Aug^{st} 1906

Dear Mrs Martindale

Jessie is writing to You herself either to-day or to-morrow.

We are both inexpressibly grieved at the account of your ill health and sufferings; and we are very much touched at your kindness in writing with your own hand all the kind wishes and the friendly words which we so much appreciate.

We do hope earnestly that a decided improvement in your health will soon take place. Pray receive for Yourself and Miss Martindale the hearty expression of our sympathy and friendship. I am dear Mrs Martindale always your very faithful friend and obedient servant

Joseph Conrad.

To William Rothenstein
Text Copy, Harvard; Unpublished

14 Addison Road. W.
21st August. [1906]

My dear Will

In three words: we are well. I ought to have written before.

Jessie came down on Saturday last very chirpy but for the game knee which hurts a good deal. Brother Jack is flourishing exceedingly and making himself agreeable all round.

I am working as usual not fast enough. Still something gets done. And you? Your house seems charming. I hope Alice is resting thoroughly and the kiddies expanding in joyful freedom away from this wilderness of bricks which oppresses Borys' and my spirit. We hope to escape from the bondage in a fortnight from this. Voilà.

Our dear love to you all big and little
Ever Yours
Conrad

P.S. You'll have to come with Alice and John to the Pent before the fine weather is over.

To John Galsworthy
Text MS POSK; Danilewiczowa

[London]
24th Augst [1906][1]

Dearest Jack

A letter to Cortina went off a day before I heard from Mrs Smith that you were in Paris.

The idea of rehearsals being so near excites me.[2] You will let me come to one of them—one day.

Brother Jack flourishes and the mother also. We will—all being well—leave your nest on the end of Augst or say 2^d Sept.

It'll be perfectly safe and we would like to get some fine weather at the Pent.

At the Pent! Where You must come if only to see Jack. So Jessie says. But if you have rehearsals every blessed day! . . . !

We are going back to no servant, no nothing. Jessie says she will manage. So be it; but she got up rather lame. However that's improving.
Our very dearest love Yours ever
Conrad.

C/o McClure Philips c^o Union Sq. New York ought to find Ford.

---

[1] The contents – rehearsals, the new baby – fix the year.
[2] Galsworthy's *The Silver Box*, his first completed play, was to open at the Court Theatre on 25 September.

To J.B. Pinker
Text MS Berg; Unpublished

[London]
[late August 1906][1]

Dear Pinker.

I have referred him to you.

If you think it worthwhile—or good policy—I would try to finish the short thing I have left (rather chaotic) at the Pent.

I am however plunged neck deep in Verloc.

Yours ever

Conrad.

To Ada and John Galsworthy
Text MS Forbes; Unpublished

[letterhead: Pent Farm]
Wednesday [5? September 1906][2]

Dearest Jack and Ada

Thanks for your permission to come of Friday. We arrived here all well, and we begin to feel at home already.

In the matter of car I would advise a local man in Dover.[3] The hotel people ought to know. I don't know anything nearer than Canterbury which would [be] difficult to arrange. There is a decent garage in Deal where they let out cars. You'll find their ad: in the little local guides for Dover and Deal which they sell at the rway stalls.

When motoring over here direct course by *high road* to Folkestone. The Alkham Valley route should not be taken unless the driver has been there before. From Folkestone go through Cheriton, Beachboro, Hitchen Hill, and at the four cross roads beyond Hitchen Hill turn sharp to *left* and then bearing to the right you will get into Postling—and from there you know the way. I will be on the lookout for you.

It's delightful to think of seeing You again. Our dear love

Ever yours

Conrad.

---

[1] On behalf of an unspecified editor in New York, M. E. Hanshaw asked for a 5,000 word story, offering £120 for delivery within a month. Conrad wrote on the back of Hanshaw's letter, which is dated 22 August 1906.

[2] Letterhead twelve, used intermittently between September 1904 and 1906. There were three homecomings to the Pent in that period: May 1905, April and September 1906; the Galsworthys were away for the first, and an extant letter [18? April] reports the second. The third was announced for 2 September; 5 September is the closest Wednesday.

[3] The Galsworthys were returning from France.

To J.B. Pinker
Text MS Berg; Unpublished

[letterhead: Pent Farm]
Wednesday [12 September
1906][1]

My dear Pinker.

Herewith 12 pp of MS. I am going on as fast as I can. Will you please instruct Moore[2] to send me all he has had typed since I saw him last.

Please send me this week a cheque for £10 for my furniture man as I want (must) order a cot from him. And another for £6, the local chemists bill.

Jack likes Verloc and finds it quite interesting from 'public' point of view. His play will be performed on the 25 or 27 I am not certain of the date. Would you get me a ticket (circle or stall?) for the first performance of *The Silver Box*. I will come up. It's a matinee of course.[3] Are you going? If so I would like to have a seat near you and compare impressions. I want to see well and hear well. It will be an interesting experiment.

Kindest regards Always yours
J. Conrad

To John Galsworthy
Text MS POSK; J-A, 2, 37 (with omissions)

[letterhead: Pent Farm]
12 Sept 06
9 am

Dearest Jack

I've got the MS. this morning and before tackling the task of the day I want to thank you for your dear and good letter.

I am no end glad you like the thing[4] generally.

The point of *treatment* You raise I have already considered. In such a tale one is likely to be misunderstood. After all you must not take it too seriously. The whole thing is superficial and it is but *a tale*. I had no idea to consider Anarchism politically—or to treat it seriously in its philosophical aspect: as a manifestation of human nature in its discontent and imbecility. The general reflections whether right or wrong are not

---

[1] The following Wednesday, Conrad thanked Pinker for fulfilling his requests.
[2] The manager at Pinker's office.
[3] Granville-Barker and Vedrenne's standard practice with a new play; having proved itself, it had an evening run in 1907.
[4] Part of *The Secret Agent*.

meant as bolts. You can't say I *hurl* them in any sense. They come in by the way and are not applicable to particular instances—Russian or Latin. They are—if anything—mere digs at the people in the tale. As to attacking anarchism as a form of humanitarian enthusiasm or intellectual despair or social atheism that—if it were worth doing—would be the work for a more vigorous hand and for a mind more robust, and perhaps more honest than mine.

The diffuseness pp *141 to 151* depending on the state of the writers health, has been felt, and shall be remedied in the measure of possibility.

As to the beastly trick of style I have fallen into it through worry and hurry. I abominate it myself. It isn't even French really. It is Zola jargon simply.[1] Why it should have fastened on me I don't know. But anything may happen to a man writing in a state of distraction. We shall see to that with great care when the tale is finished. You'll get a few pp more when Pinker returns them to me. The end is not yet tho' 45 thousand words *are*.

And was Ada *really* interested?

Our dearest love to you both.

Your

Conrad.

P.S. Brother Jack flourishes in the sole care of his mother as well (if no better) as ever. But she has no time to write—or even to call her soul her own as you may imagine. You would never think that the care of a baby not six weeks old is universally recognised as the exclusive work for one person. Brother Jack is a serene soul with a fiery temper somewhere at the back. To see that lame woman hop around with him, cook with one hand, attend to Borys (for B must not feel himself neglected in those small attentions he has been used to receive) and watch that I should not be disturbed in my work is a pretty subject but as it does not lend itself to romantic treatment I won't say any more about it.

---

[1] Conrad told St.-John Perse of a fondness for Zola (in 1912: Najder, p. 379), but he must also have regarded him as a writer who – unlike Flaubert, the master – was too hurried to care about style.

To H.G. Wells

Text MS Illinois; Unpublished

[letterhead: Pent Farm]
15 Sept 1906.
Saturday evening

My dear Wells.

The Comet[1] appeared to my naked (and surprised) eye yesterday morning. By a great effort of will I stuck to my own task till lunch time. I began my observations in the afternoon and continued at it far into the night. I've completed them this morning.

It is indeed a phenomenon!

But after observation comes computation and I can't say I am ready with that as yet. In appraising a book of that sort one must do some exact thinking and my thinking is at present in a confused state. Some rough conclusions I have arrived at and am sending them to you for what they are worth. And I will say that your "harsh and earnest youth"[2] is quite a creation: in intensity and lucidity a step beyond your other creations. And I mean this not only as to himself but more completely in everything and everybody related to his personality. As to Nettie she is beyond the shadow of doubt the most feminine of all your women and as it were the glorified quintessence of them all from poor little Weena of the old old days[3] to the girls of that lucky dog Kipps—may his shadow never grow less! My present feeling is that those two people *are* the book the whole book. I am as yet under the sheer power of your art—the compulsion of it. The day of liberation may come or may never come. Very likely I shall be dead first. But if it does come that'll be the day on which I shall marshall my futile objections as to the matters treated of in this book.[4]

This is all for the present. There is a point I would raise (not critically) if I were not feeling so confoundedly muddle headed just now. I fear being misunderstood; but I will either write to you soon or try to come over for an hour or so. Meantime I will endeavour to think it out. In a few days I will be sending you a wretched little volume of mine which is going to be shot out on the rubbish heap by Methuen on the 4th of Oct.[5] Jessie sends her best love. She is very lame but very game too, run[n]ing the show and looking after her baby singlehanded of

---

[1] *In the Days of the Comet.*   [2] Leadford, the narrator.

[3] *The Time Machine* (1895).

[4] In Wells's novel the liberation, brought about by the passing of a comet, is from traditional codes of sexual behaviour.

[5] *The Mirror of the Sea.*

course. The little chap positively hadn't* had yet a single ache of any sort in his six weeks of life. We are driven to delay his lawful meals on purpose to give him a chance to exercise his lungs. He avails himself of it with the greatest moderation. With my love to you all big and little.

Ever yours

Conrad

To John Galsworthy
Text MS POSK; Danilewiczowa

[letterhead: Pent Farm]

16 Sept

'06

Dearest Jack.

My stall is C. 7. I want to see and hear without worry and the bother of opera glasses.

My excitement is tremendous and your letter is like oil on the flames. Will you be there on the 25th?

Jessie of course can't come and is on the verge of tears.

Postman waiting.

Yours ever With our best love

J Conrad

To John Galsworthy
Text MS Forbes; Unpublished

[letterhead: Pent Farm]

17 Sep 1906.

Dearest Jack.

If you are not utterly absorbed in your rehearsals and can live without the mummers (You remember Constantin Marc in Histoire Comique[1] who couldn't) perhaps you would not mind as you pass along some street or other to look in at a watchmaker and get me a watch for Mons: B. who is entitled to it by promise on my side and performance on his.

I've directed Pinker to send You £2. At the time I was mate of the *Torrens*[2] a very good gun-metal Waterbury could be got for 40/−. I fancy I have seen oxidised case watches for boys marked at less than that in the windows. And it need not be a Waterbury. I ask you to do that thing

[1] By Anatole France (1903).
[2] 1891–3: he met Galsworthy on the second return voyage.

for me because I positively can't spare the time to go myself to Hythe or Folk'ne. Verloc exhausts my time and my energy.

Perhaps if you or Ada going along High St Kens: see something of the kind You wouldn't mind buying it for me and instructing the shop-keeper to send it on here.

Pray pardon my impudence. It should be interesting to your artistic perceptions by its very magnitude—an enormous bulk at a very low temperature. I entreat you both to look at it in that calm, detached way.

Affectionately yours

Conrad

To J.B. Pinker
Text MS Berg; Unpublished

[letterhead: Pent Farm]

Wednesday. 17 [19?] Sep^t 1906[1]

My dear Pinker.

Herewith pp 407 to 428 of Secret Agent—about 2.400 words. Remains to write the half—the dramatic half of the last chapter.[2] I have been at it the best part of last night and am in hopes of pulling it off in a creditable manner.

Many thanks for the cheque the theatre ticket and the specially bound copy of the *M. of the S.* It is the very thing but I'll wait a week or so before sending it on.[3] I don't know either what is the proper form for the inscription. Perhaps You could give me a hint?

Please let me have a cheque for £6.3.4. and another for £7. to settle accounts; also £5 for myself (open).

Jack is delighted with his cast. He works at rehearsals from 10 till five every day and is full of hope. So I reckon the performance will be interesting enough. I hope to see you there. I had to write to H. G. about his last book. I am afraid he isn't pleased.

Kindest regards

Your Conrad.

We are all well. Borys is going to a school nearby as day boy to begin with on Monday next.

---

[1] Wednesday was the 19th.

[2] As finished for serial publication, *The Secret Agent* is about two-thirds of its ultimate length; the MS of this version (Rosenbach) amounts to 627 pages.

[3] To A. J. Balfour, who had been Prime Minister when Conrad received his grant from the Royal Bounty.

To J.B. Pinker
Text MS Berg; Unpublished

[letterhead: Pent Farm]
Thursday. [20 or 27 September
1906][1]

My dear Pinker.

Many thanks for Your letter and enclosures. ——

Can I send the inscription as at* the back?

If you have any opinion as to its tact of wording it would be friendly of you to let me know. A remark on the margin would do.

Your[s] always

Conrad.

Have you—or can you—give me any idea where B. is at present. I would send off the thing at once.

I think this is too involved

To

The Right Hon. Arthur James Balfour. M.P.

this copy of a work, which has at least the merit of being short and perhaps also that of having been written in a spirit of pious fidelity to an existence already remote and to the simple men whose humble task on this earth has been faithfully performed—

is presented by the author in testimony of his feelings, genuine and profound which he finds difficult to put into such worthy words as would not suffer them to appear diminished in their warmth, character and nature.

Pent Farm.

1906.

---

[1] Close in date to the letter of '17' [19?] September. Conrad's desire to wait a week before sending off Balfour's copy makes the later date more likely.

To J.B. Pinker
Text MS Berg; Unpublished

[letterhead: 14, Addison Road,
W.]
Wednesday [26 September
1906][1]
8 am

My dear Pinker.

The play is a piece of life absolutely interesting and I rather think it will be a success. At any rate the audience yesterday was evidently held—a little surprised at times but interested and moved by the simplicity of presentation. There's not a single piece of wit, paradox or smartness in the whole 3 acts. I admire Barker's courage and I admire equally his wonderful talent of a stage manager.[2]

It's difficult to give you the idea of the purposeful artlessness of the thing. Briefly imagine Ibsen without that sort of mystic undercurrent of something which is found in his plays. A success—but of course one never knows.

Wells was there. Garnett. Hudson. Mrs Pat Campbell. I saw the head of Archer, perfectly impenetrable. Walkley gave signs of approval.[3] In the lobby I heard such words as "Queer". "Very good', and so on. The last act—the Police Court, admirably managed, gripped the house. Actors really excellent. Really. I am curious to see the papers this morning.

I am off soon—back to my task. I do so want to pull off my Verloc at last! Not that I am weary of it. Quite the contrary—but I am anxious as to the last 30 pages.

Barker sent me urgent requests for a play by two different people besides Jack himself. G. asked me whether you were in the house. I told him you would be sure to see the play later.

Yours always

Conrad

PS Please send £*10.10* to Mrs Richmond. St Leonard School. Stanford. N^r Hythe. Kent.

---

[1] The day after the opening of *The Silver Box*.
[2] During the legendary seasons at the Court, 1904–7, J. E. Vedrenne managed business and Granville-Barker artistic affairs; Shaw's plays aside, Granville-Barker also directed every production.
[3] Mrs Patrick Campbell (Beatrice Stella Tanner, 1865–1940) could count among her triumphs many roles in 'problem' plays. A. B. Walkley reviewed for *The Times* and was Archer's great rival.

To Henry James
Text L.fr. 77

[London]
[October 1906][1]

Ce livre, très cher Maitre,[2] a au moins le mérite d'être court. Est-il jamais permis de vanter son oeuvre? Je ne sais. Mais ceci est un moment d'intimité. Je ne crains pas de vous le dire, ce petit volume composé sans art est dépourvu de toute malice; vous n'y trouverez aucune philosophie, mais, peut-être, quelques sentiments des choses lointaines et des hommes simples qui ont vécu.

Ces esquisses furent tracées surtout pour mon plaisir. Ecrire pour le plaisir est une dangereuse fantaisie. Je me la suis passée au risque de provoquer des grimaces d'ennui ou des sourires plus blessants encore. Si dans cette petite préface écrite pour vous tout seul, j'en fais la confession, c'est que je suis très sûr de l'amitié dont vous m'honorez. Je sais que votre sourire s'éclairera d'une bienveillante douceur. Votre oeil ami saura distinguer dans ces pages cette piété du souvenir qui a guidé la phrase tâtonnante et une plume toujours rebelle.[3]

Translation

This book, very dear Master, has at least the merit of being short. Is one ever permitted to boast of one's work? I do not know. But this is a moment of intimacy. I am not afraid to tell you that this little volume, artlessly composed, lacks all malice; you will not find any philosophy there, but, perhaps, some feelings about distant things and simple men who have lived.

These sketches were set forth chiefly for my own pleasure. To write for pleasure is a dangerous fantasy. At the risk of provoking grimaces of boredom or even more hurtful smiles, I have ignored the fact. If within this little preface written for you alone, I make my confession, it is because I am very sure of the friendship with which you honour me. I

---

[1] Conrad sent James a copy of *The Mirror* with this inscription. James replied on 1 November: G. Jean-Aubry, ed., *Twenty Letters to Joseph Conrad* (First Edition Club, 1926).

[2] Conrad's friendship with the Master began with the presentation of *An Outcast* in 1896, reciprocated by a gift of *The Spoils of Poynton* in 1897. By writing in French, Conrad emphasized their shared devotion to the language of Flaubert.

[3] In reply, James praised Conrad's 'adorable book' in the warmest terms: 'You stir me, in fine, to amazement and you touch me to tears, and I thank the powers who so mysteriously let you loose with such sensibilities, into such an undiscovered country—for sensibility.'

know that your smile will light up with a benevolent sweetness. Your friendly eye will know how to distinguish in these pages this devotion to memory which has guided the tentative phrase and an always stubborn pen.

To Ada and John Galsworthy

Text MS Forbes; Unpublished

[Pent Farm]
Wednesday. [3 October 1906][1]

Dearest People,

Such letters! Such beautiful letters![2] This is incense indeed and I remain still a little intoxicated with the scent.

That the little book should meet with your approval is a piece of good fortune. I own I did not expect it. The intention was modest and the execution hurried tho' never careless. I had my grave doubts. Well. Now I am relieved (for I trust you both implicitly) if just a little bit overwhelmed by such a ready and delicate *comprehension* of its innermost feeling.

I await the cuttings with great impatience. Of the 'Times' article[3] I heard from (of all people in the world!) Nellie Lyons[4] who came on Friday to see us *and* the baby. I mentionned* I was in town on Tues: and she said at once. "Yes. I thought so. To Mr *Jack's play*". I am afraid she said "Mr Jack's". That's Borys' fault. He set the fashion (at the age of 3 or thereabouts). Then she mentioned the Times' article. "Very good. Very good indeed." and seemed really pleased in her obscure, inarticulate way. After adoring the baby for a time she started across the fields to meet Borys coming from school. They sat and spooned on a stile till I went out at dusk and parted them.

Life has been rather difficult this last week or so. Jessie's nerves are rather jangled and the leg very troublesome. It is a worry. It seems impossible to secure freedom for tackling the end of Verloc. I've been put off and have lost grip. Bother. Our very very dear love.

Yours affectionately

Conrad.

----

[1] Eight days after Galsworthy's première.
[2] John's is preserved in *Twenty Letters*. It reads in part: 'I think the episode in *Initiation* the finest thing you have ever written. I wept over it seated in a public seat and surrounded by natives .... The style on the whole is an advance of anything you have done. It is terser and more varied.'
[3] Walkley's hospitable review of *The Silver Box*, 28 September.
[4] Formerly a maid at the Pent.

To R.B. Cunninghame Graham

Text MS Polwarth; Watts 164

[letterhead: Pent Farm][1]
4 Oct. 1906

Très cher ami.

Incredible as it may appear to you the paper you sent was the first news of your loss.[2]

Rest assured of our most heartfelt sympathy. We would be very glad to hear how you are.

No matter how deeply one feels it is difficult to say the right thing; and for the conventional condoling phrases I have no heart. If you think of coming south it would be good to see you.

With my wife's kindest regards

Affectionately yours

J. Conrad

P.S. In a few days I'll be sending you a little book of mine just about to be published. I intend also to forward a copy to your brother[3] to whom if he is still staying with you please remember me cordially.

To J.B. Pinker

Text MS Berg; Unpublished

[letterhead: Pent Farm]
4 oct 1906

My dear Pinker.

Thanks for your letter of yesterday's date. This is good news indeed! and a great incentive to strenuous effort to retrieve my position.

Don't think, for God's sake, I am loafing with the end of Verloc. But I've told you of the domestic difficulties. Well 3 days ago a 40 acre farmer, a friendly man and his wife, let us have their young daughter at once. She had not been 24 hours with us when her little sister a dear little child which* we saw running about only the day before sickened in the evening and died before day broke. The father came to our back door at 6 in the morning crazed with grief—but he did not forget to bring the milk! The little boy brother was also ill and in a very bad way. Of course

---

[1] Type fifteen begins.

[2] Of his wife, Gabriela (originally Caroline Horsfall). She had died of diabetes in Hendaye, southern France, early in September.

[3] Charles (1853–1917), formerly a naval officer, now deputy chief inspector for the Royal National Lifeboat Institute.

all this upset my wife. Clearly there is an outbreak of enteric in the village. I had a lot of running about, going first over the fields to the school to give them warning as the stream the school cows water from is contaminated. I helped young Richmond to drive the cows away and shut the field gates then started on other peregrinations. We at the Pent are all right.

But this is bad luck. Of course all that bother made me lose grip of my end. It's awful. However the trouble is settled now. I am slowly getting hold again. I'll send you some more pages and all the type to morrow by rail. But the end I can't send you yet. Its too important to be dashed off. I am going to sit up to night and shall go on sitting tight till the thing is done. More I can't tell you. The story will be between 52 and 54 thou:—When you produce the type for an editor you may say that it is an *extended, uncorrected* copy—and if the Editor is a man of some decency of feeling You may tell him that Conrad is ready to shorten the tale for ser pub:[1] I have passages already marked in my mind for the purpose. I can take out 2 to 3 thou. words if so desired—analysis. But *no one else* must mangle the thing. In haste.

Yours always

Conrad.

To J.B. Pinker
Text MS Berg; Unpublished

[Pent Farm]
Thursday [11 October 1906][2]

My dear Pinker.

I am sending you here *17 pp*. which is all I can allow to pass out of my hands today.

I am sitting night and day over the story, stopping just short of the danger of inducing sleeplessness—for that would be fatal to further production. I can't stop after Verloc. If I could take a month off after it—that would be another matter. Over-sitting has to be paid for at some time or another. I am thinking of the books to follow.

As to this one pray remember it's rather a task. It's the first story of

---

[1] In Great Britain. In the United States, the serial had already been taken by *Ridgway's: A Militant Weekly for God and Country*; the first instalment came out on 6 October. Perhaps interest on the part of a British magazine was the 'good news' of paragraph one. In any case, *The Secret Agent* did not appear in Britain until Methuen published the book version in September 1907.

[2] The day before Lucas reviewed *The Mirror* (*TLS*, 12 October, pp. 344–5).

mine dealing with London. And the ironic treatment of the whole matter is not so easy as it looks. And the end is difficult since it just consists in extending that same ironic treatment to the bringing about and the very execution of the final murder (of Verloc by his wife). I tell you it's no joke—not to me at any rate.

If the people who want the story for a serial know my work at all, they must know also that what makes it is not story but quality. And this they can judge of fully without the last half-chap^{er}. On the other hand if the *name* is all they want the last 4–6 thou: words can make no difference. You know that I am not likely to fire off something unsuitable for general reading. You may assure them I am safe.

But I don't mean to delay a moment. Not a moment! All this beautiful weather is passing over my head and I hardly see the sun.

I get a lot of beautiful private letters about the *M of S*. To-day an enthusiastic note from Kipling. I am quite surprised.[1] But I am anxious as to the public. I want for these few deeply felt pages a good press reception. And in that too I am thinking of the books to come. What's written is written.

Lucas reviews me in the Times I suppose to morrow (Friday). If so please send me the N°.

Ford's back. I suppose You know.

Please send me a cheque for £5.10, and one for £3.8 and another for 5 too—for myself. I need them on Sat when my wife goes to Hythe.

Kindest regards Yours

Conrad.

PS <u>Do</u> telephone Methuen to send me 4 copies at once (for Newbolt, Archer, Gosse and Tarver).[2] And get also a couple bought in shops for me. I *must* have them.

---

[1] Although Kipling lived in East Sussex, he had few dealings with neighbouring writers. His note (9 October) shows that he admired 'Typhoon' as well as the new book. Besides the appreciations from Galsworthy, James, and Kipling already cited, Conrad kept letters about *The Mirror* from Garnett, E. V. Lucas, Wells, and Rothenstein; all but Rothenstein's (MS, Indiana) are in *Twenty Letters*. Conrad did not usually save his correspondence.

[2] John Charles Tarver (1854–1926), author of books on Flaubert and the Emperor Tiberius.

To John Galsworthy

Text MS Forbes; Unpublished

[letterhead: Pent Farm]
Sunday night [14? October
1906][1]

Dearest Jack

Pardon me not writing. I am trying to finish the damned story and the end is not yet. I am jeopardising an extremely good serial contract[2] but I can't help it. Perfect misery.

I'll come to talk soon about various things. Brother Jack has been indisposed slightly. Jessie is well but she can't either read or write from difficulty of focussing. We have at last two satisfactory girls. Two, for really Jessie must have a personal attendant of some sort—a kind of aide-de-camp. Borys at school.—I would have a lot to tell of that if I had the time. All the countryside takes an immense interest in the event. It's quite amazing.

I am weary—weary, but manage to give you a thought every day.

Our dear love Ever yours
Conrad.

Kipling sent me an enthusiastic little note. The Age of Miracles is setting in! Also the age of the Times Book Club.[3] The End of the world is at hand.

To J.B. Pinker

Text MS Berg;[4] Unpublished

[Pent Farm]
[mid October 1906][5]

It's exasperating! I want my books to be of uniform appearance as far as the text is concerned, at least, and surely the title page is an integral part

---

[1] The Sunday after the 11th, when Kipling's note arrived?

[2] With *Ridgway's* in New York, where the first weekly instalment had already appeared? Or with a prospective publisher in London, as may be implied in the letter of [11 October]?

[3] Founded in 1905, *The Times* Book Club offered that newspaper's subscribers the chance to borrow popular books free of charge or buy them very cheaply. In the autumn of 1906, the Publishers' Association and the Associated Booksellers began a campaign against the club's 'American' marketing methods.

[4] The MS lacks a beginning.

[5] Reviews of *The Mirror* began to appear a week after its publication on the 4th (*Daily News* on the 10th; *Outlook*, 13th; *Academy*, 20th); by the end of the month, however, Conrad could have promised the imminent end of the 'beast Verloc'.

of a book, and a dedication is too.[1] Other Am: publishers treat one decently as far as I know; but Harpers seem to be mere barbarians.

Have you any idea how *M of S* was subscribed? The reviews are really appreciative and the private letters quite enthusiastic! This book won't damage my reputation, that's certain!

_____ Hueffer was here from *Wed*: evening till Thursday afternoon. His second vol: of Fifth Queen series will be better than the first even. But he seems worried, and must be really so, because of money matters. Very delicately it is true but still he asked me whether I could pay off something of an old debt of £100 I've owed him for some years. He must be pinched indeed. I could never understand the necessity of the American trip[2] which must've been deucedly costly tho' he's a man who knows how to get value for money. I feel quite wretched and overdone not with work but with the anxiety this beast Verloc causes me. I am quite unhappy not to be able to answer your appeal to hurry up in a manner satisfactory to You. I hope no great harm's done yet to the book's value.

Kindest regards Yours

Conrad

To Alice Rothenstein

Text MS Harvard; Unpublished

[letterhead: Pent Farm]
Thursday. [18 or 25? October
1906][3]

Dear Alice,

So sorry to hear of poor Will being laid up. Thanks for your dear p-card.

Jessie is laid up with temperature too, and pains in all her joints. Jack however is well. As to myself I exist in an ineffectual sort of way. Am finishing a book and find it too much for me.

Do please drop us a word on a pc as to Will's progress. Jessie sends her dearest love to you all in which I join with all my heart

Ever yours affectionately

J. Conrad

---

[1] The U.S. edition omits both the dedication and the second half of the title: *Memories and Impressions*.
[2] Nor, after the event, could Ford. On his return, he was attacked by 'a whole flight' of bouncing cheques (Mizener, p. 126).
[3] The contents match those of the following letter.

To Elsie Hueffer

Text MS Yale; Unpublished

[letterhead: Pent Farm]
Friday. [19 or 26? October
1906][1]

Dear Elsie

Impossible to come. Jessie laid up with temp^{re} and pains in all the limbs. Borys has had tonsils—but *he* is better.

No end of worry. I am still at Verloc.

We are so awfully disappointed. Our dear love

Yours ever

J. Conrad

To J.B. Pinker

Text MS Berg; Unpublished

[letterhead: Pent Farm]
Monday. [22 or 29? October
1906][2]

Dear Pinker.

Thanks for your letter. In the matter of Am. book for Secret Agent please do what you think best. I am only thinking that Harpers have paid well for serial pub^{on} of the 2 Anarch: Stories.[3] Are they worth keeping in with? Probably any other Yank publisher would be as bad as they are. Consider the question from that point of view. But perhaps you have already done so.

What were the terms of Nostromo? Altogether the book was contracted for £900 both countries, both forms. What proportion of that amount came under the head of advance on book form in the States I don't remember. I fancy it was *£200. Book in Am 300 Book in Eng: £400 serials.* But I may be wrong.

---

[1] Letterhead fifteen: the date must fall between the Hueffers' return late in September (Mizener, p. 124) and the temporary conclusion of *The Secret Agent* at the end of October (later work on the novel was done overseas). Letters from the earlier part of October report Borys healthy and attending school.

[2] Because *Ridgway's* began the serial on 6 October, the 15th is the earliest possible Monday, but this letter more probably belongs near the frenzied end of the month. The revised knifing scene (pp. 581–616 in MS) was despatched on 2 November. A detailed analysis of the MS will appear in the Cambridge *Secret Agent*.

[3] In *Harper's Magazine*, August and December 1906. The firm did take *The Secret Agent*.

Ridgways are sending me their rag. It's awful—and it don't matter in the least. I see they are 'editing' the stuff pretty severely.[1]

I am doing the knifing scene over again. Meantime have these 20 pages typed at once please. You'll have more to morrow.

Always yours

J. Conrad.

To J.B. Pinker

Text MS Berg; Unpublished

[letterhead: Pent Farm]
Wednesday. [31 October 1906][2]
11.40 pm.

My dear Pinker

Have these pages typed.

To morrow *Thursday* I will have the end ready and will send it on either by last train in the evening or by the 7.45 am on *Friday*. Even in that last case you will have time to have the few pages typed before the American mail closes. In any case if the matter is so urgent you could send them by train to South[ampt]on to catch the *SS "New York"* which is this Saturday's mail boat. You are very patient—and I am very sorry. I would sit up to night but I am gone so stale all of a sudden that it's of no use.

But you will have your end by Friday 10 am—unless I go to pieces altogether which I don't intend to do.

Aren't you sick of me?

Yours

Conrad.

Send me meantime one cheque for £*8.10*—one for £*1.15* one for £*5*.

---

[1] Emily Dalgarno examines the mutilations in *Conradiana* 9 (1977), 50–1.
[2] The *New York* was 'Saturday's mail boat' on 3 November.

To J.B. Pinker
Text Telegram, Berg; Unpublished

[Stanford, Kent
2 November 1906
9.28 a.m.]

Bookishly London

38 pages leave by 10 train begin typing at once another 1500 words to end shall leave at noon by rail with you about 2.40 in time to be typed and catch Southampton mailboat please wire me at five oclock

Conrad

To Algernon Methuen
Text J-A, 2, 38

Pent Farm.
7 Nov. 1906.

Dear Mr. Methuen,[1]

Thanks for your letter with enclosures. I quite understand the object of a descriptive note in a catalogue or circular. I have some notion too of the methods of publishing. I am acquainted with one of the very best travellers in the trade. And as to the "notes" in question, poor W. H. Chesson[2] used to write them very skilfully for T. F. Unwin's publications—my own early novels amongst others. I have also a pretty clear idea who wrote these "notes" for Mr. Heinemann and for Messrs. Blackwood. The point is that I was never asked to furnish that sort of thing myself. And I still think that the author is not the proper person for that work.

I've a very definite idea of what I tried to do and a fairly correct one (I hope) of what I *have* done. But it isn't a matter for a bookseller's ear. I don't think he would understand: I don't think many readers will. But that's not my affair. A piece of literary work may be defined in twenty ways. The people who are serializing the *Secret Agent* in the U.S. now have found their own definition. They described it (on posters) as "A

---

[1] Algernon Methuen (originally Stedman, 1856–1924; baronetcy 1916) founded his company in 1889. Besides text-books, the source of the firm's prosperity, he published Kipling, Stevenson, and Maeterlinck; between 1906 and 1915 he brought out six Conrad titles.

[2] Wilfrid Hugh Chesson (1870–1952) was a perceptive student of Conrad's works and, as one of Unwin's readers, was among the first to see the MS of *Almayer*.

Tale of Diplomatic Intrigue and Anarchist Treachery."[1] But they don't do it on my authority and that's all I care for.

I could never have found that. I confess that in my eyes the story is a fairly successful (and sincere) piece of ironic treatment applied to a special subject—a sensational subject if one likes to call it so. And it is based on the inside knowledge of a certain event in the history of active anarchism.[2] But otherwise it is *purely a work of imagination*. It has no social or philosophical intention. It is, I humbly hope, not devoid of artistic value. It may even have some moral significance. It is also Conrad's writing. I should not be surprised if it were violently attacked. And when it is prepared for "book form" it will be 68,000 words in length—or perhaps even more.[3]

In this connection I wanted to ask you whether it would be possible to have the book set up and *galley slips* pulled off for me to work on? I would like it done very much unless the cost of such self-indulgence were ruinous. I would send the type-script at once to you.

I am very sensible of your kind attention in warning me of the 2nd impression[4] in time for corrections. There will be five—3 caused by my own faulty proof reading and 2 typographical errors. You will find them on the enclosed sheet of paper, clearly set out.

To H.-D. Davray

*Text L.fr.*77

Pent Farm
8 Nov. 1906

Mon cher Ami,

Merci pour le livre qui m'a intéressé beaucoup. C'est très gentil à vous de me l'avoir envoyé. Moi je n'écris pas dans les journaux. J'en suis très incapable.

J'ai écris à Methuen de vous envoyer le *Mirror*. Les critiques ont balancé l'encensoir avec vigueur. Je crois bien que dans le cas de plusieurs c'était avec l'intention de me casser le nez. Il y en a qui ont

---

[1] The fourth episode (27 October, p. 50) is headed: 'A Novel Dealing with the Anarchists and Revolutionaries of London, in which the Diplomatic Intrigue of a Foreign Power, together with Human Selfishness and Anarchistic Treachery, Furnish the Amazing Complications.'

[2] The attempt to blow up the Greenwich Observatory on 15 February 1894. The 'wide knowledge' came *inter alia* from Ford, from Sir Robert Anderson's *Sidelights on the Home Rule Movement* (1906) and, quite possibly, from David Nicoll's *The Greenwich Mystery!* (Sheffield, 1897): Sherry, *CWW*, pp. 205–334.

[3] The book form was half as long again as the serial.   [4] Of *The Mirror*.

saisi l'occasion de donner un coup de pied à ce pauvre *Nostromo* qui a été enterré tout vif il y a deux ans.[1] Vous vous rappelez? En dessous de ce concert de louanges je peux entendre comme un murmure: "Tenez-vous au large. N'abordez pas!" Ils veulent m'exiler au milieu de l'océan. C'est flatteur. Ils n'ont fait cela qu'à Napoléon!

Ils seront bien attrapés.

Je viens de finir un roman (?) où il n'y a pas une goutte d'eau—excepté de la pluie, ce qui est bien naturel puisque tout se passe à Londres. Il y a là dedans une demi-douzaine d'anarchistes, deux femmes et un idiot. Du reste ils sont tous des imbéciles, y compris un Secrétaire d'Ambassade, un Ministre d'Etat et l'Inspecteur de Police—personnages secondaires. Cette fantaisie sera dédiée à Wells. Et à propos de Wells son livre sur les Etats-Unis[2] est tout-à-fait chic. Il a compris un tas de choses incompréhensibles en elles-mêmes. Voilà à quoi sert une imagination comme la sienne servie par une intelligence mordante comme un acide. J'ai presque oublié de vous dire que nous avons un autre fils nommé Jack. Il est arrivé en aout. Il est fort aimable et très solide. La maman se rappelle au bon souvenir de Madame votre femme et vous envoie ses *kindest regards*.

Je suis toujours, cher Ami, le vôtre très cordialement.

Translation

My dear Friend

Thank you for the book, which interested me very much. It is very kind of you to have sent it to me. I do not write for the newspapers. I am utterly incapable of it.

I have written to Methuen to send you the *Mirror*. The critics have swung the censer vigorously. I'm strongly persuaded that in several cases it was with the intention of breaking my nose. There are those who have seized the occasion to kick poor *Nostromo*, which was buried alive two years ago. You recall? Beneath this chorus of praise, I can hear in a murmur: 'Keep to the open sea. Do not land!' They want to exile me to the middle of the ocean. It is flattering. They did that only to Napoleon.

They will be well and truly cheated.

I have just finished a novel (?) with not a drop of water in it—except the rain, which is quite natural since everything takes place in London. It contains half a dozen anarchists, two women, and an idiot. They're all

---

[1] The *Athenaeum* (27 October, p. 513), for instance, praised him for returning to his proper subject: 'When Mr Conrad writes of the sea his work is a pure delight.'
[2] *The Future in America*.

imbeciles, what's more, including an Embassy Secretary, a Minister of State, and an Inspector of Police—secondary characters. This fantasy will be dedicated to Wells. And on the subject of Wells, his book on the United States is quite smart. He has understood a heap of fundamentally unintelligible things. That's the purpose of an imagination like his, aided by an intelligence as sharp as acid. I have nearly forgotten to tell you that we have another son, named Jack. He arrived in August. He is very strong and most lovable. His mother wishes to be remembered to Madame your wife and sends you her kindest regards.

I am always, dear friend, yours very cordially.

To Edward Garnett

Text MS Sutton; G. 200

[letterhead: Pent Farm]
8 Nov. 1906

My dear Edward

Thanks for your dear letter.[1] I waited till now so as to finish my imbecile story before I spoke to you. The principal thing I have to say is that I want the plays *as soon as possible*—both plays.[2] Send them at once my dear fellow: first because I am impatient to see them anyhow—but also for the reason that just now I am especially fit to read them with something approaching understanding. How long this blessed state will last I can't say.

But what about the performance? Where are you going to try?[3] Remembering your sardonic retort "Hengler's Circus"[4] I dare not air my theory of preaching to the Gentiles in the market place. And yet I feel that I'm not utterly wrong there. But perhaps it is impracticable—perhaps there is no market place open to us even for the purpose of having oyster shells and rotten eggs thrown at our heads. The more's the pity.

Jessie sends her dear love to you all. There's something wrong with her eyes just now. I am not at all easy about her.

---

[1] Preserved in Heilbrun, *The Garnett Family*, pp. 112–13.
[2] Garnett's *The Breaking Point* and *The Feud*. He had mentioned them on 20 October in a letter praising *The Mirror* (*Twenty Letters*).
[3] Accepted at the Haymarket Theatre, *The Breaking Point* was denied a licence by the Lord Chamberlain; it received a 'private' Stage Society production in April 1908. *The Feud*, a drama of revenge in thirteenth-century Iceland, played in Manchester in 1909.
[4] An old-established circus famous for its equestrian acts (and hence its production of horse-manure?).

My very affectionate regards to Your wife. Remember me to your
boy.[1] We talk of him often here

Yours ever

J. Conrad

To John Galsworthy
Text MS POSK; Danilewiczowa

[letterhead: Pent Farm]
15 Nov 1906

Dearest Jack

Yes. I've finished Verloc, and am very sick of it. There is a month['s]
work in it yet and perhaps more. I am in a state of such depression as I
have not known for years. I don't know why but no doubt the cause is
physical tho' I can't say I am ill in any way. I feel weak however.

Edward wrote to me. He says The *Country House* is your
masterpiece—so far.

I will try to come along soon. I need the sight of you both—I can't say
how much! And the mere thought of travelling to town fills me with
dread!

Poor Jessie stands this life pluckily. I fancy we must get away if only to
Montpellier again both for her and me too. And that too scares me.

Our dearest love Ever yours
J. Conrad.

Borys is getting on very well. But he ought to go somewhere else. I feel it.
Will try to arrange it after Easter.

---

[1] David, who in connection with *The Breaking Point* later wondered: 'What was Edward's
intention? It seems at moments that his object was to punish his audience': *The Golden
Echo* (New York: Harcourt, Brace, 1954), p. 113.

To Edward Garnett
Text MS Sutton; G. 201

[letterhead: Pent Farm]
[17 November 1906][1]

My dearest Edward.

I got the play[2] at 9 this morning. I've shut myself up with it at once and I won't come out of the room. I will see no one, will let no word or thing come between it and me till I've written to you.

The conduct of the action is simply admirable. I am using here the *exact* word. Admirable from an abstract point of view. Whether you (or anybody else) has the right (I don't mean the ethical right) to throw, in practice, that quintessence of tragedy at our heads (as it were) is another question. It is the quintessence of tragedy and also the quintessence of your really amazing talent for the stage. I know a little what writing is. We come to our work attuned by long meditation, prepared, in a way, for what is to come from under our pen, by the processes of our imagination and of our intelligence and temperamentally disposed (since it is our own work) to accept its necessity—its truth. I am putting to you stupidly what you know very well. But my point is this that I don't think, my dear fellow, you have realised the firmness of mind necessary to an audience who would face your play. If the phrase weren't idiotic I would say that the play is too concentrated. It hits one exactly like a bullet. You can see it coming—I admit—but that doesn't make it easier in the least. On the contrary, it prolongs the agony and brings on that feeling of *helplessness* which I think is fatal to the effect of the play.

The poignancy of things human lies in the alternative. Grace as conceived and presented by you may be true but her position is no longer poignant. From the moment we hear and see her in the wood all hope is over. It becomes obvious that nothing Sherr[ington] can say or do is of the slightest use—unless indeed he were to tie her up hand and foot and carry her off in that way. And mind my dearest Edward you present this state of the girl as initial, fundamental. That's her character—you say. But don't think for a moment that we remain

---

[1] Garnett's dating: he had every reason to remember the circumstances of this letter.

[2] *The Breaking Point*: Duckworth brought it out in 1907 during the controversy over its being banned. On p. x, Garnett offers this summary: 'A girl, Grace Elwood, has intimate relations with her lover, Sherrington, a man whose wife has previously left him. Her father, Dr Elwood, and her lover quarrel for control of her. The girl, fearing she is *enceinte*, cannot stand the strain and succumbs. This is the tragedy. The moral, so far as there is one, is directed against the male egotism of two unseeing and self-willed men.'

indifferent. The effect is produced only too well. The effect is nightma-
rish. Whether you meant it to be so or not I don't know—but that's the
effect. The doom is not hanging over her head. It has already fallen. And
one feels that Sherr: is not the man to lift it. And what's not less
important Sherr: too is presented to us initially as utterly hopeless. One
feels him to be so. We are flung right into the middle of a situation that is
already gone *too far*.

That's her character—you say. I have a certain difficulty in grasping
it. You may tell me I don't know women—and it's very possible I don't.
But to attempt a definition she is the incarnation of submissiveness of a
submissiveness so perfect that it is inconceivable why she should not go
away with Sherr: when he asks her to do so and when it is absolutely
clear there is no alternative. One is driven to ask oneself *why* she had
given herself to Sherrington. From love? But where's her love now?
From simple submissiveness to the hand that took hold of her? But
where's her submissiveness now? These considerations are extremely
disturbing. They are the more so because one does not see *why* she
should stick to her father, like this. The man is not a terrible or a
seductive personality. It seems no personality could be terrible or
seductive enough in the situation as presented to us. Neither is he
pathetically appealing. He is not pitiful, he is not lovable, he is not
awful. Then why? Why this enslaved state? What keeps her chained so?
Sense of duty—the strength of her affection? But you can't eat your cake
and have it. If the sense of duty and the strength of affection are so
terribly effective now where were they when she gave herself to
Sherr'on? By the terms of the problem she could not have done so from
passion—because passion which is not stronger than filial piety is not
passion, it's some other thing of which I have no knowledge.

In its psychological origins the situation for me is enigmatical. If you
meant to present to us a drama of conscience then I haven't understood
your intention at all. That of course would be mainly my fault. But not
altogether—because I am no more stupid than the audience would be.
And this is a play for an audience distinctly triumphantly so. Ibsen
himself has never written a play that was so much, so perfectly in its
workmanship a play for the stage.

But what I want to point out here is the play's quality of hopelessness.
At the end of the first act we feel that everything is over. I have felt it so
strongly that I can't keep it to myself, I can't write of the play and omit
saying so. It would be the merest hypocrisy. The attitude, the words of
the girl at the end of Act 1st settle the whole business. And even

Sherrington seems to think so too. You have every right to invite us to behold this woman perish. But the impression is that she is done for already and what we are to see is the mangling of her body. The play thus misses poignancy and becomes harrowing. It is so terribly harrowing that we want to take refuge in incredulity. We ask ourselves on purpose to ease our feelings: What sort of lover is that who (under these circumstances) can't persuade her. Its inconceivable that the girl should have given herself to him and then suddenly should have become so insensible to his words, to his anguish, to his person! It isn't fate. It seems more like a spell, a mysterious spell which holds them both. And one goes on asking, what—who—cast it on them. They are done for whatever happens, no matter what anybody does, Mansell or Mrs Sherrington. They have lost footing to begin with. Its difficult to express what I mean. I must try to do it by a concrete image. We are called to look at two people crosssing a torrent—a mad rush of water—their chances are one in a thousand. We even feel that they *must* be swept off. We look at them. As long as they stand it is a poignant sight. Directly they are swept off their feet the sight ceases to be poignant, anguishing, appealing. It becomes harrowing only. My dear Edward you are inviting us to see a harrowing sight. Their characters are such that they never had a footing. And that, frankly, is incomprehensible—at least to me. For I ask myself how on earth did they get so far into the bed of that torrent?

I come back to my idea that this is a drama of conscience so subtly balanced that it escapes my comprehension. But here I am faced by the difficulty of time. The position has lasted for some time. What brings on then the crisis of conscience. The word of the doctor? of a doctor! The assurance of that man. Then it's not conscience but funk. It can't be conscience since it is plain that it is the fact of being pregnant that affects her so. And here a sheer question of fact arises. Did she really want a doctor to tell her so? Why my dear Edward a girl so afraid of the plain issue would have been in a blue funk from the first—from the first fortnight. Ten doctors assuring her that it was *not so* could not have assuaged her fears. One does not want to be a great expert in seduction to feel sure of that. And you represent her as doubting, absolutely doubting doubting the word of the doctor while she is already in a state of pregnancy advanced enough for that man to form an opinion! I warn you solemnly that no man or woman in the auditorium will believe you for a moment. She was much more likely to rush out of the consulting room to do away with herself there and then—since it is obvious she being "established" as you 'establish' her character—nothing on earth can matter. She's doomed by that funk lest the father should know. Because that's what it is. Mrs Sherr: arrival cannot possibly have anything to do with that denou[e]ment. It's simply a question of time. It's *that* which decides it: Sherr'on goes to *tell* her father—and she jumps into the river. But the thing in another two months shall become apparent anyhow—and she will jump into the river!

Thus this girl who can neither face her father nor her lover—faces death. Here my dear Edward I am—controverting the psychology of that action—I am going to say elementary things. Girl mothers have com[m]itted suicide before in the history of mankind. They have. But never from the mere fear of parental wrath or tenderness to parental anguish. To maintain that is a negation not only of love but even of mere sensuality. The suicide follows the abandonment by the lover. It is comprehensible even as caused by parental wrath in the *absence* of the faithful lover—some accidental absence. But here the lover is at hand with his person, his voice, his entreaties his devotion and his fidelity—with all the personal fascination of a man fascinating enough to have seduced *that* girl. She could not have loved him. Then why did she give herself to him?—After all it isn't the usual sort of thing in her sphere of life to go all that length out of mere casual kindness. But on the theory or reading of her character as temperamentally submissive perhaps neither the attack nor the defence were very fierce. Very well. Then surely in that passive woman, in that acquiescent and timid soul the dread of parental wrath—or of the parental sorrow if you like— and the love for the man who had conquered her (from herself alone) would have counterbalanced each other giving her poor soul a sort of awful equilibrium. After Sherr: went away she would have sat there till father and lover came back to "tear her in two" as Mansell says. But to go out and drown herself—an act of energy anyhow—never. You make it go down, your art does it; but not for long. The arbitrariness of it causes a reaction. After that come surprise—and doubt. You can't do the impossible.

A scene in which these two would be squabbling over her, the selfish fatuously selfish father and that lover whose love could not move—I won't say a mountain, but a grain of sand—a scene in which they would be pulling her to and fro till she died in their hands that is a scene my dear Edward which you could write, which you could *make* go down with tremendous effect—I am confident. And, you know, it would be quite conceivable; conceivable by the audience I mean. You are capable of that achievement.

As it is the going away of Sherrington remains inconceivable. Don't let us forget that he is her lover. He has her there. The thing is done. She has gone away from her father. All he has got now to do is to lock the doors and order the carriage. Why should he leave her alone to rush off and force himself upon the father. To what end? What can he expect? Bring him to the girl? As the thing stands now I want to know why? In the first act he wanted her to go away from her father. That was the difficulty. Now she has done it—actually has done it. Ran from her home to the house of her lover. He has got her; he has got his supreme chance. And he drops her! At first when Mansell tells him his wife had been to see the father (and as he does not know what she said there) it is comprehensible that he should rush over there to be at hand and take the girl away. But once Grace is with him there is no earthly reason that I can discover. And I am not particularly dense as a rule.

He could hardly have expected to get the old man's blessing. If he thought that the girl was going mad (and that's the first we hear of it) that was not the way to save her sanity. For if she was going mad with anything it was with the apprehension of her father *knowing*. It's a shock to see him rush off leaving her to her madness—to put his hand to it in fact.

It's absolutely marvellous tho' how for the time of the reading your skill of presentation makes one accept all this! But only for the time of reading. Directly afterwards one is positively assailed by all these questions, all these doubts and objections which do believe me I haven't sat to think out. They have rushed upon me, unexpected and anything but welcome. They have rushed upon me with such a force that I can not hold my tongue. There is no other man in the world to whom I would have written as I am writing to you now.

It is a magnificent subject. I entreat you my dear Edward to put this play in the drawer for six months or so. Then consider my objections afresh. I may be wrong. But I am perfectly sincere; and in absolute sincerity there is always a grain of truth. I care too much for your work to pass it off with a complimentary phrase; and about your work I can speak to you without fear of being misunderstood—but to you alone. These words are for no other ears. I beg of you *not* to show this letter to *any one*—but to your wife of course if she wishes to see it. No third person would understand how much affection, how much regard and respect for every line you write there is in this burst of criticism. I don't choose to be misinterpreted as I would be sure to be. The play is admirably done. I believe this, and that's all I need say to men who are strangers to your effort and to my anxiety. And you must forgive the stupidity, the inevitable stupidity that no one can steer clear of in this world. If I have not understood you I would have at least showed you how in this instance you may be misunderstood. And that knowledge may be useful too in a universe ruled mainly by fools.

With our dear love

Ever Yours

Conrad

To Edward Garnett
Text G. 210

Pent Farm
Stanford Near Hythe
Kent
20 Nov. 1906

My dear Edward.

You attach too much importance to my remarks! At the same time you do seem to be a little unreasonable—in discounting my judgement on the ground that it is delivered with the knowledge of the end! How else could I judge? You advance as a sort of objection that I reason from my knowledge of the end. I reason of course from my knowledge of *the whole*. In what way the *ignorance of the audience* is more likely to be right I don't know. I can assure you that the audience will judge—or sum up its feeling about the play—from its knowledge of *the whole*. It cannot be otherwise. To reproach me with my clairvoyance is not exactly just my dear Edward. But if it is a sin then it isn't a very great one. Moreover, referring to the same part of your letter please note that I never said the audience would be bored. I said the audience wouldn't stand it, quite another thing. And even in that I shouldn't wonder if I were totally wrong.

We must meet soon. I am just now horribly seedy and depressed. I am meditating a flight to the South if it can be arranged. I must run over to town on Tuesday next,[1] if I can, just to see you for an hour or so.

There would be much more to say about the play but frankly just now I am not up to it.

Love from us all.

Ever yours

Conrad

[1] The 27th.

To Sidney Colvin
Text MS Duke; Unpublished

[letterhead: Pent Farm]
21st Nov 1906

Dear Mr Colvin,

Perhaps if the weather is fine enough to make a drive tolerable Mrs. Colvin and yourself would come as far as the Pent—have a cup of tea and see the new baby. My wife would have put that proposal before you herself but just now there is something wrong with her eyes; a difficulty (I trust temporary) in focussing which prevents her from reading and writing.

The wind is dreadful our way and coming to see us will strike you as an experience in slumming—country, bucolic slumming. But with a little sunshine the drive is not so bad. Postling is the village to make for and once there any child would direct the driver to the Pent Farm 1/4 a mile further on.

I haven't been even thinking of writing a play tho' Barker has very kindly been encouraging me by promises of performance. As to novels I have written something which is certainly fiction of a sort but whether it's a novel or not I'll leave it to the critics to say. That won't be published till next year—winter season I suppose. Why the accurate newspaper press should credit me with 2 novels I don't know. It's one of these absurd misapprehensions of which journalists alone have the secret.

Our kindest regards. Believe me dear Mr Colvin very sincerely yours

Jph. Conrad.

To John Galsworthy
Text MS Forbes; Unpublished

[letterhead: Pent Farm]
Sunday. 11am [25 November or
2 December? 1906][1]

Dearest Jack

I sit down yet warm from the reading to say something about the book. But I can not write a long and laudatory disquisition; and if I

[1] When *The Country House* appeared in March 1908, the Conrads were overseas; this letter must follow a reading of the MS, which Conrad (to judge from the letter of that date) had not seen on 15 November. Sunday the 18th seems too soon after the heroic encounter with Garnett's play, while a date after 2 December would not fit the pattern of Conrad's movements.

could do that trick—it would be just the trick of a practised critic. What I would like to find is some short formula conveying my concentrated feeling. And I can't think of anything more illuminating to say but that the book is such as to increase my affection for you. Its quality is of the sort which lifts conception insight, vision, technique, unfailing felicity of phrase, above the plane of detailed analysis. It is in short more like some fine action—an action that irresistibly augments one's regard for you—than a piece of fine work. It's* *humanity gets home first*. Then comes its art—well nigh without reproach. The flight of Mrs Pendyce, the ride of the Squire are— but what's the good of particularising? They *are*. That's just it. Everything *is*. The whole stands admirably plastic in a peculiar light, the emanation of Your personality, a light particularly and wonderfully searching and yet never crude, never—if I may say so—indiscreet.

For a fellow craftsman it is an inspiriting book. Many a time I've laid the pages down for the sheer enjoyment derived from dwelling upon the excellence of the work. The savour of that critical presentation is never acrid. The deliberation of method, the gravity—I may venture to say—with which the task is approached make a wonderful contrast to the ironic felicity of expression. But I am falling into analysis here. And again I want a formula not emotional this time but let us say intellectual, which would resume that side of the book. And that is difficult to find. If I were limited to a single sentence I would say that at no time the confidence of the reader in the author is shaken.

This does not seem much but I assure you I mean it to stand for the recognition of very singular merit—of a very rare gift.

I think dear Jack I will run up to town next week to talk a little about the book. There is one point, a matter of detail, which does not come very readily under my pen just now. It's nothing important: but I am extremely jealous of the excellence of the book. On the other hand I am at this moment quite sure—whether my feeling will stand against calm reflexion. I'll turn it over in my mind meantime, and perhaps Thursday—would you be free in the afternoon on Thursday?

Our dear love to You both. Pardon this lame letter. My very delight with the book has trammeled my expression

ever Your

J Conrad.

To H.-D. Davray

Text MS Yale; *L.fr.*79

[letterhead: Pent Farm]

5 Dec 1906

Cher Ami

L'apparance de Karain[1] a été une delicieuse surprise. Je vous serre les deux mains bien tendrement en admirant Votre patience et ce devouement a votre tâche ingrate—ce parfait devouement qui seul vous a permis d'interpreter l'âme même de ce nuageaux récit pour les lecteurs français.

Nul ne peut connaître comme moi les difficultés de la tâche Vous Vous êtes imposée; donc personne ne peut savoir comme je le sais jusqu'à quel point Vous avez réussi. C'est tout simplement admirable!

Je reste tout etonné de cette lecture. Etonné et ému; et comme la langue française est la pierre de touche de l'expression—sinon de la pensée elle-même—je demeure affligé par les fautes que je decouvre.— Pas Vos fautes. Vous êtes parfait. Mes fautes a moi. J'examine ma forme a moi dans le clair mirroir de Votre talent et je constate qu'elle est loin d'être irreprochable. Très loin.

Vous croyez bien que je n'ai guère pensé au coté matériel de la chose. Mais puisque Vous avez jugé néccessaire de m'envoyer trente francs je vous en remercie beaucoup. Quant a ma reconnaissance pour tout le mal Vous Vous êtes donné affin de 'placer' le conte je n'en dis rien ici. Ce serait trop long.

Ecoutez cher Davray. Nous partons pour Montpellier le 16 de ce mois. Nous passerons la journée du 17 a Paris. Comme je deteste de me trimbaler avec toute ma caravane par la ville nous resterons a l'hotel de la Gare du Nord—je veux dire l'hotel *dans la Gare* même. Ce serait bien gentil si madame Davray et Vous voudriez bien venir déjeuner avec nous là, vers midi et demi le lundi 17. Nous repartons le soir même.

Qu'en dites vous cher Ami? Nous serions si heureux de vous voir. Enfin, écrivez moi un petit mot. Nous nous rappelons bien cordialement au souvenir de Madame Davray et avec mille amitiés je suis cher ami,

Tout à Vous

Conrad

---

[1] Davray's translation in *Mercure de France*, 15 November and 1 December.

Translation

Dear Friend,

The appearance of *Karain* has been a delightful surprise. I shake your two hands very tenderly while admiring your patience and this devotion to your thankless task—this perfect devotion which alone has let you interpret the very soul of this cloudy tale for French readers.

No one can know as I do the difficulties of the task you imposed upon yourself; no one then can know as I know the point to which you have succeeded. It is quite simply admirable!

I remain entirely astonished by this reading. Astonished and moved; and as the French language is the touchstone of expression—or else of thought itself—I stand distressed at the faults that I discover. Not your faults. You are perfect. My own faults. I look at my shape in the clear mirror of your talent and I declare that it is far from being irreproachable. Very far.

You well know that I have hardly thought of the material side of the thing. But since you have judged it necessary to send me thirty francs, I thank you very much. As to my recognition of all the trouble you have given yourself in order to place the tale I will say nothing about it here. It would take too long.

Listen, dear Davray. We leave for Montpellier on the 16th of this month. We shall pass the day of the 17th in Paris. As I detest dragging myself and all my caravan around the city, we shall stop at the Gare du Nord hotel—I mean the hotel *within the station* itself. It would be very pleasant if you and Madame Davray would come to luncheon with us there, about 12:30 on Monday, the 17th. We set off again the same evening.

What do you say about it, dear friend? We should be so happy to see you. So write me a little note. We remember ourselves warmly to Madame Davray and, with a thousand kind regards, I am, dear friend,

Sincerely yours,

Conrad

To Marguerite Poradowska
Text MS Yale; Rapin 184; G.&S. 107

[letterhead: Pent Farm]
7 X^bre [décembre] 1906

Très chère et bien aimée Margueritte.*

Jessie Vous a écrit il y a quelque temps. Je me demande si Vous avez reçu la lettre? Il y était question d'un accident dans les Alpes dont la nouvelle dans les journaux nous a rempli d'inquiétude. Car enfin le nom de Jean Gachet y était en toutes lettres comme une des trois victimes. Mais le message de l'Agence Reuter disait: "Membres du Club Alpin *allemand*". Donc? ... Je ne sais que penser et j'espère de tout mon coeur que cette grande douleur Vous a été epargnée.[1]

Depuis la naissance de Jack j'ai travaillé pour ainsi dire jour et nuit pour finir le roman commencé au mois de Mars a Montpellier. C'est fait. Et voilà que nous sommes a la veille de repartir pour Montpellier encore pour y passer les trois plus mauvais mois de l'année 1907.

Notre intention est de quitter Pent Farm le 16 de ce mois (Dimanche) a 11^h du matin pour arriver a Paris à 6^h 4 du soir. Comme je deteste de me trimballer par la ville avec ma caravane (y compris Jean Alexandre) nous passerons la nuit a l'hotel de la Gare même, ou au bout du compte, on est très bien. Chère et bonne donnez nous le bonheur de Vous voir le soir même et dinez avec nous a 7.30. Nous tacherons de ne pas trop Vous fatiguer avec notre bavardage.

Le Lundi j'ai invité H. D. Davray (du "Mercure") a déjeuner avec sa femme—et j'ai l'honneur de Vous y prier avec Monsieur votre frère a qui veuillez transmettre nos cordiales salutations. Nous partirons le même jour a 10.40 du soir comme l'autre fois. Envoyez nous un petit mot et dites oui. Nous Vous embrassons tous bien fort

A vous de coeur

Conrad

Translation

Very dear and much-loved Marguerite,

Jessie wrote to you some time ago. I wonder if you have had her letter? It concerned the newspaper story of an accident in the Alps which made us very anxious. For, unmistakably, a Jean Gachet was listed as one of the three victims. But the report from Reuters said: 'Members of the

---

[1] Mme Poradowska's nephew was alive and well.

German Alpine Club'. So? . . . I don't know what to think, and I hope with all my heart that you have been spared this great sorrow.

Since Jack's birth, I have worked, as it were, day and night to finish the novel begun in March in Montpellier. It's done. And here we are on the eve of setting off again for Montpellier, to pass there the three worst months of 1907.

We intend to leave Pent Farm on Sunday, the sixteenth of this month, at 11 a.m., for an arrival in Paris at 6:04 p.m. As I detest traipsing round the town with my caravan (John Alexander included), we shall spend the night at the hotel right in the station, where, when all's said and done, one is very comfortable. Kind and dear Marguerite, give us the happiness of seeing you the same evening, and dine with us at 7:30. We shall try not to wear you out with our prattling.

On the Monday, I have invited H.-D. Davray (of the *Mercure*) and his wife to lunch—and I have the honour of inviting you and your brother, to whom please send our cordial greetings. We leave the same evening at 10:40, as before. Send us a note saying yes. We hug you warmly.

Affectionately yours,

Conrad

To Count Szembek
Text *L.fr.*80; Najder 249

Pent Farm,
8 Déc. 1906.

Très cher Monsieur et Ami,

Je n'ai d'autre excuse à offrir pour notre long silence que, de ma part: travail acharné pour finir un livre, et de la part de ma femme un trouble des yeux qui l'empêchait de lire et d'écrire. Heureusement, cela c'est passé ou du moins amélioré considérablement depuis quinze jours.

Depuis la naissance de Jack, j'ai travaillé pour ainsi dire jour et nuit. Enfin c'est fait![1] Et nous sommes sur le point de partir pour Montpellier, car tous les deux et même tous les quatre nous avons besoin du soleil.

J'ai été étonné de recevoir une lettre de Cerio me demandant une lettre d'introduction pour Gorki.[2] Pourquoi moi? Je lui écrivis que je

---

[1] As well as *The Secret Agent*, 'Il Conde' – a story founded on an experience of the count's.
[2] From late 1906 to 1913, Maxim Gorky (A. M. Peshkov) lived mostly on Capri; he had been sentenced to exile after the insurgencies of 1905. Cerio: Dr Giorgio (who had treated Conrad), or his brother Dr Ignazio (who had given Conrad the run of his library).

n'avais jamais vu Gorki de ma vie. Je ne savais même pas qu'il était à Capri.

Dans notre existence retirée et travailleuse rien n'arrive de bien intéressant. Les jours passent—le temps marche vite. Voilà tout ce que j'ai à dire. Mais soyez sûr, Cher Monsieur, que nous gardons précieusement le souvenir de votre bonne amitié. Sur cette assurance, dont je suis sûr vous ne doutez pas, je vous dis au revoir, pour le moment. Je suis écrasé sous les arrièrés de ma correspondance, car, à vrai dire, je n'ai écrit une seule lettre voilà trois mois bientôt. Croyez-moi, Cher Monsieur et Ami, tout à vous bien affectueusement.

P.S.—Ma femme a l'intention de vous écrire bientôt. Borys vous envoie *his love*.

Translation

Very dear Sir and Friend,

I have no other excuse to offer for our long silence than, on my part, intense work to finish a book, and on my wife's part a disorder of the eyes which prevented her from reading and writing. Happily that has passed or at least improved considerably in the last fortnight.

Since Jack's birth, I have worked as it were day and night. At last it is finished! And we are on the verge of leaving for Montpellier, for both of us, all four even, need the sun.

I was astonished at receiving a letter from Cerio asking me for a letter of introduction to Gorki. Why me? I wrote to him that I've never seen Gorki in my life. I didn't even know he was on Capri.

In our secluded and industrious life, nothing very interesting happens. The days pass—time goes by rapidly. That is all I have to say. But be sure, Dear Sir, that we cherish the memory of your kind friendship. With this assurance, which I am sure you do not question, I say goodbye to you, for the moment. I am crushed under the backlog of my correspondence, for, to be frank, I haven't written a single letter for almost three months. Believe me, Dear Sir and Friend, very affectionately and sincerely yours.

P.S. My wife intends to write to you soon. Borys sends you 'his love'.

To J.B. Pinker
Text MS Berg; Unpublished

[letterhead: Pent Farm]
11th Dec 1906

My dear Pinker.

Please put cheques into these envelopes

Dr Rayner D. Batten   £*15.15*

Messr[s] Sharpe & Sons £11.

Batten looked after Borys a year ago. Sharpe are chemists who furnished medicines then and also this year when we were in London.

I am extremely sick of everything. Fact is I'm not at all well and feel desperately miserable. I've been like this once before, eight years ago. I was younger then, tho'.

Tell me whether there is anything from Your point of view in being agent for French authors in this country? I intend to stay in Paris two days and shall see a few people. I have already been asked questions on that point by some French authors of standing.

I will try to arrange with the *Mercure of France* for a translation of selected writings of mine. A small volume. I would like very much to see myself in French. I don't think there will be any money in it. But the fancy is strong on me.

We are going decidedly on Sunday. I have an odd feeling that Sunday will never come. Bad form of nervousness *that* is. I will come to town early on Friday. I think You had better give me £100 then and I will pay some accts remaining here and do the best I can with the rest in the way of going over and in Montpellier. I will be sending You MS from there I trust.

Yours ever

Conrad.

PS Sorry haven't stamps for these letters.

To Ford Madox Ford
Text Violet Hunt's copy, Cornell; Unpublished

Pent Farm
11 Dec 1906

Dearest Ford,

I made an effort to communicate with you by tel: yesterday but after waiting up to the limit had to rush off to attend to various matters. If I had gone to the Club[1] on the chance I would have had a sight of you.

However I am coming up on Friday once more and would dearly love to get in touch with you between 12–2 if possible. Afterwards I *must* rush off to see Rothenstein—Lucas, if possible, finishing off late with Jack if the Gals-thy's will put me up. Hope they will. I have matters to talk over with him. Then on Saturday morning I will try to give a "pose" to that miraculous young amateur photographer—you know—the fellow who photos everybody in any way illustrious.[2] I want to be illustrious too.

I feel damnably ill in my inside. It is *not* a joke. We leave on Sunday. On Monday I'll lunch in Paris with Davray. Karain in French reads surprisingly. On Monday night, we start off again.

I feel as if I were never coming back again. Most queer sensations of being no longer of this world come upon me as I sit writing. Heart thumps, head swims—nervous breakdown? very difficult to keep it away from Jessie. It's funny but startling too. Do drop me a line.

Yours trés ébranlé[3]

Conrad.

To H.-D. Davray
Text MS Yale; *L.fr*.81

20 Dec. 1906.
Riche Hotel
Montpellier

Cher ami

Un simple mot pour Vous remercier de l'envoi de Karain que j'ai reçus* hier.

Je vais me mettre aux corrections tout de suite et puis Vous jugerez en dernier lieu.

---

[1] The National Liberal?
[2] Alvin Langdon Coburn (1882–1966)? His sitters around this time included Shaw, Wells, Chesterton, and James.
[3] 'Yours most uneasily.'

C'était delicieux de Vous voir tous les deux ayant si bonnes mines et si bons pour nous. Les choses amicales que Vous avez dites m'ont remonté le moral.

Mille amitiés

Tout à Vous

J. Conrad.

Translation

Dear Friend,

Just a word to thank you for sending 'Karain', which I received yesterday.

I shall apply myself to the corrections immediately, and then you will have the final say.

It was delightful to see you both looking well and so kind to us. The friendly things you said have improved my morale.

A thousand regards.

Sincerely yours,

J. Conrad

To J.B. Pinker
Text MS Berg; Unpublished

Riche Hotel
Place de la Comedie
Montpellier
20 Dec. 1906

My dear Pinker.

We arrived here after a very tolerable journey. The P.L.M. Rway not making a reduction on family tickets except for places on the Riviera I had to pay full prices alas!

In Paris I had to lunch Davray and Gourmont.[1] Karain had produced quite a little sensation. Any sort of attempt towards an artistic expression gains a quick recognition in France. As Davray went about telling people that he was to see me on my passage through Paris several distinguished men send* me verbal messages through him. I confess I received them with pleasure. De Gourmont being one of the *Mercure*

---

[1] Either Rémy de Gourmont (1858–1915) or his brother Jean (1877–1928); both wrote for the *Mercure*, although Rémy (one of the magazine's founders) is by far the better known. Poet, novelist, playwright, and the foremost advocate of Symbolism, he touched the minds of Eliot and Pound.

band of writers called on me. All this amiability to a totally unknown man on the strength of one short story has flattered me immensely.

The "*Mercure*" is disposed to publish a *vol* of short stories next winter season.[1] *Karain—Outpost—Lagoon* and *Heart of Darkness* would make it up. The first 3 are ready now. For the *H of D* Davray would find a translator. It would be probably himself. My personal revision would be necessary but that need not interfere with my work. It would be distinctly a relaxation. As a matter of fact I sat down yesterday and finished revising Karain—just to see what I could do in that way.

Will you ascertain the sentiments of B'woods and Fisher Unwin[2] as to this plan. I don't think B'woods would object. F. U. might, as there is no money in it. I trust your powers of persuasion.

We touched, with Davray—upon the idea of literary agency in London for French Writers. He thinks the thing quite feasible tho' difficult to start at first. The initial move would be to spot well beforehand a work which would present some chance of being read in England and put into your hands at once. A work for instance like the novel just published of two young authors whose hero is as a matter of fact Kipling himself.[3]

The thing would be to get in touch with the *Authors* not the *translators*. To Davray's remark that if the authors went direct to you you would require probably some independent advice I assured him that as far as my knowledge goes you were certain to have it, and also, I haven't the slightest doubt, that of Hueffer who anyhow understands French literature thoroughly and is the *coming man* in the literary world. It's my conviction he will become a sort of sublimated Gosse before many years pass over our heads.[4]

At any rate the project is feasible; the only real question is whether it's worth the trouble. That can only be discovered by trying, I think, and in no other way.

We have become so suddenly French here that we have ventured to dispatch a box of the celebrated Montpellier sweets to Mrs Pinker. I saw the things prepared from start to finish myself. The box was packed at midnight yesterday and went off by the first post. Montpellier furnishes the whole world with those particular wares, and at this season the

---

[1] The project fell through.   [2] Publishers of the stories in question.
[3] Untraced. Louis Fabulet and Robert d'Humières collaborated on *translations* from Kipling.
[4] As editor of the *English* and the *Transatlantic Review*, Ford indeed became one of modern literature's great mediators.

artists (I can call them nothing less) work overtime with extraordinary devotion and enthusiasm.

Our best wishes go with this Frenchified offering which in its concentrated sweetness has a symbolic character on the occasion of the New Year's season.

I'll report progress with my work in my next. May prosperity attend you for long years in your domestic life and in Your strenuous work.

Yours always

J. Conrad.

To R.B. Cunninghame Graham

Text MS Dartmouth; J-A, 2, 40; Watts 164

31 Dec 1906

Riche Hotel.

Montpellier

Très cher ami.

Your letter reached me here and no proof of your friendship could have been more welcome.

I am away here from the Pent in a sort of panic before the menaces of the winter. A horrid almost suicidal depression sent me off in search of sunshine. We have found it here. The weather is cold, calm dry brilliant. I hope I will be able to work and don't want to get back with less than half a book.

And à propos of book. In December Edward Garnett said to me "I'll give you Cunninghame Graham's book[1]—but I suppose he will send it to you."—I said: "Don't give me his book. I prefer having it from him."—

The question is:

Where is the book?

This however is no reproach. It simply explains why I haven't read it yet. Mudie[2] is under instruction to send it on to me here. When it arrives I shall swallow it up at a sitting and then write to you.

We have been thinking much of You this year end. It is sad to think of you feeling your loneliness at this season—though you certainly are a man round whom many affections must be centred, many admirations and even some enmities. To you life must keep its value to the last, and the words you have written the perfect expression of your rare personal-

---

[1] *His People* (Duckworth), the latest collection of stories and sketches.
[2] The bookshop and circulating library.

ity shall be read in the far future with the *disinterested* admiration they deserve. Your magnanimous indignations and your human sympathies will be perceived as having made their mark on their time. Words worthy of you, uncompromising and sincere shall be your descendants and the servants of your memory more faithful than any child could be—for alas our children are but men like ourselves with short memories and but an imperfect fidelity to the spirit that has animated our own existence. Exceptional natures are fated to remain alone, but when they possess the gift of noble expression they have and keep a family of their own from generation to generation. Je vous serre bien tendrement les mains.[1]

Yours

Conrad

My wife's love and also love from Borys who has religiously preserved with a special care everything you have ever given him from his very babyhood.

To Ada and John Galsworthy
Text MS Forbes; J-A, 2, 39

[Montpellier]
31 Dec. 1906.

Dearest Ada & Jack

We end this year with our thoughts directed especially to you two, with the greatest affection and gratitude. May Your finding felicity in each other's happiness go hand in hand through long and serene years with the reward of men's praise for good work rightly done and contented hearts in Your unselfish lives.

The "petits cadeaux qui entretiennent l'amitié"[2] arrived safely day before yesterday to the great joy of the recipients. Jacklet seems to think the innocuous parrot the greatest joke in the world. Borys communes with the pigs every spare moment. It is considerably more than a *succès d'estime* I can assure you.

I haven't been writing yet; but I've been hatching things all the time, tho' to the outward eye presenting no difference from the other loafers on the Place de la Comedie. Jessie's eyes again trouble her but I don't

---

[1] 'I shake your hands most affectionately.'
[2] 'The little gifts that sustain friendship'.

think there is any reason for uneasiness. Otherwise we are all well and tolerably frivolous.

I have been correcting and re-writing partly the French translation of Karain, for book form. A selection of four tales Karain, Lagoon, Outpost and Heart of Darkness will make a volume which the *Mercure de France* declares its willingness to publish in winter 1907. I admit it would flatter my vanity to see myself in French—partly at least of my own translating.

But all this is not serious business of the kind that ought to engage the thoughts of a man of 48 with two kids and a wife to leave behind him—un beau jour. I wish to goodness I could get on terms with Chance[1] quickly. Each day is like a stroke of the inexorable clock to me.

Voilà. There's nothing new—except (an important exception) that I've discovered a vol. of Anatole France unknown to us—a work of his younger days. I will be sending it to you in day or two. Meantime much love from us both and affectionate thanks from B. Ever your affectionate friend and servant

Conrad.

To H.-D. Davray
Text MS Rosenbach; *L.fr.*82

Riche Hotel
Montpellier
31 Dec 1906.
11.30 pm.

Mon cher ami.

Nous terminons l'année en pensant à Vous. Le tapage du reveillon monte de la rue. Il a (le tapage) un accent méridional fort prononcé—et, comme Karain, je me remémore ma vie errante qui a commencé a Marseille—té mon bon[2]—voilà la trente et unième année qui sonne.

Votre bonne lettre arrivant ce matin nous a fait le plus grand plaisir. Nos souhaits au longues années de bonheur vont vers vous et Mme Davray du plus profond de notre coeur.

Vous recevrez bientôt Karain machiné au net. J'ai reduit les 3 premières pages d'une bonne moitié. Partout ailleurs j'ai pourchassé la phrase inutile avec zèle, j'ose le dire. Les autres corrections que j'ai faites sont telles que je voudrais faire dans le texte anglais pour une nouvelle édition.

---

[1] Both the novel and the metaphysical agency?   [2] Marseillais dialect.

Je ne sais pas l'addresse de M. d'Humières, et je ne sais pas non plus ou la trouver. Je pense qu'il a abandonné la traduction du *Nigger of the N* il y a longtemps.[1] Pensez Vous qu'on pourra faire quelque chose avec ce bouquin?

Mes hommages a Mme Devray.* Ma femme envoie milles amitiés

Tout a vous

J Conrad.

Translation

My dear friend,

We end the year thinking of you. The New Year's Eve uproar mounts in the street. It (the uproar) has a most pronounced southern accent— and, like Karain, I recollect my wandering life, which began at Marseilles—listen, my friend—there is the thirty-first year being rung in.

Your good letter, arrived this morning, gave us the greatest pleasure. Our wishes for long years of happiness go to you and Madame Davray from the bottom of our hearts.

Soon you will receive 'Karain' typed cleanly. I have reduced the first three pages by a good half. Everywhere else, I dare say that I have zealously hunted down useless phrases. The other corrections I have made are those I should want to make in the English text for a new edition.

I do not know the address of M. d'Humières, nor do I know where to find it. I believe that he gave up the translation of the *Nigger of the N*. a long time ago. Do you think it would be possible to do something with that old book?

Our regards to Madame Davray. My wife sends her best compliments.

Yours

J. Conrad

---

[1] It came out as a serial in 1909.

1907

To Ernest Dawson

Text MS Yale; *Listy* 255; Original unpublished

Montpellier.
Riche Hotel.
3 Jan 1907

My dear good friend.

Jessie could not write to you her gratitude for the lace collar which besides being very charming was the very thing she wanted just then. Her eyes have been troubling her a little. It's nothing serious but it's very annoying anyway. She is nursing Jack.

Have you heard of Jack? He arrived in August last and flourishes exceedingly. We like him very much.

I've no doubt his mamma will be writing to you in affectionate terms before very long. And the fact is my dear Ernest that we all have much affection for you—if we don't write very often.

Your jeering reference to my Gaspar Ruiz story[1] has been taken notice of. It's all very well for you to jeer. You *don't* write for a living.

I have written since a few other things which have no other merit but that of procuring bread and butter for 3 harmless persons for whom alone my work is intended really. The public is a mere circumstance. Why don't you write something to give me a chance to dig you under the fifth rib. Where's your English notion of fair play? Eh?

Jessie has turned author too. She has written a cookery book and got £25 for it from a real publisher.[2] She's puffed up with pride and I'll have to get all my friends to suppress her a bit. Nothing however but an epidemic of indigestion setting over all the United Kingdom after publication will subdue her. Love from us all to your house and heartiest wishes of peace and prosperity. Yours very affectionately

J. Conrad.

To David Meldrum

Text MS Duke; Blackburn 189

Riche Hotel
Montpellier.
4 Jan 1907

My Dear Mr Meldrum

No end of thanks for your good letter. Every word from you is valued more than you can think.

---

[1] In serial, *Pall Mall Magazine*, July–October 1906.
[2] An advance from Alston Rivers & Co. The firm did not take the book, however, and *A Handbook of Cookery for a Small House* did not make its commercial début until 1923.

Our dearest wishes for your uninterrupted prosperity. We have sent a box of preserved fruit a speciality of this town to Mrs Meldrum; but I am afraid it did not reach your house on New Years day as all the establishments here were overwhelmed with orders.

The Knife—so Complete and Magnificent—has made Borys very happy. It was good of you to think of the little Chap.

I have been so awfully depressed that I positively ran away from the Pent. Here we have found plenty of sunshine but also lots of wind. I had a small touch of influenza which stopped my writing for a few days.

I can see day light if I get two clear years before me without gout or other devilish hindrances. I am trying to pull myself together for a sustained effort.

With my wifes love to all your house in which I join.

Always yours

Conrad

To Marguerite Poradowska
Text MS Yale; Rapin 185; G.&S. 108

5 Janvier 07
Riche Hotel
Montpellier

Chère Margueritte.*

Les enfants sont enchantés! Le petit Jean embrasse son chat avec une vraie affection. Quand* a Borys Votre gentil cadeau est tout a fait a son goût. Nous allons prochainement a Palavas pour faire courir le bateau sur les ondes agitées.

Des embrassades très fortes de la part de tout le monde.

Jessie est fort occupée a confectioner son petit livre de cuisine pour lequel Alston Rivers & Cie lui offrent *700 frcs.* Ça vaut la peine et puis elle connait son sujet a fond—je veux dire la cuisine d'un menage modeste. Et puis ça l'amuse. Mille remerciements d'avoir envoyé chez Davray les deux contes.[1] C'est que Vous êtes bonne pour moi!

Davray m'a permis de faire quelques changements dans sa traduction de Karain. Me permettrez Vous d'agir de même avec l'*Avant poste du Progrès* et le *Lagune*? Le dernier surtout a besoin d'être raccourci, serré un peu—n'est-ce pas?

J'ai eu une petite grippe. Je n'a[i] pas ecrit six lignes depuis notre

---

[1] Her translations of 'An Outpost of Progress' (done by May 1900: *Letters*, 2, p. 269) and 'The Lagoon'.

arrivée ici. C'est difficile de se mettre a l'ouvrage après un mois de fainéantise absolue.

J'ai la paresse de tous les Polonais. Je prefère rêver un roman que l'ecrire. Car le rêve de l'oeuvre est toujours beaucoup plus beau que la realité de la chose imprimée. Et puis l'Anglais m'est toujours une langue etrangère qui demande un effort formidable pour être maniée.

Je Vous baise les deux mains Our dearest love to you

Tout à Vous de coeur

Conrad.

Translation

Dear Marguerite,

The children are delighted! Little John hugs his cat with real affection. As for Borys, your kind gift is entirely to his taste. We shall soon go to Palavas to sail the boat in rough seas.

Very warm hugs from everyone.

Jessie is working steadily on her little cookery book, for which Alston Rivers & Co. are offering her 700 francs. That makes the effort worthwhile, and of course she knows the subject thoroughly—I mean, cooking for a modest household. And then it amuses her. Many thanks for having sent Davray the two stories. You are very good to me!

Davray has allowed me to make some changes in his translation of 'Karain'. Will you permit me to do the same with 'An Outpost of Progress' and 'The Lagoon'? The latter especially needs to be shortened, tightened a little, don't you think?

I've had a mild case of the 'flu. I haven't written six lines since we arrived here. It's difficult to get back to work after a month of complete idleness.

I feel the laziness common to all Poles. I'd rather dream a novel than write it. For the dream of the work is always much more lovely than the reality of the thing in print. And then, English is still for me a foreign language whose handling demands a fearful effort.

I kiss both your hands. Our dearest love to you

Yours affectionately

Conrad.

To H.-D. Davray
Text MS Yale; *L.fr.*83

[Montpellier]
8 Janvier 1907

Mon cher et bon ami.

Reçu les deux nouvelles de Mme Poradowska (je veux dire traduites par . . .).

J'ai tellement maculé les bonnes pages de Karain avec de grands pâtés d'encre que je les envoie a Londres pour être ecrites a la machine.

Le tout vous parviendra dans quelques jours. Rien ne presse n'est ce pas?

J'ai en ce moment un travail qui me tient tout entier. Donc j'ai mis *La Lagune* et l' *Avant poste* de coté pour quelques jours.

J'ai eu une petite grippe, mais c'est fini. Il fait beau. Il fait paresseux surtout ici. Ce que je n'ai pas envie de travailler!! Non, vraiment; Vous qui êtes un des vaillants de ce monde Vous ne comprendrez jamais mon horreur de la plume.

Je vous serre la main

à Vous

Conrad.

Translation

My dear and good Friend,

Received the two tales by Madame Poradowska (translated by, that is).

I have so stained the clean pages of 'Karain' with great splotches of ink that I am sending them to London to be typed.

Everything will reach you within a few days. There isn't any hurry, is there?

At present, I have a piece of work which absorbs me entirely. Therefore, I have put 'The Lagoon' and 'The Outpost' aside for several days.

I've had a slight bout of 'flu, but it's over. The weather is good. Everything here makes me lazy. The fact is that I don't want to work!! No, truly; you who are one of the world's valiant men, you will never understand my horror of the pen.

I shake your hand.

Yours,

Conrad.

To Ford Madox Ford

Text Violet Hunt's copy, Cornell; Unpublished

[Montpellier]
8th January 1907

Tres cher

I am sending you with my love a pretty edition of Emaux et Camees.[1]

I don't think you have anything on your shelves of the verses of the bon poete. I haven't seen these poems since, since the days before the Deluge. How simple they were those great romantics!

I am better in this sunshine. The landscape around has a magic all bustle, all of colour alone. The villages perched on conical hills stand out against the great and sweeping line of violet ranges as if in an enchanted country. The beauty of this land is inexpressible and the delicacy of colours at sunset and sunrise beyond the power of men to imagine. Of course it must be seen now, in winter. And every day as I go about entranced, I miss you more and more. You ought to see this. And what a book of verse and prose you could find here within an hour's drive in all directions! I am drunk with colour and would like dearly to have you to lean upon. I am certain that with no other man could I share my rapture.

Work at a standstill. Plans simply swarming in my head but my English has all departed from me. Our dear love to you all.

Yours ever,

Conrad.

To Henry Hick

Text MS Texas; Unpublished

8 Jan 1907.
Riche Hotel
Montpellier.

My dear Hick.[2]

I ought to have thanked you sooner for your generous gift of Gissing's generous words.[3] I am touched by the kind thought which moved you and shall cherish this bit of paper extremely, as long as I live.

---

[1] The most notable volume of Théophile Gautier's lyrics (1852).

[2] Dr Henry Hick (1853–1932) had been Gissing's boyhood friend in Yorkshire. During the last few years before Gissing's death in 1903 they corresponded frequently. Hick practised in New Romney, not far from the Pent; Conrad may have met him through Wells, another friend.

[3] In his last letter to Hick, Gissing wrote: 'Conrad, as you know, has published some most admirable stories; his English is a miracle.' See *Henry Hick's Recollections of George Gissing*, ed. Pierre Coustillas (Enitharmon, 1973), p. 67.

May all the good attainable in this world attend you and all yours through long years of peace and content.

My wife joins me in kindest regards. Believe me my dear Hick

very gratefully yours

J. Conrad.

To J.B. Pinker
Text MS Berg; Unpublished

Riche Hotel.

8 Jan 1907.

My dear Pinker.

To day I am sending only a copy (corrected pages) of Karain in French. Please have them typed out neatly and beautifully and send them to me here for a last revision; after which I'll send them to the Mercure de France as authorised text for this volume of Tales. You may be surprised that I should ask you to do that in London; but the fact is that there's no typing office here and I don't know the address of one in Paris. On the other hand I don't want Davray to see how much I've cut up and amended his translation. I would like this done as soon as possible. And it must be done very correctly. There is an office for typing in all languages which advertises in the *Athen[a]eum*. It ought to be all right.[1]

I regret to report a small bout of influenza which put me out of action for a few days just as I had closed with the 'enemy'. The enemy is work of all kinds. I am all right now and more hopeful than I've been for a long time, really. I think, to be frank with you that a painful swollen ankle has got something to do with this improvement of my 'moral[e]'. It's just 12 months since any sign of gout showed. I don't mind a little of it if it serves to clear the brain.

Tho' I am not sending you any MS as yet there is some ready. But not enough to make it worthwhile. Please pay to me at the Credit Lyonnais here £*80* through the Cr. Lyonnais in London. I think that's the best way. And please do it this Friday as I will want the money next week to settle bills.

Have you as I asked you in my last (or one before last) sent £3 to Mrs Richmond? (St Leonard's School. Stanford N^r Hythe. Kent) I ask, as

---

[1] The Cambridge Type-Writing Agency, 10 Duke St, was staffed by women from the universities.

I've not heard from her and in the scurry of moving to a new office the matter might have been neglected.

This is all for the moment. I trust You feel at home in your new quarters and that auspicious fortune sits at your elbow within the new walls.

Ever yours

J. Conrad.

We had a delightful letter from Mrs Pinker for which our thanks.

To J.B. Pinker

Text MS Berg; Unpublished

[Montpellier]
9 Jan. 1907

My dear Pinker

Please send me *two good* fountain pens. I have shattered mine by dropping it out of a 3^d floor window.

I don't know which is the better system Waterman or Swan or another. I want something really good.

Will you be kind enough to get for me the N° of the Speaker containing my causerie on Anatole France. It was in 1904 I think but a reference to the index will be necessary as I dont remember the date.[1]

I am anxious to get hold of that article as A. France wishes to see it. It would be best to get 3 or 4 copies if obtainable.

Do tell me please whether I ever asked you to send a cheque to *Rev. F Smith* Stanford Rectory. Kent. for One guinea. I can't remember. If not I am asking you now. That is for some subscriptions promised long ago.

Pardon all this Worry

Yours

J Conrad

To R.B. Cunninghame Graham

Text MS Dartmouth; Watts 167

14 Jan. 1907
Riche Hotel, Montpellier

Très cher ami.

I've read your book[2] with the usual delight and more than the usual admiration. You are incomparable in the consistency and force of your

[1] 16 July 1904: reprinted in *Notes on Life and Letters.*   [2] *His People.*

vision, in the sustained power of expression—and You are the Great Preface Writer of the Time.[1]

Three times I've gone through your pages so vigorous, so personal and so exquisite. What a *Return of the Native* you have given us![2] *His people* is a wonderful piece of description and an amazing feat of analysis.

And so is each of these sketches—though I don't know whether *Sketches* is the right name.

As a matter of fact a new name should be invented for the form of the gems you have given to our literature.[3] They are revelations of the uncommon in feeling and expression. But that's a poor definition and I feel I could accumulate words upon words without coming anywhere near to the line of your peculiar distinction.

On the whole your quality so distinct in effect is in its essence elusive. It is not a superficial gift of brilliance, of wit, of picturesque phrase. It can't be touched by the critical finger because it lies deep. Its origin rests in the "sens profond de la vie" characterised by irony that is gentle and by a fierce sympathy.

Borys charges me to thank you infinitely for the book which arrived safely the other day.[4] He's very delighted with it. But upon the whole that boy is not a reader.

On the other hand he would spend his day on horseback if he were allowed. Just now he seems to live exclusively for riding. We went in search of a Camargue saddle.[5] Not a single one to be found in Montpellier. Arles, the riding master tells me, is the nearest place where I could see one. Our love to you. Yours always

Conrad.

To H.-D. Davray
Text MS Yale; *L.fr.*84

[Montpellier]
15 Jan 1907

Cher Ami.

Non je ne crois pas que la traduction me donnera *trop* de mal. Enfin je verrai a me debrouiller avec.

[1] Graham always led off his books with a flamboyant address to the reader, much in the manner of the seventeenth century.
[2] As in Hardy's novel, the hero of the title-story makes a sorry return to his old home.
[3] Combining features of the essay, the short story, and the descriptive sketch, his short works defy generic boundaries.
[4] In time for his ninth birthday.
[5] As used by herdsmen in the Rhône delta.

Je vais écrire a M d'Humieres demain pour lui demander des nouvelles de mon *Nigger*.

Je vais vous envoyer un numéro du *Speaker* (de l'annee 1903)[1] contenant une *Causerie of the Week* sur A. France a propos de Crainquebille.

Jetez-y les yeux et si la chose peut se faire faites la parvenir à A. France. Il lit l'anglais je pense.

Nos amitiés les plus impressées a Mme Davray

Tout à Vous

Conrad

Je suis très content d'apprendre que the *Informer* Vous plaît. Très content.

Translation

Dear Friend,

No, I don't think the translation will give me *too* much trouble. Well I'll manage.

I shall write to M. d'Humières tomorrow in order to ask him for news of my *Nigger*.

I'm going to send you a number of the *Speaker* (from 1903) containing a 'Causerie of the Week' about Anatole France, in connection with *Crainquebille*.

Cast your eyes over it and if the thing can be done, send it to A. France. I believe he reads English.

Our warmest greetings to Mme Davray,

All yours

Conrad

I am very happy to learn that 'The Informer' pleases you. Very happy.

---

[1] Actually 1904.

To Humphrey Milford
Text TS Private collection; MacShane

15 January, 1907
Riche Hotel
Montpellier

Dear Sir,[1]

Your letter reached me today only. The heading of this letter explains the delay.

I am greatly flattered by your proposal; but the writing of my own stuff is a matter of so much toil and difficulty that I am only too glad to leave other people's books alone. Years ago I looked into *Typee* and *Omoo*, but as I didn't find there what I am looking for when I open a book I did go no further. Lately I had in my hand *Moby Dick*. It struck me as a rather strained rhapsody with whaling for a subject and not a single sincere line in the 3 vols of it.

On the other hand W. H. Hudson was enthusiastic about that very book and generally the whole of Melville's work. Couldn't he write the preface you need?[2]

Pardon this suggestion. It got under the pen and I let it be.

Believe me dear Sir,

very sincerely yours,
Joseph Conrad.

To J.B. Pinker
Text MS Berg; J-A, 2, 41

[Montpellier]
25 Jan 1907

My dear Pinker.

Here's a tale of woe. Borys has adenoïds—if that's how the beastly things are called. Growths at the back of the nose. The doctor called in to see the baby noticed him standing by openmouthed and advised me to show him to a specialist. This I did and there's no doubt of it. The growth is pretty considerable and will have to be removed. Just now the boy is having a preliminary treatment. Fortunately here in the university town one can command considerable skill at comparatively small cost. In a month's time it will have to be done and the prospect is

---

[1] Humphrey Milford (1877–1952; knighted 1936) had just transferred to the London office of Oxford University Press. He was Publisher to the University from 1913 to 1945.
[2] O.U.P. did not publish Melville until 1920. Everyman's Library brought out *Typee* and *Moby Dick* in 1907 and *Omoo* in 1908.

something of a worry. But his health has been very uncertain for some time now and perhaps that was the cause of this ailing.

But this is not all. Last night at seven I had my pocket picked in a crowd around a mask[1] who had been knocked down by a tramcar. Borys and I were in the car and of course were the first in the business of picking the woman up—and my pocket book either fell out or more likely was lifted out. There were 200 frcs in it. Please send me a £10 note instanter because life without pocket money is not worth living.

I am putting the last touches to a story which I fancy you will find profitable and not difficult to get rid of either. Subject military. Title *The Duel* Epoch 1st Napoleon's wars.[2] My modesty prevents me saying that I think the story good. Action sensational. The ending happy.

Don't imagine I am neglecting *Chance*. I've done a lot to it. I won't say a big lot but just fair. Neither will I say I am very pleased with what I've done. It's just tolerable. However I plod on with that and shall see my way better presently. I've been doing the story because I may just as well be doing it as worrying about the other stuff.

I've begun my Spanish lessons. I have been also a few times to the Town Library—with an object. And the object is reading up all I can discover there about Napoleon in *Elba*.[3]

It seems that there he was surrounded by spies, menaced by murderers and threatened by revengeful Spaniards and Corsicans.

I think I've got a theme for a Mediterranean novel with historical interest, intrigue and adventure. There may be even a success in it—who knows. All I want now is to discover the moral pivot—and the thing will be done.

As a matter of fact Louis XVIII was approached with proposals to have the Emperor killed; and the Great powers were not averse to a project of kidnapping him (by some Spaniards) in the hope—I fancy— of him getting a knock on the head in the scuffle.

There's something in the subject—for a later day.[4]

Kindest regards Yours ever

Conrad.

---

[1] Jean-Aubry emends to 'man', but the victim was a woman – a 'mask' in the sense of 'reveller'?

[2] *Pall Mall Magazine*, January–May 1908 and *A Set of Six*.

[3] He was there from May 1814 to February 1815. Jean-Aubry notes that the library had only one volume on that period: Paul Gruyer's *Napoléon, roi de l'île d'Elbe*.

[4] An anticipation of *Suspense*, his uncompleted final work.

To Ford Madox Ford
Text MS BL Ashley 2945; Unpublished

[Montpellier]
25 Jan.
'07

Dearest Ford.

Jessie's cooking book is written and quite ready and corrected with general Remarks, 130 recipes and Prefaces* by yours truly[1]—all wanting to be retyped clean and nice. We shall dispatch it as papiers d'affaires Registered to you at the Nat. Lib. Club by the 30th of this month.

She's in a state of delightful excitement about it and very grateful to you the 'Onlie begetter' of this work of art like the late lamented M^r H of Shakespeare's sonnets.

My preface is a mock serious thing into which I dragged Red Indians and other incongruities. But the little book is not bad. It's about 15,000 words or a little less. Suggested title: Cooking Precepts for a Little House—or something of that kind—if editors like.

Get them to fork out of* del: of MS:[2]—in order to make her completely happy. A fur coat for Borys hangs thereby.

And a propos of Mons. B. the poor little devil will have to be scraped for adenoids if thats how the damned things are called. I had him examined by a specialist. He has not been very well. Nothing definite. Sudden temperatures and feelings of malaise. I am rather worried because he got very thin rather rapidly. Enfin!

The baby flourishes exceedingly. I am so so and don't get on very rapidly with *Chance*. Between whiles I am doing a silly short story and feel age creeping on me.

But enough of that!

What are you doing. When is Your verse coming out?[3]

An hour ago Elsie's and Rina's joint letter arrived.[4] Many thanks and much love to all your women.

It was a startling piece of news about Mrs Martindale. Please tell the gracious Señora that I will write to Hampstead[5] in a day or two.

---

[1] His Preface is reprinted as 'Cookery' in *Last Essays*.
[2] Pay an advance on delivery to Alston Rivers (L. J. Bathurst and René Byles), Ford's publishers. He was acting as go-between.
[3] *From Inland* (July 1907): all but six poems came from earlier volumes (Mizener, p. 127).
[4] Elsie and the two daughters, Christina and Katharine, were living in Winchelsea; Ford was in London (*ibid.*).
[5] To Mrs Martindale's house in Broadhurst Gardens. She died on 18 February.

I say no more or I would begin to groan and I dare say you want to do your own groaning in peace.

Une forte étreinte mon très cher.[1]

Tout à vous.

Conrad.

To J.B. Pinker
Text MS Berg; Unpublished

15 Febr 1907
Riche Hotel
Montpellier.

My dear Pinker.

Please transfer for me to the Credit Lyonnais here £85 on receipt of this letter which I suppose will reach you on the 18th.

On the same day I will be posting You a story (A Duel) which I trust will cover that amount. I am very anxious to pay as much as I can as I go. I think I will be done with that story on Monday. I am not quite sure—but then as you know I am also writing the other thing—the famous *Chance* that is going to bring a real turn of luck.[2]

As to the story You are going to receive I must tell you that the Editor of *Harpers Mag.* wrote me asking for a tale for his Summer N°—to be delivered by end of April.

I sent him a sort of synopsis of *A Duel* and referred him to you; saying that by the time he had communicated with you, you will have the story in your hands. I also promised him to ask you not to place the story in Eng^d till You had heard from him. His letter was very nice and I've no doubt it was *meant*. They ought to give a 100 for it. It's certainly as good as the Anarchist tho' very different in subject and treatment. Of that however you are the judge. All I want is to keep on doing something towards expenses here as I go, because I'll have payments to make in England by and bye.

I don't send you any *Chance*. I don't want to part with it. My desire in respect of that tale is to finish it off, each page, as I write. The prospect of revising the *Secret Agent* is not pleasant. It will have to be done however. For *Chance* I want to avoid that stage altogether. I am confident I will finish *Chance* by the end of the year. I reckon that working at the *Secret Agent* will take six weeks at least of my time. I do hope You benefitted*

---

[1] 'A big hug, my very dear [fellow].'   [2] As it did, in 1913.

by your stay on the Riviera. We are all well here. Borys rides first rate.
My Spanish progresses too

Yours always

Conrad.

To J.B. Pinker
Text MS Berg; Unpublished

[Montpellier]
20 Febry [1907][1]

My dear Pinker

Thanks for the money safely to hand.

I've received this moment copy of Secret Ag^t agreement with Harpers.
In reading it over I perceive that there is no question of any advance on
royalties. Do they absolutely refuse to give the advance?

Does Methuen give us anything for the Canadian rights or is it only
the usual 3^d p copy of the colonial edition?[2] This is simple curiosity on
my part.

With the extension of the contract to a period of 10 years we must put
up I suppose since Harpers are making such a point of it.

I will send you the signed cont^{ct} to morrow. I post this at once and at
the moment I have no envelope big enough for the other.

Yours always

J. Conrad.

PS If you get a[n] MS[3] addressed to my wife (or me) to Your care
please keep it in your office. I'll tell you the story pendent thereunto
when I see you.

To J.B. Pinker
Text MS Berg; J-A, 2, 42

[Montpellier]
26 Febr 1907

My dear Pinker

Borys has got a thundering go at measles. That fellow catches
whatever's going. I've been nursing him 2 nights now. No bronchial

---

[1] The business agenda gives the year.

[2] The colonial was always cheaper than the home edition, and yielded a smaller royalty:
in this case, threepence per copy.

[3] The rejected cookery book.

complication has supervened so far. But You ought not to be surprised if You hear that Baby's got the measles or I, or my wife or Miss Wright[1] or the maid or all of us together. It's the most damnable thing.

Send me 3 five pound notes please by post—in case of anything.

In regard of my work I am quite aware that Chance is the main thing. What I [am] concerned most about is the *good work* on that subject. You understand me. I wish to avoid having two versions. Am I to understand you want the MS of that book now as far as I've gone?

I am extremely unwilling to send it to you. There isn't quite enough to place it on the sample—the more so that it is not a story of intrigue as the Secret A might be regarded. I will make it interesting enough You may well trust me for that. But please don't place it *too soon*. I can't afford to botch such effects as my writing is able to produce. I want time. I will of course send you what is ready on my return. I wish to reach a certain point from which I will be able to dictate for a little while. All that part is maturing very fairly; and a month of dictating will give a famous share to the thing. I intend to give up the month of May to that; which month by the bye I wish to spend in London. But of that I will tell you later. Then June July, Aug. Sept. Oct in the Pent driving hard and exclusively at it will bring into view of* the conclusion which last I tell you frankly I *haven't* got as yet. But by that time it will be there.

Meantime don't imagine I am wasting time by working at the short story for Harpers or elsewhere. On the contrary I am employing the waste time—and I have told You why I am so anxious to utilise the odd hours.

Talking of Harpers. Pray tell me if (judging from draft of agreement to hand) they refuse to give me any advance. If so I dislike that attitude very much. It means that they will take the book and then for 10 months we won't see a penny of their money. Drop me a line on the subject and if you say plainly *you wish it* I'll sign the agreement as it stands, but not before.

On the occasion of G. Moore's French trans: of *Esther Waters* the *Gil Blas* (Par[isia]n daily très chic) calls me a *powerful seer of visions*.[2] This on the strength of Karaïn alone. A boom in France may have a good effect (by reverberation) at home. I am now shortening *The Duel* for

---

[1] Cousin and companion to Jessie Conrad; typist to Joseph.

[2] Gustave Kahn, 'Un réaliste anglais: George Moore', 24 February: 'Le *Mercure de France* nous révélait il y a quelques semaines, un puissant visionnaire, Conrad.' Kahn also mentions Kipling, Hardy, and Wells.

Harpers or any other magazine. I would have been ready before but for this infernal kick up with measles.

Yours ever

Conrad.

To J.B. Pinker
Text MS Berg; Unpublished

[Montpellier]
1st March 1907

Dear Pinker.

A thousand apologies. I must be getting blind. The agreement arrived just as B was sickening seriously and in the worry I only looked at it once.

I will post it to night.

B is threatened with pneumonia. It's a frightful worry. The weather however is fine. Last night he seemed better and slept quietly for some five hours.

Yours ever

Conrad

To J.B. Pinker
Text MS Berg; Unpublished

[Montpellier]
4 Mch 1907

My dear Pinker.

I feel I must write to you and it seems to me I have hardly the courage to set the thing down on paper. The doctor is just gone. You know how they talk but there is the fact that apparently Borys is menaced in both lungs. His textual words are: "This must be looked into at once." All these false appearances of pneumonia which passed off, and now this persistent bronchitis whose sounds are heard on each side under the armpits mean pht[h]isis[1] probably. The analysis will be made to morrow. The most terrifying fact in all this for me is that for the last three weeks I myself have had a suspicion of something of the kind. I would not give way to it but it has been gnawing at my vitals all that time. And now we shall see. I have a presentiment that if that is it it will

---

[1] Tuberculosis.

not last very long. But of course—as the doctor says—it may be nothing. I confess I have written the above words without conviction.

After this there's not much more to say. Don't imagine I am utterly knocked over. I feel luckily a good power of resistance within me. Strange fate. Just now when I became conscious of a fresh lease of health and life, when I feel a strenghtening* of my mental grip on my work this thing must come on!

I haven't done much for the last 4 days, but You may be assured that there will be no collapse on my part. Of course now till we know for certain all the plans I was going to write to you about are suspended. I will say no more. I needed the relief of confiding in a man of whose sympathy I am certain.

Kindest regards

Yours ever Conrad.

Agreement with Harpers posted to day.

To John Galsworthy

Text MS Forbes; J-A, 2, 43

[Montpellier]

5th Mch 1907

Dearest Jack.

I had your dear letter and we have your book[1] for which our thanks and our love. I ought to have written before—but when You have read the news I have to give you, you will not wonder I was not anxious to put pen to paper.

Borys had the measles. This would be nothing if he had not developed symptoms of pneumonia, which however passed away, leaving what appears to be bronchitis. Alas, it seems that he is threatened in both his lungs. The doctor imparted to me his fears yesterday. The most terrific part of it was this that for the last month even before he sickened for measles, I myself had a notion of something of the kind—a sort of gnawing fear which I kept from Jessie of course. A sort of slight cold with a little cough hung about him, but he rode and fenced and learned French with great zest and industry—and I was reluctant to admit my dread to myself. I had no other ground but the expression of his face which struck me one evening as he sat opposite me. We were having a

---

[1] *The Country House*, already seen in MS.

game of dominos and I had the greatest difficulty to finish the hundred. Then I went out and walked about the streets for hours. I managed to quiet myself but the impression remained. It turns out now that poor Jessie on her side had the same fears—and observed the same discretion. Then came the attack of measles with all the unexpected complications and this thing which the doctor thought was a most persistent bronchitis and now fears is something else. For the last ten days he has got dreadfully thin. We can't get him to eat more than a few mouthfuls and that only he will do for his mother's sake. His pulse keeps between 100–110 and the temperature jumps up and down in the day but is always up at night. The change in his character is also astonishing. But this won't bear being written about.

An analysis would have been made already but we can't get him to expectorate as yet, tho' he is trying his hardest in order to please me. This is the tenth night I haven't slept. I don't mean to say I have had no sleep for all that time; but I hang about his room all night listening and watching. I simply can't go to bed. Then in the afternoon I throw myself down on a sofa and sleep from sheer weariness. For four days I haven't written anything. Jessie is wholly admirable sharing herself between the two boys with the utmost serenity. She does everything for both. Borys who had been always so considerate is very exacting now. Nothing is right, good, or even possible unless his mother is there.

The analysis when it's made will put all doubt to rest—tho' indeed I've but little doubt left for my comfort now. It may be expected that this particular bout may be stopped. Then arises the question what next? It will I fear be impossible to return to England in April. Of school there can be no question just now. I have the idea that perhaps we could take him to Switzerland to some sanatorium high up for the summer and then come down to say Antibes (on the Riviera) for the winter. At his age everything can be cured. As the doctor told me "You may yet have a vigorous young fellow when he's eighteen". But meantime? I beat about for some feasible scheme of life under this new visitation. If this start is not checked soon then the whole thing won't last very long. That I feel. He doesn't complain of any pain, but he moans in his sleep most fitfully all night. I am writing this in his room. My dear Jack this is too awful for words. Jessie heroically has gone to bed—for the other must be thought of—leaving her dear love to you both. As to me I take refuge in the sense of your affection which seems more priceless in this great trouble

Ever yours

Conrad.

PS I've written to Pinker. Please tell Lucas and Edward to whom I ought to have written but I simply can not now. Give Ed. my congratulations, my wishes for the success of the play and my love. Ford too sent me his book.[1] I'll try to scrawl a line to him tomorrow.

To Ada and John Galsworthy
Text MS Forbes; Unpublished

[Montpellier]
9th Mch 1907

Dearest Jack and Ada.

I write at once to tell you the result of the first test. It is *very good*. No Koch bacilli.[2] Four other tests will take place within the next fortnight. As Moulis our doctor and prof: Grasset (a French celebrity)[3] say we must do away with every doubt—en avoir le coeur net[4]—and one test is not conclusive under the circumstances. But I think that we have now the secret of this horrible adventure.

A second eruption of measles has taken place. You understand that the first had run its course apparently and had totally disappeared. Then followed the awful 5 days of these broncho-pneumonic symptoms, child swathed in mustard plasters up to his armpits, racking incessant cough, high temperature and so on. This, note, coming after the pretty serious bronchial complication of the measles which should have passed away pari passu with the other symptoms. No medication seemed to produce the slightest effect. I could see on the 3^d day that Moulis was appalled by the extraordinary virulence of this lung attack. Last night he told me—I haven't told you half of what I thought. The little man was beaming and shaking hands with me and Jessie with the greatest effusion. As to us we can hardly stand—at least it's true of me.

The night I wrote to you, towards morning, about 3 or 4 o'clock, I went to his bed and switched on the electric light to look a[t] the boy. I could hardly believe my eyes! Between mid^{gt} and 4 another eruption had come out on head neck and body. I rang up the night waiter and sent him out to fetch Moulis who came at once. At first he was incredulous and very suspicious but by 6 in the morning the character of the eruption could not be mistaken. The fever had eased a little. Also the cough. We began to breathe then. In the evening the test note came from

---

[1] *Privy Seal*, the second part of the *Fifth Queen* trilogy.   [2] Evidence of tuberculosis.
[3] Dr Joseph Grasset (1849–1918), Professor of Clinical Medicine at Montpellier, had written extensively on the nervous system.
[4] 'To put our hearts at ease about it'.

the laboratory—and we came to life feeling very tired. It is clear that all the infection had gone into the lungs and set up all these alarming symptoms. Not once in 2000 cases does this happen I am told. Of course the child is terribly shaken. His emaciation is painful to see. Prof: Grasset saw him last night for the 3^d time, and stayed with me talking him over for an hour.

Here's a precis of the conversation: He will grow up with his medical character untainted, there is every reason to suppose. But taking into consideration his medical history for the last year (since scarlet fever) his predisposition to rapid pulse and high temp: and the peculiar contraction of the heart Dr Moulis had observed in Jany when attending him for slight 'grippe' you must be careful just now. My advice is don't take him to England now, not at all this summer if you can possibly avoid it. Go to Switzerland. Not too high. The lake of Geneva would do—Montreux, Vevey and even Geneva itself. There's a school there in every street. For August you may go a little higher to Glion for instance.

I then spoke of Champel N^r Geneva—a modest but rather well reputed hydropathic establishment where I have been twice myself in 1891 and 1894.[1] He thinks it an excellent plan. It's just out of town. He may go to some school there, have a little hydropathy under Dr Glatz, sleep with his windows open and get braced up more than in Montreux or Vevey. And again he said: I am strongly against him being taken back to England at present. But I would have no objection to you going back in winter if you like—if nothing happens in the meantime. By that time I believe he will be perfectly able to stand both the English climate and the English school life. He thinks both in fact very healthy.

So far Grasset who is coming once more to morrow, (as he says for his own satisfaction) to see Borys.

The fever is still there; but the cough is diminished and altered in character. To day he looks more like himself. The relapse of measles must run its course.

Upon reflexion I will do what I am advised to do. You know that we are not inclined to make an invalid of the boy. Last winter many a day he went to school (in Stanford) with his pulse up to a 100. But twice he had bouts of fever at the Pent and twice already here before this. He must be taken care of in the special way advised by Grasset. The idea is to set up his nerves on which he lives so much and render him less liable to catch

---

[1] And again in 1895. Hydropathy (or hydrotherapy) was a much-favoured cure; in the form of high-pressure douches, it used the healing waters externally as well as internally.

every infection. This seems reasonable. And in truth I too will want some hydropathy after this scrimmage.

As to Jessie she can not but derive some benefit too. She will have more rest than at the Pent. She will only have Jack to look after. Nellie Lyons[1] offers to come out and stay with us abroad. This is excellent and I think I will send Miss [. . .][2] we have now back to England in another fortnight. [. . .] of the whole plan? [. . .]

Ever yours

Conrad

To J.B. Pinker
Text MS Berg; Unpublished

[Montpellier]
[c. 9 March 1907][3]

Dear Pinker

Just a word to tell you the first laboratory test is very good. Four more are to be made.

The secret of this extremely virulent attack seems to be a sort of suppressed measles infecting the lungs. Another eruption has taken place the lung symptoms easing off almost at once. Of course the child is terribly shaken and most painfully emaciated. Fever is still there, but less. The cough also is nothing to what it was.

Prof. Grasset (in consultation) is coming again to morrow, when I will write you at length. We are all well, so far.

Ever Yours

Conrad

To J.B. Pinker
Text MS Berg; J-A, 2, 45

[Montpellier]
13 Mch 1907

My dear Pinker.

The second laboratory test is also negative. That's all very well but $1\frac{1}{2}°$ of fever every evening and pulse up to 110 must have some cause. One can not feel quite easy with that. And so far he won't eat anything like enough. However we are thankful for the small mercies.

[1] Formerly a maid at the Pent, and devoted to Borys.
[2] MS damaged: the first lacuna must concern Miss Wright.
[3] According to the medical news, between 9 and 12 March.

The last consultation has taken place. Textually this is what Grasset (a distinguished professor) advises.

Starting from the assumption that there is *no* tuberculosis he says however that the disposition of the lungs to get so heavily involved ought to be watched. The idea is to make the boy resistant to infection of every sort. Considering also his predisposition to temperature and quick pulse (observed by us for over a year now—ever since scarlet fever) which may be nervous phenomena he's of the opinion that the best thing for us is not to take him to England yet but proceed in a month's time to Switzerland—not too high up. Specifically he says Geneva lake would do for climate and altitude and even Geneva town itself. He pointed out to me that there is a school or two in every street almost, so he need not be idle as far as learning something is concerned. He wishes him also to have a hydropathic treatment, very thorough and prolonged, sleep with open windows and so on. I suggested then Champel a hydrotherapic establishment in the suburbs of Geneva, very modest but enjoying a considerable reputation amongst medical men. I was there myself in 1893 and 1894. Grasset and the other man seemed to think it the very thing.

They have no objection to English climate as such; only to the English climate in the present circumstances. As Grasset said: You tell me he lived a natural life in the country in the open air. Well yet this thing happened. This shows that to be braced up, made resistant to infection and so on, he wants something else, something more. I believe that what he wants he can get in Switzerland in the spring and summer months. If nothing fresh supervenes take him back to England in winter if you like. That has no importance. What's important is to brace him up thoroughly at once and fundementally,* without medicaments and invalidism. At his age everything can be mended except an actual organic defect. But when he is fourteen say it will not be so easy. You may have him ailing then till he's 17 or 18—to the great detriment of his future. In Champel he will get his proper cure with special diet and so on. He will want to be fed up. The treatment will stimulate his appetite.—Those are the conclusions of the doctor.

For myself my dear Pinker if it is to be Switzerland for him I much prefer Geneva now than Davos-Platz later on where the modern Dance of Death goes on in expensive hotels. There's nothing to prevent me writing in Champel (1/3 of my *Outcast* was written there in 1894) and the place is cheap—as such places go. I myself will not be any the worse for a course of water cure after this earthquake sort of shock. Champel has brought me round once and it may give me a fresh lease of mental life again now my health shows signs of general improvement. It is 14 months now since my last fit of gout! This is worth following up on the chance of securing permanency. But of course I am not thinking so much of myself as all that—but still.

Anyway this is what I think of doing. I want to send Miss Wright and the girl we have with us now back to England as soon as possible. On the other hand Jessie must have somebody efficient to help look after the baby. Any sort of trained nurse would be too expensive in the long run. Fortunately the servant we had with us for six years offers to come back. She will make up in devotion what she may lack in skill. She has thrown up her situation, kicked over all domestic opposition and is apparently standing bag in hand on the sea shore waiting to be called over. Of course we have accepted her offer. A quite sensible saving will be effected by having one person less in the establishment—besides the salary of Miss Wright. It will be felt in hotel bills and travelling ex: and also in other little ways. Poor Nellie is not an expensive servant. We will have however to fit her out in proper clothing here: a matter of 100 to 150 frcs. We think it very much worth while, the more so that we have a positive affection for the girl who came to us first at the age of 16, quite a child.

I want to start with the other two on the 21st of this month. I will have to go as far as Paris with them and put them into the boat train there, Miss Wright is such a fool. Can't be helped. The uncle of the other will see her off in Dover and I will be at the station in Paris to meet her and start back at once for Montpellier. I leave at 7 pm one day and am back at 10 pm the next. I hope Borys will be up by the 20th and the extra rooms where he was isolated given up by then. So far baby has escaped both the epidemic of measles in the town and the contagion at home.

I will have to ask you to do for me a good many things for which accept my apologies in advance. And first of all do get me a 42 in *basket trunk* (covered) of fair quality. You pass a shop of the kind on your way along the Strand I think. Please instruct the people to paint J. C. on the top and dispatch it *at once* by rail carriage paid to Mr *W. E. S. Graham. Stanford. Westenhanger Station S. E. R.* He's the girl's uncle and she will pack into it a lot of things we shall want from the Pent. Also please send a cheque for £5 to Miss N. Lyons c/o Mr *W. E. S Graham. The Drum inn. Stanford. Hythe. Kent.* It's important that the trunk should be in Westenhanger by the 18th inst.

To me please send off the usual *£80* cheque on Friday to settle bills here on Monday the 18th. I was in hopes that the proceeds of the Harper's story could go to the general fund; but as it is I must ask you to let me have them specially to meet the expences* extraordinary connected with Borys's illness and our change of plans. I propose to meet from it also our travelling to Geneva when the time comes and keep the rest in reserve, for I am afraid now of the unexpected. Let us set it at a hundred. Send me then *sixty* on <u>Monday</u> early and I will call on the balance later. I say Monday because I will post to you the serial version of the Duel on Sat: and you ought to get it on that day. But it would be nicer and more sure if you sent everything at once in one draft on Friday. I want very much to start Miss Wright and the girl off on the 20th or the 21st at the latest.

Towards the end of *Mch* I will begin to send you early pages of *Chance* in MS. For the last 3 days I have written 500 words pr day but it will take some work to bring the whole production to that average. Don't be disgusted if the MS dribbles in very thin at first. I will have to correct on my own dismal scribble and that takes time. It's no use parting with stuff which may require weeks of correcting work. Moreover when I have it by me a lucky idea occurs and is set down in its place; whereas when the MS is not there it is lost because my brain has no storage room.

The *Duel* will complete a very full vol: of short stories. It is always a reserve. I don't say anything more about it but if need arises it could be used to wind up my affairs at the Pent. Its sure to be worth £200 or so and I think that some £90 would settle everything there. The house must be kept on yet. It's £27 a year taxes included.

But of all that later. I don't think *Chance* will be delayed by a single day. I shall buckle to it exclusively. I don't want to see the proofs of the *Agent* till June when the other had* been shoved well forward.

Your[s] affectionately

J Conrad.

PS Thanks for your letter. I knew we would have your sympathy.

To J.B. Pinker
Text MS Berg; Unpublished

[Montpellier]
16 Mch '07

My Dear Pinker.

I've sent you by rg^d packet 70 pp of duel. Miss Wright discovers she hasn't any more typing paper—or thinks she hasn't. She's off her chump. Cant send my scrawl. It's illegible but at any rate in a day or two I will either copy it myself or the paper will be found. I didn't want to miss the post.

Thanks for your let[t]er. Do you suppose me above the usual weaknesses of humanity? Who's the *my editor* of your letter who's going to look at Chance? I am curious. You should be either more discreet or less mysterious. I would never have asked you how you were dealing with the stuff but now of course I want to know very much. It reads as if you kept an editor on the premises. Where do you chain him up.

B is not himself yet of course. He begins to eat but his pulse keeps up. I try to forget all this.

You need have no doubt of *Chance* being ready in the times mentionned.*

Do tell me in two words how the two books of H[ueffer] and Jack are really doing. H's is very good work. Amazing in fact. Of the other you know my opinion.

Yours always

J Conrad.

To John Galsworthy
Text MS POSK; Danilewiczowa

[Montpellier]
19 March '07

Dearest Jack

Our thanks to Ada and You for Your dear letters. Borys begins to feed decently but he's coughing still, a dry hacking cough most disagreeable to hear. The second laboratory test is favourable also.

Of course the boy is very far from being himself yet.

It is decided we go to Champel (Geneva) from here, end April. I feel confoundedly shaken up and can only work with terrific effort. I need not tell you I am disgusted at what I manage to do. My dearest Jack I read the C[ountry] H[ouse] with perfectly unalloyed delight. What does the press say? I won't say much here for we have talked this "remarkable piece of work" (in journalese) over several times before.[1] I can only say that it came to me in book form with a freshness, with a force, with an authority which simply amazed me. Upon my word I don't think I knew how good how admirably good it all was till this last reading in print. I have hugged myself with delight all along the pages. There are no holes in this stuff. It is wonderfully woven wonderfully coloured wonderfully fitted to the subject.

Have you got a spare copy of the play[2] you could let me have for a week? To see your work would comfort me in my miserable despondency about my own.

I've managed to drop a line to Ford. I haven't heard from him since leaving Eng*ᵈ*. Is he well?

My congratulations on the reprise of the Silver Box.[3] Let me know how it goes down with the general public. I want to know.

Enough for the evening. I feel very stupid just now.

Ever yours

J Conrad.

Jessie will be writing to Ada soon. Our dear love to her and you.

To Robert d'Humières
Text MS Vaugelas; Guérin

23 Mars 1907
Riche Hotel
Montpellier.

Cher Monsieur.

Votre lettre qui me trouve ici m'a fait grand plaisir. J'étais tellement convaincu de l'ingratitude de la tâche que Vous Vous êtes imposé[4] que je n'aurai été nullement surpris d'apprendre que Vous l'aviez abandonné. Je suis d'autant plus heureux d'entendre que le livre au titre funeste est déjà a moitié traduit et que Vous comptez continuer.

Cherchiez-vous la santé, le repos ou seulement une distraction dans le voyage que Vous venez de faire? Avec de la chance on trouve de tout dans le monde. Le difficile est d'avoir de la chance. J'espère que la fortune Vous a été propice dans Votre course a travers les longitudes.

[1] See the letter of [25 November or 2 December 1906].
[2] He had finished *Joy* in January (Marrot, p. 208).
[3] Whose matinée success had earned a run of evening performances.
[4] Translating *The Nigger*: it appeared in *Le Correspondant*, 25 August–10 October 1909.

J'éprouve cher Monsieur le plus vif désir de Vous voir: d'abord pour Vous serrer la main avec la reconnaissance que vos paroles amicales m'inspirent et puis pour admirer 'de visu' l'homme qui n'a pas craint de se colleter avec mon Nègre. Mais voilà ou nous en sommes.

Notre garçon ainé a fait une maladie ici. Cela a debuté par une rougeole pour finir par des complications assez menaçantes du côté des poumons. Enfin nous avons des inquiétudes. Par l'avis du médecin nous restons ici jusqu'a la fin Avril et puis nous allons en Suisse. Pas bien loin cependant: a Champel près Geneve ou il y a un etablissement Hydrotherapique sérieux. Ce n'est qu'en Sept^{re} que nous penserons a rentrer en Angleterre—par Paris naturellement. A cette epoque sans doute Vous serez absent de Paris. Mais tout de même je suis bien décidé de ne pas laisser finir cette année sans me faire connaître personellement a Vous.

Si Vous re-voyez M. Henry James 'notre bon maitre' dites lui un mot affectueux de ma part, je Vous en prie.

Croyez cher Monsieur que je suis on ne peux plus sensible a l'honneur que Vous faites à l'oeuvre et a l'écrivain. Permettez moi de me souscrire ici Votre reconnaissant ami

Joseph Conrad.

Translation

Dear Sir,

Your letter, which found me here, gave me great pleasure. I was so convinced of the thanklessness of the task you imposed upon yourself that I would not have been at all surprised to learn you had abandoned it. I was even happier to learn that the book with the distressing title is already half translated and that you count on continuing.

Were you looking for health, relaxation, or simply distraction in the journey you have just made? With luck, one finds everything in the world. The difficulty is in having luck. I hope fortune has been favourable in your journey across the longitudes.

I feel, dear Sir, the keenest desire to see you: first, to shake your hand with the gratitude that your friendly words inspire in me, and then to admire face-to-face one who is not afraid to grapple with my *Nigger*. But that's where we stand.

Our elder son has fallen ill here. It started with measles only to end with menacing complications in the lungs. In short, we are worried. On the advice of the doctor, we shall stay here until the end of April and then we are going to Switzerland. Not too far, however: to Champel, near Geneva, where there is a serious hydrotherapeutic establishment. Only in September do we think of returning to England—by way of Paris of course. At that time of year you will surely be away from Paris. But all the same, I am fully decided not to let this year pass without getting to know you personally.

If you see Henry James again, 'our good master', give him an affectionate word from me, I beg of you.

Believe me, dear Sir, that I could not be more sensible of the honour you have afforded the work and the writer. Allow me to sign myself here as your grateful friend,

Joseph Conrad.

To H.-D. Davray

*Text L.fr.*85

24 Mars 1907
Riche Hotel
Montpellier.

Cher Davray,

Borys a été bien malade, ça a débuté par une rechute de rougeole pour finir avec une complication assez menaçante du côté des poumons. Il en reste en ce moment des inquiétudes. Par l'avis des médecins ici nous restons à Montpellier jusqu'à fin Avril et puis nous allons à Champel près Genève. Je ne pense pas que nous rentrions en Angleterre avant le mois de Septembre—si tout va bien.

Dans un jour ou deux je vais vous envoyer *Karain* et *La Lagune* au net tous les deux. Je viens de recevoir une lettre aimable de M d'Humières. Il s'est amusé à faire le tour du monde en treize mois. Mais le *Nigger* est à moitié traduit et il est en train d'y travailler en ce moment.

J'ai bien mal travaillé ici jusqu'à présent. Enfin—on verra à se rattraper.

Bien à vous.

P.S.—Rappelez nous tous, y compris Jack, au bon souvenir de madame Davray. Ma femme envoie ses amitiés.—Borys ses salutations. Il n'est que peau et os le pauvre petit diable. Il tousse encore. Enfin l'analyse au laboratoire (il y en a deux) donne un bon résultat. On en fera deux encore pour en avoir le coeur net. A un moment donné ça avait l'air de tourner mal.—je ne vous dis que ça.

Translation

Dear Davray,

Borys has been very ill, having begun with a relapse of measles, ending with a distinctly threatening complication in the lungs. Some anxiety still remains. On the advice of the doctors here, we shall remain at Montpellier until the end of April, and then we shall go to Champel, near Geneva. I don't think we'll return to England before September—if all goes well.

In a day or two I'll send you 'Karain' and 'The Lagoon', both clean copies. I've just had a friendly letter from M. d'Humières. He has diverted himself by going around the world in thirteen months. But the *Nigger* is half translated and he's working on it now.

I have worked very badly here up till now. So—we shall see about catching up.

Sincerely yours.

P.S.—Remember all of us, Jack included, to Mme Davray. My wife sends her regards—Borys his greetings. He is nothing but skin and bones, the poor little devil. He still coughs. At last, the laboratory analysis (there are two of them) yields a good result. There will still be two more in order to put our minds at rest. At one point it looked as though things would turn out badly—enough said.

To J.B. Pinker

Text MS Berg; Unpublished

[Montpellier]
[March 1907][1]

Dear Pinker.

Pray settle for me the bills here enclosed and in addition a cheque for £.*2.18.0.* to Mrs Foulds. 5 Meath Road. Ilford. Essex. with simply the words "by Mr Conrad's instructions". another for £ *1.10* to Mrs C. Finn Postling, Hythe Kent.

Thanks very much

Yours

Conrad.

---

[1] The month and year of receipt pencilled in at Pinker's office.

To J.B. Pinker

Text MS Berg; Unpublished

Riche Hotel
Montpellier
8 Ap. 1907

My dear Pinker.

I've been beastly ill without being laid up.

The MS[1] goes by the same post. I tried to copy it clear and did do some pages. I dare say an intelligent typist will find his way through it.

Pray send on receipt of this a cheque for £2.3 *to* Mr D. West, 145 High Street Hythe. Kent

I want him to have it by the 11th as promised.

Balance due to Miss E. *Wright*

17 Moreland R^d. East Croydon
£6.16.0

Mrs J. George.[2] Reynolds Farm Hawkhurst. Kent. £2.2.

Mrs C. Finn Postling Hythe. Kent. £3.

She's the caretaker of Pent Farm and keeps the dog and cat for Borys.

My head seethes with ideas but I am dead tired not with the work but with the infernal stress under which it is done. I wish I had that careless, sunny nature people talk of in connection with Stevenson. But then Stevenson perhaps—but never mind.[3]

I will be writing extensively in a day or two. Don't expect the first batch of Chance before the end of this month.

Ever yours aff^ctly

Conrad.

---

[1] Of 'The Duel', without the closing pages. He had intended to post the MS on the 3rd (telegram, 2 April, Berg).
[2] Jessie's mother? Hawkhurst is about thirty miles from the Pent.
[3] Conrad thought Stevenson a meretricious writer: *Letters*, 2, p. 371.

To John Galsworthy
Text MS Forbes; Marrot 211 (in part)

Riche Hotel.
Montpellier
12 Ap. 1907

Dearest Jack.

I didn't write before because I was finishing something. That does not mean I didn't read the play[1] at once. I've read it more than once the very first day, then many times since in whole and in parts—and my admiration for the innefable* Colonel and the adorable Miss B has done nothing but grow and grow. Other improvements disengaged themselves from my reading: the first of them being that the ironic treatment is very complete. I contemplated it with the attention it seemed to me to deserve (and with some mistrust. But let that pass) and discovered that it was full of felicitous touches in a way that might almost be called continuous. My envy of your achievement was great thereat. The symmetrical arrangement of the four couples—the old couple—the young couple—the irregular couple—and the couple to be—with Miss B unpaired fluttering around extorted my admiration too. And I don't know whether the crowning irony of presenting us the Joy & Dick idyll in that section was rigidly intended or not but at any rate it is there—in the end of Colonel's idyll. For no doubt he began like Dick with Mrs Colonel who no doubt would have been very much like Joy under the special circumstances.

Altogether the feeling of this piece of work being successfully done increases on examination. The objections arise only to vanish before the clever handling. And this is about the greatest proof of soundness—if not the only one: because a play that would give no rise to objections as it goes on would not be going on—would be non-existent in fact. The delicacy of observation is greater than in the S[ilver] B[ox] or perhaps the sentiments observed are of more delicate kind. It matters not which, since the observer is equal to every fineness that comes in his way. And the whole action though multiple hangs together in a wonderful way—a result that I don't know whether to ascribe most to your skill or to your sincerity.

Upon the whole turning the pages of that play, here and there, I suspect every time that there is more in it than I ever will be able to see perhaps. The scene between Mother and daughter: H'm! H'm! Phew! Exactly so! One wonders at the depth of passion in that tree climbing

---

[1] *Joy*, produced in September 1907.

young lady—till one realizes the insight of presentation—the illuminating power of youthful egoism and the strenght* of youthful res[s]entiment.[1] And she is a delightful goose (tho' geese don't perch on trees I believe—unless wild?) and all this is very good very good. And I shouldn't wonder in the least if it were to fetch the public immensely.

The only weakness of the play as a whole (and I don't know that it is a weakness—or a defect) is a slight effect of wrangling. But I don't know that it is wrong or whether it is available at all. All the people talk *directly* to the point, and the cryptic subacid interferences of Miss B. intensify this wrangling impression. The question arises whether a play could be written when everybody would be talking round the point?

But I won't go into this inquiry now. I feel remarkably stupid to day, having finished a story of some 30000 w. only late last night. It's a thing of no consequence.

Borys does not look so very bad now. He is very an[a]emic. His heart is under observation; the cough has disappeared but the pulse persists. He's got very spoiled during his illness but he's a good little chap at bottom. Jack flourishes very much and is a very amusing little cuss. Jessie is fairly well but an[a]emic also for the present. We must go to Champel it appears. I am very tired—with an undercurrent of worry and dread keeping me irritable. To work is a terrible effort. And it's done. The effort I mean. And as usual there isn't enough to show for it. There never is. I'll never work fast enough. Meantime my 50th year is approaching!

Could you my dear Jack inquire at your bookseller's whether there has appeared a book entitled *Animal Artizans** (Studies of Birds and Beasts).[2] The Author's name I fancy is *C. J. Cornish*. If so do please get it sent over to me at once for Mons. B. If anything ever makes that boy take to reading it will be books of that sort. I ask you because you are the most trustworthy of friends and I want the book at once.

Jessie's dear love to you both. Is there a chance if [you] go on the Cont this year of your passing through Geneva? Is there? It's on the way to most places.

I see in casually obtained D Chr^cle the reception of *S. B.* on first evening was very good.[3] My congratulations. With love to you [...][4]

                                                    Yours ever

                                                                    J. Conrad

---

[1] The French word chosen for its Nietzschean overtones?
[2] Newly published by Longmans, Green.
[3] The *Daily Chronicle* reviewed *The Silver Box* on 9 April.   [4] Word illegible.

PS I will send play over in a day or two only. Want to read it again.

PPS At the moment of closing comment this tribute from a special specialist and his wife. Also I have just seen ad[t] of LARGE edition of Country House.[1] I am made happy by all these things.

To J.B. Pinker
Text MS Berg; Unpublished

[Montpellier]
13 Ap. 1907

My dear Pinker

On the 11th I sent off the end pages of the Duel. They were not included in the first lot by mistake.[2] Things are rather in a confusion here.

Please send me, on receipt of this, draft on Cr. Ly[ais] as usual for £80 and also the £40 as arranged at the same time. I am not exactly certain when we will leave here. Snow is falling in Lyon and no doubt in Geneva too. The Hydropathic in Champel will not be open till May 5th I believe. I will be writing to them in a few days to make arrangements for a prolonged sojourn.

I am revising the pages of Chance I shall begin sending you. I will send them in small batches 10 or so at a time. So if any should get lost the disaster would not be crushing.

Unless I am very much mistaken you will find no difficulty in placing the Duel. It's too long for Harpers and I can't shorten it. The game's not worth the candle. Perhaps you have already had the idea to send them that story *Il Conde*. Just the thing for a magazine's summer no.[3]

I am glad to hear Jack's play pleased Mrs Pinker and Yourself. There's a lot in Galsworthy.

I am very much possessed by the idea of striking a blow for popularity. Various notions pass through my head and I would like to have your opinion on them. On the other hand I don't want You to think that I am passing my time in making plans. It is not so. I am steadily

---

[1] Galsworthy's new novel was reprinted twice in March and once in April.

[2] He probably did not finish them until the early hours of the 11th ('late last night' in the letter of the 12th). At 1.20 p.m. on the 11th, he sent a telegram (Berg) announcing that the last batch had left.

[3] In the U.S., *Forum* took 'The Duel' (July–October 1908), and *Harper's Magazine* took 'Il Conde' (February 1909).

hammering at *Chance*. But I want to have something inside of me when that is done—something ready to come out.

I am writing to-day with a heavy heart to the Rector of Beaumont School[1] to say that Borys can't join this next half-term. He's under treatment now here. Morning frictions, salt baths, medicines, special diet. It's rather horrible. He's an[a]emic and very nervous. Pulse constantly near 100, but he looks much more like himself. I am well now. I felt extremely seedy for 10 days or so. Our kind regards

Yours

Conrad.

To William Heinemann
Text MS Heinemann; Unpublished

Riche Hotel
Montpellier.
France
15 April '07

My dear Heinemann.

You must forgive the delay in answering your letter. When it arrived our oldest boy was very ill. Our anxiety was prolonged for many days. Afterward I myself felt extremely knocked up and too languid to do anything.

No proposal in any sort of tangible way has been put before me either by McClure, directly or, by Pinker. In a most roundabout way (which I need not specify) some rumour of something of the kind being thought of in America came to my ears—I attached no importance whatever to it. This was last Sept I think. I haven't given it a moment's consideration. Indeed there was nothing to consider. In the last letter I had from P only 4 days ago there's not a word about McClures or their agent.

The hitch as to Rescue is caused by my necessities not by P's machinations.[2] Nothing can happen in regard to the disposal of that book without my consent. So far I can't devote all my time to it—and my spare moments are rare and only too short. I am very much distressed by this.

I don't exactly understand what Mr Corrigin[3] (of whom I've never heard) has been suggesting to you. If my reading of your letter is correct

---

[1] The Roman Catholic college near Windsor. Borys would have joined the preparatory division.
[2] Since 1898, McClure had held serial and Heinemann book rights for *The Rescue*.
[3] One of McClure's employees?

he has given you the option to take over this dismal contract. You don't say on what conditions? And of course I don't pretend to ask—but it seems to me that they can't expect you to do more than take over the sum they have advanced. You can't doubt my preference for your firm over any other; but whether I am bound to two firms or only to one it can make no difference to my firm resolve to finish that book as soon as a pronounced selling success will give me the necessary leisure. That's the crux of the affair. The will is there and perhaps the ability to make something tolerable of it too. No one and nothing can influence me adversely except *la force des choses*. This is all I can say. With kindest regards to yourself and Pawling

Yours sincerely

J. Conrad

To J.B. Pinker
Text MS Berg; Unpublished

Riche Hotel
Montpellier
3 May 1907

My dear Pinker

Thanks for the typecopy of the few pages of Chance which I've received yesterday.

I've been knocked over by an attack of gout—the first now for 18 months: left hand and wrist. Four days in bed. I got up yesterday and am very shaky. Nerves all to pieces. But all that wont last very long. I am going to try a radical treatment this time and am even thinking of going to Contrexéville[1] for 21 days in July. It's worth while to try. They tell me here I am by no means hopelessly tainted, the best proof being the slightness of the attack after such a long interval—comparative slightness be it understood.

I am almost too shaky to write this letter. What I['ve] got to say is this:

The proofs of Sec^t. Ag^t will be given back end June not before. You know my dear Pinker that I wish to do my best but I cannot do better. I must *see* that story. The mere notion of you sending the proofs to Harpers puts me in a fever of apprehension. *Don't do it* for goodness's sake. You know it was always understood the book had to be worked upon thoroughly.

---

[1] A spa in the Vosges.

Send me £100 by the 13th of this month as I wish to leave on the 15th for Geneva. You will hear from me fully in a day or two. Meantime with kindest regards

Yours ever

J Conrad.

To J.B. Pinker
Text MS Berg; Unpublished

6th May '07
Riche Hotel
Montpellier.

My dear Pinker.

I was not in a fit state to write you fully last time. I am getting better rapidly tho' I can't use my hand as yet. It's extremely bothersome. But the head is getting clear and that's the main thing. The weather is horribly wet here and poor Borys has started coughing again. I can hear him now; it's a sound that robs me of my composure in a great measure. I am anxious now to get away from here but it seems that the weather has turned very cold about Lyons and Geneva. However we start from here on the 15th. I find that to get away from here and arrive in Geneva with a little money in hand I will want £25 that I asked you for. Please send it on.

The supply of MS of Chance was stopped by my gout as you must have guessed. I'll start on again in a very few days, a few pages at a time. Do not take the trouble to send the type back to me at once. Every fortnight or even every month will do. I am correcting as I copy from my first MS.

I am writing to the Postmaster in Stanford to forward me the proofs of S.A. which he must have been keeping as I've seen nothing of them so far. Are they galley slips as it was arranged?

Do not doubt for a moment that I will do all I can to get the S.A ready for the printer soon. If there is hurry I will leave off Chance completely for a fortnight or so. I suppose it will be just as well. My only anxiety was to get Chance forward—you understand. The S.A. however has its importance as a distinctly new departure in my work. And I am anxious to put as much "quality" as I can in that book which will be criticised with some severity no doubt—or *scrutinised* rather, I should say. Preconceived notions of Conrad as sea writer will stand in the way of its acceptance. You can see this Yourself.

Does Methuen think the work has any chance of getting at the public? If so I quite understand that every effort should be made to get it ready early. What do you think Yourself? I am thinking as I've told you before of striking a blow for popularity. The fate of the S.A. may be instructive from that point of view.

Yours ever

Conrad.

PS Please send at once cheque for £3 to L. E. Straughan. The Post Office. Stanford. Hythe. Kent on Mr Conrad's acct/. Also £*1.1* to Mudies 48 Queen Victoria Street office.

To John Galsworthy

Text MS Forbes; J-A, 2, 47

Riche Hôtel

Montpellier.

6 May

1907

Dearest Jack

I didn't write before because of horrid gout. It has come back after an interval of 18 months and has depressed me frightfully.

No luck.

I am glad you think I've done something. It's but 30 000 words of rubbishy twaddle—and it's far from enough. Very far. I am sinking deeper and deeper. The state of worry in which I am living—and writing—is simply indescribable. It's a constant breaking strain. And you know that materials subjected to breaking strain lose all elasticity in the end—part with all their 'virtue' on account of profound molecular changes. The molecular changes in my brain are very pronounced. It seems to me I have a lump of mud, of slack mud in my head. The only bright spot in my existence is Your success. I am glad to hear you are about to tackle the subject of your fourth play. That's the way! Now You must affirm yourself by sheer weight of your work. But the intention of going then to a novel is also very good. What novel? We are going to Champel près Genève on the 15th. I will send you the address of the hotel.

I am suffering a good deal of pain yet in my left wrist. Have been in bed, feeling very beastly for five days. The nervous collapse is consider-able. Cant react somehow. I drag about with an arm in the sling hopeless, spiritless without a single thought in my head. Borys is coughing a lot and I own that the sound robs me of the last vestiges of composure. I don't mean to say that I show this. I don't. But you and Ada may be told.

Jessie, what between the two boys and myself, has her hands very full. She sends her tender love. Little Jack thrives. He's a joyous little soul.

We have no house to come back to. Of course there is the Pent. The difficulty would be to get away from it. I don't see my way to anything just now. The only thing perfectly clear is that we can't live there any longer.

Thanks ever so much for the book received a fortnight ago.

With dear love to you both

ever yours

Conrad.

To Robert d'Humières
Text MS Vaugelas; Guérin

6 Mai 1907
Riche Hotel
Montpellier

Cher Monsieur

Un atroce accès de goutte au poignet m'a empêché de repondre a Votre bonne et amicale lettre.

Nous partons pour Genève le 15 de ce mois. Ce sera une vraie joie de Vous voir.

Nous tâcherons de nous loger a l'hotel de la Roseraie a Champel.[1] Même si nous sommes forcés de prendre gite ailleurs un mot a cette adresse me trouvera toujours

A bientôt donc cher Monsieur

bien a vous

J. Conrad.

Translation

Dear Sir,

An excruciating attack of gout in the wrist has prevented me from answering your kind and friendly letter.

We leave for Geneva on the 15th of this month. It will be a delight to see you.

---

[1] His lodging on previous visits.

We shall try to stay at the Hotel de la Roseraie in Champel. Even if we are forced to take lodgings elsewhere, a word to this address will always find me.

Until we meet, dear Sir

Yours truly

J. Conrad.

To J.B. Pinker
Text MS Berg; Unpublished

[Montpellier]
8 May 1907

My dear Pinker

Many thanks for your letter. I am anxious to have the S.A. come out this year so as to have the next clear for *Chance* and the Vol of short stories.

Will not end of June do for delivering the last sign^{re} of the SA? It is the last third of the story that wants expanding, writing up, making effective. The rest would need merely style corrections.

I am beginning to copy again the pp of *Chance*. You will be getting them in a thin stream very soon.

Yours ever

Conrad.

To J.B. Pinker
Text MS Berg; Unpublished

[Montpellier]
11 May 1907

My dear Pinker

I have pulled myself together at last after my gout. The head is clear, tho' the nerves are jangled; but there's not much to wonder at in that. To-morrow (Sunday) Borys is going to be examined again by Prof Rausier[1] and another man. His cough has come back 3 weeks ago. There will be another laboratory test on Monday. It is like living in a nightmare. It is impossible to shake off the oppression of that thing.

I am awaiting the proofs of the S.A. They will no doubt turn up on Monday. Please drop me word at the *Hotel de la Roseraie Champel près Genève* if end June will be time enough to secure early publication.[2] I am

---

[1] Georges Rauzier (1862–1920).
[2] Methuen published *The Secret Agent* on 10 September.

bound to do all I can not to delay the publication. And I will do it too. It's only a question of arranging my work. If I have till end July to get the *SA* ready for press I need not interrupt my work at *Chance*. If you must have the *SA* corrected by the 15 June (say) I can manage that too I think. In any case you may rest assured that Chance will be ready by end Nov.

The *SA* must not be put off till next year. I am spending too much money to afford that delay. You must have some of your advances back this year.

You remember I asked you some time ago whether you could find a situation for a lad we used to have and who enlisted on leaving us. He is now in England with a good character from the army and good testimonials also as mess-waiter. He would be good in the stables as well as in the house.

Please send cheque for £*2.10* to the Rev. F. Smith. Stanford Rectory N^r Hythe. Kent.

I will write to you on arrival in Geneva and shall send then some MS.

Yours ever

Conrad.

To J.B. Pinker
Text MS Berg; J-A, 2, 48

[letterhead: Hôtel de la Poste
Genève]
18 May 1907

Private

My dear Pinker

Thank you very much for the money sent. If I telegraphed on the 14^{th1} it was because our rooms were let already and had to be vacated, moreover I had a compartment* reserved in the train for the 15th. I have miscalculated my expences* in Montpellier and must ask you to send frcs *1100* by means of Credit Lyonnais to Mr *Joseph Ducaillar* Riche Hotel Montpellier, in the course of the week. I left that much in his debt. And please don't scold me because I have just now as much as I can bear. Here I am stranded again with baby at its last gasp with whooping cough. It began in Montpellier. We started by medical advice counting

---

[1] 'Have you sent the money I must retain seats in my train tomorrow Tuesday please wire' (telegram, 13 May, Berg).

on the change of climate to check the disease but it has developed on the road in a most alarming manner. The poor little devil has melted down to half his size. Since yesterday morning he has had a coughing fit every quarter of an hour or so and will not eat anything. We'll have to resort to artificial feeding very soon. Of course la Roseraie Hotel won't take us now. We stick here isolated at the end of a corridor. Really I haven't got my share of the commonest sort of luck. I suppose Chance will have to pay for all this. But if you think I ought to come home I will do so as soon as baby can travel, and will let my cure go to the devil. Borys of course has whooping cough too but very mildly. Still it isn't good for him. My dear Pinker I feel that all this is almost too much for me.

I am trying to keep a steady mind and not allow myself to dwell too much on the cost of things or I would go distracted.

The proofs of *S.A.* have reached me and I have almost cried at the sight. I thought it was arranged beyond doubt that I was to have *galley slips* for my corrections. Instead of that I get the proofs of set pages! Apart from the cost of correction which will be greatly augmented through that there is the material difficulty of correcting clearly and easily on small margins. And upon my word I don't want just now any extra difficulties put in the way of my work. I am hurt at Methuen disregarding my perfectly reasonable wishes in such a manner. If Alston Rivers can always furnish galley proofs to Hueffer Methuen could well do that much for me. I feel their carelessness in this matter as a slight. Please tell them on the telephone from me that I have no photograph to send them. They bother me for that.

In the circumstances after reflecting on the best way of dealing with the S.A. I think I *must* curtail my corrections as much as possible. I have begun to correct and shall be sending you the first signatures as I finish them off. Meantime I shall lay *Chance* aside entirely—either the writing or the copying. The delay won't be long. Don't let Your editor in the States slip away. Promise him a big lot of stuff by Sept^{er}. You can do that safely.

The *S.A.* approached with a fresh eye does not strike me as bad at all. There is an element of popularity in it. By this I don't mean to say that the thing is likely to be popular. I merely think that it shows traces of capacity for that sort of treatment which may make a novel popular.

As I've told you my mind runs very much on popularity just now. I would try to reach it not by sensationalism but by means of taking a widely discussed subject for the *text* of my novel. Apart from religious problems the public mind runs on questions of war and peace and labour. I mean war, peace, labour in general not any particular way or any particular form of labour trouble.

My head is in such a state that I don't know whether I make my idea clear. In short my idea is to treat those subjects in a novel with a sufficiently interesting story, whose notion has come into my head lately. And of course to treat them from a modern point of view. All this is vague enough to talk about but the plan in my mind is fairly definite. I will hurry on with that directly I've done with *Chance*. There is no time to lose.

Please drop me a line here on receipt of this. I feel most awfully lonely and am putting all my trust in you to let me t[h]rough.

Yours ever

J Conrad.

To J.B. Pinker
Text MS Berg; Unpublished

[letterhead: Hôtel de la Poste]
May '07
19th evening

My dear Pinker.

I think that in 2 or 3 days the baby will be sufficiently better to be moved. The Champel people have consented to take us in as they have an annex to their hotel where we can be isolated in a way. I am anxious to bring the bill here to an end as soon as possible. Also at the Roseraie I will be able to start work in earnest. You had better send me £*10* at once in case of some more trouble. A postal order sent in a *not* registered letter would do best.

When I look at the proofs of the *SA* I feel exasperated with Methuen. The utter contempt shown for my wishes and my instructions is galling. If it had been the merest fancy I think that Conrad was worth attending to. But you know it was no mere author's caprice. I had hurried the thing on in the hope of having every facility to give it a properly finished shape later on.

I hope Borys will begin his cure this week. If it had not been for him I would start for England to-day with a light heart. The poor baby is absolutely exhausted and I think that it is only my wife's fierce determination to hold on to him that kept him alive. He has not virtually been out of her arms for the last sixty hours. A very clever young swiss doctor has the case in hand.

I am sick of everything—just a little. But that will wear off.

Yours ever

J. Conrad

To J.B. Pinker
Text MS Berg; Unpublished

Saturday 25 May. 07
Hotel de la Roseraie
Champel
près Genève

My dear Pinker

I send you by this post 64 pp of corrected proof. On Monday I will post some more; by Thursday you will get half the book and I believe that the whole will be in your hands by the end of this month. Let Methuen set up the corrections and forward you the revises in two sets. One set you will be able to send to US as it comes in. The other please forward to me as I wish to look over the revise for the English edition which will be standard one. This last remark applies to all my work. The English edition is the authoritative one in case of future reprints. Please my dear Pinker bear that in mind; for you will have the care of my literary reputation when I am no longer there to fuss about things myself. But truly I don't fuss about much. I haven't the heart for it. You will understand better what I say when I tell you that since the day before yesterday Borys is laid up with rh[e]umatism. If you laugh at this news I won't take it ill. I am ready to laugh myself tho' on the wrong side of my mouth. Both ankles are involved so far, but the fever is moderate about 100°—no more. Thats a good feature. And the boy turns out as plucky as can be with the pain. When you think that at the same time he has the whooping cough which jerks him all over when it comes on (about once every hour) you may imagine what he has got to stand in the way of torture: for the pain of a rh[e]umatic joint when moved is horrible.

The baby is mere skin and bone. He was so bad at the hotel de la Poste that we had to get oxygen for him and so on. Since we came here (last Thursday) the change of air and being out in the garden of this place all day has done him lots of good. He feeds now properly. It's a question of time with him now.

Coming home at once is out of the question now. I reckon then on three more months here. I think I can manage here on £60 a month including doctor and my own cure. But let us say £200 for the 3 months and another hundred to pay the people about the Pent. By end Aug^st the S.A. will be out in book form and bring in more than that. Besides I have upon the whole got on so well in planning *Chance* that it is quite possible it may be finished in three months from now. You know I always can work best from June to October. And even if Chance is not finished till October it will be always something substantial to make a fresh start on—with better luck I hope.

I was greatly disappointed at not having heard from you this week. Please my dear fellow when you receive this on Mond: or Tuesday wire me over £20 through Cook's office. They lay themselves out for that kind of thing. If you have already [. . .]¹ the £10 I had asked you for then wire over only ten more. And pray write me a [. . .] whether I can count on the amounts suggested above. I want to work in [. . .] security. Pardon my long letters.

Yours ever

Conrad.

To J.B. Pinker
Text MS Berg; Unpublished

[Champel]
[late May 1907]²

My dear Pinker

Your good and friendly letter arrived on Sat after I posted mine to you. I am sorry I ever mentionned* my disappointement* at your silence. One gets to feel tender as if flayed, in the midst of worries—but I spoke in sorrow only.

You know what further developments I've been favoured with. Well Borys since 3 am to day is free from pain, but of course remains powerless as to the use of his feet. The other joints have escaped—it seems fever gone. Perhaps it was a purely accidental attack? But the truth is that ever since the fatal measles he showed at times red patches on elbows, knees and ankles. He would also casually mention pains here and there—wondering how he managed to strain so his knee or wrist or thumb. But of course neither he nor we made anything of it.

I send you the *SA* up to p *160*—half the vol. Let them get on with

---

¹ MS torn.
² Between 25 May, when the 'good and friendly letter' arrived, and 1 June, when the next set of proofs went off.

that. The second half will take more time. But I promise you not to linger over it more than a decent regard for my work requires. I still fancy that by end May I will be able to turn to Chance to the exclusion of everything else.

Thanks very much for the money. I[f] you think I didn't writhe at the sight of my acct/ You must think me singularly callous. All the beautiful plans of settling down modestly and quietly to work with renewed health have been knocked over by all these alarums and excursions. Yet I needn't give up. But all that I will write of later on.

The tale vaguely indicated to You takes consistency slowly, during the hours of idleness.

I must start on it at *once* at *once* after Chance.

> Yours very afftely
>
> J Conrad

To William Rothenstein
Text MS Harvard; J-A, 2, 50

> 28 May. 07
> Hotel de la Roseraie
> Champel
> Genève

Dear Will.

You must forgive me—us—our long silence. I am ashamed and tired of sending tales of woe—endless, everlasting—to my friends. And there is never anything else to say.

We went to M'pellier for some 3 months—not from self indulgence but to make sure, to confirm if possible the improvement which a first visit there caused in my gouty state. Our intention was to return in March, send Borys to school settle down to work with renewed strenght* and better hopes.

Early in Febr^y Borys fell ill with measles. An attack of extreme severity and made remarkable by the very exceptional case of a relapse. Lung complications set in—with an aspect so menacing that I may say we have looked the very spectre in the face. When I tell you that all this dragged for weeks, boy wrapped up in mustard poultices, racked with cough, consultations, long faces, laboratory tests and so on you may imagine how we felt. However—in the language of the official analyst: les Bacilles Koch n'existent pas. But the boy came out so shaken up that the return to England was for the moment out of question. The medical authorities advised us to take him to Switzerland to set him up and regain generally his constitution by a course of hydropathy. We selected Champel and waited in the south for the beginning of the season—

We waited nursing him up slowly into some strength when at the end of April the luckless little devil caught whooping cough. The baby too. However we started for here. And we are here! I wonder the people took us in. Poor baby is simply melting away in our hands. It's a heartbreaking business to look at him. But this is not all. Four days ago Borys who has never been really himself since that attack of measles got laid hold of by an attack of rh[e]umatism in both ankles. Comprenez-Vous? He's being stuffed with salicilate.

Fortunately the fever is not very high about 100° and he's as plucky with the pain as it is possible to be. And all this time with a whooping cough which jerks him all over as he lies in bed. I break into cold perspiration whenever I hear him cough for I know how horrible is the pain of a jarred rh[e]umatic limb.

Voilà. Jessie has been simply heroic in the awful Montpellier adventure never giving a sign of anxiety not only before the boy but even out his sight; always calm serene, equable, going from one to the other and apparently never tired though cruelly crippled by her leg which is not in a good condition by any means. But how long she will last at it I dont know. I caught her the other evening dropping a tear over little Jack. He's indeed a pitiable object to see.

But enough of this. What will happen next I don't know. I managed to finish a 30000 words story (since the New Year) and going on with a new novel and am preparing for the press (in book form) the one I finished for serial publication last October. And all this does not amount to much. I need not tell you I am ruined for this year by all these complications. All my plans are knocked on the head, plans of work, hopes of a publishing success. And next year I'll be fifty!—No! we did not write; we thought of you often tho'; and you must never doubt our affection for dear Alice for yourself and your dear chicks. Ever Yours

Conrad.

PS Jessie will drop a line to Alice very soon. Just now she hardly ever has the baby out of her arms night or day. I'll let you know how we get on next week. Don't be angry.

To J.B. Pinker
Text MS Berg; Unpublished

Saturday
1st June. 1907.
Hotel de la Roseraie
Genève.

Private

My dear Pinker.

I've wired twice asking you for a telegraphic transfer of £10 through Cook's or the Post off.[1] To my first wire on Wed: I had an answer by letter yesterday suggesting I made some mistake. To the other sent off at 10 am. (yesterday) no answer came during the day.

The fact is that having paid bills at Hot: de la Poste and one week here I am without a penny; and I am anxious to begin my cure which I cannot do without first seeing the Champel doctor (fee at once) and taking a series of tickets which must be paid for in advance. I must also tell you that I suffer from periodical eruptions of gouty eczema and it appears that the hot water treatment cannot be begun while it is on. In fact it would not be a safe thing to do. Just now I am free from it but certain nervous sensations make me fear it will come on soon. Once on the beastly thing lasts 2 or 3 weeks. I was and am very anxious to check it if possible by the treatment.

I tell you the miserable tale so that you should know it was no senseless whim of mine. I am not throwing away. Please my dear fellow on receipt of this wire over* the sum demanded *at once*. I've only six francs in my pocket for all fortune. It's awkward.

I acknowledged last week your good autograph letter. We are very grateful to you for your sympathy. The baby is not well. He seems too ill for the disease he's suffering from, and we fear there may be something else. We shall see. Borys is no longer in pain now but can't use his feet yet.

I send you to day corr^d proof *SA* up to p 288. The remaining few pages and the additional stuff inserted into the first text I keep by me over to morrow (Sunday). I will post it on Monday evening all complete. The end is rounded properly—the theme is developed and concluded decently. I will have no reason to be ashamed of the book and the

---

[1] 28 May: 'Please effect the transfer asked for in my letter of Saturday last'; 31 May: 'Please wire over ten pounds by Cook letter and completed proofs go tomorrow' (Berg).

Americans will have no excuse for any delay in publication. What effort all this has cost me under the circumstances You may easily guess.

I beg you to attend to the *revise* being sent to me soon *in two sets*. I ask you to do this as a friend not as an agent. When the date of pub: is fixed you will let me know without delay, please!

I am thinking of dedicating the vol to Wells. I hinted something of that to him already. The full title I wish to run like this:

THE
SECRET AGENT.
A Simple Tale

I dont want the story to be misunderstood as having any sort of social or polemical intention.

I'll attack *Chance* next Tuesday if all goes well—or rather no worse than at present. I feel mentally pretty fit.

Yours

Conrad.

4 pm This moment Cooks telephone here that the money is here many thanks. I send this so that you should learn the reason of my urgency. J. C.

To J.B. Pinker
Text MS Berg; Unpublished

[Champel]
Sat. 1^{s[t]} June. [1907] 5.30 pm

My dear Pinker,

I recollect suddenly that I've forgotten to chapter the batch of proofs send* off an hour ago. Tear off this part and send the note below to Methuen at once, or better still slip it into the envelope containing the proofs if that is not gone yet from Your office when you receive this.

Apologies

Yours J. C.

To J.B. Pinker

Text MS Berg; Unpublished

5 June '07
Hotel de la Roseraie
Genève.

My dear Pinker

A reg^d envelope containing printed and MS pp of *SA.* goes by the same post with this.

It isn't quite the end yet. All but however and you may rest assured I will not be behind the time first named (10th to 15th June) in getting the book ready.

I haven't the material time to be quicker. Borys is now powerless in both hands. He suffers a great deal. He's also very helpless as You may imagine. Can't even sit up without help. I've to look after him. I am having the ghastliest time imaginable. Nursing hinders me in my work not only intellectually but materially. I set down the pen in the middle of a phrase and have to go to him. And to look at him is not exactly composing to the mind. I come back to my paper as if out of a nightmare and don't remember what I wanted to say.

This thing drags, the temp: fluctuating between 100–101½. Doctor every day for this must be watched. I find that I won't be able to manage on £60 *per month* here. I must have eighty as (nominally) in Montpellier. But here I have good hopes not to go beyond that. Please my dear fellow see to it that I get £40 on *Wednesday next here.* If I see that I can do with less next fortnight you may be sure I won't ask for more than absolutely necessary, under the circumstances. I've begun my own cure which makes me sleepy and tired at first. I've to drink 2 frcs worth of mineral water per day too!—I am atrociously unhappy but this is not the time to give up. Kindest regards

Ever your

Conrad.

PS Please send me the money by draft on the *Credit Lyonnais* as you did for Montpellier. It's the nearest place to me, and I haven't a minute to spare for anything.

PPS Mention what's happening to me to Hueffer and Jack when you see them. I write to no one but you because I can't—absolutely can't find time for the hastiest scrawl.

To John Galsworthy
Text MS POSK; J-A, 2, 51 (with omissions)

6 June '07
Hotel de la Roseraie
Genève.

Dearest Jack

Jessie sent off a short letter to Ada yesterday I think.

Borys is very plucky with the pain. I believe he cried a little to his mother once but never before me who am his principal attendant. It's I who break into a cold sweat when I hear a beastly fit of whooping cough shaking him all over—with his four rh[e]umatic joints. However there is* only three now: both wrists and one elbow. He has no more pain in his feet but they are of no use whatever as yet. This has been going on for a fortnight nearly; the temperature from 100° to 101°. He hasn't lost his pluck but he's losing his spring and lies very quiet and resigned all eyes as to his face and skin and bone as to the body. I read to him all day and attend to him the best I can with one arm; because my left since my last gout isn't much use; and what I can do with it is done at the cost of a good deal of pain. Now and then I steal an hour or two to work at preparing the Secret Agent for book form. And all this is pretty ghastly. I seem to move, talk, write in a sort of quiet nightmare that goes on and on. I wouldn't wish my worst enemy this experience.

Poor little Jack has melted down to nothing in our hands. He, however, seems to have turned the corner. But all his little ribs can be seen at a glance. To day he smiled very distinc[t]ly the first time in the last 30 days or so, and with a pathetically skinny little paw reached for my nose-nippers. I mention these favourable symptoms lest you should think this letter unduly pessimistic.

From the sound next door (we have three rooms) I know that the pain has roused Borys from his feverish doze. I won't go to him. It's no use. Presently I shall give him his salicylate take his temperature and shall then go to elaborate a little more the conversation of Mr Verloc with his wife. It is very important that the conversation of Mr Verloc with his wife should be elaborated—made more effective, don't you know—more true to the situation and the character of these people.

By Jove I've got to hold myself with both hands not to burst into a laugh which would scare wife, baby and the other invalid—let alone the lady whose room is on the other side of the corridor.

To day completes the round dozen of years since I finished Almayer's Folly!

And in this connection how is Edward? What about his play? I have

had no letter from any one since your last. And I've written to no one
except to Pinker—and just a word to Rothenstein for decency's sake.

My love to you both. This letter requires no answer. But indeed you
may write all the same, write of yourselves, of your work of the subject of
the last play and of the novel which is to follow.

Ever Your

Conrad

To John Galsworthy

Text MS Forbes; Unpublished

[Champel]

9 June 07

Dearest Jack

Thanks* dear Ada for her good letter to Jessie. It *is* a comfort to know
one is thought of by people one loves.

After 15 days nearly of rheumatic fever, yesterday pleurisy set in on
the right side. Consultation took place at 2 o'clock and from then till
evening the two doctors hung about ready to puncture him should his
breathing get worse. They were reluctant to do it explaining to me that
in his then state if they were to draw off a pint or two there would be as
much liquid once again in a couple of hours. Of course if he had not
been able to breathe it would have had to be done. They put him in a
hot-water pack and waited. The fever eased up and they went away.
This morning as I write this it is certainly easier; and of course as the
pleurisy set in the pains in his joints left him in a great measure.

He sends his love to you both in a weak but cheerful voice.

The doctors hope now that they will be able to carry the cure out by
re-absorption. But of course for a few days yet we can't feel safe an hour
ahead and he has to be constantly watched for changes of temperature.
The rh[e]umatic fever is undoubtedly the after effect of the scarlet fever
(18 months ago). Ever since that time he has been what he called
'straining' his joints, knee, ankle, wrist—and wondering how he did it.
It was that no doubt. Now the measles shook him up his resisting power
was weakened and out it came. All this ruined me mentally and
materially this year. The cure recommended by Grasset for him can not
be carried out. Everything is knocked on the head—every plan made
and every hope of quick work. Well! So be it. Our dear love

Ever yours

Conrad.

PS I had half a mind to call you to look over the revise of Secret Agent. But Ada says you are overdoing it. Don't dear Jack. Don't work a wilting brain unfairly. And dislocate your mental powers. Not too many people and things. I suppose the doctors say that much?

To Elsie Hueffer
Text Violet Hunt's copy, Cornell; Unpublished

Hotel La Roseraie, Génève
9th June 1907

Dear Elsie

Thanks for your good letter. It is pleasant to know one is missed. Dear Ford. Tell him that I need a long talk. I long for it as the Arab for a drop of water in the desert.

I don't know my dear Elsie what you heard from Mrs Rothenstein. Borys has got rheumatic fever and yesterday pleurisy set in. This morning he is easier but he is very ill. It's no time to think of travelling, either home or towards Italy.

His convalescence won't be even in sight for a fortnight yet. Meantime he has got to be watched and attended to constantly. The doctors hang about ready to puncture him if it should become necessary. At the same time both the watches are taken. I don't leave him an inch or a minute.

I haven't materially the time to say more.

Our best love to you both and the dear girls.

Yours always

Conrad.

To J.B. Pinker
Text MS Berg; Unpublished

[Champel]
11 June [1907]

My dear Pinker

I send you in an open envelope registered, pp 8 to 17 (incl:) MS of *SA*.[1]

I couldn't get more ready. Pleurisy declared itself on Sat: with poor Borys. We had a consultation on Sunday and all that afternoon the two

[1] Expansion of the original text.

doctors hung about ready to make a puncture should his breathing get worse.

However he improved towards the evening of Sund: It was materially impossible for me to do more as I must attend him. He's very helpless with his rh[e]umatic joints tho' the pains left him almost entirely since the pleuresy* supervened. To write at his bedside is not so very easy. You understand that.

The origin of his rh[e]umatic fever is obviously in the leavings of the scarlet fever (18 months ago). I am happy to be able to say that the heart remains unaffected so far. But who knows what to-morrow may bring forth?

Pretty hard lines this! Thanks for the revises ever so much. I had two batches. You're a dear fellow. My next to you will contain both MS and print and the end of all shall be in your hands by the 15th. I keep well enough luckily. Baby improves greatly.

I shall expect to have drafts from you to-morrow which is my pay day at this hotel. Some MS will go to morrow eve[n]ing and the rest on Sat.

Affectly your

Conrad.

PS.   I managed to write to Jack & to Ford.

To John Galsworthy
Text MS Forbes; Unpublished

[Champel]
Wednesday. [12 or 19 June
1907][1]

Dearest Jack

Your letter is "bully".

Give a careful consideration to the component parts of the "A Commentary" vol.[2] I don't for a moment pre-judge its interest. The danger lies in what the Genl Pub^c may think *monotony*.

You see What I mean?

Congratulations to dear Ada on the *Seven Songs*.[3] I wish I were there to hear them.

---

[1] The 're-absorption' of Borys's pleurisy gives the approximate date.

[2] A series of sketches intended as social criticism; originally written for the *Nation*, they appeared as a book in 1908.

[3] Ada Galsworthy set a number of poems to music (Mottram, pp. 19–20).

Borys' state on the whole favourable today. Re-absorption goes on. No other trouble discovered on examination this morning.

    Our dear Love to you all

Ever Yours

J. Conrad.

To Elsie Hueffer

Text Violet Hunt's copy, Cornell; Unpublished

[Champel]

15 June 1907

My dear Elsie

    With our greatest love and thanks for your touching offer we should not ask you to come here unless things were much worse. Indeed dear Senora they are bad enough, but mostly in the way of anxiety. His helplessness is passing away.

    The questions before us are:

    Is the pleurisy *bacillary* or the consequence of rheumatism?

    Is the rheumatism itself of a *bacillary* character or the sequence of scarlet fever (18 months ago)?[1]

    The *bacillary* rheumatism does not yield to salicylate. This one has apparently yielded as far as pains in the joints are concerned. But the fever *will* not leave him. It has all the character of hectic fever. Temp. below normal at 8 a.m. and running up to $100\frac{1}{2}$–$101\frac{1}{2}$ between noon and four o'clock. After touching $101\frac{1}{2}$, it leaves him sometime during the night.

    But the persistence of the fever is fairly accounted for by re-absorption of the pleurisy which goes on slowly.

    Generally, we've got to watch and wait. To-day sounds of bronchitis have been heard on auscultation. The cough is terrific. We are in the 18th day. Your sympathy at this distance comforts us much. Jessie is very grateful to you both. Her dear love. Have you got our letter written from Montpellier? Somehow with you two I *don't* feel as if I were making myself a nuisance when talking of our misfortunes and terrors. One has a complete faith in you and Ford. I'll try to write to him. I am now preparing the Sec. Agt for book form with what effort you may guess.

Ever yours affectionately

J. Conrad.

---

[1] Pleurisy, rheumatic and scarlet fevers could all result from the same streptococcal infection.

To Katherine Sanderson

Text MS BU; Unpublished

16 June [1907]
Hotel de la Roseraie
Geneva

Dear Mrs Sanderson.[1]

Your letter reaches me only to day after being delayed at the Pent and then in Montpellier. I cannot well express to you our profound distress at the news You give me. Human sympathy stands powerless before such a tragic bereavement—but I know that you and Yours look for consolation to that Faith which enables the believer to bear a mountain of sorrow with the supreme strength of hope and resignation.

I would come over at once to see dear Ted without delay.[2] But alas! we are detained here by the serious illness of our boy Borys. Rh[e]umatic fever complicated by pleurisy. He's been ill 3 weeks and the end is not yet. There's no saying what the end will be. Please give my dear love to Ted. I know he will accept the message for your sake however unworthy of forgiveness I may appear to his sight.

Please dear Mrs Sanderson give us news how his wife is and also let us know how Mrs Macfarlane is going on. One needs all the grace of God to go through life with becoming fortitude.

Give my affectionate remembrance to all the members of the family and believe me always dear Mrs Sanderson

your most affectionate friend and
servant

J. Conrad.

To John Galsworthy

Text MS Forbes; J-A, 2, 52 (in part)

[Champel]
17 June '07

Dearest Jack

Borys does not get on at all. Symptoms of a bronchitis at the top of left lung have declared themselves since the 15th. And there is the pleurisy

---

[1] Ted's mother (née Oldfield, c. 1843–1921), 'whose warm welcome', according to Conrad's dedication of *The Mirror*, 'and gracious hospitality extended to the friend of her son cheered the first dark days of my parting with the sea'. As well as looking after Conrad's well-being, she encouraged his development as a writer. Almost all his letters to her were destroyed (information from Mrs C. E. Taylor).

[2] He must have been on leave from Africa, perhaps because of the bereavement.

too. With this a hectic fever well characterised and rapid emaciation with a cough. This is his 22 day in bed. Things could not look much more ugly. Another doctor is coming this afternoon.

I am keeping up but I feel as if a mosquito bite were enough to knock me over. Good God! If I were to get it now what would happen! As it is I don't know very well what will happen. It will be nothing good anyway—even at best. And how to face it mentally and materially is what keeps my nerves on the stretch.

I thought I told You I was getting the Secret Agent ready for book form. There was an additional chapter to write.[1] That's done. 2 chapters to expand—which I am now trying to do.

Impossibility to get away from here. Dread of going back to the Pent; a sort of feeling that this is the end of things at the end of twelve years' work—all this does not help me much in making Mr & Mrs Verloc effective for the amusement of a public—which won't be amused by me at all.

Generally, the position does not stand being thought about. So no more of it. Our dear love to you both

Yours ever,

Conrad.

PS I will look at the allegory to-night. Don't give up too much of your time to Massingham.[2] There are other ways to serve the nation. This isn't advice. It's a sudden thought which occurred to me. A government—believe me—is either the expression of a people's character or an illustrated commentary on the same. Are we allied with Russia so much as that? I haven't seen a paper French or Engl^{sh} for the last 3 weeks.

---

[1] Chapter Ten.

[2] Henry William Massingham (1860–1924), a Liberal (and eventually Labour) journalist. He edited the *Daily Chronicle* (1895–9) and the *Nation* (1907–23). In the latter, he had just published Galsworthy's 'The Alliance: An Allegory' (8 June, pp. 555–6), an objection on moral grounds to the impending Anglo-Russian *entente*.

To J.B. Pinker

Text MS Berg; Unpublished

[Champel]
Thursday Morning [20 June
1907][1]

My dear Pinker.

In reply to yours of the *18*th MS pp 1–29 (more will be dispatched to-day) follows on the *p 294* of proof.

I've send* it to you in 3 lots. The first lot pp 1–7 went with a portion of corrected proof properly marked where the insertion begins. It was sent like the others in an open envelope and registered as *papiers d'affaires* but I cannot give you the date.

I was sure you had it and I still hope it will turn up either at Methuens or at the printers.

That it went to you I am sure as I post everything myself. Let a search be made. Still, accidents will happen, but it seems unlikely that that particular batch should have gone astray.

I will write to you tomorrow.

Ever yours

Conrad.

To J.B. Pinker

Text MS Berg; Unpublished

[Champel]
23 June '07[2]

My dear Pinker.

Things don't go well here. At the end of thirty days' fever we have the greatest difficulty in keeping up his strength.

I send you in a separate envelope pp 30–36 (incl) of *SA*. I give you my word that I *can't* get on quicker. I shall work desperately to night and on Sunday if the slight turn for the better apparent this morning is maintained. There's not much to do now. If I manage it I will wire you the word *Finished* some time in the course of Monday next. I hope I will.

Please let me have £40 for *Wednesday* next *here* by the same way as last time.

What about the pp *1–7* which you think are missing? I am a bit anxious but of course I could replace them

Yours ever

J. Conrad.

[1] Between Pinker's letter of the 18th and Conrad's of the 23rd.   [2] 22 changed to 23.

To J.B. Pinker
Text MS Berg; Unpublished

[Champel]
26 June [1907]

My dear Pinker

Thanks for the money.

Borys is better after 32 days of bed, so far. His palate lips and tongue are in such an awful state that we can nourish him only on Brand's meat essence and Valentine's meat juice, with milk of course. He's a miserable object skin and bone.

I have had lumbago—a short fit; but so severe that I could not get out of bed.

All right now. I am sending pp of SA to morrow. I am doing all I can and worrying more than is good for me

Yours ever

J. Conrad

To John Galsworthy
Text MS POSK; Danilewiczowa

[Champel]
27 June 07

Dearest Jack.

Just a word before the post goes to tell you that we had two days already without fever.

I waited 24 hours before writing the good news to make sure.

Love from us all to you both.

Ever Yours

J Conrad

Soon a long screed about all sorts of things

To J.B. Pinker
Text MS Berg; Unpublished

[Champel]
1st July '07

My dear Pinker.

I send to day another batch of pp SA. I am going on as fast as I can. A couple of days more ought to do it. Borys has been moved to a couch yesterday after 33 days in bed. The convalescence will be long I fear.

My income tax will have to be paid as the In^d Rev^{ne} Dept are hunting me up. Also the bills in Kent. Meantime please send a cheque for £3.3 to Mrs *J. George*. Reynolds Farm Hawkhurst Kent and for £*10* to *Miss A. Sex*[1] 17 Moreland Road East Croydon.

Yours always

J. Conrad.

To J.B. Pinker
Text MS Berg; Unpublished

Saturday.
27 July '07
Hotel de la Roseraie
Génève

My dear Pinker.

Up to the morning of writing 10ΛM I have received no money.[2] If I had it was my intention to remove to day to the mountain hotel on Salève in order to help along the boy's convalescence. But perhaps we will be able to manage without that move. He's picking up fast.

Please send me on receipt of this letter two cheques one for frcs *540* in the name of Monsieur *A. Habel* the other for *150 frcs* in my own name. These are to settle with the doctors. It was impossible for me to pay them as I went along. There are more than 80 visits. The boy was in utmost danger for some five weeks. Special food had to be given him, for his mouth, throat & palate were in such a state that he could not swallow any ordinary food. He lived on Brands Essce and Valentine's meat juice for days and days and that cost over eleven frcs every day. It had to be done.

I won't enlarge. It was the most awful time I've ever had.

The Secret Agent as it stands is a work of some mark. I have told You before why I attached a special importance to having it as well done as I could. I've lost a month extra over it. Under the circumstance I don't think I've done badly.

I am preparing the revises to send back to you. The lot I have now I

---

[1] Jessie's Aunt Alice, who lived with Miss Wright, the typist. Borys remembered her as 'a handsome old lady of imposing presence ... highly intelligent and a brilliant conversationalist' (*My Father*, p. 13).

[2] Three telegrams from July have survived (Berg): 'Manuscript posted. Please send usual amount on Tuesday. Borys menaced by relapse' (8th). 'Finished dispatch by early train tomorrow pray send draft as usual' (22nd). 'End pages in two lots marked A and B left yesterday thanks for letter writing' (25th).

will post on Monday. Hurry up the balance of proofs. For those end pages I'll want *no revise*. One correction will do. Hurry up Methuens. I want to get on with *Chance* now, and before that I must clear my mind entirely of the *Sec Ag*ᵗ.

The next 12 months will be the time to make a really heroic effort. I feel strong mentally. My little cure has done me good. But I am worried incessantly with the thought of the future. I will write to you of my plans in a day or two. I am anxious to get away from here as soon as possible and set to work repairing the disasters of these months. Write to me without fail.

Yours always

Conrad.

PS You will begin to receive MS of *Chance* in a few days.

To John Galsworthy
Text MS Forbes; J-A, 2, 53

30 July '07
Hotel de la Roseraie
Génève

Dearest Jack

At last I can tell You that Borys's convalescence may be considered as ended. The period of picking up strength has begun. We had various alarums—but that seems all over now. It has been altogether a ghastly time—from the 15ᵗʰ May to the 15ᵗʰ July. In that time I've written roughly speaking 28 to 30000 words in order to make a decent book of the *Secret Agent*. I think it's pretty good—for what it is. The pages you've marked for cancellation (or cancelling?) in the typescript are retained, after a proper amount of thinking over. They fall in pretty well with the ironic scheme of the book—and the public can skip if it likes.

We return soon. My health is comparatively good but my anxieties have been increased by all that happened in the last four or rather five months. We shall try to pick up the old existence somewhere nearer London than the Pent. But everything is difficult in my position. I look forward with dread to an effort which, I fear, from the nature of things, can never any more be adequate.

It shall be made of course, but the feeling itself is against the probability of success. Art, truth, expression are difficult enough by themselves—god knows!

I am anxious to see You. Let it be soon after my return. But I don't suppose You'll be in London then. I don't know exactly the plan of your movements. Of Your allegory we shall talk when we meet.

Our very dear love to You both

Yours ever

Conrad.

To J.B. Pinker
Text MS Berg; J-A, 2, 54 (with omissions)

30 July 1907
Hotel de la Roseraie
Geneva

My dear Pinker.

Thanks for the money. The book I think is a book to produce some sensation. I don't say it is good but I say it is the best I could do with the subject. In the 2 months of the boy's illness I managed to write into it some 26–28000 words. After that I imagine I can do anything; for you can have no idea of my mental state all that time. Besides the anxiety for the child there was the tearing awful worry of the circumstances.

We must end this damnable outing now as soon as possible. I have been trying to think out everything. I can't come back to the Pent unless all that's owing there is paid, as I told you before. I'll send you a list here. A hundred will do I fancy to cover it all except the income tax.

After getting back to the Pent the great thing will be to get away from there as soon as possible, and make a fresh start.

There will be the house hunting. Perhaps we may get something near Ashford to make the moving less expensive.[1] If You hear of any inexpensive sort of house in the country near London make a note of it for us.

We have been calculating everything and we have arrived at a budget £664 a year counting the house for £50. In this Borys' schooling is included. He can't go yet to Beaumont but perhaps we could place him as day boy somewhere. There is a school in Ashford which would do for six or nine months or so. But these are details. Adding to the above sum £126 for (alas!) the doctor (better be prepared for that infernal side of my existence) we arrive at £800 for the 12 months. If we can do with less so much the better but I dare not say less. Now for the next 12 months

---

[1] A distance of only ten miles.

work: that is Chance (completed) and another novel I dare to hope you will obtain £*1600*. That is the basis of my calculation.

I reckon 4 months for *Chance* counting from 1st of Augst for I am not going house hunting as You may imagine. At the Pent I will go to work. But it is of the utmost importance for me to get settled for good. Moreover the Pent is damnably expensive to live in. The idea is to have no bills. One spends always more than one intends to do. But all this will not be possible till we've got clear of the place.

I think I can say safely that the *Secret Agent* is *not* the sort of novel to make what comes after more difficult to place. Neither will it I fancy knock my prices down. *Chance* itself will be altogether different in tone and treatment of course, but it will be saleable I believe. By the end of Sept^{er} you will have a really considerable lot of it to show. Of course it will not be on popular lines. Nothing of mine can be, I fear. But even Meredith ended by getting his sales.[1] Now, I haven't Meredith's delicacy and that's a point in my favour. I reckon I may make certain of the support of the Press for the next few years. The young men who are coming in to write criticisms are in my favour so far. At least all of whom I've heard are. I don't get in the way of established reputations. One may read everybody and yet in the end want to read me—for a change if for nothing else. For I don't resemble anybody; and yet I am not specialised enough to call up imitators as to matter or style. There is nothing in me but a turn of mind which whether valuable or worthless can not be imitated.

It has been a disastrous time. You must help me settle down now on an economical basis. It will cost something to do that but that once done 3 years of close sitting will do the trick. I'll be then 52 and not worn out yet as a writer. Without exaggeration I may say I feel renovated by my cure here—and considering the adverse circumstances this seems a good sign. I am anxious to get back and drive on.

We could start from here on the 10th. I would like to start on that date. To fetch me home after settling here I will require £*80*. The sooner you let me have that the better. I would go on the 8th providing always You pay the people in Kent before I return in accordance with the enclosed list. Of course all the proceeds of SA will go but right from my return the fixed limit of £800 will be strictly adhered-to. It must be. No more trips abroad. I am sick of them.

Always yours

Conrad.

[1] With *Diana of the Crossways* (1885), George Meredith's thirteenth novel, commercial was added to critical success.

To H.G. Wells

Text MS Illinois; Najder (1970)

30 July '07
Hotel de la Roseraie
Genève

Dear old H G.

I've just finished the book form text of the *Secret Agent* which for better or worse is to be published in September next I think. I propose to dedicate that masterpiece to You. Considering that the time passes and that I am not likely to improve much by keeping on this earth I think the moment for that small proof of very great affection to be given has come.

Hereby I ask for permission!

The inscription to run like this

To
H. G. Wells
The Chronicler of Mr Lewisham's Love
The Biographer of Kipps and
The Historian of the Ages to Come
This Simple tale of the XIX Century
is affectionately inscribed.

I submit the above to your approval. If it's withheld for some reason, well then, the simple To H. G Wells will do.[1] But pray observe that in this definition I have stated what the perfect Novelist should be— Chronicler Biographer and Historian.

Perhaps You may have heard that Borys has been very ill twice since February last. Measles complicated with an atrocious and alarming bronchitis first and then R[h]eumatic fever with pleurisy. Thirty odd days in bed this last go! It was a ghastly time.

I wrote however.

All these things kept us out abroad till now. I am perfectly ruined in every respect just now. Not an idea in the head—not a shekel in the pocket not a grain of confidence in my breast. We will leave this place on the 8th or 10th of next month for the Pent. The boy is picking up his strength now. Jessie joins me in dear love to you both and to Your dear chicks.

Ever your

Conrad.

---

[1] 'Inscribed' became 'offered'; otherwise the full dedication stood.

To J.B. Pinker
Text MS Berg; Unpublished

[Champel]
Saturday
3. Aug '07

My dear Pinker

Thanks for the cheques. I have also received some proofs from Methuen which I have corrected and sent back the same day by the five o'clock post. Thus they ought to have them by the afternoon of the next day.

I long to get away from here. The place is odious to me; and the whole thing with its anxieties and expense sits on me like the memory of a nightmare.

You've seen me through it nobly. But I have the sense of the reality sufficiently developed to feel very anxious as to my position—almost intolerably anxious.

I hoped to be back in Eng^d early in April! You know how this came about. They were all dinning it into me that Switzerland was absolutely necessary for the boy. As a matter of fact he would I suppose have been just as ill in England.

My only hope now is to finish *Chance* early in December. I cling to it desperately. It must be done! And another novel *must* be finished by August next. I have got the idea in my head. A good idea too. But of that later.

Meantime the sum to which I mean* strictly limit myself may appear to You too high. I've fixed the amount at 800 on purpose to give a margin for the unexpected. The idea is that you should send a cheque every week for the household expenses at the rate of 300 a year—say six pounds a week. Then every quarter there would be the rent—B's schooling etc—but all to fall strictly within the limit, as it has been estimated, and not a penny more. If we can save on the estimate so much the better.

But I must get away from the Pent, first of all. The costs of moving—and, still more heavy I fear, the expenses of looking for a house will all have to come out of the sum mentionned.* They will only bear on its distribution. However we may secure a farm-house I see being advertised near Ashford at £40. Miss Capes also is looking for something suitable in the direction of Winchester.[1] Perhaps we may

---

[1] She lived in the city.

have a bit of luck and be able to move off in September, without too much hunting.

A little furniture to be bought on the instalment plan is also included in the amount I've fixed for myself for the next three years. From your own estimate of what you can do with my work I think that at the end of that time I will balance my acct with You or very nearly so. As I don't think that the *S. A.* will affect adversely my prices and as *Chance* seems to shape well for a certain public I don't see any reason to despair. But I feel sometimes on the verge of it thinking how all my plans have been knocked on the head.

Yours always

Conrad.

To J.B. Pinker

Text MS Berg; Unpublished

[Champel]
Monday [5 August 1907]¹

Dear Pinker

Here's the last of the proof. Try to have a corrected set sent to the States. If the money *or the public* ever comes to us it will be from there. We must treat them well.

—— You have now my long letter. I wish to add to it the following considerations.

In May (when I arrived here) my debt to you was what it was. And there were then the advances for book form (£500 in all) to come in. Since then I have spent (*including what I've* asked you *for, to see me home*) £276.

The position is no more appalling now than it was in May.

I don't defend myself. I only point out to you the fact that strictly speaking I have not in these unlucky months increased my indebt[ed]-ness. I have alas eaten up over half of the book rights. And a lot of fun I had out of it too.

With a book on the eve of appearing and another Volume ready if you like* (or if we must) make use of it² *don't* my dear fellow knock me over. There's nothing I desire more than to fall in with Your severest plans for bringing about a more tolerable state of things. I suffer from it quite as

---

1 The only Monday between the 'long letter' of 30 July and the return to England on 10 August.

2 'Il Conde' and 'The Duel' had not yet appeared in magazines; early publication of *A Set of Six* would sacrifice their potential earnings.

(

much as you do. Don't you think that I ever consider the accumulated indebt[ed]ness!

Above all don't keep me here with the expenses going on.[1] Miss Capes writes that she has looked up two modest houses near Winchester. Some £30 a year. She is going to inspect them for us. But you understand that no move of any kind will be made till You are fully informed of it and declare that the cost may be incurred. I mean this to be so—for my own sake as well as your own.

Yours

Conrad

If you get pp of *Chance* for typing keep the type in your office till I call for them.

To J.B. Pinker

Text MS Berg; Unpublished

[letterhead: Pent Farm]
Tuesday.
13 Aug '07

My dear Pinker.

In the terms of your letter of the 6th Aug '07 (in which the strict limit of £600 a year is established) I reckon that this year begins on the *10th* of this month the day of our arrival here. In other words that I may reckon on £600 between this and the 10th Aug*st* 1908—I on my side writing in that time 80 000 words *at least*; this 80 000 words being the words of a *novel* not short stories.

This I believe is your idea. In mentioning the number of words I hereby solemnly declare that I don't mean to limit my output in any way. I think I am quite capable of 100 000 words, and I need not protest of my willingness to do as much as in me lies every year. I only want to know if you accept that number *at the worst*.

Tell me also my dear fellow whether the cost of moving to our new house is to come out of that amount. I am under the impression that it is not. I intend to ask for estimates from a firm in Winchester (say) and another in Ashford, also from one in London and accept the lowest.

As you are going away for a few days I will ask you to send me a fortnights household money (as I want now to pay here as we go) say £*12*

---

[1] On the 7th, Conrad wired: 'Please advise me today if may expect leave here tomorrow or Friday' (Berg).

or if you prefer leave instructions to send one cheque for £6 on Friday next and another on the following Friday. Besides that please send me at once one cheque for £5 for my travelling expenses as I must go to Winchester on Thursday next by arrangement with Miss Capes to see the house. Also one cheque £5 in the name of Mrs *C. Finn* to pay the woman who looked after the house and boarded the dog for the last eight months. I will enter these amounts as the first drawn under the new dispensation. I send you the guide book and I hope you will have the best possible time on your wise holiday.

Ever your

Conrad

PS You'll find on your return some few pages of *Chance* typed. Please remind Methuen to send me a set of corr*^{d}* proofs as soon as possible. Can I have a typed copy of *Duel* for a day or two to look at?

To Harriet Mary Capes

Text MS Yale; Unpublished

[Pent Farm]
Aug 13 1907

Dear Miss Capes.

You are infinitely good to us!

I write in haste to tell you that nothing short of absolute impossibility would prevent us from coming to live in Your neighbourhood. King Charles' cottage as described by you seems wholly delectable.

Jessie (to her great sorrow) has decided to send me alone to Winchester. Travelling with the baby and the maid is such a heavy and expensive business. She is reasonable. Moreover if we all came it would mean bringing Borys too. We would be an unmanageable crowd. So I will come alone with full powers to negociate* and conclude.

May I come to Winch'er at one o'clock. The well known gravity of my character encourages me to ask you to lunch with me "en camarade". Then we could drive out to Colden Common see the Cottage and return in time for me to catch a train about 5 or 6 for London where I must see the painter Rothenstein on that evening.

The postman's waiting. Our dear love. Awaiting your permission to come on that day I am always Your very affectionate friend and servant.

J. Conrad.

To J.B. Pinker
Text MS Berg; Unpublished

[Pent Farm]
14 Augst '07

My dear Pinker.

I forgot yesterday to speak to you of my income tax business.
Please have the enclosed paper filled in claiming exemption for insc^e.
I've been assessed at £800. Its about time this was paid.

I have signed the form 38 but have no particulars here. The In^d Rev^{ne} letter enclosed here will explain what they want.

Yours ever

J. Conrad

To Harriet Mary Capes
Text MS Yale; Unpublished

[letterhead: Pent Farm]
Tuesday 20th Aug
1907.

Dear Miss Capes

I have been infinitely worried ever since my return from the delightful visit to you. A dead set had been made at me by two doctors and half a dozen friends—the object of it being to force me away from the southern counties altogether. I daren't resist their threats and entreaties. I simply dare not. It's so important that for the next couple of years I should keep well! All the future hinges on that. So we are going to try* find something inland—on the Midland line perhaps. Thus if gout comes on with the winter I shan't hear the odious "I told you so."

We feel both profoundly unhappy at this change in our intentions. We have hesitated for the last two days. I suppose I must own to a certain cowardice: a couple of doctors a literary agent a posse of wise men make a strong combination. It's one great howl: Don't! So be it.

Pray believe that if [I] give up the plan of living somewhere within touch of you it is not from any exaggerated notion as to the value of my work. It is not from regard for literature. It is from regard for wife and boys for whom I must write as much as I can. They'll want it all. And the sands are running out!

I am writing to your good Agent. I ought perhaps to have written yesterday but I hadn't the heart.

Thus a cherished desire is thrown away for the sake of, so called, health. And probably it does not matter in the least where one lives. I shall, most likely, be laid up in the usual way for the usual number of days. I am disgusted with myself. Jessie is resigned—as ever—and more sorry than she can express. We have nothing in view; but the first tolerable farmhouse that turns up between London and Bedford we shall take—and be done with it. The savour is out of the thing.

Borys has caught an atrocious cold. It's worrying to us. Baby is well. Jessie will be writing to you to morrow I think. We are hanging on here practically without a servant and she has her hands full. She sends meantime her thanks for the portrait and her very best love.

I will keep you informed of what is happening to us and am in sorrow always your most affectionate friend and servant

J. Conrad.

To William Rothenstein

Text MS Harvard; *Listy* 259; Original unpublished

[letterhead: Pent Farm]

21 Aug '07

Dearest Will.

Ever so many thanks for Your dear letter which welcomed me here. It was quite brotherly in its helpfulness. Your appreciation is a great item in the capital with which I work. One requires a fund of belief in oneself to do any artistic work and you pay a genuine contribution to that account which is always on the verge of being exhausted.

I was going through the town on a house hunting expedition when I proposed a descent upon You. I have to fit things into each other as much as I can being damnably short both of shekels and of time. I have some hopes of my new book which is coming out next month. It's very different from anything I ever wrote before—and millions of miles away from the Mirror that Mirror of which you speak in a manner perfectly angelic. You shall get your copy in due course and have another opportunity to be as angelic again as you please. But before this happens we shall have seen each other no doubt.

We are in treaty for a jolly old Farmhouse 2½ miles from Luton (Beds). The Midland runs trains there in 45 minutes[1] and a good many of them in the day. I shall feel much nearer you when we get settled there. If all goes well we shall be moving on or about the 20th—of next month. Could a small visit be arranged then for poor Jessie who is hungry and thirsty

---

[1] Closer to London than the Pent was by a full hour.

for the sight of dear Alice and the Children? Of her affection for your own person you need not doubt. On the subject I can say no more.

Poor Borys has to be watched very carefully for at least a year to come. It's a great anxiety both immediate and for the future. My sands are running out. I should like to see him started in the right way—and started soon.

As to myself I am well. I only wish to get settled and be at work again. It's twelve years since I've published Almayer's Folly—my first book. It's about time for the greater public to discover me, if they mean at all to become aware of my existence. In other ways I've been more than repaid for the honesty of my intentions by friendships such as yours. But there are the children and the poor woman—pretty near a cripple; it's no use shutting one's eyes as to that. There are moments when my thoughts are not exactly of a rose colour!

Enfin! Che sarà sarà. In another 16 months I will be 50 years old.[1] But there's life in the old dog yet.

Ever yours

Conrad.

PS Best love to Alice who lives in the Wonderland of your works. I want a peep therein very badly. And hugs all round to your chicks of whom we talk so often here.

To John Galsworthy
Text MS Forbes; Unpublished

[letterhead: Pent Farm]
24 Aug '07

Dearest Jack

I expect to tear out from Methuen a set of proofs in a day or two.

I've been thinking of your offer to review the novel; and of course I've been thinking of it with gratitude. Cold reason however founded upon a general distrust of mankind prompts me to say:—better not. For your opinion I do care very much; but I can hear it privately. A word or two of friendly criticism I've the right to demand from you. I am impatient to hear it. But a public pronouncement over your signature I think unadvisable for both our sakes.

I've read Hueffer's portrait of Mr John Galsworthy several times.[2] It is interesting mostly as the portrait of Mr Hueffer himself. As I have my

---

[1] Much sooner: he would turn 50 on 3 December.
[2] In *Tribune*, 10 August.

own strong conception of J. G. I can't say I've been greatly edified. Looked upon abstractedly the thing is distinctly good.

I've been unprofitably busy house-hunting: I mean unprofitably from a literary point of view. Otherwise my efforts are crowned with success. Subject to analysis of well water I think we are fixed. It is a farmhouse of ample proportions and amiable aspect. It's 2½ miles from Luton and 30 from London. The Midland runs trains in 45 minutes and a good many of them in the day. I'll feel much nearer to you when we get settled there. Height: 500 ft soil: clay and gravel.

The great thing is to get in and start work. It isn't easy. Perhaps we may manage it by the 20th of next month.

Meantime we are hanging on here in disorder and destitution with no servant but the faithful Nellie, without lad, without trap without anything. Baby Jack has a recrudescence of whooping cough with signs of croup and bronchitis peeping out. The doctor has seen him today. On the other hand Borys is improving visibly.

Jessie is very tired. She sends her dear love but has no time to write. She is making ready for the move with great enthusiasm. I feel fairly well—but not so well as when you saw me. I am very anxious to get on with *Chance* but cant make a fresh start.

Ever yours

Conrad.

Advise dear Ada of my affection. I've for her a very interesting book on Rousseau[1] which I will send on very soon—or bring in my hand as soon as you get back to town; for I want to see her very much.

I send this to your town address as I can't lay my hands on your last letter.

To J.B. Pinker
Text MS Berg; Unpublished

[letterhead: Pent Farm]
Saturday 31st Aug. '07

My dear Pinker.

I trust you came home refreshed from Your trip. I am very curious to hear how it went on, and if Mrs Pinker and Eric have enjoyed the tour. I shall probably look in on Tuesday at Talbot House for a few minutes on my way to Luton.

---

[1] Rousseau was to haunt *Under Western Eyes.*

Now I want to tell you that I've done some pretty severe house hunting, yet not so bad as I feared would be necessary. I discovered quite unexpectedly by means of a not particularly attractive adv*ent* a farm house near Luton 2½ miles from the station and 30 from London. The Midland run several 40–45 minute trains in the day; and the slow ones take no more than one hour from Luton to St Pancras. The fares there and back cost 5/– which is less than a single journey from the Pent. The house is not big but roomy for its size with a walled garden in front. There is also an excellent kitchen garden with fruit trees, properly fenced and with a door to it which locks—so that one may expect some good from it. The position is excellent 500 ft above sea level on clay and gravel. The well is 200 ft deep and, I imagine, quite safe as far as the purity of water is concerned. The last tenant—a barrister from London—lived there 2½ years. I've 'bated the rent down to £60 rates and taxes included. This is really cheaper than some of the £50 houses I've inspected and even some at £45—not anything as convenient as this one is and with rates and taxes to pay. Taking into consideration the expense and loss of time involved in a further search I don't think I've done so badly in securing this place which is called 'Someries'. It is on that plutocrat Wernher's estate of Luton Hoo.[1]

What seduced me most was the nearness to town combined with perfect rural isolation. I want to be in closer touch with everybody. It will be quite possible for people I care for to come and see me for the day and even for an afternoon. There are about 27 decent trains either way in the 24 hours.

I am anxious to get in on the 15th of this month. They are fitting in a bathroom for us and staining the floors. The loss of days is even more appalling to me than the loss of pounds sterling. And it was impossible to sit down seriously to work. All I've done was mere nibbling at it. I must get settled soon and forget myself in my tale. I've asked for moving estimates and expect to get them by Monday next.

                                                    Yours ever

                                                                J Conrad

I send you agreements with Aston[2] & Methuen. By the bye, I went and worried out a set of pages from Methuen just in time to discover a

---

[1] Sir Julius Charles Wernher (1850–1912), born in Germany, made a Transvaal fortune from gold, diamonds, and scrip. He now lived in London and Bedfordshire, where he had filled Luton Hoo with his art collection.

[2] Unidentified: perhaps associated with the *Pall Mall Magazine*, which was to publish 'The Duel'.

beastly typographical blunder affecting the two last chapters. It's incredible carelessness! However I think I was in time. One can trust no one.

To Alice Rothenstein
Text MS Harvard; Unpublished

[letterhead: Pent Farm]
1ˢᵗ Sept 1907

Dear Alice

That precious baby of ours is still coughing with distinct whoops. It isn't safe to bring him near your chicks, and his precious Mama instructs me to let you know at once that a visit to you is out of the question for the present. She is very sorrowful about it as You may imagine. However we are going (next week) to live much nearer London. We have taken a farmhouse near Luton, 2½ miles from the station. There is a good service, something like 30 trains in the 24 hours, and a good many of them do the distance in 40 minutes. We cherish the hope of seeing much more of you dear people than it has been possible in the past. It may even happen that you shall have to remonstrate with me on the frequency of my visits.

For the moment I am busy getting a longish (and stupidish) story ready for the Pall Mall; but I will be soon knocking on your door. Is the Hampstead Station of the new tube[1] anywhere near the aforesaid door? Or any other station? I've no notion of the topography of your part of the world. A hug to Your great man. Love from us all to your houseful. Always Your devoted servant

J. Conrad

To J.B. Pinker
Text MS Berg; Unpublished

[Hythe, Kent][2]
4ᵗʰ Sept: 07

My dear Pinker

I am on my way to lunch with Wells.

I've signed the agreement as to the new house and we are going in next week. Please send a cheque for £3.3 to Mʳ B. Cole c/o Messrs: Cumberland & Sons Luton (Beds).

[1] On the line from Camden Town to Golders Green, opened in June.
[2] Conrad wrote under the cancelled letterhead of the White Hart Hotel.

The best tender for moving we had is for *34.17.3*. I shall want that cheque on Thursday next[1] and will come for it to your office on Tuesday or Wednesday as we go through London on our migration.

The weekly £6 due this Sat please send in two cheques—one for £5 and another for £1.

I am disgusted at the unsettled state of my mind. But it'll be soon over now

Yours ever

J Conrad

To J.B. Pinker
Text MS Berg; Unpublished

[letterhead: Pent Farm]
8th Sept. [1907]

My dear Pinker.

Thanks for weekly cheques. The *S.A.* is coming out on the *12*th. So I am advised by Methuen.

Please send off on Monday before 5 oclock if possible the cheques as per list, to clear my wife out. I shall be in London on Tuesday and see [you] in Your office. I shall sleep at Galsworthy's that night. Jessie will spent* Wednesday night in London. On Thursday we are going in—at last.

Yours ever

J Conrad.

Mrs B. Palmer. £*1.4.10* Mr Epps £*1.1*. Mrs E. Hills £*1*. Mr. R. Johnson *1.10* Mr E. Marshall *3.14.2* J. Conrad £5

To Harriet Mary Capes
Text MS Yale; Unpublished

[Pent Farm]
[10 September 1907][2]

Dear Miss Capes

Just a word to tell you that we are leaving Pent Farm to day on our way to the new home. It is in Bedfordshire 40 minutes from St Pancras and many times a day. It is 2½ miles from Luton: a farmhouse of a rather

---

[1] The 12th.   [2] Postmark.

cosy sort without distinction of any kind, but quite 500 ft above the sea—which is what we both want. Its name is Someries.

We expect to be there on Thursday next. Jessie will spend one night at the inn in Stanford and one in London. The poor girl is very tired but otherwise fairly well.

And the day of our entering upon our new house is the day of publication for my new novel. If I can get my author's copies on the 12th the very first one shall be for you.

These are the last words I shall write in the old house. We leave it with our t[h]oughts directed to you in great regard and affection and in the hope that You will be our first visitor in our new abode. Jessie'll write to you next week and meantime sends her dear love. Always your affectionate friend and servant

J. Conrad.

To J.B. Pinker

Text MS Berg; Unpublished

[letterhead: 14, Addison Road]

1907

12 Sept

My dear Pinker.

My wife is going to day to Someries at 11 o'clock. I'll stay on in town till 4: but as I cannot get to Your office this morning I'll ask you to post to Jack Galsworthy a cheque for £8, being the £6 of this week's payment advanced, and 2 extra for expenses. Please send also to Messrs Norman & Staccy 118 Queen Victoria St. EC a cheque for £5 first payment for the furniture which thereafter is to be of £2.5 monthly for the period of two Years, on the 14th of each month.

I have no doubt of my ability to terminate Rescue[1] parallel with my other work providing there is sufficient inducement. Do my dear fellow approach this affair as soon as you can. Till I hear of it from you I'll* nothing to distract my attention from Chance.

Yours always

Conrad

---

[1] Conrad's long-deferred novel, whose rights Heinemann had already bought; it appeared in serial in 1919.

To John Galsworthy
Text MS Forbes; Unpublished

Someries
Luton
15 Sept 1907

Dearest Jack

We have been living here in a most awful mess of things camping in a rout of furniture, on a heap of rubbish in the utmost distress. The workmen were in the house still. The pump still to pieces, and one of the vans had not arrived. As usual Jessie worked while I went about raving and tearing my hair.

If it had not been for the restful time she had in London thanks to you she would have been completely knocked up.

To finish me off what with Fords catastrophe[1] and my own worry I've got a bout of gouty eczema which drives me to distraction. It does not lay me up however or else the end of all things would come.

B. goes to school on Thursday. I don't think it's a very famous arrangement but no doubt it will do for the present. The people are stupid but obviously very decent.

On the subject of the thumping row we had just before I left you I will say nothing just now. My brain seethes with other matters by no means as interesting and ever so much less profitable. At bottom we want the same thing. It is a difference of policy but as neither of us two is likely to have charge of the foreign affairs very soon we may let our differences stand over till we meet.[2]

Your copy of the S.A. is here but I can't find a piece of string to tie it up with. I can find nothing. I've only found the ink this morning.

I've written to Ford telling him that if he thinks that a legal attack upon me will force P's hand[3] to go ahead without compunction, I could say nothing else. But at the same time I know very well that he will do no good for himself. I don't see how he can. All he may do is to knock me over completely and utterly and even knock me out of house and home, since a clause of the agreement terminates my tenancy in case of bankruptcy or composition with creditors. My past work and my policies are mortgaged up to the hilt to P anyhow. As to my future work once my position with P is destroyed I don't see how it is to be produced;

---

[1] Elsie Hueffer had undergone a kidney operation; Ford was desperately short of money (Mizener, p. 130).

[2] Differences over the future of Russia?

[3] A manoeuvre to obtain more money from Pinker, thereby enabling Conrad to pay his debts to Ford.

as I don't suppose the old farmer will let me browse on his stubble with my little family—for the love of God.

My conduct to Ford is not so base as it looks. I had certainly a windfall (official) in the Italian year,[1] but even with that and what I got from P I just squeezed through. Five months I *could not* work. Then came Borys' scarlet fever. I was very ill myself too, that Dec^er as you may remember. Still I managed to keep going slowly; but I am certain that if I had not gone to Montpellier that winter I would have gone to pieces. The only thing I may reproach myself with is the journey South this Year. But no one could foresee what would happen there! On a review of my position P thought it justifiable the more so that I expected to bring Chance 3 parts done from this fatal excursion. You may imagine how I raged to feel myself stopping back into the everlasting hole. I've done what work I could but all the same I've come back ruined again for a time. I am too weary for words.

And again there is writing under pressure pumping for dear life—before me. I would rather die than be ill again but as a matter of fact I can't afford either. I will have to pump till the handle breaks or the ship goes down under me. But I am humiliated and dismayed nevertheless at the necessity.

Yet I can tell you one thing—that all this mental and moral wretchedness would be like nothing to me if I had written or felt it in me to write a work so genuine in inspiration so lofty in expression as your last play; so true in sentiment so poignant in its dramatic force. The meanest understanding the bluntest feeling must be touched from one end of the land to the other by a piece of art so deeply felt and so masterfully presented.

When I think of you having written *Strife*[2] I am almost consoled. Our dear love to you both.

Ever yours

J. Conrad.

---

[1] The government grant in 1905.
[2] Galsworthy had finished a draft in April; the play was produced in 1909.

To W.H. Chesson
Text MS Rosenbach; Unpublished

Someries
Luton
Beds
16th Sept '07

My dear Chesson[1]

You are a very live critic. As to your civility it's simply immense! Joking apart I can not refrain from telling you of the pleasure your review has given me.

Since you recognise in me some virtuosity in my art you may imagine my delight at finding an ear like yours so alive, so unerringly aware of every shade and modulation of the tune. From what you say I perceive that nothing escaped you—literally from the title page to the very end—nothing! I am assured of it. Think what that assurance means to the writer. It is the rarest, the most fortunate experience. You may say, with the Emperor Trajan, that you have not wasted your day.[2]

Your penetrating criticism not only informs the public (if the public *can* be informed) but enlightens the author about himself. Till I have* read your article I was not aware that "the bizarre—or that which is idiotic with force and egotism" (jolly definition)—exhilarated Mr Conrad.[3] I was not aware; but since you've written it I see that it is so. Henceforth I shall understand the true cause of that sort of grim satisfaction with which I wrote certain passages in this and other books.

So thanks for all Your good words and especially for the good words about the form.[4] Now that you have seen that as well as everything else, I may confess I took special pains with it.

Yours sincerely grateful[ly]

J. Conrad

---

[1] As a reader for Fisher Unwin, Wilfrid Hugh Chesson (1870–1952) was among the first to see the MS of *Almayer* and appreciate its promise. As a newspaper reviewer, Chesson contributed several perceptive appraisals of Conrad's fiction. 'With Mr. Conrad in Soho', the review of *The Secret Agent*, appeared in the *Daily Chronicle* on 13 September.

[2] Marcus Ulpius Traianus, born in Spain, was Roman Emperor from 98 to 117.

[3] Chesson particularly enjoyed the untended pianola that rounds off the anarchist conclave with 'The Blue Bells of Scotland'.

[4] 'A masterpiece in narrative, in which every event is a link in a chain ... perfection of form'.

To Henry James
Text MS Harvard; J-A, 2, 55

Someries
Luton
Beds.
20 Sept 1907.

Très Cher Maître.

I am sending you my latest volume. Receive it with the indulgence which cannot be refused to a profound and sincere sentiment prompting the act. The covers are deep red I believe. As to what's inside of them I assure you I haven't the slightest idea. That's where Hazzlit's* Indian Jug[g]ler has the pull over a writer of tales. He at least knows how many balls he is keeping up in the air at the same time.[1]

I've heard from the Imperatively Necessary Pinker of your kind inquiries. To know that your thought is sometimes turned towards me and mine is deeply comforting. Perhaps the I. N. P. told you that this year in France we had—in the words of the parrot—'a hell of a time'. In 8 months poor Borys managed to achieve two serious illnesses. Enfin!

Notwithstanding that he only got up from the last 7 weeks ago I took him up yesterday to a small school in the neighbourhood. And I miss him exceedingly to-day.

We have abandonned* the Pent to its green solitudes—to its rats. Here's a chapter closed. The new one opens much nearer London—less than 40 minutes—and many times a day. When You come up for your London Period you must extend it episodically as far as the Someries—any day when the conjunction of the planets and Your inclination point favourably to my request. N'est ce pas? You would not deprive the boy of the privilege of boasting to his descendants that he has seen Henry James under his father's roof. It would be downright cruelty considering what a scant store of glamour I am likely to leave him otherwise.

A Vous de coeur

J. Conrad.

---

[1] In 'The Indian Jugglers' (*Table-Talk*, vol. 1, 1821) Hazlitt marvels at the jugglers, who can keep four balls in the air at once: 'Instead of writing on four subjects at a time, it is as much as I can manage to keep the thread of one discourse clear and unentangled.'

To William Rothenstein
Text MS Harvard; Unpublished

Someries
Luton.
24 Sept 1907

Dearest Will.

Thanks for your letter. To find *one* reader like [you] is reward enough for a pen-worker. And its well it is so, for no two could be found with such vivid sympathy such almost miraculous comprehension of artistic aim and an intelligence so ready to grasp the slightest tones of intention.

I am sorry I shan't see You soon. But good luck and easy labour to you!

Our dear love to you all

Yours ever

J. Conrad

To J.B. Pinker
Text MS Berg; Unpublished

Someries
Wednesday. [25 September
1907][1]

My dear Pinker

Its just as well. I wasn't in a state to travel and see stage plays.[2] D[r] Tebb was here yesterday and my thoughts were far from playful.

I don't think I will be able to come on Friday. I am pretty bad but *at work all the time.*

Yours always

J. C.

Have you seen a slating of SA in Country Life?[3]

---

[1] Between the *Country Life* review and the letters of [27 September].

[2] The opening of Galsworthy's *Joy* on the 24th?

[3] By 'Z', 21 September, pp. 403–5; reprinted in *Critical Heritage*, pp. 186–9. The reviewer missed the book's sardonic tone, complained about its psychological analyses, and found it inflated and digressive. 'The book might fairly be described as a study of murder, by a writer with a personality as egotistical as that of Mr. Bernard Shaw, only lacking in the wit and humour which goes some way to justify the existence of the latter.'

To John Galsworthy
Text MS Forbes; J-A, 2, 57

Someries. Luton
Friday. [27 September 1907][1]

Dearest Jack

What you say of the reception of *Joy* confirms me in the dismal conviction that a work of art is always judged on other than artistic grounds, in this imperfect world.[2] I imagine how much your altruism is aware of your actors' disappointment. But actors have compensations of their own for such misadventures. I ask myself however whether you do not exaggerate the magnitude of the misadventure aforesaid.

And in any case it does not matter. Besides we must see yet what the *public* will do. It does not always endorse the verdict of the critics. I regret bitterly not having been in the house for the première. I sit here and fret and keep on exasperating myself thinking of Your work and mine. No matter. Bad as it is to see one's work misunderstood the murmurs against *Joy* shall be drowned in such a shout around *Strife* as this country has not heard for a hundred years or more. That is not only my conviction but my feeling—an absolutely overpowering feeling. You've got only to sit tight and watch your glory approaching.

Of all the criticisms I've seen only the D.T.'s.[3] It is condemnation of course—the condemnation of a man who is mainly disconcerted. He—(they) expected you to write *The Silver Box* for ever and ever. Being disconcerted he can not see the higher artistic quality of *Joy*. It is a yelp of astonishment more than anything else. It is of course possible that *Joy* is less theatrical (in the proper sense) than *The SB*. I can't tell, not having seen the performance. But it is possible. The good creatures would naturally resent that with all the force of their simple feelings. Not seeing the surface qualities they expected they cried out—a chorus.

To tell you the real truth I had a suspicion that something of the kind might happen. I had it in Montpellier as I read the play. But I said nothing of it to you. I spoke about the play which is good—and not about the critics—who are what they are. It seemed to me clear that the qualities of *The SB* being on the surface and the qualities of *Joy* being

---

[1] Between the opening of *Joy* on the 24th and Garnett's review of *The Secret Agent* on the 28th.

[2] Galsworthy's new play, produced at the Savoy by Granville-Barker, had a very bad press (Marrot, pp. 208–10; Dupré, pp. 141–2).

[3] The *Daily Telegraph* (25 September 1907) found 'no story in it, except such as might be written on a sixpenny-piece'; it was 'not a good play or even a play at all'.

hidden deep in the interaction of delicate feelings there was that risk to
run. You have run it. It had to be.

I demur to Your saying that it is good for one. It is neither good nor
bad. In the phraseology of Mr Vladimir I am inclined to ask "Why are
you saying that—from morality—or what?"[1] Your activity having
become as it were an ingredient of my mental life, I can judge with the
intimacy of a kindred spirit and with the detachment of a separate
individuality. It is just nothing to one—the one being You. The
superficiality of blame can in no sense be more valuable than the
superficiality of praise. You've had both—for indeed *The S.B.* had a
sufficiency of the latter. But there is in your work the sort of merit which
escapes the standards of current criticism with its formulas of thought
and its formulas of expression.

Nevertheless that merit will always be felt present under the vain
words babbling of success or failure. It is Your possession—and the rest
is just nothing.

In *Strife* that merit, that 'virtue' of Your gift, the hidden essence of
your great talent reaches an extraordinary force of feeling and an
amazing felicity of conception—a thing infinitely greater than mere
felicity of expression. Of that last it can be said that it is just to the
conception—and no more can be said. Thus nothing jars that obscure
sense of the fitness of things we all carry in our breasts—and the whole
drama develops its power over our emotions irresistibly and harmoni-
ously, to a point where the shallowest mind must receive the impression
of depth and the stoniest heart the impression of pity.

Jessie sent some flowers to Ada yesterday. We are settled—up to a
certain point. Settled enough at any rate to be ready for your visit. I am
very anxious to see you before You leave town—and I am not fit to travel
feeling extremely anyhow. That's the reason I don't ask for a seat yet. I
had a friendly letter from Lucas and another from Graves[2] about the
S.A. Not a word from Edward[3] tho'. I suppose he thinks I don't care.
He's wrong. I do ... Do you really mean that the *SA* has made a mark?
And what is *making a mark*? Our dear love. Au revoir soon. Ever Your

J Conrad.

---

[1] "'What do you want to make a scandal for?—from morality—or what?'" (*The Secret
Agent*, p. 227).

[2] Identified by Jean-Aubry as Alfred Percival Graves (1846–1931), Robert's father. An
Irish poet and editor and a leader of the Celtic renaissance, he put together several
anthologies of Welsh and Irish literature.

[3] Garnett.

To J.B. Pinker
Text MS Berg; J-A, 2, 56

[Someries]
Friday. [27 September 1907][1]

My dear Pinker.

Thanks for Your letter ever so much. I was not unduly impressed by the Country Life slating. I could write a jolly sight better slating myself of that book—something that *would* get home onto its defects.

As to *A Duel* I think that McClure's notion is not half bad.[2] How would that move affect the chances of vol form publication *here* by and bye? Of course vol of short stories in the States could not include that one. If the conditions they propose are good I should say: Yes! Certainly. I like you to advise me of what is being done but you understand very well that the decision rests always with you. My position is this: While I am writing I am not thinking of money. I couldn't if I would. The thing once written I admit that I want to see it bring in as much money as possible and to have as much *effect* as possible.

Talking of effect: Is the S. A. producing any on the public? I wish I knew, mainly for this reason that if there's going to be a second edition soon (or at all) I would like to correct a few horrid misprints there are—if that can be done.

Graves wrote me a nice letter a day or two ago. Who is the Buchan you mention in yours? Is he John Buchan who used to write in B'wood 3 years ago?[3] Graves is a good friend to have—apart from being a sympathetic person to know. Lucas wrote me too with enthusiasm. A J. Dawson also—only yesterday. But from Ed. Garnett I haven't heard privately tho' I know he is to review the book somewhere. This is ominous. I am not well enough to ask You to arrange a meeting with D[r] Robertson Nicoll[4] yet, but I should like to have a sight of him. Is Ford's book[5] gone into 2[d] edition already as I hear—not from him tho'. Jack's play has been abused all round I am informed. I dreaded something of

---

[1] Between the *Country Life* review and Garnett's review on the 28th.
[2] In 1908, McClure brought out 'The Duel' as a discrete volume, *The Point of Honor: A Military Tale.*
[3] In one of John Buchan's early contributions to the magazine, Conrad detected 'naiveness of an appalling kind or else a most serene impudence' (*Letters*, 2, p. 216). By 1907, Buchan had become a partner at Thomas Nelson & Sons.
[4] William Robertson Nicoll (1851–1923, pseudonym Claudius Clear), the Scottish critic, founder and editor of the *Bookman*, an arbiter of respectable literary taste.
[5] *An English Girl*, published earlier in the month, one of five Ford titles appearing in 1907.

the kind. Still that means nothing. His triumph with *Strife* will be all the greater.

Kind regards
Yours always

J. Conrad.

PS   You will see what one exposes oneself to with photographs. Here I am with Legallienne like a gorilla with an angel.[1] It makes me sick to see myself facing that creature. Not to speak of Lang's perfidious little joke under the heading of Literature. Just look at N° of the Ill. Lond: News.—No more photos! Please!

To J.B. Pinker

Text MS Berg; Unpublished

[Someries]
Sunday ev^g [late September or early
October 1907][2]

My dear Pinker

I send you complete proof of A Duel. The title I've changed as follows: *The Duel. A military story.* It will be also more suitable for the small vol form in the States.

Do get the P[all] M[all] M[agazine] people to pull off *two corrected* sets of galley slips. One of them we could send to McClure presently. The other I would [. . .][3] to keep by me for the time of book-form publication here.

But after all even one set would do. I would like to have it for a few days before it goes to America.

I conclude the *SA* is being already reprinted? Is that so?

Jack who has seen some MS pp of *Chance* thinks well of it. Yes. The Duel well illustrated and delicately got up will make a nice sort of bijou volume. I am much pleased with the McClure idea.

Yours always

Conrad

---

[1] Andrew Lang presided over a literary page, 'At the Sign of St. Paul's', in the *Illustrated London News*. On 5 October (p. 514), a characteristically sombre picture of Conrad faced a characteristically exquisite one of the belletrist Richard Le Gallienne (1866–1947). Conrad must have seen an advance copy of the issue.

[2] The possible dates are 29 September, 6 or 13 October. Conrad accepted the McClure proposal on 27 September; by 15 October he knew that *The Secret Agent* had indeed gone into a second edition.

[3] Word left out on starting a new page.

PS Please send out to buy a copy of *S.A.* for me. I want the 1st ed: if possible—to present.

To J.B. Pinker
Text MS Berg; Unpublished

[letterhead: Talbot House]¹

Monday. [30 September 1907]²

My dear Pinker.

I can't wait as Jack and Mrs Jack are coming to see us this afternoon I must rush home.

Last week I havent had* a cheque. As it did not come this morning either I ran up to inquire—the cause not being clear to me. I suppose over-sight. But this is just it. The fact is my dear fellow that I am not certain how I stand in the disposal of the amount agreed between us.

This is not conductive* to that serenity necessary for due production of interesting fiction. I have been most damnably bothered out of my composure by several things and I think I must make a clean breast of it to you at once as I see no way out of it unless by your help.

What I['ve] got to say is that you must raise the amount for the twelve-month by sixty pounds—that is *I must* ask you for that: What You will say I don't know: I submit however that it will be worth Your while to stretch the point and make the £600 into 660. That however is not all. I want the extra amount I am asking for now—as follows in cheques 1. for £15. 1. for £6.5. Two *for* £4 1. for £3.8 1. for £5. 1 for £2. = total *37.13.** The rest one for £15. and one for 2 one for 3. would do about 20th Oct.

This is of course apart from the principal amount of £600. of which I keep account. £6 every week and a cheque from time to time as I ask for it.

Pray stretch a point. This will clear me completely and make life a different thing altogether. I was thinking of borrowing the money somewhere and paying it off in monthly instalments (spread over 2 years). *But* before I try I wish you would tell me what you are disposed to do.

Of course I am ready to disclose all particulars. Anyway you will know how the money is spent. But I haven't the time to tell you all this now. I must bolt away for St Pancras.

---

¹ Pinker's office stationery.
² The day of the Galsworthys' visit, which can be dated from the next letter.

They tell me at Methuens that *The SA* is going "very well, very well indeed".

We have stuff for a vol of short stories without the *Duel*. In view of my request perhaps Meth: would like to publish it say in Jany. Surely we could get £120 down for it—60 for me and 60 for you. Don't refuse me finally without looking at that side of the position; because really I need the relief for which I ask. I am going on with *Chance* tho' I'm seedy

Yours

Conrad

Pray post £6 and at any rate the extra 4 to night

To J.B. Pinker
Text MS Berg; Unpublished

[Someries]

Tuesday. [1 October 1907][1]

My dear Pinker

Galsworthy was here yesterday with his wife. A very intelligent analytical appreciation of *Joy* (by Walkley I suppose) in the *Times* has cheered him up.[2] I don't think he was hipped. He was surprised more. He has too much character to be seriously upset over this.

Your letter struck me very much. I am sending it on to Jack to see and I am sure it will please and interest him very much. It has pleased and interested me—mainly as a revelation of J. B. Pinker's mind. We think there alike in the main, tho' our point of view is not identical—as indeed it could not be. I suspect that You have a much better grip on what the play really is than I have. I am not surprised that the critic failed to convince you. The official criticism—professional criticism—is mainly a matter of special jargon with very little individual thinking behind it. Now you can, and You do, think individually—that's clear to me.

G. is off to Devonshire on Saturday for a month I believe.

I received a letter yesterday morning which caused me to come over to see you. God is my witness I didn't want to bother you. Thanks very much for your PS which I take as an affirmative to my request.

Jack tells me there is a very good review of SA. by Garnett in last Sat's *Nation*. The damned press cutting Agency has not sent it on yet.

If (as a financial expedient) You arrange for a vol of short stories say in Jany next I propose that it should consist of: *Gaspar Ruiz: 3 parts. The*

---

[1] The Tuesday after Garnett's review.   [2] Quoted by Marrot, p. 209.

Anarchist. The Informer. The Brute. Il Conde. equivalent to seven short stories—say 57–60 thousand words. Anyway there would be as much matter as in many of Wells's volumes at 6/-.

There would remain for the nucleus of another vol *A Duel.* 30[000] words.[1] And in this connection it strikes me that I have material for another military story about the same length and we could publish the two together when the time comes. It would be something distinctive. Military stories of a hundred years ago.[2] See?

I sat up with *Chance* last night pretty late. That's nothing. What's bad is that when I do go to bed I don't go to sleep as I used to do. But that's only temporary and I am getting considerably better.

Jack approves of the house. When *are You* coming to have a look round? Do come before the weather goes to pieces—any [. . .][3] and in the time most convenient to You. You might come for instance by the 12.15 for lunch and get away early enough to give a look into your office before going home if you wanted to. There's a train at 3. and another at 3.50. But of course it would be nicest if you could stay till the 5.22 arriving St Pancras at 6. Or you could come later in the afternoon to dine and sleep—or dine without sleeping. I don't ask you formally to meet any one but just to come to see us this time and have a look round and a chat. The weather still holds but it won't last long I fear—so don't put it off a minute longer than You can help.

Yours always

J. Conrad

To Ford Madox Ford

Text MS BL Ashley 2923; *Listy* 261;
Original unpublished

Someries
Luton
1st Oct. '07

Dearest Ford.

It is as I thought. In many respects—and from an absolute point of judgment—the book[4] is simply magnificent. There's no doubt of it: for

---

[1] In *A Set of Six*, the 31,000 words of 'The Duel' joined the 52,000 words of the other stories.
[2] An anticipation of 'Prince Roman'? (Conrad began this story in 1908 as part of *A Personal Record*, and finished it in 1910.)
[3] MS torn.
[4] *An English Girl*, completed in May and published in September, a novel drawing on Ford's transatlantic adventures.

the feeling one has is that this sort of thing could not have been done otherwise.

And it is a big thing. The more one thinks of it the better is seen the really amazing magnitude of intention and the measure of success. The psychology of two great nations one European the other extra European absolutely contained in the scheme of a novel—carried out with a delicacy of insight and breadth of view which simply makes me gasp! You've done it. I say nothing of the ingenuity of the means. I admire in silence.

In the way of criticism I would say that the conversations (when Don is being talked about) are inspired by such delicate alert thinking that sometimes (for an ordinary reader) an effect of mysteriousness is produced. I think you will understand what I mean. The girl is superlative. The father most interesting and amusing (and by the bye he's a genial invention for concreting the inner meaning of many things) Canzano most delicately picturesque and sympathetic. Augustus a pathetic devil très tapé and the Bishopess simply priceless. Don himself[1] suffers from being the peg—but that could not be avoided. A peg there had to be and at any rate hes *not* a wooden peg. Loin de là. In fact on[e] can only say Well! well! well!

And let me tell you that the westward passage is done most admirably in its atmosphere, in its detail in the pictorial glimpses of the sea. These last are delightful. L'oeil d'un poète qui serait peintre aussi.[2]

And of course the book in a curious indefinable way has a delicate distinction, something ingeniously individual and exceptional, even, I mean, amongst your own other work. I need not tell you that I am profoundly in sympathy with its feeling. Drop me a line.

Ever Yours

Conrad.

---

[1] Don Collar Kelleg, an American crusader.
[2] 'The eye of a poet who might also be a painter.'

To Edward Garnett

Text MS Free; G. 211

Someries.
Luton.
1 Oct 1907

Dearest Edward.

I only heard from Jack yesterday of your review in the Nation.[1] I sent to the Railway Station today for the No.

It makes a fine reading for an author and no mistake. I am no end proud to see you've spotted my poor old woman.[2] You've got a fiendishly penetrating eye for one's most secret intentions. She *is* the heroine. And you are appallingly quick in jumping upon a fellow. Yes O! yes my dear Edward. That's what's the matter with the estimable Verloc and his wife: "the hidden weakness in the springs of impulse".[3] I was so convinced that something was wrong there that to read your definition has been an immense relief—great enough to be akin to joy. The defect is so profoundly temperamental that to this moment I can't tell *how* I went wrong. Of going wrong I was aware even at the time of writing—all the time. You may imagine what a horrible grind it was to keep on going with this suspicion at the back of the head.

You must preach to me a little when we meet—and even pray over me if you only will. Unless you think I am past praying for.

Sitting here alone with the glowing lamp in this silent, as yet strange house, I feel a great affection for you—and a great confidence in your judgment. Twelve years now—just a round dozen my dear—since I hear[4] your voice in my ear as I put aside each written page. Yes. A great affection and an absolute confidence.

Ever yours

J. Conrad.

When are you coming to see me in my new surroundings? Let it be soon. Any day. Any week. It'd really be no trouble to come over here and sleep one night before going to the Cearne at the end of your London

---

[1] Unsigned, 28 September, p. 1096; reprinted in *Critical Heritage*, pp. 191–3. Garnett praises 'Mr. Conrad's ironical insight', and 'his serene impartiality', seeing in the book 'the profound and ruthless sincerity of the great Slav writers'.

[2] Winnie Verloc's mother.

[3] They 'are less convincing in their actions than in their meditations ... at certain moments they become automata'.

[4] 'Since I began to hear'.

spell.[1] Only let me know the day because I want to meet you at the station. Remember me very affectionately to your wife. Jessie sends her dear love.

To Edward Garnett
Text G. 212

[Someries]
Friday [4 October 1907][2]

Dearest Edward.

Thanks for your letter. I've been expecting the appearance of the play and the attack on the censor with impatience.[3]

Of course I'll write something since you think it may do good in the endeavour to get us rid of a bitter absurdity.[4] Only I don't think my word will have any weight at all. I've been so cried up of late as a sort of freak, an amazing bloody foreigner writing in English (every blessed review of S.A. had it so—and even yours[5]) that anything I say will be discounted on that ground by the public—that is if the public, that mysterious beast, takes any notice whatever—which I doubt. You understand that having the novel of Mr B. Fry and his mamma for the fireside and Mr Hall Caine's "Christian" for their evening out[6] they are not insensate enough to bother their heads about an absolutely incomprehensible controversy. They won't. Most of them have never heard of the Censor of plays and when they hear of his existence they will become at once instinctively his warm partisans. He is an institution, a respectable institution; he is an obvious and orderly fact; he satisfies the common mind and soothes the common cowardice.

---

[1] Garnett worked in town during the week, leaving for his house in the country on Fridays.

[2] Between the letters of 1 and [8] October.

[3] Plays for public performance required a licence from the Lord Chamberlain; the job of inspecting them for traces of blasphemy, indecency, or disrespect for crowned heads devolved upon the Examiner of Plays, G. A. Redford, a retired bank-manager. When Redford threatened to deny *The Breaking Point* a licence, Garnett sent him an angry but eloquent letter (actually written by William Archer, 10 August 1907). As part of his campaign against censorship, Garnett published both letter and play.

[4] Earlier in the year, Redford had renewed his veto of *Mrs Warren's Profession*; his latest victim was Granville-Barker's *Waste*.

[5] Garnett had started his review: 'It is good for us English to have Mr. Conrad in our midst visualising for us aspects of life we are constitutionally unable to perceive.'

[6] *The Christian*, the dramatization of a novel by Hall Caine (for Conrad one of the most depraved of authors) was inspiring London audiences. *A Mother's Son*, by Beatrice Fry and her husband, the footballer, cricketer, and world long-jump champion C. B. Fry, was being assiduously promoted by the publisher of *The Secret Agent*.

Andrew Lang[1] will tell them perhaps that he is a historical survival and that'll capture their imaginations. To have a court official standing by to warn off criminal attempts on the delicacy of their morality will appear to them flattering—and natural too. For morality must be protected. That is self evident. Such protection is worthy in every sense and mostly in this that its existence in the corporeal shape of the Censor expresses the great fact of national self righteousness. Which fact is great and praiseworthy and very English.

On the other hand the public will learn of your existence. They will hear your name, and Chesterton's, and Galsworthy's and Archer's and, say, mine too and 40 other names.[2] They will perceive dimly that we are not stockbrokers, not clerks, not manufacturers or bankers, or lawyers, or doctors or bishops or cricketers or labour members, or scavengers, or company directors. We will in short appear to be unauthorised persons. Some Andrew Lang or other will tell them, or rather insinuate to them, that we are vulgar rogues and vagabonds. They'll accept this as a luminous statement for various self evident reasons one of them being that it'll save them trouble. A controversy is troublesome to the public mind. A controversy on the liberty of art is doubly troublesome because to that mind it is incomprehensible. When we say: Art, that public mind thinks (if it thinks at all) of water colour landscape as practised by their aunts, sisters, sweethearts. Thus our words are bound to sound to them fearfully unintelligible or abominably perverse.

Of course Lord A.[3] and the Licenser of plays take themselves seriously. They think themselves guardians of public morality. In this belief they have with them the public opinion in so far as it is not public indifference. The day this support is withdrawn from them they will become ashamed of their functions and the censorship of plays will disappear.

I will take the line of the Policeman if you like: but frankly I don't think it is a good line. It is of course workable but I'll confess to you that it does not run in the way of my convictions. You say: *The Censor should be a policeman etc.* But my conviction is that the Censor should *not be at all.* You say: *change* the policeman. But who is to judge of his discrimination? How is he to be found out? Who is to dismiss him? Who is to be trusted with the power to nominate him? Where are you going to find the tact,

[1] Andrew Lang (1844–1912), the Scottish poet, editor, translator, historian, and student of folklore and mythology. He was unsympathetic to modern literature.

[2] On 29 October, *The Times* published a letter of protest signed by 71 writers, including Hardy, Ford, James, Meredith, Swinburne, Yeats, and Conrad.

[3] Viscount Althorp, the Lord Chamberlain.

the wisdom, the breadth of mind, the artistic sense, the philosophical impartiality of thought, the wide intellectual sympathy, the humanistic and the brazen self-confidence necessary for such a post, for you can't draw a hard and fast line for him. He can't be a policeman he must be a magistrate, a high functionary—the supreme judge of form in art, the arbiter of moral intention. No. That function is impossible. The pretence to exercise it is shameful as all disguised tyranny is shameful. That's how I feel about it. The institution should be attacked on moral grounds as a cowardly expedient.

Yours ever

Conrad

To J.B. Pinker
Text MS Berg; Unpublished

Someries
Luton
6 Oct '07

My dear Pinker.

Thanks very much for the weekly cheque and the other cheques for £*15.5. 3.8. 4. 2. 6. 5.* making altogether £*35.13* out of the extra sum I've asked for.

I am getting into stride and expect to attain a pretty fast gait very soon

Kindest regards
Ever yours

J. Conrad.

To R.B. Cunninghame Graham
Text MS Dartmouth; J-A, 2, 59; Watts 169

7th Oct 1907
Someries
Luton
Beds.

Très cher ami.

I am sorry you've left town already. We have just got into this new house and were anxious to see you under its fairly weather-tight roof. It is very accessible from London: many trains and some under 40 minutes and only 2½ miles from Luton. Its a farmhouse on the Luton Hoo Estate belonging to that knight errant Sir Julius Wernher. A flavour of South

Africa and Palestine hangs about our old walled garden—but it is not intolerably obtrusive.

I am glad you like the *S Agent*. Vous comprenez bien that the story was written completely without malice. It had some importance for me as a new departure in *genre* and as a sustained effort in ironical treatment of a melodramatic subject—which was my technical intention.

Mr Vladimir was suggested to me by that scoundrel Gen: Seliwertsow whom Padlewski shot (in Paris) in the nineties.[1] Perhaps you will remember as there were peculiar circumstances in that case. But of course I did him en charge.

Every word you say I treasure. It's no use: I can not conceal my pride in your praise. It is an immense thing for me however great the part I ascribe to the generosity of Your mind and the warmth of your heart.

But I don't think that I've been satirizing the revolutionary world.[2] All these people are not revolutionaries—they are shams. And as regards the Professor I did not intend to make him despicable. He is incorruptible at any rate. In making him say "madness and despair— give me that for a lever and I will move the world"[3] I wanted to give him a note of perfect sincerity. At the worst he is a megalomaniac of an extreme type. And every extremist is respectable.

I am extremely flattered to have secured your commendation for my Secretary of State and for the revolutionary Toddles.*[4] It was very easy there (for me) to go utterly wrong.

By Jove! If I had the necessary talent I would like to go for the true anarchist—which is the millionaire. Then you would see the venom flow. But it's too big a job.

I have been thinking of your empty house. We must steel our hearts. Living with memories is a cruel business. I—who have a double life one of them peopled only by shadows growing more precious as the years pass—know what that is. I have had the new ed. of Sta. Teresa[5] sent

---

[1] 18 November 1890. The former head of the Third Section of Russian police came to Paris to co-ordinate activities against the Nihilists; his assassin, who fled to America, was alleged to have connections with the French police (Baines, p. 331; *Listy*, p. 265; Watts, p. 171).

[2] As his contributions to the militant press reveal, Graham stood farther to the left than he had in the nineties.

[3] P. 309.

[4] 'Toodles' and Sir Ethelred – who bears more than a passing resemblance to Sir William Harcourt, Liberal Home Secretary from 1880 to 1885. As an M.P. (1886–92), Graham sat as a scandalously dissident member of the same party.

[5] Gabriela Cunninghame Graham's life of the saint in a posthumous edition for which her husband had written a new preface (Eveleigh Nash, 1907).

down for a leisurely re-reading. It seems no end of years since I read first this wonderful book—the revelation for the profane of a unique saint and a unique writer. Tempi passati!

My wife sends her affectionate regards. We had a most atrocious time abroad—both children ill and Borys very seriously too. He is at a little preparatory school in Luton now. Do let me know when you are coming south again. Toujours à vous de coeur

J. Conrad.

To Edward Garnett
Text J-A, 2, 59; G. 215

[Someries]
Tuesday 4pm. [8 October 1907][1]

Dear Chief,

(For you are the Cabecilla of the brave Guerillos)[2]—here's my escopette ready to go off. I've loaded it with a handful of pretty nasty slugs. Do you see to it that it is fired off properly by some steady hand. And look here: no censorship! It's *that* or nothing. I could not make it shorter. I am long because my thought is always multiple—but it is to the point anyhow. And I haven't spoken from a literary point of view. *You* can do that admirably. But as I love you I'll allow you to shorten what's necessary. Indeed the thing wants looking through carefully in proof. Only don't take the gems out. No gem must be taken out.[3] I am proud of my powers of stately invective combined with the art of putting the finger to the nose. It's a fascinating mixture. Don't you go Censoring it too much. Your sagacious letter (one would think a piece of Macaulay)[4] was not much to the point. You remember always that I am a Slav (it's your *idée fixe*) but you seem to forget that I am a Pole. You forget that we have been used to go to battle without illusions. It's you Britishers that "go in to win" only. We have been "going in" these last hundred years repeatedly, to be knocked on the head only—as was visible to any calm intellect. But you have been learning your history

---

[1] The 'escopette' (blunderbuss) went off in the *Daily Mail*, 12 October.

[2] 'Chief of the brave rebels': in *Nostromo*, Conrad uses *guerrillero*, the standard form.

[3] Garnett 'cut out two or three of the most extreme passages', for instance the following remarks on the Examiner: 'He must not even know that his grotesque existence is a direct insult to forty-five million more or less of souls certainly neither more nor less pure than his own, most of them more intelligent—all of them more worthy.' For the text of the cuts, see Garnett, p. 216, n. 1.

[4] A piece of high-minded eloquence, that is, in the grand Whig manner.

from Russians no doubt.[1] Never mind. I won't say any more or you'll call it a mutiny and shoot me with some nasty preface perhaps. I am now going to inspect your manner of carving into small pieces the Censor of Plays. Book just arrived.

Ever yours

Conrad

Note: if you wish it typed send to *Pinker* with enclosed note. Talbot House Arundel Street

To the *Daily Mail*
Text Daily Mail, 12 October 1907, p. 4[2]

[Someries]
[c. 8 October 1907][3]

A couple of years ago I was moved to write a one-act play and I lived long enough to accomplish the task. We live and learn. When the play was finished I was informed that it had to be licensed for performance. Thus I learned of the existence of the Censor of Plays. I may say, without vanity, that I am intelligent enough to have been astonished by that piece of information, for facts must stand in some relation to time and space, and I was aware of being in England—in the twentieth-century England. The fact did not fit the date and the place. That was my first thought. It was, in short, an improper fact. I beg you to believe that I am writing in all seriousness and am weighing my words scrupulously.

Therefore I don't say inappropriate, I say improper—that is, something to be ashamed of. And at first this impression was confirmed by the obscurity in which the figure embodying this, after all, considerable fact had its being. His name was not in the mouths of all men, far from it. He seemed stealthy and remote. There was about that figure the scent of the Far East, the peculiar atmosphere of a mandarin's back yard, and the mustiness of the Middle Ages, that epoch when mankind tried to stand still in a monstrous illusion of final certitude attained in morals, intellect, and conscience.

---

[1] By no means a figure of speech: the Garnetts had many friends among the refugee community.
[2] With substantial revisions and additions, this piece appears in *Notes on Life and Letters* as 'The Censor of Plays: An Appreciation'.
[3] Circumstances give an approximate date.

It was a disagreeable impression, but I reflected that probably the Censorship of Plays was an inactive monstrosity; not exactly a survival, since it seemed obviously at variance with the genius of the people, but an heirloom of past ages, a bizarre and imported curiosity preserved because of that weakness one has for one's old possessions, apart from any intrinsic value; one more object of exotic virtu, an Oriental potiche, a Magot Chinois[1] conceived by a childish and extravagant imagination, a grotesque idol provoking wonder and derision but allowed to stand in stolid impotence in the twilight of the upper shelf.

Thus I quieted my uneasy mind. Its uneasiness had nothing to do with the one-act play. The play was duly produced, and an exceptionally intelligent audience stared it coldly off the boards. It ceased to exist. It was a fair and open execution. But, having survived the freezing atmosphere of that auditorium, I continued to exist, labouring under no sense of wrong. I was not pleased, but I was content. I was content to accept the verdict of a free and independent public, judging after its conscience the work of its free, independent, and conscientious servant—the artist.

Only thus can the dignity of artistic servitude be preserved—not to speak of the bare existence of the artist and the self-respect of the man. I shall say nothing of the self-respect of the public. To the self-respect of the public the present appeal against the Censorship is being made, and I join in it with all my heart. For I have lived long enough to learn that the monstrous and outlandish figure, the Magot Chinois, whom I believe to be but a memorial of our forefathers' mental aberration, that grotesque potiche, works! The absurd and hollow creature of clay seems to be alive with a sort of (surely) unconscious life worthy of its traditions. It heaves its stomach, it rolls its eyes, it brandishes a monstrous arm, and with a censorship, like a bravo of old Venice with a more carnal weapon, stabs its victim from behind in the twilight of its upper shelf.

This Chinese monstrosity, disguised in the trousers of the Western Barbarian, and provided by the State with the immortal Mr. Stiggins's plug hat and umbrella,[2] is with us. It is an office—an office of trust, and from time to time there is found an official to fill it. He is a public man. The least prominent of public men, the most unobtrusive, the most obscure, if not the most modest.

But, however obscure, a public man may be told the truth if only once in his life. His office flourishes in the shade, not in the rustic shade beloved of the violet, but in the muddled twilight of men's imperfect

[1] A tall vase and a porcelain monkey.   [2] See *The Pickwick Papers*.

apprehension, where tyranny of every sort flourishes. Its holder need not have either brains or heart, no sight, no taste, no imagination, not even bowels of compassion.[1] He needs not these things. He has power. He can kill thought, and incidentally truth and incidentally beauty, providing they seek to live in a dramatic form. He can do it, without seeing, without understanding, without feeling anything, but[2] of mere stupid suspicion, as an irresponsible Roman Caesar could kill a senator. He can do that, and there is no one to say him nay. He may—what might he not do! There has been since the Roman Principate nothing in the way of irresponsible power to compare with the office of the Censor of Plays.

But this is England in the twentieth century, and one wonders that there can be found a man courageous enough to occupy the post. It is a matter for meditation. Having given it a few minutes, I come to the conclusion in the serenity of my heart and the peace of my conscience that he must be either an extreme megalomaniac or an utterly unconscious being.

The Censor must be unconscious. It is one of the qualifications for his magistracy. The other qualifications are equally easy. He must have done nothing, expressed nothing, imagined nothing. He must be obscure, insignificant, and mediocre—in thought, act, speech, and sympathy. He must know nothing of art, of life—and of himself. For if he did, he would not dare to be the Censor!

Frankly, Sir, is it not time to knock the improper object off its shelf? It has stood too long there. Hatched in Pekin (I should say) by some board of respectable rites, the little caravan monster has come to us by way of Moscow, I suppose. It is outlandish. It is not venerable. It does not belong here. Is it not time to knock it off its dark shelf with some implement appropriate to its worth and status, say with an old broom handle.

Joseph Conrad

---

[1] In the King James version, 'bowels of mercies': Colossians 3.12.
[2] The revised text has 'out'; the archaism may have been intentional or a misreading of Conrad's hand.

To the Rev. Robert P. Downes

Text MS Berg; Unpublished

Someries
Luton
Beds
8 Oct. 1907

Dear Sir.[1]

Pray do not suspect me of discourtesy. I hate to have my portraits published. The one or two that turn up from time to time in illustrated papers are youthful indiscretions coming home to roost to my great vexation. A writer lives sufficiently in his pages. And anyway I have no photograph of myself in the house.

Believe me very faithfully Yours

Jph. Conrad.

The Editor of *Great Thoughts*

To J.B. Pinker

Text MS Berg; Unpublished

[Someries]
Tuesday. [8? October 1907][2]

My dear Pinker.

Thanks for everything. I had Reynolds here.[3] I decidedly think there is a lot in that young man. I also like him for certain qualities he has, which are not on the surface it is true, but which are there all the same.

I am toiling on.[4] J.C Tarver[5] who lives not far from here has asked me to go and see him but I won't move till some day next week. I want to put on a spurt. Time passes with frightful rapidity. So does the money. I am terrified.

Your[s] ever

J. Conrad

R. tells me that Galsworthy's play got home on you. At least I understood him so.

---

[1] Robert P. Downes, Ll.D., edited *Great Thoughts from Master Minds*, a weekly compendium of reprinted stories, essays, and quotable quotations, price sixpence. Child readers were eligible for the Great Thoughts Pansy League.

[2] Received by Pinker '10/07': the stationery (Pent letterhead, cancelled) and the reference to *Joy* suggest a date early in the month. On the 1st Conrad had just been to London; on the 15th, he was there again: this letter came at a more sedentary moment.

[3] Stephen Reynolds, author, social critic, and, by recent choice, Devonshire fisherman.

[4] The letter accompanied some pages of *Chance* (note on letter made in Pinker's office).

[5] Author of a study of Flaubert; he lived in Woburn Sands, about 15 miles away.

To J.B. Pinker
Text MS Berg; Unpublished

[Someries]
10 Oct '07

My dear Pinker.

Of course. That's what we meant. Come any day the spirit moves You and the sun shines. If you wire in the morning and catch the 12.15 pm. you will find a lunch of a modest kind.

Please send the enclosed to R[obertson] N[icoll]. I like his review in the Reader[1] and I am telling him so.

Yours always

J Conrad.

I wrote a fierce denunciation of the Censorship of plays in the form of a letter to the Editor. Garnett wishes to ram it into the Dy Mail—if not the Nation will take it.

To J.B. Pinker
Text MS Berg; Unpublished

[Someries][2]
10 Oct. '07

My dear Pinker.

With the exception of my first 2 books I think, the publishing house of Baron Tauchnitz has refrained from publishing any of my work.[3] Meantime it had acquired almost every piece of rubbishy fiction You may think of that fell from the press. Considering the literary value of my work as determined by the concensus* of critical opinion in England and the U.S. I have accustomed myself to look upon my exclusion in the light of a distinction.

I am not inclined to forego this distinction for the sake of £20. I recognise the special, eminent, standing of Baron Tauchnitz's collection. But I have my own standing too. I can not allow a publishing House so much in the public eye to take two of my early works, then ignore seven as if they were unworthy or unfit to have a place in that

---

[1] *Reader*, 5 October, pp. 513–14. Nicoll was impressed by the banality of Verloc's wickedness and by 'the sedate and unflinching composure with which the characters are handled'. He called Conrad the most powerful stylist since the Brontës.

[2] Like several others of the period (e.g. to Downes, 8 October), this letter is written on Pent stationery, type fifteen. Sometimes, as here, the old address was not deleted.

[3] Tauchnitz, a Leipzig publisher, sold paperback editions of books in English throughout the continent. The two Conrads were *An Outcast* (1896) and *Tales of Unrest* (1898).

great (and undiscriminating) collection—and suddenly offer to include the tenth.

And the books that can't be found in the *Collection of British Authors* under Baron Tauchnitz's imprint include the *Nigger*, *Youth*, *Lord Jim*, *Mirror of the Sea* the very corner stones of my reputation, the best part of seven years of my literary life!

As a friend You'll understand my feeling. To be excluded from the Tauchnitz Collection *is* a distinction for Joseph Conrad whose place in English Literature is made. To come at the call of Baron Tauchnitz after 8 years of neglect is not to be thought of. None of my work shall appear *with my consent* in the Tauchnitz collection unless the head of that eminent firm agrees to include at least four works mentionned* above, which he was ill-advised enough to neglect.

As my agent I beg you to put my view before the representative of Baron Tauchnitz in this country in order that the Firm should be *fully* advised of my decision.

I am my dear Pinker
Always yours

J. Conrad

PS Can you work this line? I need not tell you that I feel very strongly in that matter. The above is written so that you could communicate it in full where it would get home. I really & truly feel that I had rather not unless the other books were there too.

Of course if you think I *must* take the money! Anyway I don't think that to be in the Collection is very good from a business point of view. It must affect the sale of royalty copies in a measure.

Have you the stomach for that negociation?* I believe you are quite up to the diplomatic feat. We want only to be very dignified. Of course I would renounce my part of remuneration for the four books—B'wood would want something no doubt. Should T. have his knife in Heinemann you could make concessions. Drop the Nigger for instance—and be content with 3 books. Or else we could put forward *Nostromo*. But it is really absurd that *all* the body of my work should be out of the Collection. It's insulting.[1]

JC

---

[1] None of the proposed titles was published in Conrad's lifetime. Nevertheless, *The Secret Agent* appeared in 1907 and *A Set of Six* in 1908.

To Sidney Colvin
Text MS Buffalo; Unpublished

[letterhead: Someries]
11 oct. 1907

Dear Colvin

I won't even attempt to say what your letter is to me. I have been miserably nervous about the book but you reassure me right royally. Your judgment being for me above suspicion in point of conviction, of art and of taste, the generous words of your approval have a very special value in my sight.

The nicest part of your letter is the promise to come and see us under our new roof. It goes without saying that the choice of the day rests with you—only let it be soon. I would venture to suggest next Saturday—unless you have an insuperable objection to sleeping out of your own bed if only for one night?

The puritanism of the Midland Rway discourages Sunday travelling—to Luton at any rate. You would have to start from St Pancras at *9.30* am which is I fear uncomfortably early. The next train after that is at *1 pm* arr: Luton *2.12* an absurd time altogether. It would make too a very imperfect inside of a day—the return trains being *8.8* pm and *9.54*.

But if You could come by one of the Sat: afternoon trains as *3.50* arr: here *4.29* or *4* arr here *4.48* or even *5.10* arr *6.3* we could have two distinct varieties of talk—the evening talk and the morning talk and by leaving here at 2.37 on Sunday you could be *home* at 4.15. I hardly dare suggest a full week end lest you should get bored. I've ever the consciousness of not being amusing—not like poor dear Mark Twain the favourite of mining camps and Royal Palaces.[1]

My wife, who thanks you for your message and sends her kindest regards to Mrs Colvin and yourself, is very urgent that you should take the risk. A word on a pc during the week will bring me to the station to meet you. We are two miles out of town. Please remember me to Mrs Colvin.

Yours cordially

J. Conrad.

---

[1] Samuel Langhorne Clemens (1835–1910), who had already lost a daughter, was further saddened by the death of his wife in 1904. In the summer of 1907, when he came to England to receive an honorary degree from Oxford, he was cheered by the stevedores of Tilbury and made welcome at Windsor Castle.

To H.G. Wells
Text MS Illinois; Unpublished

[letterhead: Someries]
Saturday [12 October? 1907][1]

My dear good H. G.

I am delighted with your letter since in effect it seems to tell me that I've done what I deliberately tried to do.[2]

Yes. That return is—looks—fishy.[3] Quite so. I would like to defend it but I can't remember how I did argue myself at the time into a belief in its absolute rightness. Nothing escapes your eye! Your good words close my little flutter. It has lasted just a month. The reception was distinctly good. One man only called it indecent trash—bad art and rotten morality.[4]

You must come to see us in our new home. I feel jaded but keep on writing convulsively what seems to me most dismal nonsense. Borys is at a little school in Luton and comes home for week ends. Jessie who is jubilant at your commendation of the S[ecret] A[gent] is pretty well and sends her dear love. Baby is very much alive but won't talk. With great affection for you both

Ever yours
J Conrad.

To J.B. Pinker
Text MS Berg; Unpublished

[letterhead: Duckworth & Co]
[15? October 1907][5]

My dear Pinker

My wife has been furnishing me with pocket money & cigarettes and paying wages out of her six pounds weekly housekeeping money pretty nearly since we came home. I think that now we are settled down it is only fair to put her right so that she may start fair and show what she can do. The whole lot including servant's wages up to date amounts to £9.18 by her acct/. I dare say I've spent a little too much on myself but there

---

[1] Saturday 12 October would be 'just a month' after publication of *The Secret Agent*. This may be the first appearance of Someries letterhead one.

[2] In a novel dedicated to Wells.

[3] Mrs Verloc's return to the shop in the final chapter?

[4] The *Country Life* reviewer complained of Verloc's being 'decent in his indecency, and honest in his dishonesty': 'Mr. Conrad ... is naughty, without being at all nice.'

[5] Received by Pinker '10/07', written on Garnett's office stationery. Sent, perhaps, after lunch with Garnett on the 15th; they had not met earlier in the month.

are things she bought for the house—small things that run up in a most damnable way. Please send me £10 anyhow. I would like to know how much of the £660 agreed upon I have drawn. Perhaps Your cashier could give me a rough note. I mean to stick to the agreement and I want to see whether my own note of money spent is correct. As I told you before I intend (and think I can) squeeze in *The Rescue* into the year's work if any sort of arrangement can be made with H[einemann] and McC[lure].

Yours Always

J. Conrad

To Ford Madox Ford
Text Violet Hunt's copy, Cornell; Unpublished

[Someries]

Wednesday 15 [16] October

1907[1]

My dear Ford

I was in town yesterday and at about 12.30 telephoned to the Club asking if you were there. The reply being "No" I went on then to the Mont Blanc where I found the usual crowd.[2]

I was too damnably done up to do anything except going home early in the afternoon. Forgive me not looking you up. Edward told me "*The Girl*"[3] had a real sound success.

We are both in our second Editions—*savez vous?*

I am very much anyhow. Do come over! I don't get on at all.

Render me the service of getting for me the "Figaro" and the "Le Journal" of the *16th October* and send them on here—*voulez-vous?*[4]

I asked Marshall[5] to come over here and see me some time next week.

---

[1] The 15th was a Tuesday; the Mont Blanc circle did not meet on Mondays.

[2] Edward Garnett presided over Tuesday (and sometimes Wednesday) lunches in the upper room of this Gerrard St restaurant. Among the regulars were Hudson, Belloc, Chesterton, W. H. Davies, Stephen Reynolds, and R. A. Scott-James; they were often joined by Galsworthy and Ford. In later years, Conrad would have seen such friends there as Muirhead Bone, Perceval Gibbon, and Richard Curle.

[3] *An English Girl.*

[4] At this period, Conrad took a pronounced interest in Parisian newspapers (e.g. the letter to Pinker of 30 December). The issues he wanted have no literary relevance, and he would hardly have known in advance about the acts of political mayhem that shadow their pages. What he did know in advance were the dates of the big lottery drawings.

[5] Archibald Marshall, a partner in Alston Rivers; until Northcliffe suddenly shut it down, he had edited the *Daily Mail* book supplement, the location of a series of Ford's literary portraits.

He'll be very much bored, I fear. Give him my address please so that he can write me the day.

Ever yours miserably,

J. Conrad.

To J.B. Pinker
Text MS Berg; Unpublished

[letterhcad: Someries]

24 Oct [1907][1]

My dear Pinker.

Will you please let me have now the balance of the £60 you have so kindly consented to advance (as extra) this year. It is still £25.

Would you be good enough to send £15 (cheque) to Mr *Richard Hogben Robus. Lyminge. N^r Folkestone. Kent.* And of the rest send me cheques for £2.*10.* £4 £6.*11* which is 3 more than stipulated but which I need to make up the payments.

Many thanks

Yours J Conrad.

To John Galsworthy
Text MS Forbes; J-A, 2, 62

[letterhead: Someries]

24 Oct '07

Dearest Jack

I am glad Ada and you found the story[2] tolerable. This in fact is my idea of historical romance put into a short form to try my hand at it.

I've not been able to get from P your article on myself.[3] I am interested but neither anxious nor impatient: for I've a great confidence in your judgment and I enjoy in anticipation the reading of something about myself which I know is truly felt and warmly expressed.

My article on the Censor was not bad: stately invective and co[nte]mptuous derision (vulgo: thumb to the nose) mingled in skilful doses to express an honest indignation. What You've seen of it was only the shadow of a shade. It was first censured by Edward (by permission I admit) and afterwards by the Dly Mail gang—whoever they are—as too

---

[1] Letterhead one and the need to pay off the owner of the Pent give the year.
[2] 'The Duel'.
[3] 'Joseph Conrad: A Disquisition', *Fortnightly Review*, April 1908, vol. 89, pp. 627–33; reprinted in *Critical Heritage*, pp. 203–9.

long I suppose. And length is an element of force—an influence in itself. Else why do we all yearn for long reviews? But I dare say I was not gentlemanly enough (being very much in earnest) and as the sagacious Edward observed "we mus[t]n't provoke a reaction in his (the Censor's) favour." I didn't see the matter in the same light, but I did not discuss the point for fear that Edward (who declares himself Irish)[1] should tell me that (as a Slav) I know nothing of the English temper in controversy. To me it seems that if the cause be good the blows should be stout and that if you mean to down a man you don't avoid hitting him under the jaw for fear of "provoking a reaction". In so far the Censor is estimable. He in his 12 years of office was not afraid of "provoking reaction". I suppose he knew what he was doing when he choked off Annunzio that dreary, dreary saltimbanque of passion (out of his original Italian of which I know nothing) and Maeterlin[c]k the farceur who has been hiding an appalling poverty of ideas and hollowness of sentiment in wistful baby-talk—two consecrated reputations, not to speak of the sacrosanct Ibsen,[2] of whom like Mrs Verloc of Ossipon, I prefer to say nothing. The refusal to pass Barker's play[3] in the face of the first attack increases my esteem for that imbecile. But his office is an ugly anachronism a thing per se unworthy and should be abolished on that ground: not because it stands in the way of Messrs: Annunzio, Maeterlin[c]k and Ibsen or even E. Garnett and G. Barker. I therefore mentionned* not one of these gentlemen but tried to overwhelm the institution by an attack on its contemptible and ridiculous character pushed on ruthlessly it is true but based strictly on the dignified declaration (I like it much) whose copy you sent me. I thought it was going to be real warfare—but I fear it's nothing more deadly than a literary flutter. Anyhow, ask Edward to send or show you the original draft which (I am told) he has kept by him—in the muniment chest of the Cearne (that celtic stronghold) for the wonder of future ages—I presume.

Incidentally too I've learned that after 12 years of work (spoken of by the public press in the way you know) Mr J. Conrad can not command

---

[1] His mother, Olivia Narney Singleton, came from County Clare, but Edward's declared Irishness was also a matter of political sympathy.

[2] Ibsen's *Ghosts* fell under the ban in 1891; Maeterlinck's *Monna Vanna* was forbidden because a stage direction requires the heroine to appear clad 'only in a mantle'; D'Annunzio's *La Città morta* was considered too dangerous for London audiences even (or perhaps especially) when performed in the original Italian by Eleanora Duse. D'Annunzio's Nietzschean dramas and Maeterlinck's Symbolist fantasies had a devoted contemporary following; the latter author won the Nobel Prize in 1911.

[3] *Waste.*

space for a 1000 words in a newspaper not even for once: and that he [is]
to be cut about by the Dly Mail young man in the same way Mr Jones' or
Mr Robinson's (of Maida Vale or Finsbury) letters to the Editor are. As
I don't suffer from swelled head this sort of medicine nauseous, has not
done me any good.

The S.A. has run his little race with the moderate triumph of two
editions. I go on with Chance convulsively as a jaded horse may be
made to gallop—and I fear it's all extravagant trash—the trash and
extravagance of despair. Pages *must* be written—so I write them—and I
haven't even the comfort to think I am writing them fast enough.

Our love. When are you coming back?

Ever Yours

J. Conrad.

To John Galsworthy
Text MS POSK; J-A, 2, 63

[letterhead: Someries]
29 Oct 1907

Dear Jack.

The reading of your article soothed my spirit of profound discontent.
The thing is magnificently all right in its general considerations. As to
their application to my personality it is not for me to say. A too
protesting modesty would be uncivil to You. To show all my gratifi-
cation would be perhaps indecent. But since your friendship is too
sincere to deal in anything but truth I will tell you that I am glad the
truth is *this* and no other. There are sentences I would bind about my
brow like a laurel wreath and rest content.[1]

I won't say any more just now. I want to come very soon and talk to
you. I would ask you at once to eliminate the word aristocracy, when
you see the proof. The name has never been illustrated by a senatorial
dignity which was the only basis of Polish aristocracy. The Equestrian
Order is more the thing. Land-tilling gentry is the most precise
approach to a definition of my modest origin.[2] As English publications
reach far and wide notwithstanding the Censorship,[3] I am anxious not

---

[1] For example, about Conrad's oeuvre: 'The writing of these ten books is probably the
only writing of the last twelve years that will enrich the English language to any great
extent.'

[2] The Polish term is *szlachta*; this class made up about ten per cent of the nation (Najder,
Chronicle, p. 3).

[3] Here, the Russian kind.

to be suspected of the odious ridicule of passing myself for what I am not. I'll talk to you more of that when we meet. The correction I ask for will spoil the sentence as it stands; but in that respect I may express the doubt whether ship-life though pervarded* by a sort of rough equality is truly democratic in its real essence.

In "Typhoon" (not *The*) the name is *McWhirr* instead of McGrath. The name of the old boy in "The End of the Tether" is *Whalley*.

I am glad it's going to be a real fight. The *protest*[1] as I've said is really first rate full of dignity in sentiment and phrasing.

What did Murray write in the Nation?[2] Good?

I feel excited at the idea of You preaching a crusade. Do you really mean preaching with the living voice? Where? How? When?

In haste for post.

Our dear love to you both

Yours ever

J Conrad.

To Elsie Hueffer

Text Copy, Lamb;[3] Unpublished

Someries
Luton,
Sunday evening [Autumn
1907?][4]

Dear Auntie Elsie

I write the obligatory letter for Jessie, who besides entertaining Jack[5] is harbouring a great ache in her heel—however I've seen them worse.

The terms of the letter need not be obligatory—our sentiments being of spontaneous, independent, sincere and original type. The two days in W[inchelsea] have been delightful.

I am quite unable to say anything really pretty in the way of thanks

[1] The letter in *The Times*, 29 October, signed by 71 authors, among them Conrad.

[2] Censorship 'misses the vicious man and hits the reformer': 26 October, p. 117. To the campaign, Gilbert Murray brought both his dionysiac energies and his authority as a student of Greek theatre.

[3] A copy made by the late Katharine Lamb, the Hueffers' younger daughter.

[4] If the Someries address is correct, autumn 1907 is the only feasible period; by December, the Hueffers had left Winchelsea for good (Ford, in any case, only came down at weekends: Mizener, p. 130). When sold in 1928, the letter was supplied with a date not recorded on the copy, 17 March 1902, but a surviving MS fits that date more precisely (*Letters*, 2, p. 393). Were it not for the address, however, the tone and contents of this text would point to 1901 or 2 rather than 1907. The date stays tentative.

[5] Galsworthy or the baby?

and have mislaid my polite "letter writer" which expresses itself with great force & elegance; but pray believe in our gratitude.

Will you kindly tell the domestic despot that I have written a good many pages on Saturday, none to-day, and contemplate a field day for to-morrow. My immortal productions you had gratified me so much by asking for, leave on Monday evening addressed to your honoured hands. My love to the chicks & and to the authors of their being.

Your most faithful servant,
J. Conrad

Jack sends friendly greetings and contemplates a visit to you before very long.

To J.B. Pinker
Text MS Berg; Unpublished

[letterhead: Someries]
Thursday evening [Autumn
1907][1]

My dear Pinker.

Thanks for both your letters. I had no idea one of my galley slips sets was a revise. I shall send it to you tomorrow morning.

As to the title. I have no invention for that sort of thing. Besides no other title would do so well to my mind the story being the story of a duel or at any rate a duelling story. The psychology of every single being in it hangs on the practice of duelling. Besides if I were to change the title for the P.M.M. I would have to stick to it later on for book form—and that would not please me at all.

I defy any man to find a better title for a story which is all duel and nothing but a duel. There is in it to start with no feud, no quarrel, no rivalry. Whatever sentiments come into it they all flow out from duelling pure and simple—in all its naked absurdity I think the title must stand.

Yours ever
J. Conrad

---

[1] The *Pall Mall Magazine* began 'The Duel' in January; the Someries letterhead came into use in mid or late October. Any Thursday between then and late November would be possible.

To Alice Rothenstein
Text MS Harvard; Unpublished

[letterhead: Someries]
1st Nov. 1907

My dear Alice.

The trains on Sunday are a bitter mockery. We hoped to see you here on Saturday for lunch. But since Sunday it must be here is the dismal tale.

You can start either from Finchley Road *9.45* am or West Hampstead *9.47* am. arriving Luton *10.53*. Over an hour's run—whereas on week-days the distance can be made under 40 minutes!

Can You manage to start as early as that?

If you can—*do*. For after that there is no train till *1.13* pm from Finchley Road or *1.15* from W. Hampstead, arriving Luton 2.12. After that hour Luton is cut off from civilization till 6 in the evening!

I shall be at the station of course whichever train you choose. Please send wire on enclosed form because a letter would not reach us till Sunday morning and I must know on Sat: to order the trap to come here for me first.

You can return by a train at 8.8 pm reaching W. Hampstead at 9.11. We shall have an early dinner.

Au revoir—then. Jess is in a sort of fever of expectation. Borys will be home from school. *Do* bring darling John. We are all right now. Our love. Yours with devotion

Conrad

To E.L. Sanderson
Text MS Yale; Unpublished

[Someries]
6 Nov '07

Dearest Ted

Just a word before I feel that you are far away again[1]—and I send it today lest it should miss you if I waited till tomorrow.

Please tell your wife with my most affectionate regards that I have tried to give Jessie some idea of the children to the best of my ability: the intelligence and charming vitality of Kitty the darlingness of poor invalid Biddy—she has a dear voice too—and the sterling worth of Ian.

---

[1] Back in Kenya.

He's the most sympathetic little man I've ever met in my life. I felt in touch with him as if he were my own.

I am advised this morning by Methuen that the two books have been sent to you, so my mind is at rest. I only regret I could not write Your name and mine on the fly leafs.

The platform of Elstree Station is becoming for me a sort of hallowed ground. There you talked to me of your engagement and showed me the ring. Yesterday we paced it together and in the few minutes before the parting I felt what a great part you and yours have in my life. At my age if not a[t] yours one may be permitted to grow sentimental a little—at times. But enough!

To our next meeting then. We may grow older. Days do count—they even count up. Time wears down the edge of fine sensations—but I fancy our friendship is too solid to show signs of decay if we both lived to a hundred. May every blessing attend you and all that are dear to you.

Yours ever

J. Conrad

PS. Give my love to your mother please.

PPS I send you an* Yankee Mag^{ne} with a story of mine which is not so bad in workmanship I fancy though otherwise a trifle.[1] Read the story in the train and throw the magazine out of the window.

To Deshler Welch

Text MS Dartmouth; *Listy* 267; Original unpublished

[letterhead: Someries]
7 Nov '07

Dear Mr. Welch.[2]

I fear I have nothing interesting to tell you. I am at work now at a novel called *Chance* its action taking place at sea. It is rather a discursive sort of thing—by no means what the reviewers call "a well-told story." It will be finished I hope by the end of the year.[3] When and how it is to be published I know nothing whatever. This part is the exclusive concern of my friend Mr Pinker.

He tells me that Messrs. McClure think of publishing early next year

---

[1] The most recent American publication was 'The Brute' in the November *McClure's Magazine*.

[2] Deshler Welch (1854–1920), journalist and author, worked for the New York *Tribune* and founded *Theatre Magazine*.

[3] Set aside in favour of *Under Western Eyes*, it was not finished until March 1912.

a long short story of mine in a small vol—something like the form in which *Typhoon* was published 3 years ago I think by Messrs Putnam & Sons. I like the idea very much. The story (which is to appear, soon, serially, in the P.M.M.) is entitled *The Duel. A Military Story* and the title describes it exactly.[1]

I have enough short stories—some published serially in the US—others only on this side—to make a vol. of. They are a fairly varied lot written without malice—nothing to be ashamed of, nothing to crow about either.

This is all I can tell you as to what's done and doing. Of my plans I can say nothing definite. I am thinking of a big novel with London for background and of another which is nothing less than European in scale. But you had better say nothing of that for fear of exciting my "large American Public" unduly.

Believe me
Yours faithfully
J. Conrad

To J.B. Pinker
Text MS Berg; Unpublished

[letterhead: Someries]
Tuesday [12 November 1907][2]

My dear Pinker.
Thanks very much for your letter received this morning. Please send me a cheque to Mr J. Webdale £2.5 one to Miss D. Hatton[3] for *1.13.4* one for myself for *one pound*.

S. Colvin wrote me an admiring letter. He wants to come and see me. Everybody wants to come and see me—except you it seems. If the Kaiser's coming to Guildhall stops business to morrow (Wednesday) why shouldn't you come here to lunch if the day is fine—or even if it isn't. There is a train at 12.15. Send a wire on receipt of this sudden suggestion.

Ford was here too. Is it true that the SA is in the 3^d edition.
Yours always
J. Conrad

[1] McClure published it as *The Point of Honor*.
[2] The day before the Kaiser's visit to the City of London.
[3] Mr Webdale kept a warehouse in Luton; Miss Hatton is unknown.

To J.B. Pinker
Text MS Berg; Unpublished

[Someries]
[c. 20 November 1907][1]

My dear Pinker.

No luck. I have been sleepless for nearly a week and in a state of nervous irritation, unbearable to myself and others.

S. Colvin came for the week and did me good in a measure by a tremendously complimentary state of belief in my work. S.C. is a good friend to have.

Please send me a cheque for *18/6* and another for £1.5.

Post waiting

Yours

Conrad

To John Galsworthy
Text MS Forbes; Unpublished

[letterhead: Someries]
Wed^sy 27 Nov '07

Dearest Jack

Your letter found me in bed with gout—alas. I've been beastly ill and I am not much better yet. Ever since we came here I have been hindered in my work—in the work on which I have depended so much. It's fatal. I have pra[c]tically done nothing since end August. Not that I haven't tried! God knows.

I don't know whether I shall be able to come on the 10^*th*. No doubt my foot will be swollen yet then. I can't sleep—at last. It was bound to come. This trying to break through a stone wall is getting too much for me. What sort of mind could I bring to your gathering? I am glad your appreciation goes into the Fortnightly. This my best success amounts to 4,300 copies of which 1500 are colonial edition. Love to dear Ada

Ever your

Conrad.

---

[1] Marked '11/07' in Pinker's office. On 12 November, Colvin had not begun his week's visit; on the 22nd, Conrad's gout returned.

To J.B. Pinker
Text MS Berg; Unpublished

[letterhead: Someries]
28 Nov 1907

My dear Pinker

After I left you last Friday[1] I felt a twinge of gout on the stairs. By the time I got home I felt thoroughly ill and I've only got out of bed this morning. No luck. Still it was a light attack as they go and I am less depressed now. Still I should not be able to be present at the 'evening meal'—on your birthday I suppose, though the convocation letter does not say. I am very sorry. My best wishes will be with you on this as on any other day of the year but with a special reference.

I trust you had a good time on your Irish journey but I am afraid you could not have had a good return passage.

Kindest regards
Yours always
J. Conrad

PS I am starting my writing to day again. I could cry when I think of the many wasted days this year. Do go and see my portrait[2] soon.

To William Rothenstein
Text MS Harvard; Unpublished

[letterhead: Someries]
28 Nov 07

Dearest Will.

I was delighted with Your Italian letter and grateful for it too. I heard from S. Colvin you were back and I would have tried to come over but an attack of gout laid me up eight days ago. I got up this morning but the foot is monstrously swollen yet. Goodness only knows when I'll be able to leave home.

I am weary of my silly life.

Can't You snatch a day or ½ a day and come over to see me. I shan't weep before you and it may very well be that I'll find the moral strength to smile. Come for lunch—or for dinner or for the night. We do long for a sight of you.

Our dearest love to you all

Ever yours
J Conrad.

---

[1] The 22nd.   [2] By Rothenstein?

To Ada and John Galsworthy
Text MS Forbes; Unpublished

[letterhead: Someries]
Saturday [30 November or 7
December 1907][1]

Dear Ada and Jack

Our loving thanks for the lantern—the most sympathetic piece of wrought copper I have ever seen in that shape. We went about (I sorely hobbling) trying it all over the place and deriving much enjoyment from successive hangings. The dining room won't do because of the heavy wheelspokes shadows on the walls with a great hub of shade resting on the table. The effect is romantically sinister. It must be the hall where the effect is picturesque. The exact spot where Your gift is to be suspended we haven't decided upon yet. The argument and experiments shall be continued to morrow, Monsieur B putting his oar in as usual.

I am glad you have had the idea of providing me with a lantern for the beginning of my 50th year.[2] You may depend on it I shall try to keep the light in it going as long as I can.

Your malicious little dig at me dear Jack as to me being afraid of failing in social brilliance at your dinner misses its mark. It is not brilliancy that was in question but the merest decency. I am not afraid of not being brilliant enough—the difficulty is to keep my wits together in some sort of social shapeliness. For upon my word I feel myself sometimes going mad with worry and apprehension—feeling ill and powerless in my craft, with but little hope of things ever getting better. It's the instinct of the wounded animal that keeps me to my hole. But I will come, I will come. I want to see you two. Our dear love.

Ever Your

J Conrad.

To William Rothenstein
Text MS Harvard; Unpublished

[letterhead: Someries]
2 Dec '07

Dearest Will

We shall expect You on Thursday. But do come for the night. There

---

[1] Conrad's birthday fell on 3 December; the impending dinner was on the 10th.
[2] He was just ending it.

are trains in the morning early enough for a man of your noble
independence—as the 9.32 which stops at Kentish Town where you can
connect for Hampstead.

Meantime drop us a pc:

With love to all

Yours ever

J Conrad

To J.B. Pinker
Text MS Berg; Unpublished

[letterhead: Someries]

4 Dec. 1907

My dear Pinker.

I send you a few pages more of Chance for typing.

I took your hint of trying to start a short story. You will have it after
Xmas.—It should help with the bills. It's the one about the revolutionist
who is blown up with his own bomb.[1]

C. Scott of the London Mag.[2] has written me asking for a story. I
don't know whether it's good for me to appear in a periodical of that
sort. Curtis Browne[3] has approached me with a proposal from France to
translate the *S.A.* I referred him to You but at the same time I said that
I would have to be satisfied as to the quarter from which the proposal
comes, before I authorised a translation. I am not anxious to be
translated anyhow.

Please have this acct/ of Norman & Stacey[4] attended to—if the Nov[er]
instalment has not been paid yet. Send me a cheque for £5.7 I owe my
wife for advances out of her housekeeping money.

I am free of pain and my head's pretty clear. This was a light and airy
fit of gout; but I haven't been out yet. Yours always

J Conrad.

---

[1] The origin of 'Razumov', the short story that grew into *Under Western Eyes*?
[2] Clement Scott, formerly the much-feared drama critic of the *Daily Telegraph*.
[3] Curtis Brown, the American-born agent, one of Pinker's principal competitors.
[4] They had furnished Someries.

To William Rothenstein
Text MS Harvard; Unpublished

[letterhead: Someries]
4 Dec. '07

Dearest Will

Certainly. Let it be Saturday.[1] Get a week-end ticket—you'll save 50% which is always agreeable. Drop me a line to name the train. If You can catch the 12.15 pm from St Pancras Borys will meet you at Luton Station on his way from school for his week end at home.

Our love

Yours Conrad.

To John Galsworthy
Text MS Forbes; Unpublished

[letterhead: Someries]
Monday [9 December 1907?][2]

Dearest Jack

I propose to arrive at Your Castle between 4–5 with my bag. If there is anything to say against that please speak on telephone to Pinker's office where I will be sometime in the morning

With great love

Yours Conrad

To William Rothenstein
Text MS Harvard; Unpublished

[Someries]
12 Dec '07

Dearest Will.

This is wholly admirable![3] After this nothing more can be said. But you may be certain that every phrase of so noble and simple construction, so pregnant with the sincerities of your artistic faith has its humble response in my mind and heart.

It is a wonderful plea of self-expression. I've always suspected that in Rothenstein the painter we have lost a stylist of an absolutely pure verbal inspiration. This pronouncement upon the faith of the artist is art

---

[1] The 7th.
[2] Letterhead one puts the date between October and March. The eve of Galsworthy's dinner on the 10th is a likely occasion.
[3] An unidentified speech.

in itself, the lofty precept and the memorable example in one. This speech—worthy in its unstained single-mindedness to be an allocution to little children contains the heart of an eternal verity, the first and the last word of artistic salvation.

I look to you, dear Will, with a still greater, if possible, confidence in Your genius and with a renewed warmth of friendship in the augmented pride of that affection which links our thoughts, our convictions and our feeling.

Ever Yours

Conrad.

To J.B. Pinker

Text MS Berg; Unpublished

[letterhead: Someries]

Thursday. [12 or 19 December 1907][1]

My dear Pinker

I send you in a hurry *10* pp of *Razumov* the first of the two short stories. It is quite possible that you will get the *rest* (say 35 pp) by Monday or Tuesday.

All the pp of *that* story will be marked R to avoid confusion with other MS pp.

Please have what I send here typed at once and the type (*with MS.*) posted back to me say on Sat. if possible.

Do you think it worth while to sound Courtney[2] as to taking that story?

I believe the Fort.ly Rev is going to publish short stories.

In haste

Yours Conrad.

---

[1] On 4 December, Conrad expected to send 'Razumov' after Christmas; by the 23rd, he had sent 30 pages.

[2] W. L. Courtney (1850–1928), editor of the *Fortnightly Review* since 1894, and literary editor of the *Daily Telegraph*.

To J.B. Pinker
Text MS Berg; Unpublished

[Someries]
Monday [23 December 1907][1]

My dear Pinker
  I sent MS of Razumov up to p. 30. More shall follow immediately after the holidays.
  Will there be anyone in the office on Friday or Sat.
  Send me £2. I've no cash in the house
                                    Yours always
                                              J. Conrad.

To J.B. Pinker
Text MS Berg; Unpublished

[letterhead: Someries]
Monday 30 Dec
'07

My dear Pinker.
  I send You some 20 pages of Razumov. It isn't the end. More shall follow to-morrow.
  It's a more difficult job than I thought and unluckily (but I am never anything else) I've had gout since Boxing day. It never interrupted my writing but it has not helped it forward either. I am rapidly improving. What's most killing is the depression which goes with it. One requires a certain elasticity, cheerfulness of mind to get on fast and easily. The pain was insignificant.
  I've been doing some more too to Chance. I haven't been idle—and that's something.
  Reynolds was good company both to me and Borys. There's a lot in that young man. Borys' school report extremely good—"determined and intelligent worker".
  Mrs Pinker's charmingly friendly letter has been extremely appreciated by my wife. Pray thank her from me for making so much of a very small matter. I trust you are all well in disregard of this beastly anti-hunting weather. May luck attend your steps in the coming year
                          Kindest regards
                                    Yours Conrad.

---

[1] The question about Friday and Saturday gives a date just before the Christmas holidays.

_PS_ *Please* procure for me *le Petit Journal* of the *first* and 2^d of January when they come out[1]

---

[1] See n. 4 to the letter of 15 [16] October, and the close of the letter to Szembek, 16 May 1905.

SILENT CORRECTIONS TO THE TEXT

The following slips of the pen have been silently corrected.

Missing full stop supplied

5 Jan. 1903: after 'com[missi]on of 10%'; [11 Jan. 1903]: after '(. . . answer for nothing)'; [6] Feb. 1903: after 'four instalments ready', after 'book somewhat'; 16 March 1903: after 'pull through', after 'a copy royalty'; 22 April 1903: after 'your father is better'; [April? 1903] (to Ford): after 'with my suggestions'; [May or June? 1903] (to Ford): after 'overwhelming', after 'Post here'; 6 June 1903: after 'the June month'; [8 or 15? July 1903]: after 'before my gaze', after 'love to you all'; [early Aug? 1903] (to E. Hueffer): after 'entre parenthèses'; 22 Aug. 1903 (to Pinker): after '(. . . confidentially you understand)'; 11 Sept. 1903: after '(except a Saturday)'; [7 or 14 October 1903]: after 'terrible time'; [early November 1903] (to Ford): after 'I think', after 'ground of our motives'; 21 Dec. 1903 (to Casement): after 'plus d'Europe'.

[early Feb? 1904] (to Pinker): after 'carry matter further', after 'rights reserved strictly', after 'illustrated at 10/6'; [24? Feb. 1904]: after 'going on well'; [25? Feb. 1904]: after ' "*Missing*" ', after ' "*Stranded*" '; 2 March [1904]: after '*P.M.M*'; 29 March 1904: after 'height of my influenza'; 5 April 1904: after '(Watson and C°)'; 15 April 1904: after '*Mirror of the Sea*'; [25? April 1904]: after 'to take the papers'; [15 June 1904]: after 'otherwise untrustworthy'; 3 July 1904: after 'We shall meet soon', after 'love to you all'; [24 Aug. 1904]: after 'to catch my train'; 1 September 1904: after 'brandy and soda', after 'write soon'; [2 Sept. 1904] (to Pinker): after 'received this morning'; 18 Oct. 1904: after 'for corrections', after '(Strand Story)', after 'a sea-paper', after 'for the Quar-[ter]ly'; 25 Nov. 1904: after 'better to night'; 30 Nov. 1904: after 'opening one just now'; 1 Dec 1904 (to Lucas): after '(save the mark!)'; [1 Dec. 1904] (to Pinker): after 'up to 22 Dec'; [2? Dec. 1904]: after 'famously'; 21 Dec. 1904: after '(M[irror] of the S[ea])'.

4 Jan. 1905: after 'drew £*245*', after 'sum of £*1597*'; [9 Jan. 1905]: after '3 weeks after publication'; 29 Jan. 1905 (to Galsworthy): after 'No more just now'; 5 Feb. 1905: after 'earliest possible moment'; 15 Feb. 1905:

after 'reach of the voice'; [c. 6 April? 1905]: after 'received safely';
12 April 1905: after 'effect of the influenza', after 'a grip on things', after
'2ᵈ class carriages', after 'Dynamite Ship story', after 'on that large
amount'; 22 April 1905 (2nd to Pinker): after 'hands without reserve'; 9
May 1905: after 'far away from You', after 'a sort of "four"'; 12 May
1905: after 'text and tone'; 30 June 1905: after 'in the *Fortnightly*', after
'Borys too'; 20 Sept. 1905: after '25 pounds', after 'all these demands';
22 Oct. 1905 (to Pinker): after 'of the Standard'; 22 Nov. 1905: after
'knocked on the head'.

1 Jan. 1906: after '*Informer* myself tomorrow'; [4 Jan. 1906] (to Galsworthy): after 'or very near that'; 11 Jan. 1906 (to Galsworthy): after 'to
begin in June'; 16 Jan. 1906: after 'another for £2.10'; 18 Jan. 1906: after
'body of the work'; 23 Jan. 1906 (to Archer): after 'savour of impertinence'; 23 Jan. 1906 (to Pinker): after 'the papers tonight', after 'see
the proofs through'; 31 Jan. 1906: after 'love to you both'; 7 Feb. 1906:
after 'all this toil'; 21 Feb. 1906: after 'is less trouble'; [mid March?
1906] (2nd to Pinker): after 'will be better', after 'for the Outlook'; 28
March 1906: after 'received two days ago'; [4? June 1906]: after 'must
have been influenza'; 7 July 1906: after 'about the 28th'; 4 Aug. 1906 (to
J. Wells): after 'Brother Jack', after 'middle of September'; 4 Aug. 1906
(to A. Rothenstein): after 'comfortably located'; 14 Aug. 1906: after
'years and meditate'; 16 Aug. 1906: after 'sympathy and friendship';
[late Aug. 1906] (to Pinker): after 'referred him to you', after 'neck deep
in Verloc'; 16 Sept. 1906: after 'C.7', after 'oil on the flames'; 17 Sept.
1906 (to Galsworthy): after 'for 40/-'; 17 [19?] Sept. 1906: after 'on
Monday next'; [3 Oct. 1906]: after 'great impatience', [11 Oct. 1906]:
after 'send me the Nᵒ', after 'goes to Hythe'; [17 Nov. 1906]: after 'I am
confident', after 'her father *knowing*'; 20 Dec. 1906 (to Pinker): after 'my
work in my next'.

4 Jan. 1907: after 'little Chap'; 5 Jan. 1907: after '*700 frcs*'; 8 Jan. 1907
(to Pinker): after 'might have been neglected', after 'all for the moment',
after 'within the new walls'; 25 Jan. 1907 (to Ford): after 'to all your
women', after 'Mrs Martindale'; 20 Feb. 1907: after 'for the other'; [c. 9
March 1907]: after 'all well, so far'; 16 March 1907: after 'on the
premises', after 'are really doing'; 19 March 1907: after 'in this stuff'; 8
April 1907: after 'by the same post'; 13 April 1907: after 'in placing the
Duel'; 6 May 1907 (to Pinker): after 'from here on the 15ᵗʰ'; 8 May 1907:
after 'style corrections'; 18 May 1907: after 'began in Montpellier', after

'let me t[h]rough'; 5 June 1907: after 'composing to the mind', after '£60 *per month* here', after 'in Montpellier', after 'to spare for anything'; 11 June [1907]: after 'MS of *SA*'; [12 or 19 June 1907]: after '"bully"'; 17 June 1907: after 'what will happen'; [20 June 1907]: after 'the *p 294* of proof'; 26 June 1907: after 'Thanks for the money', after 'skin and bone'; 1 July 1907: after 'long I fear'; 27 July 1907: after 'without fail'; 30 July 1907 (to Pinker): after 'from here on the 10th'; [5 Aug. 1907]: after 'Some £30 a year'; 14 Aug. 1907: after 'time this was paid'; 12 Sept. 1907: after 'extra for expenses'; [25 Sept. 1907]: after 'to come on Friday'; [30 Sept. 1907]: after '(spread over 2 years)', after 'tell you all this now'; 1 Oct. 1907 (to Garnett): after 'for the No', after 'Any week'; 7 Oct. 1907: after 'you like the *S Agent*', after 'in the nineties', after 'I treasure', after 'steel our hearts'; 10 Oct. 1907 (2nd letter): after 'Tauchnitz's collection'; 1 Nov. 1907: after 'Luton *10.53*'; [c. 20 Nov. 1907]: after 'another for £1.5'; 27 Nov. 1907: after 'God knows'; 28 Nov. 1907 (to Rothenstein): after 'a sight of you'; [12 or 19 Dec. 1907]: after 'publish short stories'; 30 Dec. 1907: after 'shall follow to-morrow'.

Dittography
25 April 1905 (to Wells): a second 'thought' after 'for a moment that your'; 8 May 1905: a second 'it' after 'I rewrote'; 16 May 1905 (to Gosse): a second 'as' after 'I shall look upon'; 28 Nov. 1905: a second 'no' after 'in which there is'; 22 March 1906: a second 'you' before 'may imagine that effort'; [25 Nov. or 2 Dec. 1906]: a second 'moment' after 'I am at this'; 8 April 1907: an 'is' after 'She's'; 6 May 1907 (to Galsworthy): a second 'you' after 'I am glad'; 13 Aug. 1907 (to Capes): a second 'we' before 'could drive'; 21 Aug. 1907: a second 'for a' after 'We are in treaty'.

Other
Quotation marks supplied:
1 Oct. 1903: after 'manque de vraisemblance'; 20 Oct. 1905: after 'only of H.G. Wells', after 'Man is not final'; 5 March 1906: after 'acct/'; 29 March 1906 (to Ford): after 'cat of a public'.

Bracket supplied:
2 Jan. 1903 (to Ford): after 'Famiglia'; [early August? 1903] (to E. Hueffer): at the very end; [early Feb? 1904] (to Pinker): after 'serial rights'; 13 Jan. 1905: after 'these early episodes'; 18 Jan. 1906: after 'commemorative paper on Nelson'.

Bracket deleted:
[early Feb? 1904] (to Pinker): before 'serial rights'; [26 Aug. 1904]: before 'may date on Monday'.

Colon supplied:
[early Feb. 1904] (to Pinker): after 'as follows'; 3 May 1907: after 'say is this'.

Semi-colon supplied:
4 Jan. 1905: after 'the sum £*1352*'.

Comma supplied:
22 April 1905 (to Pinker, 2nd letter): after 'Prothero'; 15 July 1905 [1901]: after 'the case when I work'; 28 March 1906: after 'really excited'; [5? Sept. 1906]: after 'Cheriton'; [11 Oct. 1906]: after 'Newbolt'; [17 Nov. 1906]: before 'Mansell or Mrs Sherrington'.

Dash supplied:
[8 Jan. 1903] (to Elsie Hueffer): after 'dragging about of tables etc etc'; [early Sept. 1903] (to Ford): after 'masterpieces etc etc'.

CORRIGENDA, Volume 2

Page xiii: 'The Rev. Foy F. Quiller-Couch'; xv and *passim*: 'Danile-wiczowa'; xxix: 'Anne Elizabeth Bontine'; xxix: Brooke (née Rodick, 1856–1920); xxix: de Brunnow born 1865; xxxi: revised biography of Mrs Graham in Volume Three; xxxii: Kliszczewski (c.1849–1932); xxxiii: Pawling died 1922; xxxiv: Watson (1858–1928); xxxiv, Zagórska: delete dates; Plate 13, caption: 'by R.H. Sauter'.

34, n. 1: 'in the *Torrens*'; 80, n. 2; 'John Charles Tarver'; 90, n. 6: '(1868–1938)'.

105, l. 30: 'la dedands*"'; 106, n. 2: '(1849–1903)'; 195, provenance: delete '*101*'.

245, n. 5: '1833?'; 265, n. 2: '*Loch Etive*', 267, translation, l. 11: 'how sales are going'; 270, translation, l. 5: 'Nieuwpoort'; 271, 273: MSS now in NLS; 281, l. 1: 'I shall no longer be there'; 294, n. 2: 'They saw him'.

332, 378, 387: letters to Ford in Goldring.

400, l. 26: 'le marin qu'il vous faut'; 410, l. 15: 'your small women'; 466, n. 2: '*Litteratursällskapet*'; 470, n. 2: 'In the name of God'.

(Index II) 478, *Lord Jim*: add 166–9; 480: add Juvenal, 303; 481, Meldrum: add 62; Milner, Sir Alfred; Nieuwpoort; 482, delete *Evening* from *Glasgow Herald*; add *Glasgow Evening News*, 186; 483: Tarver, John Charles.

INDEX I

In Index I, which identifies recipients, only the first page of each letter is cited.

In Index II, an index of names, run-on pagination may cover more than one letter. References to ships are consolidated under 'Ships'; references to newspapers and magazines under 'Periodicals'. References to works by Conrad appear under his name.

A full critical index will appear in the final volume.

Recipients

INDEX II

Names of people, places, ships, organizations and publications

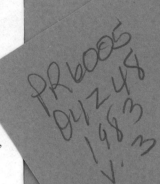